# COMBINATION TABLE

| # | Combination | page | | # | Combination | page |
|---|---|---|---|---|---|---|
| 1 | □ □ □ □ □ □ | 261 | | 33 | ○ ○ □ □ □ □ | 302 |
| 2 | ○ ○ ○ ○ ○ ○ | 262 | | 34 | □ □ □ □ ○ ○ | 304 |
| 3 | □ ○ ○ ○ □ ○ | 263 | | 35 | ○ ○ □ □ □ □ | 305 |
| 4 | ○ □ ○ ○ ○ □ | 265 | | 36 | □ ○ □ □ ○ ○ | 307 |
| 5 | □ ○ □ □ ○ □ | 266 | | 37 | □ □ ○ □ □ □ | 308 |
| 6 | ○ □ ○ □ □ □ | 267 | | 38 | □ □ ○ □ □ □ | 309 |
| 7 | ○ □ ○ ○ ○ ○ | 269 | | 39 | ○ ○ □ ○ □ ○ | 311 |
| 8 | ○ ○ ○ ○ □ ○ | 270 | | 40 | ○ □ ○ □ ○ ○ | 312 |
| 9 | □ □ □ □ ○ □ | 271 | | 41 | □ □ □ □ ○ ○ | 313 |
| 10 | □ □ ○ □ □ □ | 273 | | 42 | □ ○ ○ ○ □ □ | 315 |
| 11 | □ □ □ ○ ○ ○ | 274 | | 43 | □ □ ○ □ ○ ○ | 316 |
| 12 | ○ ○ ○ □ □ □ | 275 | | 44 | ○ □ □ □ □ □ | 317 |
| 13 | □ ○ ○ □ □ ○ | 277 | | 45 | ○ ○ ○ ○ □ ○ | 319 |
| 14 | □ □ □ □ ○ □ | 278 | | 46 | ○ □ □ ○ ○ ○ | 320 |
| 15 | ○ ○ ○ □ ○ ○ | 279 | | 47 | ○ □ ○ □ □ ○ | 321 |
| 16 | ○ ○ ○ □ ○ ○ | 281 | | 48 | ○ □ □ ○ □ ○ | 322 |
| 17 | □ ○ ○ ○ □ ○ | 282 | | 49 | □ ○ ○ □ □ ○ | 324 |
| 18 | ○ □ □ ○ ○ □ | 283 | | 50 | ○ □ □ □ ○ □ | 325 |
| 19 | □ □ ○ ○ ○ ○ | 284 | | 51 | □ ○ ○ ○ □ ○ | 326 |
| 20 | ○ ○ ○ ○ □ □ | 286 | | 52 | ○ ○ □ ○ ○ □ | 328 |
| 21 | □ ○ ○ □ ○ □ | 287 | | 53 | ○ ○ ○ ○ □ □ | 329 |
| 22 | □ ○ □ ○ ○ □ | 288 | | 54 | □ □ ○ □ ○ ○ | 330 |
| 23 | ○ ○ ○ ○ ○ □ | 289 | | 55 | □ ○ ○ □ ○ ○ | 332 |
| 24 | □ ○ ○ ○ ○ □ | 291 | | 56 | ○ ○ □ □ ○ □ | 333 |
| 25 | □ ○ ○ □ □ □ | 292 | | 57 | ○ □ □ ○ □ □ | 334 |
| 26 | □ ○ □ ○ ○ □ | 293 | | 58 | □ □ ○ □ □ ○ | 336 |
| 27 | □ ○ ○ ○ ○ □ | 295 | | 59 | ○ □ ○ ○ □ □ | 337 |
| 28 | ○ ○ □ □ □ ○ | 296 | | 60 | □ □ ○ ○ □ ○ | 338 |
| 29 | ○ □ ○ ○ □ ○ | 297 | | 61 | □ □ □ ○ ○ □ | 340 |
| 30 | □ ○ □ □ ○ □ | 299 | | 62 | ○ ○ □ □ ○ ○ | 341 |
| 31 | ○ ○ □ □ ○ ○ | 300 | | 63 | □ ○ ○ ○ □ ○ | 342 |
| 32 | ○ □ □ □ ○ ○ | 301 | | 64 | ○ □ ○ □ ○ □ | 344 |

# DICTIONARY OF
# DREAMS

*Didier Colin*

# DICTIONARY OF
# DREAMS

**INTERPRETATION AND UNDERSTANDING**

3,500 interpretations to understand
the true meaning of your dreams

Graphic design by Michel Méline
Layout by Jean-Pierre Jauneau
English edition designed by Chris Bell
Cards designed by Philippe Jacquemin

© 1995 Hachette Livre (Hachette Pratiques: Vie Pratique)
© Hachette Livre (Littérature générale: Livres Pratiques), 1994
This edition published by
Hachette Illustrated UK, Octopus Publishing Group,
2–4 Heron Quays, London E14 4JP

English translation produced by JMS Books LLP
Translation © Octopus Publishing Group

A CIP catalogue for this book is available from the British Library

ISBN: 184202 184 2

Printed in China

*'A dream benefits those who keep it in their heart, but it is a disaster for those who do not understand it.'*

attributed to Tanuatamun, Egyptian Pharaoh
of the XXVth Dynasty, who reigned from 663–656 BC

*'They will tell me I talk about things I have never experienced but only dreamed – to which I might reply: it is a lovely thing to dream such dreams! And besides, our dreams are much more our experiences than we believe – we must relearn about dreams! If I have dreamed thousands of times about flying – would you not believe that when I am awake I also possess feelings and needs giving me an edge on most people...'*

Friedrich Nietzsche

# Contents

Introduction 8

Practical guide to dreams 14

How to use this book 19

Glossary of symbols 33

Dictionary of symbols 51

Interpretations and predictions 259

Bibliography 347

# Introduction

'Those who dream of the banquet may weep the next morning, and those who dream of weeping may go out to hunt after dawn. When we dream we do not know that we are dreaming. In our dreams we may even interpret our dreams. Only after we are awake do we know that we have dreamed. But there comes a great awakening, and then we know that life is a great dream.'

*Chuang Tzu, Taoist philosopher (399–295 BC)*

*You may wonder how the languages of tarot, astrology and dreams can be interpreted in conjunction with each other, but this is indeed the case.*

*Dreams, tarot and astrology share a common language – the language of symbols – that can be interpreted in different ways but requires the use of the much-neglected skill of intuition.*

*Through our intuition, our intellectual memory, we can draw on the enormous potential of the collective conscience, barely a fraction of which we access in ordinary life.*

*The Tarot is made up of a number of Arcana, whose symbols allow us access to the constantly changing pattern of events and circumstances that surrounds us and which we create or excite, whether knowingly or not. Interpreting Tarot cards helps us to exercise our free will and to view the consequences, deliberate or involuntary, of our own actions, while helping us to assess the role played by our own destiny – of which we may also be aware or unaware.*

*Astrology, on the other hand, is made up of a zodiac, again expressed in symbols, which affords us a comprehensive, panoramic view of the world in which we live. By focussing on a unique instant in the heavens – the moment of our birth – we can pinpoint the key trajectories that govern and reveal the nature of our individual personality and its future development. The probable events and circumstances revealed by a celestial map merely support the individual in his or her development and fulfilment.*

*And finally we come to dreams, which seem to represent a double life lived during sleep, a life full of unlikely, irrational, fantastic, wonderful or tragic adventures, in which the dreamer enjoys the privilege of being both actor and spectator. The adventures are full of lively and impressive symbols, viewed in four dimensions within a world peopled by both the extremely realistic and the wildly imaginative. Decoding the language of the symbols of dreams depends much more upon intuition than strict analysis, for here we come into direct contact with our true selves: nature, soul and spirit.*

*To sum up all three languages: it is probably helpful to define the language of Tarot as a support structure in our daily life, through which the state of the soul or conscience can be accessed at a given point in time; this makes it a wonderful tool in meditation. The language of astrology helps us to know ourselves and assess just how conscious we are of the roles played by our own free will and destiny. The language of dreams encourages us to get in touch with ourselves in our totality – every aspect of what and who we are.*

*The three disciplines complement each other, all sharing the common language of symbols and all focussing on the same goal – self-fulfilment or access to the path that leads there.*

*You will find it helpful to write down your dreams in a notebook; when you return to them, you will be able to see that each dream is unique. It seems that we can instantly recognize our own dreams by their individuality, underlining just how intimate and privileged our relationship is with them. It is through dreams that we express the most generous and benevolent aspects of our nature.*

*Every individual's dream life is unique, making it impossible to give general or common interpretations to particular dreams; similarly, it is not feasible to create an interpretative structure applicable to a variety of people whose dreams feature a particular concept or symbol. However, the language used to describe dreams is by its very nature universal and can offer a basic vocabulary from which, through association, cross-checking and intuition, we may be able to give general interpretations, based on analogy and good sense.*

*In order to help you interpret your own dreams in this fashion, I have adopted a reference system based very heavily on analogy. Before being hijacked by computers and other modern forms* of communication, this parallel language (analogue) was always (and still remains) the code common to all esoteric doctrines and practices as well as to the divinatory arts.

This book cannot provide answers to all your questions or contain every possible subject or interpretation. What I attempt to offer are interpretations inspired by my own experience, by my knowledge and intuition of the realm of dreams. By using the many entries, the proposed technique and the divinatory game contained in the book, you can develop your own interpretations, day after day.

There is no magic formula or universal knowledge that can be applied to answer all your questions. This book aims to put you on the right path to the solutions and the clarification you need – both of which are actually within yourself. The future cannot be predicted. Only the intelligent and intuitive part of our soul holds the key that enables us to open the doors of our conscious world and to shed light on it. Dreams are the language of the soul and when we dream our soul speaks the language of truth, warning or informing us. In this way dreams can be predictive.

*For more than twenty years, I have been trying to unlock the mysteries of the soul and to discover more about the deep psychology and psychopathology of human beings. What I have tried to do here is to offer you a possible reading of the great book of dreams. It is for you to find your own interpretation, for while there may be one book of dreams and of life for everyone, each individual's interpretation is unique. To discover, acknowledge and celebrate one's difference, one's style, is to live, to be awakened and illuminated by Life itself. The individual is separate and unique and yet part of the greater whole at the same time, and this is what we can describe as the ultimate communication – communion.*

*Our dreams reveal this state of communion. The future as revealed by dreams is that of a time out of time, where everything comes together in us, where the past, the present and the future are one, where our wildest dreams come into being because they are what we are. This future is promised to us. It lies within us and awaits our discovery. By dreaming and interpreting those dreams we come closer to it.*

# Practical guide
# to dreams

## DO DREAMS REVEAL OUR FUTURE?

Premonitory dreams, or those that warn us of a fact or event before it occurs, are often compensatory dreams. I call them 'dreams of moderation' because of the reassurance and sense of calm they can give us. They are easy to interpret.

Other more obscure and confused dreams contain information or messages that are harder to decode. They reveal mistakes in our behaviour or actions and shed light on ways we can change our attitudes and become more aware of why we do certain things. We get to know ourselves better as a result.

These dreams project us into the future for a very simple reason – the unconscious is unaware of the division between past, present and future. It is only upon awakening the morning after a dream or during the days that follow that we can appreciate the lessons contained in our dreams. An alternative title for this book could be *Dreams and Your Future*, because it is our future or, more exactly, what we will become that dreams tell us about. However, I believe it is important to stress that the 'future' we are discussing is not definite or destined. It is not written on a tablet of stone, but is as yet undetermined, simply a probable or potential future. Our dreams warn us of the foreseeable consequences of our actions. It is nevertheless clear that if we can learn from these warnings, we can influence what is to come. In this way our dreams help us to exercise our free will.

## DO ALL OUR DREAMS HAVE MEANING?

According to scientific research, it appears that one night's sleep is made up of four or five phases, in the course of which we are able to dream. It is therefore likely that we dream at least once during the night.

It does not necessarily follow that we are able to remember the content of our dreams or indeed the fact that we have dreamed at all. However, we may sometimes have confused or blurred impressions of two or three dreams during our waking hours. Which of these contains a message? Why should we select one dream over another? It is quite legitimate for you to ask questions of this nature, as not every dream is charged with the same level of meaning.

According to traditional oneiromancy (theory of dreams), dreams experienced during the first half of the night or during the day (for example, during a siesta) are not particularly important. They rarely contain key or profound information and can be described as 'dreams of digestion' or dreams of compensation, or even premonitory dreams, warning us with their symbols of an imminent fact or event. Such 'dreams of digestion' can cause nightmares. A slow or difficult digestive process, and the energy involved, can be the catalyst for visions of destruction, catastrophe, murder or violent death. On the other hand, dreams that occur during the second half of the night, especially those just before you wake up, often contain important messages. It is to these dreams that we need to pay most attention.

## CAN WE CONTROL OR DIRECT OUR DREAMS?

Certain yoga techniques can help us to control our dreams or at least to be perfectly conscious of them, experiencing them in a semi-wakened state. However, such practices are not advisable for those without experience in the technique. If you attempt such a technique without proper monitoring or surveillance, or with the wrong motives, you risk very harmful psychological consequences.

It is nevertheless possible to employ a safe way to experience this state of 'waking dreams', as practised by some yoga experts. Before falling asleep, try to empty yourself of your day-to-day thoughts and worries and relax your muscles; when you feel calm, concentrate your mind on a specific matter, a particular question to which you seek an answer, without letting your imagination intervene. If your thoughts wander, try to rein them in and bring them back to the subject in question, focussing on it like a fixed point in your mind. If your powers of concentration are intense enough, if only for a moment, you will manage to establish a line of communication, pass on a message, or ask yourself the question. Your dream will provide a response and you will then be able to interpret it using the explanations contained in the dictionary of symbols (p. 51). There you will find the answer you have been looking for.

## SHOULD WE REVEAL OUR DREAMS TO OTHERS?

Your dreams are intimate things and belong to you. Try not to reveal them to others or to confide in those whom you do not trust implicitly. Nowadays, we tend not to appreciate the value of our dreams and the helpful, if not healing, messages they carry. By failing to attach sufficient value to them, we do not treat them with respect, discussing them all too freely as a result. We find ourselves divided between what we consider to be a childish, naïve tendency to attach too much significance to them – a sceptical view of all things to do with the world of dreams – and an automatic reflex that that makes us seek a meaning in them at any cost. In *Dreams and their Islamic Interpretation*, Toufi Fahd, a researcher at CNRS[1], said that a dream deserves as much respect as its interpretation and should be told only to an expert or adviser in the field and never to a stranger or enemy; otherwise it is in danger of losing all its value. The interpreter of dreams should possess good qualities, including religious beliefs, memory, piety, clemency, discretion and silence in the presence of things of which they are ignorant; they should

1 National Centre for Scientific Research in France

avoid gossiping or boasting about what they hear in confidence and should never divulge it to others.

Those practising esoteric arts should consider these words. If you know of a dream interpreter in possession of all these qualities, consult them by all means but otherwise keep your dreams to yourself. If you want to interpret your own dreams or those of someone close to you, you know what you must aspire to, in order to be worthy.

## HOW DO I RECOGNIZE A PREMONITORY DREAM?

As I have already mentioned, all dreams can be described as premonitory due to their function as warnings. However, should we fear that a dream of a catastrophe or accident involving a loved one will actually come true? It is important not to over- or underestimate the content or, indeed, the power of our dreams. Don't overestimate them, as it is rare for a dream to become reality, but do not underestimate them, as the thoughts of someone who has dreamed of a specific event – thoughts charged with both positive and negative energy – have the force to bring it about. Each and every one of us has a creative energy, which is not fundamentally positive and which, if activated, usually unconsciously, may set in motion real events in our lives; it can be the catalyst for circumstances that realize the hopes or anxieties we have felt in our dreams. We should not neglect our capacity both to receive and project, an ability we sometimes exploit through excessive intervention or unchecked dependence.

We are usually able to recognize a premonitory dream instantly, or when an event or fact experienced in a dream manifests itself in our everyday life – hence the value of keeping an account of our dreams, which should be dated. You can then look at your notes on the dream and say to yourself 'how extraordinary, that is exactly what I dreamt!'

How to be aware of having had a premonitory dream is another matter entirely. These can sometimes happen before a natural disaster or a collective trauma, such as an earthquake or war. We know that animals sense danger and our dreams spring from the same natural instincts. However, there are no strict rules to distinguish between a dream that warns of an event that will occur in our life and a dream that teaches us about our spiritual state, our feelings, behaviour and personal development.

A tendency to believe that a dream inevitably predicts a real eventuality stems from a lack of confidence and emotional resources in oneself and one's life.

In conclusion, I offer two reflections that stem from my experience of interpreting my own dreams and from studies in traditional oneiromancy:

**1** Do not dramatize your dreams, over-emphasizing upon the spectacular or extraordinary aspects that can accompany a premonitory dream.

**2** Do not force events, do not tempt fate, do not defy your destiny by trying to replicate at all costs the content of your dream in real life. From dream to reality is but a step, tempting but dangerous to cross.

## WHAT IS THE POINT OF OUR DREAMS?

The purpose of our dreams is to clarify, illuminate and awaken us – to shed so much light on our consciousness that the dream ceases to play a key role, one upon which we depend. It is because our consciousness is buried deep or obscured by our rational minds that we dream. By dreaming, we are reconciled with ourselves, reconnected with reality – we are *awakened*. It is not the dream that is a lie, but the absence of the dream – except when we no longer need to dream, when we are in a state of perfect consciousness and absolute truth. The Kaushitaki Upanishad[1] goes further in describing this state of returning to one's centre or core, as we will in death: '*When a man sleeps without dreaming, he becomes one with breath: speech and all words, sight and all forms, hearing and all sounds enter him*'.

1 Upanishad: any of the sacred Sanskrit treatises on theology and metaphysics that form the basis for Hindu philosophy and faith (dating probably to before AD 500).

# How to use this book

In order to interpret the meaning of the symbols in your dreams and to understand what they reveal or predict, just follow the detailed instructions below:

## DISCOVERING THE MEANING OF THE SYMBOLS IN YOUR DREAMS

### 1 Keep a dream diary

Dedicate a notebook or diary to keeping a record of your dreams. Write a brief, clear account and make sure you date each entry. Avoid using elaborate language and don't worry too much about noting down every detail. Keep your account simple and stick to the key facts.

DREAM DATED 10TH JANUARY

I take an unusual path back to my house. There's a sled on the road, which I have to negotiate. I climb up, using a ladder. When I reach the summit and prepare to set off down the slope, I notice that it is really unsteady and suspended in a void.

To illustrate the process of identifying the symbolic content of a dream, here is my account of a dream that I had on 10 January:

'I take an unusual path back to my house. There's a sled on the road, which I have to negotiate. I climb up, using a ladder. When I reach the summit and prepare to set off down the slope, I notice that it is really unsteady and suspended in a void.'

19

## 2 Recognizing the symbols in your dream

Each dream contains one or more symbolic elements (an object, person, animal etc.); they hold the key to its meaning and need to be identified in order for the significance of the dream to be fully understood.

You may find it hard to recognize these symbols at first, but you will soon realize how obvious they are when you write down or discuss your dream. The moment you put them into words, their importance will jump out at you.

It sometimes happens that, on waking, we cannot remember the details or sequence of events in our dreams, but during the course of the day an image or a particular aspect of the dream persistently come to mind. It is this aspect of the dream that carries the greatest symbolic meaning, and thus demands attention.

When you have successfully identified the symbols, note them in your diary in order of appearance:

For example, the symbols in my dream that caught my attention immediately were:

1   path

2   road

3   sled

4   ladder

5   summit

6   slope

7   void

# 3 Using the glossary of symbols

Turn first to the glossary of symbols, starting on p. 33. This will refer you to the relevant 'symbol-words' that are interpreted in the dictionary of symbols. Look up the words in the glossary of symbols in the order in which they first appeared in the dream.

• If your dream features a concept that is a symbol-word, look up the appropriate entry in the glossary (where it will appear in capital letters), which will refer you to the relevant page in the dictionary of symbols. There you will find the explanatory text.

• If your dream does not feature a symbol-word, you will find it next to the corresponding symbol-word (in lower case letters) that refers you to the relevant page.

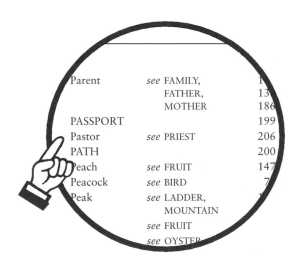

| Parent | *see* FAMILY, | 1 |
| | FATHER, | 13 |
| | MOTHER | 186 |
| PASSPORT | | 199 |
| Pastor | *see* PRIEST | 206 |
| PATH | | 200 |
| Peach | *see* FRUIT | 147 |
| Peacock | *see* BIRD | 7 |
| Peak | *see* LADDER, | |
| | MOUNTAIN | |
| | *see* FRUIT | |
| | *see* OYSTER | |

Again taking my dream as an example, look up the seven aspects in order of appearance:

## 1 PATH

PATH                              p. 200

Write down the word 'PATH' in your dream diary, along with the corresponding page in the dictionary of symbols, so that you can consult the relevant text later.

## 2 ROAD

Road        *see* STREET    p. 232

'Road' corresponds to the symbol-word STREET, which you will find on p. 232 of the dictionary of symbols.

Again, note the symbol-word and page number in your dream diary.

### 3 SLED

| Sled | *see* LADDER, | p. 171 |
|------|---------------|--------|
|      | MOUNTAIN      | p. 186 |

'Sled' corresponds to two symbol-words: LADDER and MOUN-TAIN. You will find them on pp. 171 and 186 of the dictionary of symbols. Note the entries and corresponding page numbers in your dream diary, after the previous entry.

### 4 LADDER

You have already highlighted the ladder as the third element. Write down the word and page number again so that you can look up the relevant text once more.

### 5 SUMMIT

| Summit | *see* LADDER, | p. 171 |
|--------|---------------|--------|
|        | MOUNTAIN      | p. 186 |

'Summit' corresponds to two symbol-words, LADDER and MOUNTAIN, which you have already identified as the third element of the dream and which you will look up once more in the dictionary of symbols. Write down the two symbol-words and the relevant corresponding pages in your dream diary.

### 6 SLOPE

| Slope | *see* MOUNTAIN | p. 186 |
|-------|----------------|--------|

You have already identified the symbol-word MOUNTAIN as the third and fifth elements of the dream and you will look up the relevant text once more. Write down the symbol-word and relevant page in your dream diary.

### 7 VOID

| VOID | | p. 248 |
|------|--|--------|

Write this final symbol-word and its corresponding page number in your dream diary, after the preceding entries. From the seven elements, you have found five symbols: PATH, STREET,

LADDER, MOUNTAIN and VOID in the following chronological order:

| 1 | PATH | p. 200 |
|---|------|--------|
| 2 | STREET | p. 232 |
| 3 | LADDER | p. 171 |
|   | MOUNTAIN | p. 186 |
| 4 | LADDER | p. 171 |
| 5 | LADDER | p. 171 |
|   | MOUNTAIN | p. 186 |
| 6 | MOUNTAIN | p. 186 |
| 7 | VOID | p. 248 |

All you have to do now is to consult the dictionary of symbols.

*DREAM DATED 10TH JANUARY 1993*

*I take an unusual path back to my house. There's a sled on the road, which I have to negotiate. I climb up, using a ladder. When I reach the summit and prepare to set off down the slope, I notice that it is really unsteady and suspended in a void.*

PATH p.200
STREET p.232
LADDER p.171
MOUNTAIN p.186
LADDER p.171

LADDER p.171
MOUNTAIN p.186
MOUNTAIN p.186
VOID p.248

---

NB Dreams often contain elements that appear to have no obvious connection, but in fact they can be linked to a single symbol-word. This is the case with Sled, Ladder and Summit, all of which are connected to LADDER, and with Summit and Slope, which relate to MOUNTAIN.

---

## 4 Consulting the dictionary of symbols

Following the order in which the different elements appeared, read the relevant text to find the aspect that corresponds with your own situation. Then write it down in your dream diary. Again using the example of my dream, follow the stages:

### 1 PATH

Having read all the text relating to this word symbol, I establish that the second paragraph corresponds to my own situation and copy it into my dream diary.

2   You are following an unknown or unusual path: you have already changed course, direction or decision, in theory if not in practice. Alternatively, you will follow another path to reach your goals or you will change direction altogether.

## 2   STREET

Two paragraphs correspond to my dream – paragraphs No. 4 and No. 8. I copy them into my dream diary:

4   You are walking calmly on the road: you will forge ahead, slowly but surely, taking no risks, believing in yourself and fate.

8   A wall, or some other unexpected obstacle, blocks your way: unexpected difficulties will compel you to take a break from a situation, or give up.

> **NB** It is not uncommon to find two paragraphs that relate to one situation, so make sure you read all the text.

## 3   (3, 4 and 5) LADDER

Paragraph No. 1 of this symbol-word relates to the situation revealed in my dream by the sled, ladder and summit, and so I copy them into the dream diary:

1   You climb a ladder with ease: this heralds progress and self-confidence.

## 4   (3, 5 and 6) MOUNTAIN

Paragraph No. 4 of this symbol-word relates to the situation revealed in my dream by the sled, ladder, summit and slope. I then copy them into my dream diary:

4   You reach the summit with ease, without stopping on the way, and descend the other side without difficulty: you will overcome an obstacle or make some progress in your life rapidly and easily.

5   VOID

Paragraph No. 3 of this symbol-word relates to my situation and I copy it into my dream diary.

3   You fall into the void: you are about to discover something that is essential to your personal development or you will experience a major change or disruption that may throw you off balance for a while.

NB Each paragraph relating to a situation revealed in a dream can be interpreted in one or more ways. If it has several interpretations, choose the one that relates most closely to your current circumstances and their likely development.

## 5 Analyzing the information

Having noted the relevant text, you can then analyse it in a way that will help you highlight the key points in your dream.

Similarly, once you have made this analysis, write it down in your dream diary, as simply and clearly as you can. You will then be able to appreciate the situation to which your dream refers – past, present or future.

Let's go back to the example of my dream to illustrate this process:

• The text relating to the first symbol-word (PATH) heralds a change of mind or direction.

• The text relating to the second symbol-word (STREET) encourages me to move forward, confidently and easily, to solve a problem or negotiate a new phase in my life.

• The text for the third symbol-word (LADDER) talks of progress and self-confidence.

- The explanation for the fourth symbol-word (MOUNTAIN) denotes a phase in my life that I will negotiate with confidence and ease.

- Finally, the fifth symbol-word (VOID) refers to a major change, a revelation or new awareness.

## ANALYSIS

Analysis of all this information indicates a change of 'course, direction or decision ' (No. 1), together with a belief 'in self and fate' (No. 2), which will allow me to progress despite 'unexpected difficulties' (No. 2).

I can then 'climb with ease ... progress and self-confidence' (No. 3) enabling me to 'reach the summit with ease' (No. 4).

However, my dream warns me that things won't stop there. Once this period has passed, I will feel drawn to undergo 'a major change or disruption' (No. 5).

## CONCLUSION

I will change my behaviour and develop as a result, overcoming unexpected hurdles. Solving this problem will lead to an important change in my life – a change that is much bigger than myself.

## WHAT YOUR DREAM CAN TEACH YOU OR PREDICT

You are now able to identify the circumstances to which your dream refers and, with the help of the divinatory game, you can also uncover the useful lessons and predictions that the dream holds.

The game is made up of 24 perforated cards:

| 6 upright triangles | 6 squares | 6 inverted triangles | 6 circles |

## 1 Choose your cards

Shuffle the cards on a table and choose six, selecting every fourth card:

- count 1, 2, 3, 4 and lay the fourth card on the table, face down

- count 5, 6, 7, 8 and lay the eighth card on the right of the first card, face down

Continue counting the cards in this way until you have selected six cards (the fourth, eighth, twelfth, sixteenth, twentieth and twenty-fourth.)

## 2 Turn the cards over

When put together, the six symbols before you form a configuration that is made up of one or more upright triangles ▲, squares ☐, circles ○ and/or inverted triangles ▼.

For example: ☐ ☐ ☐ ▲ ☐ ▼

It would be possible to select six identical symbols – for example, six circles or six upright triangles – but this does not affect the quality of your draw in the least. However your card draw sums up, it always corresponds to the predictions and directions of your dream.

## 3 Convert your draw

In order to interpret the information revealed by your draw, you need to convert the six symbols in front of you, using the conversion table below:

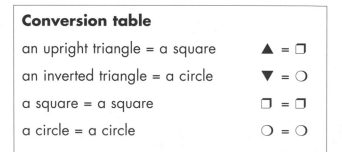

**Conversion table**

| an upright triangle = a square | ▲ = ☐ |
| an inverted triangle = a circle | ▼ = ○ |
| a square = a square | ☐ = ☐ |
| a circle = a circle | ○ = ○ |

Therefore, the combination that results from the conversion of your card draw will be composed of squares and/or circles.

For example, let us imagine my configuration looks like this:

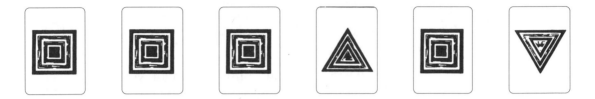

Using the conversion table, translate the cards into combinations of circles and/or squares:

| | | |
|---|---|---|
| a square = a square | ☐ = ☐ | |
| a square = a square | ☐ = ☐ | |
| a square = a square | ☐ = ☐ | |
| an upright triangle = a square | ▲ = ☐ | |
| a square = a square | ☐ = ☐ | |
| an inverted triangle = a circle | ▼ = ○ | |

The combination corresponding to the draw looks like this:

NB If the combination of figures in your draw is composed entirely of squares and/or circles, there is no need to convert it. In this case go straight to p. 31*

## 4 Find the predictive content of your draw

In order to do this, you will need to refer to two things:

• firstly, the combination you have just converted (our example above: □ □ □ □ □ ○)

• secondly, the original configuration of your draw, before you converted it ('pre-conversion', as in our example above: □ □ □ ▲ □ ▼)

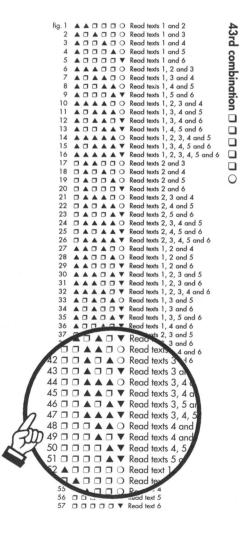

fig. 1  ▲ ▲ □ □ □ ○  Read texts 1 and 2
2  ▲ □ ▲ □ □ ○  Read texts 1 and 3
3  ▲ □ □ ▲ □ ○  Read texts 1 and 4
4  ▲ □ □ □ ▲ ○  Read texts 1 and 5
5  ▲ □ □ □ □ ▼  Read texts 1 and 6
6  ▲ ▲ ▲ □ □ ○  Read texts 1, 2 and 3
7  ▲ □ ▲ ▲ □ ○  Read texts 1, 3 and 4
8  ▲ □ □ ▲ ▲ ○  Read texts 1, 4 and 5
9  ▲ □ □ □ ▲ ▼  Read texts 1, 5 and 6
10  ▲ ▲ ▲ ▲ □ ○  Read texts 1, 2, 3 and 4
11  ▲ □ ▲ ▲ ▲ ○  Read texts 1, 3, 4 and 5
12  ▲ □ ▲ ▲ □ ▼  Read texts 1, 3, 4 and 6
13  ▲ □ □ ▲ ▲ ▼  Read texts 1, 4, 5 and 6
14  ▲ ▲ ▲ ▲ ▲ ○  Read texts 1, 2, 3, 4 and 5
15  ▲ □ ▲ ▲ ▲ ▼  Read texts 1, 3, 4, 5 and 6
16  ▲ ▲ ▲ ▲ ▲ ▼  Read texts 1, 2, 3, 4, 5 and 6
17  □ ▲ ▲ □ □ ○  Read texts 2 and 3
18  □ ▲ □ ▲ □ ○  Read texts 2 and 4
19  □ ▲ □ □ ▲ ○  Read texts 2 and 5
20  □ ▲ □ □ □ ▼  Read texts 2 and 6
21  □ ▲ ▲ ▲ □ ○  Read texts 2, 3 and 4
22  □ ▲ □ ▲ ▲ ○  Read texts 2, 4 and 5
23  □ ▲ □ □ ▲ ▼  Read texts 2, 5 and 6
24  □ ▲ ▲ ▲ ▲ ○  Read texts 2, 3, 4 and 5
25  □ ▲ □ ▲ ▲ ▼  Read texts 2, 4, 5 and 6
26  □ ▲ ▲ ▲ ▲ ▼  Read texts 2, 3, 4, 5 and 6
27  ▲ ▲ □ ▲ □ ○  Read texts 1, 2 and 4
28  ▲ ▲ □ □ ▲ ○  Read texts 1, 2 and 5
29  ▲ ▲ □ □ □ ▼  Read texts 1, 2 and 6
30  ▲ ▲ ▲ □ ▲ ○  Read texts 1, 2, 3 and 5
31  ▲ ▲ ▲ □ □ ▼  Read texts 1, 2, 3 and 6
32  ▲ ▲ ▲ ▲ □ ▼  Read texts 1, 2, 3, 4 and 6
33  ▲ □ ▲ □ ▲ ○  Read texts 1, 3 and 5
34  ▲ □ ▲ □ □ ▼  Read texts 1, 3 and 6
35  ▲ □ ▲ □ ▲ ▼  Read texts 1, 3, 5 and 6
36  ▲ □ □ ▲ ▲ ▼  Read texts 1, 4 and 6
37  □ □ ▲ □ ▲ ▼  Read texts 2, 3 and 5
...  Read texts ... 3 and 6
...  □ □ ▲ ▲ □ ○  Read texts ... 4 and 6
42  □ □ ▲ □ ▲ ○  Read texts 3 ...
43  □ □ ▲ □ ... Read texts 3 a...
44  □ □ ▲ ▲ ▲ ○  Read texts 3, 4 ...
45  □ □ ▲ ▲ □ ▼  Read texts 3, 4 ...
46  □ □ ▲ □ ▲ ▼  Read texts 3, 5 an...
47  □ □ ▲ ▲ ▲ ▼  Read texts 3, 4, 5...
48  □ □ □ ▲ ▲ ○  Read texts 4 and...
49  □ □ □ ▲ □ ▼  Read texts 4 and...
50  □ □ □ ▲ ▲ ▼  Read texts 4, 5 ...
51  □ □ □ □ ▲ ▼  Read texts 5 ...
52  ▲ □ □ □ □ ○  Read text 1
53  □ ▲ □ □ □ ○  Read te...
54  □ □ ▲ □ □ ○  Read tex...4
55  □ □ □ ▲ □ ○  Read ...
56  □ □ □ □ ▲ ○  Read text 5
57  □ □ □ □ □ ▼  Read text 6

*43rd combination □ □ □ □ □ ○*

**a** Firstly, consult the combination table at the front of the book (printed on the inside cover pages), where combination Nos. 1–64 are illustrated. Next to each combination you will find a page number directing you to the text on the relevant combination in the section on interpreting and understanding your dreams (from p. 259 onwards).

**b** You now need to refer to the table that appears alongside this section. Fifty-seven pre-conversion configurations (numbered 1–57) appear alongside each of the combinations. Look for the one that corresponds to your pre-conversion draw, and against it you will find a direction to the relevant text, where the context for the advice and predictions contained in your dream will be explained.

In the example we have been using, the combination (□ □ □ □ □ ○) can be identified as No. 43 (of the 64 possibilities illustrated in the combination table). This entry refers you to p. 315 and to the pre-conversion configuration table for the 43rd combination, where you will find the 57 configurations of this combination.

The pre-conversion configuration from our initial draw (symbols) can be identified as No. 49 and this refers you to texts 4 and 6 of the 43rd combination (p. 315):

**4** Your anxious nature drives you to constant activity. But by forcing events and manipulating circumstances as you do, you generate messy situations and endless obstacles and difficulties, without even realizing it. You would be well advised to calm down and stop stubbornly insisting on intervening in everything. But will you be able to take this advice on board?

**6** You are to be applauded if you have made efforts to resolve serious difficulties, to put a stop to a negative situation, or to correct or improve yourself. However, make sure that you have gone into everything in great depth and have not overlooked a detail that could turn out to be critical and dangerous. Only then can you be satisfied and sure of your results.

## It is not always necessary to convert your draw*

If your draw is composed entirely of squares or circles, there is naturally no need to convert it – it is already a combination.

All you need to do is refer directly to the combinations at the back of the book and find the one relevant to your draw. You need only read the opening paragraph and not the following six texts, since the opening paragraph relates exclusively to draws that do not require conversion.

Let's take the following draw as an example:

This draw does not need to be converted – it is made up entirely of squares and circles and is therefore already a combination.

Consult the combination chart (featuring 64 combinations) at the front of the book and pinpoint the one that relates to the draw. It points you to combination No. 54, which you will find on p. 329.

You need to read only the opening paragraph, not the six texts that follow.

### 54th combination ▢ ▢ ○ ▢ ○ ○

The feeling of being in sympathy with someone is a free and spontaneous emotion to which you can abandon yourself unreservedly. To become something deeper and more lasting, it must be left to develop naturally. In fact, violent emotions rarely lead to solid relationships, but to break-ups and an unstable and turbulent emotional life.

### IMPORTANT FOOTNOTE

• Never make more than one card draw per dream.

• If, having assessed the counsels and advice revealed by the symbolic content of your dream and by your card draw, you still feel the need for more information, this is because you have not yet assimilated fully the directions you have been given. Be patient, with yourself and with the information, and the meaning will come to you eventually.

• You may sometimes find that two or three dreams carry the same meaning. Do not be surprised by this. It only goes to show that you have yet to appreciate the full significance of the messages they are transmitting. That is why these messages are repeated in your dreams until you have grasped them completely and drawn the relevant conclusions.

# Glossary of symbols

## A

| | | |
|---|---|---|
| Abbey | *see* PRIEST | 206 |
| Abdomen | *see* BODY (19) | 79 |
| ABSCESS | | 53 |
| ABSENCE or ABSENT FRIENDS | | 53 |
| Abyss | *see* VOID | 248 |
| ACCIDENTS | | 54 |
| Accordion | *see* MUSICAL INSTRUMENTS | 188 |
| Accuse | *see* JUSTICE, LAWYER | 168 172 |
| ACROBAT | | 54 |
| ACTOR and ACTRESS | | 55 |
| Admiral | *see* OFFICER | 196 |
| ADULTERY | | 55 |
| Age | *see* BIRTHDAY | 76 |
| AIRPLANE | | 56 |
| Airport | *see* AIRPLANE | 56 |
| ALCHEMIST | | 57 |
| ALCOHOL | | 58 |
| Alley | *see* PATH | 200 |
| ALPHABET | | 58 |
| AMBASSADOR | | 58 |
| Amulet | *see* TALISMAN | 236 |
| ANCHOR | | 59 |
| ANGEL | | 59 |
| ANGER | | 60 |
| Animal | *see* specific animal in dream | |

| | | |
|---|---|---|
| Ankles | *see* BODY (32) | 79 |
| ANT | | 60 |
| ANTELOPE | | 60 |
| ANTENNA | | 60 |
| ANTIQUES DEALERS and ANTIQUES | | 61 |
| Anvil | *see* HAMMER | 158 |
| APARTMENT | | 61 |
| Apocalypse | *see* CATASTROPHE | 111 |
| APPLAUSE | | 63 |
| Apple | *see* FRUIT | 147 |
| Apricot | *see* FRUIT | 147 |
| APRON | | 63 |
| AQUARIUM | | 63 |
| ARCH | | 64 |
| ARENA | | 64 |
| Arm | *see* BODY (15) | 79 |
| Armchair | *see* POSTURE, VELVET | 206 246 |
| ARMY | | 65 |
| ARROW | | 66 |
| Assassin | *see* MURDER | 188 |
| Asylum | *see* FOOL/LUNATIC/ MADMAN | 145 |
| ATHLETE | | 66 |
| ATTIC | | 67 |
| Autumn | *see* GARDEN, TREE | 151 242 |

| | | |
|---|---|---|
| Avenue | *see* STREET | 232 |
| Awning | *see* CURTAIN | 127 |
| AXE | | 67 |

## B

| | | |
|---|---|---|
| BABY | | 67 |
| Baby's bottle | *see* BABY, | 67 |
| | MILK | 183 |
| Back | *see* BODY (22) | 79 |
| BAG | | 67 |
| Baker | *see* BREAD | 100 |
| BALCONY | | 68 |
| Ball | *see* GAMES and TOYS, | 150 |
| | RACKET/BAT, | 208 |
| | SPHERE, | 227 |
| | SPORT, | 229 |
| | WOOL | 256 |
| Ball | *see* DANCE | 127 |
| Ballet | *see* DANCE | 127 |
| Banana | *see* FRUIT | 147 |
| Bank | *see* CHEQUE, | 115 |
| | MONEY | 184 |
| BANKRUPTCY | | 68 |
| BAPTISM | | 69 |
| Barometer | *see* MEASURING | |
| | INSTRUMENTS | 179 |
| BARREL | | 69 |
| Barrel organ | *see* MUSICAL | |
| | INSTRUMENTS | 188 |
| Basket | *see* FRUIT, | 147 |
| | BAG | 67 |
| BATH | | 69 |
| BATS | | 71 |
| Beach | *see* SEA | 217 |
| BEANS | | 71 |
| BEAR | | 71 |

| | | |
|---|---|---|
| BEARD | | 71 |
| BEAVER | | 72 |
| Bed | *see* POSTURE | 206 |
| Beehive | *see* BEES, | 73 |
| | HONEY | 162 |
| BEER | | 72 |
| BEES | | 73 |
| BEGGAR | | 73 |
| BELL | | 73 |
| Belly | *see* BODY (19, 36) | 79 |
| BELT | | 74 |
| BENCH | | 74 |
| Bible | *see* BOOK | 97 |
| BICYCLE | | 74 |
| Billiards | *see* GAMES and TOYS, | 150 |
| | SPHERE, | 227 |
| | TABLE | 236 |
| BIRD | | 75 |
| Birth | *see* BABY, | 67 |
| | CHILDBIRTH | 116 |
| BIRTHDAY | | 76 |
| Bishop | *see* PRIEST | 206 |
| BISON | | 76 |
| BITE/BITING | | 76 |
| Black | *see* COLOUR | 120 |
| Blackberry | *see* FRUIT | 147 |
| BLANKET | | 77 |
| Blaze | *see* CATASTROPHE, | 111 |
| | CELLAR, | 113 |
| | FIRE | 139 |
| Blessing | *see* BAPTISM, | 69 |
| | PRIEST, | 206 |
| | MARRIAGE | 178 |
| BLIND ALLEY/DEAD END | | 77 |
| Blind | *see* BLINDNESS, | 77 |
| | CURTAIN | 127 |

| | | |
|---|---|---|
| BLINDNESS | | 77 |
| Blonde | see CORN, | 123 |
| | HAIR | 157 |
| Blood | see BODY (38) | 79 |
| Blowpipe | see ARROW, | 66 |
| | BOW, | 98 |
| | CATAPULT | 111 |
| Blue | see COLOUR | 120 |
| Boa constrictor | see SNAKE | 225 |
| Boar | see PIG | 201 |
| BOAT | | 78 |
| BODY | | 79 |
| Bolt | see KEY | 169 |
| Bomb | see EXPLOSION | 136 |
| Bones | see BODY (33) | 79 |
| BOOK | | 97 |
| Boots | see SHOES | 221 |
| BOTTLE | | 98 |
| BOW | | 98 |
| BOWL | | 99 |
| BOX | | 99 |
| Boy | see CHILD | 116 |
| BRACELET | | 100 |
| BRACES | | 100 |
| Braid | see HAIR, | 157 |
| | SPIRAL | 229 |
| Branch | see TREE | 242 |
| BREAD | | 100 |
| Breastfeeding | see BABY, | 67 |
| | BODY (18) | 79 |
| Breasts | see BODY (18) | 79 |
| BRICK | | 101 |
| BRIDGE | | 101 |
| Bronze | see METAL | 181 |
| BROOM | | 102 |
| Brown | see COLOUR | 120 |
| Brush | see COMB, | 122 |
| | HAIR, | 157 |
| | PAINTER | 199 |
| Bubble | see SPHERE | 227 |
| BUCKLE or EARRINGS | | 102 |
| Buddha | see GOD(S) | 155 |
| Buffalo | see BULL, | 102 |
| | OX | 198 |
| BULL | | 102 |
| Bullfight | see ARENA, | 64 |
| | BULL | 102 |
| Burglary | see THIEF | 239 |
| BUSH | | 103 |
| BUSINESS CARD | | 103 |
| Butcher | see MEAT | 180 |
| BUTTER | | 103 |
| BUTTERFLY | | 103 |
| BUTTONS | | 104 |

## C

| | | |
|---|---|---|
| CABBAGE | | 104 |
| CADUCEUS | | 104 |
| Cage | see BIRD, | 75 |
| | LION, | 175 |
| | ZOO | 258 |
| Calculator | see COUNTING | 124 |
| CALENDAR | | 105 |
| CAMEL | | 105 |
| CAMERA | | 105 |
| CAMPING | | 105 |
| CANDLE | | 106 |
| CANNON | | 106 |
| Canoe | see BOAT | 78 |
| Canvas | see PAINTER | 199 |
| CAPE | | 107 |

| | | |
|---|---|---|
| CAR | | 107 |
| Cardinal | see PRIEST | 206 |
| CARESS | | 109 |
| Carnation | see FLOWER | 142 |
| CARROT | | 110 |
| CART | | 110 |
| Cash | see MONEY | 184 |
| Castanets | see MUSICAL | |
| | INSTRUMENTS | 188 |
| CASTLE | | 110 |
| CAT | | 110 |
| CATAPULT | | 111 |
| CATASTROPHE | | 111 |
| Caterpillar | see BUTTERFLY, | 103 |
| | WORM | 256 |
| CAULDRON | | 112 |
| CAVE | | 112 |
| CELLAR | | 113 |
| CEMETERY | | 114 |
| CENTAUR | | 114 |
| CENTRE | | 115 |
| Chain | see PRISON, | 207 |
| | SPIRAL | 229 |
| Chair | see POSTURE | 206 |
| Champagne | see BOTTLE, | 98 |
| | WINE | 254 |
| Check | see CHEQUE | 115 |
| Cheeks | see BODY (4) | 79 |
| CHEESE | | 115 |
| CHEQUE | | 115 |
| Cherry | see FRUIT | 147 |
| Chess | see GAMES and TOYS | 150 |
| Chest | see BODY (18) | 79 |
| CHESTNUT | | 115 |
| CHILD | | 116 |

| | | |
|---|---|---|
| CHILDBIRTH | | 116 |
| CHIMNEY/FIREPLACE | | 117 |
| CHOCOLATE | | 117 |
| Christ | see CROSS, | 125 |
| | GOD(S) | 155 |
| CHRISTMAS | | 117 |
| Chrysanthemum | see FLOWER | 142 |
| Church | see TEMPLE | 238 |
| Cinema | see SHOW | 222 |
| CIRCLE | | 118 |
| Circus | see ACROBAT, | 54 |
| | ARENA, | 64 |
| | CLOWN, | 118 |
| | MAGIC, | 177 |
| | SHOW, | 222 |
| | ZOO | 258 |
| Climbing | see LADDER, | 171 |
| | MOUNTAIN, | 186 |
| | TOWER | 240 |
| CLOCK | | 118 |
| Clogs | see SHOES | 221 |
| Clothes | see COSTUME | 123 |
| Cloud | see RAIN, | 208 |
| | SKY | 223 |
| CLOWN | | 118 |
| Coach | see TRAIN, | 241 |
| | UNDERGROUND/ | |
| | SUBWAY | 245 |
| COAL | | 119 |
| COAT | | 119 |
| Cobra | see SNAKE | 225 |
| COCK | | 119 |
| COCKROACH | | 119 |
| COFFEE | | 120 |
| COFFIN | | 120 |
| Colonel | see OFFICER | 196 |

| | | |
|---|---|---|
| COLOR/COLOUR | | 120 |
| COMB | | 122 |
| COMBAT | | 122 |
| Comet | see STAR | 230 |
| COMMUNION | | 122 |
| Compass | see MEASURING INSTRUMENTS | 179 |
| Concert | see SHOW | 222 |
| CONSTRUCTION SITE | | 122 |
| Cooking, cooked | see FISH, KITCHEN, MEAT | 140 170 180 |
| Copper | see METAL | 181 |
| CORAL | | 123 |
| CORN | | 123 |
| CORNERS | | 123 |
| Corpse | see FUNERAL | 150 |
| Corridor | see TUNNEL | 244 |
| COSTUME | | 123 |
| COUNTING | | 124 |
| COUNTRY | | 124 |
| COUPLE | | 125 |
| Courtyard | see CENTRE, CIRCLE, GARDEN, SQUARE | 115 118 151 230 |
| CRAB | | 125 |
| Cradle | see BABY, BOAT | 67 78 |
| Crater | see MOUNTAIN | 186 |
| CRIB | | 125 |
| CROCODILE | | 125 |
| CROSS | | 125 |
| CROSSROADS | | 126 |
| Crow | see BIRD | 75 |
| CROWN | | 126 |
| Crying | see TEARS | 237 |
| CRYSTAL | | 126 |
| Cul-de-Sac | see BLIND ALLEY/ DEAD END | 77 |
| Cup | see BOWL, GLASS | 99 154 |
| CUPBOARD | | 126 |
| Currant | see FRUIT | 147 |
| CURTAIN | | 127 |
| Cutting | see KNIFE | 170 |
| Cyst | see ABSCESS | 53 |

**D**

| | | |
|---|---|---|
| Dagger | see KNIFE | 170 |
| DAM | | 127 |
| DANCE | | 127 |
| DATE | | 128 |
| Date | see FRUIT | 147 |
| Daughter | see CHILD | 116 |
| Dawn | see LIGHT, SUN | 174 234 |
| Deaf | see BODY (6) | 79 |
| Death | see FUNERAL | 150 |
| DEBT | | 128 |
| DEER | | 128 |
| Demon | see DEVIL | 129 |
| Departure | see SUITCASE, TRAIN | 234 241 |
| DESERT | | 128 |
| DETOUR | | 129 |
| DEVIL | | 129 |
| Diamond | see CRYSTAL, STONE | 126 231 |
| Dice | see GAMES and TOYS | 150 |
| Dinosaur | see MONSTER | 185 |

| | | |
|---|---|---|
| DIRECTION | | 129 |
| Disease | *see* BODY, | 79 |
| | DOCTOR, | 130 |
| | HOSPITAL | 164 |
| DISGUST | | 130 |
| Disk | *see* CIRCLE | 118 |
| DIVER | | 130 |
| Diving | *see* BATH, | 70 |
| | SEA, | 217 |
| | VOID, | 248 |
| | WATER | 250 |
| Divorce | *see* COUPLE | 125 |
| DOCTOR | | 130 |
| DOG | | 131 |
| Dollar | *see* MONEY | 184 |
| Dolphin | *see* FISH | 140 |
| Dominoes | *see* GAMES and TOYS | 150 |
| DONKEY | | 131 |
| DOOR | | 132 |
| Dough | *see* BREAD | 100 |
| Dove | *see* BIRD | 75 |
| Downpour | *see* RAIN | 208 |
| DRAGON | | 132 |
| DRAWER | | 133 |
| DRAWING | | 133 |
| Dress | *see* COSTUME | 123 |
| Drinking | *see* BEER, | 72 |
| | BOTTLE, | 98 |
| | COFFEE, | 120 |
| | FRUIT, | 147 |
| | GLASS, | 154 |
| | MILK, | 183 |
| | WATER, | 250 |
| | WINE | 254 |
| Driving | *see* CAR | 107 |
| DROWNING | | 133 |

| | | |
|---|---|---|
| Drum | *see* MUSICAL | |
| | INSTRUMENTS | 188 |
| Duck | *see* BIRD | 75 |
| Duel | *see* COMBAT, | 122 |
| | SWORD | 235 |
| Dustbin | *see* RUBBISH | 213 |
| Dustman | *see* RUBBISH | 213 |
| Dwarf | *see* IMP/GOBLIN/ELF | 167 |

### E

| | | |
|---|---|---|
| Eagle | *see* BIRD, | 75 |
| Ears | *see* BODY (6) | 79 |
| East | *see* DIRECTION | 129 |
| ECLIPSE | | 134 |
| Eel | *see* FISH | 140 |
| EGG | | 134 |
| Eight | *see* NUMBER | 193 |
| Elbow | *see* BODY (15) | 79 |
| ELECTRICITY | | 135 |
| Electricity | *see* MEASURING | |
| meter | INSTRUMENTS | 179 |
| ELEPHANT | | 136 |
| Eleven | *see* NUMBER | 193 |
| Entrance | *see* DOOR | 132 |
| Envelope | *see* POSTMAN, | 205 |
| | WRITING | 257 |
| Exam | *see* SCHOOL | 216 |
| EXCREMENT | | 136 |
| Exit | *see* DOOR, | 132 |
| | MAZE | 179 |
| EXPLOSION | | 136 |
| Eye(s) | *see* BODY (5) | 79 |

### F

| | | |
|---|---|---|
| FACTORY | | 137 |
| FAME | | 137 |

| | | |
|---|---|---|
| FAMILY | | 138 |
| Fat | see BODY (19) | 79 |
| FATHER | | 138 |
| Father Christmas | see CHRISTMAS | 117 |
| FEATHER | | 138 |
| Feet | see BODY (31) | 79 |
| Felt | see HAT, | 160 |
| | WRITING | 257 |
| FEVER | | 139 |
| Fig | see FRUIT | 147 |
| Film | see SHOW | 222 |
| FINE | | 139 |
| Fingers | see BODY (17) | 79 |
| Fir | see CHRISTMAS, | 117 |
| | TREE | 242 |
| FIRE | | 139 |
| FIREFIGHTER | | 140 |
| Firework | see FIRE | 139 |
| FISH | | 140 |
| Fishing | see FISH | 140 |
| Fist | see BODY (16) | 79 |
| Five | see NUMBER | 193 |
| FLAG | | 142 |
| Flame | see FIRE | 139 |
| Flood | see CATASTROPHE, | 111 |
| | CELLAR, | 113 |
| | WATER | 250 |
| FLOUR | | 142 |
| FLOWER | | 142 |
| FLY | | 144 |
| FLYING | | 145 |
| Flute | see MUSICAL | |
| | INSTRUMENTS | 188 |
| FOG | | 145 |
| FOOL/LUNATIC/MADMAN | | 145 |

| | | |
|---|---|---|
| Forehead | see BODY (2) | 79 |
| FOREST | | 146 |
| Fortune | see MONEY, | 184 |
| | TREASURE | 242 |
| Forty | see NUMBER | 193 |
| FOUNTAIN | | 146 |
| Four | see NUMBER | 193 |
| FOX | | 146 |
| FRIENDS and FRIENDSHIP | | 146 |
| FROG | | 147 |
| FRUIT | | 147 |
| FUNERAL | | 150 |
| Fur | see COAT | 119 |

**G**

| | | |
|---|---|---|
| Game | see HARE, | 159 |
| | HUNTING, | 165 |
| | RABBIT | 208 |
| GAMES and TOYS | | 150 |
| GARDEN | | 151 |
| GARLIC | | 151 |
| Gauge | see MEASURING | |
| | INSTRUMENTS | 179 |
| Gazelle | see ANTELOPE | 60 |
| Gesture | see BODY (15) | 79 |
| GHOST | | 152 |
| GIANT | | 153 |
| GIFT | | 153 |
| GIRAFFE | | 154 |
| Gladiator | see ARENA | 64 |
| GLASS | | 154 |
| Glove | see BODY (16) | 79 |
| GLUE | | 154 |
| GOAT | | 155 |
| GOD(S) | | 155 |

| | | |
|---|---|---|
| Gold | *see* METAL | 181 |
| Gondola | *see* BOAT | 78 |
| Goose | *see* BIRD | 75 |
| Gooseberry | *see* FRUIT | 147 |
| Gorilla | *see* MONKEY | 185 |
| GRAIN | | 155 |
| Grape | *see* FRUIT, | 147 |
| | WINE | 254 |
| GRATER | | 156 |
| Green | *see* COLOUR | 120 |
| Grey | *see* COLOUR | 120 |
| Grotto | *see* CAVE | 112 |
| GROUND/SOIL/EARTH/LAND | | 156 |
| GUARD | | 156 |
| Guitar | *see* MUSICAL | |
| | INSTRUMENTS | 188 |
| GUN | | 157 |

**H**

| | | |
|---|---|---|
| HAIR | | 157 |
| HAMMER | | 158 |
| HANDKERCHIEF | | 158 |
| Hands | *see* BODY (16) | 79 |
| HANGING | | 159 |
| HARBOUR | | 159 |
| HARE | | 159 |
| HARLEQUIN | | 160 |
| Harmonium | *see* MUSICAL | |
| | INSTRUMENTS | 188 |
| Harp | *see* MUSICAL | |
| | INSTRUMENTS | 188 |
| Harvest | *see* CORN, | 123 |
| | GRAIN | 155 |
| HAT | | 160 |
| Head | *see* BODY (1) | 79 |

| | | |
|---|---|---|
| Hearse | *see* CAR, | 107 |
| | FUNERAL | 150 |
| Heart | *see* BODY (34) | 79 |
| HEDGEHOG | | 161 |
| Heel | *see* BODY (31) | 79 |
| Heliotrope | *see* FLOWER | 142 |
| HELL | | 161 |
| Helmet | *see* HAND | 79 |
| Hen | *see* BIRD, | 75 |
| | EGG | 134 |
| HERO | | 161 |
| Hill | *see* MOUNTAIN | 186 |
| Hips | *see* BODY (25) | 79 |
| HOLE | | 162 |
| HONEY | | 162 |
| Hopscotch | *see* GAMES and TOYS | 150 |
| Horn | *see* MUSICAL | |
| | INSTRUMENTS | 188 |
| HORSE | | 162 |
| Horseshoe | *see* HORSE | 162 |
| HOSPITAL | | 164 |
| Hot-air balloon | *see* SPHERE | 227 |
| HOTEL | | 164 |
| HOURGLASS | | 164 |
| HOUSE | | 164 |
| Hundred | *see* NUMBER | 193 |
| HUNTING | | 165 |

**I**

| | | |
|---|---|---|
| ICE | | 166 |
| Ice-skating, ice-skater | *see* ICE | 166 |
| IDENTITY CARD | | 166 |
| IMP/GOBLIN/ELF | | 167 |
| INHERITANCE | | 167 |

| | | |
|---|---|---|
| Ink | *see* WRITING | 257 |
| Inn | *see* HOTEL | 164 |
| Insect | *see* ANT, | 60 |
| | BEES, | 73 |
| | BUTTERFLY, | 103 |
| | COCKROACH, | 119 |
| | FLY, | 144 |
| | LADYBIRD/ | |
| | LADYBUG, | 172 |
| | SPIDER, | 228 |
| | WASP | 249 |
| Intestines | *see* BODY (37) | 79 |
| Iris | *see* FLOWER | 142 |
| Iron | *see* METAL | 181 |
| Ironworks | *see* FIRE, | 139 |
| | METAL | 181 |
| ISLAND | | 167 |
| IVY | | 167 |

**J**

| | | |
|---|---|---|
| Jacket | *see* COSTUME | 123 |
| Jam | *see* CAULDRON, | 112 |
| | FRUIT, | 147 |
| | SUGAR | 233 |
| JELLYFISH | | 167 |
| Jesus | *see* CROSS, | 125 |
| | GOD(S) | 155 |
| Jewellery | *see* BRACELET, | 100 |
| | BUCKLE or | |
| | EARRINGS, | 102 |
| | CROWN, | 126 |
| | NECKLACE, | 190 |
| | RING, | 210 |
| | STONE, | 231 |
| | TALISMAN, | 236 |
| | TREASURE | 242 |
| JOURNALIST | | 168 |
| Judge | *see* JUSTICE | 168 |

| | | |
|---|---|---|
| JUGGLER | | 168 |
| Jungle | *see* FOREST | 146 |
| JUSTICE | | 168 |

**K**

| | | |
|---|---|---|
| KANGAROO | | 169 |
| KEY | | 169 |
| Kidneys | *see* BODY (24) | 79 |
| King | *see* FAME | 137 |
| KISS | | 169 |
| KITCHEN | | 170 |
| KITE | | 170 |
| Kneeling | *see* BODY (30), | 79 |
| | POSTURE, | 206 |
| | PRAYING | 206 |
| Knees | *see* BODY (30) | 79 |
| KNIFE | | 170 |
| Knitting | *see* WOOL | 256 |
| Knot | *see* ROPE, | 212 |
| | SHOES | 221 |

**L**

| | | |
|---|---|---|
| Laboratory | *see* ALCHEMIST | 57 |
| Labourer | *see* GROUND/SOIL/ | |
| | EARTH/LAND, | 156 |
| | PEASANT | 200 |
| LACE | | 171 |
| LADDER | | 171 |
| LADYBIRD/LADYBUG | | 172 |
| Lake | *see* BATH, | 69 |
| | WATER | 250 |
| LAMA | | 172 |
| LAMB | | 172 |
| Lamp | *see* LIGHT, | 174 |
| | OIL | 197 |
| LAWYER | | 172 |

| | | |
|---|---|---|
| Lead | *see* METAL | 181 |
| Leech | *see* BITE/BITING, | 76 |
| | BODY (38) | 79 |
| Legs | *see* BODY (29) | 79 |
| Lemon | *see* FRUIT | 147 |
| Letter | *see* POSTMAN, | 205 |
| | WRITING | 257 |
| LIFT or ELEVATOR | | 173 |
| LIGHT | | 174 |
| Lighthouse | *see* LIGHT, | 174 |
| | TOWER | 240 |
| Lightning | *see* STORM | 232 |
| Lilac | *see* FLOWER | 142 |
| Lily | *see* FLOWER | 142 |
| Lily of the valley | *see* FLOWER | 142 |
| LIMPING | | 174 |
| Line | *see* QUEUE | 207 |
| LION | | 175 |
| Lips | *see* BODY (9) | 79 |
| Little finger | *see* BODY (17) | 79 |
| Liver | *see* BODY (35) | 79 |
| LIZARD | | 175 |
| LLAMA | | 175 |
| Lock | *see* KEY | 169 |
| LOCOMOTIVE | | 175 |
| Lorry | *see* CAR | 107 |
| Lottery | *see* GAMES and TOYS, | 150 |
| | STREET | 232 |
| Lotus | *see* FLOWER | 142 |
| LOVE | | 176 |
| LOVER | | 176 |
| Luggage | *see* BAG, | 67 |
| | SUITCASE | 234 |
| Lumberjack | *see* AXE, | 67 |
| | TREE | 242 |

| | | |
|---|---|---|
| Lying down | *see* POSTURE | 206 |
| LYNX | | 177 |

**M**

| | | |
|---|---|---|
| Mackerel | *see* FISH | 140 |
| MAGIC | | 177 |
| Magician | *see* MAGIC | 177 |
| Man | *see* MEN and | |
| | WOMEN | 181 |
| MAP | | 177 |
| Marble | *see* GAMES and TOYS, | 150 |
| | SPHERE | 227 |
| MARRIAGE | | 178 |
| Marsh | *see* WATER | 250 |
| Mascot | *see* TALISMAN | 236 |
| Mask | *see* CLOWN | 118 |
| Mass | *see* BAPTISM, | 69 |
| | FUNERAL, | 150 |
| | MARRIAGE, | 178 |
| | TEMPLE | 238 |
| Match | *see* ARENA, | 64 |
| | COMBAT, | 122 |
| | SPORT | 229 |
| MATCHES | | 178 |
| Mayor | *see* FAME | 137 |
| MAZE | | 179 |
| MEASURING INSTRUMENTS | | 179 |
| MEAT | | 180 |
| MEDAL, LOCKET | | 180 |
| Melon | *see* FRUIT | 147 |
| MEN and WOMEN | | 181 |
| MERRY-GO-ROUND | | 181 |
| METAL | | 181 |
| Meteorite | *see* STAR, | 230 |
| | STONE | 231 |
| MICROPHONE | | 182 |

| | | |
|---|---|---|
| MICROSCOPE | | 182 |
| Middle | *see* CENTRE, | 115 |
| | NUMBER | 193 |
| Midwife | *see* CHILDBIRTH | 116 |
| MILK | | 183 |
| MILL | | 183 |
| Miller | *see* MILL | 183 |
| Milometer/ | *see* MEASURING | |
| odometer | INSTRUMENTS | 179 |
| Mimosa | *see* FLOWER | 142 |
| Mine | *see* CAVE, | 112 |
| | TUNNEL | 244 |
| Minister | *see* FAME | 137 |
| Mirage | *see* DESERT | 128 |
| MIRROR | | 183 |
| MOLE | | 184 |
| MONEY | | 184 |
| Monk | *see* PRIEST | 206 |
| MONKEY | | 185 |
| MONSTER | | 185 |
| MONUMENT | | 185 |
| MOON | | 185 |
| Mosque | *see* TEMPLE | 238 |
| Mosquito | *see* BITE/BITING, | 76 |
| | FLY, | 144 |
| | WASP | 249 |
| MOTHER | | 186 |
| Motor | *see* CAR | 107 |
| Motorcycle | *see* BICYCLE | 74 |
| MOUNTAIN | | 186 |
| Mouth | *see* BODY (8) | 79 |
| MOVING HOUSE | | 187 |
| MUD | | 187 |
| Mule | *see* DONKEY | 131 |
| MURDER | | 188 |

| | | |
|---|---|---|
| MUSEUM | | 188 |
| MUSHROOM | | 188 |
| Music | *see* MUSICAL | |
| | INSTRUMENTS, | 188 |
| | SINGING, SONG | 222 |
| MUSICAL INSTRUMENTS | | 188 |
| MUSTARD | | 190 |

## N

| | | |
|---|---|---|
| NAIL | | 190 |
| Nails | *see* BODY (17) | 79 |
| Nape of neck | *see* BODY (3) | 79 |
| Narcissus | *see* FLOWER | 142 |
| Neck | *see* BODY (12), | 79 |
| | NECKLACE | 190 |
| NECKLACE | | 190 |
| NEEDLE | | 191 |
| NEST | | 191 |
| NET | | 192 |
| Nightingale | *see* BIRD | 75 |
| Nine | *see* NUMBER | 193 |
| North | *see* DIRECTION | 129 |
| Nose | *see* BODY (7) | 79 |
| Nostril | *see* BODY (7) | 79 |
| Notebook | *see* PENCIL, | 201 |
| | WRITING | 257 |
| NUDITY | | 192 |
| NUMBER | | 193 |
| Nurse | *see* HOSPITAL | 164 |
| Nut | *see* FRUIT | 147 |

## O

| | | |
|---|---|---|
| Oar | *see* BOAT | 78 |
| Oasis | *see* DESERT, | 128 |
| | ISLAND | 167 |

| | | |
|---|---|---|
| Obstacle | see BLIND ALLEY/ | |
| | DEAD END, | 77 |
| | WALL | 248 |
| Ocean | see SEA, | 217 |
| | WATER | 250 |
| OFFICER | | 196 |
| OGRE | | 197 |
| OIL | | 197 |
| Olive | see FRUIT | 147 |
| One | see NUMBER | 193 |
| ONE-EYED | | 198 |
| Onion | see PLANT | 203 |
| Opera | see SHOW, | 222 |
| | SINGING, SONG | 222 |
| Orange | see COLOUR, | 120 |
| | FRUIT | 147 |
| Orchestra | see MUSICAL | |
| | INSTRUMENTS, | 188 |
| | SHOW | 222 |
| Orchid | see FLOWER | 142 |
| Organ | see MUSICAL | |
| | INSTRUMENTS | 188 |
| Overall | see APRON | 63 |
| Owl | see BIRD | 75 |
| OX | | 198 |
| OYSTER | | 198 |

**P**

| | | |
|---|---|---|
| Pagoda | see TEMPLE | 238 |
| PAINTER | | 199 |
| Painting | see COLOUR, | 120 |
| | PAINTER, | 199 |
| | SCHOOL, | 216 |
| | SLATE, | 224 |
| | SPONGE | 229 |
| PARACHUTE | | 199 |

| | | |
|---|---|---|
| Paradise | see ANGEL, | 59 |
| | GARDEN | 151 |
| Parent | see FAMILY, | 138 |
| | FATHER, | 138 |
| | MOTHER | 186 |
| PASSPORT | | 199 |
| Pastor | see PRIEST | 206 |
| PATH | | 200 |
| Pavement | see STREET | 232 |
| Peach | see FRUIT | 147 |
| Peacock | see BIRD | 75 |
| Peak | see LADDER, | 171 |
| | MOUNTAIN | 186 |
| Pear | see FRUIT | 147 |
| Pearl | see OYSTER | 198 |
| PEASANT | | 200 |
| Pebble | see STONE | 231 |
| Pen | see WRITING | 257 |
| PENCIL | | 201 |
| Pendulum | see CLOCK | 118 |
| Peony | see FLOWER | 142 |
| Pepper | see SALT and PEPPER | 214 |
| Petrol | see CAR | 107 |
| PHOTOGRAPH | | 201 |
| Piano | see MUSICAL | |
| | INSTRUMENTS | 188 |
| PIG | | 201 |
| Pike | see FISH | 140 |
| PILL | | 202 |
| Pilot | see AIRPLANE, | 56 |
| | OFFICER | 196 |
| Pineapple | see FRUIT | 147 |
| PIPE | | 202 |
| Pipes | see MUSICAL | |
| | INSTRUMENTS | 188 |
| PIRATE | | 203 |

| | | |
|---|---|---|
| Pistol | *see* GUN | 157 |
| Plait | *see* HAIR | 157 |
| Plan | *see* MAP | 177 |
| PLANE TOOL | | 203 |
| Planet | *see* SPHERE | 227 |
| PLANT | | 203 |
| PLAYING CARDS | | 204 |
| Plum | *see* FRUIT | 147 |
| POISON | | 204 |
| Policeman | *see* OFFICER, | 196 |
| | STICK | 231 |
| Pond | *see* BATH, | 69 |
| | WATER | 250 |
| Poor | *see* BEGGAR | 73 |
| Pope | *see* FAME, | 137 |
| | PRIEST | 206 |
| POSTCARD | | 205 |
| POSTER | | 205 |
| POSTMAN | | 205 |
| POSTURE | | 206 |
| Pot | *see* CAULDRON | 112 |
| PRAYING | | 206 |
| Pregnancy | *see* BABY, | 67 |
| | BODY (19), | 79 |
| | CHILDBIRTH, | 116 |
| | MOTHER | 186 |
| President | *see* FAME | 137 |
| PRIEST | | 206 |
| Prince | *see* FAME | 137 |
| PRISON | | 207 |
| PROSTITUTE | | 207 |
| PUPPET | | 207 |
| Pursuit | *see* MONSTER, | 185 |
| | TIGER, | 239 |
| | UNDERGROUND/ | |
| | SUBWAY | 245 |

| | | |
|---|---|---|
| Puzzle | *see* GAMES and TOYS, | 150 |
| | MAZE | 179 |
| Pygmy | *see* IMP/GOBLIN/ELF | 167 |
| Pyramid | *see* LADDER, | 171 |
| | MOUNTAIN, | 186 |
| | TRIANGLE | 244 |

**Q**

| | | |
|---|---|---|
| Queen | *see* FAME | 137 |
| QUEUE | | 207 |
| Quiver | *see* ARROW, | 66 |
| | BOW | 98 |

**R**

| | | |
|---|---|---|
| Rabbi | *see* PRIEST | 206 |
| RABBIT | | 208 |
| Race | *see* BICYCLE, | 74 |
| | CAR, | 107 |
| | RUNNING, | 214 |
| | SPORT | 229 |
| RACKET/BAT | | 208 |
| RADIO | | 208 |
| Raft | *see* BOAT | 78 |
| Rail | *see* TRAIN | 241 |
| Railway | *see* LOCOMOTIVE, | 175 |
| | TRAIN | 241 |
| RAIN | | 208 |
| RAINBOW | | 209 |
| Raincoat | *see* RAIN | 208 |
| RAKE | | 209 |
| RAM | | 210 |
| Raspberry | *see* FRUIT | 147 |
| RAT | | 210 |
| Raw | *see* FISH, | 140 |
| | MEAT | 180 |
| Ray | *see* FISH | 140 |

| | | |
|---|---|---|
| Red | *see* COLOUR | 120 |
| Referee | *see* ARENA, | 64 |
| | JUSTICE, | 168 |
| | SPORT | 229 |
| Rescuer | *see* DROWNING | 133 |
| Revolver | *see* GUN | 157 |
| Ribs | *see* BODY (21) | 79 |
| Rice | *see* GRAIN | 155 |
| RIDER | | 210 |
| RING | | 210 |
| Ring finger | *see* BODY (17) | 79 |
| River | *see* BATH, | 69 |
| | BOAT, | 78 |
| | WATER | 250 |
| Road | *see* STREET | 232 |
| ROBOTS | | 211 |
| ROCKET | | 211 |
| ROOF | | 212 |
| Room | *see* HOUSE, | 164 |
| | MONEY, | 184 |
| | SHOW | 222 |
| ROPE | | 212 |
| Rose | *see* FLOWER | 142 |
| Route | *see* STREET | 232 |
| RUBBISH | | 213 |
| Ruby | *see* RING, | 210 |
| | STONE | 231 |
| RUG | | 213 |
| Ruler | *see* MEASURING | |
| | INSTRUMENTS | 179 |
| RUNNING | | 214 |

**S**

| | | |
|---|---|---|
| Sabre | *see* SWORD | 235 |
| Sadness | *see* TEARS | 237 |
| SALAD | | 214 |
| Salmon | *see* FISH | 140 |
| Salt | *see* SALT and PEPPER | 214 |
| SALT and PEPPER | | 214 |
| Sandals | *see* SHOES | 221 |
| Santa Claus | *see* CHRISTMAS | 117 |
| Sapphire | *see* RING, | 210 |
| | STONE | 231 |
| Sardine | *see* FISH | 140 |
| Saturn | *see* RING, | 210 |
| | SPHERE | 227 |
| Saucepan | *see* CAULDRON | 112 |
| SAW | | 215 |
| Saxophone | *see* MUSICAL | |
| | INSTRUMENTS | 188 |
| SCAFFOLDING | | 215 |
| SCALES | | 215 |
| SCHOOL | | 216 |
| SCISSORS | | 217 |
| SCORPION | | 217 |
| SEA | | 217 |
| SEAL | | 218 |
| Seal | *see* RING | 210 |
| Season | *see* GARDEN, | 151 |
| | TREE | 242 |
| SECT | | 218 |
| Seed | *see* CORN, | 123 |
| | GRAIN | 155 |
| Seven | *see* NUMBER | 193 |
| Sexual organs | *see* BODY (26) | 79 |
| SHADOW | | 218 |
| Shark | *see* FISH | 140 |
| SHEEP | | 219 |
| Shell | *see* SPIRAL | 229 |
| SHEPHERD | | 219 |
| SHIELD | | 219 |

| | | |
|---|---|---|
| SHIP | | 220 |
| Shipwreck | *see* BOAT, | 78 |
| | CATASTROPHE, | 111 |
| | SHIP | 220 |
| SHIRT | | 220 |
| SHOEMAKER | | 220 |
| SHOES | | 221 |
| Shooting star | *see* STAR | 230 |
| SHOP | | 221 |
| Shopkeeper | *see* SHOP | 221 |
| Shoulders | *see* BODY (14) | 79 |
| SHOUTING | | 222 |
| SHOW | | 222 |
| Shower | *see* RAIN | 208 |
| Sidewalk | *see* STREET | 232 |
| SIEVE | | 222 |
| Silhouette | *see* MEN and WOMEN | 181 |
| SINGING, SONG | | 222 |
| SIREN | | 223 |
| Sitting | *see* POSTURE | 206 |
| Six | *see* NUMBER | 193 |
| Skeleton | *see* BODY (40) | 79 |
| Skin | *see* BODY (39) | 79 |
| Skirt | *see* COSTUME | 123 |
| SKY | | 223 |
| Skyscraper | *see* TOWER | 240 |
| SLAP | | 224 |
| SLATE | | 224 |
| Sled | *see* LADDER, | 171 |
| | MOUNTAIN | 186 |
| Slope | *see* MOUNTAIN | 186 |
| Small | *see* BABY, | 67 |
| | CHILD, | 116 |
| | IMP/GOBLIN/ELF | 167 |
| Smoke | *see* CHIMNEY/ | |
| | FIREPLACE, | 117 |
| | FIRE, | 139 |
| | PIPE, | 202 |
| | TOBACCO | 239 |
| SNAIL | | 224 |
| SNAKE | | 225 |
| Sneezing | *see* BODY (7) | 79 |
| SNOW | | 225 |
| SOAP | | 226 |
| Socks | *see* BODY (31), | 79 |
| | SHOES | 221 |
| South | *see* DIRECTION | 129 |
| Space | *see* STAR, | 230 |
| | VOID | 248 |
| SPADE | | 226 |
| SPECTACLES | | 226 |
| SPEECH | | 227 |
| Speedometer | *see* MEASURING | |
| | INSTRUMENTS | 179 |
| SPHERE | | 227 |
| Spice | *see* SALT and PEPPER | 214 |
| SPIDER | | 228 |
| Spine | *see* BODY (23), | 79 |
| SPIRAL | | 229 |
| Spirit | *see* IMP/GOBLIN/ELF | 167 |
| SPONGE | | 229 |
| SPOON | | 229 |
| SPORT | | 229 |
| SPOTS | | 230 |
| Sprain | *see* BODY (32) | 79 |
| Spring | *see* GARDEN, | 151 |
| | TREE, | 242 |
| | FOUNTAIN, | 146 |
| | WATER | 250 |
| SQUARE | | 230 |

| | | |
|---|---|---:|
| SQUIRREL | | 230 |
| Stadium | *see* ARENA, | 64 |
| | SPORT | 229 |
| STAR | | 230 |
| Station | *see* TRAIN | 241 |
| Steel | *see* METAL | 181 |
| Steering wheel | *see* CAR | 107 |
| STICK | | 231 |
| Sting | *see* BEES, | 73 |
| | HOSPITAL, | 164 |
| | WASP | 249 |
| Stomach | *see* BODY (19, 36) | 79 |
| STONE | | 231 |
| STORM | | 232 |
| Stranger | *see* MEN and WOMEN | 181 |
| Strangling | *see* BODY (12) | 79 |
| STRAW | | 232 |
| Strawberry | *see* FRUIT | 147 |
| STREET | | 232 |
| Subway | *see* UNDERGROUND | 245 |
| SUGAR | | 233 |
| SUITCASE | | 234 |
| Summer | *see* GARDEN, | 151 |
| | TREE | 242 |
| Summit | *see* LADDER, | 171 |
| | MOUNTAIN | 186 |
| SUN | | 234 |
| Swallow | *see* BIRD | 75 |
| Swamp | *see* WATER | 250 |
| SWAN | *see* BIRD | 75 |
| Sweater | *see* WOOL | 256 |
| SWEET | | 235 |
| Swimming | *see* BATH, | 69 |
| | DROWNING, | 133 |
| | WATER | 250 |

| | | |
|---|---|---:|
| SWING | | 235 |
| SWORD | | 235 |
| Synagogue | *see* TEMPLE | 238 |

## T

| | | |
|---|---|---:|
| TABLE | | 236 |
| Tablecloth | *see* CIRCLE, | 118 |
| | SQUARE, | 230 |
| | TABLE | 236 |
| TAIL | | 236 |
| TALISMAN | | 236 |
| Tango | *see* DANCE | 127 |
| Tape measure | *see* MEASURING | |
| | INSTRUMENTS | 179 |
| TAR | | 237 |
| Target | *see* BOW, | 98 |
| | GUN, | 157 |
| | HUNTING | 165 |
| TAX | | 237 |
| TEA | | 237 |
| TEARS | | 237 |
| Teeth | *see* BODY (11) | 79 |
| TELEPHONE | | 237 |
| TELEVISION | | 238 |
| Tempest | *see* BOAT, | 78 |
| | CATASTROPHE, | 111 |
| | STORM, | 232 |
| | WATER | 250 |
| TEMPLE, church, mosque, pagoda, synagogue | | 238 |
| Ten | *see* NUMBER | 193 |
| TENT | | 238 |
| Theatre | *see* SHOW | 222 |
| Thermometer | *see* MEASURING | |
| | INSTRUMENTS | 179 |
| THIEF | | 239 |
| Thighs | *see* BODY (28) | 79 |

| | | |
|---|---|---|
| Thin | *see* BODY (19) | 79 |
| Thistle | *see* FLOWER | 142 |
| Thorn | *see* FLOWER | 142 |
| Thousand | *see* NUMBER | 193 |
| Three | *see* NUMBER | 193 |
| Throat | *see* BODY (13) | 79 |
| Throat-cutting | *see* BODY (13) | 79 |
| Thumb | *see* BODY (17) | 79 |
| Ticket | *see* MONEY | 184 |
| TIGER | | 239 |
| TOBACCO | | 239 |
| Toes | *see* BODY (33) | 79 |
| Toffee | *see* SWEET | 235 |
| Tom-tom | *see* MUSICAL INSTRUMENTS | 188 |
| Tongue | *see* BODY (10) | 79 |
| Tools | *see* HAMMER, | 158 |
| | PLANE TOOL, | 203 |
| | RAKE, | 209 |
| | SAW, | 215 |
| | SPADE | 226 |
| TORCH | | 240 |
| TOWER | | 240 |
| Toy | *see* GAMES and TOYS | 150 |
| TRAIN | | 241 |
| Trash | *see* RUBBISH | 213 |
| TREASURE | | 242 |
| TREE | | 242 |
| Trial | *see* JUSTICE, | 168 |
| | LAWYER | 172 |
| TRIANGLE | | 244 |
| Trombone | *see* MUSICAL INSTRUMENTS | 188 |
| Trousers | *see* COSTUME | 123 |
| Trout | *see* FISH | 140 |
| Trumpet | *see* MUSICAL INSTRUMENTS | 188 |
| Trunk | *see* SUITCASE, | 234 |
| | TREASURE | 242 |
| Tulip | *see* FLOWER | 142 |
| Tuna | *see* FISH | 140 |
| TUNNEL | | 244 |
| TURTLE | | 244 |
| Twelve | *see* NUMBER | 193 |
| Twenty-one | *see* NUMBER | 193 |
| Two | *see* COUPLE, | 125 |
| | NUMBER | 193 |

**U**

| | | |
|---|---|---|
| Umbrella | *see* RAIN | 208 |
| UNDERGROUND/SUBWAY | | 245 |
| UNICORN | | 245 |
| Union | *see* MARRIAGE, | 178 |
| | RAINBOW, | 209 |
| | RING | 210 |
| URINATING | | 245 |

**V**

| | | |
|---|---|---|
| VALLEY | | 246 |
| Vampire | *see* BODY (38), | 79 |
| | BITE/BITING | 76 |
| Veins | *see* BODY (38) | 79 |
| VELVET | | 246 |
| Vertigo | *see* VOID | 248 |
| VETERINARIAN | | 246 |
| Vicar | *see* PRIEST | 206 |
| Violet | *see* COLOUR, | 120 |
| | FLOWER | 142 |
| Violin | *see* MUSICAL INSTRUMENTS | 188 |

Violoncello      see MUSICAL
                     INSTRUMENTS      188
Viper            see NEST,            191
                     SNAKE            225
VIRGIN                                246
Vision           see Practical guide
                     to dreams         14
VOICE                                 247
VOID                                  248
Volcano          see MOUNTAIN         186

# W

Walking          see FOREST,         146
                     LIMPING,        174
                     PATH,           200
                     RAIN,           208
                     ROOF,           212
                     STREET          232
WALL                                 248
WAR                                  249
Washing          see BATH             69
WASP                                 249
Watch            see CLOCK           118
WATER                                250
WATERFALL                            251
Weapon           see BOW,             98
                     CANNON,         106
                     CATAPULT,       111
                     GUN             157
WEASEL                               251
WEATHERVANE                          251
Web              see SPIDER          228
Wedding          see MARRIAGE        178
WELL                                 251
West             see DIRECTION       129
WHALE                                252
WHEEL                                252

WHEELBARROW                          253
White            see COLOUR          120
Will             see INHERITANCE,    167
                     LAWYER          172
WINDOW                               253
WINE                                 254
Wing             see AIRPLANE,        56
                     BIRD,            75
                     FLYING          145
WITCH                                254
WIZARD                               254
WOLF                                 255
WOOD                                 255
Woodcutter       see AXE,             67
                     TREE            242
WOOL                                 256
WORM                                 256
WOUND                                256
WRITING                              257

# X, Y, Z

X-RAY                                258
YAWNING                              258
Yellow           see COLOUR          120
Zero             see NUMBER          193
ZOO                                  258

# Dictionary
of symbols

*'Dreams surely are difficult, confusing, and not everything in them is brought to pass for mankind. For fleeting dreams have two gates: one is fashioned of horn and one of ivory. Those which pass through the one of sawn ivory are deceptive, bringing tidings which come to nought, but those which issue from the one of polished horn bring true results when a mortal sees them.'*

Homer (*c.*700 BC), The Odyssey

# ABSCESS

The actual location of the abscess is of great significance. Look up the entry for the affected part of the body.

1    You discover you have an abscess: you are aware of a problem or a situation that has occurred, which must be resolved or taken a step further. Alternatively, you are making yourself very anxious (creating 'bad blood') and need to lance the abscess by saying what is on your mind before things get worse.

2    Your abscess is being lanced: you are being helped to resolve a problem or to sort out a conflict. Alternatively, you may be forced to ask for help.

3    You lance your abscess yourself: the problem worrying you is not too serious and can be resolved easily.

4    It is a large abscess: you are preoccupied by your concerns and can no longer ignore them.

5    It is a small abscess: your problem is not serious or you are inclined to ignore it.

6    Your body is covered in abscesses: you have become very tense recently and it is time to put a stop to this and take serious action to resolve your problems.

7    You are in the presence of someone with one or several abscesses: someone you know will confide in you about their concerns and worries and will need your support. On the other hand, this person has an ulterior motive and is not as well intentioned as may at first appear.

8    You lance another person's abscess: you are in control and able to resolve an external situation of which you are a part; or you are in a position to help or relieve another person in your circle.

# ABSENCE or ABSENT FRIENDS

1    You sense or experience the absence of someone close to you: you need to assess your moral, emotional or financial dependence on this person. It could mean you have a false idea of the person or that you are not seeing him/her in their true colours; it could be that he/she is not in the place where you are looking.

**2** You are absent yourself: you are not happy with what you are doing at the moment and you want to escape and do something different. Alternatively, you realize that life goes on and that the earth will continue to revolve without you.

# ACCIDENTS

**1** You meet with an accident: you are on the wrong path or you are unaware of the risks that you are taking. Only a physical or emotional disruption in your life can help you realize that you must stop, take more care or reverse. However, this event is avoidable since your dream warns of the risk you will run if you do not change your course.

**2** You cause an accident: you have made or are about to make a mistake or an unwise move. The dream warns that it would be better not to do this.

**3** You witness an accident: this signifies that you will have a narrow escape from danger or from a perilous situation in which you were involved without thinking.

**4** An accident happens in broad daylight: an unexpected event will be a lesson to you. Alternatively, you will be in a position to avoid it.

**5** An accident occurs at night: this may be an unavoidable shock, possibly the only way to make you appreciate that you are on the wrong course and need to put a stop to this situation.

# ACROBAT
### (see also MAGIC, p. 177; SHOW, p. 222; ZOO, p. 258)

**1** You are performing acrobatics: you are unconsciously taking risks; your situation is precarious and insecure, or you are walking a tightrope (in the true sense of the word 'acrobatics' – walking on tiptoe).

**2** You watch someone else performing acrobatics:

• if it is a stranger: this indicates that you need to realize the insecurity of your position. Alternatively, you are taking risks without thinking;

• if the performer is one of your friends or family: he/she is not as stable, balanced or loyal as you think or might wish. This person is in a difficult situation but will try to keep up appearances.

3   You are watching acrobats: your own thoughts and feelings are involved and are not under control. Although the situation may appear attractive from the outside, it is still not as stable as you might wish.

## ACTOR and ACTRESS

1   You dream of being an actor or an actress in a play or film: this denotes a very useful self-awareness. The dream makes you both spectator and actor at the same time. More often than not, in a dream we play out a scene, an action or a situation while also being privileged witnesses. This mirrors our own daily lives, although we are not always aware of this. In order to understand the meaning of such a dream and the lessons it contains, it is important to analyze the situation or the scene depicted in the play or film in which you are acting together with the nature and importance of the roles themselves.

2   You are a famous actor or actress: clearly you cannot be this celebrity in real life but a part of you identifies with this person. Certain elements within yourself are similar, and it is these that play, or will play in the future, the most significant role in your life. It is up to you to detect the positive or negative nature of these elements in your personality and bring them to the fore, to centre stage, in your life.

## ADULTERY
### (see also LOVER, p. 176)

1   If you are committing the act of adultery:

•   this is a compensatory dream, expressing a suppressed, unacknowledged desire;

•   your feelings or your relationship with your partner may be a source of dissatisfaction to you at the moment. Rather than acknowledge or integrate this situation and face up to it, you have a tendency to run away. Therefore, in betraying your partner, you are betraying yourself.

2    If you are the victim of adultery:

• in most instances, this dream indicates anxiety, repressed feelings, fear that your partner does not love you or uncertainty about how to seduce or please him or her;

• let yourself be guided by the instinct which alerts you to feeling this distance from or indifference to your partner. Otherwise, misunderstandings or things left unsaid will damage your relationship.

3    You witness an act of adultery in your dream: you will be the victim of a betrayal or deception by someone you know, who will be dishonest about his or her true intentions.

# AIRPLANE

1    If you are boarding a plane: this is a good sign and denotes that things are developing smoothly and you will reach your goals in due course. You will be facilitated by favourable events.

2    You are the pilot: you must be adroit, vigilant and authoritative in order to reach your goals and achieve your ambitions. Your progress remains firmly in your own hands.

3    The flight encounters difficulties:

• if you are a passenger: it denotes that you will go through a period of turbulence, uncertainty and difficulty, the result of unforeseen and disconcerting events or circumstances. However, you will actually benefit in terms of development;

• if you are the pilot of the plane: it is important that you do not confuse speed with haste. You need to wait until you hold a winning hand before making an important decision. You should scrutinize all the elements of the situation in order to avoid insurmountable obstacles along the way.

4    If the take-off is difficult: this means that you are excessively preoccupied with mundane or down-to-earth matters. You are unable to separate yourself from mundane detail, in order to see the big picture from above. Alternatively, you are involved in a project that will not get off the ground or a situation that will not progress.

5    If you dream of a problematic landing: this signifies that you have distanced yourself for too long from the material or moral

obligations that face you. Returning to reality and the constraints of your current situation is potentially painful or difficult.

6  If the plane goes into free fall: this heralds a fall from a great height, a disappointment or an abrupt confrontation with reality, either because you were deceived by your circumstances or because you became carelessly confident. It could be the result of unthinking enthusiasm, great haste or arrogance.

7  If the plane loops the loop: you will take unnecessary risks, or, despite your skill, everything you are engaged in right now will amount to little or astonish your friends and family.

8  If the plane crashes:

• and you are the victim of a dreadful air catastrophe: be prepared for upheaval in your life, an emotional, mental or material disruption caused by circumstances or events. Your projects and plans will undoubtedly be open to question;

• and you emerge unharmed from an air catastrophe: whatever upheaval or shock occurs in your life, not only will you not suffer as a result but you will be relieved by the consequences;

• and you are responsible for an air disaster: the message of this dream is similar to the interpretation given in paragraph No. 6.

9  If your plane is hijacked: this signifies that circumstances or events beyond your control will force you to have a change of heart, direction or plan.

## ALCHEMIST

1  If you dream of an alchemist working in his laboratory: expect profound transformations in your life, in yourself or in those around you; these will be good or bad, depending upon the atmosphere there. However, in all cases you must bear in mind that these transformations are useful and necessary, possibly vital.

2  You are an alchemist: you are in a state of psychological and emotional transformation. Your ideas are changing and developing. If you wish it, you can bring together and combine all the elements available to you in order to transform your existence, turn a page in your life or change yourself completely. However, be aware that

these changes depend entirely upon you, on your will and your capacity to exploit your own potential and your current circumstances.

# ALCOHOL
## (*see also* BEER, p. 72 and WINE, p. 254)

1   If you are drinking mild alcohol: this foretells good news or the discovery of the ideal solution to a problem. Alternatively, moderation is the only remedy for your current illness or condition.

2   If you are drinking strong alcohol: you will hear unexpected, exciting and drastic news, whether pleasant or unpleasant will be revealed by other elements in your dream. Alternatively, you must use the greatest and most effective means possible to resolve a problem that is currently preoccupying you. If this is a health issue, you should focus on it without delay.

3   If you are drinking moderately: this dream is a warning to employ moderation and not exaggeration in your actions and to be circumspect and impartial when listening to what others have to tell you.

4   You are drinking excessively: you tend not to listen when people are talking to you or you are unable to appreciate the consequences of the words spoken around you.

# ALPHABET

To see, draw or read an alphabet in your dream is an encouragement to be flexible, receptive and attentive in the way you appreciate and respond to your environment. It urges you to make an effort to listen carefully to what others say to you and in turn to communicate your own ideas, thoughts and feelings to them clearly.

# AMBASSADOR

1   You meet or entertain an ambassador: you will receive a letter or news of a distant relative or someone whom you have not seen for a long time or with whom you have lost contact. It can indicate that you will have the means to resolve a situation that has been preoccupying you, to find the necessary compromise or make the required arrangements. Alternatively, you will need to

be diplomatic, flexible and understanding in order to achieve your goal.

2   You dream you are an ambassador: it signifies that you have all the necessary attributes and advantages to play the role of mediator or to accomplish a task that is of great importance to you. However, you should not forget that the ambassador is a messenger of peace and of war, and that, should your negotiations fail, you may have to act strongly or even violently; you will be required, at least, to take firmer or more radical action.

## ANCHOR

1   If you see, find or drop an anchor: it is time for you to come to a halt, to take a pause in your life and to stop being so influenced by other people. You need to cease being a pawn and to become more active in the game of life. You are being granted a lucky sign, as long as you know how to exploit your own inner potential and natural abilities.

2   You are raising the anchor: you will undertake a fruitful action, embark upon a journey or move house. This change in your circumstances will cause more changes and transformations in your life than you had anticipated or even hoped for. On the other hand, you may be tempted to let yourself go, to relax and to relieve your tensions by expressing your thoughts clearly and revealing your true nature.

## ANGEL

1   You see an angel in your dream: this is good news, signifying a birth, a creation or a great happiness that you will experience.

2   You are among angels: whatever your current concerns or problems, you will manage to resolve them and emerge from the situation. This difficult and testing period in your life will enable you to develop and live in happier and more pleasant circumstances. In short, great joy awaits and you will be in heaven.

3   You dream you are an angel: this is a wonderful dream, signifying that your imagination and positive thoughts and feelings will help you to transcend reality, take your life to a higher level and overcome those things that make you afraid or stall your progress. Take advantage of this powerful moment.

# ANGER

**1**   You are angry: this is usually a compensatory dream that expresses your disagreement with another person or with a situation that preoccupies you. At the same time, the dream advises you to act more firmly and state your thoughts more clearly.

**2**   You see an angry person: someone in your circle is concealing his or her true colours or holding a grudge against you.

# ANT

To dream of ants or an anthill signifies advantages or profit to come, the direct result of your own hard work and ingenuity. It could herald feelings of anxiety, nervousness or heightened sensitivity; if you destroy an anthill it means that all your efforts are in danger of turning to nothing.

# ANTELOPE

**1**   You see an antelope or a herd of antelopes in the wild: this is a sign of good fortune, of potential riches, of wonderful revelations and inspired, inventive ideas.

**2**   You see an antelope in a cage or a zoo: this reinforces your inability to use your imagination to the full or to exploit your natural potential. There are two reasons for this: either you will find yourself in a situation with no escape or which does not permit you to fulfil your potential, or you will not exercise your own powers to act.

**3**   You see an antelope being eaten by other animals: beware of potential enemies, the danger of theft or the loss of a precious possession, an original idea or a business you have created.

**4**   You are chasing an antelope: this dream means that you will receive winnings or a significant profit. It can denote that you will have a great idea.

# ANTENNA

Seeing one or several antennae indicates that you should be aware of your natural receptivity or that you should exploit it to enable you to be permanently in contact with the outside world, whether at a distance or in close proximity. The dream reinforces the vital role of intermediary that all of us can play, together with the great wealth of information and external forces that we can grasp, absorb and transmit in our turn. It advises you to open up yourself to the outside world and to use all your five senses to appreciate, experience and understand what is happening and what will happen around you in the near future.

## ANTIQUES DEALERS and ANTIQUES

1    You are in an antiques shop: here you are accessing the most conservative part of your personality, the part that refuses to expand and develop, to accept natural change in people and objects. The antique furniture and pieces found in this shop represent the baggage of your past that you have stored and preserved within you. The dream is an announcement that the time has come to take stock and decide what you value and what can be junked. It can indicate that you will be confronted by an old situation, which you thought had been settled long ago but which will return to the forefront.

2    You spot a piece of furniture or a precious item:

• you acquire this object or piece of furniture: its symbolic significance in your dream is of great importance (see the relevant symbol in the glossary of symbols). Such objects reveal a fact or an event from your past with which you identify and which you can integrate in your present life, a genuine point of reference and support for your deep psychological and personal development. The act of acquisition shows that you are aware of the object's value and you will use it well;

• you steal the item: the lessons to be learnt are the same as in the previous paragraph, but the theft signifies that you do not understand that you can obtain what you want on your own merit and through the use of your own potential, that you think things will not come to you in the normal way or that you do not believe you deserve them.

## APARTMENT

A dream of an apartment or the interior of a house takes you back to your inner life, its characteristics and evolution. If you can remember the way the rooms were arranged in the apartment in your dream, try to reconstruct how they appeared, if only approximately. The geometric pattern of your room plan will help you interpret the symbolic significance of your subconscious.

1    You are visiting an apartment: you are made aware of the enclosed universe in which you are evolving, and this allows you to redefine and rediscover yourself and to develop fully and calmly within the context in which you find yourself. It denotes a realistic and lucid attitude.

2    You are renting an apartment: you are in an unstable or temporary situation, and this dream advises you to avoid settling down for the moment, to call things to a halt and enjoy a pause before continuing on your path.

3    You are buying an apartment: you feel the need to plant your roots and settle down somewhere, to put down your bags and mark out a territory that gives you an identity.

4    You dream of being in an empty, uninhabited apartment: it will be helpful if not vital to empty yourself of preconceptions and cast a fresh eye on your situation.

5    If you dream of being in an apartment filled with furniture and objects, this signifies that you are full of ideas, imaginative thoughts and inspiration which you don't know what to do with, that you do not exploit or that are simply useless.

6    You find yourself in a dusty, dirty, dilapidated apartment that may have been uninhabited for some time: you pay too much attention to worldly appearance and to social life. You need to reflect and withdraw in the near future. The dream can also signify some psychological disturbance that, if left unattended, could, sooner or later, have quite serious consequences for your inner well-being. It could indicate a need to take preventive or curative measures.

7    You are in a luxury apartment: you do not remotely appreciate the psychological, mental or spiritual resources that you have at your disposal. However, you possess all the resources necessary to develop and fulfil your desires and ambitions.

8    If you dream of being in your parents' apartment or your childhood home: whatever your age or your current situation, this dream

warns that your thinking and behaviour are framed according to the tenets learned during your childhood or from your parents. You have changed your external context but not your internal one.

## APPLAUSE

1   If you are applauding: this denotes future joy, euphoria and enthusiasm.

2   If you are being applauded: you will require help, approbation or recognition of your qualities and merits.

## APRON

1   If you dream you are wearing an apron or overalls: this signifies that you will take certain precautions before starting something; it might mean that you will receive a job offer or begin a new career, or else you will show yourself to be modest and reticent about expressing your feelings or desires.

2   If you see an apron or overalls: this means a change of job or career, or that you will end a situation that you find inconvenient or dissatisfying; possibly you will not pursue a relationship any further.

## AQUARIUM
### (see also FISH, p. 140)

An aquarium reveals confused, agitated and unproductive thoughts, or an acute sensitivity and contradictory feelings. It also indicates a personality that is closed in on itself, impenetrable and unable to express intense, albeit passive, feelings.

1   If the water in the aquarium is clear: you will see yourself clearly and, even if you feel constricted and constrained, you will always be able to regenerate.

2   The water in the aquarium is cloudy: this is a sign of self-deception or an inability or unwillingness to exploit fully your own potential and inner resources. You refuse to acknowledge and reveal your true self. The dream can also herald a confused, difficult, unsatisfying or deceptive situation in which you will find yourself or which you will have to resolve.

3   If the water is spilling out of the aquarium: you will be unable to control or contain your emotions. Depending on the context in which the aquarium appears in the dream, it is a sign of great joy or great sadness.

4   If the aquarium contains very little water: it is a sign that you are unable to empty yourself of emotional clutter and transform your inner self or to achieve an important change. Alternatively, it can mean that you lack the vital resources and energy to do this. Take care to recharge your batteries.

5   If the aquarium is empty: it means that you are reaching the end of your resources but this dry spell makes you open and flexible enough to refill your inner reserves with a new and fresh source of energy. This may lead to a new development in your life.

6   If the aquarium is damaged or shatters: it is a sign that you are about to undergo a beneficial and liberating shake-up, both spectacular and amazing. You will abandon your reserve and let yourself go totally or excessively.

# ARCH

If you see or pass beneath an arch: this dream denotes that you will be saved in extremis from a difficult situation and that you will emerge unharmed, surviving a catastrophe undamaged and protected by the arch. It signifies a safeguard.

# ARENA
### (see also CENTRE, p. 115; CIRCLE, p. 118)

1   You are sitting in the terraces of an arena or stadium: you will find yourself caught up in a situation over which you have no control; you will have to be satisfied with remaining on the fringes of the action, playing the role of spectator.

2   You are in an arena or a stadium: the time has come for you to act openly, to show what you are capable of and to clearly demonstrate your strengths to others.

3   You are alone in an empty arena or stadium: you must be aware of the limits in which you can act; you can be either the catalyst in a situation or its focus. In order to achieve this status, however, you will have to make a decision without the support or approval of others.

**4** You enter an arena or a stadium: you are about to reach your goals, to embark on your chosen path or to break through to the heart of a matter. You may be offered a job or new activity.

**5** You are leaving a stadium or arena: if you have just completed a task or mission, this denotes that you should leave without regret and with no looking back. It can also announce a change in your place of residence, a new workplace or the loss of a job.

**6** You are watching a match, fight or show in an arena or stadium: you will witness or be implicated in a controversy or conflict within your circle.

**7** You take part in a match or combat held in an arena or stadium: you will be the cause of an intense discussion or conflict in the near future. You will be heavily implicated in this situation, and even if you are not on the winning side, you will learn from the outcome. However, if there is neither winner nor loser in your dream, this means that the discussion will have had no purpose or the conflict is not about to be resolved.

**8** You are watching a bullfight: this signals the need to be ready give up something or to sacrifice the convictions and principles or the excessively emotional responses which lead you to act in an impulsive, aggressive or violent manner.

**9** You take part in a bullfight: you don't know how to let go, to trust to your good sense, to let yourself be guided by your instinct and to express yourself simply and spontaneously. This dream advises you, therefore, to change your attitude, not to sacrifice what is best in you.

## ARMY

**1** If you see or attend a march-past: you will act with great discipline and rigour, or you will be on the defensive. The dream may also signal that you are impervious to other people's ideas, principles and convictions when they differ from your own. You will experience a certain satisfaction exhibiting your strength and force, your power over others. It may be necessary to face a difficult or conflict situation in which you need to adhere strictly to the rules.

**2** If you see or take part in the combat: you will find yourself involved in a struggle, a conflict or challenge, the outcome of which is yet to be determined. However, you will act or respond energetically, whatever the outcome. The dream may herald an illness, the nature of which will be clarified by the region, location or spot where the war or combat occurs (see the relevant entry in the glossary of symbols). Alternatively, it can signal an internal struggle or rupture, or a choice or commitment arising from necessity rather than desire, which you will resist.

3   If you see a decimated army: this denotes that you will not reach your goals, or, should you do so, it will be at the cost of a great sacrifice or significant losses.

4   If you see a victorious army: this signals that you will emerge from a period of struggle or conflict and finally achieve peace, well-deserved rest and a period of calm. It can also herald success and a personal triumph.

5   If you see a vanquished army: it is a sign of release, liberation and recovery or of a victory gained over yourself against your combative instincts or your destructive emotions.

# ARROW

1   You shoot one or more arrows: you are or will be drawn towards a very precise target and will not rest until you have reached it; or your words will be somewhat hostile and aggressive although frank and straightforward.

2   One or more arrows are shot at you: those close to you or around you will be free with their criticism and sarcasm, which is bound to sting you.

# ATHLETE

The athlete represents heroism, competitiveness, the supremacy of physical force, willpower and courage. If you dream that you are an athlete, it is either a sign of arrogance, self-satisfaction and presumption or an encouragement to take action, to embark on a project, to dare, or to exploit all your resources in order to achieve something very close to your heart or to attain a specific objective. It can also be the sign of an ability to surpass yourself, to execute a spectacular, unusual or courageous deed.

# ATTIC

1   You are in a well-organized, clean attic: your thoughts and opinions, your beliefs and principles are so organized and ordered that you are fully able to exploit your intellectual resources.

2   You are in a disorganized, dirty and dark attic or one littered with old objects and papers: your current behaviour is based on outdated and inappropriate tenets. Alternatively, you will soon have to confront a situation or an issue from the past that you should have resolved long since.

3   You are clearing out your attic and removing all the rubbish: you will feel the need to put the various aspects of your life in order.

# AXE

If you see or use an axe in your dream, it is a sign of rage, upheaval, an irrepressible urge, or of an unexpected and liberating event or radical decision. It can also predict a peaceful but certain resolution to the problem, thanks to your own courage and willpower.

# BABY
### (*see also* CHILDBIRTH, p. 116; MILK, p. 183)

To dream of a baby heralds a birth, a new creation, inspiration or situation. It can mean the adoption of a different type of behaviour, the birth of a new awareness or state of mind that will develop and change your view of things. Alternatively, you have total confidence in your environment and feel completely at ease within it.

# BAG

1   You see a bag:

- if it is your own bag: you attach too much importance to what other people think of you;

- if it is somebody else's bag: you will have dealings with someone questionable, or whom you will want to know better.

2   Someone gives you a bag: this means you will be linked with, or married to, somebody who is of a higher social standing than yourself or substantially wealthy.

**3** You have a bag full of photographs or things that belong to different people: you view others with a consistently critical eye; or you are possessive and exclusive in your relationships, which makes you more likely to use people, or monopolize their attention.

**4** You are stowing an important document or something precious in your bag: your success is guaranteed. You will achieve whatever you want.

**5** If your bag is very full, or you are having trouble finding something in it: you will be plunged into a difficult or confusing situation, or a complicated relationship.

**6** Delving around in the bottom of your bag: this means that you will discover a secret or become aware of some important matters; alternatively, you will be caught in the act and will have to own up to what you have done.

**7** If you are emptying your bag: you are finally going to say exactly what is on your mind and in your heart, with no beating about the bush.

**8** Removing unusual objects from your bag: this indicates that you will prove that you can face up to any situation and that no one can catch you out, because you are highly resourceful.

**9** If you see someone carrying your bag, or one like it: someone will try to steal from you, cheat you or deprive you of something that is rightfully yours.

## BALCONY

To dream that you are on a balcony signifies that you observe the external world but lack the courage to become part of it. It is an indication of circumspection, reflection and wisdom. Alternatively, it means that you fear the outside world and others, that you lack self-confidence and have difficulty in expressing yourself and revealing your personality outside your usual milieu.

## BANKRUPTCY

**1** You go bankrupt: you will succumb to depression or bouts of depression that will threaten to sap your energy and damage your well-being. You need to take preventive measures.

**2** Your employer goes bankrupt: you lack initiative, autonomy and experience, weaknesses that could lead you to question your professional situation. You need to be more independent and to take greater risks.

# BAPTISM

**1** If you are attending a baptism: it could mean that you are about to enter a new phase in your life or that you will gain your independence. Alternatively, you will participate in the creation of something new.

**2** If you are being baptized: this can herald a gain or reward. Alternatively, it signifies that you will emerge from a difficult situation or emotional challenge regenerated, more advanced and renewed. On the other hand, it could mean that you will find yourself at liberty to act honestly and freely.

# BARREL
## (*see also* WINE, p. 254)

**1** A barrel: this is a sign that your professional skills, competence and tenacity will be put to the test; or that you will be successful, and deservedly so, but you will need plenty of patience.

**2** A leaking barrel: you feel your actions are in vain, or that you are working on a pointless, interminable and exhausting task.

**3** You are making a barrel: it will take a long time for your business to be profitable but you will achieve your ends; possibly – like a good wine – you will improve with age.

**4** You dream of lots of barrels: you will find yourself in an enviable financial situation; another interpretation is that you will undergo a long spell of peaks and troughs before things come right.

# BATH
## (see also DROWNING, p. 133; SEA, p. 217; WATER, p. 250)

**1** You are bathing in a bath: you want to purify yourself, to rid yourself of the past and to turn a page in your life in order to be reborn and to embark upon an entirely new path. Is this possible?

Ask yourself this question. Alternatively, if you are about to enter the bath, it means you will act, take the initiative or assume responsibility.

2    You are bathing in a swimming pool: if you want something in your life to change, you will have to jump in with other people, relax and have confidence in yourself and in events around you. You will feel more secure psychologically as a result, better able to give yourself up to your feelings and to a sense of tenderness.

3    You are swimming in the sea: this signifies a need to go back to your roots, to empty yourself of preconceptions about yourself and things around you and to allow yourself to be carried by events. The dream advises you to slow down, relax and let go.

4    You are bathing at midnight: you are currently in a difficult situation or a painful period in your life. However, this dream reveals that you still have hidden resources and that you can regenerate yourself enough to face your own taboos and trust in your own intuition and memory. You need to look back to your past for the answers and solutions to current difficulties.

5    You are bathing in a river or stream: have faith in time and allow circumstances and events to evolve of their own accord, to develop spontaneously, while remaining true to yourself, whatever happens. Time solves many problems.

6    You are bathing in a pond or small pool: you will be worried or preoccupied by an old situation or one that you have allowed to stagnate through negligence or lack of clear-sightedness and which you need to clear up.

7    You are bathing in a lake: you are entering a fruitful, fertile period, full of inspiration and beneficial or happy events. Take advantage of this phase in your life.

8    You are taking a cold bath: people or events will not be helpful, but this situation will act as a stimulus and help you to see things clearly.

9    You are taking a warm bath: you will let yourself go, doing only what is absolutely necessary or required. You won't be able to resist the temptation to drift.

## BATS (animal)

If you see one or several bats, you will place yourself in a situation with no exit; or you will have one or more mad, reckless ideas that you will find hard to control. It can also mean that you will have dealings with envious, jealous, harmful or threatening people.

## BEANS

1   You sow beans: this indicates financial gain to come, which will bring prosperity and security sooner or later; or you will have an intense love affair.

2   You pick beans: your ambitions will be fulfilled as planned.

3   You eat beans: your financial situation will be less advantageous than expected and this will lead to debates and arguments with those around you.

## BEAR

1   If you see a bear in your dream: you will meet someone rough, surly and difficult, but who is actually very kind and well meaning deep down.

2   You hunt a bear: you tend to boast about a plan that is close to your heart, without being sure you are capable of seeing it through.

3   A teddy bear: this denotes that you are shying away from a feeling or desire that might force you to face up to your responsibilities.

## BEARD

1   To dream that you have a beard has one of the following interpretations:

   • for a woman: your words are harsh and unreasonable and others find you unapproachable and severe;

   • for a man: you give the impression of being in control of your feelings and you possess great amounts of energy or strong will. You are able to exert an influence over your circle;

   • for both a man and a woman: the longer the beard, the more meaningful the elements of the dream. Alternatively, the dream can herald challenges and difficulties that you must overcome by exploiting both experience and strength of character.

2    You are developing or growing a beard: this heralds a need to show patience, wisdom and maturity; conversely, should the beard grow too quickly, it signifies a lack of lucidity and knowledge.

3    You are sporting a trimmed beard or are shaping and combing it: this is a sign of vanity, self-satisfaction and self-sufficiency. It denotes a superficial life, too full of hollow words and empty promises.

4    You are shaving or trimming your own beard: it means that you will feel the need to bring matters to a head, to clarify your situation and show yourself in your true colours; you will not want to hide your thoughts and opinions. Alternatively, you will wait for the correct moment to act.

5    You are having your beard shaved or trimmed: this means that you will lose out in a situation or lose power. It can mean that you will be forced to pay your debts but you will recover what you pay out in due course.

6    You are wearing a false beard: this shows a lack of courage, will and determination; you talk big but act little.

7    You have dealings with someone wearing a false beard: someone is lying or will lie to you. Alternatively, you should not heed the hypocritical or spiteful words, the lies and slander being bandied around by someone in your circle.

## BEAVER

The appearance of a beaver in your dream indicates your awareness of your dual nature and heralds a long and laborious task ahead, such as the purchase or construction of a house.

## BEER
### (see also ALCOHOL, p. 58; WINE, p. 254)

1    You are drinking beer: this heralds energy, enthusiasm and courage. If you get drunk, however, it denotes that you will become presumptuous or fall under evil influences.

2    You are spilling beer: this signifies a loss of vital energy or an end to aggressive behaviour.

# BEES
## (*see also* HONEY, p. 162)

1   You see a bee, or a bee is buzzing around the room in which you find yourself: this signifies future happiness, an experience of joy and good fortune or a positive opportunity. It promises that a happy event will occur within your family or home environment.

2   You are stung by a bee: this also signifies joy, happiness and good fortune, which will come as something of a surprise, or even shock, causing you concern.

3   You see a swarm of bees: this signifies joy and happiness, honour and recognition or promises the possibility of recompense or popularity.

4   You see a hive: this is a sign of order, calm, peace, stability and organization – it represents a tranquil, ordered life.

# BEGGAR

1   You see a beggar: you are or will be frustrated in your emotional life or in the attempt to achieve your goals, either because you lack generosity and cannot simply let yourself go, or because you refuse to express your true feelings – pride prevents you from asking for what you need.

2   You are a beggar: your false humility will fool no one; you will know exactly how to succeed in your business or affairs.

# BELL

1   You hear bells ringing: this is a good omen, a sign that you will hear good news. Alternatively, someone you know will express their discontent or will reproach you for something. This dream can denote dissatisfaction with your own words or deeds or the imminent need to undertake an important task; you will understand that the time has come to tackle this.

2   You are ringing the bells: you are communicating your love of life and your happiness to your friends, while inviting them to share in this joy.

## BELT

1   You are putting on a belt: this is a sign of ease, comfort, security and fidelity.

2   The belt is too tight: you will be forced to make economies, slow down, reduce your outgoings; the dream cautions prudence in your financial situation.

3   The belt is too loose: your position is not as secure as you may think or you may not be able to keep your promises or commitments.

4   The belt is old: this is a sign of financial insecurity or infidelity.

5   You are wearing a pretty, decorated belt: you will be rewarded or honoured. Alternatively, you will play a key part in a situation or assume the role of head of the family.

6   You are wearing a metal belt: others think you are either too authoritarian or on the defensive. It can mean that you will remain indifferent to the events around you in the near future.

## BENCH
### (*see also* POSTURE, p. 206)

If you are sitting or lying on a bench, this signifies a precarious or temporary situation or a moment of anticipation and uncertainty.

## BICYCLE

Whatever the context of your dream, riding a bicycle indicates the will, desire, power and energy demanded to move forward, to take your destiny in your own hands and to give your projects and ambitions the necessary impetus. It is a manifestation of the attributes needed live a full and energetic life.

1   You are cycling in emptiness, in a vacuum: you lack reality; you are deluding yourself and chasing shadows.

2   You are cycling uphill with difficulty: this indicates that you will encounter problems in achieving your objectives.

3   You have dismounted due to the steep hill: you will experience a fallow period, a relief from tension or a reduction of your effort and input in a project.

4    You are travelling rapidly downhill on your bike: continue on your chosen path but be aware of the risks involved.

5    Your brakes have failed: this dream counsels prudence either because you will no longer be in control of the situation or in control of yourself.

6    You win a cycling race: this indicates that you will be the victor in a difficult situation or a competition, or you will have the last word.

7    You fall off your bicycle: you will not achieve your goals.

# BIRD

Every species of bird (lark, dove, swallow, blackbird, nightingale, etc.) carries its own particular message. Here, the focus is on birds in the general sense, rather than on particular species and their characteristics.

1    You dream about a bird: someone is about to play an important role in your life or career:

   •    if it is a migratory bird: this person will be fickle and indecisive, and either lives abroad or travels widely; he or she is only passing through;

   •    if it is a bird of prey: this person will be greedy, domineering, demanding and a loner, or else a tenacious and dangerous enemy;

   •    if it is a wader: this person will be proud and rich, or from a more privileged background than your own;

   •    if it is a domestic fowl (or a grouse, pheasant, partridge, etc.): this person will be hard-working, productive and generous, but will lack intelligence and an open mind;

   •    if it is a mountain bird: this person will be intelligent, clear-sighted and cunning, but also an opportunist who takes life as it comes and lets others take charge.

2    You dream about a species of bird that is either unknown or you do not recognize it: an exceptional, astonishing person will come into your life – a true original you may not be able to live without.

**3** If you hear a bird singing: you will hear some surprising news; you may find a new romance, or someone will declare their love for you.

**4** A bird in a cage: you will meet or fall in love with someone who belongs to another; you may not be able to do what you want, or you are now the prisoner or victim of a situation that you brought about yourself.

**5** A bird flies into a house through open windows: a happy event will take place at home or in another area of your life; or a new love will come into your life and take you up to new and unimagined heights.

**6** To dream about an injured bird: you just cannot forget a disappointment or a sad event; or you may have to help or comfort someone who has been disappointed in love.

**7** You see a bird fly away: you are going to make a new start, or you are going on a journey. Alternatively, a relative, a child or someone close to you will leave their home, their family or their natural environment, or else will distance themselves from you.

## BIRTHDAY

A birthday celebration heralds a gift that you will receive or should give. It can mean that you need to face an important stage in your life, that an advantageous proposal is going to be put to you or that you will receive a promotion shortly.

## BISON

**1** You see a bison or a herd of bison: it is sign of material prosperity, emotional fulfilment or spiritual well-being.

**2** A single bison or a herd is pursuing you: this heralds a happy event that you have sensed without crediting it or about which, strangely enough, you have been anxious.

## BITE/BITING

**1** An animal bites you: you will be the victim of a betrayal or you are in the grip of a hidden vice or secret passion, from which you cannot free yourself.

**2**   A child bites you: you will have dealings with someone who is too possessive and jealous; alternatively, you will take a new interest in or have a strong feeling for someone, which will seem quite harmless to you at first but will become more and more important in your life.

**3**   An adult bites you: someone will seek to profit from or exploit you in some way, taking advantage of your qualities and abilities or inspiration from your behaviour; possibly you will become smitten with someone or fall prey to a sudden passion.

**4**   You bite someone: you cannot rein back your possessive and aggressive instincts or you will demonstrate clearly but also violently the hold that you have over someone in your circle.

## BLANKET

**1**   You are lying under a thick blanket: you are too exclusive and possessive, or the feelings others have for you are both stifling and restricting.

**2**   You are hiding or you are naked beneath a blanket: you are trying to hide the truth, to jealously guard your secrets and plans.

## BLIND ALLEY/DEAD END

If you find yourself in a dead end, it signifies your need to retrace your steps, despite your stubborn instinct to keep moving forwards in search of an answer – an answer that simply is not there. Retreat or surrender is not dishonourable when there is no other choice.

## BLINDNESS
### (*see also* ONE-EYED, p. 198; STICK, p. 231)

**1**   If you dream that you are blind: it denotes a future self-deception and a failure to see the true nature of things. You will refuse to admit or appreciate reality – or more precisely, your own reality – insisting upon being guided by your desires and impulses.

**2**   You are or become blind but you feel a sense of well-being and relief: by stepping back from your current situation or external affairs, you will be able to see things in a different light and appreciate people and life more profoundly.

3   You become blind and this grieves you: this signifies an excessive dependence upon the world of appearances and on your external, superficial relationships. You may also be too attached to material possessions.

4   You are blinded by an excessively bright light: this denotes that you will be the victim of your passions, desires, emotions and uncontrolled instincts. Alternatively, you will allow yourself to be blinded or overwhelmed by illusory circumstances or impressive-sounding but insubstantial propositions.

# BOAT
### (see also SHIP, p. 220)

1   You see an empty boat floating or drifting in calm waters: you are confidently allowing yourself to be cradled and carried by soothing and calm circumstances or events in your life.

2   You see an empty boat floating or drifting in troubled waters: your nonchalant and lax attitude could put you in a dangerous or unstable situation. Alternatively, wait for stormy times to pass, things will return to normal in due course.

3   You are rowing a boat through calm waters, your courage, determination and efforts will lead you to your goal;

   • you are heading down river: you are steering your vessel well in favourable circumstances; you are on course;

   • you are heading up river: you will have only your own strength to rely on in battling against winds and tides to reach your final goal.

4   You are rowing a boat in troubled waters: this indicates that you are in an unstable, eventful phase of your life with an uncertain outcome. You may be prey to contradictory thoughts or strong emotions that can upset the balance of your situation or convictions.

5   You are floating or drifting in a boat with no oars: you will have to relinquish your autonomy and rely on the fulfilment of your destiny through belief in it and in yourself.

6   You are rowing in a boat with other rowers: you will find the help or support you need. Alternatively, you will participate in a communal, social or humanitarian action.

# BODY

## THE HEAD (1)

1   You have a large head: you will tend to dramatize a situation or exaggerate a problem. This is a sign of inflated behaviour or ideas.

2   You see someone with a large head: you will benefit from a stroke of luck, a good opportunity.

3   You feel that your head is separated from your body: you will feel that your ideas or projects cannot be realized; this dream may denote the end to your worries and anxieties or the recovery from an illness, or can herald a sudden passion or a destabilizing impulse.

4   You hit your head: do not throw yourself headlong into an adventure or enterprise beyond your capacity. You will lack clear-sightedness or you will dig your heels in to no avail.

## THE FOREHEAD (2)

1   Your forehead is very large: you will need to summon all your resources and your intellect to face a difficult situation or confront your adversaries.

2   Your forehead is wounded: you may be prevented from defending yourself or facing a difficult or problematic situation.

## THE NAPE OF THE NECK (3)

1   You have a pain in the nape of your neck: you are being obstinate for no reason or in vain – relax or give up.

2   You have a broken neck: if you are too audacious, reckless or presumptuous, your progress will be interrupted.

## THE CHEEKS (4)

1   You have red cheeks: despite your fears or lack of self-assurance, you will easily achieve your goals (*see also* SLAP, p. 224).

2   You have pale cheeks: you will have worries or concerns.

### THE EYE OR EYES (5)

1   Light eyes: these reveal sincere emotions.

2   Dark eyes: these denote betrayal or hypocrisy in someone.

3   If you are making eyes at someone: you will be overwhelmed by your feelings, or you will be influenced by your emotions, resulting in a lack of objectivity in your judgment.

4   You are staring: you will be tempted to impress your circle but you will not be taken seriously.

5   You can see into the distance: this denotes clear-sightedness and objectivity together with a penetrating intellect.

6   Your eyes are shut, you are having problems with your sight or feel you are going blind: you trust too much in appearance and refuse to accept reality. You are shutting your eyes (*see also* BLIND-NESS, p. 77; ONE-EYED, p. 198) or you are trying to isolate yourself from the outside world and its propensity to cause you anxiety or to distract you from your goals.

7   You feel you are under scrutiny by one or more eyes: you have a bad conscience or are to blame for a situation; whatever the case, you are not at peace with yourself.

### THE EARS (6)

1   Your ears are large or increasing in size: you will hear something that will go straight to your heart, particularly if you are a woman.

2   Your ears are cut off: you will feel powerless due either to a refusal to listen to reason or to an inability to act or react as you would wish.

3   Your ears are blocked or hidden under a hat, cap or hood: you will be unable to believe what people say to you or to trust in someone around you.

4   Your ears have been removed: you will be particularly attentive and receptive to others.

5   Your ears are injured or diseased: you will hear malicious words that will be painful or annoying; or you will be deceived in love.

**6** You are or become deaf: you will become increasingly insensitive or closed to the ideas of others and will lose confidence both in yourself and in life; this dream advises you to change your attitude.

**7** You find yourself among deaf people or you are talking to them: you will feel misunderstood; people will not listen to or believe you. Alternatively, your demands and needs will not be heard or met.

## THE NOSE (7)

**1** You have a large nose: this is a sign of vanity, pride and a desire to impose your will on others. It demonstrates an attachment to material possessions and worldly goods together with a certain sensuality and greed.

**2** You have a small nose: this denotes discretion, intuition and great sensitivity.

**3** Someone else has a large nose: you will have dealings with an indiscreet or dishonest person.

**4** You are wearing a false nose: your instincts are wrong and you should not trust them; possibly you will deceive those around you about your desires and intentions.

**5** You see someone wearing a false nose: you will come across someone who is not what they claim to be and who makes serious errors of judgement.

**6** You have a nosebleed: this often indicates financial or material loss or the sapping of vital energy.

**7** You sneeze: you will hear good news or be forgiven for a mistake that you have made. Alternatively, any health issues will soon be remedied or doubts about your ability to succeed will prove to be unfounded.

## THE MOUTH (8)

**1** Your mouth is closed: choose your words with care and avoid saying anything that could cause you harm or future regret.

**2** Your mouth is open: do not believe everything people say to you; treat others' words with a pinch of salt.

**3** You have a full, sensual mouth: you cannot disguise your sensuality or greed.

**4** You cover your mouth with your hand: you will be torn between your thirst for knowledge, your desire to investigate a situation more deeply and your indolence or laissez-faire (*see also* YAWNING, p. 258).

## THE LIPS (9)

**1** Your lips are smiling or sensuous: you will experience happiness or be carefree and serene.

**2** You lips are down-turned or pinched: you will be unable to relax and enjoy life; or you will have dealings with someone sceptical and difficult.

**3** Your lips are chapped or wounded: your feelings have changed.

**4** You have a dominant upper lip: you can rely on your friends or you will receive support from influential people.

**5** You have a dominant lower lip: you will be unable to avoid being the victim of envy, treachery or indiscretion.

## THE TONGUE (10)

**1** You stick your tongue out: a difficult period to come will require you to economize; or you will not get what you want. Alternatively, you do not take your current situation seriously or you make fun of those around you.

**2** Someone sticks their tongue out at you: others are not completely honest about what they think of you; or promises will be made that cannot be kept. This dream can also mean that someone you know will tell you what they wish.

**3** Your tongue grows longer: think before you speak; it may mean that you will foil your critics or convince others of your sincerity.

**4** Your tongue has been cut off: you will be prevented from expressing, explaining or defending yourself. You will bite your tongue, with beneficial results.

**5** You burn your tongue: things that you long to say are not necessarily to your benefit. Hold your tongue and you will avoid saying words you regret.

6   Your tongue is heavy or painful: you will be tempted to spread malicious gossip or slander, unless you are the victim or target of it yourself.

## THE TEETH (11)

1   You have fine white teeth: your strong will, mental equilibrium and dynamic, positive attitude will bring you luck and success.

2   Your teeth are poor, damaged, fragile and uneven: you lack self-confidence or you waste your energy and willpower. Alternatively, you have harmful relationships.

3   You lose one or more teeth: this heralds a loss, disappointment or upheaval; it can also denote fatigue, a lack of physical power or energy. If you lose an incisor, this involves a daughter or sister, if a molar, an uncle or aunt. On the other hand, if you lose a canine tooth, it signifies you yourself (if you are a man) or your husband or father (if you are a woman). This dream can also signal radical change in your family environment or a change of address.

4   If you lose a wisdom tooth: you will be tempted to lose your cool within your family or in a situation relating to a member of your family.

5   You have one or more teeth removed: an upheaval will occur but will turn out to be a great relief in the end.

6   You have a decayed tooth: you have allowed a situation or relationship to stagnate or deteriorate through failing to act or react at the right moment; you will suffer the consequences. It can denote the need to be doubly careful to avoid being the victim of your own negligence.

7   One or more teeth grow bigger: this signifies greed, unfulfilled wishes and unexpressed, repressed desires that might spill over and overwhelm you.

8   You have toothache: you will know exactly what you want and no one will be able to prevent you from carrying out your decision. The dream can herald financial difficulties or that you will give in to angry or passionate feelings.

**9** You have false teeth: your financial provisions will prove to be inadequate. You will have dealings with a dishonest person or one who will not keep his promises.

## THE NECK (12)

**1** A strong, straight, elegant neck: denotes integrity, uprightness and fidelity as exemplified either by you or by someone with whom you are in contact or in a relationship.

**2** A small, fine, fragile neck or one that is sunk into the shoulders: signals that your ambitions and projects are beyond your means or that you will have dealings with an untrustworthy or presumptuous individual. Alternatively, you will lack imagination or vision in a situation or relationship.

**3** Your neck is swollen or painful: someone you know will reveal their feelings towards you or you will be surprised by your own.

**4** A scarf or other item of clothing is tied tightly around your neck: you will be deeply involved in a relationship or situation.

**5** You are being strangled: you will be forced to express your desires and thoughts, fulfil your ambitions or assume your full responsibilities. The dream can herald an obligation to pay your debts or take on a heavy burden in order to achieve your goals. Alternatively, you are now and will be in the future both anxious and distressed.

**6** You strangle someone with your bare hands: your arguments will convince another person to tell you what he or she is really thinking, to put their cards on the table and make their intentions clear.

**7** You strangle someone with gloved hands: you will try to avoid being implicated in some business and to keep your hands clean in order to get what you want from another, but you will not be able to avoid it.

**8** You are strangling someone with a rope, scarf or other item: you are fearful of someone else's intentions towards you. This can also indicate that you know that someone close to you has something very important to say or reveal and this is causing you concern – you would prefer them to remain silent (*see also* ROPE, p. 212).

## THE THROAT (13)

1   Your throat is dry: your desires will not be satisfied; or you will not be able to express your thoughts clearly due to your fear of the consequences or of being misunderstood.

2   You have a burning sensation or an irritation in your throat: you will openly take someone for a ride, unless they manage to do it to you first. Your own intentions or those of others will be in poor taste.

3   You feel a knot or lump in your throat: this heralds anxiety due mostly to a lack of self-confidence or confidence in those around you. It is vital that you should express your thoughts and fears freely and clearly.

4   Your throat has been cut or you are cutting someone's throat: this signals sudden violence or an injustice of which you will be the cause or victim.

## THE SHOULDERS (14)

1   You have broad shoulders: you take on too many responsibilities, assume too many obligations and feel the weight of both.

2   You have narrow shoulders: you are anxious about being overwhelmed by your responsibilities and afraid that you are not up to it.

3   The right shoulder: for a man, this denotes a supportive wife or girlfriend; for a woman, it represents psychological or moral obligations in relation to those close to her.

4   The left shoulder: for a man, this denotes psychological or moral obligations to those near to him; for a woman it represents the husband or friend who will come to her aid.

5   You offer your shoulder to lean on: you will help someone resolve a difficult situation.

6   You are holding someone by the shoulders or someone is holding you by the shoulders: you will help another person or you will receive support yourself.

7   You shrug your shoulders: you will express your disapproval of or lack of interest in a situation or in someone you know.

## THE ARMS (15)

**1** You have long arms or your arms grow longer: you will benefit from an act of generosity, affection and consideration. It can also denote an increase in your circle of friends or your influence.

**2** You have short arms: despite your enthusiasm and willpower, you will not achieve your goals; or you will not be able to rely on any help.

**3** You raise your arms: you will be unable to act without the agreement of others or without submitting yourself to certain influences; you will lose your free will.

**4** Your right arm has been cut off: this signals the loss of your power and free will or the loss of a friend.

**5** Your left arm has been cut off: you will lack imagination, creative freedom and entrepreneurial spirit; or you will be freed from an enemy or adversary.

**6** You have one arm or you see a one-armed person: you will feel powerless, unable to act or react in a given situation; possibly you will have dealings with someone who demands your help or intervention in their situation.

**7** Your arms feel heavy: you will be tired or faced with a difficult situation.

**8** You have one or two broken arms: this denotes conflict and disagreement with one or more of your friends.

**9** You knock your elbow: this signals an emotional upheaval or some surprising news.

**10** You are signalling to someone with your arms: you will be forced to ask for help; don't hesitate or it will be too late.

**11** Someone is signalling to you with their arms: someone you know wants to communicate with you or expects something from you, but you are not listening or you don't understand.

## THE HANDS (16)

**1** You have beautiful hands: you will demonstrate skill, knowledge and practicality.

**2**   Your hands are bent: your words will be twisted and your acts or intentions misconstrued.

**3**   Your hands are dirty: you have yet to resolve a long-standing problem or find a solution to a difficulty linked to your past; you will have to face these sooner or later, since they are affecting your current actions.

**4**   You are afraid of getting your hands dirty: you will hesitate to embark on an adventure or affair, about which you are doubtful; or you will refuse to help.

**5**   You are washing your hands: you refuse to take part, give your opinion or to involve yourself in a situation. This can also herald prestigious personal success.

**6**   You have burnt one or both hands: you will have dealings with malevolent people or jealous friends. Alternatively, by wanting to help certain friends, you risk falling into a trap.

**7**   You are shaking hands with someone: you can count on the unconditional help or support of your friends or relations.

**8**   Your hands are tied or chained: you will be powerless, trapped in a situation or left with no choice but to wait.

**9**   Your hands are swollen: you are in danger of conflict with your friends.

**10**   Your hands have been cut off: if this concerns your right hand, it denotes treachery to come from a man claiming to be your friend; if it is your left hand, it indicates treachery by a woman who calls herself a friend. If both hands are cut, you will be betrayed or duped by a couple. It can also herald a break-up or the loss of a friend, associate or situation that you felt you had under control.

**11**   You are wearing gloves: this is the sign of an active, prestigious social life and the respect of your friends and relations. It can denote an obsequious character who hides his or her true nature or a lively, flexible, subtle character who can adapt to all situations.

## THE FINGERS AND NAILS (17)

The meaning of your dream can be interpreted differently, depending on whether your thumb, index, middle, ring or little finger plays a dominant role.

1    The thumb represents your desires: an injured thumb denotes an unsatisfied desire, an impossible dream or a project that will not come to fruition as planned. A missing thumb reveals a feeling of powerlessness, lack of fulfilment or frustration. A deformed or misshapen thumb is a warning of a problem with your sight or understanding.

2    The index finger represents your moods – your joy or sadness: a wounded index finger indicates an inability to make a choice. It can represent anxiety or a tendency to harbour grudges, repress your emotions or suppress your anger. A missing index finger reveals that you will soon shed your sadness and fear. A raised index finger heralds a tendency to take a stand, make your opinion known or express yourself clearly. A deformed or misshapen index finger warns of a problem with your gall bladder.

3    The middle finger symbolizes your will: a wounded middle finger indicates indolence or a lack of will and tenacity. A missing middle finger heralds an end to your dark thoughts, whereas a raised middle finger represents a happy and smiling nature. A deformed or misshapen middle finger warns you of a malfunctioning spleen or pancreas.

4    The ring finger denotes your emotions: if injured, it indicates conflict or disappointment in your relationship with your partner or a latent hypersensitivity. If your ring finger is missing, you will reveal a secret, be free to indulge a deep passion or discover that a particular fear is unfounded. A raised ring finger indicates that you will give vent to your feelings. A misshapen or deformed ring finger is a warning of a problem with your liver.

5    The little finger denotes your feelings: an injured little finger indicates heartache or misunderstandings. If your little finger is missing, it means the end of a love affair. A raised little finger heralds a period of truce in a difficult emotional relationship, or a future ability to appreciate others and understand your situation, relationship and feelings more clearly. A misshapen or deformed little finger warns of heart problems or high blood pressure.

6    Long or growing nails: herald unrealistic projects or ambitions well above your means.

7    You have painted nails: you are overly tempted to trust appearances and see things superficially.

**8** You file your nails: you will have financial difficulties or will need to economize. This can also mean an urgent need for a fierce defence of your rights or prerogatives.

**9** You cut your nails: your profits or benefits will diminish, or you will lose your combative edge. This may indicate a lack of self-confidence in the future.

**10** You lose your nails: you will suffer financial losses; you will not profit through a lack of aggression, opposition or resistance.

## THE CHEST, TORSO, BREASTS (18)

**1** Your torso is bare: you will not be afraid to express your sentiments clearly; you will wear your heart on your sleeve and reveal your sincerity and authenticity.

**2** You see a man with a naked torso: if he is someone you know, you can trust this person because he is open; if it is a stranger, you will feel a deep and sincere affinity for someone you meet.

**3** You see a bare-breasted woman: if you know the woman, this foretells a kind-hearted female who will help, support or protect you. If she is a stranger and you are a man, it is the expression of a future desire for a woman you know or, alternatively, it heralds a sensual rather than sentimental encounter or adventure. If the woman is a stranger and you are a woman, it reveals a future need to be more in harmony with your ideas and thoughts, to be calmer and closer to those you love and who love you.

**4** You see a woman with beautiful breasts: a woman close to you is generous, thoughtful, kind and attentive; or you will have a lovely surprise and your desires will be fulfilled.

**5** You see a woman with very large breasts: this is a sign of prosperity for your family but it is also an indication of a generous and flourishing nature, of vitality and great happiness.

**6** You are caressing a woman's breasts or you are breastfeeding: you need to surrender yourself to your emotions.

**7** You see a woman whose breasts are heavy with milk: this is a sign of potential wealth, profitable enterprises or situations or an increase in your financial rewards.

**8** You see a woman breastfeeding: this heralds joy, happiness, harmony or emotional fulfilment in your relationships with your partner or family (*see also* BABY, p. 67).

### THE ABDOMEN (19)

**1**   You have a flat, smooth abdomen or you see someone with such an abdomen: you will have meagre resources or you will conceal your profit or possessions. It can also mean that you lack vitality and joie de vivre.

**2**   You have a round, fat abdomen or you see someone with such an abdomen: your profits will increase; or it may be an expression of your reliable and resourceful nature and your ability to influence your friends and impose your strong and slightly overwhelming personality. It could also be a manifestation of your vitality and love of life.

**3**   You see a pregnant woman: you will hear good news or you will improve your financial situation and increase your material gain.

### THE NAVEL (20)

**1**   You see or display your navel: you have a self-centred, egocentric character and lack of objectivity and generosity. Alternatively, you will not rest until you uncover the deep or hidden reasons behind your actions, desires and current preoccupations.

**2**   You see the navel of another person: this is the core, the root cause of the problem that is currently preoccupying you, and you will become aware that you are not alone in encountering such difficulties.

### THE RIBS (21)

**1**   You see your ribs: you will experience a period of restriction or the need to make economies.

**2** You see someone else's ribs: someone you know will ask for your help.

**3**   You have a cracked or broken rib: worries or concerns caused by a woman in your circle will confront you or this woman will have material or health worries herself

## THE BACK (22)

1   Your back is bare: you will disapprove or disagree on something.

2   Your back is painful: you will be betrayed or deceived by someone you know or you will doubt their honesty or trustworthiness.

3   You turn your back on someone: you will be unaware of or refuse to confront a delicate or difficult situation. Alternatively, your close relationship with a friend or relation will deteriorate.

4   Someone turns their back on you: either a particular person will remain indifferent to your desires or projects or you will make an impossible demand.

## THE SPINE (23)

1   You have a deformed or painful spine: this reveals a weak character, a lack of willpower or an unstable situation.

2   You have a straight spine: this indicates a stable, solid, faithful and balanced character.

## THE KIDNEYS (24)

1   You have a pain in your kidneys: this heralds a problem within the family or particularly onerous responsibilities. It can also indicate a weak character.

2   You have damaged or diseased kidneys: your progress will be cut short, you will be unable to reach your destination or fulfil your goals.

## THE HIPS (25)

1   You have splendid hips: this is a sign of good health, well-being, generosity or longevity.

2 You have narrow hips: this indicates an introverted character lacking in generosity, openness and flexibility; it can signal failing health.

3   One or both hips are broken: your excesses and lack of self-restraint will be your downfall.

## THE SEX ORGANS (26)

**1**   You have male sex organs: if you are a woman, this indicates a sign of a strong wish to assert yourself and great self-confidence and decisiveness. If you are a man and the genitals are disproportionate, it denotes excessive confidence, and abuse of power and authority; it warns that you will be blinded by your own desire.

**2**   You have female sex organs: if you are a man, this indicates that you are in control of your instincts and emotions.

**3**   You have both male and female genitals: this both symbolizes and helps you to understand the ambivalence of your own personality and that of others; it points to the duality of life itself, and in particular that of men and women. Behaviour in both sexes can be masculine and feminine without implications of sexual ambiguity; by possessing two sets of sexual organs you can enjoy the sensitive, emotional and receptive side of your nature together with the active, creative and positive aspect, thereby achieving a sense of wholeness or fulfilment.

**4**   You are caressing your genitals: this is often a compensatory dream, which is easily interpreted; it can also reveal an element of narcissism and self-satisfaction, a tendency to be self-sufficient but emotionally immature, and a fear of expressing your true self and desires.

**5**   You are displaying your genitals: this indicates a lack of self-confidence or an indication of the need for other people, or of their approval, in order to undertake or complete something that is very close to your heart.

**6**   You have a sexual relationship with someone you know: whether you are a man or a woman, this heralds a desire for reconciliation with this person, for a good relationship with him or her or for agreement with their ideas. It may denote a wish to be this person, to be in their position or to be identical to them.

**7**   You have a sexual relationship with a stranger: this is an expression of your desire for independence, for clear demarcation from your family or social environment, for the opportunity to take on your desired responsibilities and risks.

**8**   You have several genitalia or someone else has: you have a deep need for a sensual and emotional attachment or a thirst for absolute love.

9    You are invited to or attend an orgy: this reveals idealism, a desire to devote yourself entirely to a common or collective cause, to sublimate your own desires in order to devote yourself to others.

## THE BUTTOCKS (27)

1    Attractive naked buttocks: these are a sign of fertility, generosity, prosperity and affluence.

2    Small naked buttocks: these denote energy, dynamism and impulsiveness (*see also* HIPS, p. 91).

## THE THIGHS (28)

Depending on whether they are open, closed, flabby or firm, thighs reveal whether you give in to or resist your desires, influences or the will of others.

## THE LEGS (29)

1    You have splendid healthy, muscular or tapering legs: you possess the willpower or intellect needed to control your energy, impulses and psychological or professional development. This is a good omen and encourages you to stick to your current path without diversion.

2    You have fragile legs with pins and needles or high blood pressure: you are or will become the victim of your desires and feelings and unable to control them. The dream is a warning that you are on the wrong path and that your thoughtless behaviour could have damaging consequences in your life.

3    You have broken one or both of your legs: your impatience or lack of inner balance will bring difficulties and obstacles into your life.

## THE KNEES (30)

1    You have painful knees: your overweening pride restricts your inner and external development.

2    You have injured knees: your self-esteem has been or will be dented.

3    You are wearing kneepads: your pride results in a tendency towards self-protection and isolation. If you remove the pads, it is an indication of humility and recognition of your weaknesses.

## THE FEET (31)

1    You have bare feet or walk barefoot: you are or will be in a precarious, restrictive and difficult situation, in particular with relation to your finances and possessions. It can also mean that you neglect or waste your own energy and creativity, or that you know how to be modest and humble, something that will help you to develop both internally and externally. An additional interpretation is that you need to be more realistic and to maintain contact with strong, stable values.

2    You have large feet: this indicates your desire for worldly goods.

3    You have small feet: you will have a long way to go before reaching your goals or destination.

4    You have dirty feet: your vital energy is failing and it would be wise to have a general check-up.

5    You have one or more wounds on your feet: this has the same significance as the previous entry, but it can also denote contradictory or unrequited desires.

6    Your feet are deformed: you lack self-confidence or self-awareness. Alternatively, you will experience feelings of shame, confusion and disappointment.

7    You are washing your feet: you will pay for your mistakes, and things will return to their natural order (*see also* BAPTISM, p. 69).

8    You are washing the feet of someone else: here you are expressing secret desires and emotions towards this person, or you will help them to escape from a difficult situation or rectify their mistakes.

9    You have broken one or both feet: you are in such a weak psychological and emotional state that you could easily be the victim of an accident or fall. The dream warns you to take great care.

10   Your feet have been cut (off): you will be prisoner of a situation.

**11** You stamp your feet: this denotes impatience, anger, disagreement or refusal to act. It could also herald great joy (*see also* SHOES, p. 221).

## THE ANKLES (32)

**1** To sprain or break one or both ankles indicates a mental fatigue or weakness, poor decision-making, difficult relationships with those around you, upheaval in your social environment or a lack of communication.

## THE TOES (33)

**1** You have sprained or broken one or several toes: you are impatient and irritable. Alternatively, in spite of your tenacity or stubborn behaviour, you will be forced to let go of or give up something.

**2** You have deformed toes: you risk making errors in your future deeds or decisions. Take extra care.

## THE HEART (34)

**1** You can feel your heartbeat: you will have difficulty mastering your emotions or you will enjoy a new romance.

**2** You have a bad heart or a heart murmur: you are under pressure or hypersensitive. The dream is a warning to relax and remain calm.

**3** You see your own heart: do not doubt your feelings or those of someone close to you.

**4** You see your heart bleed: you feel unloved or emotionally wounded.

## THE LIVER (35)

**1** You have liver problems: you will experience very strong emotion or you live in fear of a crisis or upheaval in your situation or circle of friends. Alternatively, you will feel envy, jealousy, bitterness or anger.

**2** You see your own liver: this is a sign of emotional balance and physical health.

## THE STOMACH (36)

**1**   You have a bad, painful or heavy stomach: this indicates that you harbour grudges or refuse to accept changes within or around you. It could mean that you are rejecting your vitality and joie de vivre or are unable to flourish to your full potential. An alternative interpretation is that you will lack assurance or confidence in your means.

**2**   You see your stomach: this denotes your inner balance and sense of proportion, your temperate, measured nature.

## THE INTESTINES (37)

**1**   Your intestines are blocked or painful: you will tend to confuse problems, to be unable to separate and analyze issues in order to resolve your difficulties. Alternatively, you will refuse to say what you think.

**2**   You have diarrhoea: you will have an emotional upheaval or you will be overwhelmed by anger.

## THE VEINS (38)

**1**   You see your veins or they are swollen and bulging: your boldness will pay off, allowing you to achieve your goals; you may feel sadness and temporary nostalgia.

**2**   Your veins are hardly visible: you lack opportunity in your enterprises or projects; someone you know may cause you sadness or fear.

## THE SKIN (39)

**1**   You have beautiful, smooth, healthy skin: this indicates a love of life, unclouded happiness and a peaceful, serene existence; it also points to an opportunity worth seizing.

**2**   You have a damaged or diseased skin: you will be unable to hide or channel your concern and anxieties; you will sense your diminishing vital energy. The dream advises you to take care of your general health.

**3**   You skin is soft: this indicates the softness and delicacy both of your character and emotions.

**4** Your skin is rough or hard: you appear very reticent and unreceptive to the feelings and ideas of others.

**5** Your skin is dull, tanned or black: you will be unable to hide your desires or intentions, or you will wish to be seductive and pleasant.

**6** You have yellow skin: you are afraid or will fear to make a decision, take action or commit yourself.

**7** You have red skin: you will be incapable of concealing your joy and enthusiasm, your passionate and idealistic character.

**8** You are very thin, merely skin and bone: by reducing your expenditure and exploiting all your resources and potential, you will achieve your objectives.

## THE SKELETON OR BONES (40)

**1** You see your own skeleton or someone else's: this heralds a situation or relationship that will come to an end or a page in your life that you will turn. Alternatively, it denotes a need to be more consistent and active for your plans and ambitions to come to fruition.

**2** You see or feel your bones under your skin: you will be overwhelmed by work.

**3** You have a bone disease: your plans will not mature, your ambitions and initiatives will prove to be utopian or ill-founded.

## BOOK

**1** You read a book: your imminent autonomy will be matched by your responsibilities, or an important revelation will bring about major change in your future and personal development. Alternatively, you will meet someone who will play a key role in your life.

**2** You are reading an old book: it is time to put your ideas in order, to redefine your motivations, which have been blurred through your neglect, laziness or indifference.

**3** You read a book with a number of blank pages: you know the limits to your actions, the motives which drive you and the circumstances which prompt you – all you have to do now is act in order to stamp your style and authority on things.

# BOTTLE

If the bottle contains a message, genie, elixir or a potion fit for the gods, it is a good omen.

1    The bottle is full: it foretells good news, temporary happiness, clear-sightedness and intuition.

2    The bottle is empty: it indicates temporary absence or a passing frustration.

3    The bottle has been discarded: it denotes a plea for help or an important message, sent or received; it can mean news coming from afar or a revelation about to be made.

4    The bottle is broken: this reveals a fading hope, a disappointment or a frustration.

# BOW
### (*see also* ARROW, p. 66; GUN, p. 157; HARE, p. 159; HUNTING, p. 165; RABBIT, p. 208)

1    You see or possess a bow: this is a sign of physical or mental strength, of intellectual power that you can exploit freely.

2    If you dream of a bow in a quiver full of arrows: this foretells a developing situation or a pregnancy.

3    If you prepare your bow to hit a target:

•    if the target is close and easily visible: you will reach your goal, or your words are frank, direct and will hit the bull's-eye;

•    if the target is in the distance and unclear: you will hope to travel, or you will show yourself to be very ambitious. Alternatively, you may try to attain an ambiguous goal without being sure of reaching it. It may mean that what you say will be useless, your words will not be heard;

•    if you are hunting: you owe your achievements and gains to your own merits, efforts and skills. It can also mean that you make a judgement or speak your mind about someone in your circle (represented in your dream by the animal you are hunting – see the relevant animal in the glossary of symbols). It is equally possible that your dream is the expression of a desire that you will feel or display when meeting this person (see next point);

• if the target is human: someone in your circle will be impressed by your perspicacity, knowledge, lucidity or candour.

4   You break a bow: you surrender the use of your powers or strength or you refuse to speak or listen to the truth.

5   You make a bow: you will give yourself the means to exercise a power or authority. This can also herald a union or a marriage.

## BOWL

The contents of the bowl are important and you need to look up the relevant entry in the glossary of symbols.

1   A full bowl: this reveals that you are or will be in full possession of your means and will experience a period of wealth and abundance – albeit temporary – or that you will know how to profit from circumstances or to motivate yourself in order to reach your goals. It may signal that you will achieve satisfaction and fulfilment or that you must see your projects through to their conclusion.

2   An empty bowl: this denotes a need for love, understanding, tenderness, a chance to share and exchange feelings; the bowl symbolizes a demand or plea that will certainly be heeded and answered soon.

3   A broken or upturned bowl: this is an expression of exasperation often caused by your excessively passive or permissive behaviour. The dream is a warning to be proactive rather than laissez-faire.

## BOX

If a box plays an important role in a dream, it signifies a secret, a mystery or enigma concerning you or your life. Perhaps someone is hiding something from you or preparing a surprise for you; maybe you conceal things about yourself. Whichever the case, the contents of the box should be examined.

**1**   The box is empty: either you are harbouring illusions or false notions or you will not find what you are seeking, you are on the wrong path.

**2**   The box is full of different items: you have a surfeit of ideas, desires and confused, incoherent feelings, of which you should divest yourself.

**3**   The box is locked: you will refuse to see or appreciate what is happening within or around you.

**4**   The box is open: a secret will be revealed or you will discover very important facts relating to you.

## BRACELET

**1**   If you are wearing one or several bracelets on your forearm: you are too dependent on those close to you, on your family and friends; it can also indicate the advent of problems in your relationships with them.

**2**   If you are wearing bracelets on your wrist: the dream indicates a lack of firmness and determination and a tendency to dwell on your past. It can mean that you will have financial difficulties due to mistakes made in dealings with others, in controversial contracts or poor management.

**3**   If you are wearing one or more bracelets on your ankle: it denotes a current or future lack of free will. You are constrained by circumstances or by material or moral obligations.

## BRACES

A dream of seeing or wearing braces alerts you to certain mistakes that you have made and to the need to modify your behaviour or change your attitude. It counsels more conformist, appropriate responses in order to avoid reproach by others.

## BREAD
### (*see also* FLOUR, p. 142)

**1**   You are making bread: you will have lots of work to do, but you will feel highly motivated and are sure to reap excellent rewards.

**2**   You are eating hot, crusty golden bread: business matters will be fully satisfying, highly profitable and full of promise for the future.

**3**   Eating dry bread: this signifies that your financial situation will be worrying or very difficult, but this will probably be because you have lacked courage or tenacity in the past.

**4**   Someone steals your bread: you will lose a good job, or you will have to cope with some unexpected expenditure that will upset your finances.

**5**   You have a meal with no bread: you must be very patient if you want to achieve your goals.

**6**   Eating bread with the crusts cut off: this is a warning that you will have to prove yourself before you get what you want, or get where you want to be.

# BRICK
### (see also WALL, p. 248)

The appearance of one or more bricks in a dream is often a sign of prosperity for your family or household. It sometimes heralds the acquisition of a home or property but also underlines the protective and provident way in which you care for those close to you.

# BRIDGE

**1**   You see a bridge: you can depend on a solid and reliable situation; or you will come into contact with a very strong character who has a determined, powerful nature and a good understanding of human relationships. Alternatively, whatever is preoccupying you now will slowly but surely change – just give it time.

**2**   You are crossing a bridge: you are about to go through an important stage in your life, or you will be reconciled with a relative, friend or neighbour.

**3**   You see a burning bridge: once you have made a choice or taken a decision there will be no going back; it could mean that an agreement or contract will fall through, or that a partnership or marriage will not go ahead.

**4**   You see a bridge collapse: you will have a serious disagreement with one or more people, or break off all contact with him/her/them.

# BROOM

The appearance of a brush or broom in your dream is a sign of self-protection, of regeneration, an independence of spirit and an ability to transform yourself and develop of your own accord.

1   You are sweeping your home or a house: this signals happiness and prosperity for your family, your home and yourself. Alternatively, it heralds a happy change or a useful transformation within your family or household.

2   You are sweeping outside or in front of your door: your situation and relationships will need a clean sweep, a clarification.

3   You are flying on a broom: you will succumb to instincts, hasty impulses and blind or fervent desires. You will allow yourself to be swept along.

# BUCKLE or EARRINGS

1   You are fastening or unfastening a buckle on a belt: you are giving in to or repressing your feelings, sensuality or impulses (*see also* BELT, p. 74).

2   Earrings: they should be seen as an encouragement to pay more attention to what others have to say. Alternatively, they symbolize your ability to distinguish the real from the false and to recognize the truth, to understand the unspoken. They may signal that you are in a state of anticipation or readiness for love or they may foretell the arrival of a gift from a woman.

# BULL
### (*see also* ARENA, p. 64; OX, p. 198)

1   To dream of a bull means you will meet somebody with a powerful, possessive, materialistic and wild character. Alternatively, both sides of your nature will be given free expression – your wild, untamed side and your feeling, loyal side – or you will need to gain control of a situation, and study it very seriously and with extreme confidence.

2   A raging bull foretells that you will irritate somebody who is pernickety, realistic, obstinate and probably also selfish. This person appears to be calm and level-headed, but this is a front, and

underneath there lies a rather violent character; or else you will be unable to control your anger, or will reveal yourself to be very unforgiving.

3    If you are being charged or gored by a bull, beware of someone in your circle who bears a long-standing grudge against you; this dream can also augur difficulties or problems in a work or family relationship.

## BUSH

If you see or fall into a bush in your dream and you are male, it means a woman loves or desires you. If you are female, it indicates the idealism of your feelings. It is also the sign of a lively, imaginative and productive mind. If the bush is prickly, you will experience a great passion or sensual love that will be both difficult and painful. It can also signal worries and problems in relationships, or conflict with one or more women of your acquaintance.

## BUSINESS CARD

1    If it is your own card: it shows that you are preparing for an important event and want to show yourself in your best light.

2    If the card belongs to someone else: it reveals that others respect and love you and that you will soon learn this.

3    If the card is blank: it means that you will be free to act as you please.

## BUTTER

Butter is a sign of wealth, prosperity, fertility or profit. However, if the butter is melting, your prosperity is at risk of dissolving like snow in the sun. You are advised to act wisely and cautiously. If you are suffering from an illness, it heralds the prescription of an effective remedy that will bring about a speedy recovery.

## BUTTERFLY

1. You see a butterfly: an important change will take place in your life, or you will to behave in a careless, lackadaisical manner.

**2** You are chasing a butterfly: you love someone who is unfaithful or inconstant. Alternatively, your emotional relationships lack continuity or depth. If you catch the butterfly, someone you meet will change your love life and the way you behave when in love.

**3** You see or own a collection of multi-coloured butterflies: you like to charm and to be courted, but you do not know how to love, or you do not want to be in love.

## BUTTONS

**1** If one or more buttons is missing from your clothes: whether you like it or not, you will be unable to conceal your true thoughts for very long and others will be able to read you like an open book. It can mean that you are about to abandon your distrust of someone in your circle or that you feel defenceless and ready to let go.

**2** If you see a large number of buttons: you are aware of the futility and relative value of money and of the fleeting, illusory nature of worldly goods.

**3** If you see cufflinks: they denote awareness of a need to keep up appearances while still remaining determined and steadfast.

## CABBAGE

**1** You see a cabbage: this heralds an imminent birth or good health.

**2** You plant a cabbage: this foretells longevity, an excellent physical condition and great energy.

**3** You eat a cabbage: this is a sign that you should think about your health and perhaps take preventive measures.

## CADUCEUS

A caduceus, or winged staff entwined with serpents, is the emblem of Mercury, the messenger, subsequently associated with healing. To see a caduceus in your dream is a portent of recovery from illness or of concern about your health; it can announce a future union or marriage. Alternatively, it heralds sensual pleasure and passion or fertility and the early stages of pregnancy.

# CALENDAR

The appearance of a calendar reveals that you are conscious both of the passing of time and the perpetual cycle of life. The regular pattern and cycle of seasons is punctuated by constant change and endless transformation and the calendar represents the paradox of simultaneous birth and death, the origin of all life on earth. What you do with the calendar in your dream plays an important role in understanding what you do with your time; it reveals whether this notion of time is part of your consciousness or rejected as a result of anxiety.

# CAMEL

1    You see a camel: this heralds an imminent feeling of sadness, loneliness or isolation. Alternatively, someone you know will become indifferent or unapproachable.

2    You are riding a camel: it signifies that you will set off on a voyage or that, in a new phase of your life, you will feel that you can rely only on yourself.

# CAMERA
### (see also PHOTOGRAPH, p. 201)

If you dream of using a camera, this signifies that you should focus and concentrate upon a precise subject in order to see things as they are rather than how you wish them to be. You will then be in a position to view and appreciate reality in a defined and limited context, while trying to remain objective. If the camera you are using in your dream is defective or if the photographs that you take using the equipment are blurred or badly framed, you can clearly see the need to focus in your own life.

# CAMPING
### (see also TENT, p. 238)

Camping is a representation of the way in which we install our-selves temporarily in a place in order to rest, enjoy a break or await patiently a particular event or thing. Think of the transient nature of your present situation; what you are involved in at the moment is no more than a stage in your life, a passing moment.

If you are camping in a calm, beautiful environment, you will enjoy an especially beneficial period, experience an idyllic situation or an ideal relationship – but only temporarily. The dream warns you not to put down roots in this situation or to make the relationship an end in itself; instead, you should realize that this is just one phase in your life.

# CANDLE

1   A lit candle can have a number of meanings:

- if the flame is weak: events in your life will follow their usual pattern and you will feel calm, patient and self-aware;

- if the flame is strong: this indicates that events in your life are shooting ahead and you will be enthused by an exciting situation or an inspired idea.

2   An extinguished candle: it means that you lack joie de vivre and enthusiasm and are not exploiting your potential. Alternatively, you know something you will not reveal and you are refusing to communicate your knowledge or your skill, which means you are of no use to anyone. Finally, it could be that there is a touch of eccentricity in you that is begging to be released and expressed.

# CANNON

1   If the cannon is directed towards you: it indicates that you are living in fear of a crisis or conflict that is directly linked to you; if it points in the opposite direction, this fear concerns someone connected to you.

2   If you fire the cannon or order it to be fired: it heralds well-deserved recognition or reward; it may also signal good news or a birth among your friends.

3   If you hear cannon fire, it can have a variety of meanings:

- several fusillades in a war situation: this signals a concern or threat felt by you or an approaching problem or conflict that you will have to face, sooner or later;

- a single shot: this foretells surprising news.

4   If several cannon are in action: a necessary yet beneficial crisis or rupture is heralded.

# CAPE

If you are wearing a cape, it means that you are draped in your dignity, protected and cosseted by your ideas and principles. If you hide behind your cape in order to travel incognito, it signifies that you do not show your true self and that you seek to allay suspicion about your intentions or your personality.

# CAR

If a car appears very clearly in your dream, try to take note of the shape and colour of the vehicle.

1  If you are driving the car: this stresses the importance of your responsibility for the events and circumstances of your life. The way in which you drive is an indication of your clear-sightedness, prudence and your good or bad behaviour.

2  If you are driving a car with ease on a wide, clear road without obstacles: your path is clear and you can proceed confidently and safely.

3  If you are driving a car with difficulty on a narrow road or one full of traps: your path in life is narrow and you will have to overcome many obstacles before achieving your goal.

4  You are zigzagging along the road: you are unsure of how or where to direct yourself, or you will behave in a somewhat unreliable and frivolous or downright thoughtless way.

5  You are driving in fog: you should take extra care since you do not know where you are or where you are going (*see also* BLINDNESS, p. 77).

6  You are driving a new vehicle: you will be able to demonstrate your ability by taking a new position or assuming a new responsibility. Alternatively, you will receive a reward or an encouragement for your achievements and skills.

7  You are driving an old or second-hand vehicle: this denotes a lack of freedom and independent action; it can also indicate that your progress or projects will be slowed down or curtailed. Perhaps your means do not match your desires and ambitions.

**8**   You are driving at speed: you are impulsive and determined and will go straight to your objective.

**9**   Your car breaks down:

•   due to a mechanical fault: elements and events outside your control but caused by past mistakes and negligence are in danger of compromising your plans, ambitions or desires;

•   due to a lack of petrol: you will lack foresight or you will overestimate your power. Whichever is the case, your plans are in danger of being brought to an abrupt halt.

**10**   You are driving a stolen vehicle: you will suddenly change your mind, direction, view, decision or behaviour.

**11**   You cause an accident: you need to take care – a physical or mental shock is inevitable unless you change your attitude, behaviour and manner. The dream does not foretell an accident in which you or others will be fatally wounded, but it acts as a warning against excessive, exclusive or unilateral behaviour and advises you to change course or take time to reflect and see things more clearly.

**12**   You are the victim of an accident: an unexpected or unforeseeable event threatens to occur in your life, bringing your plans or progress to an abrupt halt. You need to be aware of this and be doubly careful.

**13**   Your car is showing signs of age or damage: you should take great care of your general health in the future. It can also mean that you are using inappropriate measures in your current situation.

**14**   Your car loses a wheel: the assumptions on which you will proceed or develop are unreliable, or you need to attach less importance to practical and concrete reality and more to the less rational, more creative and spiritual values.

**15**   You do a 180-degree turn: you will reach a turning point in your life or you will have to make an abrupt volte-face or reverse. Whichever the case, expect a phase in your life during which you will need to face important decisions and changes.

**16**   You are driving on the wrong side of the road: you will need or want to escape well-trodden paths and routine, predictable behaviour. Alternatively, your imagination and independent spirit (and even your contradictory side) will become increasingly important in your life.

**17** You allow yourself to be overtaken by other vehicles: you will fall into bad company whom you should not trust. The dream can also signify that you will be caught out or trumped despite your confidence in yourself and your resources.

**18** You are a passenger in the car, seated next to the driver: you will be driven to giving advice or help to someone in your circle. Alternatively, it may be you who will need the support of one of your friends to put you straight or to achieve something.

**19** You are a passenger in the back of the car: you will allow yourself to be guided or driven by circumstances or events in your life.

**20** If you pass your driving test: you will receive the power or authorization ('the green light') to undertake or achieve a desired project. You will be fully responsible for your decisions and deeds, together with their consequences.

**21** If you fail your driving text: this signifies a lack of will, tenacity, autonomy or independent spirit.

**22** If you dream that you are driving without a licence: you will do anything to achieve your goals: break rules, take risks, do impossible things.

**23** You car has no brakes: it will be too late to halt your momentum, to give up your intended project – you will be forced to see it through to the end, whether you wish to or not.

**24** Your car has had a collision and its bodywork is damaged: you are incapable of concealing from others or from yourself the shock, wounds, and psychological and emotional ordeals that you have suffered.

## CARESS

**1** If you are caressing someone: you feel the need to provoke reactions in others, or, conversely, that you fear their response and are trying to keep them calm.

**2** If you are being caressed: people are flattering you and appear to appreciate and love you, but you are need to check other aspects of your dream in order to ascertain if these feelings are sincere. Alternatively, you need the recognition of others to stimulate and reassure you.

## CARROT

1 A dream of one or more carrots: this is the manifestation of your current desires, impulses and motivation.

2 If you are eating raw carrots: it can herald the loss of your voice or the advent of a respiratory problem or a developing pulmonary illness that requires preventive action. It can be the sign of a surprising event, which will literally take your breath away or leave you speechless.

3 If you are eating cooked carrots: it can be a warning of a physical or psychological fear or of a lack of energy and dynamism.

## CART

If you see or push a cart, it is an encouragement to sow before you reap, to pull up your sleeves and work hard. Alternatively, it is a sign of union or pregnancy.

## CASTLE

1 You see a castle: this is a symbol of your pride, sense of honour or automatic self-defence mechanism in dealings with others and with the outside world; you will learn from your experiences in the dream.

2 You are living in a castle: your pride and ambition is in danger of leading to a certain state of isolation and emotional frustration; you need to be more aware of these tendencies within you.

3 You are in a besieged castle: you sense danger and fragility in the defences that you have constructed between yourself and others; you fear these walls may fall and leave you unprotected and exposed. However, take comfort from this – it is all to the good.

## CAT

To see a cat is an indication that you will land on your feet again, whatever your current situation; you will find your place in the world once more as things return to their original order. Alternatively, it is a warning of a relationship with someone cunning, subtle, apparently friendly but untrustworthy; he or she is in danger of deceiving or betraying you.

## CATAPULT

**1** You hurl a missile from a catapult: you will be critical, acerbic and aggressive.

**2** You see or are given a catapult: you will display such a rebellious and contradictory spirit that those trying to communicate with you may be tempted to give up.

**3** Missiles are hurled at you from a catapult: you will be the target of critical, malicious or wounding remarks.

## CATASTROPHE

A catastrophe, whether explosion, fire, earthquake or tidal wave, denotes an important and necessary upheaval in your life or behaviour. It reveals self-awareness or personal development that cannot happen without a catalyst, such as a shock, rupture, loss or failure. The message contained in this dream is comparable to that revealed by the XVI card of the Major Arcana in Tarot, the House of God (the Tower), which predicts an inevitable rupture or the downfall of someone who has acted unilaterally and followed the wrong path, with presumption and imprudence. A reversal of the situation is required to enable the person involved to transform his/her behaviour and life for the better. However, it is important to remember that the predictive role played by a dream is a warning of upheaval, a sudden event or a challenge to your circumstances. It encourages a wise and measured response with regard to your situation or actions, direct or indirect, short or long term.

**1** If you emerge safe and sound from a catastrophe: it can be interpreted in two ways, depending on the circumstances in your dream:

• whatever the upheaval or the changes around you, you will remain largely untouched by them;

• the upheaval or changes around you or provoked by you will not be dramatic enough to change you, whatever your situation.

**2** If you are the victim of a catastrophe: it heralds a change in attitude or situation, dictated by certain circumstances; you will suffer the consequences.

# CAULDRON

1   You see a full cauldron: this is the expression of active forces that are bubbling up in you; it indicates mental activity and great potential within you, which is demanding to be expressed. It can also be a sign of abundance and prosperity for you and your family.

2   You see an empty cauldron: you are too passive or you may feel that everything you do is to no avail and that you are of no use to anyone. Alternatively, the dream can mean that you will fail to keep your promises and engagements or that someone who behaves similarly will deceive you. Lastly, it signifies that you are willing to undertake or execute a new challenge in your life but you do not know yet what this is.

3   You see an upturned cauldron: this is a warning that your ideas, projects and undertakings to date are in danger of being suddenly challenged, compromised or spoiled.

# CAVE

1   You are in a cave: this indicates an event or project in the pipeline or an imminent change in your family or professional circumstances.

2   You are leaving a cave: you are ready to act, take responsibility and look firmly to the future. If you are in any doubt about your readiness, the dream acts as a strong encouragement for you.

3   The cave is dark, cold and threatening: you may be the victim of a betrayal or deception by someone you know. Alternatively, you are fearful of the future and resistant to change, thereby running the risk of retreating into yourself.

4   The cave has a narrow entrance:

  • if you are trying to enter the cave: this indicates that your desires and ambitions will not match your circumstances. Alternatively, you will be unable to effect the changes you want without putting in a good deal of effort and patience;

  • if you are trying to leave the cave: you are afraid to take the plunge, to move forward, to take on your responsibilities alone or to embark on a new project. However, you can get there in the end.

5   You live in a cave: you must not lose hope. You may make an important discovery or a new and happy event will occur very shortly in your life, helping you to progress and develop.

6   You find a precious item or treasure in a cave: you will experience a new feeling or enjoy a surprising, defining encounter; you will begin a new, stimulating and enriching relationship. Alternatively, you will enjoy a stroke of luck or a unique opportunity or a happy coincidence or a wonderful chance will occur in your life (*see also* TREASURE, p. 242).

## CELLAR

The sight of a cellar brings to the surface the very depths of your being. You are entering the universe of your own vital instincts, both creative and destructive.

1   The cellar is dark: unable to control your instincts, you are deluding yourself or will do in the future; this can cause dramas and repeated failures and you need to be aware of this.

2   The cellar is light: you find solutions to problems within yourself; or you are able to shed sufficient light on a difficult and painful situation by using your past experience as a reference. Alternatively, it can mean that you are not deceiving yourself.

3   The cellar is dirty or cluttered: you make no effort to have a clear understanding of your own character, or you are indulging in a certain moral lassitude. It could be that a painful affair or difficult situation – caused by your own weakness or the negligent behaviour of those close to you – is about to surface and will require clarification and resolution.

4   You search for or find a valuable object or essential item in the cellar: this is a sign of wealth, prosperity, and material and spiritual contentment gained by exploiting your own resources and inner strength. Your successful personal qualities are based on solid and durable principles.

5   The cellar is flooded: unknown to you, your feelings or anxieties threaten to overwhelm you. Alternatively, you are currently involved in a stifling or frustrating relationship but refuse to admit it.

**6**   The cellar is on fire: you are suppressing a strong desire, which is eating away at you from inside and threatens to be your downfall if you ignore or give in to it. Alternatively, this may be a warning to avoid reacting with anger or becoming inflamed by a cause that you think important.

# CEMETERY
## (see also FUNERAL, p. 150)

**1**   You are walking in a cemetery: you are nostalgic and seek to return to your past; but you realize that you cannot turn back the clock; news of death may reach you but will not surprise you.

**2**   You are locked in a cemetery: your nostalgia for the past, for a time that has gone, prevents you from living in the present and envisaging the future. You are becoming anxious and isolated as a result. Being locked in the cemetery indicates the need to realize the past is dead and buried forever, with no chance of return.

**3**   You find yourself by the grave of someone close to you, who is not in fact dead: if the person is ill, this heralds an imminent recovery; if he or she is worried, it foretells an end to their concerns. On the other hand, if the person has changed dramatically, either you are unwilling to admit it or you have yet to notice it. An alternative interpretation is that a distance or difference of opinion separates you from this person, and yet you are close to them in your thoughts and feelings.

**4**   You find yourself by the grave of someone who died long ago: this person is not responsible for the rupture of the emotional or psychological links that connected you, it is you who are no longer receptive to them. Alternatively, someone you know who has a direct or indirect connection with the deceased, will help you bring about an important change within yourself or your life.

# CENTAUR

**1**   You see a centaur: you will have dealings with someone whose uncontrolled feelings and desires will attract or seduce you; or your own unbridled passion is trying to reveal and express itself freely.

**2**   You are a centaur: you experience, currently or in the future, brutal or uncontrollable reactions and it will be hard for you to hear reason and calm down.

## CENTRE
### (see also CIRCLE, p. 118)

1    You are in the centre: you are at the heart of a situation and totally responsible for its development. Alternatively, you aspire to get to the core of yourself and those around you and to exploit all your potential.

2    You are looking for the centre: you are searching in all directions but you are unable to grasp or bring about a coherent pattern to your life at the moment. You need to pause and take stock in order to discover your true self or your way forward.

## CHEESE

A dream in which you see or eat cheese signals good health, well-being and vitality; it can denote a potentially advantageous and healthy financial or material situation, but one that you should exploit more fully. It could also warn that you may make too much of a minor event or unimportant matter.

## CHEQUE

1    You write a cheque: you are ready to give your word, show the colour of your money or play your hand in a situation.

2    You receive a cheque: your current situation is promising and shows potential, but as yet nothing has been achieved.

3    You cash a cheque: you can trust your present situation or be confident that someone you know will keep his or her promise.

## CHESTNUT

If you dream of a chestnut it is a sign of clear-sightedness, satisfaction and security in material and financial matters. However, if you are throwing chestnuts or if they land on your head, this means conflict or disagreement over money. On the other hand, if you eat them, it is a sign of success, reward and financial gain to come.

# CHILD
### (see also BABY, p. 67; CHILDBIRTH, p. 116; MOTHER, p. 186)

1   You see a child: girl or boy, it is your inner child that you see; it may be a sign that your behaviour is childish, infantile or that you lack simplicity, spontaneity and imagination.

2   A child gives you advice: you need to act or respond in a simpler, less dramatic, less rigid way and to take yourself less seriously.

3   You see a child asleep: this represents the sleeping child inside you, awaiting a wake-up call. When this happens it may make you happier, calmer and more carefree. Alternatively, you may soon lead a very serene existence.

4   You see a group of children playing together: there will be much excitement and enthusiasm around you, or your friends will prove undisciplined and rowdy.

5   You play with children: you will succeed in all your enterprises, simply and with ease, or you will not take your ideas, actions or circle very seriously.

6   You console a child: you will experience harm or grief but you will keep it to yourself; alternatively, you are not sufficiently aware of your own sensitivity or that of others with whom you have relationships.

7   You are with a badly disciplined, excitable child, who is disruptive or annoying: you must abandon your childish behaviour, act with responsibility and independence – in effect, it is time to grow up.

8   You see or take care of a sick child: you have lost your spark and your carefree, joyful spirit, but it is not too late to recover them. This dream could also mean that you feel helpless in the face of a difficult situation.

# CHILDBIRTH

1   You dream that you are giving birth: this does not necessarily indicate the birth of a child or a suppressed desire to have a child. It can signify the arrival of a new element in your life, a new dimension or a fresh understanding that has resulted from a period of gestation or extended reflection alongside an increased inner maturity. It can indicate a new situation that you will bring about, a

promise that will be realized or a project that will become concrete. The conditions in which the birth takes place should not be given undue consideration – what counts is the act of giving birth itself.

2   You are present at a birth: good tidings or news of a birth will reach you. It may be that you will learn of something new in your life or in your circle of friends. Alternatively, you will have a good idea, be inspired or have some success in one of your creative undertakings in the near future.

## CHIMNEY/FIREPLACE

1   You see smoke emerging from a chimney: you will hear news or rumours that you will doubt but which are true; or you will soon be able to give vent to your feelings.

2   You are sitting in front of a fireplace or you are burning wood: this is a sign of domestic tranquillity but also of passions brewing or slumbering within you.

3   You are sitting by an unlit fireplace: the future of your family situation worries you or you feel a certain malaise or lassitude in your household.

## CHOCOLATE

Seeing or eating chocolate is a sign of good physical and mental health together with a gentle, understanding and accommodating nature.

## CHRISTMAS

1   You are celebrating Christmas: a happy event or new experience is on the way.

2   You are celebrating Christmas, although it is not Christmas Day: you will receive a magnificent gift, or a wish is about to come true. Alternatively, a happy event or new experience will come earlier than you anticipated.

3   You see Father Christmas: this is a sign that you have kept in touch with your inner child. It may mean that you tend to indulge in wishful thinking but do not let yourself be taken in by it, or that you will encounter someone who is naïve but full of kindness and good intentions.

## CIRCLE

1    You are inside a circle: you feel protected from external events and at ease with yourself; you have no desire to leave your current situation.

2    You are outside a circle: you feel rejected, unloved and partially excluded from the society in which you live. Alternatively, you will experience a loss or leave a particular situation.

3    You are going round in circles: you cannot find a way out or a solution. You need to move outside the circle of your current ideas, relationships or regular activities (*see* ARENA, p. 64).

4    You are drawing a circle: if you try to control a situation or to limit its potential, you will only damage your own strengths or become more introverted.

5    You are at the centre of the circle: (*see* CENTRE, p. 115).

## CLOCK

1    To dream of a clock, pendulum, watch or alarm clock that has stopped or broken indicates that you are out of sync with events, either acting prematurely or intervening too late. The dream is a warning to ensure the time is right before embarking on any action.

2    You hear a clock, pendulum or alarm clock ringing: the time has come to act, choose or decide.

## CLOWN

1    You are disguised as a clown: you will feel rejected and misunderstood; or you will show a different, hitherto hidden aspect of your character.

2    You are playing the clown: you will be inclined not to take things seriously, to underestimate the dramatic nature of your situation or to distance yourself from those close to you.

3    You see a clown: you will learn something new, hitherto unsuspected, about a matter or situation that has been preoccupying you. It could be that someone in your circle will deceive you about his or her true intentions.

## COAL

1   You see, discover or collect coal: this is a sign of good fortune or a piece of luck, but it also puts you on notice that the energy and qualities you possess are not currently being exploited. You must face the tasks that will allow you to achieve your goals.

2   You keep yourself warm with coal: you are living on your reserves and need to beware your tendency to consume all your energy without thinking.

## COAT

1   You are wearing a new coat, or a warm, comfortable fur or leather coat: you are well protected; your position is comfortable and secure, financially as well as emotionally.

2   You are wearing an old or mended coat: contrary to what you might think, you will not be as well protected or supported as you would like; alternatively, you will act with false modesty that will not deceive anyone.

3   Someone offers you a beautiful coat: you will achieve your ambitions and succeed in business and in your dealings with people.

## COCK

1   You see a cock: this is a sign of the pride, vanity and self-satisfaction that you display in your behaviour or which is exhibited by someone with whom you are currently involved.

2   You hear a cock crowing: you will soon hear some important news; or you will be in a position to undertake or realize a new idea that is dear to you or an ambitious project.

## COCKROACH

1   If you see one or more cockroaches: you will have dealings with one or several deceitful people. Alternatively, you will be victim of malicious gossip or libel or receive some bad news. The dream can also mean a disappointment or discouragement.

2   If you kill one or more cockroaches: slander which you will hear or of which you will be the subject cannot touch you; it may

be that you will act firmly, overcome depression and shake off your dark thoughts.

3   If you find one or more cockroaches on your body or clothes: it is time to act, to stop being guided by fixed and inflexible ideas, and to change your attitude and situation by rejecting outdated behaviour to which you cling.

## COFFEE

1   You are drinking coffee: this indicates that you need a stimulant or tonic; it warns you to be more vigilant and attentive. It can also mean that you will hear inspiring or pleasant words.

2   You see coffee grains: unrealistic ideas and thoughts are fragile or bitter; they need to be adapted to circumstances. Only then can they stimulate or inspire.

## COFFIN

1   You see a closed coffin but you don't know if there is a body inside: you have a presentiment that important changes will occur in your life but you do not know what form these will take; you cannot see how they will help you move on from your past.

2   You see an empty coffin: you are feeling anxious without reason or are prey to dark, morbid or discouraging thoughts. Alternatively, you are in a relationship that is nearing its end and this is causing you concern.

3   You see a coffin containing a corpse: now is the time to turn a new leaf and look to the future.

4   You are lying in a coffin or the coffin is meant for you: you are ready to embrace all the new developments in your life, even if it means drawing a line through your past and abandoning your current situation or way of life.

## COLOUR

Each colour has its own individual interpretation. To help you integrate their significance into the wider context of your dreams, we give here the various symbolic meanings of colours in different contexts.

1   Black: signifies renewal through renunciation, oblivion, instinct, primitive life, necessary clarification as well as obscurity, adversity, sterility, finality, chaos, uncertainty, anxiety and jealousy.

2   Blue: symbolizes gentleness, receptivity, understanding, well-being, flexibility and adaptability, the conscience and the spiritual life. It also represents the unreal, dreams of utopia, incoherent and confused feelings.

3   Brown: represents realism, stability, humility, respect, discipline, moral fortitude and duty together with sadness, depression, servitude, material or moral obligations, fixed notions and authoritarianism.

4   Green: stands for hope, awakening, inspiration, aspirations, regeneration, healing, peace and clear-sightedness but also flexibility, carelessness, negligence, corruption and madness.

5   Grey: symbolizes balance, neutrality, wisdom, fairness and the unconscious as well as melancholy, boredom, drunkenness, confused ideas and ignorance.

6   Orange: stands for pure, ideal, sublime, absolute love, the union of souls and bodies; it also represents marriage, fidelity, debauchery, excess and lust.

7   Red: symbolizes a thirst for knowledge and power, action, creation, excitability, desire, impulse, passion and a love of life as well as perversion, secrets, hidden mysteries, the impulse towards creative or destructive power, anger and violence.

8   Violet: represents lucidity, reflection, inner equilibrium (psychological, moral and emotional), communication, exchange, the cycles of life and renewal; it also indicates instability, doubts, lack of inner equilibrium, inability to accept change and transformation.

9   White: represents purity, openness, gestation, birth, the beginning or the end as well as coldness, indifference, things yet to be revealed or completed and the invisible, imprecise and shapeless.

10 Yellow: represents the light of truth, authenticity, initiation, intuition, memory, faith, eternal life, fertility, dynamic and radiant intellect as well as deceit, lies, betrayal, disappointment, blindness, cowardice and the world of appearances and illusion.

## COMB
### (see also HAIR, p. 157)

**1** You are using a comb: what you are about to do will not be very enjoyable, or you will feel totally unmotivated and indifferent towards whatever it is you are doing; it may be that you will achieve the impossible in order to offload your worries or solve your problems.

**2** Someone else is using a comb: you will meet someone far too superficial, who looks ideal but lacks depth.

**3** Someone offers you a comb: you are going to quarrel with a relative or friend.

**4** You lose your comb: your ideas will be mixed up and your business affairs will be complicated.

## COMBAT

**1** You witness combat: you will be unable to remain indifferent to the problems and conflicts that are taking place around you and into which you will be dragged, sooner or later. Alternatively, take care of your health; this dream could denote that your body is battling for your health or that you need to fight illness.

**2** You take part in combat: you will encounter brutal adversaries and you will have to do battle to reach your goals or maintain your position.

## COMMUNION

**1** You are taking Communion: you sincerely want to have relationships that are simpler, calmer and more harmonious. You want to feel more secure in your relationships with those around you.

**2** You are attending a Communion Service: your projects will come to fruition or your wishes will be granted.

## CONSTRUCTION SITE

If you are crossing, find yourself in, or work on a construction site, you are in a transitory phase of your life. Some of your projects are coming to fruition but your situation is still unclear. You need to pay attention to the roots you are currently putting down in order to ensure that you are establishing a solid foundation.

# CORAL

Seeing a coral bed foretells skin reactions, you will feel hyper-sensitive or your nerves will feel on edge. Alternatively, this may indicate a deep suffering that you find difficult to contain or to hide.

# CORN
## (see also BREAD, p. 100; FLOUR, p. 142)

1   You see, give or receive an ear of corn: a happy event or an advantageous transaction will occur in your life. Alternatively, you will give or receive a reward that makes you very happy.

2   You see a sheaf or field of corn: this is a sign of prosperity, abundance and happy, fruitful relationships.

3   You see one or many grains of wheat: this heralds a necessary sacrifice that will prove worthwhile in the end.

# CORNERS

If you find yourself in an enclosed space with corners, it signifies a need to appreciate the limits within which you can or should act constructively in order to achieve the best results. It can also mean that you will encounter temporarily insurmountable obstacles, which will force you to reflect and to see things differently. Alternatively, you will come to understand that it is necessary to round off those corners, to show flexibility in order to achieve one's aims. The dream can also advise you to act in a less aggressive manner, to be less defensive and more open, with your innermost heart and spirit alert to the world and its progress.

# COSTUME
## (see also ACTOR and ACTRESS, p. 55; AMBASSADOR, p. 58; CLOWN, p. 118; COLOUR, p. 120; HARLEQUIN, p. 160; OFFICER, p. 196; PRIEST, p. 206)

1   You are wearing a new suit or new clothes: someone will make you an advantageous proposal and you will want to look your best,

display all your assets and potential and play your trump cards in order to seize this opportunity.

2    You are wearing a suit or garments that are worn, threadbare or old-fashioned or that you have not worn for a long time: you are hiding your true nature. Your constant reference to the past and your conservative tendencies prevent you from living in the present and being true to yourself.

3    You are wearing an unfinished suit or incomplete garments: you will behave capriciously, with good or bad consequences, depending on whether the different elements of your clothing match each other.

4    You change your suit or clothes: you can no longer dissimulate; others now know what you are, what you think and what you want.

5    You are wearing clothes that do not belong to you and that are inappropriate for your situation or character: you feel uneasy about yourself, disoriented, out of place and inadequate. It is important that you get in touch with your true nature.

## COUNTING

1    You are counting on your fingers: this is a sign of moral concern, material insecurity or a lack of self-confidence.

2    You are doing your accounts: you will have to put your affairs in order or pay a debt; or you should express your thoughts and feelings once and for all.

## COUNTRY

1    If you dream you are in a foreign country: you will soon be faced with an entirely new situation in which you will have to show imagination and initiative, quickly put aside your prejudices or pre-conceptions and change the way you do things.

2    If you feel like a foreigner in your own land: you will feel uneasy in your normal social milieu, or feel out of place or unsociable. This dream can also indicate that you will not achieve your goals, or that you will not be heard or understood in your natural environment or social milieu.

## COUPLE

1   If you see or form part of a happy, united couple: this is a sign of inner harmony or it marks the beginning of a period of feeling totally in tune with yourself.

2   You see or are part of a mismatched, disunited couple: you will behave in a way that you don't approve of deep down and this will create inner tension and conflict.

## CRAB

1   You see a crab: you have or will have dealings with someone who is very sensitive, shy, unapproachable but very possessive; or you will sidestep an issue to obtain what you want or to reach your goals.

2   You see several crabs: you will come in contact with hypocrites or your situation or relationships will deteriorate.

## CRIB

To see a crib signals joy, happiness, birth and prosperity.

## CROCODILE

1   You see or are pursued by a crocodile: you will have dealings with a malevolent person. Alternatively, someone will pursue you doggedly, doing everything possible to win you over, but you will be able to question his or her real motives.

2   You kill a crocodile: you will face adversity alone but will attain success.

## CROSS

1   You see a cross: you are at a crossroads; you will have to make a choice, but you have all the advantages on your side.

2   You are wearing a cross: you are currently experiencing a difficult or testing period, but you will soon come through it, provided you remain steadfast and face up to the situation, challenging both good and bad influences along the way. In other words, you are the best and only person to solve your problems.

**3**  You are kneeling before a cross: take courage in both hands and continue on the right path.

## CROSSROADS

If you find yourself at a crossroads in your dream, this indicates that you exercise your free will in order to choose your way, to embark upon a new route or to give a new direction to your life.

## CROWN
### (*see also* FAME, p. 137)

**1**  You are given a crown or tiara: you can be certain of reaching your goals sooner or later; your enterprise will succeed or you will be entrusted with new responsibilities.

**2**  You are wearing a crown: this denotes imminent material, social or professional success.

## CRYSTAL

**1**  You see crystal: this reflects the purity and sincerity of your emotions and intentions; it may herald your clear-sightedness and your desire to speak and know the truth. It can also denote imminent recovery from illness or health issues.

**2**  You are given or wear a diamond: this is a token of friendship, love, of sincere and requited emotion and deep, stable and lasting relationships.

## CUPBOARD

**1**  If you see an old cupboard: this denotes a confrontation with a past situation or an old story in which you played a key part and in which you certainly made mistakes. You probably thought it was over and done with and firmly in the past, but this is not the case, as the presence of this old piece of furniture in your current dreams indicates.

**2**  If you see a new or modern cupboard: your generosity and sociability hide many things, notably old-fashioned attitudes, which lie stored in the cupboard but will emerge sooner or later.

3   You see a cupboard with a locked door: this dream underlines the difficulty you experience in living in the present, accepting your current situation or acknowledging a tendency to conceal your feelings and jealously guard your secrets.

4   You see a cupboard with one or both doors open: the contents of the cupboard are of vital significance. You need to pick out the item(s) in the cupboard and consult the relevant entry in the glossary for their meaning; remember that the objects should be seen and interpreted within the context of your past and your inner life. If the cupboard is empty, it is a warning against loss or theft in your family or home.

## CURTAIN

1   Dreaming about open curtains, or that you are opening curtains: this signifies clarification about your job or life in general; or somebody around you will tell you a secret or reveal something.

2   Dreaming about curtains that are closed, or closing them yourself: this symbolizes the end of a situation or relationship; this dream can also mean that you will refuse to face the truth, however incontrovertible the facts may be.

3   A theatre curtain opening: heralds an important event that will be essential to your personal development or crucial to your future.

4   A theatre curtain closing: announces the end of a chapter in your life: you will turn the page.

## DAM

Seeing a dam in your dream indicates tensions or inhibitions. However, these can be positive or creative, since they will inevitably cause a reaction or release productive, dynamic energy. Should the dam break, this indicates that your long repressed tensions and feelings are on the point of breaking free and may overwhelm you.

## DANCE

1   You are dancing alone: you will find it hard to make a decision or you will enjoy new and varied activities.

2   You are dancing with a partner: you will find someone in your circle very attractive and will be unable to resist temptation.

**3** You see someone dancing: you will be courted by someone you know or whom you will soon meet; alternatively, someone in your circle will be unsure of what they want and will need you to make the decision for them.

## DATE

**1** You see a date that relates to an event from your past: an identical situation or event will confront you. The dream warns you to take appropriate action.

**2** You see a date from history: consult reference books to find out which event or situation this date relates to; it should throw some light on your current or future situation.

**3** You see a date that is in the future: this relates to the conclusion of a matter or problem that is currently preoccupying you. It heralds the end of a project, mission or affair.

**4** You see a date in the future that you know is fateful: be assured that this does not foretell an imminent mishap or fatality; instead, it encourages you to live life to the full and enjoy it day by day without too much concern for the future.

## DEBT

If you dream that you owe money or anything else to someone you know, you feel morally indebted to this person. If he or she is a stranger, it denotes an imminent encounter with someone to whom you will be indebted.

## DEER

To see, hear or hunt a deer denotes birth, fertility or prosperity for you or someone you know. It can also signify good news, the clarification of a situation, a feeling of relief or an encounter with an exceptional, unusual person in whom you will place your trust; this person will teach you stimulating, enriching, even primordial things.

## DESERT

**1** You see a desert: this heralds a time of solitude during which you will have to rely entirely upon your own resources.

**2** You are walking in the desert: take advantage of a few moments of solitude to get back in touch with yourself and recharge your batteries; you need or will need this renewed energy. Alternatively, your future words or deeds will be in vain; others will not hear, see or follow you.

**3** You see or discover an oasis: you will experience a period of rest, calm and respite; however, the dream advises you to keep going, since this represents no more than a stage on your journey.

**4** You see a mirage: this heralds the loss of your illusions, which is all to the good; you will soon get to the heart of the matter, the core of reality.

## DETOUR

**1** You make a detour to reach a specific destination: you lack simplicity and openness and you do not listen to others' advice, resulting in a failure to reach your goals as quickly as planned.

**2** You make a detour without knowing your destination: you are not clear, precise or organized enough in the planning or execution of your projects, thereby losing precious time.

## DEVIL

**1** You see or meet the devil: dangerous experiences or illicit adventures will tempt you, or you will fall under a malevolent or dishonest influence.

**2** The devil pursues or threatens you: you will have trouble getting out of a difficult, painful or restrictive situation. Alternatively, others will do all in their power to prevent you from achieving your goals.

## DIRECTION

**1** You are heading east: you will take an entirely new direction; you will undertake or execute a new project; a birth, creation or fortunate change will take place in your milieu.

**2** You are heading west: you will bring a matter to conclusion; you are all set to reach your goal and get what you want. This is a favourable time for personal development.

**3**   You are heading north: worrying or testing times await and are inevitable; you are heading towards a difficult path, one that is painful and testing but good for your development.

**4**   You are heading south: you will enter a splendid period in your life, during which your wishes will be fulfilled.

**5**   You change direction abruptly: an unexpected, unforeseeable and inevitable event beyond your control will force you to change your plans and bring about a reversal in your situation.

**6**   You don't know which direction to take: your indecision is not necessarily a bad thing, since you have to make an important decision and should take time to reflect upon it before acting.

## DISGUST

If you feel disgust, you will not rest until you extricate yourself from a difficult situation that incites your complete disapproval. An alternative interpretation is that you will harbour grudges that may harm your health.

## DIVER

If you dream about a diver or that you are wearing a wetsuit: you will go through a period of introspection, and will feel the need to intensify your relationships, your feelings and your sense of self; another interpretation is that you will have to work in secret for a time, in order to reach the goal you have set yourself.

## DOCTOR

**1**   You consult a doctor: this dream shows that you are determined to find a solution to your problems, whatever they are; you are ready to do whatever it takes to achieve this; it could also mean that you must not hesitate to ask for wise advice to help you achieve your aims.

**2**   You consult a doctor, knowing that you are not ill: you are worrying for nothing and you need no one's help to make the decisions that face you or to do what you have to do.

**3**   You are a doctor: serious illnesses demands serious measures; you will achieve your aims in your professional life, or in financial matters, but it will be a struggle; alternatively, someone will consult you and you will know exactly the right thing to do.

## DOG

1   You have a dog on a lead: you are in control of your instincts but you are still not happy. Alternatively, you will be held to certain obligations that will deprive you of your freedom and autonomy.

2   A dog bites you: someone you know harbours deep animosity for you and is in danger of harming you. Be on your guard.

3   You are stroking a dog: the dream questions whether you ought to trust those in whom you have confidence.

4   You see a dangerous dog: you will be either the victim or perpetrator of slander or malicious gossip that you do not know how to resist.

5   A dog is following you: someone in your circle whom you consider (now or in the future) to be untrustworthy will become a good and faithful friend.

## DONKEY

1   You see a donkey and you feed or stroke it: you aspire to a simpler life, to be true to yourself rather than hide behind appearances. You want to live at peace with yourself and with others. Alternatively, you will help or support an ungrateful person.

2   You mount a donkey: through modesty, patience and genuineness you will obtain what is rightfully yours. You will do what you have to, or you will achieve your goal – simply and without fuss.

3   You mount a donkey but cannot control it: this signifies that you will confide in a person or persons who are unworthy. It may be that your personality is more complex than you think or are prepared to reveal, but you will not listen to what others have to say on this subject and keep everything to yourself.

4   You mount a donkey, but it refuses to move: you lack confidence in yourself and faith in life. Despite your determination to proceed, your situation remains stagnant. The dream is advising you to let go, to stop keeping things to yourself and to change if circumstances require it.

# DOOR

1   If you dream of a door that is:

- closed, and you are inside: you refuse to be open with others, to say what you think or clearly express your wishes and intentions (Is this a good or a bad thing? Only you know the answer.) Alternatively, you will meet someone who refuses to accept their responsibilities and just likes to sit back and take things easy, or the outcome or solution on which you are depending cannot come about unless you take action;

- closed, and you are outside: if you do not act or react at the right time, or if you do not change your attitude, you will find the door closed in your face and no one will listen to you or help you; it can also mean that you will hesitate before making a decision about integrating into a new environment or going through a major stage in your life;

- open, and you are inside: you will have an unexpected visitor, or you are waiting for something new to come along, but nothing will happen until you resolve to change your routine habits and your daily grind, and confront reality or the outside world. Alternatively, anything is possible, as you are well aware, although you are free to close the door if you choose; the dream might equally indicate that you will glimpse a way out of your problems, or find a solution to them;

- open, and you are outside: you will receive an invitation, or you will do something new, change your career or get a new job that, in time, will prove lucrative.

2   If you dream you are knocking at a door: this signifies that you have an important initiative or decision to take.

3   If you are entering through a door: you are about to embark upon a significant stage of your life.

4   If you are going out through a door: you will find a solution to your problems.

# DRAGON

1   You see a dragon: you are not fully aware of the power of your cool temperament, strength of character, psychic power or your

energy, all of which will enable you to achieve your most ambitious goals; the dream signals that nothing will come between you and your ambitions.

2   You fight with a dragon: you will need to do battle to overcome difficulties and conflict or to get the better of an aggressive, malevolent person.

3   You see a sleepy dragon: you need to beware the storm of passion that is brewing within you; sooner or later, it may well rise up and upset your equilibrium or the stability of your position.

## DRAWER

1   An empty drawer denotes that a secret will be revealed to you or that you may be the victim of an indiscretion or a robbery or might have financial difficulties.

2   If you dream that you are rummaging in a drawer full of clothes or other items: facts or events from the past, that you thought had been settled for good, will become priority issues once again.

3   An item of furniture with many drawers indicates that a situation or relationship will turn out to be far more complex than you originally thought.

4   You find a secret drawer: you will discover something upsetting; alternatively, you will find hidden resources within yourself that you had neglected or never knew were there.

## DRAWING
### (see also PENCIL, p. 201)

1   You are drawing: you will make all kinds of plans and projections; you will need to execute them, but just how to do this will become clear in a future dream.

2   You see or are shown a drawing: you have no choice but to accept things as they are.

## DROWNING

1   If you are drowning: you are suffering the consequences of your own mistakes, but you tend to blame others for them. Alternatively,

you try to disguise your true intentions or to spread confusion around you. However, this attitude will not help you to resolve your problems or escape a difficult situation you feel is dragging you further and further down.

**2**   You are saved from drowning: you will finally escape from a difficult situation that seemed to offer no way out; or you will be able to count on the generous, spontaneous and selfless help of someone in your circle.

**3**   You save someone else from drowning: you will remain clear-sighted, lucid and calm in the face of difficult circumstances; or you will spontaneously offer help to someone who will be extremely grateful.

## ECLIPSE

**1**   You see an eclipse of the sun: your father (regardless of whether you are male or female) or your husband (if you are a woman) will cause you problems, either due to a sudden conflict between you, to a testing situation or a health issue. This dream may herald an abrupt disappointment or frustration, a loss or a period of emptiness.

**2**   You see an eclipse of the moon: your mother or one of your children (regardless of whether you are male or female) will be the object or cause of concern, either as a result of health problems or a sudden questioning of your relationship. It can denote that, owing to a lack of tact and flair in taking advantage of a situation, you will fail to achieve what you want or you will lose something. Alternatively, a project or a wish will not be realized.

## EGG

**1**   You dream about an egg, or an egg plays a significant role in your dream: this shows that you make yourself out to be more naïve or honest than you really are; or that an important event is in the pipeline, either in the family or at home – perhaps the birth of a baby, or a creation of another kind – or that you aspire to live in perfect harmony with those around you.

**2**   You are collecting eggs from a nest: you will make money, or your business affairs will prosper, or you will hear some excellent news about your family or home.

3    You see yourself putting eggs in a basket: this is a sign that you wish to gain maximum benefit from all the elements, assets and advantages at your disposal, with the minimum of risk; or that you may be too selective in your behaviour. However, by opting for all or nothing – 'putting all your eggs in one basket' – you risk losing everything.

4    You break one or more eggs: in order to get what you want, or for your plans to come to fruition, you must make certain sacrifices, call certain things into question, change your ways and take risks; or else this dream is an omen that a plan or deal will not come off.

5    You smash one or more eggs: this indicates that you will have to be extremely vigilant and take every precaution in a delicate situation or a deal that is far from in the bag.

6    You steal or hide an egg: you will try to hide the truth or cover something up.

7    Someone gives you some eggs: you will get the chance to strike some great deals; someone may give you money, or someone will share their true feelings or wishes with you.

8    You peel a hard-boiled egg or break its shell: you will lack generosity; you will refuse to acknowledge a fact or event that takes place within your family or household, or you will come across as a miserly person.

9    You dream of a hen laying eggs: this is a guarantee of great financial success.

10   You see, are offered or eat a chocolate egg in your dream: you will experience all the pleasures of mutual love and shared feelings. These will be very enjoyable, but whether they will be deep and lasting is another matter.

# ELECTRICITY

1    A power cut or interruption: this warns of an abrupt decline in tension or vitality or that an emotion or relationship will suddenly be open to question.

2    You get an electric shock or electrocute yourself: you will see stars soon, the result of a bolt from the blue in love or inspiration. This heralds an unexpected and exciting event.

# ELEPHANT

1   You see or encounter an elephant making slow and quiet progress: you will be wooed by someone or seized by a desire to please or seduce, to excite passion in a partner or stranger. Alternatively, someone you know will show great control despite having a forceful, even violent nature.

2   You see an angry or charging elephant: you will feel passionate feelings, irrepressible desire or a brutal, violent reaction to your partner or someone you know; or you will have difficulty mastering your impulses, controlling your emotions and resisting the temptation to be angry.

3   You ride an elephant: your emotional relationships are solid, reliable and calm, reinforced by your power, equilibrium and effectiveness. You will master with admirable skill all the resources to hand so that you can face any situation with remarkable sangfroid.

4   You see a herd of elephants: you will harbour grudges or bitterness that could eventually explode into sudden anger, upheaval or breakdown.

5   You see elephants performing in a circus: you will boast about your strength, courage and calm, but others won't take you seriously.

# EXCREMENT

1   You tread in excrement: your finances or situation will improve after concluding a favourable deal; or, should you lose your balance or footing, you will be tempted to profit by dishonesty instead.

2   You are soiled by excrement: some of your past actions or reactions will affect your behaviour or your present situation.

# EXPLOSION
### (see also CATASTROPHE, p. 111)

1   You see an explosion: a crisis, mood swing or feeling of anger will arise among your friends. Alternatively, you are over-emotional at the moment and about to crack or your concerns are ill founded. In fact, an upheaval or crisis in your personal or professional life seems inevitable.

**2**   You witness an explosion involving a number of victims: honourable exit from a difficult or critical situation will be possible, with minimal collateral damage.

**3**   You are the victim of an explosion: you will be angry, suddenly and violently disagreeing with or disapproving of someone you know. Alternatively, you will be unable to avoid sharp and abrupt criticism or rejection by one or more of your acquaintances.

# FACTORY

A factory signifies that you will participate in a joint project. It can also symbolize major upheaval and activity in your work or family life, or that you will need to work hard to get what you want.

# FAME
### (*see also* ACTOR and ACTRESS, p. 55; LOVE, p. 176)

**1**   You are in the presence of one or several celebrities: on the one hand, this underlines the importance of the message contained in your dream and, on the other, makes it clear that in the end there is no point concealing yourself.

**2**   You are in the company of one or more officials (heads of state, ministers etc.): this encounter is connected with the principles that govern, direct or influence your daily behaviour. Depending on the type of relationship you have with these people in your dream, you will be able to detect if you feel at one with yourself or not, if you are able to expand or express your personality or are inhibiting it. Alternatively, the dream heralds a mission with which you will be entrusted, a key role you will be asked to play or a project that will be executed sooner or later. The dream is an encouragement to achieve your goals.

**3**   You are a head of state, minister or official person: you will have a tendency to overestimate your means, potential, personality or opportunities.

**4**   A king or queen receives you (*see also* SUN, p. 234): this is a sure sign that your skills and qualities will be recognized and rewarded. Alternatively, you will achieve your objectives very rapidly.

**5**   You are a king or queen: you must display courage, will and determination; possibly you will take your mission too seriously.

Alternatively, you will be proud or arrogant or will have to play the role of mediator between apparently irreconcilable parties, with firmness and determination.

## FAMILY

**1**   You are with your family, surrounded by those you love, in a happy, joyful atmosphere: you tend to idealize your family relationships, in order to compensate for disappointments or frustration in this context. Alternatively, a happy event will soon occur in your family circle.

**2**   You are with your family but the atmosphere is tense: you lack autonomy or the ability to act totally independently. Possibly you will experience a need for psychological, emotional or moral equilibrium.

## FATHER

**1**   If you dream about your father: whether he is alive or dead, this is primarily a reminder of the nature of your relationship, and all that might have been left unsaid or misunderstood. The dream can also be an expression of your need to assume certain responsibilities and to take charge of your life. Another interpretation is that at present you are charmed or influenced by someone whose personality seems uncannily similar to that of your father – whether real or idealized.

**2**   If you dream about a father with his children: whether you are male or female, you are going to have to assume the role of head of the family.

## FEATHER

**1**   You see or are offered a feather: you will experience a fleeting moment of happiness; it may be that your current feelings will not last, or that someone loves you less than they pretend; or else you may receive a nice letter or hear some cheering news.

**2**   You see feathers flying in the wind: you will be fickle or unfaithful in your emotional relationships, which will probably be many and various, or you will find it hard to contain your anger or animosity towards someone who has tricked you or stolen from you.

**3** You are wearing feathers: you have style and panache but your bravery or daring are more for effect than effective.

## FEVER

A fever indicates a state of high excitement resulting from a fascinating project or a very promising situation; or that you will experience a new, heightened emotion. It could also indicate that your general health is or will be fragile and feverish – you may be counselled to take precautions.

## FINE

**1** You have to pay a fine: wrongly or rightly, you will feel at fault for a past act or will have to suffer the consequences of a mistake you have made. Alternatively, you fear being penalized for no reason or that you will be blamed for something in the near future.

**2** You pay up honourably: if your health is poor, you will soon recover. If you are in conflict with someone, you will soon become reconciled. If it is more a question of being judged or condemned unfairly, your honour is about to be restored.

## FIRE
### (*see also* TORCH, p. 240)

**1** You see a bonfire: you will enjoy happy and hopeful times; or you will express your joie de vivre, enthusiasm and your warm, joyful nature.

**2** You see a small fire: your actions and relationships lack generosity, warmth and passion. Alternatively, you will lack vitality and energy – recharge those batteries.

**3** You try to kindle a small fire: you will do everything in your power to motivate yourself or to encourage those around you but it will not be easy.

**4** You see a blaze: despite yourself, you will be caught up in the enthusiasm or blazing excitement that will ignite among those around you.

**5** You light a blaze: you will be fired with enthusiasm in your actions, ideas and emotions, but you risk making mistakes or behaving erratically with incalculable consequences.

6    You fight a fire or try to extinguish it: the dream questions your willingness or ability to dampen the flame of your desires and heightened emotions. If you suppress your emotions, you risk being consumed by their inner fire.

7    Flames surround you: you will have no choice but to face up to the passions that you have, willingly or otherwise, unleashed.

8    You see a firework display: your feelings are illusory or your projects unrealistic.

## FIREFIGHTER
### (see also CATASTROPHE, p. 111; FIRE, p. 139; LADDER, p. 171)

If you see one or many firefighters in a dream, you have a problem that urgently needs to be resolved; alternatively, you may find it difficult to contain your desires, passions and irrational impulses.

## FISH
### (see also WHALE p. 252)

1    You see one or many fish in clear shallow water: you are happy with yourself, at ease in your surroundings and in your element.

2    To dream of one or many fish in cloudy or deep water: means that your hopes will be dashed, or that you feel that you do not fit in with the people around you, and are uneasy about your friends and relationships.

3    If you dream of seeing or catching a big saltwater fish:

• dolphin: you are going to make a new friend, or that you will meet someone full of goodwill, on whom you will be able to rely in any circumstances; it could be that someone will guide you along the road to success, or that a reliable person will help you in your work or a quest;

• ray: you will encounter somebody whose physical appearance you may find shocking, but whose feelings and integrity will surprise you; alternatively, your intuition may turn out to be well-founded;

• giant sardine: something which seems trivial or insignificant now will turn out to have unexpected advantages or major benefits for you; or that you will have dealings with someone who, sooner or later, will have an important job or will have set their sights on one;

• shark: this is a sign that you will come across someone who will do anything to get what they want and may entangle you in dangerous situations; or that you will not be able to control or hide your aggression, greed or impatience;

• tuna: you will do some fantastic deals, or that, if you ask for a rise, you will get it.

4   If you dream of seeing or catching a freshwater fish:

• eel: a plan will fall through or that, despite your best efforts and goodwill, you will miss out on a deal or an opportunity; you may meet someone who shirks their responsibilities, does not keep promises or will leave you;

• pike: you will encounter a tough adversary who will eventually submit to your will;

• salmon: this is a sign that someone will contribute to your personal development; or that you will make a very important discovery that will change your view of the world, and perhaps even change the course of your life;

• trout: you probably feel you are swimming against the tide and acting differently from everyone else, but that your efforts will prove highly successful; or that you will meet an extraordinary person – a nonconformist who will greatly enrich your life.

5   If you see or catch small fish in your dream: you will have minor worries or problems.

6   You are eating fresh or raw fish: this indicates that good things are coming your way or that you are going to see a marked improvement in your financial situation.

7   You are eating fried fish: this indicates that your family situation will be slightly worrying; it may foretell problems in your relationship with a brother or sister, or a brother or sister may find themselves in a worrying situation.

## FLAG
### (*see also* COUNTRY, p. 124)

1    You are carrying a flag: your merits and qualities will be unanimously recognized and valued.

2    You see a flag: expect a conflict in your relationship with friends or neighbours.

3    You tear up or burn a flag: you or others will question your convictions and beliefs.

## FLOUR

1    You see bags full of flour: you will make substantial financial gains and will be able to spend liberally, or happy times with loved ones lie ahead.

2    You are covered in flour: what you do or embark upon will provoke disapproval or malicious gossip from people you know.

3    You are rolling around in or you fall in flour: libellous words or persistent adversaries will get the better of you.

## FLOWER

1    You pick flowers: you will behave in a rather carefree or happy-go-lucky fashion, but you may well be misled by events or unwittingly drawn into a difficult, testing situation. Alternatively, you will rely too greatly on appearances or will allow yourself to be influenced by the opinions others have of you (or vice versa).

2    You give flowers: the flowers represent your feelings, offered sincerely or spontaneously to someone else. They can also indicate that your inability to express your feelings to others or to confide freely and easily in them may lead to half-truths and a lack of real communication.

3    You receive flowers: this is proof of the affection others have for you and heralds a happy and calm phase in your emotional life.

4    If a particular flower appears in your dream or plays a significant role, it can be interpreted in a variety of ways:

•    carnation: a new friendship awaits, or relationships with friends and close relatives will be rewarding. The dream may signify an invitation to a fashionable event or that you can be deceived by nothing or nobody;

• chrysanthemum: your current situation or relationships are solid and durable or you will have contact with an uncomplicated and spontaneous person who is both reliable and discreet. It can signify that your dreams and projects will be fulfilled in the long term. Alternatively, you will be preoccupied by your own health or that of someone close to you;

• heliotrope: a revelation or important discovery will alter your beliefs and perhaps lead to a transformation of your life itself or you will be caught up in turbulent emotions and fond feelings – in other words, love is in the air and in your thoughts;

• iris: whatever your problems and concerns, you will come through effortlessly; if you are unwell, this dream signifies a certain and surprising recovery. If you are dealing with conflict, clashes or disagreement, the dream foretells reconciliation;

• lilac: you will have a romantic relationship or a love affair or someone will declare their love for you;

• lily: you will be loved but your romantic relationships will be passionate, even turbulent. Alternatively, you will receive significant promotion or an honorary position;

• lotus flower: your sensuality is heightened and has an inevitable influence upon your future behaviour and choices. The dream can also signify accord, harmony and constancy in your relationship, or that you will slowly realize the fugitive, illusory nature of worldly things – and that it is therefore better not to make too much of them;

• mimosa: you are encouraged and advised to hang on to your own beliefs and convictions which you have forged and proved over time; or perhaps, in a difficult or critical situation, you will appreciate the need to see things through to the end, aided by the certainty that something new lies round the corner and that nothing is forever;

• narcissus: someone will try to dupe you with flattering but insincere words, or you will have dealings with someone vain and egocentric. A period of idealistic behaviour may be signalled, during which you sublimate your own feelings and relationships;

• orchid: you will encounter a demanding and selective perfectionist; your initiatives and actions will bear fruit but only temporarily. Alternatively, the dream may herald the birth of a child, your own or that of someone else;

• peony: you will come into contact with a shy, modest or even over-emotional person who will not dare to reveal his/her feelings for you. Alternatively, you will lack self-confidence and underestimate either your own feelings or those of others;

• rose: this heralds happiness, a blossoming both of your relationships and your life in general; the colour of the rose can tell you more (*see also* COLOUR, p. 120); a yellow rose, for example, can reveal sincere emotion or a betrayal of affection or heartbreak;

• thistle: you will have dealings with a hostile and aggressive person or you are feeling defensive and, should you be the target of others' aggression, will give as good as you get. Alternatively, conflict with those around you may be inevitable, or you will need to take some form of tonic or pick-me-up;

• tulip: you will meet a superficial and gullible person, or you should beware of setting too much store by appearances. This can signify a need to intensify your relationships or feelings (*see also* COLOUR, p. 120);

• violet: you will meet someone shy who will not or does not know how to express their feelings; or you will be haunted, disturbed or even paralysed by memories of your past relationships or love life.

## FLY

1  You hear or see a fly buzzing around you: your life or your current situation will seem far too static, which will make you impatient with it; someone may try to provoke you or make life impossible for you. This dream could indicate that you will be too easygoing, leading certain people to take advantage of your goodness and generosity.

**2** You are in a room full of flies buzzing around: you will have something on your mind, or you will be plagued by obsessive ideas that you can't get rid of, or you will be disturbed and bothered by greedy and troublesome people. You are warned to think well before confiding in those around you; in fact, take care because you could find your thoughts and opinions broadcast indiscreetly.

**3** A fly bites you: a spiteful person whom you did not think capable of harming you will reveal himself to be aggressive and dangerous; you may become angry suddenly and for no apparent reason.

**4** You kill one or several flies: backbiting or jealousies won't touch you – you can handle them with ease.

## FLYING
### (see also AIRPLANE, p. 56; BIRD, p. 75; BROOM, p. 102)

If you are flying, you will experience a happy moment or an indescribable joy; alternatively, you will be freed from everything that is tying you down, specifically from a cumbersome, frustrating and restrictive situation; it may be that you are deceiving yourself – but sooner or later you will have to come back down to earth.

## FOG

If you are walking, driving or navigating in fog, it is clearly an indication that you don't know where you are at the moment or how to escape the uncertainty both around and within you. It is not necessarily a negative dream, since it may well announce a period of transition full of promise and hope from which you will emerge a refreshed and greater person.

## FOOL/LUNATIC/MADMAN

**1** You see or meet a fool: you will make unexpected profits that you will spend recklessly; or you lack wisdom and constancy in your emotional relationships, your concepts or your projects.

**2** You are mad: your feelings and desires will lead you to act or respond in an irrational, insane fashion. Alternatively, you will feel out of kilter with your environment, alienated or in conflict with those around you.

**3** You are surrounded by lunatics or in a lunatic asylum: you will be involved, implicated or dragged into an absurd, audacious, senseless undertaking.

## FOREST
### (see also TREE, p. 242)

**1** You walk or stroll in a forest: there are unresolved issues and unfinished business in your life and environment that, without proper attention, may take you by surprise or elude you. The dream also signifies a need to get back in touch with your own instincts, the real power of which you have yet to realize.

**2** You get lost in a forest: you will be imprisoned by your own instincts, desires and emotions, which could, sooner or later, have unfortunate consequences, in your business or your life.

## FOUNTAIN
### (see also WATER, p. 250)

**1** You see a fountain: a happy event or new situation will stimulate you to renewed vitality and love of life; or you will behave in an irrational, even crazy way, but it will do you a great deal of good.

**2** You drink from a fountain: you will long to return to your roots and get back in touch with basic, simple and reassuring values.

## FOX

**1** You see a fox: you will meet someone whose feelings or intentions are neither sincere nor honest; or you will reveal yourself to be quite casual, and extremely seductive and convincing, when it comes to getting what you want.

**2** You are hunting or catching a fox: you will thwart a conspiracy against you; or you will unmask the dubious intentions or dishonest behaviour of somebody in your immediate circle.

## FRIENDS and FRIENDSHIP

**1** You dream of a friend: this is always a good sign and heralds the arrival of help, support and protection; it may signify a feeling of emotional and spiritual well-being and happiness.

2    You make a new friend: this indicates that you will find the right environment, the emotional and spiritual balance you require in order to be more aware and open to new horizons and values.

3    You are surrounded by friends: this signifies a sense of being carefree, a period in your life that is enjoyable and from which you can fully benefit.

4    You feel a great affinity for someone: this reveals a need to deepen a relationship, to be less self-centred, less selfish and to focus on a particularly dear person or his/her circle. It is a sign of the need for union and solidarity.

5    The appearance of a partner in your dream: this can indicate the imminent arrival of news about this person. The nature and contents of the message depend upon the context, actions, backdrop and circumstances of the dream itself.

## FROG

If you see one or more frogs, you will soon have the opportunity to change your circumstances. However, an invasion of your living quarters by the frogs signifies that events or situations beyond your control will delay this transformation.

## FRUIT

1    The kind of fruit you dream of picking or eating is important:

•    apples: emotional happiness and fulfilment will come your way; or new or renewed self-awareness will help you see your current situation or life in general more clearly;

•    apricots: these promise improved finances or deep happiness in love; they can also foretell heightened sensuality and a very active sex life;

•    bananas: the financial rewards you anticipated will come your way; your sensuality may intensify;

•    blackberries: you will encounter one or more people whom you can trust or with whom you will be associated; you may embark on a productive endeavour or an interesting voyage. This dream can also herald prestige in your professional environment, thanks to your experience and skills;

- cherries: your relationship with your partner will blossom or you will enjoy rewarding encounters with new people. Bitter cherries portend unhappy love affairs;

- dates: someone will attempt to seduce or woo you. Alternatively, your hard-won gains will not be as substantial as you estimated;

- figs: your professional or financial situation will improve slowly but surely or you will be able to realize a project close to your heart. Alternatively, you may be tempted by a new love affair, one whose development and outcome are uncertain;

- gooseberries: your emotional relationships will be rather tense or difficult, but this is not necessarily threatened. Alternatively, your efforts and patience will be rewarded and your love life will be successful;

- grapes: these promise a time of prosperity and material gains. An encounter with someone new, or the start of a new love affair, may be heralded;

- lemons: you will be too demanding of others or you will feel unable or unwilling to live up to the high expectations they have of you. The dream may indicate that your hard work will not be in vain and that you will achieve your goals in the end;

- melons: whatever your worries and preoccupations, things will not only return to normal but improve, thanks to your goodwill, your receptive and understanding nature and your good sense;

- nuts: you will spend more time talking than doing. Alternatively, your professional relationships will weigh heavily on your shoulders or you will dislike your working environment. The dream may signal substantial extra work and responsibility but that your efforts will be rewarded, or that you will meet someone who is surly, tough and hard to get to know but who will turn out to be sensitive, pleasant and well disposed towards you;

- olives: you will be the victim of your own emotions or your love life may prove mysterious and complicated but you will enjoy challenging the norms;

- oranges: you will find yourself in a difficult situation, exit from which will demand great patience; health issues may require you to take a rest. You could receive an offer of partnership or union, the chance to embark on a major journey or to meet someone from a warm country;

- peaches: you will be impulsive, impatient, possessive and emotional or your own playful or provocative emotions will get the better of you;

- pears: you will be invited to a religious ceremony – a marriage or a funeral. Alternatively, an unexpected but life-defining event will occur or you may have dealings with someone friendly and pleasant who turns out to be rather naïve, with a tendency to delude others as well as themselves;

- pineapple: you will be invited to a very pleasant event or you will enjoy a period of carefree happiness;

- plums: nothing you may say or do can help you; possibly your projects will not succeed in the way you had hoped; a desire will remain unsatisfied or a sentiment unreciprocated;

- raspberries: you will spend happy moments with your friends;

- strawberries: you will not rebuff advances or turn down proposals made to you; you will not be able to resist the temptation of a mad love affair, should it arise;

- tomatoes: a secret relationship or affair will be discovered and disagreements or conflict will inevitably follow; you may meet someone who is shy and reserved, afraid to express his/her true thoughts or feelings.

2   You see a basket of fruit: positive and profitable times are ahead. Alternatively, someone will demonstrate their affection for you and you will feel loved and appreciated by your friends and family.

3   You see, pick or eat unripe fruit: you will be disappointed with the outcome of a situation or your relationships with friends will be superficial, insincere and unfulfilling.

4   You are making or eating jam or cooked fruit: you are preparing yourself slowly but surely for a significant and beneficial change in your life, and you are right to do so: it will come in its own good time.

# FUNERAL
### (*see also* CEMETERY, p. 114)

1    You attend a funeral: you are on the brink of a huge change in your life; or you will be too absorbed with thoughts of material, practical matters. Alternatively, a good opportunity will come your way or a situation will arise that demands your control before you can bring about an important change.

2    You attend the funeral of a friend or someone dear to you: the person in question will encounter serious problems, which may also affect you.

3    You attend your own funeral: the time has come for change; willingly or otherwise, you must turn your back on the past, start a fresh page in your life and prepare to face the future. If there are many people at your funeral, you can rest assured that this change will meet with the approval of others. If you are alone (or nearly), you will find you have only yourself to rely upon.

# GAMES and TOYS
### (*see also* PLAYING CARDS, p. 204)

1    Chess: a conflict with those around you demands logic, clear-sightedness and a feisty, intelligent spirit.

2    Children's toys: you will act in an immature, irresponsible way, refusing to assume your proper responsibilities.

3    Dice: you leave too much in your life to chance, destiny or external events, instead of taking responsibility for it yourself. This can leave you at the mercy of fate, at the risk of being buffeted by events without the possibility of influencing them.

4    Dominoes: patience, perseverance and discipline will be required to enable you to exploit your potential and reach your target.

5    Hopscotch: natural, spontaneous and straightforward behaviour will lead you to your goals.

6    A puzzle or riddle: you will be tempted to make things pointlessly complicated or to be unclear and imprecise when you speak. Try to express yourself more simply.

7   Snooker or billiards: your relationship with money is complicated. This is why your financial situation is shaky. Treat money as a means, an instrument, rather than an end in itself, and things will improve.

## GARDEN

1   You stand or walk in a well-kept garden: everything seems to be in perfect order in your life at the moment. You should take full advantage of all your resources.

2   You stand or walk in a neglected garden: you are, or will be, rather slapdash or careless. You are more interested in the superficial or cerebral than the simpler and more vital aspects of life; you need to reassess your situation.

3   You stand or walk in a garden:

   • in spring: a new love or more harmonious relationships are round the corner; your hopes for emotional fulfilment will not be in vain;

   • in summer: the summer gardens herald happiness, fulfilment and the granting of your dearest wishes;

   • in autumn/fall: although you refuse to acknowledge it, you know that the end of a particular phase in your life is nigh and this makes you anxious or sad;

   • in winter: you are gradually becoming aware of your deepest desires and turning your back on the material and temporal aspects of life; the winter garden helps you to understand that the answers to all your questions are to be found within yourself, nowhere else.

4   You are trapped in a deserted garden: you have achieved a certain amount of balance, but it is based on self-interest and egotism. Instead of making you more generous, sympathetic and dependable, it has distanced, even isolated you from others.

## GARLIC

1   You smell or eat garlic:

   • this indicates angina, influenza or fever, all of which you can curb. The act of seeing, smelling or eating the garlic in your dream has a preventive or remedial significance;

- it indicates a recovery from illness or the end of a conflict.

2    You see cloves of garlic: this is a sign of protection or a positive and healthy instinct for self-protection.

# GHOST

1    A dream in which you see, meet or talk to a ghost or phantom can be interpreted in a number of ways, depending on the following contexts:

- if the deceased person is a close relative or someone whom you knew well: this person's spirit is still very much in your heart and in your thoughts, either because of your receptive, sensitive nature or your need for that person (or vice versa). In any case, the dream alerts you to the presence of this person and to the fact that something is expected from you. In other words, the apparition is saying 'help me to help you' or, if you prefer, 'help yourself by allowing heaven to assist you through me'. This sort of dream often comes just before a major change, a serious test or great happiness;

- if the ghost is a stranger: this unknown person's spirit is trying to get a message, through you, to someone of your acquaintance to whom the deceased was close, but cannot reach; you must relate your dream to this acquaintance, whom you will surely meet the following day, as its message is addressed to him or her rather than to you;

- if someone still living appears as a ghost: as you well know, this person is close to your heart and thoughts; you have deep affinities which you feel strongly and will shortly be able to affirm.

2    A dream in which you are frightened or threatened by a ghost or phantom can also be interpreted in a number of ways:

- if it is a close relative or someone you knew well when alive: the loss of this person has meant you have been unable to resolve relationship, emotional or other difficulties; their appearance in your dream helps you to understand that it is not too late to do this;

- if it is a stranger: the fear aroused in you by the appearance or aggressive behaviour of this person comes from within yourself; you need to learn from it and change your behaviour;

- if the ghost is someone who is still alive: you do not like this person and, unconsciously, you wish them dead or rather, out of your life, but the dream reveals that this would not resolve the conflict or disagreement between you.

## GIANT

1   You see a giant: your ideas and ambitions are beyond your power; or you will experience an overwhelmingly powerful emotion.

2   You see a walking giant who destroys everything in his path due to his enormous size: the outcome of your efforts will not match your intentions, either because you overestimate your ability or because you are unable to control your emotions.

3   You fight with a giant or are pursued by one: a bold plan will succeed only with considerable and seemingly insuperable difficulty, but remember you hold all the trump cards.

4   You are friends with a helpful and pleasant giant: you will succeed in your ambitions with the support of an influential person or organization.

## GIFT

1   You are giving a gift: this shows that you are ready to make an important decision, to give of your best and offer your trust.

2   If you receive a gift: it foretells a new job or engagement. It could also signal that you will be invited to play an important role or take on a great responsibility. A token of love or a proof of friendship may come your way (see also BIRTHDAY, p. 76).

3   You are disappointed not to receive a gift: rightly or wrongly, you will feel unloved or unappreciated. It may mean that you will be involved in a delicate situation or experience a tricky period in your life, during which you must not make any mistakes or show any weakness.

## GIRAFFE

Dreaming of a giraffe promises contact with someone aloof and indifferent. If the giraffe is running, it means that this person will escape your clutches; feeding the animal symbolizes the nurturing of your own pride.

## GLASS
### (see also CRYSTAL, p. 126; MIRROR, p. 183; SPECTACLES, p. 226; WATER, p. 250; WINE, p. 254)

1   You are in a room full of glass objects: let your actions be as pure, clear and simple to understand as your intentions or ideas and all will be well; this dream promises you that.

2   You break glass: this signifies that a plan – which was probably unrealistic, or in which you had little faith – will not come off or that a completely unexpected opportunity will present itself, though you will find it disconcerting or paradoxical.

3   You see, are holding or are offered an empty glass: you will not get all that you want, but this also signals another step along the road to success, or towards achieving what you want; alternatively, you will have high hopes of a new relationship and will make yourself readily available.

4   You see, are holding or are offered a full glass: you will enjoy yourself in good company; you may hear pleasant news or learn something interesting.

5   You are clinking glasses: you will be disillusioned or bitterly disappointed, largely due to your lack of clarity and objectivity about a project into which you will unthinkingly, enthusiastically or naively allow yourself to be drawn.

6   Breaking a glass: this heralds an unavoidable split.

## GLUE

If you are using glue, this signifies confrontation with your emotional dependency and your difficulty in acting independently and detaching yourself from someone close to you. You find it hard to live without this person or are unable to draw a line under your past.

# GOAT

The appearance of a goat in your dream is a reference to an intelligent, independent and capricious woman. It can herald a sudden, unexpected event or piece of information that will have emotional consequences.

# GOD(S)

1   You witness or hear the voice of God: this is a sign of joy, happiness, protection and inner fulfilment.

2   You pray to or implore God: you crave greater harmony in your inner or outer life or you seek protection, support or approval.

3   You are among the gods: the gods are with you; this is a sign of luck and success in your enterprises, of joy and happiness in your life.

4   You are in the presence of a god, goddess or mythical figure: you are inclined to suppress some aspects of your behaviour or your feelings, thoughts and instincts.

5   You fight against a god: you will undertake a task that is ambitious or audacious, an act that represents a form of defiance. You need to be aware of just how powerful and resourceful you are.

# GRAIN
### (*see also* CORN, p. 123)

1   You see piles of grain: this dream heralds advantageous circumstances, imminent financial gain or an inheritance; it can also represent your rich strain of imagination and creativity that you could exploit if you wanted.

2   You sow grain in the soil: your current projects will come to fruition, but only in the long term and with patience and perseverance; you may have to agree to sacrifice something in order to achieve your goals.

3   You throw seeds or grain to the wind: you lack both precision and coherence in your current work or the planning of future projects; despite this, some of your plans will succeed but only in the long term.

**4**   You eat uncooked grain: you will waste your advantages and profits by reckless and wasteful behaviour.

**5**   You eat cooked grain: profits are coming your way.

## GRATER

To see or use a grater indicates that a project or initiative will not come off, that you will wear yourself out completely or that you will see a relationship or a business deal through to the very end.

## GROUND/SOIL/EARTH/LAND
### (*see also* CORN, p. 123; DESERT, p. 128; GRAIN, p. 155; HOLE, p. 162; PEASANT, p. 200; PLANT, p. 203; SPADE, p. 226)

**1**   You see rich, fertile soil: you have a great many potential resources at your disposal, both internal and external; it is up to you to make the best use of them and to exploit them.

**2**   You are working the soil: you will experience an emotion so strong that it will pierce you to your very core; alternatively the tables will be turned in a certain situation or a project or task will require substantial effort, patience and tenacity on your part.

**3**   You are walking barefoot on firm ground: you will demonstrate a realistic attitude whatever the circumstances, keeping your feet firmly on the ground.

**4**   You hold earth in your hands: you will fully enjoy the fruits of your labours; alternatively, the real, material things in life give you greatest satisfaction.

**5**   You see or are walking on virgin soil: you have free will and will reap what you sow.

**6**   You inherit or own a plot of land: you will need to double your efforts, or persevere with what you are doing, if you want to keep what you have acquired and retain your material possessions.

## GUARD

A dream of a guard or caretaker, who forbids you to enter somewhere you need to be or hinders your access, signifies a hitherto unknown problem or unforeseen obstacle that prevents you from achieving what you have set out to do. Alternatively, it may warn that you need to be aware of and conquer a major obstacle in your path in order to reach your target.

# GUN
### (see also HUNTING, p. 165)

1   You are pointing or shooting a gun at somebody: you feel rebellious, betrayed or hurt, and are in danger of overreacting; alternatively, somebody in your circle has something you want but your stubborn attempts to procure it will not have the desired effect.

2   Someone is pointing or shooting a gun at you: you will be the target of criticism or general disapproval; or someone will try to take your place or get you dismissed.

3   You are carrying a gun: you will reveal your true intentions or feelings sooner or later.

4   You are firing a gun: you are aware that it is not always appropriate to speak the truth; if you speak before you think, your words could cause embarrassment in a delicate situation.

# HAIR

1   You have long hair: it indicates physical strength, intelligence and receptivity.

2   You have short hair: it shows weakness, a lack of intelligence and receptivity, a limited understanding and a tendency to prejudge.

3   You are untangling your hair: you will make an effort to see things more clearly but it will not be easy; your desires and ambitions will be hard to realize or satisfy.

4   You are combing your hair: you will try to keep up appearances but you will find it hard to hide your true desires and ambitions.

5   You are having a haircut: you will be disappointed, betrayed or hurt by someone close to you; or you will lose money or become bankrupt or unemployed. It is important to remember, however, that a dream warns of an event or action that may occur in your life but that can be prevented as a result of the warning. On the

other hand, it often represents the fear of such an event rather than its inevitability. It is essential to read the Introduction and Practical guide at the beginning of this book.

**6**  You are washing your hair: your fears and anxieties will be unfounded and you will be able to dispense with them easily.

**7**  You have white hair: this is a sign of wisdom, experience and clarity and indicates imminent respect and consideration for you.

**8**  If you dream of having hair of a different colour to your own, it is a sign that you will change your social circumstances or your current situation.

**9**  Someone is pulling your hair: others are seeking or demanding things from you that are beyond your strength and means. Do not allow them to take advantage of you.

**10**  You have combs, clips or ribbons in your hair: your professional or social skills and qualities will be recognized and duly rewarded.

**11**  You are losing your hair: you have a lively, young, imaginative, inventive, enthusiastic and enterprising spirit or you will soon meet someone who possesses these qualities.

**12**  You are wearing a wig: you are easily influenced; possibly your ideas and convictions are too superficial.

**13**  You are bald or see a bald man or woman in your dream: you will not go unnoticed but instead you will be appreciated for your true qualities. Alternatively, you may receive substantial rewards or advantages.

## HAMMER
### (*see also* NAIL, p. 190)

If you see or use a hammer, you need time to understand something and accept reality such as it is; it may be that you will achieve your aims through patience, perseverance and courage.

## HANDKERCHIEF

**1**  You use a handkerchief to blow your nose: have you made a mistake? There is nothing for it but to admit it and learn from it; perhaps you will be caught out and will be harshly reproved.

**2**   You use a handkerchief to dry your tears: something that you thought was a big drama or deception will turn out to be insignificant and quickly forgotten.

**3**   You find a handkerchief: you will cause or have caused someone pain but doubtless without choice or intention; alternatively, you have committed yourself to undertake an important task and you must not forget it.

## HANGING

**1**   To dream of someone being hanged: danger, inconvenience or disappointment is in store. Alternatively, somebody will become too dependent on you or you will have dealings with somebody who talks too much and will not be able to keep their mouth shut.

**2**   If you are being hanged: circumstances will compel you to take on certain tasks or obligations that will prove gratifying or will do you credit, but they will be burdensome and deprive you of free will. Alternatively, whether due to people or circumstances, you may feel there is a gun against your head and you will have no choice but to comply with whatever demands are made of you.

**3**   To be hung up by your feet: you are going to find yourself trapped in a situation. You will feel paralysed and powerless and, for a while, will just have to wait for a way out to present itself. Your own mistakes have got you into this situation.

**4**   To dream you have been condemned to death by hanging: this foretells a change of job, career or place of work.

## HARBOUR

If you see a harbour in your dream, or are walking around one, this indicates that after a difficult and troubled period in your life you will have a well-deserved rest, a period of respite when you can recharge your batteries. It can also mean that the goal you have set yourself will soon be reached.

## HARE

**1**   You see one or more running hares: you will have to confront and respond to inevitable but completely unexpected events with both speed and efficiency. Alternatively, you will not let yourself be affected by the panic and chaos that will spring up around you.

2   You hunt or catch a hare: an unexpected opportunity will come your way or you will be able to take advantage of a rare chance to achieve something (*see also* HUNTING, p. 165).

## HARLEQUIN

If your dream features a harlequin or you are disguised as Harlequin, this image represents an aspect of your personality. You appear to be someone who wastes his/her energy and skills, hiding behind the mask of old-fashioned principles and received ideas and behaving in an unstable, indecisive and unpredictable manner. Nevertheless the character represented by Harlequin is that of someone potentially brimming with original ideas, plans, desires and ambitions, all of them easier to dream up and debate than to put in place. If Harlequin himself appears (or a character or person reminiscent of Harlequin), it is a sign of a desire to integrate mind-body-spirit principles. This union is essential to achieve balance, fulfilment and happiness.

## HAT

1   If the hat you are wearing is:

•   classic or neutral in style: you appear to be someone who is balanced and discreet but lacking in a certain spontaneity or sincerity;

•   original or ridiculous in style: you have far-fetched or fantastic ideas; or you don't take life seriously;

•   made of straw: your ideas are frivolous and futile, your feelings are spontaneous but volatile and unstable;

•   a beret, cap or helmet: you have fixed ideas beyond which you do not venture;

•   a bonnet: you are too naïve or unworldly; you refuse to acknowledge the gravity of a situation;

•   ecclesiastical in style: you have a noble, generous and ambitious spirit or you will become increasingly preoccupied by considerations of a moral, mystical or spiritual nature;

- a rain hat: you refuse or you will be unable to keep cool, remain clear-headed or face facts;

- a sun hat: you will be able to contain your impatience and succeed whatever and wherever you choose.

2   You are given a hat: this signifies a poisoned chalice, a way of implicating you in a matter or a mistake that has been made.

3   You are trying on various hats: your ideas and desires are changeable, unstable and easily influenced. Alternatively, you will hesitate between several choices or options that are presented to you.

4   You have lost your hat: you are no longer sure of your situation; or you could well lose, forget or misplace something in the near future through deliberate negligence or imprudence. You need to be on your guard.

## HEDGEHOG

1   You see a hedgehog: you will encounter an aggressive or tense character or you will soon become irritable and defensive yourself, overreacting to the slightest thing.

2   A hedgehog pricks you: you will fall prey to someone egoistic who is indifferent to your needs or well-being; your naïveté will let you down.

## HELL

To see yourself in hell or entering it indicates that you blame yourself for certain mistakes in your relationships or that you will experience testing times that are the logical and inevitable outcome of past errors.

## HERO
### (*see also* FAME, p. 137)

To dream of a hero, of being a hero or of acting heroically indicates your tendency to idealize your actions and your life or to depend on the approval and respect of others for your sense of self-worth and ability to achieve your goals.

# HOLE
### (*see also* WELL, p. 251)

**1**   You fall into a hole: you will forget or mislay something; you may have a blackout, a sudden drop in blood pressure or a fainting fit. Watch your blood pressure and take care of yourself. Alternatively, someone will try to catch you out or mislead you.

**2**   You are in a hole: you live too much alone, isolated and shut away from the world, and because of this nothing much will happen in your life; alternatively, you will find yourself trapped by certain contingencies, obligations or responsibilities; you may have to face up to the consequences of a mistake you have made.

**3**   You are digging a hole: you will channel your efforts and energy into establishing a stable and secure situation for yourself, or you will take out a loan.

**4**   You are filling in a hole: you will be forced to settle your debts and sort out your financial situation.

# HONEY
### (*see also* BEES, p. 73)

In your dream you are eating honey. If you are ill this indicates a speedy recovery; it may indicate that your business affairs will go well and you will gain in some way.

# HORSE

**1**   You are trotting on a horse: this is a sign that you are in control and that you will have a normal, healthy and happy love- or sex-life. Alternatively, it is a promise of good fortune, accession to power or to a position of authority, or social and professional promotion. Your merits will be recognized.

**2**   You are galloping on a horse: this dream reveals your physical power and determination to satisfy your desires at all costs or fulfil your ambitions with all haste.

**3**   Your horse bolts: this dream underlines your enthusiasm, your irrepressible and unconsidered impulses and your inability to contain, control or calm yourself.

**4**  Your horse rears up: you will have difficulty controlling your instincts and mastering your impatience but you should manage it eventually with enough good will. Alternatively, you should not let go of the reins or be discouraged, as you will finally overcome your difficulties.

**5**  You are riding bareback: you need to face reality; you may feel deep desire for someone in your circle.

**6**  You fall off the horse: your hopes and projects are in danger of sudden collapse; you may make a mistake and suffer the consequences very soon.

**7**  You are jumping over obstacles on your horse: your courage, strength of will and energy will enable you to overcome all the obstacles in your path and reach your final target.

**8**  You are riding a wild horse: this reveals your independent spirit, your desire for autonomy and the irrepressible nature of your personality.

**9**  You see a white horse: this is a good omen and a sign of clear conscience and an enjoyment of life.

**10**  You see a black horse: this is a sign of profit, gain or advantage obtained through more or less legal means. Alternatively, it heralds an upheaval, the loss of psychological balance or a radical departure in your life.

**11**  You see a horse with a multi-coloured coat: this denotes a strong sexual appetite and a powerful energy that needs to be released. It can mean that a current affair has great potential.

**12**  You see a winged or flying horse: an imminent voyage or good news awaits; your merits will be rewarded or recognized.

**13**  You see one or several riders:

* if you are a woman: you will meet someone or become involved in new relationships;

* if you are a man: you will hear important news that will require quick decisions; or you will try to become involved in a new social environment or a new relationship.

**14**  You are sitting astride a horse or an object of some kind: you are or will be in a precarious, unstable or uncomfortable situation for some time to come but do not lose hope; stay determined to see it through to the end by showing flexibility and understanding.

## HOSPITAL

**1** You are convalescing or receiving treatment in hospital: events or circumstances beyond your control will compromise your plans.

**2** You are a member of a hospital team: your loyalty to your friends damages or will damage your personal development, spirit of independence or ability to achieve your goals; you may soon be required to resolve a difficult family or household issue.

## HOTEL

If you dream that you are staying in a hotel, it signifies that you are in a period of transition, a temporary and insecure phase during which it is better to think in the short rather than long term. Alternatively, circumstances will force you to keep your emotions or activities under wraps for a while.

## HOURGLASS

You have very little time left to complete a task, keep a promise or do what is necessary to get what you want. Alternatively, an event or change is imminent.

## HOUSE
### (see also ATTIC, p. 67; CAVE, p. 112; MOVING HOUSE, p. 187; WINDOW, p. 253)

**1** You see a fine house with a simple façade: you will feel at ease with yourself but you won't put yourself forward or try to stand out from the crowd.

**2** You see a house with a very elaborate façade: you set too much store by appearances – your own in particular – instead of looking at the real truth behind situations and people. The dream does not judge your behaviour but acts as a warning.

**3** You see a house with a neglected façade: you attach no importance to appearances; or you feel ill at ease with yourself. Alternatively, you will seek to change your appearance or give yourself a new look.

**4**  You see a house with a dilapidated roof: your thoughts will be muddled or you will be too gullible.

**5**  You see an empty house: you lack curiosity and imagination and are not good with people; you may not be open to the ideas and feelings of others.

**6**  You are in a house that is full of furniture and objects of different styles: you are brimming with ideas and projects but take care – too much can often result in too little.

**7**  You build your own house: you are making slow but sure progress and your long-term success will be commensurate with your skill, your experience and your merits.

**8**  You demolish your house: if needs must, you are ready to start again from scratch – and you are right, since in this fashion you will at one stroke overcome all obstacles in your path.

**9**  Your house is on fire: you need to act or respond urgently either because this is a very rare opportunity or because an inevitable clarification can throw light on your situation. Alternatively, you may succumb to desires and passions that will consume and exhaust you (*see also* FIRE, p. 139).

# HUNTING
**(*see also* ARROW, p. 66; BOW, p. 98; GUN, p. 157; HARE, p. 159; LION, p. 175; RABBIT, p. 208)**

In order to grasp the full meaning of this dream, it is important to check the entry in the glossary for the symbolic significance of the hunted animal. You should also pay attention to the weapon you are using.

**1**  You are tracking an animal or game: this indicates your personal search or intellectual and spiritual enquiry. It can denote the projects or ambitions that you want to fulfil.

- if the animal or game escapes you: you are unlikely to achieve your goals;

- if you catch the animal or have it in your sights: it indicates that the fulfilment of your ambitions relies upon your actions; you are about to reach your goal.

**2** You kill the animal or game: you will have to rid yourself of the negative influences around you or distance yourself from one or more harmful people. Alternatively, you will find the answers to your problem and you will know exactly what you should do.

# ICE

**1** You see an icy landscape: only time and patience will resolve a future impasse. Alternatively, you will become resigned or indifferent to events or people around you.

**2** You are ice-skating: a situation or relationship will come to a standstill; whatever your concerns or preoccupations, the dream counsels a calm and passive response.

**3** You smash some ice: you will do all in your power to ensure harmony and resolve conflict among your friends.

**4** You eat an ice-cream: you try to hide your sensitivity and your feelings, but your need for tenderness and gentleness will be too strong; alternatively, you will have dealings with someone who appears indifferent but who will turn out to be very sensitive.

# IDENTITY CARD
## (*see also* PASSPORT, p. 199)

**1** If you lose or have lost your identity card: it is a manifestation of your lack of self-confidence or of a lack of self-awareness. It can mean that you will be the victim of a theft or that you will lose your papers (identity or otherwise); it can indicate the loss of something you have had for many years or an item of great sentimental value.

**2** If in your dream you have a false identity card: it can mean that you are lying about or hiding your true character or that you are living a double life. It can indicate that you are unable to say what you think or that your words will not be believed.

**3** If the photograph on your identity card is not of you: it denotes that you are too easily influenced or that you like to identify with someone else. It can signify that you have a dual personality or lead a double life but are unable to hide it (*see also* PHOTOGRAPH, p. 201).

## IMP/GOBLIN/ELF

If you see one or more goblins, your intuition and imagination will be enlivened and stimulated by events or people around you; you may behave in a somewhat unstable way in your emotional relationships with others. The dream may warn that you will be involved with people or circumstances that are not what they seem and that you will be deceived thereby. Alternatively, you will experience an inner restlessness and agitation that will weaken your energies and damage your equilibrium.

## INHERITANCE

If you come into an inheritance, it signifies your tendency to rely too heavily upon others or on outside forces to sort out your finances. You need to acknowledge that your material comfort depends on you alone, on your enterprise and willpower.

## ISLAND

1   You see or discover an island: after emerging from a difficult, confused and unstable phase in your life, you will to be able to take time out to organize yourself and to plan your future.

2   You live on an island: you need to be alone for a while; you may appear aloof and inaccessible to others.

## IVY

1   You see climbing ivy on the front or walls of a house: you are faithful and constant in your emotional relationships, but your own feelings or those others have for you are possessive, exclusive and stifling. Sooner or later they will cause tension or conflict.

2   You see climbing ivy on a tree trunk: you can rely on the deep and sincere feelings of someone who seems very attached to you.

## JELLYFISH

You are swimming among jellyfish, or you step on or see several jellyfish: you tend to enjoy feeling guilty and to regard your past mistakes with a certain complacency, without really learning a lesson from them. This dream advises you to confront facts without being too hard or too easy on yourself, so that your life can move on.

## JOURNALIST

1   You meet or deal with one or more journalists: someone you know or are about to meet will show interest in you and will support your projects.

2   You are a journalist: you will witness an event but refuse to get involved. You will be powerless to change something in your life – all you can do is verify the facts.

## JUGGLER
### (see also ACROBAT, p. 54)

To dream of juggling indicates that you are struggling to stay balanced, despite your various skills. Your current situation is precarious and demands that you take it more seriously or you will lose your footing.

## JUSTICE
### (see also LAWYER, p. 172)

1   You attend a trial: you will need to pay close attention to a situation, in which you will become involved sooner or later. Instead of playing the blame game as you tend to, try to understand the reasons behind your actions and motives.

2   You are on trial: you have made too many concessions or bad decisions in your dealings with others or in your own life. You feel guilty and need to acknowledge your mistakes.

3   You are a judge: you will have to make a difficult decision or impose your authority, whether you want to or not.

4   You are found guilty during a trial: you are only too aware of the mistakes you have made and can therefore make amends appropriately.

5   You are found innocent during a trial: everything will turn out well, so you don't need to worry; a dispute or conflict with someone will be resolved quickly, indeed it is in your interest to effect this at your earliest opportunity.

# KANGAROO

To dream of a kangaroo signifies a happy and flourishing home life but also indicates the spontaneity, instability and extravagance of your own character or that of another person with whom you are in contact.

# KEY

1   You see or find a key: you will learn or uncover a secret or you will find the solution to a problem that is currently worrying you. Alternatively, you will be able to enjoy a moment of freedom, do as you wish or embark upon a journey alone.

2   Someone gives you or trusts you with a key: the dream advises you to rely more on your intuition and instincts and warns that you are not exploiting these to their full advantage. You may be entrusted with the mission of resolving a delicate situation, utilizing methods of which you alone know the secret. Another interpretation is that people will confide in you.

3   You have lost your keys: you refuse to solve a problem or accept the solutions proposed to you. If you have lost your car keys, you will refuse to assume your responsibilities, to take action or make a decision or to change something in your life or behaviour. If you have lost the keys to your house or apartment, it's a question of a problem at home or in your family and your inability to face the difficulties within your household. You will be unable to find the answer to a crucial problem.

# KISS

The person whom you are kissing or who is kissing you, and the feelings that this engenders, should be considered very carefully when interpreting this dream.

1   If you are being embraced:

•   and you enjoy the kiss and like the person who is kissing you: you will benefit from help, enjoy moral or emotional support, receive a declaration of love or a proof of sincere and unselfish friendship. Alternatively, you may be involved with someone affectionate but possessive;

• but you don't enjoy the kiss or like the person who is kissing you: don't trust outward demonstrations of affection. You may become involved with a hypocrite or be the victim of betrayal.

2 If you are kissing someone: you are spontaneous, sincere, ready to give your trust, rightly or wrongly; perhaps you feel a strong desire to get close to or to possess someone. Alternatively, you seek to devote yourself to a cause, to be committed or to be emotionally or psychologically involved in a situation or relationship.

## KITCHEN

1 You are in the kitchen: this is an expression of a real love of life, a taste for simple and healthy pleasures; it may be a warning that you need to make some major changes in your family environment or current situation.

2 You are cooking: your future depends to a significant degree on your current deeds – be careful of your words and actions. It is important to be vigilant.

## KITE

To dream of one or more kites is a sign of protection and support or a benevolent intervention that will save and preserve you whatever happens.

## KNIFE

1 You have or use a knife: you are in danger of conflict, upheaval or separation.

2 You threaten someone with a knife: quarrels, disagreements and conflict with people you know are inevitable.

3 Someone threatens you with a knife: you will be the victim of betrayal, slander or defamation.

4 You cut yourself: you will not win your arguments or solve disagreements. It is an indication that you will have to suffer the consequences of your own aggressive instincts and rebellious instinct as a result.

# LACE

1    You are wearing lace: you will reveal your secrets, thoughts and desires but you should remain vigilant; be careful whom you trust or you risk disappointment.

2    You see someone else wearing lace: do not trust or confide in this person, who guards secrets jealously, harbours insincere emotions and threatens to harm you.

# LADDER

1    You climb a ladder with ease: this heralds progress and self-confidence.

2    You climb a ladder with difficulty: your inner or outer evolution is slow but sure. The dream encourages you to pursue your development without slacking.

3    You climb a ladder but never reach the top: the goal you have set yourself is beyond your means or power. Alternatively, you have chosen a very long route to your destination.

4    You deliberately walk under a ladder, either from bravado or playfulness: you are prepared to take risks with no concern for the consequences, good or ill, of your acts.

5    You walk under a ladder unintentionally: you need to assume your responsibilities and be prepared for the consequences of your actions or you will soon make a regrettable mistake.

6    You see or are given a ladder: you will find the answer to a painful or difficult problem or the outcome of a troublesome situation.

7    You carry or transport a ladder: you hold the answer to the problem currently preoccupying you; you just need to put it into practice.

8    You descend a ladder: you are about to renew contact with reality and to face facts rather than indulge in self-delusion. Alternatively, a situation will prove to be less promising than you thought.

9    You fall off a ladder: you will be interrupted suddenly and stopped dead in your tracks.

# LADYBIRD

The appearance of a ladybird is a portent of good news. If it lands on you, someone will declare their affection for you; if there are several ladybirds, you will realize that happy events come in pairs or more, not just singly.

# LAMA

To see a lama, or Tibetan monk, heralds an important decision, requiring you to be completely honest in your dealings with both yourself and others (*see also* PRIEST, p. 206).

# LAMB

A lamb in a dream signifies purity, innocence, liberty, lightness and grace. The lamb brings you into contact with the purest and most genuine aspect of your self, the part that is unsullied by any bad thought or deed.

This 'lamb-like' aspect of your self is immortal and yet subject to endless change. It is completely receptive, which makes it gentle, but it is not submissive or slavish. To be 'as gentle as a lamb' does not necessarily mean you are gullible, passive and without initiative. The innocence of the lamb makes it incorruptible. Whatever your concerns, current anxieties, problems or difficulties or your responsibilities and tasks, the presence of a lamb in your dreams is a true revelation, a sign of grace and pardon, assuring you that you will emerge unscathed and all the better for your experiences and trials. This is true on the condition, naturally, that you do not sacrifice the lamb, the most precious part of yourself that is within you, unless it were to nourish yourself.

# LAWYER
### (*see also* JUSTICE, p. 168)

1  You see or have dealings with a lawyer: a significant change or event concerning your family situation, home or property is imminent.

2  You visit a lawyer to hear a will being read: you will receive an unexpected windfall, your income will increase, or your

professional and financial situation will improve; a close relative or someone in your social circle may want to clarify their position or their relationship with you.

3    You dream you are drawing up or signing your own will: this is a sign of longevity and a happy and peaceful old age; it could signify that you will feel the need to clarify or review your situation or to get to know yourself better and be more honest with yourself.

4    A lawyer is defending you: it signifies that you blame yourself or are too self-critical. The appearance of the lawyer in your dream is a call to be less hard on yourself and to be aware that your current behaviour stems from a lack of inner clarity that can mean you are intolerant of others. The dream can also herald the need for a discussion, explanation or clarification if you want to make yourself understood and for things to return to normal.

5    You are acting as a lawyer: you will have to intervene in a difficult or delicate matter, to defend a cause or concept that is close to your heart or to take up the defence of someone in your circle. Alternatively, you feel that you have made a mistake and you want the opportunity to justify yourself.

## LIFT or ELEVATOR

1    If you dream that you are in a lift going up: you will progress, develop, gain promotion or a reward or enjoy a stroke of luck.

2    You are in a lift going down: you will enter a regressive or depressive phase of your life. Take this message on board and let things take their course the better to bounce back when the time is right.

3    You are in a lift that is shooting up like a rocket: you will be tempted to see or deal with matters with a certain aloofness, to ignore the humdrum routine of daily life, in order to dominate the situation and for an easier life.

4    You are in a lift that is descending in free fall: this dream has a number of interpretations. It can mean that you will be forced to come down from your pedestal or you will have to look deep into yourself and explore the darker aspects of your personality, which you have to date refused to acknowledge and integrate.

Alternatively, you will enter a listless, spiritless and depressive phase in your life and this dream encourages you to react now to avoid being engulfed by it.

## LIGHT
### (see also CANDLE, p. 106; OIL, p. 197; SUN, p. 234)

1　You see an intensely bright or blinding light: light will be shed on your problems; the answers may be right in front of your eyes but you do not see them. Alternatively, the truth will out.

2　You see a feeble or flickering light: you doubt yourself and your beliefs, or your ideas and imagination will fail to clarify your situation.

3　You switch on the light or an electric lamp: you will suddenly see everything clearly, both within and around you, or you will help someone see the light about his or her own situation. Alternatively, you will have an excellent idea that will clarify your position or your dealings with others.

4　You turn out the light or an electric lamp: for reasons that are obscure, you will refuse to allow yourself certain pleasures, which would do you good. The dream can denote an unwillingness to face facts or to see the truth or that your original ideas and plans will not come to fruition.

## LIMPING
### (see also BODY, p. 79)

1　If you are limping in your dream: it is a sign of psychological imbalance or an emotional complication (double life, betrayal, break-up, unrequited affection). Alternatively, it can underline a moral feebleness or a material or financial instability. It can herald an important revelation or preface a disturbing event that will force you to reconsider your position and put your harmony, integrity and ambitions in question. It can signal a moral, ideological or spiritual conversion.

2　If you see or meet someone with a limp: it denotes that you will soon receive a surprising message, an unexpected letter or some extraordinary news.

# LION

**1**   You see a lion in the wild: a proud, strong and untamed person, who has both courage and willpower, will enter your life. Your own pride will make you inflexible and poorly adapted to your circumstances, or you will give free rein to your instincts and desires.

**2**   You see a caged lion: you will learn how to protect yourself from your own instinct to dominate and take complete control. Alternatively, you will have contact with an untameable character or a dangerous adversary whom you will succeed in convincing or conquering.

**3**   A lion chases you: you will be unable to contain your lust for power and need to dominate, but sooner or later you will suffer the inevitable consequences.

**4**   You hunt a lion: you will embark upon a bold, ambitious or dangerous adventure; take precautions and assess your means and strengths before you do so (*see* HUNTING, p. 165).

# LIZARD

To see a lizard denotes an encounter with a wise, attentive and enlightened person or that you will soon be able to take a holiday or a well-deserved rest. It can also denote the birth of a boy in your family or among your friends.

# LLAMA

Seeing a lama indicates that you will have dealings with a gullible, aggressive and surly character, who pretends to be friendly and well meaning (*see also* CAMEL, p. 105).

# LOCOMOTIVE
### (*see also* TRAIN, p. 241)

**1**   You see or drive a steam locomotive: your projects and plans are theoretical rather than practical, but they express your need to escape to horizons new. The dream can denote an inclination to leap headlong into a situation or relationship, blinded by your enthusiasm.

**2**  You see or drive an electric train: you will do everything in your power to get physically or spiritually close to someone dear to you. Alternatively, you will embark upon a voyage that will prove life changing or a person you have yet to meet will play an important role – be prepared, he is on his way.

## LOVE

**1**  You dream that you love a stranger: this denotes that a new and unexpected event will occur in your life. It will cause great happiness or euphoria, albeit temporary.

**2**  You dream that a stranger loves you: this confirms your worth is recognized and is proof of the esteem in which others hold you. You may experience a new relationship or feelings that are new to you.

**3**  You are in love with a famous person: you underestimate your own qualities and the nature of your feelings and your ability to love. It can also mean that you are an idealist and are emotionally unfulfilled.

**4**  A famous person expresses love for you: you underestimate the feelings that someone has for you or your feelings are unrequited. Alternatively, you will experience a hopeless love affair.

## LOVER
### (see also ADULTERY, p. 55)

**1**  For a woman:

* a dream of having a lover: in most cases this should be seen within the context of fantasies. It is usually a dream of compensation and balance. However, its symbolic significance must not be ignored. The lover represents the masculine side of your personality, with which you wish to be united in order to free yourself from all forms of emotional dependence. The dream indicates a desire for emotional and psychological fulfilment, particularly if it occurs frequently. It also denotes a wish to recognize or rediscover in yourself and your life a true representation of your masculine side, whose integration is essential to your balance;

* if your husband or partner has a mistress in your dream: this is an expression of a foreboding you refuse to acknowledge

or of an unjustified concern, which is hereby exorcized. It can indicate a secret desire to play this role yourself in order to seduce your partner again.

2   For a man:

• a dream of having a mistress: this should be seen within the same context as a woman's dream of a lover. It has the same symbolic significance, except that it represents the feminine side of the man's personality;

• if your wife or partner has a lover: the dream has the same but inverse meaning as for a woman (see above).

## LYNX

Dreaming of a lynx indicates dealings with a cunning, lively, enigmatic character, who always insists on having the last word and may well be a thief. Alternatively, you will see the world very clearly – nothing will escape your notice, including the real motives of those around you. If the lynx bites or attacks you, your health may be in danger and you should take precautions.

## MAGIC
### (*see also* ACROBAT, p. 54; JUGGLER, 168)

1   You watch magic tricks being performed: someone will deceive you or you will delude yourself about a project or relationship that will prove a disappointment.

2   You are performing magic tricks: you will manage to convince others of certain facts, but you won't fall for them or for anything else yourself.

## MAP

The kind of map in your dreams is significant:

• you consult a normal map: you don't really know where you are at the moment. You will need advice and guidance to find your way or to choose a new direction in your professional or emotional life; or, you will soon have the opportunity to travel. It may mean that you can come up with unusual plans or projects;

• a relief map: this indicates that your plans are very ambitious or that they will exceed your expectations;

• an old, damaged or torn map: this denotes that you have to depend on your own resources to follow your path or make decisions. Alternatively, it can mean that your plans and ambitions lack precision and will be hard to realize;

• a treasure map: this encourages you to focus on what is essential in yourself and in your life, whatever your given situation. You need to concentrate on a precise objective, and in that way you will achieve goals well beyond your hopes;

• a sky chart: this reveals that you live in your dreams rather than in reality, expecting manna to fall from heaven along with good fortune and luck. It is not impossible, but not everything that falls from the sky is fortunate, and the dream warns you of this.

## MARRIAGE
### (*see also* COUPLE, p. 125)

1   You attend a wedding: someone will make you an interesting proposal or partnership contract; you may have a defining emotional experience.

2   You get married: this indicates prosperity and excellent emotional relationships, particularly within the family; if you are already married, you will be nostalgic for the idyllic engagement period.

## MATCHES

1   You light a match: this indicates that you will have a good idea or that you are taking or will take a good initiative. However, you should take care to act or react quickly and demonstrate skill and speed.

2   The match fails to light: this means that you are about to take a pointless risk or to be enthusiastic about what you (wrongly) think is a good idea.

3   You are unable to extinguish it: you are obsessed by a fixed idea. You need to integrate it, admit it into your life or act upon it otherwise it could get totally out of control.

**4**  You burn your fingers with a match: you will find it difficult to contain yourself, to resist a temptation or desire.

**5**  You see a full box of matches: you have good ideas, great initiative and substantial intellectual and moral resources. However, your enterprises will be too ephemeral.

**6**  You see an empty box of matches: you are low in resources, ideas, imagination or vital energy; undoubtedly you have done too much recently. The dream is advising you to be cautious and to recharge your batteries.

**7**  You are opening a box of matches the wrong way and they are spilling onto the ground: your ideas lack constancy and coherence or, on the other hand, your ideas are too ordered, organized and methodical. Whichever is the case, a different order or an unexpected outcome will emerge, a new, original and unforeseen idea. In order for this to happen, however, it is vital that you keep an open mind and rethink your values, certainties and convictions.

## MAZE

If you stroll in or are lost in a maze, your ideas and beliefs are leading you astray. Think less and act more.

## MEASURING INSTRUMENTS
### (*see also* SCALES, p. 215)

The kind of measuring instrument you dream of, either seeing or using it, has the following meanings:

**1**  Barometer: the measurements shown indicate how your emotional life and your family and social relationships will develop.

**2**  Compass: you will not be able to extricate yourself from a difficult situation if you continue your current directionless behaviour; you need to take radical measures.

**3**  Electricity meter: its indicators reveal the level of tension or harmony in your current circumstances together with the likelihood of future disruption.

**4**  Gauge: you assess the feelings or intentions of someone whom you doubt; the measurements may reflect your own feelings and intentions, which you question. Alternatively, your financial situation will prove worrying.

5   Milometer/odometer: you can assess your past and future progress towards the ultimate target.

6   Ruler: you need order and structure in your life and you must clearly define your limits in order to achieve your goals.

7   Speedometer: by consulting this instrument you will learn whether the pace of your life will increase or decrease or whether you have already reached cruising speed.

8   Tape measure: you will take all necessary precautions and assess your chances, your means and your skills with precision before embarking on a new enterprise or tackling someone.

## MEAT

1   Eating raw meat: indicates that you will manifest your instincts and desires in an aggressive, even slightly brutal, way, or that newfound energy will make you dynamic and hardy.

2   Eating cooked meat: means you will temper your desires and your possessive nature or that your financial or material situation will give you great satisfaction.

## MEDAL, LOCKET

1   You win or are awarded a medal: this indicates personal success of some kind, or that your abilities and efforts will be rewarded. It heralds a promotion or entry into an exclusive circle.

2   You lose a medal: if you are unable to exploit what is given to you, it will be taken from you.

3   You are wearing a locket: you can depend upon the unconditional support of someone close to you.

4   You find or are given a medallion: a very good-hearted person, whom you have not yet met, will soon enter your life and play a key role in your personal development.

5   You lose a medallion: someone close or a family member will disappear from your life.

## MEN and WOMEN

1   You see or meet a woman you don't know:

•   if you are a man: the dream heralds an encounter, a relationship or a liaison with a woman that you have not yet met and who will mean a great deal to you;

•   if you are a woman: a woman whom you have yet to meet will bring great joy or play a key role in your life.

2   You see or meet a man you don't know:

•   if you are a woman: this signifies that you will meet a man who will turn your life – romantic, social or professional – upside down;

•   if you are a man: a man as yet unknown to you will be a big influence on your development or will give you unconditional support.

3   You see or meet strange women or men: those you see or meet share your ideas and beliefs. The dream tells you that you are not alone in thinking this way and offers comfort and support.

## MERRY-GO-ROUND

You see or ride on a merry-go-round in your dreams. Your obsessive feelings and negative thoughts are making you go round in circles. This dream warns you to get off the merry-go-round before you become ill. Start behaving in a less childish and more responsible way and express yourself more clearly and frankly.

## METAL

The appearance of an object or something metallic emphasizes your psychic potential, the transformative power that is within you and that tends to manifest itself in your worldly life. The metal as well as the nature of the object itself must be examined in order to understand fully the message contained in your dream.

1   Bronze: you can rely on certain people, have complete confidence in a particular situation or will have to prove your self-discipline; alternatively, you will fall prey to your own weakness and desires.

**2** Copper: the objectives you aspire to will spur those around you to help you obtain what you want. This dream can also denote that you will be rescued from a very difficult situation from which you did not think you would be able to escape, or that you will feel a sense of nostalgia for something or someone.

**3** Gold: your frankness and magnanimity earn you esteem and recognition from those close to you; you are or will be idealistic and a perfectionist in matters of love. It can herald prosperity or a tendency to rely too heavily on appearances, with bitter disappointment as a result.

**4** Iron: you will display great will and determination in all trials, but you might be well advised to be a little more flexible and receptive when going through the necessary changes in your life or situation. Alternatively, you will benefit from a great stroke of luck or a unique occasion. It may denote a very combative and inflexible nature.

**5** Lead: you are about to undergo a painful experience from which it is imperative that you learn a lesson. You may feel as though everything around you is stagnating and you are going nowhere, but you will have no choice in the short term other than to be patient. Alternatively, in spite of appearances, your professional situation or personal relationships will develop favourably, while your emotional life will undergo a complete transformation.

**6** Silver: if you are a man, this indicates that a woman's feelings for you are genuine; if you are a woman, you will experience strong and pure feelings for a man with prospects of a certain social standing, or you will be appreciated for your honesty and integrity.

## MICROPHONE
### (see also SINGING, SONG, p. 222; SPEECH, p. 227)

If you are speaking into a microphone, you will have a chance to say loud and clear what you have been thinking deep down for a long time – no one will be able to ignore you.

## MICROSCOPE

If you are using a microscope, you will get bogged down in the detail of something or you will make a mountain out of a molehill.

# MILK

1   You drink milk: you will be enchanted and delighted by someone's smooth-talking ways or you will be appreciated and protected by those you love.

2   You knock milk over or see it spilled on the ground: you will dramatize a minor situation.

3   You boil milk: the problem that is worrying you at the moment will turn out to be less serious than you had feared. Alternatively, you will find it hard to control your emotions.

4   You see a woman breast-feeding: you will be able to rely on the feelings and well-meaning advice of a woman friend.

# MILL

1   You see a windmill: your ideas and ambitions will be noble and generous but utterly unrealistic. It may be that you will have dealings with someone who is very talkative or talks bigger than he acts, or that your future will depend entirely on circumstances.

2   You see a watermill: either your income will increase or circumstances and new relationships will sustain your ideas and beliefs.

3   You are a miller, or you have dealings with a miller: if you need financial assistance in order to achieve something very important to you, you must show that you can be ambitious and generous; the attempts of others to harm you will backfire.

# MIRROR

1   You are looking at yourself in a mirror: something will force you to do some soul-searching and to take a closer look at yourself. Alternatively, if you are a man, either you will have a son very like you or you will have some worries in your professional life; if you are a woman, either you will have a daughter who will bear a close resemblance to you, or you will have a rival.

2   You see yourself in a mirror; you know that it is you but you don't recognize yourself: there is a real difference between the way you see yourself and the way you are in reality. This dream advises

you to get to know yourself better; or that your current situation and activities don't match your ambitions and desires. You need to take this on board.

3    The mirror in which you are reflected is broken: a particular hope or dream will not be fulfilled; in time you will learn to conquer your weaknesses and correct your errors and, in order to do this, you can count on someone's unconditional support.

## MOLE

A mole represents a home-loving, fearful or miserly person coming into your life. Alternatively, someone will reveal to you the secret intentions or actions of another or you will be closely watched without your knowledge; it could indicate that it will take a lot of persuasion to make you face the truth or that – after a long and difficult transitional period – you will gain a position of responsibility or a hoped-for reward.

## MONEY

1    You see, receive or have money: you will make some small gains and will have several different jobs or activities, but they won't last long and certainly won't enable you to stabilize your financial situation; the latter is at risk of becoming even more precarious and uncertain for a time.

2    You see, receive or have foreign currency: you will receive a loan or some kind of financial aid that you need, or your income will increase thanks to a new activity or opportunity to do something in a field other than your own.

3    You find some old coins: you do not exploit your potential to the full. If you were to do so, not only would you become more fulfilled, but your financial situation would also improve (*see also* TREASURE, p. 242).

4    You see, receive or have several banknotes: be careful, you could find money slipping through your fingers, either because you will be confronted with unforeseen expenses, because you have to pay your debts or because you will be wasteful and extravagant.

5    You see bundles of banknotes: you aspire to live beyond your means and doubtless will have the opportunity to do so. However,

you will do well to consider that this affluence will not solve all your problems.

## MONKEY

A monkey symbolizes a meeting with somebody who is a bit of a joker or whom others do not take seriously; nevertheless, you will soon realize that there are two sides to this person. Another interpretation of this dream is that a child close to you will be extremely fidgety and boisterous, and will take up a lot of your time; it may be that you are being advised to act sensibly but not to take yourself so seriously, or that you will meet somebody who appears pleasant but turns out to be a flatterer or cheat, who could well take you for a ride.

## MONSTER

You see a monster in your dream. Whatever its shape or form, the monster is a manifestation of an overwhelming, undisclosed anguish that you need to express. By giving you a fright that you won't quickly forget, this dream alerts you to the problem and warns you to get to the bottom of it. It can herald a meeting or a relationship that won't be without risk.

## MONUMENT

If you see or visit a monument, you will be rewarded for something, or will succeed in your affairs or enterprises, but this success could mark the end of your progress or development. Try to look further ahead, be more ambitious or optimistic.

## MOON

1   You see the full moon: this signifies a rewarding emotional life, popularity, prestige, recognition of merit, idealism, hypersensitivity, creative inspiration or a birth.

2   You see a crescent or waxing moon: you will come up with an original idea or an artistic creation whose realization will bring you enormous satisfaction. Renewed vitality, both physical and mental, may be indicated.

**3**   You see a waning moon: your goals will not be met; you will lack inspiration, or you will be involved with pointless concept. Alternatively, you will feel depressed, tired and below par.

**4**   You see the moon turn or dance in the sky: you will find yourself in a dangerous and insecure position or you will act in a thoroughly irrational way, for which you will suffer the consequences, unless you put a stop to it immediately.

**5**   You see an eclipse of the moon: someone you know will vanish from your life or you will discover that a person you admired greatly is not as perfect as you had imagined.

**6**   You see several moons in the sky: you are an idealist, a dreamer and you seek unconditional love and respect from those around you. You are imbued with a deep need for union but this cuts you off from reality, whether external or internal. The dream can also indicate that you will fall under the influence of vague and illusory ideas.

## MOTHER

**1**   You are in touch with your mother: whether your mother is still alive or not, this dream takes you back to your relationship with her, to the things left unsaid and misunderstandings unresolved. However, it may also indicate your need for the maternal love that you lack or cannot express. It can herald a happy event in your family life or your role in reconciliation.

**2**   You see a mother with her child or children: your loved ones will demonstrate their sincere affection for you (*see also* CHILD, p. 116).

## MOUNTAIN

**1**   You see a mountain: you will become thoughtful and rather idealistic or you will experience a period of calm and serenity or well-earned rest.

**2**   You see a mountain chain: you will experience conflicts and dissension with others or powerful adversaries will get in your way.

**3**   You climb a mountain: the path towards achieving your aims will be long, difficult and laborious but when you get there you will owe nobody anything and you will have thoroughly deserved your success.

**4** You reach the summit with ease, without stopping on the way, and descend the other side without difficulty: you will overcome an obstacle or make some progress in your life rapidly and easily.

**5** You descend a mountain: you will obtain satisfaction and people will recognize your qualities and worth.

**6** You see a volcano erupting: you won't be able to stop yourself becoming angry or overwhelmed by your emotions, you will become a victim of your desires, instincts and passions; your behaviour may provoke criticism or a violent reaction on the part of someone near to you.

**7** You see an extinct volcano: you are brimming with turbulent emotions inside and feel as if you will explode at any moment; perhaps you are walking on eggshells, or you will experience a situation that could become explosive. Be careful.

## MOVING HOUSE

To move house in your dream denotes upheaval in your projects. Alternatively, it can mean that you will be the catalyst for a great change in your situation or life that brings with it a new element or the opportunity to set off on the right foot once more. It can also indicate crazy and illogical behaviour.

## MUD

**1** You are walking through mud: this reveals the confusion in your current situation, its difficulties and complications, which are in danger of overwhelming you or bogging you down. Alternatively, others will do all they can to discourage you or to ensure you do not succeed.

**2** You fall in the mud: this indicates that you get bogged down in your own ideas, imagination and endless initiatives, which never lead to anything concrete, real or tangible. It may be that you will fall into a rut or be trapped in a tricky situation. It can also represent the promise of a recovery or the certainty of finding within yourself all that is required for your regeneration.

## MURDER

**1**   You witness a murder: you bear a grudge against someone, but this dream has more to do with trying to conquer your own negative feelings than with the person in question; you are turning a new page in your life, whether you like it or not.

**2**   You are murdered: someone in your circle or an associate is suffocating and inhibiting you. This dream advises you to react energetically and to assert your own personality more firmly.

**3**   You commit a murder: you know full well that one person's happiness can be another's pain; thus you will profit from an opportunity to someone else's detriment; you may refuse to accept or admit something important.

## MUSEUM

If you visit or walk around a museum looking at the exhibits, you will feel inspired, imaginative and creative or you will be led to take stock of the events of the past or of your relationship with your family and your roots.

## MUSHROOM

**1**   You see or pick an edible mushroom: it is a sign of healthy and stimulating relationships; you may have pleasant and dynamic new encounters. It can also herald an imminent attraction for the opposite sex – you may be overwhelmed by choice on that score.

**2**   You see or pick poisonous mushrooms: it means that you will be the victim of slander or gossip or that you will have dealings with untrustworthy, possibly malevolent characters. Alternatively, you will have a difficult and disappointing love affair.

## MUSICAL INSTRUMENTS

The type of instrument you see or play in your dream has the following meanings:

**1**   Accordion: all the excitability, turbulence and action in your life will leave you breathless; alternatively, you will be able to increase your modest means through your skill and knowledge.

**2** Barrel organ: you will have dealings with a difficult, wild and uncontrollable person or you will feel a sense of nostalgia, clinging to old memories.

**3** Castanets: a thorny issue will cause you headaches but you will resolve it eventually; you may fail to contain your passionate instincts.

**4** Drum: you will make a lot of noise about nothing or a mountain out of a molehill; your arguments may fall on deaf ears. This dream may signal a shocking, disruptive event that will ultimately prove beneficial and bring you great comfort.

**5** Flute: you will fall for the charms of a seductive character; or you will experience bitter disappointment and regret. Alternatively, pleasure and passion will come into your life.

**6** Guitar: you will be over-sensitive and emotional or you will fall in love.

**7** Harmonica: you will think very seriously about embarking upon a major voyage or going to live in distant parts; alternatively, you will have a meaningful but fleeting encounter with someone.

**8** Harp: you will demonstrate inner equilibrium and self-control or you will fall in love at first sight. This dream can also herald dealings with a woman who appears sweet and accommodating but who will prove to be materialistic and self-interested.

**9** Horn: enjoyment and fulfilment are on the cards.

**10** Organ or harmonium: you will witness or participate in a religious ceremony; it might indicate that you seek harmony in your emotional life but are somewhat idealistic. Alternatively, a life-changing event will occur or you will have to do all in your power to maintain equilibrium in your life.

**11** Piano: you will need to use all your skill to avoid dissonance and false notes in your dealings with others; despite your virtuosity and energy, you will not receive credit for what you do.

**12** Pipes: no one else is interested in your thoughts and actions, or you will encounter someone whose fine words or good humour will please you greatly, although you perceive their intentions are less pure than they seem. Alternatively, something is reaching its natural end and needs either to be renewed or replaced.

**13** Saxophone: you will be inclined to bear grudges, to keep trotting out ancient grievances; you may find yourself in fresh contact with someone with whom you lost touch a long way back.

**14** Tom-tom: ignore malicious gossip and keep confidences; a secret or surprising piece of news will reach you. Alternatively, you will hear in advance about a tricky situation or major upheaval and will be able to deal with it properly as a result.

**15** Trumpet: you will soon discover the verdict of a judicial affair in which you are implicated, directly or indirectly or your achievements will soon be recognized and rewarded. You may be the object of discussion or receive a plea for help.

**16** Violin: your enthusiasm and love of life will communicate itself to others or you will have dealings with a manic-depressive, whose mood swings are as dramatic as they are unpredictable. Alternatively, you will need to show great discipline in your projects and planning.

**17** Violoncello: you will be deeply disturbed by what others say or do in your name or on your behalf; or you will tend to concentrate on your own feelings and desires.

## MUSTARD

You see, you eat or you upset some mustard: you will fall victim to your own impatience and irritability; you will be on edge or will give way to anger.

## NAIL

**1** You see one or several nails: you are in danger of conflict with those who contradict you.

**2** You are hammering in nails: you will have dealings with rivals, competitors or powerful antagonists. Alternatively, you will take a stubborn stand in a litigious affair with no guarantee of achieving your goal or winning the case (*see also* HAMMER, p. 158).

## NECKLACE

**1** You are wearing a necklace: your relationships are harmonious and happy, based on powerful and solid emotions. This means fidelity and a flourishing love life; or that you will be entrusted with a delicate task or confidential mission.

2    You are given a necklace: you will ask someone to marry you or someone will propose to you.

3    You see a pearl necklace: this is a sign of your honesty, loyalty and openness (or that of the person wearing the necklace in your dream). Alternatively, you will become prosperous (*see also* OYSTER, p. 198).

## NEEDLE

The threaded needle puts you on course, giving you direction. Following the thread will enable you to 'sew', to collect the pieces of fabric and create the patchwork. The needle is an instrument of reunion, reconciliation and repair.

1    If you find a needle or use a needle in your dream:

- you are bringing together all the different aspects or pieces of your present life. If you are in conflict with one or more people in your circle, the needle signifies the possibility of reconciliation;

- it is the promise of union or marriage.

2    If you prick yourself with a needle: you are self-deluding, careless, naïve or presumptuous; only a sudden shock ('a prick') will bring you out of your torpor and back to reality.

3    Someone gives you a needle:

- take careful note of other aspects of your dream: these will contain important information that will 'orient' you, that is, guide you and point out the correct path;

- alternatively, you will receive good advice or some useful help on choosing the right way to achieve your goal, by playing all your trump cards.

## NEST

You find a nest:

1    Ant's nest: this indicates serious upheaval at home, or the start of major home improvements.

**2** Bees' nest: your home or family life is sure to become a hotbed of activity, with profitable results.

**3** Bird's nest: your family situation will remain precarious and uncertain or you will move house, possibly not by choice. Alternatively, this dream counsels that if you are patient and persevering, you will eventually achieve all that you wish for, or that you will soon get your independence (*see also* BIRD, p. 75).

**4** Caterpillar's nest: some major, positive changes will take place within the family or at home.

**5** Mouse's nest: a somewhat blithe, carefree attitude will prevail at home.

**6** Squirrel's nest: this means either that your family situation has a safe future, or that you will hear of a marriage or birth in the family.

**7** Termites' nest: you may think seriously about buying, restoring or building a house or else someone will seek to disrupt your home or family life.

**8** Vipers' nest: you will have enemies within your own family.

**9** Wasps' nest: disagreements or arguments are about to break out within your family or household. Alternatively, you will meet a group of aggressive, unkind people, so watch out.

## NET

To see or fall into a net is symbolic of a trap that may be set for you and into which you risk falling headlong. It can also herald a total dependence upon a situation or person.

## NUDITY

**1** You dream that you are naked in a public place: this is an indication that you will be forced to show your true colours, reveal all your weaknesses and be honest and genuine; alternatively, you will feel extremely ill-at-ease at a social gathering or you will lack self-confidence.

**2** You are naked in your dream and there are other naked people around you: a sign that your relationships with those around you will be mutually honest and open.

3   You are with someone who is naked: this means that someone will open their heart to you and you will be able to trust them too.

4   You see a very attractive naked man or woman: this signifies that you idealize your feelings and desires, but this does not make them any less intense or urgent.

# NUMBER

Numbers that appear to you in dreams are often secret combinations that are revealed to help you solve certain problems and find practical solutions, both psychological and material. The number that you see in your dream may therefore be interpreted as an opportunity, fate, destiny, a challenge or a big gamble. This is why traditional oneiromancy (the interpretation of dreams), would advise you to 'play' this number, because it could prove to be a source of material gain. But, most importantly, the interpretation of the number is the key to your psychological and spiritual development. Clearly, an exhaustive list of possible number combinations cannot be given here.

You dream about one of the following numbers:

1   Zero: you will have to start from scratch at work or at home. Alternatively, all the elements you need to begin or see through a new project will be at your disposal, or you will show yourself to be particularly receptive to others (*see also* CIRCLE, p. 118).

2   One: you must show courage, determination, daring and originality and rely on no one but yourself. In other words, you will have to take on a leadership role, or you will win a competition, or a lucrative alliance or association will be achievable.

3   Two: conflict and discord will be unavoidable; it may be that, whatever your actions, you will be able to play for both teams or exploit fully your ambivalent nature. Alternatively, you will have to make an important choice; you will have your ups and downs, or your financial situation will prey on your mind.

4   Three: you will have lots to do; your relationships will be stimulating and fulfilling, and you will feel extremely communicative and full of curiosity; you may become increasingly aware of the assets and advantages you possess. You may hear some happy news, such as the birth of child, or your heart will be torn

between two people and you will find it difficult to choose (*see also* TRIANGLE, p. 244).

5    Four: your deeply sensitive nature will probably make you more realistic and less trusting; your family or home situation may be a source of worry, or you are reaching the end of an era (*see also* SQUARE, p. 230).

6    Five: you will be in complete control of your situation and take full advantage of all your assets. Alternatively you will find yourself at the heart of a personally advantageous situation, or you will be idealistic and seek perfection in your love life or emotional relationships, or a union or marriage may be on the cards (*see also* CENTRE, p. 115).

7    Six: you need to take a firm decision, or to make up your mind, once and for all, about which way you are heading. If not, you will be forever swaying between contradictory feelings, events or circumstances. The number six can also indicate that you will be called on to play the role of intermediary in a delicate situation, or that you will successfully extricate yourself from a situation that is currently preoccupying you.

8    Seven: your courage, determination and willpower will bring you the success you crave or enable you to get what you want, or you will be the architect of a great change in your life. It could mean that you will achieve the impossible in order to maintain balance in your situation or harmony in your relationships, or you will engage in a lucrative transaction or take out a loan; you may tie up a profitable contract, deal or alliance.

9    Eight: you have come full circle. If you want to get out of a dead-end situation you will have to react decisively and challenge everything around you; this number can also signify that you will be the victim of your own impulses and desires, or that you must be strict and disciplined with yourself to achieve your goals or restore order to your situation. Someone may leave you something in a will.

10  Nine: your thoughts or pursuits will prove fruitful and help you to complete an important task or mission. This, in turn, will allow you to create something new and original in your life; you may be about to enter a necessary period of transition, during which time you will be left to your own devices, or you will be nobody's fool,

but your lucidity will be of little use; perhaps your professional or social situation will expand in some way, which will broaden your horizons, either geographically or intellectually.

**11** Ten: you will obtain precisely what you expect or hope for, or that you have devoted yourself to for some time – proof of your social and professional success; you may be in for more ups and downs, but you will have free will, and be able to move things along in a positive and beneficial way; or you will be ambitious, tenacious and implacable, making no concessions when you are convinced you are right about something.

**12** Eleven: you will demonstrate an independent but perhaps also an unstable state of mind, make outrageous remarks and tend towards excessive and provocative behaviour. Alternatively, you will make new friends or form new bonds, or you will concoct or implement a daring plan; you may make a mistake, by being over-enthusiastic, overindulgent or undisciplined, or your psychological and physical state will give you cause for concern.

**13** Twelve: you will find yourself in a difficult situation with no way out, probably as a result of your own mistakes, or you have explored every aspect of a situation and will soon have to move on.

**14** Thirteen: a radical change will take place in your life; you will reap what you have sowed, or you will have an exceptional stroke of luck. It could be that you will end a situation or relationship.

**15** Twenty-one: your wishes will come true and exceed all expectations; or you will embark on a great journey or adventure that will change the course of your life. This dream can also denote that you aspire to perfection in life.

**16** Twenty-two: you will be the victim of your own impulses, changeability and passions; you may have an unexpected encounter or give in to panic; you may be going on a short journey.

**17** Thirty-six or three hundred and sixty: whatever you are hoping for or expecting is at least a year away; alternatively, you will not delude yourself or give your trust lightly.

**18** Forty: you will be extremely distressed by a painful event or difficult circumstances, but when you come through the experience you will have grown as a person and will feel reinvigorated; you may have to make a sacrifice, isolate yourself or simply give up if you want to get out of a difficult situation.

**19** One hundred: you will enjoy complete success in your professional or social life.

**20** One thousand: unclouded happiness, you will feel complete, your personality will blossom and your dearest wishes will come true.

**21** Ten thousand: your actions will bear fruit, your business affairs will be profitable, and your financial situation comfortable. In short, on a material level, everything will go swimmingly; everything will come together, you will be in harmony with the people around you and at one with yourself.

# OFFICER

If you dream of one of the following:

**1** Police officer: you are probably feeling guilty about mistakes you have made, and that you have not yet learned from; alternatively, you really must respect certain rules or knuckle down if you want to achieve your goals and get what you want; it could be that a stranger you meet in exceptional circumstances will help you to get back on track.

**2** Army officer: you will have to take on some heavy responsibilities or you will be entrusted with an important mission; in a contentious or confusing situation, you will be advised to act tough and make a firm and final decision – in other words, adopt a military attitude; you may gain the support of an influential person.

**3** Naval officer: your plans and business deals will come off, so long as you keep things on an even keel, do not steer off course and brave the wind and tides with vigilance and perseverance. Alternatively, the future of your family situation or a company will rest entirely on your shoulders.

**4** Air force officer: make sure your objectives are well defined if you want to achieve your goals or obtain something you hold dear. Another interpretation could be that you will have to aim higher and be more ambitious and daring if you want to fulfil your dreams or that you are going to have to make some serious decisions that may seem drastic to you. However, you will have no choice in the matter.

5    Astronaut: you will hurl yourself into a venture without really weighing up the consequences. This will mean that, sooner or later, destiny, circumstances or other people will determine your future. This dream can also indicate that you are divorcing yourself from reality, which will not help you to better yourself socially, psychologically or spiritually, or that, sooner or later, your stubborn and self-centred nature will leave you isolated and alone.

## OGRE
### (see also GIANT, p. 153)

To dream of an ogre denotes that an extreme, unsatisfied, obsessive desire you can no longer control is gnawing away at you, or that an obsession or your extreme or selfish behaviour is stifling or destroying your sensitivity and emotions. This dream is a warning that, if you do not change your attitude, sooner or later your seriously depleted energy resources will lead to health problems.

## OIL

1    You see oil in a bottle or other vessel: you will have dealings with one or more influential people who will support you in a delicate situation. Peaceful and happy times with your family are ahead.

2    You knock over some oil: you tend to take on too much, to reconcile the irreconcilable and do the impossible; this can be a dangerous attitude.

3    You drink oil: you will try to soften harsh words or disagreeable news; perhaps others will try to make you believe in something unlikely or deceive you unwittingly. If you care about your well-being, you need to look after health – take action now.

4    You see an oil lamp: someone – almost certainly a woman – is in your heart and your thoughts, or someone dear to you will help clear up a mystery, resolve a problem or shed light on your inner self.

5    You rub aromatic oil on a part of your body, or all over: you will experience a moment of total relaxation and of feeling carefree and released (see also BODY, p. 79).

## ONE-EYED
### (*see also* BLINDNESS, p. 77, BODY, p. 79)

**1**   You can see with your right eye: this denotes reason, logic and realism in your current acts and thoughts. However, you are behaving in a unilateral way that lacks objectivity.

**2**   You can see with your left eye: instinct and intuition guide you but you are acting unilaterally and you lack objectivity.

**3**   You meet or are involved with a one-eyed person: however paradoxical or unlikely it may seem, you are capable of being immensely clear-sighted and lucid about yourself and others. You can both see and understand people beyond external appearances, but your perceptiveness causes you anxiety and fear.

## OX

The ox is the expression of your physical strength and your dedication to work together with your courage and determination, consciously or unconsciously, to put aside your own selfish feelings. It is a portent of the excellent results you will achieve if you demonstrate resolute and fruitful patience. It can also act as a warning to take time to assimilate and understand what is happening both within and around you at this time.

## OYSTER

**1**   You open or eat oysters: renewed energy and vitality lie ahead, or your love life will be rich, rewarding and passionate but you will get more from the relationship than you give to it.

**2**   You find a pearl in an oyster you are eating or opening: although your romantic and sex life is currently rather unstable, you will enjoy an unexpected and important encounter, fall in love or experience a completely new emotion.

**3**   You are unable to open an oyster: someone you know will be indifferent to you and your emotions or will stubbornly refuse to express their feelings or opinions.

**4**   You are given a pearl: someone will demonstrate real and deep affection for you, to which you will not be able to remain indifferent. This could herald a proposal of marriage or union or that the sincere feelings someone has for you will help you achieve a greater sense of emotional harmony and peace. Alternatively, you will regain your love of life and happiness.

## PAINTER
### (see also COLOUR, p. 120)

You see a painter working on:

1   A portrait of a man or woman you do not know: you will meet someone who will prove to be a decisive force in your life. You have a premonition about this meeting, but it will only happen in its own good time.

2   A portrait of you: someone close to you will help you to see yourself more clearly, or to make the most of qualities you never knew you had. Alternatively, someone is thinking about you and will make you an interesting offer.

3   A landscape: you will feel nostalgic.

4   An abstract painting: your ideas will be muddled or your plans will be impossible to see through.

5   A painting that you recognize as a masterpiece: you will enjoy great success in an area that is particularly important to you.

## PARACHUTE
### (see also VOID, p. 248)

To dream you are using a parachute signifies that, whether you like it or not, you will be forced to take the plunge – in other words, make an important decision. But this dream also warns you to take all the necessary precautions to ensure you have a soft landing. It could mean that you have been avoiding reality lately and it's now time to get your feet back on the ground although here, again, be careful.

## PASSPORT
### (see also IDENTITY CARD, p. 166)

1   You dream of your passport or you open it: you will go on a journey. It can also mean that you will have carte blanche to do whatever you like, and to come and go as you please.

**2**   You show your passport to a customs official: you will have to go through an important stage in your life, but the transition will neither be smooth nor easy.

## PATH

**1**   You are walking along a clearly marked path: you are self-confident and sure of your destiny, carving out your own particular route in life and certain of reaching your goals sooner or later.

**2**   You are following an unknown or unusual path: you have already changed course, direction or decision, in theory if not in practice. Alternatively, you will follow another path to reach your goals or you will change direction altogether.

**3**   The path unrolls before you as you progress: you will exercise free will and determine your own future.

**4**   You are walking along a path in the fog: you are sure of nothing and your future is uncertain; you need to take extra care (*see also* FOG, p. 145).

**5**   You can see the end of the path: you are about to cross an important threshold in your life or experience a defining change. It can denote an imminent achievement of your goals.

**6**   You stop or look behind you on the path: you are anxious and lack confidence in yourself and your actions. Alternatively, facts and events relating to your past will curtail your progress.

**7**   The path becomes more and more narrow as you proceed: you will encounter difficulties.

**8**   The path becomes progressively wider as you proceed: you will enter a fruitful period in your life, during which you will exceed in your enterprises even more than you hoped.

## PEASANT

**1**   If you see peasants working in the fields: you will reap precisely what you have sowed, both in your love life and in your professional life. Another interpretation is that no one will hand you anything on a plate or make your task any easier, but your efforts and hard work will pay off.

**2** If you see yourself as a peasant: you probably seem a bit boorish or unsociable to those around you or else you have a long and difficult task to carry out, which you will take on without any fuss.

# PENCIL

**1** You see or write with a pencil: you will hear some good news or receive a pleasant letter.

**2** You draw with a pencil: you are being encouraged to exploit your creativity and your original ideas or to define your plans more precisely.

# PHOTOGRAPH
### (*see also* CAMERA, p. 105; MIRROR, p. 183; PAINTER, p. 199)

**1** You see a photograph of yourself: you need to stop pulling the wool over your eyes and to see yourself as you really are.

**2** You see a family photograph: your family situation will be a source of worry or even your main worry; alternatively, you feel that your family situation or relationships at home are stagnating.

**3** Someone is photographing you: someone is thinking about or has feelings for you or is including you in their plans; if you do not know who this person is, you soon will.

**4** You are taking photographs: you are trying to make time stop, but you cannot prevent everything from changing around you.

**5** You are ripping up photographs: you wish to draw a line under your past – but will you be brave enough? Either this, or someone dear to you will cause you distress.

# PIG

**1** To dream of a pig: you will meet someone who is unyielding, choosy and excessive, someone who makes no concessions; the dream may indicate that you should pay more attention to your body's needs and feelings, which you seem to be neglecting in favour of your intellect or mental state.

**2** Being chased or harassed by a pig or wild boar: foretells that someone greedy, insatiable, coarse, vulgar or nasty will pursue you relentlessly or that you will not be able to resist gluttony or excess, or that your selfish behaviour will do you no good.

3   Hunting or catching a wild boar: means that a wild, difficult and indomitable person will eventually take up your cause or share your views, or that a good opportunity or a stroke of luck is on the cards.

## PILL

1   You see, are prescribed or are given pills: you are about to hear some unpleasant news. Alternatively, your general health may need to be thoroughly checked. Another interpretation of this dream is that you will not have the last word in a discussion or dispute.

2   You give pills to somebody else: means that you will hear bad news, or that you will have to break bad news to someone you know.

3   You take a multi-coloured pill, or one that you know to have fantastic therapeutic or energizing properties: you will have a life-enhancing experience, enjoying boundless pleasure in complete abandonment to your desires.

## PIPE
### (see also TOBACCO, p. 239)

1   If you are smoking a pipe in your dream: home is where you feel at your best, where you can truly relax and recharge your batteries; it could also signify that, although you say nothing, this does not mean you do not have an opinion.

2   If you see somebody else smoking a pipe: someone will try to deceive you or lure you into a trap, or you will meet a rather timid, stay-at-home type.

3   Breaking a pipe: heralds an unexpected event that will bring you great joy; alternatively, you will lose a job or break all ties with somebody. Although this may not pleasant, all will turn out for the best.

## PIRATE

To see or be a pirate indicates that you are in tune with your rebellious, invincible, untamed nature; you feel a sense of revolt against your social environment, your circle of friends or the world in which you live. You believe that you will find your true self and inner satisfaction by playing the outlaw, by embarking on adventures or living according to your own rules.

## PLANE TOOL

If you see or are using a plane in your dream, you need to smooth over the problems or obstacles that get in your way; or, either in your relationships or your work, you need to demonstrate precision and skill.

## PLANT

Every plant has its own particular properties or qualities. We could look at the effects of individual plants on our physical and mental health, or study their symbolic meanings one by one. However, as with flowers, fruits, trees, birds, and so on, a comprehensive study of the symbolism behind every single variety of plant would fill an entire book on its own. Consequently, there is only room here to discuss plants in general as they appear in our dreams. For a more complete and precise interpretation of your dream, you should consult a book dedicated to plants and their various properties.

1   To dream of a healthy plant: this is a sign of good future health and vitality, or indicates that your work or business situation is blooming. It can also mean that a child will give you complete satisfaction.

2   You dream of a wilting plant: this means your health will cause concern or even alarm, and you will soon need a medical examination or treatment. Alternatively, you may have to take tough action to rectify a situation or you will be concerned about the health or development of a child.

3   You are looking after a plant: your care and kind attention will earn you the respect and gratitude of your peers. Alternatively, your family situation will evolve and blossom slowly but surely.

**4**   A present of a plant: heralds a new responsibility or promotion.

**5**   Putting a plant in the ground: this is a sign that you will need to perform a highly delicate operation in which there will be no room for error.

**6**   An exotic plant: indicates that a stranger, from a faraway place or simply from a different environment to your own, will come into your life and bring about some changes.

## PLAYING CARDS
### (see also GAMES and TOYS, p. 150):

**1**   If you are playing cards and winning: this signifies that your candour and frankness will be an asset or that you will reach your goals.

**2**   If you dream you are playing cards and losing: this is an indication that, despite your skill, judgement, perceptiveness and willingness to take risks, you won't attain your goals or have the last word. The dream warns you to stop.

**3**   If you are cheating at cards: it means that you are not playing the game and are preoccupied by the outcome of your current situation.

**4**   If you are playing Patience: this is a warning to be patient and tenacious in order to achieve your ambitions or be successful in your business.

## POISON

**1**   You dream that you have been poisoned: you must immediately look after your health, go for a medical examination or see a good doctor; it could mean that many problems are poisoning your life. The only way to improve your situation is quickly to eliminate whatever is causing you trouble or hampering your development.

**2**   You are poisoning someone: despite your good intentions, you are probably leading someone astray or even harming them, or you resent someone and this feeling is eating away at you.

**3**   Someone is poisoning you: this indicates that someone will say bad things about you, and you will suffer the consequences unless you are more vigilant and perceptive.

# POSTCARD
## (see also POSTMAN, p. 205; WRITING, p. 257)

1   If you receive a postcard: it means that good news is coming your way or that you have a tendency to delude yourself.

2   If you write or send a postcard: this means that you have a moral obligation to someone and it is to this person that you are sending the card. Alternatively, you are faced with a mission or obligation and you want to be rid of it as soon as possible; or you may have something you want to say but dare not.

# POSTER

1   If you see a poster: this foretells a discovery or the awareness of an important fact or event in your life.

2   You are putting up a poster: you wish to say or express something important to those around you, but you do not know how to do this or how to attract their attention.

3   You rip up or remove a poster: you refuse to reveal your true self or you do not take the opportunity to express yourself and your thoughts in order to be recognized finally by others.

4   You see a wall covered in posters: you have much to say and explain, to demonstrate and to give, but you do not know where to start.

5   You see your name on a poster: whether you wish it or not, you will be involved in a situation or matter in which you will have to play your role.

# POSTMAN

1   You see or meet a postman: you impatiently expect (or will await) a letter or some news but it will take its time.

2   The postman gives you a letter: you will hear surprising news or news that will be the catalyst for an important event in your life.

3   The postman gives you several letters addressed to you: if you have any doubt of the respect and approval others feel for you, this will soon be dispelled; or you will not act without the approval and support of others in your circle.

## POSTURE

1   You are lying:

   • on a bed: you will feel at ease, relaxed, happy with yourself and with your life – everything will go your way;

   • on the ground: it will not take much to make you happy and content; alternatively, you may go back to square one, but you will not mind doing so.

2   You are sitting:

   • on a chair: your current position or situation will remain uncomfortable, precarious and uncertain and you are probably going to have to work hard to consolidate it; or you are preoccupied with religious or spiritual matters;

   • in an armchair: you will find yourself in quite an easy, comfortable situation and will be in a strong position; keep working to get to that point, because you are on the right track; another interpretation could be that you are too complacent about your situation or that you are inclined to rest on your laurels;

   • on the ground: you will show yourself to be calm, confident, self-assured and well-balanced.

3   Kneeling: you are going to need help or you may have to prove your humility, let go of some of your privileges and loosen your grip on people and things.

## PRAYING

1   You are praying: a sign that you need help, or that, to get what you want, you must have faith in yourself and in life; alternatively, your prayers will be answered and your wishes will come true.

2   You see someone praying: someone will need your help or support in an urgent and delicate matter, or you will grudgingly give in to demands made by someone you know.

## PRIEST

If you dream about a priest or clergyman, it means you probably wish to forgive yourself for something, but you dare not admit it, or that you are blaming yourself for a mistake that could easily be rectified; it may be that you will hear of a birth, marriage or death.

## PRISON

1   If you dream about a prison: it means that, if you do not change your attitude, behaviour or direction, you could well end up trapped in a situation with no way out. However, this situation can be avoided, because the dream comes as a warning.

2   If you dream of being in prison: there's no doubt that you are a prisoner of your jealous feelings and your emotional dependencies, which are paralysing you, depriving you of personal freedom and moral, material and psychological autonomy; this dream alerts you to the fact that, somewhere within you, you have the keys to free yourself and to be who you really are; another interpretation is that you will find yourself in a dead end situation for a while, powerless to act or react, unable to do anything but hang on patiently and sit it out; your worries, problems and day-to-day troubles may make you feel as if you were in prison – try to broaden your horizons.

## PROSTITUTE

To dream of a prostitute signifies that you will meet someone – not necessarily a woman – who will stop at nothing to get what they want.

## PUPPET

To dream of a puppet is a sign that you will meet someone fickle or capricious whom you will clearly not be able to trust. Alternatively, someone you know will be completely dependent on you; this dream can also mean you are completely at the mercy of circumstances or of others' will and decisions.

## QUEUE

If you dream that you are standing in a queue: your time will come, but just stay calm and be patient for now.

# RABBIT

**1** You see one or more rabbits: this is a sign of fertility, prosperity and great activity. Alternatively, it indicates a tendency on your part to spread yourself too thinly, taking on too much at one time. It can foretell dealings with a greedy and impatient person.

**2** You hunt or catch rabbits: this denotes an opportunity to realize a longed-for project. It can also indicate that a young or dynamic person will play a key role in your future life.

# RACKET/BAT

If you dream you are looking at or using a tennis racket, table tennis bat, cricket bat etc., you will enter into a fierce discussion or argument whose outcome will be uncertain. It could also mean that you will be presented with an opportunity that you must seize immediately, or that you will need to make a quick decision, or possibly that unforeseen, unsettling circumstances will require you to act shrewdly, intelligently and with foresight.

# RADIO

If you see or listen to a radio: you will receive some surprising news; alternatively outside events or circumstances will strongly influence your behaviour or the decisions you are about to make.

# RAIN

**1** Walking in the rain means that, whether you like it or not, you will be forced to take risks.

- if the rain is light: you will have lots of worries, problems, trials and tribulations, and your daily life will seem tiresome and difficult;

- heavy rain: this means that an unexpected event or encounter will bring changes to many areas of your life or will change your ideas or convictions;

- torrential rain: this means you will be unavoidably involved in situations or problems that you previously thought to be no concern of yours;

• a shower: this means you will be unburdened of your worries or fears as if by magic.

2   You are walking in the rain under an umbrella: by being too protective, or staying on the defensive, you will be slow to act and therefore unable to seize good fortune and opportunity when it comes along.

3   You are walking in the rain wearing a raincoat: whatever your worries or problems, they will not sap your morale or undermine your choices or decisions.

4   You are watching the rain through a window: you will be extremely hesitant when it comes to taking risks, replying to an invitation, accepting a proposal or seizing an opportunity.

# RAINBOW
## (see also BRIDGE, p. 101)

1   You see a rainbow: this dream puts you in touch with your vital and spiritual energies, with your inner strength, which is split into seven distinct but unified components, representing a bridge between the visible and invisible worlds. This type of dream often announces a happy event, a new perspective in your life, a great joy that will come to you soon. If you have this dream during a difficult period in your life, you can be sure that you will soon emerge from it.

2   You pass under a rainbow: you will encounter a period of peace, calm and tranquil happiness during which your wishes will be granted.

3   You walk on a rainbow: if you advance from left to right you will undergo a period of transition leading to favourable material or physical conditions, if you walk from right to left, the transition relates to enhanced spiritual and metaphysical values.

# RAKE

To see or use a rake in a dream means that you will not rest until you find what you are seeking, you will show tenacity in your quest, and will get what you want in the end; alternatively, your extravagance, gullibility or recklessness may put you in a risky financial situation.

## RAM

The appearance of a ram in your dream reveals a strong desire or an impulsive, aggressive urge. It can also indicate pride or a lack of objectivity and lucidity on your part. It can herald a project that will soon materialize. The sacrifice of a ram is a sign of the abandonment, voluntarily or otherwise, of this urge, pride or project.

## RAT

1   You see a rat: someone in your circle will try to harm you or you will fall into a trap. However, this dream acts as a warning to you and thereby ensures that you can avoid it; alternatively, you will have dealings with a miserly person.

2   You are chased or bitten by a rat: your emotional relationships will be disappointing, or you will become involved with a person who is too possessive, choosy, jealous and passionate; or you will be the victim of a robbery or burglary.

## RIDER

If you see a horse rider, it symbolizes your noble, generous ambitions and your romantic, idealistic nature. It reveals a need to dream, to experience unusual adventures, to transcend the real world to a higher, deeper or more absolute plane. It can also herald a great love or a deep passion.

## RING

1   You are given or you find a ring: this signifies alliance, union, marriage or reconciliation. It denotes shared feelings and unalloyed happiness.

2   If you find or have rings of different sizes and shapes: you will have an emotional choice to make, an important decision to reach, an agreement to endorse or a contract to sign.

3   If you break or smash a ring, willingly or unwillingly: this denotes anger, rebellion, explosive emotional tension and even betrayal and rupture.

4   If you have lost your wedding ring: you doubt your emotional

relationships, your feelings or those of your partner. Alternatively, you will encounter conflict with your partner or have a disagreement with an associate or someone in your circle. The dream reveals a lack of clarity about your own feelings, which will give rise to confusion and psychological disharmony.

5    If you find a ring in your dream: expect a happy event, great joy or recompense, certainly some kind of gift, donation or inheritance.

6    If the ring you find is broken or you put back together a broken ring: it appears you will have difficulty finding peace, harmony and union in your life, both within yourself and with those around you. However, your good will and clear-sightedness can help you. On the other hand, you may succeed, slowly but surely, in becoming reconciled with someone or, despite being currently single, you will ultimately find a partner.

7    You receive a ring as a gift: this denotes a future promotion, reward or material profit in the form of goods. It may mean that you will be entrusted with a mission. Alternatively, you will be in a position to exercise power.

8    If someone gives you a ring: you will be ready to give away or share your possessions. You aspire to union, to be understood or you wish to share your power.

9    You lose a ring in your dream: this is a sign of material loss or unhappy events. It can herald general difficulties or a break with your circle or environment.

## ROBOTS

To dream of one or several robots is to confront your own attitudes, your automatic responses, your tendency to stick rigidly to the same principles and processes whatever the circumstances. The person or people represented by one or more robots in your dream will help you to detect and understand the nature of these automatic reflexes that govern your behaviour and attitudes.

## ROCKET

1    If a rocket lifts off: it promises achievement of your goals.

2    If you are inside a rocket on lift off: it indicates that your

projects and objectives may well be too ambitious or that you are ready for anything in order to achieve your target as quickly as possible.

3   If you see a rocket on its launcher: it signifies your readiness to embark upon a bold project or it promises some surprising news.

## ROOF

1   You dream that you are perched on or walking along rooftops: this means that you will be guided by your ideas, convictions, ambitions and intelligence, or that you will reach the pinnacle of your career.

2   You hear someone walking on the roof of your house: you will be influenced by a third person, or will espouse his or her ideas and convictions to the detriment of your own; alternatively, a sad or painful event may occur in your life.

## ROPE

1   You see a rope: you are about to have an emotional encounter or form a new relationship.

2   You climb a rope: you will find an unexpected, fortunate answer to a situation or problem that currently seems insoluble.

3   You descend a rope: even if you are in a precarious, uncertain situation, you will be able to re-establish yourself and put your best foot forward once again.

4   You see a hanging rope:

   •   and you suspend or hang yourself from the rope: you will come through your problems; you will soon be able to take control of your situation;

   •   and you swing on it: despite the constraints or trials that you are currently facing, you do not take your situation very seriously. It can also indicate that the lack of concern that you demonstrate could have damaging consequences;

   •   destined for someone else: you are wrong not to feel implicated in a certain matter, sooner or later you will become involved;

• destined for you: you will manage to emerge from a difficult, painful, testing situation, but not without great effort. You will be greatly relieved as a result.

5    You are tying knots in a rope: you seem to be master of your own destiny but you are not self-deluding and you know how to learn from your experiences, mistakes and successes.

6    You are untying a rope: your understanding, perspicacity and tolerance will allow you to solve a problem.

7    You are tied with a rope: you are a prisoner of your own emotional ties, material dependency or needs and unfulfilled desires. You need to be aware of this situation.

8    You have a rope tied around your neck: from now on, you need to take full responsibility and respect your commitments. Alternatively, this heralds a union, a marriage or a contract that may involve material or financial considerations.

## RUBBISH

1    Your house or apartment is filled with rubbish: there are people around you who wish you harm, or your relationships are unhealthy or damaging to your personal development.

2    You dream about dustmen collecting or emptying refuse: it is time to let go of the things that are ruining your life, or to free yourself from the tasks or obligations that are getting you down.

3    To dream about a rubbish dump: this warns that you will feel dangerously complacent about certain unhealthy or useless things you have eliminated from your life, although you are not entirely clear of them yet.

4    Falling into a trash heap: signifies that your tendency to over-indulge or let things wash over you may well have serious short- or long-term repercussions.

## RUG

1    You see a small, fairly thick rug: you will be worried by material and financial considerations, or your income will be modest.

2    You see a large rug: your finances will be quite comfortable.

**3**    A worn rug: indicates that your material resources have nearly run out, and you will probably be forced to take out a loan or request financial help.

**4**    You are sitting on a rug: you will become too attached to material possessions, or to reality and will find it hard to let go.

**5**    You are lying on a rug: someone will talk or think about you, or will make you an interesting proposition; you may experience some sort of shock or upset which will leave you completely at a loss or else a tough adversary will get the better of you.

**6**    A rug that is on fire, or that has been left out in the sun: this heralds a missed opportunity; it might also denote that you will be unable to act or react as you had planned.

## RUNNING

**1**    You are running for no particular reason or simply for pleasure: events in your life are about to take off and you will reach your goal ahead of schedule.

**2**    You are running to escape someone or something: you will search far and wide for something that is under your nose or within easy reach.

**3**    You take part in a race: with increasing frequency, you will feel the need to assert yourself within your family, social or professional environment.

## SALAD

To dream of seeing or eating salad can have various interpretations: you may have trouble extricating yourself from a confusing, messy situation or promises made to you will not be kept. It could mean that you will encounter an untrustworthy person or persons, or that you are too modest, and will need to prove yourself and demonstrate your worth if you wish to be noticed or to achieve the position you deserve.

## SALT and PEPPER

**1**    You see or eat salt: you feel that your life is rather boring, monotonous and in need of a dash of something new and unusual;

otherwise, you lack enthusiasm, love of life, self-confidence or optimism. An increase in your finances may be heralded, but it will be one that does not cause you great joy.

2    You see or eat pepper: an unanticipated event adds a little spice to your life or you will feel irritable, volatile and vulnerable. Alternatively, you will hear disappointing, frustrating or unpleasant news.

## SAW

1    You see a saw in your dream: you will not be able to avoid a separation or break-up, that you will receive some surprising news or that you will find yourself in a difficult, uncomfortable, shaky situation.

2    Sawing wood: is a sign that, out of boredom, you will probably cause some sort of disruption or split, either at work or in your love life.

## SCAFFOLDING

1    You see scaffolding: your enterprises will take time to come to fruition, demanding both perseverance and courage. Alternatively, the plans and projects of others will stand in your way.

2    You are standing or working on scaffolding: your courage, patience and skills will be put to the test, but if you work unceasingly you will reach your goals.

3    You fall off some scaffolding: you have been moving too fast without seeing the big picture; you will be forced to abandon your plans or at least to reflect upon and refine them before pursuing them further.

## SCALES

1    If you see a set of scales: it heralds the imminent arrival of emotional or material harmony, of balance in your relationships, of a sense of order, wisdom and justice in your life.

2    If you see an old set of scales: it is a signal of a conflicted situation that you will need to weigh up and judge according to old-fashioned values that are rigorous but correct.

3    If the scales are balanced: you can trust your own judgement or rely on the harmony and stability of your situation.

4    If the scales lean to the right: it means that you give too much emphasis to material goods, to the active life and to the rational and concrete side of things. Alternatively, you will make a biased and uncompromising judgement.

5    If the scales lean to the left: dreams, feelings and sentiments play too large a role in your life, causing an imbalance. A tendency to reconcile the irreconcilable prevents you from being fair and impartial in your thinking.

6    If the pans of the scales swing from one side to the other in a perpetual balancing act: your doubts, uncertainties and lack of assurance are making you indecisive, unstable and fickle. The dream advises you to stop weighing up the pros and cons, but to make a choice or a decision.

# SCHOOL

1    You find yourself back at a school desk: this dream is a warning to you not to settle for what you already know, because you still have much to learn. Alternatively, you have not yet learned from your experiences and circumstances. The school in your dream symbolizes the 'school of life' to which you need to return.

2    You are a schoolteacher: you have the situation well under control but you need to deploy all your resources to achieve your goals. This dream may denote the self-discipline and authority that will be needed if you want to assert yourself in your social or professional environment and get what you want. If you do not take this on board you will lose status.

3    You sit an exam and:

• pass: nothing is certain or finalized in your current situation, but you do hold all the trump cards; you will succeed as long as you are willing to accept certain obligations along the way;

• fail: you overestimate your ability or potential or your plans need revision and correction.

4    You skip school: you will need to relax and take time out; an

unexpected, paradoxical fact may incite you to adopt different behaviour, shed preconceptions and see things from a new, imaginative angle.

## SCISSORS

Seeing or using scissors foretells a break with or separation from a person or situation, of which you are the cause or victim, depending upon other information revealed in the dream.

## SCORPION

If you see, are threatened by or bitten by a scorpion in your dream, this augurs suicidal behaviour – in other words, you are in danger of doing precisely the opposite of what you should if you want to extricate yourself from a difficult or problematic situation; be sure to take note and learn from this dream. Alternatively, you may come across somebody who bears a grudge against you. This person's hostility is strong, and you would be well advised to distance yourself or take swift action against them.

## SEA
### (see also BATH, p. 69; BOAT, p. 78; WATER, p. 250)

1    You see the sea on the horizon: a new and happy event will give you the chance to blossom; this in turn will expand your horizons – geographically, socially or culturally.

2    You are by the sea: you are on the threshold of a new phase in your life, but you are still frightened of taking the plunge and embarking upon a new adventure.

3    You are at sea: you are conscious of and receptive to the things going on around you, but you will still do everything you can to steer your own course without being tempted to divert from it.

4    You are underwater: your own intense feelings overwhelm you and you are submerged in contradictory emotions and the diffuse and confusing influences of those around you. You would be well advised to raise your head above the water in order to see yourself clearly and to take stock of your situation. In this way you should become more independent in your actions and ideas.

## SEAL

Dreaming about a seal heralds a situation so rich in potential that the possibilities will be endless. Alternatively, you will have dealings with somebody who is slightly clumsy and awkward, but full of energy and goodwill, or that you will feel oppressed or you may have respiratory problems.

## SECT

You belong to a sect, are invited to join a sect or you refuse to embrace its cause means that your ideas and opinions are rigid and dogmatic. They are getting you nowhere or isolating you. It may be that you will be highly suggestible to and easily influenced by the ideas or opinions of those around you, to such a degree that you feel stifled by them, or that obsessive thoughts or grudges may make you ill.

## SHADOW
### (*see also* TREE, p. 242)

1   If you see your own shadow in a dream: you lack self-confidence, you underestimate yourself and are selling yourself short. You are capable of much more. Alternatively, you will find a faithful friend.

2   A menacing shadow: you are fearful, anxious and suspicious for no apparent reason. This is preventing you from living your life, letting yourself go, trusting people and having faith in yourself and in life.

3   You dream you are chasing your own shadow: this is an indication that you are deluding yourself, chasing rainbows or searching far and wide for something that is right under your nose or within easy grasp.

4   To dream of shadow puppets: too often you will take things at face value, so there is a danger you will be betrayed or conned.

5   You see the shadow of a familiar figure: you are haunted and obsessed by the thought of someone who is either close to you now, or has gone away; alternatively, this dream may be warning you about something important (*see also* GHOST, p. 152).

# SHEEP

**(see also LAMB, p. 172; RAM, p. 210; SHEPHERD, p. 219; WOOL, p. 256)**

**1** You see a sheep: you will be involved with someone free-spirited, wayward and undisciplined; it may be that, contrary to all expectations, you will suddenly give way to anger or reveal your idealism or ambition.

**2** You see a flock of sheep: those around you seem too passive and submissive, in need of a serious shake-up. Alternatively, if you allow things to muddle on as they are, they will soon collapse into disorder.

**3** You eat lamb or mutton: you will be inclined to make an effort to become wiser, even to make sacrifices; people may try to flatter you, lulling you into a false sense of security with their smooth words.

**4** You see sheared sheep or sheep being sheared: this indicates someone is seeking to exploit you, to steal from you or to cheat you in some way.

# SHEPHERD

**1** If you see or meet a shepherd: it is a sign that you need help, advice, moral support or guidance. Alternatively, you will meet someone worthy of your trust and confidence and this person will be able to guide you well.

**2** You are a shepherd: you will have to accomplish a mission, play a key role in something or take on some new responsibility in the near future.

# SHIELD

If you are hiding behind a shield or should a shield play a key role in your dream, it signifies that protection, help or support will be offered to you, a favour will come your way or you will extricate yourself from a difficult situation. Alternatively, it is the expression of your defensiveness and your tendency to protect yourself from others, from the outside world and sometimes from yourself.

## SHIP
### (*see also* BOAT, p. 78)

1   If you are at sea under clear skies: this denotes that your good qualities and noble aspirations will be rewarded. It may also indicate that you should not hesitate to prove your courage and initiative, or to widen your intellectual, social or professional horizons. Alternatively, it could herald a future relationship with a powerful or influential person, who could give you support.

2   If the ship in which you are travelling takes on water, runs aground or is shipwrecked: you may encounter a setback of some kind, lose a job or find your projects put in question.

3   You are the captain of the vessel: you have the situation well under control and you can maintain your course.

## SHIRT

1   You wear an attractive or new shirt: you feel confident and at ease with yourself; you will receive sincere proof of love and affection.

2   You are wearing an old, torn or dirty shirt: you are not at ease with yourself; those around you will disappoint you or you will be the victim of an emotional deception.

3   You remove your shirt or someone removes it for you: you will not hold on to your current possessions or goods or someone you know will betray you or try to rob you of them.

4   Someone offers you a shirt: this is a sign of love, union or shared intimacy with someone very dear to you.

5   You are washing a shirt: you feel the need for a change, to turn over a new leaf and improve your current circumstances.

6   You are changing your shirt: you do not know what you want, you are indecisive, unreliable or unfaithful or you will be tempted to form a new romantic liaison.

## SHOEMAKER

To see a shoemaker denotes a happy romantic encounter through an intermediary (a friend or someone close to you); you will undertake a project that will give you great satisfaction.

# SHOES

1   You are trying on or wearing new shoes: you will exert a level of authority or superiority over those around you, taking charge of a situation and asserting yourself to the full. Alternatively, you will enjoy a flourishing relationship.

2   You are wearing old shoes: you rely upon outdated, old-fashioned principles, which are preventing you from achieving your full potential.

3   You are wearing odd shoes: you are not as sure of yourself as you would like to appear or you resist the dreamy, fantastical side of yourself.

4   Your shoes are too narrow, badly fastened or hurting you: you are on the wrong path or you lack energy, resolve and determination; you may be in an uncomfortable, difficult, unfulfilling situation.

5   You have lost your shoes or they don't fit: you are at odds with yourself or with the way you live. This may signify a hesitation to move forward, to grasp the nettle and impose your will.

# SHOP

To dream of being in a shop signals exchanges, relationships and discussions, the content and outcome can be interpreted according to the circumstances and discoveries in the dream.

1   If you are the sales person or owner: it indicates that you will know how to sell yourself and defend your cause or interest. Alternatively, you should listen to what others have to say and be more flexible and helpful so that they pay greater attention to you and your ideas.

2   If you are the customer: it signals that you should quickly do all in your power to achieve your goals and move in the direction of your target – otherwise you are in danger of being pipped at the post.

3   If you are window-shopping: this is an indication that you know neither what you are looking for nor what you want. It can mean that you will not reach your goals or execute your unique ideas or that you don't feel any great attachment to worldly goods.

Alternatively, your relationships with others are too superficial and you spread yourself too thinly.

## SHOUTING

1   You shout: you will soon hear some bad news.

2   You hear someone shouting: someone you know will have problems and will ask you for help.

## SHOW
### (see also ACROBAT, p. 54; ACTOR and ACTRESS, p. 55; CLOWN, p. 118; MAGIC, p. 177; MUSICAL INSTRUMENTS, p. 188)

To dream that you are watching a show means you will witness an event that you feel does not involve you (especially if the dream is about a play); or, particularly if the dream is about a film, you will find yourself in a situation about which you will have some illusions; if it is a concert, people who have come together for a common purpose will invite you to join them; whether you are receptive to their invitation depends on how much you enjoy the concert.

## SIEVE

To see or use a sieve indicates that you pay attention only to things that you find pleasing flattering or comforting. Perhaps you are inattentive, absent-minded or clumsy. Alternatively, you are unable to concentrate on an important topic that is worthy of your interest.

## SINGING, SONG

1   You are singing:

• a happy tune: you will hear some good news or you will be successful in business;

• a sad tune: you need to shed a heavy burden and let yourself go. Alternatively, you will receive some bad news;

• in public: depending on the nature of the song and the general atmosphere in your dream, this can mean that you will be able to unite and rally together those around you in your cause or you will sow seeds of discontent around you;

- alone, in your home or in a remote place without an audience: you have a heavy heart but are unable to express your feelings or confide in anyone.

2   You hear someone singing:

- in a familiar voice: you will hear news of someone you have not seen for a long time; or you will take up abandoned studies;

- in an unfamiliar voice: you will be tempted to embark on a new path or follow a different course. This may herald a new form of learning that will challenge and upset your life and its principles.

## SIREN

1   A dream of sirens singing: intimates that words or proposals which appear to be well-meaning, agreeable and pleasant could easily lull you into a false sense of security and lure you into a trap, with unforeseen consequences. Be on your guard! Alternatively, you may be nursing illusions but do not like to hear it, or you will fall prey to a feeling so intense and romantic that nothing else will matter.

2   If you see a siren: you will be charmed before you can realize it; a romantic relationship may prove confusing or will end in uncertainty, leaving you dissatisfied and frustrated.

## SKY
### (see also STAR, p. 230; STORM, p. 232)

1   You see blue sky: it is a sign of well-being, unalloyed joy and happiness.

2   You see a cloudy sky: you will be uneasy, anxious or tormented. Alternatively, you are not happy with your current life.

3   You see a threatening sky: you will experience concerns and worries; difficulties will circle around you.

4   You see a stormy sky: a social or general issue will make you very angry or inclined to revolt; you may witness an upheaval that

does not affect you (it often relates to an unexpected occurrence that affects people in general rather than you directly or you alone).

5   You see a starry sky: you will achieve your goals or keep a promise that is dear to you.

6   You are in heaven: you will experience great joy or be honoured, respected or applauded by your peers.

## SLAP

1   Someone slaps you: you will regret your actions or attitude towards someone, or you will suddenly realize that you have made a mistake and are about to suffer the consequences.

2   You slap someone: you will express your disagreement but it will not help to resolve the situation.

## SLATE

1   You see or find a stone or tile made of slate or dream of the slate roof of a house: you will be insensitive and deaf to the ideas and feelings of others.

2   You are writing in chalk on a blackboard: this is a sign of frankness, honesty and authenticity but also of the inability to cheat, lie or deceive.

3   You are writing in chalk on a child's slate: this dream encourages you to adopt a simpler, more direct and spontaneous form of expression, to rely more on your instinct and to act in a well defined context or a precise situation.

## SNAIL

1   You see a snail: patience, perseverance, constancy and courage will be needed to achieve your goals.

2   You see a snail retreating into its shell: this signifies a tendency to live your life on the defensive, to be introverted and hermit-like. Alternatively, someone is only too willing to offer their services and be there for you whenever you need them.

3   You eat snails: you need to show more patience, more consistency and greater depth in your emotions and actions.

# SNAKE

1   If you dream about a snake: you will encounter someone treacherous and cunning; you may undergo a crisis of conscience which is painful but necessary and liberating; it could mean that your vital energy will be regained, or your psychic senses awakened.

2   If you dream of being threatened or bitten by a snake: you are about to find out that, unbeknown to you, somebody sly and underhand has bccn trying to harm you for some time, or you will be forced to justify yourself against malicious gossip or slander. It may be that you will find out something that will come as a big shock – but this is the price of truth, and perhaps you have been evading it too long.

3   If snakes are slithering all around you: your relationships are muddled, complicated and unhealthy and things need to be clarified; alternatively, you have, or soon will have, feelings of anxiety or disappointment that will not go away. This dream advises you to relax and let go, because tension is highly likely to affect your well-being.

4   If, in your dream, you see or own a pet snake: this means you are very intuitive and are able to guess the outcome of a situation or read other people's moods; this is an invaluable skill, but you must not use it to wield power over or influence others. Alternatively, you will win over somebody whose intentions towards you were less than honourable, or else somebody wild, fascinating and quite influential, who inspires fear and respect, will become your ally.

# SNOW
## (see also ICE, p. 166)

1   If you see snow falling: you will hear some good news.

2   If you see a snow-covered landscape: either you will enjoy some very happy times in the company of family or loved ones, or you will show yourself to be rather cold and indifferent to the feelings of others and the interest they take in you.

3   If you dream you are having a snowball fight: an apparently trivial dispute could seriously escalate or become more acrimonious.

**4**   If you see a snowman: someone you know, whether close to you or not, will be completely indifferent to your feelings, wishes, worries or moods.

## SOAP

To dream of soap signifies that you will be implicated in a contentious issue, but will be cleared of all blame and come up smelling of roses; alternatively someone will lecture you or criticize you harshly.

## SPADE
### (*see also* GROUND/SOIL/EARTH/LAND, p. 156)

**1**   If you dream you are using a spade to dig a hole: it means you are going to get to the bottom of a specific problem or question, digging deep until you find the root cause and all becomes clear. Alternatively, you will try to rid yourself once and for all of something that is weighing you down, or you will attempt to cover up a shady affair in which you are implicated.

**2**   If, in your dream, you are using a spade to move earth around: you are going to come into money or make some significant gains.

**3**   To see somebody else using a spade: means you will be the target of spiteful or insulting remarks, or malicious gossip.

**4**   A spade lying on the ground: is a sign that you are likely to take a tumble, or to be proved wrong in an argument.

## SPECTACLES

**1**   You wear spectacles: things will appear confused and blurred but circumstances will force you to confront matters.

**2**   You wear spectacles that are not yours: you base your actions and thoughts on someone else's values and they have nothing to do with your true convictions. You are in danger of making grave mistakes as a result, since what is right for others is not necessarily so for you.

**3**   You have lost or broken your glasses: you have refused to face the truth and to see yourself as you are, with the result that your view of the world is blurred and inaccurate. It is not too late to admit and correct your mistakes.

## SPEECH

1   You make a speech: it could be that you are a little too sure of yourself or slightly presumptuous and vain.

2   You hear a speech: you will fall under the spell of fine but hollow words.

## SPHERE
### (see also GAMES and TOYS, p. 150; MOON, p. 185; SUN, p. 234)

1   If you dream about a planet, it's best to look up the characteristics of the different planets – Mercury, Venus, Jupiter, etc. – in a book on traditional astrology. However, this dream could mean that you are rather dreamy and unrealistic; if it features an undiscovered planet, you will have some new and genuinely revelatory experiences.

2   To see or play with a ball heralds an opportunity that should be seized, or indicates that you will create your own luck by means of your skill or clear-sightedness.

3   A balloon represents fragile or short-term enthusiasm or goodwill; alternatively, you will let yourself be guided by circumstances, or reveal yourself to be gullible and indecisive.

4   A globe means you will take stock of all the elements at your disposal or that you will consider every aspect of a situation.

5   If you are drawing or measuring a sphere, this means you will attempt to broaden the way you think and act or that your business affairs or professional life will blossom.

6   A crystal ball denotes that only your clear-sightedness and powers of concentration can help you to escape a difficult situation, and to act or react appropriately and effectively.

7   To dream that you are making a ball out of paper, cloth or any other material signifies that you will find it hard to keep calm and hold your temper.

# SPIDER

**1**   Seeing one or several spiders can have a number of meanings depending upon their context. The following interpretations apply if you see the spider(s):

- on the ground or floor: by having ideas that are too realistic or concrete or by seeing things in a way that is too matter-of-fact, you compensate for your dark thoughts and anxieties. The spider or spiders represent these thoughts;

- climbing up the wall: your ideas, feelings and relationships are troubling. An unusual event will take you by surprise and even alarm you. Be more aware of your behaviour, deeds and reactions, in particular in relation to those close to you;

- walking on the ceiling: you will not manage to accept, recognize or understand your unusual ideas, unexpected reactions and strange behaviour. You will surprise yourself by acting or reacting in a strange or unusual way.

**2**   One or more spiders inspire great fear or great revulsion in you: this reveals a weakness within yourself, your circle and your situation, the result of negligence, clumsiness or lack of clarity. The fear and repulsion caused by the spider(s) is a wake-up call to become more aware, an alarm bell that should encourage you to take prompt action.

**3**   You find yourself surrounded by spider's webs: a long-standing situation or one that you have allowed to worsen by failing to act at the right moment will confront you.

**4**   You see a spider weaving its web: this signifies a trap that threatens without your knowledge. It can also denote the risk of falling into a trap of your own making (but the dream warns you of this fate).

**5**   You dream of a magnificent spider's web: you are or should be aware of the fragility and transience of life. The dream is also a warning not to allow yourself to be trapped in a maze of ideas, speculations and intellectual convictions, all of which may be stimulating and attractive but which cut you off from reality, from your instinctive responses and even life itself (*see also* MAZE, p. 179).

**6** You are in a place that is full of spider's webs and you are covered by them: this dream signals difficulties, obstacles, a route full of pitfalls and traps or a tricky situation from which you will find it hard to escape.

# SPIRAL

A spiral indicates that you will cause some sort of disruption, or experience a radical change, in the near future; it can also mean that you are currently undergoing a psychological or spiritual revolution.

# SPONGE

To see or use a sponge signifies difficulty in coming to terms with or banishing past events from your thoughts – things you would rather forget. It can also mean that you will meet a failure, rebuff or trial with silent passivity.

# SPOON

**1** You see a spoon: someone will make an attractive, advantageous proposal to you or offer you an invitation.

**2** You have a spoon in your hand: your desires will remain unsatisfied or you will demand certain things in vain.

**3** You are eating with a spoon: you need to take your responsibilities on board and see them through to the end.

# SPORT
## (see also ARENA, p. 64; CAR, p. 107; COMBAT, p. 122; RUNNING, p. 214)

**1** You dream that you are engaged in some sport: this indicates that your adversaries will play fair in a work-related competitive situation or heated discussion; alternatively, you are heading for some highly turbulent times, or you may have to take risks and stick your neck out to get what you want or realize your ambitions.

**2** To dream of watching sport means that you will be asked to take sides in a difficult or contentious situation, or in a work-related contest.

## SPOTS

If you have an outbreak of spots, this foretells the imminent lifting of a great weight from your shoulders, leaving you free to speak your mind, shed your anxieties and forget your fears. It could also herald a significant financial gain resulting from past actions. Lastly, it could mean that you will feel bad-tempered and thin-skinned, with nerves on edge.

## SQUARE
### (see also CENTRE, p. 115)

No matter what the environment (house, apartment, garden, courtyard, field etc.), if it is square in shape, you are involved in a material, tangible, concrete and visible reality. The square is both a magical and restrictive shape, magical because it gathers everything together, and restrictive because it encloses things. To escape, you need to discover its centre rather than its four corners or exits, thereby finding yourself. Thus, if you find yourself in a square place, it denotes immersion in the physical and material reality of the world, in balance or in tension, depending on the circumstances of your dream. Whichever the case, such a dream always represents the quest for the centre, and all that this represents and reveals.

## SQUIRREL

The appearance of a squirrel in your dream is an encouragement to act or react more spontaneously, instinctively or intuitively, living for the present but with an eye on the consequences of your actions. It can also herald improving finances and a more secure financial or material situation.

## STAR

1   A shooting star: is a warning to remember the temporary and fleeting nature of all things. It can denote the imminent granting of a wish or fulfilment of a desire, or indeed news of a birth.

2   An intensely bright star: indicates that a meeting or conversation with someone will lead you to change course in your life. It could also herald circumstances that favour the realization of your

plans or the blossoming of your love life. Alternatively, you will find new inspiration for ideas and projects.

3   A star-studded sky: you will feel truly integrated among your circle of friends, while remaining fully yourself, independent and open. It could also herald an invitation to join a rewarding social scene where you will encounter interesting people.

## STICK

1   You are walking with a stick: this is a sign of wisdom, vigilance, tenacity and realism.

2   You are carrying a stick in your dream: it is a sign that a certain power will be invested in you or a mission entrusted to you.

3   You are leaning on a stick: you can rely confidently upon material support. Alternatively, the dream can foretell the end of your current solitary state.

4   You are walking in the dark using a stick to guide you: this is a warning to take great care. You will have to rely on yourself alone, feeling your way forward, inch-by-inch, step-by-step, taking every precaution along the way (*see also* BLINDNESS, p. 77).

## STONE
### (*see also* CATAPULT, p. 111)

1   If you dream you are sitting on a stone: you will show tenacity and determination and you will stick to your guns no matter what.

2   If you dream you are carving stone: you will create or set up something important, constructive and lasting.

3   You are moving one or many stones: you will be involved in a collective venture or social initiative.

4   A stone falling from the sky: heralds an unexpected, unforeseeable, unavoidable event that will disrupt your plans and cast doubt on many aspects of your life.

5   Someone is throwing stones at you: you will be blamed, judged and accused.

6   You are throwing stones: your initiatives and actions will be pointless or unproductive.

7    You find a rare stone: a project you are about to carry out or firm up will be long lasting.

# STORM
### (see also RAIN, p. 208; SKY, p. 223)

A storm brewing or breaking out signifies that a disruptive but liberating event or crisis is imminent. It is unavoidable, but once it has passed you will feel a great weight has been lifted from your shoulders.

# STRAW

If you dream that you are lying on a bed of straw, you will lose your job, or your financial situation will become a source of great worry. Alternatively, your immediate future will be full of uncertainty and danger.

# STREET

1    You are walking in a deserted street: to achieve your goal you will have to rely on no one but yourself; or else you are going to feel somewhat lonely, underestimated or misunderstood.

2    You are walking in a noisy, crowded street: there will be some confusion within and around you, but this will not prevent you from sticking to your path.

3    You are walking in the middle of the street: you feel completely self-assured, well balanced, at ease with yourself and in charge of your life.

4    You are walking calmly on the pavement: you will forge ahead, slowly but surely, taking no risks, believing in yourself and fate.

5    You are pacing up and down on the pavement: either you are impatient, or you will be quick to take risks, lay yourself bare and push yourself forward, in order that other people recognize your qualities or to get what you want.

6    You step off the pavement and walk in the road: you are casual and nonconformist and will break with routine.

7    You are crossing the street:

• if you cross from the right-hand side of the pavement to walk on the left: you will come to depend more on your instinct and intuition than on your sense of reason, and this will be a step forward;

• if you cross from the left-hand side to walk on the right: you do as reason dictates and thereby show that you are realistic and clear-thinking;

• crossing the road at a pedestrian crossing: signifies that you will accept unreservedly the forthcoming change in your life, but will not take unnecessary risks;

• crossing the road without paying attention to the traffic: indicates that you are enthusiastic, daring and energetic, but that you could well take unnecessary risks;

• if you are helping somebody else cross the road: you have some valuable advice or a useful lesson to impart to someone; alternatively you will help someone to implement an important change in their life.

8 A wall, or some other unexpected obstacle, blocks your way: unexpected difficulties will compel you to take a break from a situation, or give up.

# SUGAR

1 If sugar appears in your dream: you will meet somebody who is kind and affable, but who could well be a hypocrite; or you will discover that you are less fragile and vulnerable than you thought or feared.

2 If you break a sugar cube in a dream: you will be the victim of malicious gossip or cruel remarks; alternatively, you disapprove of the attitude of somebody in your circle and will make your feelings known.

3 If you are adding sugar to food or drink: you will benefit from an opportunity or else you will act with your own self-interest in mind, regardless of the concerns, needs or wishes of others.

4 A sugar bowl: is a sign that somebody will try to make you lose your position or job or will attempt to have you eliminated from a competition.

# SUITCASE
### (see also BAG, p. 67)

1   A closed suitcase: means you will be going on a journey or moving house.

2   An open suitcase: indicates that someone around you will leave you or go travelling, or that your secrets will be revealed.

3   You are carrying an empty suitcase: this signifies that your knowledge, life experience and personal values lack depth and intensity. Consequently, there is a serious danger that when you need to draw on them you will feel frustrated or ill prepared.

4   You are carrying a heavy suitcase: your knowledge, ideas and convictions are more of a hindrance than a help and are weighing you down; you may be too attached to your past and this will hold you back when you want to move on, move house or make an important change in your life.

5   If you own or are carrying an elegant suitcase: you seem to attach more importance to outward appearance than to content; consequently you will not worry too much about your inner life, so long as you can keep up appearances. An alternative interpretation is that you carry all your assets with you, but you may not be aware of them.

6   If you own or are carrying an old suitcase: you care little about what people think or say about you. You hold on to certain values, feelings or ideas and are not prepared to drop them.

# SUN
### (see also LIGHT, p. 174; SKY, p. 223)

1   You are watching a superb sunrise: this is a clear sign of happiness or success for you or your family. It also heralds the dawn of a new era in your life, or offers assurance that a certain situation will be clarified, and that light will be shed on everything that was previously hidden.

2   You are watching a sunset: a situation or relationship is about to end, but this is just one stage of your life because, sooner or later, the sun will rise again; alternatively, a worry or problem to do with your father may soon turn out to be critical.

3   You are sunbathing: you will receive a reward or promotion.

4   You have sunstroke: you will pay the price for being too vain or for having unrealistic ambitions.

5   You are blinded by the sun: sometimes the truth is not good to hear, see or understand, which you will learn to your cost; or perhaps you will be blinded by enthusiasm, naivety, elation or infatuation.

## SWEET

To see or eat sweets in a dream warns you to be careful, in case you are handed a poisoned chalice, or that words and promises may be untrustworthy. You may need to beware and correct your own potentially childish, irresponsible and egocentric attitudes.

## SWING

1   You are swinging on a swing: you don't worry about the passing of time; you let yourself be carried along by unfolding events or by fate. You feel at ease in your time and place, you travel at your own pace and appreciate that everything has a natural beginning and end and that life has inevitable highs and lows. Alternatively, this dream sometimes denotes, requited feelings or a heart that beats ever faster in time with the increasing rhythm of the swing.

2   You see a motionless swing or you are sitting on a swing without moving: you want time to stand still. You are worried about the future and you are rooted in the present, or you will refuse future changes although transformation is inevitable.

## SWORD

1   You have a sword in your belt: you will be on the defensive and, rightly or wrongly, are steeling yourself for another person's aggressive behaviour. Alternatively, you will be entrusted with a delicate mission that may require a certain amount of struggle.

2   You have a sword in your hand: if required, you will be determined to do battle to achieve your aims; or your efforts will be finally recognized, following your struggles.

**3** You are fighting a duel: you know how to defend your rights and prerogatives, to rebuff attacks, intimidation and controversy. The dream may warn of a dispute with someone close to you.

**4** You are stabbed with a sword: you will be the victim of unexpected betrayal or aggression or you will not have the last word in a debate, argument or conflict.

## TABLE

**1** If you are seated at a table: you will receive an invitation or you will speak your mind, even though some people may not like what you say.

**2** Laying the table: signifies that you are impatiently waiting or preparing for an important event affecting your family or home life, or that you intend to clarify your family situation.

**3** A round table: means that someone will tell you a secret or you may be invited to a rather exclusive gathering; alternatively, you will have a delicate problem to solve, or you will be affected by a joint decision to be made.

**4** If you are sitting at a glass-topped table, or you can see beneath the table: someone will try to lead you astray or make you a dishonest proposition; alternatively, you are about to discover the true intentions of somebody in your circle.

## TAIL

To catch or hold an animal by its tail means that your financial situation will be a source of worry; possibly you will find it difficult to control your instincts, urges and impatient nature, or you may try to hold on to someone who will evade your clutches sooner or later.

## TALISMAN

**1** To dream of a talisman or lucky charm: indicates that you will live in fear of not succeeding at something you hold dear, or that you will need help and protection or moral or spiritual support.

**2** Wearing or being given a talisman: is a guarantee of satisfaction in all areas of your life.

# TAR

Treading on tarmac reveals your own pessimism about the future and your lack of self-confidence; if you walk or fall on newly-laid tarmac, it heralds an encounter with someone who wants to do you harm, block your way or demoralize you.

# TAX

1   You discover or hear that you have to pay heavy taxes: you lack independence in your emotional or material life. The compromises you make in order to keep things in balance are becoming more taxing, making you increasingly unable to act or think freely.

2   You discover or learn that you don't have to pay tax: long-standing material or moral obligations will suddenly be lightened or will vanish; you may expect a drop in your earnings or profits.

# TEA

Making or drinking tea signals that you will play an active role in the preparations for a wedding, contract or alliance.

# TEARS

If you have tears in your eyes, you will experience deep and sincere feelings for someone; you may need to relax and let yourself go, releasing some of the current pressure you are under.

# TELEPHONE
### (see also VOICE, p. 247)

If a telephone plays an important role in your dream, it means you will live a double life, or will do whatever it takes to keep a relationship secret or anonymous; if there is no dial tone, or the call is abruptly cut off, this either symbolizes your refusal to express fully what you think, or means that you will find yourself on the receiving end of a break-up; if the telephone rings and you do not want to answer it, this indicates that you will not respond to appeals made by certain people around you, or that you will not listen to advice or warnings that are lavished upon you.

## TELEVISION

If you dream that you are watching television, you prefer not to get involved in the events and circumstances of your life, and tend to be unconcerned by what happens around you. You often put up a wall of critical objectivity between yourself and other people, which isolates you and makes it difficult for you to bond or form relationships. If you dream that you are on a television set, or are taking part in a television programme, it shows that you feel the need to tell everyone loud and clear what you are thinking, or to express an opinion that you feel is essential or decisive for you and your future.

## TEMPLE,
### church, mosque, pagoda, synagogue
*(see also* BAPTISM, p. 69; FUNERAL, p. 150; MARRIAGE, p. 178;
PRAYING, p. 206; PRIEST, p. 206)

1  If you see a temple in your dream: you will need to think carefully before you act or make an important decision, weighing up all the pros and cons; alternatively, whatever your current emotional or material problems, this dream urges reconciliation or solidarity.

2  If you enter a temple: you will become aware of something that is absolutely fundamental to your development and will probably be a decisive factor in your future; you may feel the need to free yourself of doubt, in order to act with total confidence and good faith.

3  A ruined temple: this is a sign that, ultimately, not much will remain of a relationship, a feeling or a situation to which you attached great importance or that held a significant place in your life; this dream can also indicate a new start.

4  If you are inside a temple full of worshippers: you can rely on the support, help or solidarity of your family, friends and acquaintances.

## TENT

Seeing or being inside a tent in a dream symbolizes a desire for travel, escape or change; it can also signal a period of transition and uncertainty for your family or for the members of your household;

or else you need to take a step back or bow out of some sort of joint action or enterprise. (*See also* CAMPING, p. 105)

## THIEF
### (*see also* ANTIQUE DEALERS AND ANTIQUES, p. 61; CAR, p. 107)

1   If you are the victim of a theft: either a project that is dear to your heart will not succeed, or a relationship will come to an abrupt end or a powerful emotion will throw you completely off balance.

2   An encounter with a thief: this signals that you are tempted to illicit, risky or nonconformist behaviour; alternatively, you will meet someone with dishonest intentions, but they will not fool you.

3   If you are the thief: you are aware that your current behaviour, particularly in your love life, is neither right nor fair, or you will desire or fall in love with somebody who is married.

## TIGER

1   If you see a tiger: your words and actions will be perfectly consistent; to put it another way, you will keep your promises and do precisely what you say; you may meet an aggressive, choosy or envious person or you may soon give vent to a savage, cruel streak lurking somewhere within you.

2   If you see a tiger that is tame or in a cage: you are in contact with somebody wild and uncontrollable whose behaviour will always be unpredictable, or you are reining in your warlike, aggressive instincts. Is this a good or a bad thing? Only you know the answer.

3   You dream of being chased by a tiger: someone wild, despotic and aggressive will pursue you.

## TOBACCO
### (*see also* PIPE, p. 202)

1   You dream of tobacco (cigarettes, cigars or rolling tobacco): your business affairs will be prosperous or your earnings will increase; alternatively, your love life will be vibrant, intense and stormy, or unequivocal success is on the way.

**2** You are offered tobacco: someone will confess their passionate desires or feelings to you or will pull out all the stops to make you admit to something; you may be in for a shock or an upset, or you will meet someone with a violent nature.

**3** You are surrounded by smokers: you feel oppressed and ill at ease in your family or work environment; or else you do not like the ideas or intentions of the people around you.

**4** You are chain-smoking: you are, or soon will be, very much on edge.

**5** You are smoking a cigar: you will behave in a casual, carefree manner that will not please everybody.

**6** You see someone smoking a cigar: you will feel envious of someone.

## TORCH

**1** You are carrying a torch: you can be assured that people appreciate, respect, love and confide in you; you may be convinced that you have an important task or mission to accomplish and you fear that you are not worthy of, or up to it.

**2** You see someone carrying a torch: a secret will be revealed to you, or you may not receive the promotion, task or position of trust you desire.

**3** Someone carrying a torch gives or entrusts it to you: others will try to persuade you, or you will be asked to transmit a secret or be implicated in a confidential matter.

**4** You attend a torchlight procession: you will know how to clarify your current situation or you will learn whatever you wish to know.

## TOWER

**1** A tower in your dream augurs the eventual realization of an ambitious plan; it can indicate a lack of freedom in your actions, thoughts and decisions.

**2** If you are standing at the top of a tower: you will have a panoramic, global view of everything in your life, and will therefore be master of your own destiny; alternatively you take no risks, and are careful about everything to do with yourself; it may be that you have a premonition of impending danger or that a stranger will come into your life.

3   You climb to the top of a tower: you are too proud, and may therefore find yourself isolated.

4   A tower that is on fire or collapsing: this heralds a drastic but inevitable shock, disruption or upheaval. Alternatively it indicates that you are going to lose a job, or that your plans will come to nothing.

# TRAIN
## (see also LOCOMOTIVE, p. 175)

1   You see a passing train: time is slipping away and you feel nothing interesting or significant is happening in your life. This may be because an opportunity has passed you by, or because you fear you will miss your date with destiny, perhaps because, in life and relationships, you are not fully committed. Alternatively, you will hear news of somebody who is far away, or you will meet somebody new.

2   You miss your train: you will miss an opportunity or refuse to get involved in a relationship or situation.

3   You are travelling first class: you will be extravagant or live beyond your means in the near future.

4   You are travelling on a small train: you are modest and discreet, you go your own way without drawing attention to yourself, and that suits you just fine.

5   You are travelling on a big train: there will be great unrest, and you may have to face and deal with a number of problems and difficulties in your family situation.

6   You are involved in a train crash: you will not reach the goal you have set yourself; alternatively, an unforeseen shock will call into question certain aspects of your life.

7   You are waiting for a train at a station: you are waiting for the resolution of a matter that concerns you, because you know that it will be crucial to your future.

## TREASURE
### (see also CAVE, p. 112; MAP, p. 177)

Finding treasure in a dream means that a happy, or important and beneficial event will take place in your life; it might also indicate that your financial prospects and opportunities are excellent, or that you will realize your intellectual, emotional or spiritual blessings or will come to appreciate the true worth of someone close to you.

## TREE
### (see also FRUIT, p. 147)

The tree is the symbol of life, of thinking, active mankind.

1   If you dream of a tree in spring: this indicates that you are entering a new cycle in your life. You will be able to undertake a fresh course of action or realize a new goal close to your heart. You will feel full of hope, imagination, enthusiasm and vigour.

2   If you see a tree in summer: you will master and fully exploit all the resources at your disposal both within you and in your life. You will encounter a period of accomplishment and fulfilment. Take advantage of it.

3   If you dream of a tree in autumn: it signals the end of a cycle in your life during which you will feel the need to shed all that you consider useless, uninteresting or futile, in yourself or in your environment. In this way you will reap what you have sown. This sign sometimes heralds wealth, profit and gain in the future, all due to actions and enterprises undertaken in the past.

4   If you dream of a tree in summer: it means that you will undergo a period of being solitary and left to your own devices. You should rely solely upon yourself and upon your own experience. You need to develop internally, to become stronger psychologically and spiritually. The dream sometimes announces a task or test that will force you to develop and rely on your own strengths, to rediscover your own roots.

5   If you see an uprooted tree: this is a sign of a rupture in your natural, domestic, social or cultural environment, such as leaving your home country, your childhood town or your family home. It can also announce the death, whether physical or symbolic, of a

member of your family: if you break all contact with a relative, for example.

6    If you see a tree struck by lightning: this denotes a climate of exacerbated tension, which will explode in abrupt, violent or devastating outbreaks of anger possibly directed at you. On the other hand, you may anticipate an unexpected event or an accident.

7    If you see a tree fall (cut down by a saw or an axe): it denotes a sudden and marked obstacle to the progress of your plans or a collapse of your projects. It can also denote an inability to realize what is really close to your heart.

8    If you see a tree in flames: this means that you are living in a climate of tension and extreme feelings and that you are burning up all your energies recklessly, literally 'consuming yourself' and thereby risking your inner equilibrium. The dream can be the harbinger of the latent feverish state that you are in, a condition that could easily worsen. Do not neglect your health and take preventive action to preserve it.

9    If you dream of a dead tree: you hang on to elements and values that are no longer relevant, clinging to the past without giving due consideration to the present. In this way you are losing your sense of perspective and your ability to move forward. You need to turn a page in your life to prevent your current situation remaining stagnant and sterile.

10    If you shelter under a tree:

• as protection from the sun: you lack self-confidence and fear to expose your true self. You seek protection but sooner or later you will have to leave your hiding place and move into the spotlight;

• as protection from the rain: you are fearful of getting wet, of taking risks, of moving forward and acting independently. However, if you wait for the rain to stop before doing so, it will be too late.

11    You are sitting under a tree: you will be able to demonstrate your wisdom and patience, and you will base your decisions on proven stable and solid values. This will prove fruitful, sooner or later, and should give you confidence.

12    You are climbing up or perched in a tree:

• you are close to the trunk: you will not lose contact with what you consider to be your true values and will protect them from corruption by the external, social world. You can continue to develop and grow without fear;

• you are on a branch, far from the trunk: whatever your current social or personal status, you are in an unstable, uncertain, unreliable situation – like a bird on a branch that can escape only by falling or taking flight.

## TRIANGLE
### (see also CAVE, p. 112; MOUNTAIN, p. 186; NUMBER [Three], p. 193)

1   An upright triangle: encourages you to see your plans through to their conclusion, when success is guaranteed or your dream is achieved; it may indicate that you should be active, energetic and determined in achieving your ambitions or satisfying your desires.

2   An inverted triangle: means you will need to show caution, reserve, wisdom and temperance; you may be greatly inspired and particularly receptive to other people, or will show evidence of a fertile and productive imagination.

## TUNNEL

1   To dream of walking into a tunnel: announces a painful, testing time in your life. However, you will be spurred on by the hope that there are brighter days to come and will eventually find a solution to your problems.

2   You are inside a tunnel: you feel as though you will never find a way out of your problems.

3   You come out of a tunnel: you will find a happy solution to your problems, or you will extricate yourself from a difficult situation, or see a marked improvement in your life.

## TURTLE

To dream of a turtle signifies that you are stubborn and tenacious in any circumstances, or that you may not necessarily choose the most direct route or the simplest solution to achieve your ends or get what you want; it may indicate that you will meet someone who is vulnerable, hypersensitive, suspicious and slow to make up their mind or get involved; it could be that you will meet somebody of a certain age who will be a good influence, and will advise and protect you.

## UNDERGROUND/SUBWAY
### (see also MAZE, p. 179; TRAIN, p. 241; TUNNEL, p. 244)

**1**  You are on an underground train: you will have to go through several stages before you achieve your objectives or reach your goal. Alternatively, a project or an enterprise that is currently under way will be transformed or take shape in conditions or circumstances that are very different to those you had envisaged.

**2**  You just miss a train: an event or a business deal will take place without you but in spite of your disappointment, you will decide it was for the best.

**3**  You are walking in or are lost in the underground tunnels: your projects will be called into question. It seems that, whatever the circumstances of your current situation, you are about to go astray or take a wrong turning.

**4**  You are being pursued through the tunnels: a particular fear or anxiety, or a sense of foreboding will force you out of your shell and make you express your doubts and objections.

## UNICORN

A dream of a unicorn indicates that you act from a deep sense of justice, honour and purity, which will protect you and earn you the respect of your peers. Alternatively, you will have a wonderful, deep love affair with someone you feel is your soul mate.

## URINATING

**1**  You dream that you are urinating: this means you will feel a deep sense of relief and a sudden release of all tension, or that you will find a way to pay off all your debts, and ease your financial situation.

**2** You see someone else urinating: somebody you know will fritter his/her money away, or else you will be repaid money owed to you.

## VALLEY

**1** You see a beautiful, lush, sun-drenched valley: good times lie ahead; you are about to enter a very happy stage of your life; on a material level, everything will be rosy and you will not want for anything for a very long time; alternatively, whatever your worries or problems, you will soon be able to make a fresh start.

**2** You see a murky, misty or ominous-looking valley: you are about to enter a difficult and testing stage of your life that will try you to your limit.

## VELVET

You dream you are wearing velvet or sitting in a velvet-covered chair which signifies that you will act with confidence and determination, but also with tact and sensitivity; you may hide your desires, plans or intentions, the better to satisfy them when the opportunity arrives; you will achieve what you want with the minimum of difficulty and risk (this dream actually indicates there is no point in worrying, since success is guaranteed); alternatively, your charm, or your powers of seduction, will make you irresistible.

## VETERINARIAN

Your instincts are unhealthy, repressed or inhibited; you will have plenty of physical work to do in the future.

## VIRGIN

**1** You have a vision of the Virgin Mary, you see a statue of her, or hear people talking about her: your ideas, thoughts and feelings may be confused but you must force yourself to think clearly. Alternatively, you will soon learn of a mission, task or responsibility that you will have to carry out alone; it may be that a woman who is attentive, devoted and aware of the practicalities of everyday life will play an important role in your life, or else you will develop a strong sense of conscience that will seriously impact upon your behaviour and your life in general and that will, little by little, modify your view of the world and your relationships with other people.

2    A meeting or other involvement with a young girl: means you will experience a new and very precious feeling, or it heralds an important change in your behaviour, which will allow you to take on or achieve something new in your life.

# VOICE
### (see also SHOUTING, p. 222; SINGING, SONG, p. 222; SPEECH, p. 227)

1    You are speaking but your lips do not move and no words are coming out: something that you dare not express, that you conceal or keep to yourself will be revealed or made public sooner or later without your knowledge.

2    You are speaking in a voice not your own: you will speak out about things that others think but dare not say, or your words will not be a true reflection of what you think and believe.

3    You have lost your voice: you have spoken too much and acted too little; consequently no one will listen to you any more or believe what you say.

4    You are speaking but no sound emerges: your world will be turned upside down by a strong emotion, an event or a shock.

5    You hear a quiet voice: you will hear good news or comforting words.

6    You hear an authoritarian voice: you lack flexibility and understanding with regard to yourself and others, and are therefore in danger of making errors of judgement or behaving in the wrong way.

7    You hear a voice calling out to you: you will discover a vocation or gift that you never knew you had, or a quality that you had neglected. Alternatively, you will have a delicate task or mission to complete, or will have to take full responsibility for your imminent actions and choices.

8    You hear voices, murmurs or whispers: someone will try to hide something from you; you may be the victim of spiteful remarks or you may accidentally discover a secret.

# VOID
### (*see also* HOLE, p. 162)

1    You are walking on the edge of a void and feel that you are about to fall in: you lack self-confidence, balance and self-control; the dream may indicate that you will find yourself in a dangerous, unstable situation.

2    You walk confidently on the edge of a void: you will find it easy to get through an important, delicate or difficult stage in your life; alternatively, an absence or loss will do nothing to hamper your personal development, and will not impede your business affairs or your life in general.

3    You fall into the void: you are about to discover something that is essential to your personal development or you will experience a major change or disruption that may throw you off balance for a while.

4    You are looking into the void:

• feeling giddy: circumstances will bring unavoidable change or disruption;

• not feeling at all giddy: you will think twice before opting for change or you will keep your cool, whatever risks you take.

# WALL
### (*see also* BLIND ALLEY/DEAD END, p. 77;
### MAZE, p. 179)

1    There is an insurmountable wall in front of you: you will be confronted by an impossible obstacle, or you will have to abandon an over-ambitious plan. The dream may warn that you will be forced to make an important decision that will affect your future.

2    You attempt to climb a wall: whatever the obstacles that are in your way, don't be discouraged as they won't prove insurmountable; you will try to escape from a particular situation or a relationship that is weighing you down.

3    You see a wall that has fallen into ruins: your self-protective mechanism is no longer effective or suited to your current life.

4    You see someone building a wall: the differences of opinion and misunderstandings that you experience with others are growing and threatening to get worse.

5    You are building a wall: you will refuse to make concessions or compromises with yourself or others, but as a consequence you will be more and more isolated.

# WAR
### (see also ARMY, p. 65; COMBAT, p. 122; OFFICER, p. 196)

1    You know or discover that war has been declared: you will hear bad news that requires prompt action, or you will suffer the results of a psychological shock. The dream may be a warning to be more vigilant and keener to impose your will on a disruptive environment.

2    You are resisting the occupying forces of an enemy army: you feel the weight of your material and moral obligations but you know that soon you will be free of them. Alternatively, you are too authoritarian and dominating, and the dream indicates that this behaviour is not part of your true nature and that you disapprove of it at heart. It may also indicate a threat to your vital energy from a virus or illness, a threat you can tackle now thanks to the dream's warning.

# WASP

1    A wasp buzzes around you, threatening to sting you: someone you know and trust implicitly at the moment will turn out to be aggressive or may even threaten to do you harm. On the other hand, your emotional relationships will be stimulating and lively if not harmonious and serene.

2    You see or uncover a wasp's nest: beware of those currently around you, socially, professionally or at home. The dream warns that you could fall prey to those who are not well-disposed towards you and may mean you harm. Alternatively, you have negative thoughts and desires that could well lead you to act greedily or violently.

3    A wasp stings you: you will be betrayed.

# WATER
### (see also BATH, p. 69)

1   You see water or a stretch of clear, limpid water: you will feel calm and serene – all will seem perfectly clear and calm.

2   You see a stretch of clear, calm water but you know it is very deep: your opinions, suppositions and morals inhibit your instinct; beware the deep waters within you and what they contain or conceal.

3   You see a stretch of calm, cloudy water: worry, anxiety or black thoughts plague you at the moment but you keep them to yourself; you need to achieve inner clarity.

4   You see water or a stretch of dirty, muddy or stagnant water: your present concerns and worries threaten to submerge you; it is time to clarify your inner thoughts and external relationships and to appreciate and admit that people, and indeed life itself, are inevitably and inescapably a mixture of the pure and the impure. Alternatively, your general health needs resolving; your vitality is either precarious or repressed, and a check-up with appropriate treatment could help.

5   You see a stretch of rough, troubled water, ruffled by strong or even violent winds: a current relationship or situation will cause you problems or you will hear frustrating news.

6   You see or cross a marsh or swamp: you have made an error of judgement in your calculations or your forecasts; nothing is proceeding as planned and you will be forced to make a U-turn in a project or abandon it altogether, before it founders.

7   You see a flood: you will be swamped by external events or problems in which you play only an indirect role but one that forces you to respond. Your feelings and emotions, whether contained or impassioned, threaten to overwhelm you. You will be unable to control them.

8   You are the victim of a flood: your emotions and anxieties are slowly taking you over and you will find it impossible to escape them. Difficult and frustrating events will soon confront you, the direct result of a failure to control your feelings and instincts.

9   You walk on water: your relationships, emotional and psychological life are now serene, harmonious and balanced, as a result of which you will be able to continue on your planned path with ease.

## WATERFALL

If you see a waterfall or are under one, it is a warning of certain events that will happen simultaneously. The waterfall is a good omen: you will experience great comfort in the future.

## WEASEL

A weasel is an indication that you are artful, crafty, shrewd and ready to use every excuse or subterfuge to achieve your aims. It may signal that someone you know will behave in this manner. If you are bitten or attacked by a weasel, you will be the victim of this person's pressing but hypocritical demands.

## WEATHERVANE

To dream of a weathervane underlines your own indecision, gullibility and uncertainty; alternatively, you will encounter someone unsure of their goals.

## WELL

1   You see a well: someone is hiding something from you. Either he or she is not telling you the truth, or else they are giving you only a vague or incomplete version of the truth; you may feel enriched after meeting someone highly cultured or deeply spiritual.

2   You see a dry well or cesspool: a person whom you thought generous or receptive will turn out to be selfish and greedy, and you will get nothing from them; a relationship may go nowhere and disappoint you, or a job or business deal will prove unproductive, or you will be mentally and physically exhausted, and probably in need of a pick-me-up or a bit of a rest.

3   You see a well with clear water: the more favourable your circumstances, the more you will exploit them successfully, and the more your opportunities and prospects will improve; the dream could also mean that a relationship will become increasingly

enriching, stimulating and productive, or that you will discover the whole truth about a deal, a situation or a person.

4    You fall into a well: do not try to find out about something that is no concern of yours; remember that sometimes the truth is best left hidden – otherwise you may suffer the consequences.

5    You go down a well: at present you are probably caught in a situation that seems difficult or inescapable. But appearances can be deceptive, because this dream announces a happy conclusion, an end to your worries and even great long-term success.

6    You are drawing water from a well: your family situation or your business affairs will prosper; or you will discover a new source of income.

# WHALE

The appearance of a whale indicates a necessary period of transition or gestation in your life.

1    If you enter the mouth of the whale or a whale swallows you: this can mean that even if you do not wish to submit to a period of transition or necessary gestation in your life, circumstances will force you to do so. Alternatively, you will be submerged by or absorbed into a depressive state. The dream can also signify that you are on the brink of involving yourself in a dangerous situation.

2    If you emerge from a whale or are expelled from it: it is a signal that the moment has come and that you must escape this period of transition immediately, hurl yourself into the waters of experience and face up to your responsibilities. You must enter resolutely a new period in your life.

3    If you are hunting a whale: see the entry for ARCH, page 64.

# WHEEL
## (see also BICYCLE, p. 74; CAR, p. 107; MILL, p. 183)

1    A paddle wheel or windmill: is a sign that a positive and beneficial life change is on the way, which will help you to evolve.

2    A wheel of fortune: indicates yet more highs and lows to come, or that you will put your life in the hands of fate or circumstances.

3   To dream about the wheel of a vehicle: this means that you will help someone perform a difficult task or assist in carrying out his or her plans.

4   The wheel of a chariot or cart: is a sign that you will suffer the consequences of your past mistakes.

5   If you see or are using a spinning wheel: you are going to be master of your own destiny and enjoy complete free will. Be sure to think carefully before you act and weigh up your chances of success.

## WHEELBARROW

1   If you are pushing an empty wheelbarrow: it indicates that you are in charge of your own destiny and that you may act as you please. Your life will evolve with ease.

2   If the wheelbarrow you are pushing is full: this is a sign that you should assume your responsibilities and make proper use of your energy and potential to proceed towards your goals.

3   If you are pushing a full and very heavy wheelbarrow: it denotes a current lethargy and lack of enthusiasm, a feeling of being overwhelmed by your responsibilities. However, the dream encourages you to follow your chosen (and correct) path.

4   If the wheel on the barrow fails: it is a signal that your efforts are in vain or that you will be the victim of an accident, ill health or an abrupt interruption to your plans. These effects may result from a failure to take the necessary precautions and an overestimation of your power. The dream counsels wisdom and advises you to take stock, reflect and be flexible.

## WINDOW

1   You see an open window: this presages fulfilment of your hopes, wishes and desires.

2   You see a closed window: you will feel the need to expand your horizons and see things from a different angle, but neither your circumstances nor friends will help you in this.

3   You lean out of the window: you will not be able to count on any help from others in the imminent future. Alternatively, your advice or warnings will be ignored.

**4** You look out of the window: you will allow yourself to become too involved in family or social events; they threaten to cause you bitter disappointment.

**5** You jump out of the window: you will be tempted to behave excessively or desperately, to panic and lose control, of yourself or of the situation.

## WINE
### (*see also* ALCOHOL, p. 58; BARREL, p. 69; GLASS, p. 154)

**1** If you are drinking wine in a dream: you will feel enthusiastic about a person or situation; you may feel alternately happy and sad for no apparent reason.

**2** Drawing wine from a barrel: this means you will create a situation, or begin a relationship, that you must accept fully and see through to the end.

**3** If you see or are given lots of bottles of wine in a dream: you will soon experience great joy and pleasure.

**4** If you see or are given a carafe of wine: you will probably be forced to use unconventional or illegal methods to get what you want or else somebody will make you a shady or illicit proposition.

**5** If you are offered a glass of wine: you will be respected and honoured for your skills and qualities.

## WITCH
### (*see also* BROOM, p. 102; MAGIC, p. 177, WIZARD, p. 254)

You will be involved with someone who is deceitful, dangerous and perverse, who will try to influence or manipulate you; it may be that a trap will be laid for you, or that an important discovery you are about to make will give you influence or power. The question is, what will you decide to do with it?

## WIZARD
### (*see also* BROOM, p. 102; MAGIC, p. 177, WITCH, p. 254)

You hold all the trump cards, and will prove yourself to be shrewd, imaginative and capable when solving problems or overcoming difficulties; alternatively, you will meet someone who is unsettling but attractive and interesting, and who will probably hold a certain fascination for you, or will shake up your opinions and make you change your ways.

## WOLF

1   You see wolves: enemies or powerful adversaries threaten you, or you need to watch out for people masquerading as your friends.

2   You hear one or several wolves howling: someone is laying a trap for you but you will be warned of it in time. If you are vigilant and careful, you will not fall into it.

3   You are pursued or attacked by a pack of wolves: it will be impossible to avoid conflict or dispute and you will find it incredibly hard to maintain your position.

## WOOD
### (see also FIRE, p. 139; FOREST, p. 146; TREE, p. 242)

1   You are collecting deadwood: don't trust what you have heard or will soon hear. Alternatively, you will shed without regret certain things from your past that you have hung onto for no good reason.

2   You are collecting green wood: you will encounter a deceitful or unhealthy group of people in whom you will invest your trust unwisely. Alternatively, you will act prematurely and will fail to achieve anticipated results. It may be that you will be unable to hold on to what you have got at present.

3   You are cutting wood: this signifies that your current efforts will bear fruit later or that you will exploit cannily, one after another, all the elements you have at your disposal in order to achieve greater efficiency and productivity in the long term. It is a sign of the foresight and economy that you will display.

4   You are touching wood: you will feel the need to be in contact with basic, simple human values. A stroke of luck or an unexpected opportunity may be signalled.

## WOOL

1   You are spinning wool: you will discover the deep and real roots of a problem that preoccupies you and the solution will follow.

2   You are knitting or weaving: you will be inspired to improve your finances. The dream can herald a happy or important event. Alternatively, your courage and determination will help you to become secure and stable financially.

3   You see balls of wool: financial gain is coming your way, or your economical ways will be appreciated.

4   You are wearing woollen clothes: whatever your worries, you will feel safe and protected – someone will comfort you.

## WORM
### (see also BUTTERFLY, p. 103)

1   To dream of an earthworm: this means you will find yourself impoverished, without resources or in a precarious situation, or that you will encounter someone fragile and vulnerable, or weak and unworthy of respect.

2   Wriggling worms: these indicate parasites – people who will try and take advantage of you, to exploit your generosity or naivety; alternatively, someone will try to make you reveal something you do not want to make public.

3   A glow-worm: this signifies a glimmer of hope in a difficult time of your life; it can also mean that you will hear surprising news or discover a secret, or that you will have a bright idea, an inspiration or make a discovery.

4   You find a worm in a piece of fruit or something you are eating: a deal or situation in which you are about to invest is unsound; think carefully before you get involved.

## WOUND
### (see also BODY, p. 79)

1   You are wounded: the significance of a dream about being wounded depends greatly on the location of the wound (hand, arm,

leg, foot, head etc.). The part of the body involved plays a key role in its interpretation and you should look up the relevant part in the glossary. A wound to the chest is often the expression of heartache or disappointment, whereas a wound to the head signals a blow to your pride and self-esteem.

2    Your wound will not heal: this signifies an inability to recover from a blow to your feelings or mental state, which has left you vulnerable. Alternatively, you still harbour resentment.

3    Your wound heals, leaving only a scar: you will be injured, shocked or disappointed, but it will be all to the good, since it will be the cause of your recovery from a much more serious illness.

4    You wound someone else: this is a warning that, whether deliberately or otherwise, you may be lacking in tact or understanding in your dealings with someone around you.

## WRITING
### (see also PENCIL, p. 201)

1    You write a letter: you will be inclined to have set ideas or definite feelings by which you live, to make your intentions and convictions clear and to stick by them. Alternatively, if you are signing a contract or agreement, you should be clear from the beginning about the implications, leaving nothing to chance; if the letter is addressed to another person, you must make your thoughts abundantly clear with no delay.

2    You are writing a book: you need to be more direct and less circuitous in your expression or your thoughts. It can mean that you are or will be master or mistress of your own destiny – keep this in mind.

3    You are writing with an old-fashioned pen, a fountain pen or using an inkwell: your plans are prepared with patience, wisdom and thoughtfulness or you will hear of a birth or, indeed, give birth yourself to a project close to your heart. If you frequently dip your pen in the inkwell, it denotes anxiety or indecision about the creation of an enterprise, and you will need to go over everything again. To spill the ink heralds failure through a lack of application or patience in the finalization of your plans – again you will have to go over them once more. Finally, if you knock over the inkwell, an anticipated birth or new venture will not happen.

**4** You are writing with a ballpoint or felt-tip pen: you will not put enough weight or conviction behind your words, opinions or arguments; or you will lack precision and perseverance when developing your plans.

**5** You see someone writing or writing to you: take note of suggestions or confidences made to you and advice offered before you take action, but don't lose sight of your own beliefs.

## X-RAY

**1** If you dream you are looking at an X-ray of somebody you know: it means you will learn that this person has health problems, or that you will see this person in a new light.

**2** If you dream you are having an X-ray done or you see your own X-ray: it means that you will no longer be able to hide your intentions, desires or feelings, or that your health will give cause for concern.

## YAWNING

To yawn in a dream denotes a state of grace, a precious and privileged moment in your life during which you can relax, let yourself go, indulge yourself. Alternatively, it can be a sign of anxiety or a lack of clarity and interest in your current status or actions.

## ZOO

If you dream that you are walking around a zoo, you will soon find yourself in an environment that will seem strange, paradoxical or disconcerting; alternatively, you may appear self-assured, well-balanced and at the peak of your powers, but in reality your instincts and desires are shackled by your sense of reason and by convention, principles and propriety.

# Interpretations and predictions

'*Brighter stars will rise on some voyager of the future – some great Ulysses of the realms of thought – than shine on us. The dreams of magic may one day be the waking realities of science.*'

Sir James George Frazer,
*The Golden Bough*

# 1st combination □ □ □ □ □ □

At present you are preoccupied by ideas, speculations and possibilities. For these to become reality you need to look ahead, to consider your projects in the long term in order to put in place everything necessary to make your plans work.

**1** You will not get what you want just yet. Do not wear yourself out or lose your ambition by setting your sights on immediate results at any price. You will succeed in time. Until then, be content to follow your path patiently and to remain constant in your choices. Do not let yourself be distracted by circumstances beyond your control, whether favourable or disappointing

**2** You are in the right place, in the position which suits your qualities and skills, so have complete confidence in what you are doing and make the most of your talents. You are conscientious, honest and efficient, and, little by little, this will enable you to get where you want to be. These qualities, expressed spontaneously, can only have a positive effect on the people around you and on your future.

**3** Your affairs and activities will soon make progress. Consequently, the danger is that you will be overwhelmed by events, or find yourself drawn into a maelstrom of different projects and plans, without taking time to rest and recharge your batteries. Do not automatically give in to overriding ambition. Accept your responsibilities, but remain sensible and cautious, and you are certain to succeed.

| fig. | | | | | | | |
|---|---|---|---|---|---|---|---|
| 1 | ▲ | ▲ | □ | □ | □ | □ | Read texts 1 and 2 |
| 2 | ▲ | □ | ▲ | □ | □ | □ | Read texts 1 and 3 |
| 3 | ▲ | □ | □ | ▲ | □ | □ | Read texts 1 and 4 |
| 4 | ▲ | □ | □ | □ | ▲ | □ | Read texts 1 and 5 |
| 5 | ▲ | □ | □ | □ | □ | ▲ | Read texts 1 and 6 |
| 6 | ▲ | ▲ | ▲ | □ | □ | □ | Read texts 1, 2 and 3 |
| 7 | ▲ | □ | ▲ | ▲ | □ | □ | Read texts 1, 3 and 4 |
| 8 | ▲ | □ | ▲ | □ | ▲ | □ | Read texts 1, 4 and 5 |
| 9 | ▲ | □ | □ | □ | ▲ | ▲ | Read texts 1, 5 and 6 |
| 10 | ▲ | ▲ | ▲ | ▲ | □ | □ | Read texts 1, 2, 3 and 4 |
| 11 | ▲ | □ | ▲ | ▲ | ▲ | □ | Read texts 1, 3, 4 and 5 |
| 12 | ▲ | □ | ▲ | ▲ | □ | ▲ | Read texts 1, 3, 4 and 6 |
| 13 | ▲ | □ | □ | ▲ | ▲ | ▲ | Read texts 1, 4, 5 and 6 |
| 14 | ▲ | ▲ | ▲ | ▲ | ▲ | □ | Read texts 1, 2, 3, 4 and 5 |
| 15 | ▲ | □ | ▲ | ▲ | ▲ | ▲ | Read texts 1, 3, 4, 5 and 6 |
| 16 | ▲ | ▲ | ▲ | ▲ | ▲ | ▲ | Read texts 1, 2, 3, 4, 5 and 6 |
| 17 | □ | ▲ | ▲ | □ | □ | □ | Read texts 2 and 3 |
| 18 | □ | ▲ | □ | ▲ | □ | □ | Read texts 2 and 4 |
| 19 | □ | ▲ | □ | □ | ▲ | □ | Read texts 2 and 5 |
| 20 | □ | ▲ | □ | □ | □ | ▲ | Read texts 2 and 6 |
| 21 | □ | ▲ | ▲ | ▲ | □ | □ | Read texts 2, 3 and 4 |
| 22 | □ | ▲ | □ | ▲ | ▲ | □ | Read texts 2, 4 and 5 |
| 23 | □ | ▲ | □ | ▲ | □ | ▲ | Read texts 2, 5 and 6 |
| 24 | □ | ▲ | ▲ | ▲ | ▲ | □ | Read texts 2, 3, 4 and 5 |
| 25 | □ | ▲ | □ | ▲ | ▲ | ▲ | Read texts 2, 4, 5 and 6 |
| 26 | □ | ▲ | ▲ | ▲ | ▲ | ▲ | Read texts 2, 3, 4, 5 and 6 |
| 27 | ▲ | ▲ | □ | ▲ | □ | □ | Read texts 1, 2 and 4 |
| 28 | ▲ | ▲ | □ | □ | ▲ | □ | Read texts 1, 2 and 5 |
| 29 | ▲ | ▲ | □ | □ | □ | ▲ | Read texts 1, 2 and 6 |
| 30 | ▲ | ▲ | ▲ | □ | ▲ | □ | Read texts 1, 2, 3 and 5 |
| 31 | ▲ | ▲ | ▲ | □ | □ | ▲ | Read texts 1, 2, 3 and 6 |
| 32 | ▲ | ▲ | ▲ | ▲ | □ | ▲ | Read texts 1, 2, 3, 4 and 6 |
| 33 | ▲ | □ | ▲ | □ | ▲ | □ | Read texts 1, 3 and 5 |
| 34 | ▲ | □ | ▲ | □ | □ | ▲ | Read texts 1, 3 and 6 |
| 35 | ▲ | □ | ▲ | □ | ▲ | ▲ | Read texts 1, 3, 5 and 6 |
| 36 | ▲ | □ | □ | ▲ | □ | ▲ | Read texts 1, 4 and 6 |
| 37 | □ | ▲ | ▲ | □ | ▲ | □ | Read texts 2, 3 and 5 |
| 38 | □ | ▲ | ▲ | □ | □ | ▲ | Read texts 2, 3 and 6 |
| 39 | □ | ▲ | ▲ | ▲ | □ | ▲ | Read texts 2, 3, 4 and 6 |
| 40 | □ | ▲ | □ | ▲ | □ | ▲ | Read texts 2, 4 and 6 |
| 41 | □ | □ | ▲ | ▲ | □ | □ | Read texts 3 and 4 |
| 42 | □ | □ | ▲ | □ | ▲ | □ | Read texts 3 and 5 |
| 43 | □ | □ | ▲ | □ | □ | ▲ | Read texts 3 and 6 |
| 44 | □ | □ | ▲ | ▲ | ▲ | □ | Read texts 3, 4 and 5 |
| 45 | □ | □ | ▲ | ▲ | □ | ▲ | Read texts 3, 4 and 6 |
| 46 | □ | □ | ▲ | □ | ▲ | ▲ | Read texts 3, 5 and 6 |
| 47 | □ | □ | ▲ | ▲ | ▲ | ▲ | Read texts 3, 4, 5 and 6 |
| 48 | □ | □ | □ | ▲ | ▲ | □ | Read texts 4 and 5 |
| 49 | □ | □ | □ | ▲ | □ | ▲ | Read texts 4 and 6 |
| 50 | □ | □ | □ | ▲ | ▲ | ▲ | Read texts 4, 5 and 6 |
| 51 | □ | □ | □ | □ | ▲ | ▲ | Read texts 5 and 6 |
| 52 | ▲ | □ | □ | □ | □ | □ | Read text 1 |
| 53 | □ | ▲ | □ | □ | □ | □ | Read text 2 |
| 54 | □ | □ | ▲ | □ | □ | □ | Read text 3 |
| 55 | □ | □ | □ | ▲ | □ | □ | Read text 4 |
| 56 | □ | □ | □ | □ | ▲ | □ | Read text 5 |
| 57 | □ | □ | □ | □ | □ | ▲ | Read text 6 |

1st combination □ □ □ □ □

**2nd combination**

○
○
○
○
○
○

| fig. | | | | | | | |
|---|---|---|---|---|---|---|---|
| 1 | ▼ | ▼ | ○ | ○ | ○ | ○ | Read texts 1 and 2 |
| 2 | ▼ | ○ | ▼ | ○ | ○ | ○ | Read texts 1 and 3 |
| 3 | ▼ | ○ | ○ | ▼ | ○ | ○ | Read texts 1 and 4 |
| 4 | ▼ | ○ | ○ | ○ | ▼ | ○ | Read texts 1 and 5 |
| 5 | ▼ | ○ | ○ | ○ | ○ | ▼ | Read texts 1 and 6 |
| 6 | ▼ | ▼ | ▼ | ○ | ○ | ○ | Read texts 1, 2 and 3 |
| 7 | ▼ | ▼ | ○ | ▼ | ○ | ○ | Read texts 1, 2 and 4 |
| 8 | ▼ | ▼ | ○ | ○ | ▼ | ○ | Read texts 1, 2 and 5 |
| 9 | ▼ | ▼ | ○ | ○ | ○ | ▼ | Read texts 1, 2 and 6 |
| 10 | ▼ | ▼ | ▼ | ▼ | ○ | ○ | Read texts 1, 2, 3 and 4 |
| 11 | ▼ | ▼ | ▼ | ○ | ▼ | ○ | Read texts 1, 2, 3 and 5 |
| 12 | ▼ | ▼ | ▼ | ○ | ○ | ▼ | Read texts 1, 2, 3 and 6 |
| 13 | ▼ | ▼ | ▼ | ▼ | ▼ | ○ | Read texts 1, 2, 3, 4 and 5 |
| 14 | ▼ | ▼ | ▼ | ▼ | ○ | ▼ | Read texts 1, 2, 3, 4 and 6 |
| 15 | ▼ | ▼ | ▼ | ▼ | ▼ | ▼ | Read texts 1, 2, 3, 4, 5 and 6 |
| 16 | ▼ | ○ | ▼ | ▼ | ○ | ○ | Read texts 1, 3, and 4 |
| 17 | ▼ | ○ | ▼ | ○ | ▼ | ○ | Read texts 1, 3, and 5 |
| 18 | ▼ | ○ | ▼ | ○ | ○ | ▼ | Read texts 1, 3, and 6 |
| 19 | ▼ | ○ | ▼ | ▼ | ▼ | ○ | Read texts 1, 3, 4 and 5 |
| 20 | ▼ | ○ | ▼ | ▼ | ○ | ▼ | Read texts 1, 3, 4 and 6 |
| 21 | ▼ | ○ | ▼ | ○ | ▼ | ▼ | Read texts 1, 3, 5 and 6 |
| 22 | ▼ | ○ | ▼ | ▼ | ▼ | ▼ | Read texts 1, 3, 4, 5 and 6 |
| 23 | ▼ | ○ | ○ | ▼ | ▼ | ○ | Read texts 1, 4 and 5 |
| 24 | ▼ | ○ | ○ | ▼ | ○ | ▼ | Read texts 1, 4 and 6 |
| 25 | ▼ | ○ | ○ | ▼ | ▼ | ▼ | Read texts 1, 4, 5 and 6 |
| 26 | ▼ | ○ | ○ | ○ | ▼ | ▼ | Read texts 1, 5 and 6 |
| 27 | ○ | ▼ | ▼ | ○ | ○ | ○ | Read texts 2 and 3 |
| 28 | ○ | ▼ | ○ | ▼ | ○ | ○ | Read texts 2 and 4 |
| 29 | ○ | ▼ | ○ | ○ | ▼ | ○ | Read texts 2 and 5 |
| 30 | ○ | ▼ | ○ | ○ | ○ | ○ | Read texts 2 and 6 |
| 31 | ○ | ▼ | ▼ | ▼ | ○ | ○ | Read texts 2, 3 and 4 |
| 32 | ○ | ▼ | ▼ | ○ | ▼ | ○ | Read texts 2, 3 and 5 |
| 33 | ○ | ▼ | ▼ | ○ | ○ | ▼ | Read texts 2, 3 and 6 |
| 34 | ○ | ▼ | ▼ | ▼ | ▼ | ○ | Read texts 2, 3, 4 and 5 |
| 35 | ○ | ▼ | ▼ | ▼ | ○ | ▼ | Read texts 2, 3, 4 and 6 |
| 36 | ○ | ▼ | ▼ | ▼ | ▼ | ▼ | Read texts 2, 3, 4, 5 and 6 |
| 37 | ○ | ▼ | ○ | ▼ | ▼ | ○ | Read texts 2, 4 and 5 |
| 38 | ○ | ▼ | ○ | ▼ | ○ | ▼ | Read texts 2, 4 and 6 |
| 39 | ○ | ▼ | ○ | ▼ | ○ | ▼ | Read texts 2, 4 and 6 |
| 40 | ○ | ▼ | ○ | ○ | ▼ | ▼ | Read texts 2, 5 and 6 |
| 41 | ○ | ○ | ▼ | ▼ | ○ | ○ | Read texts 3 and 4 |
| 42 | ○ | ○ | ▼ | ○ | ▼ | ○ | Read texts 3 and 5 |
| 43 | ○ | ○ | ▼ | ○ | ○ | ▼ | Read texts 3 and 6 |
| 44 | ○ | ○ | ▼ | ▼ | ▼ | ○ | Read texts 3, 4 and 5 |
| 45 | ○ | ○ | ▼ | ▼ | ○ | ▼ | Read texts 3, 4 and 6 |
| 46 | ○ | ○ | ▼ | ○ | ▼ | ▼ | Read texts 3, 5 and 6 |
| 47 | ○ | ○ | ▼ | ▼ | ▼ | ▼ | Read texts 3, 4, 5 and 6 |
| 48 | ○ | ○ | ○ | ▼ | ▼ | ○ | Read texts 4 and 5 |
| 49 | ○ | ○ | ○ | ▼ | ○ | ▼ | Read texts 4 and 6 |
| 50 | ○ | ○ | ○ | ▼ | ▼ | ▼ | Read texts 4, 5 and 6 |
| 51 | ○ | ○ | ○ | ○ | ▼ | ▼ | Read texts 5 and 6 |
| 52 | ▼ | ○ | ○ | ○ | ○ | ○ | Read text 1 |
| 53 | ○ | ▼ | ○ | ○ | ○ | ○ | Read text 2 |
| 54 | ○ | ○ | ▼ | ○ | ○ | ○ | Read text 3 |
| 55 | ○ | ○ | ○ | ▼ | ○ | ○ | Read text 4 |
| 56 | ○ | ○ | ○ | ○ | ▼ | ○ | Read text 5 |
| 57 | ○ | ○ | ○ | ○ | ○ | ▼ | Read text 6 |

4   You are now at a crossroads in your life. You have two options: either to engage with the outside world and with society, and to embark upon solid material projects, or you can take time out for yourself, step back from the outside world and concentrate on your personal development. There is nothing wrong with either choice. It's up to you to decide which works best for you, and to make your decision with full knowledge of the facts.

5   In terms of your personal development, this is an excellent time for compatibility and interaction. You are fully in tune with your environment and in harmony with those around you. Take advantage of this privileged phase in your life to begin or accomplish something that is dear to your heart, and to surround yourself with people whose ideas, aspirations and ambitions match your own.

6   It seems as if you have taken too much for granted or have overestimated your strength, options and means. Your vaulting ambition or excessive pride may lead to disappointment or failure, which will be nobody's fault but your own. However it is not too late to reconsider your behaviour and to make a more modest and fair assessment of reality.

# 2<sup>nd</sup> combination ○ ○ ○ ○ ○ ○

It is crucial that you take circumstances into account, trust your instinct and let yourself be guided by what is happening in your life. These are the preconditions for carrying your cherished plans and projects through to a successful conclusion.

1   A situation or relationship is on its last legs, or is gradually breaking down, and you do not realize it. However this state of affairs can be reversed. You just need to be more aware of it and to act or react appropriately. Forewarned is forearmed.

2   You must act and behave according to your convictions, your secret thoughts and your true motivations, in order that your behaviour is clear, consistent and comprehensible to those around you. In this way you will get what you wish as well as the approval and understanding of your associates.

3   You are not yet at the point where you can reap the benefits, rewards or esteem that you are entitled to expect. But your time will come, and you can be confident that your present actions, even if they are not currently appreciated, will prove highly profitable for you in the long term.

4   You are advised to act with extreme discretion: in your current position, the slightest move you make could be misinterpreted and could work against you. For now it is better to abstain from any action and avoid drawing attention to yourself. Keep a low profile, you will be less likely to encounter setbacks or disappointments.

5   You will soon achieve a promotion or a new job that you have set your sights on, or else you will have a key role to play. However, despite your enviable position, you will not have complete independence in your choices and actions. Your success in the matter therefore depends essentially on

being able to prove your discretion, conscientiousness and honesty.

6   To rule is to serve. In other words, if you are in a position where you can exert power it is best to hold yourself in check, because you could cause a dangerous clash. Instead, assume your responsibilities, show unswerving devotion and be receptive to whatever is thrown at you.

# 3<sup>rd</sup> combination ❑ ○ ○ ○ ❑ ○

Your current situation is muddled, but full of opportunity and promise. It is important that you keep a cool head, make allowances and find associates who will help you to see clearly, or will work with you to realize your plans or wishes.

1   Do not attempt to fulfil your dreams at all costs, or to force matters in order to reach your goal. Instead, take time to think and, together with people who can help or support you, to assess your chances of overcoming the obstacles along your way, and of conquering your current difficulties.

2   You will not achieve the results you expect just yet, but other opportunities will probably come along unexpectedly. So do not reject them, even if they come from unexpected places, or from someone to whom you do not feel close. Accept them as good omens and wait for the moment when you can achieve your true objective.

**3rd combination**

| fig. | | | | | | | |
|---|---|---|---|---|---|---|---|
| 1 | ▲ | ▼ | ○ | ○ | □ | ○ | Read texts 1 and 2 |
| 2 | ▲ | ○ | ▼ | ○ | □ | ○ | Read texts 1 and 3 |
| 3 | ▲ | ○ | ○ | ▼ | □ | ○ | Read texts 1 and 4 |
| 4 | ▲ | ○ | ○ | ○ | ▲ | ○ | Read texts 1 and 5 |
| 5 | ▲ | ○ | ○ | ○ | □ | ▼ | Read texts 1 and 6 |
| 6 | ▲ | ▼ | ▼ | ○ | □ | ○ | Read texts 1, 2 and 3 |
| 7 | ▲ | ▼ | ○ | ▼ | □ | ○ | Read texts 1, 2 and 4 |
| 8 | ▲ | ▼ | ○ | ○ | ▲ | ○ | Read texts 1, 2 and 5 |
| 9 | ▲ | ▼ | ○ | ○ | □ | ▼ | Read texts 1, 2 and 6 |
| 10 | ▲ | ▼ | ▼ | ▼ | □ | ○ | Read texts 1, 2, 3 and 4 |
| 11 | ▲ | ▼ | ▼ | ○ | ▲ | ○ | Read texts 1, 2, 3 and 5 |
| 12 | ▲ | ▼ | ▼ | ○ | □ | ▼ | Read texts 1, 2, 3 and 6 |
| 13 | ▲ | ▼ | ▼ | ▼ | ▲ | ○ | Read texts 1, 2, 3, 4 and 5 |
| 14 | ▲ | ▼ | ▼ | ▼ | □ | ▼ | Read texts 1, 2, 3, 4 and 6 |
| 15 | ▲ | ▼ | ▼ | ▼ | ▲ | ▼ | Read texts 1, 2, 3, 4, 5 and 6 |
| 16 | ▲ | ○ | ▼ | ▼ | □ | ○ | Read texts 1, 3 and 4 |
| 17 | ▲ | ○ | ▼ | ○ | ▲ | ○ | Read texts 1, 3 and 5 |
| 18 | ▲ | ○ | ▼ | ○ | □ | ▼ | Read texts 1, 3 and 6 |
| 19 | ▲ | ○ | ▼ | ▼ | ▲ | ○ | Read texts 1, 3, 4 and 5 |
| 20 | ▲ | ○ | ▼ | ▼ | □ | ▼ | Read texts 1, 3, 4 and 6 |
| 21 | ▲ | ○ | ▼ | ○ | ▲ | ▼ | Read texts 1, 3, 5 and 6 |
| 22 | ▲ | ○ | ▼ | ▼ | ▲ | ▼ | Read texts 1, 3, 4, 5 and 6 |
| 23 | ▲ | ○ | ○ | ▼ | ▲ | ○ | Read texts 1, 4 and 5 |
| 24 | ▲ | ○ | ○ | ▼ | □ | ▼ | Read texts 1, 4 and 6 |
| 25 | ▲ | ○ | ○ | ▼ | ▲ | ▼ | Read texts 1, 4, 5 and 6 |
| 26 | ▲ | ○ | ○ | ○ | ▲ | ▼ | Read texts 1, 5 and 6 |
| 27 | □ | ▼ | ▼ | ○ | □ | ○ | Read texts 2 and 3 |
| 28 | □ | ▼ | ○ | ▼ | □ | ○ | Read texts 2 and 4 |
| 29 | □ | ▼ | ○ | ○ | ▲ | ○ | Read texts 2 and 5 |
| 30 | □ | ▼ | ○ | ○ | □ | ▼ | Read texts 2 and 6 |
| 31 | □ | ▼ | ▼ | ▼ | □ | ○ | Read texts 2, 3 and 4 |
| 32 | □ | ▼ | ▼ | ○ | ▲ | ○ | Read texts 2, 3 and 5 |
| 33 | □ | ▼ | ▼ | ○ | □ | ▼ | Read texts 2, 3 and 6 |
| 34 | □ | ▼ | ▼ | ▼ | ▲ | ○ | Read texts 2, 3, 4 and 5 |
| 35 | □ | ▼ | ▼ | ▼ | □ | ▼ | Read texts 2, 3, 4 and 6 |
| 36 | □ | ▼ | ▼ | ▼ | ▲ | ▼ | Read texts 2, 3, 4, 5 and 6 |
| 37 | □ | ▼ | ○ | ▼ | ▲ | ○ | Read texts 2, 4 and 5 |
| 38 | □ | ▼ | ○ | ▼ | □ | ▼ | Read texts 2, 4 and 6 |
| 39 | □ | ▼ | ○ | ▼ | ▲ | ▼ | Read texts 2, 4, 5 and 6 |
| 40 | □ | ▼ | ○ | ○ | ▲ | ▼ | Read texts 2, 5 and 6 |
| 41 | □ | ○ | ▼ | ▼ | □ | ○ | Read texts 3 and 4 |
| 42 | □ | ○ | ▼ | ○ | ▲ | ○ | Read texts 3 and 5 |
| 43 | □ | ○ | ▼ | ○ | □ | ▼ | Read texts 3 and 6 . |
| 44 | □ | ○ | ▼ | ▼ | ▲ | ○ | Read texts 3, 4 and 5 |
| 45 | □ | ○ | ▼ | ▼ | □ | ▼ | Read texts 3, 4 and 6 |
| 46 | □ | ○ | ▼ | ○ | ▲ | ▼ | Read texts 3, 5 and 6 |
| 47 | □ | ○ | ▼ | ▼ | ▲ | ▼ | Read texts 3, 4, 5 and 6 |
| 48 | □ | ○ | ○ | ▼ | ▲ | ○ | Read texts 4 and 5 |
| 49 | □ | ○ | ○ | ▼ | □ | ▼ | Read texts 4 and 6 |
| 50 | □ | ○ | ○ | ▼ | ▲ | ▼ | Read texts 4, 5 and 6 |
| 51 | □ | ○ | ○ | ○ | ▲ | ▼ | Read texts 5 and 6 |
| 52 | ▲ | ○ | ○ | ○ | □ | ○ | Read text 1 |
| 53 | □ | ▼ | ○ | ○ | □ | ○ | Read text 2 |
| 54 | □ | ○ | ▼ | ○ | □ | ○ | Read text 3 |
| 55 | □ | ○ | ○ | ▼ | □ | ○ | Read text 4 |
| 56 | □ | ○ | ○ | ○ | ▲ | ○ | Read text 5 |
| 57 | □ | ○ | ○ | ○ | □ | ▼ | Read text 6 |

**3** Your qualities alone will not be enough to solve your current problems. Your desire to resolve them inadequately will only aggravate the delicate situation you are in. It would be wiser to follow the advice you are being offered, and to abandon your single-minded desire to obtain something that would only be a source of trouble and disappointment.

**4** Everything encourages you to forge ahead, make a choice or take a decision. However, through lack of self-confidence or reckless pride, you will be tempted to shy away from action, from asking for the help you need, or from expressing your desires. There is no shame in demanding what is owing to you, or in asking for support or protection – especially if you know where to find it.

**5** Despite your sincere wish to do the right thing, your goodwill, generous decisions and positive actions cannot flourish in your present difficult emotional situation. Instead, be content to persevere, to remain true to your convictions while waiting for the situation to change, for the problems to fade, and to gain the trust of those around you.

**6** It seems that you are as quick to express your enthusiasm as to show your discouragement at the first sign of any small obstacle or minor setback. So get a grip on yourself, and do not feel demoralized by adverse circumstances. You must not allow yourself to be diverted from your goal, before you have taken the first steps towards reaching it, or you will end up with nothing.

# 4<sup>th</sup> combination ○□□○○○□

It is not good to be too curious; it's also a weakness to lack curiosity. Similarly, someone who squanders his knowledge unreservedly, or without regard for the attention or quality of his audience, is as inexcusable as one who systematically withholds information.

**1**   You must take a firm stance, without appearing strict and inflexible. This is particularly true if you are involved with children, or people who are unprepared or unwilling to take their place in society or in the working world, those who refuse to take life seriously or to shoulder their responsibilities.

**2**   You are involved with people whose unreasonable, or even senseless, behaviour could have disastrous consequences for you, or exert a bad influence on those around you. However, show extreme tact, kindness and magnanimity and you will be able to temper their extreme attitudes and take the situation in hand.

**3**   Do not confuse servitude with servility. You may be devoted to somebody whom you respect, admire or envy, but do not try to become a carbon copy of them, or of what they represent for you. By the same token, it is not up to you to put yourself forward or to give more than is required of you. Be satisfied with your role, accept it completely, and wait until you are asked before making any response.

**4**   Avoid rash speculation, and keep your overactive imagination in check, because it

| fig. 1 | | | | | | |
|---|---|---|---|---|---|---|
| 1 | ▼ ▲ ○ ○ ○ □ | Read texts 1 and 2 |
| 2 | ▼ □ ▼ ○ ○ □ | Read texts 1 and 3 |
| 3 | ▼ □ ○ ▼ ○ □ | Read texts 1 and 4 |
| 4 | ▼ □ ○ ○ ▼ □ | Read texts 1 and 5 |
| 5 | ▼ □ ○ ○ ○ ▲ | Read texts 1 and 6 |
| 6 | ▼ ▲ ▼ ○ ○ □ | Read texts 1, 2 and 3 |
| 7 | ▼ ▲ ○ ▼ ○ □ | Read texts 1, 2 and 4 |
| 8 | ▼ ▲ ○ ○ ▼ □ | Read texts 1, 2 and 5 |
| 9 | ▼ ▲ ○ ○ ○ ▲ | Read texts 1, 2 and 6 |
| 10 | ▼ ▲ ▼ ▼ ○ □ | Read texts 1, 2, 3 and 4 |
| 11 | ▼ ▲ ▼ ○ ▼ □ | Read texts 1, 2, 3 and 5 |
| 12 | ▼ ▲ ▼ ○ ○ ▲ | Read texts 1, 2, 3 and 6 |
| 13 | ▼ ▲ ▼ ▼ ▼ □ | Read texts 1, 2, 3, 4 and 5 |
| 14 | ▼ ▲ ▼ ▼ ○ ▲ | Read texts 1, 2, 3, 4 and 6 |
| 15 | ▼ ▲ ▼ ▼ ▼ ▲ | Read texts 1, 2, 3, 4, 5 and 6 |
| 16 | ▼ □ ▼ ▼ ○ □ | Read texts 1, 3, and 4 |
| 17 | ▼ □ ▼ ○ ▼ □ | Read texts 1, 3, and 5 |
| 18 | ▼ □ ▼ ○ ○ ▲ | Read texts 1, 3, and 6 |
| 19 | ▼ □ ▼ ▼ ▼ □ | Read texts 1, 3, 4 and 5 |
| 20 | ▼ □ ▼ ▼ ○ ▲ | Read texts 1, 3, 4 and 6 |
| 21 | ▼ □ ○ ▼ ▼ ▲ | Read texts 1, 3, 5 and 6 |
| 22 | ▼ □ ▼ ▼ ▼ ▲ | Read texts 1, 3, 4, 5 and 6 |
| 23 | ▼ □ ○ ▼ ▼ □ | Read texts 1, 4 and 5 |
| 24 | ▼ □ ○ ▼ ○ ▲ | Read texts 1, 4 and 6 |
| 25 | ▼ □ ○ ▼ ▼ ▲ | Read texts 1, 4, 5 and 6 |
| 26 | ▼ □ ○ ○ ▼ ▲ | Read texts 1, 5 and 6 |
| 27 | ○ ▲ ▼ ○ ○ □ | Read texts 2 and 3 |
| 28 | ○ ▲ ○ ▼ ○ □ | Read texts 2 and 4 |
| 29 | ○ ▲ ○ ○ ▼ □ | Read texts 2 and 5 |
| 30 | ○ ▲ ○ ○ ○ ▲ | Read texts 2 and 6 |
| 31 | ○ ▲ ▼ ▼ ○ □ | Read texts 2, 3 and 4 |
| 32 | ○ ▲ ▼ ○ ▼ □ | Read texts 2, 3 and 5 |
| 33 | ○ ▲ ▼ ○ ○ ▲ | Read texts 2, 3 and 6 |
| 34 | ○ ▲ ▼ ▼ ▼ □ | Read texts 2, 3, 4 and 5 |
| 35 | ○ ▲ ▼ ▼ ○ ▲ | Read texts 2, 3, 4 and 6 |
| 36 | ○ ▲ ▼ ▼ ▼ ▲ | Read texts 2, 3, 4, 5 and 6 |
| 37 | ○ ▲ ○ ▼ ▼ □ | Read texts 2, 4 and 5 |
| 38 | ○ ▲ ○ ▼ ○ ▲ | Read texts 2, 4 and 6 |
| 39 | ○ ▲ ○ ▼ ▼ ▲ | Read texts 2, 4, 5 and 6 |
| 40 | ○ ▲ ○ ○ ▼ ▲ | Read texts 2, 5 and 6 |
| 41 | ○ □ ▼ ▼ ○ □ | Read texts 3 and 4 |
| 42 | ○ □ ▼ ○ ▼ □ | Read texts 3 and 5 |
| 43 | ○ □ ▼ ○ ○ ▲ | Read texts 3 and 6 |
| 44 | ○ □ ▼ ▼ ▼ □ | Read texts 3, 4 and 5 |
| 45 | ○ □ ▼ ▼ ○ ▲ | Read texts 3, 4 and 6 |
| 46 | ○ □ ▼ ○ ▼ ▲ | Read texts 3, 5 and 6 |
| 47 | ○ □ ▼ ▼ ▼ ▲ | Read texts 3, 4, 5 and 6 |
| 48 | ○ □ ○ ▼ ▼ □ | Read texts 4 and 5 |
| 49 | ○ □ ○ ▼ ○ ▲ | Read texts 4 and 6 |
| 50 | ○ □ ○ ▼ ▼ ▲ | Read texts 4, 5 and 6 |
| 51 | ○ □ ○ ○ ▼ ▲ | Read texts 5 and 6 |
| 52 | ▼ □ ○ ○ ○ □ | Read text 1 |
| 53 | ○ ▲ ○ ○ ○ □ | Read text 2 |
| 54 | ○ □ ▼ ○ ○ □ | Read text 3 |
| 55 | ○ □ ○ ▼ ○ □ | Read text 4 |
| 56 | ○ □ ○ ○ ▼ □ | Read text 5 |
| 57 | ○ □ ○ ○ ○ ▲ | Read text 6 |

**5th combination**

| fig. | | | | | | | |
|---|---|---|---|---|---|---|---|
| 1 | ▲ | ▲ | □ | ○ | □ | ○ | Read texts 1 and 2 |
| 2 | ▲ | □ | ▲ | ○ | □ | ○ | Read texts 1 and 3 |
| 3 | ▲ | □ | □ | ▼ | □ | ○ | Read texts 1 and 4 |
| 4 | ▲ | □ | □ | ○ | ▲ | ○ | Read texts 1 and 5 |
| 5 | ▲ | □ | □ | ○ | □ | ▼ | Read texts 1 and 6 |
| 6 | ▲ | ▲ | ▲ | ○ | □ | ○ | Read texts 1, 2 and 3 |
| 7 | ▲ | ▲ | □ | ▼ | □ | ○ | Read texts 1, 3 and 4 |
| 8 | ▲ | □ | □ | ▼ | ▲ | ○ | Read texts 1, 4 and 5 |
| 9 | ▲ | □ | □ | ○ | ▲ | ▼ | Read texts 1, 5 and 6 |
| 10 | ▲ | ▲ | ▲ | ▼ | □ | ○ | Read texts 1, 2, 3 and 4 |
| 11 | ▲ | □ | ▲ | ▼ | ▲ | ○ | Read texts 1, 3, 4 and 5 |
| 12 | ▲ | □ | ▲ | ▼ | □ | ▼ | Read texts 1, 3, 4 and 6 |
| 13 | ▲ | □ | □ | ▼ | ▲ | ▼ | Read texts 1, 4, 5 and 6 |
| 14 | ▲ | ▲ | ▲ | ▼ | ▲ | ○ | Read texts 1, 2, 3, 4 and 5 |
| 15 | ▲ | ▲ | ▲ | ▼ | □ | ▼ | Read texts 1, 3, 4, 5 and 6 |
| 16 | ▲ | ▲ | ▲ | ▼ | ▲ | ▼ | Read texts 1, 2, 3, 4, 5 and 6 |
| 17 | □ | ▲ | ▲ | ○ | □ | ○ | Read texts 2 and 3 |
| 18 | □ | ▲ | □ | ▼ | □ | ○ | Read texts 2 and 4 |
| 19 | □ | ▲ | □ | ○ | ▲ | ○ | Read texts 2 and 5 |
| 20 | □ | ▲ | □ | ○ | □ | ▼ | Read texts 2 and 6 |
| 21 | □ | ▲ | ▲ | ▼ | □ | ○ | Read texts 2, 3 and 4 |
| 22 | □ | ▲ | □ | ▼ | ▲ | ○ | Read texts 2, 4 and 5 |
| 23 | □ | ▲ | □ | ○ | ▲ | ▼ | Read texts 2, 5 and 6 |
| 24 | □ | ▲ | ▲ | ▼ | ▲ | ○ | Read texts 2, 3, 4 and 5 |
| 25 | □ | ▲ | □ | ▼ | ▲ | ▼ | Read texts 2, 4, 5 and 6 |
| 26 | □ | ▲ | ▲ | ▼ | ▲ | ▼ | Read texts 2, 3, 4, 5 and 6 |
| 27 | ▲ | ▲ | □ | ▼ | □ | ○ | Read texts 1, 2 and 4 |
| 28 | ▲ | ▲ | □ | ○ | ▲ | ○ | Read texts 1, 2 and 5 |
| 29 | ▲ | ▲ | □ | ○ | □ | ▼ | Read texts 1, 2 and 6 |
| 30 | ▲ | ▲ | ▲ | ○ | ▲ | ○ | Read texts 1, 2, 3 and 5 |
| 31 | ▲ | ▲ | ▲ | ○ | □ | ▼ | Read texts 1, 2, 3 and 6 |
| 32 | ▲ | ▲ | ▲ | ▼ | □ | ▼ | Read texts 1, 2, 3, 4 and 6 |
| 33 | ▲ | □ | ▲ | ○ | ▲ | ○ | Read texts 1, 3 and 5 |
| 34 | ▲ | □ | ▲ | ○ | □ | ▼ | Read texts 1, 3 and 6 |
| 35 | ▲ | □ | ▲ | ○ | ▲ | ▼ | Read texts 1, 3, 5 and 6 |
| 36 | ▲ | □ | □ | ▼ | □ | ▼ | Read texts 1, 4 and 6 |
| 37 | □ | ▲ | ▲ | ○ | ▲ | ○ | Read texts 2, 3 and 5 |
| 38 | □ | ▲ | ▲ | ○ | □ | ▼ | Read texts 2, 3 and 6 |
| 39 | □ | ▲ | ▲ | ▼ | □ | ▼ | Read texts 2, 3, 4 and 6 |
| 40 | □ | ▲ | □ | ▼ | □ | ▼ | Read texts 2, 4 and 6 |
| 41 | □ | □ | ▲ | ▼ | □ | ○ | Read texts 3 and 4 |
| 42 | □ | □ | ▲ | ○ | ▲ | ○ | Read texts 3 and 5 |
| 43 | □ | □ | ▲ | ○ | □ | ▼ | Read texts 3 and 6 |
| 44 | □ | □ | ▲ | ▼ | ▲ | ○ | Read texts 3, 4 and 5 |
| 45 | □ | □ | ▲ | ▼ | □ | ▼ | Read texts 3, 4 and 6 |
| 46 | □ | □ | ▲ | ○ | ▲ | ▼ | Read texts 3, 5 and 6 |
| 47 | □ | □ | ▲ | ▼ | ▲ | ▼ | Read texts 3, 4, 5 and 6 |
| 48 | □ | □ | □ | ▼ | ▲ | ○ | Read texts 4 and 5 |
| 49 | □ | □ | □ | ▼ | □ | ▼ | Read texts 4 and 6 |
| 50 | □ | □ | □ | ▼ | ▲ | ▼ | Read texts 4, 5 and 6 |
| 51 | □ | □ | □ | ○ | ▲ | ▼ | Read texts 5 and 6 |
| 52 | ▲ | □ | □ | ○ | □ | ○ | Read text 1 |
| 53 | □ | ▲ | □ | ○ | □ | ○ | Read text 2 |
| 54 | □ | □ | ▲ | ○ | □ | ○ | Read text 3 |
| 55 | □ | □ | □ | ▼ | □ | ○ | Read text 4 |
| 56 | □ | □ | □ | ○ | ▲ | ○ | Read text 5 |
| 57 | □ | □ | □ | ○ | □ | ▼ | Read text 6 |

could lead you to do the wrong thing, deceive yourself, or undertake shaky or insubstantial projects that are bound to fail. But will you heed this advice and follow it to the letter?

**5**   Despite your considerable experience you are always receptive to good advice offered by trustworthy, competent people. This mixture of deference and healthy curiosity can only have a positive impact on your personal development and on your future.

**6**   When somebody behaves in a reprehensible, careless or thoughtless fashion, and they refuse to listen to reason, your only recourse is to react firmly so that they can weigh up the consequences of their actions. However, any penalty inflicted, no matter how well deserved, should only be used as a preventive measure. Punishment should not be an end in itself, but a lesson this person should take on board to adapt their behaviour.

# 5<sup>th</sup> combination □ □ □ ○ □ ○

For now, you will just have to sit back and wait. But this does not mean that you have to remain inactive while you are waiting. From now on, you can get ready to face the events that are sure to come along, while not trying to provoke or challenge them.

**1**   You sense that something is about to happen – that events in your life are about to step up a gear. Your premonition is correct, which is why you should calmly prepare for battle. Avoid situations that might hamper your independence or prevent you from acting or reacting as you would wish when the time comes.

2   Your situation is deteriorating, and the current emotional climate weighs heavily on you. In such cases everyone is inclined to blame the nearest person, but what you need to do is to ignore unkind words, and not to respond by trying to defend yourself or by fighting back. If you pay no heed, they will soon stop.

3   You are in a difficult and dangerous situation. You have tried to extricate yourself by acting or reacting prematurely, and you did not see your resolution through. The intention was honourable, but regrettably you did not stick with it. Consequently, proceed with extreme caution and remain resolute if you want to break the impasse.

4   This is a serious situation. You should not underestimate it, but neither should you magnify it: if you dramatize it unnecessarily or react prematurely you will only make matters worse. Stay calm if possible, and do not overstep the mark, and you will be able to escape this testing situation.

5   Your situation is not easy but take advantage of any moments of respite to regroup, to prepare for your intended course of action. By learning how to recharge your batteries whenever you get the chance, you will feel better equipped to confront your difficulties and reach the goal you have set yourself.

6   You feel as though your situation is desperate, and that all your attempts to escape it have been futile. However, an imminent and unexpected happy event will help solve your problems. Greet it with joy and seize the opportunity without asking unnecessary questions; you will be glad you did.

# 6th combination ○ ▢ ▢ ○ ▢ ▢

In a situation of conflict that seems to offer no way out, compromise, however disadvantageous, is better than going to court. Therefore it is a good idea to demonstrate your good faith and intentions before the conflict degenerates. However, if everybody's rights and responsibilities are clearly defined from the outset, all possible causes of conflict can be avoided.

1   If you are at odds with somebody, assess your strengths and arguments carefully against those of your opponent. If you feel that your opponent is in a stronger or more influential position than you, it would be pointless to pursue any conflict. The wise thing would be to settle your differences speedily.

2   You are engaged in a struggle that is beyond your means or your capabilities. Your opponent is in a stronger position than you. This being the case, it would be sensible to abandon the fight, because it is already as good as lost, and can only result in unfortunate consequences, both for you and for everyone around you.

**6th combination**

| | | | | | | | |
|---|---|---|---|---|---|---|---|
| fig. 1 | ▼ | ▲ | ○ | □ | □ | □ | Read texts 1 and 2 |
| 2 | ▼ | □ | ▼ | □ | □ | □ | Read texts 1 and 3 |
| 3 | ▼ | □ | ○ | ▲ | □ | □ | Read texts 1 and 4 |
| 4 | ▼ | □ | ○ | □ | ▲ | □ | Read texts 1 and 5 |
| 5 | ▼ | □ | ○ | □ | □ | ▲ | Read texts 1 and 6 |
| 6 | ▼ | ▲ | ▼ | □ | □ | □ | Read texts 1, 2 and 3 |
| 7 | ▼ | □ | ▼ | ▲ | □ | □ | Read texts 1, 3 and 4 |
| 8 | ▼ | □ | ○ | ▲ | ▲ | □ | Read texts 1, 4 and 5 |
| 9 | ▼ | □ | ○ | □ | ▲ | ▲ | Read texts 1, 5 and 6 |
| 10 | ▼ | ▲ | ▼ | ▲ | □ | □ | Read texts 1, 2, 3 and 4 |
| 11 | ▼ | □ | ▼ | ▲ | ▲ | □ | Read texts 1, 3, 4 and 5 |
| 12 | ▼ | □ | ▼ | ▲ | □ | ▲ | Read texts 1, 3, 4 and 6 |
| 13 | ▼ | □ | ○ | ▲ | ▲ | ▲ | Read texts 1, 4, 5 and 6 |
| 14 | ▼ | ▲ | ▼ | ▲ | ▲ | □ | Read texts 1, 2, 3, 4 and 5 |
| 15 | ▼ | □ | ▼ | ▲ | ▲ | ▲ | Read texts 1, 3, 4, 5 and 6 |
| 16 | ▼ | ▲ | ▼ | ▲ | ▲ | ▲ | Read texts 1, 2, 3, 4, 5 and 6 |
| 17 | ○ | ▲ | ▼ | □ | □ | □ | Read texts 2 and 3 |
| 18 | ○ | ▲ | ○ | ▲ | □ | □ | Read texts 2 and 4 |
| 19 | ○ | ▲ | ○ | □ | ▲ | □ | Read texts 2 and 5 |
| 20 | ○ | ▲ | ○ | □ | □ | ▲ | Read texts 2 and 6 |
| 21 | ○ | ▲ | ▼ | ▲ | □ | □ | Read texts 2, 3 and 4 |
| 22 | ○ | ▲ | ○ | ▲ | ▲ | □ | Read texts 2, 4 and 5 |
| 23 | ○ | ▲ | ○ | □ | ▲ | ▲ | Read texts 2, 5 and 6 |
| 24 | ○ | ▲ | ▼ | ▲ | ▲ | □ | Read texts 2, 3, 4 and 5 |
| 25 | ○ | ▲ | ○ | ▲ | ▲ | ▲ | Read texts 2, 4, 5 and 6 |
| 26 | ○ | ▲ | ▼ | ▲ | ▲ | ▲ | Read texts 2, 3, 4, 5 and 6 |
| 27 | ▼ | ▲ | ○ | ▲ | □ | □ | Read texts 1, 2 and 4 |
| 28 | ▼ | ▲ | ○ | □ | ▲ | □ | Read texts 1, 2 and 5 |
| 29 | ▼ | ▲ | ○ | □ | □ | ▲ | Read texts 1, 2 and 6 |
| 30 | ▼ | ▲ | ▼ | □ | ▲ | □ | Read texts 1, 2, 3 and 5 |
| 31 | ▼ | ▲ | ▼ | □ | □ | ▲ | Read texts 1, 2, 3 and 6 |
| 32 | ▼ | ▲ | ▼ | ▲ | □ | ▲ | Read texts 1, 2, 3, 4 and 6 |
| 33 | ▼ | □ | ▼ | □ | ▲ | □ | Read texts 1, 3 and 5 |
| 34 | ▼ | □ | ▼ | □ | □ | ▲ | Read texts 1, 3 and 6 |
| 35 | ▼ | □ | ▼ | □ | ▲ | ▲ | Read texts 1, 3, 5 and 6 |
| 36 | ▼ | □ | ○ | ▲ | □ | ▲ | Read texts 1, 4 and 6 |
| 37 | ○ | ▲ | ▼ | □ | ▲ | □ | Read texts 2, 3 and 5 |
| 38 | ○ | ▲ | ▼ | □ | □ | ▲ | Read texts 2, 3 and 6 |
| 39 | ○ | ▲ | ▼ | ▲ | □ | ▲ | Read texts 2, 3, 4 and 6 |
| 40 | ○ | ▲ | ○ | ▲ | □ | ▲ | Read texts 2, 4 and 6 |
| 41 | ○ | □ | ▼ | ▲ | □ | □ | Read texts 3 and 4 |
| 42 | ○ | □ | ▼ | □ | ▲ | □ | Read texts 3 and 5 |
| 43 | ○ | □ | ▼ | □ | □ | ▲ | Read texts 3 and 6 |
| 44 | ○ | □ | ▼ | ▲ | ▲ | □ | Read texts 3, 4 and 5 |
| 45 | ○ | □ | ▼ | ▲ | □ | ▲ | Read texts 3, 4 and 6 |
| 46 | ○ | □ | ▼ | □ | ▲ | ▲ | Read texts 3, 5 and 6 |
| 47 | ○ | □ | ▼ | ▲ | ▲ | ▲ | Read texts 3, 4, 5 and 6 |
| 48 | ○ | □ | ○ | ▲ | ▲ | □ | Read texts 4 and 5 |
| 49 | ○ | □ | ○ | ▲ | □ | ▲ | Read texts 4 and 6 |
| 50 | ○ | □ | ○ | ▲ | ▲ | ▲ | Read texts 4, 5 and 6 |
| 51 | ○ | □ | ○ | □ | ▲ | ▲ | Read texts 5 and 6 |
| 52 | ▼ | □ | ○ | □ | □ | □ | Read text 1 |
| 53 | ○ | ▲ | ○ | □ | □ | □ | Read text 2 |
| 54 | ○ | □ | ▼ | □ | □ | □ | Read text 3 |
| 55 | ○ | □ | ○ | ▲ | □ | □ | Read text 4 |
| 56 | ○ | □ | ○ | □ | ▲ | □ | Read text 5 |
| 57 | ○ | □ | ○ | □ | □ | ▲ | Read text 6 |

**3** Do not try and lay claim to something that does not belong to you, be it a project or a material possession, whether or not you made any contribution towards its achievement or acquisition. This kind of attitude can only cause dissent and would propel you into a delicate situation. You can only take credit for something in which you invested your own personal qualities, and then it can never be taken away.

**4** Your anxious nature lies at the root of your doubts or discontent. To put an end to these feelings you are tempted to behave or react to those around you brutally or excessively. You cannot justify this attitude, so your best course of action is to give it up.

**5** If you find yourself involved in a clash or serious conflict with no obvious way out, appeal to someone whose integrity and objectivity will make him or her a fair and trustworthy mediator. If you are in the right, you will easily be vindicated. Whatever happens, you will be glad this person has intervened.

**6** You have achieved your ends and been proved right. However, you will very soon realize that this was a hollow victory, because you will have to defend yourself constantly against attack. You will not get a minute's peace and your opponent will be forever testing your patience and good faith.

# 7th combination ○ □ ○ ○ ○ ○

You are in a situation where you have tried everything in order to resolve matters and allow them to return to normal; now you have no choice but to go into battle. However, to succeed you must have legitimate reasons and to win support you must observe certain rules.

**1** You are planning to embark upon a delicate and dangerous struggle. Be very sure of your objectives and motives. Then surround yourself with competent helpers and give everyone a clearly defined task or mission. Success can only be achieved if you establish a guideline for everybody to follow to the letter.

**2** You are committed to defending a cause that concerns not only you but also everyone involved with you, and the outcome is still uncertain. For this reason it is essential that you remain involved, even if you assume a role or responsibility that allows you to step back from the fray. If people feel you are committed, they will follow you blindly.

**3** You are engaged in a battle that you risk losing through lack of cohesion and discipline. It is good for everyone to voice their opinion about the best course of action, but too many chiefs and not enough Indians is a dangerous state of affairs. In this situation an experienced person should make firm decisions that must be supported by all, otherwise confusion will lead to failure.

**4** You are engaged in a struggle or fight which is impossible to resolve. If you stubbornly persist on trying to reach your

| fig. | | | | | | | |
|---|---|---|---|---|---|---|---|
| 1 | ▼ | ▲ | ○ | ○ | ○ | ○ | Read texts 1 and 2 |
| 2 | ▼ | □ | ▼ | ○ | ○ | ○ | Read texts 1 and 3 |
| 3 | ▼ | □ | ○ | ▼ | ○ | ○ | Read texts 1 and 4 |
| 4 | ▼ | □ | ○ | ○ | ▼ | ○ | Read texts 1 and 5 |
| 5 | ▼ | □ | ○ | ○ | ○ | ▼ | Read texts 1 and 6 |
| 6 | ▼ | ▲ | ▼ | ○ | ○ | ○ | Read texts 1, 2 and 3 |
| 7 | ▼ | ▲ | ○ | ▼ | ○ | ○ | Read texts 1, 2 and 4 |
| 8 | ▼ | ▲ | ○ | ○ | ▼ | ○ | Read texts 1, 2 and 5 |
| 9 | ▼ | ▲ | ○ | ○ | ○ | ▼ | Read texts 1, 2 and 6 |
| 10 | ▼ | ▲ | ▼ | ▼ | ○ | ○ | Read texts 1, 2, 3 and 4 |
| 11 | ▼ | ▲ | ▼ | ○ | ▼ | ○ | Read texts 1, 2, 3 and 5 |
| 12 | ▼ | ▲ | ▼ | ○ | ○ | ▼ | Read texts 1, 2, 3 and 6 |
| 13 | ▼ | ▲ | ▼ | ▼ | ▼ | ○ | Read texts 1, 2, 3, 4 and 5 |
| 14 | ▼ | ▲ | ▼ | ▼ | ○ | ▼ | Read texts 1, 2, 3, 4 and 6 |
| 15 | ▼ | ▲ | ▼ | ▼ | ▼ | ▼ | Read texts 1, 2, 3, 4, 5 and 6 |
| 16 | ▼ | □ | ▼ | ▼ | ○ | ○ | Read texts 1, 3 and 4 |
| 17 | ▼ | □ | ▼ | ○ | ▼ | ○ | Read texts 1, 3 and 5 |
| 18 | ▼ | □ | ▼ | ○ | ○ | ▼ | Read texts 1, 3 and 6 |
| 19 | ▼ | □ | ▼ | ▼ | ▼ | ○ | Read texts 1, 3, 4 and 5 |
| 20 | ▼ | □ | ▼ | ▼ | ○ | ▼ | Read texts 1, 3, 4 and 6 |
| 21 | ▼ | □ | ▼ | ○ | ▼ | ▼ | Read texts 1, 3, 5 and 6 |
| 22 | ▼ | □ | ▼ | ▼ | ▼ | ▼ | Read texts 1, 3, 4, 5 and 6 |
| 23 | ▼ | □ | ○ | ▼ | ▼ | ○ | Read texts 1, 4 and 5 |
| 24 | ▼ | □ | ○ | ▼ | ○ | ▼ | Read texts 1, 4 and 6 |
| 25 | ▼ | □ | ○ | ▼ | ▼ | ▼ | Read texts 1, 4, 5 and 6 |
| 26 | ▼ | □ | ○ | ○ | ▼ | ▼ | Read texts 1, 5 and 6 |
| 27 | ○ | ▲ | ▼ | ○ | ○ | ○ | Read texts 2 and 3 |
| 28 | ○ | ▲ | ○ | ▼ | ○ | ○ | Read texts 2 and 4 |
| 29 | ○ | ▲ | ○ | ○ | ▼ | ○ | Read texts 2 and 5 |
| 30 | ○ | ▲ | ○ | ○ | ○ | ▼ | Read texts 2 and 6 |
| 31 | ○ | ▲ | ▼ | ▼ | ○ | ○ | Read texts 2, 3 and 4 |
| 32 | ○ | ▲ | ▼ | ○ | ▼ | ○ | Read texts 2, 3 and 5 |
| 33 | ○ | ▲ | ▼ | ○ | ○ | ▼ | Read texts 2, 3 and 6 |
| 34 | ○ | ▲ | ▼ | ▼ | ▼ | ○ | Read texts 2, 3, 4 and 5 |
| 35 | ○ | ▲ | ▼ | ▼ | ○ | ▼ | Read texts 2, 3, 4 and 6 |
| 36 | ○ | ▲ | ▼ | ▼ | ▼ | ▼ | Read texts 2, 3, 4, 5 and 6 |
| 37 | ○ | ▲ | ○ | ▼ | ▼ | ○ | Read texts 2, 4 and 5 |
| 38 | ○ | ▲ | ○ | ▼ | ○ | ▼ | Read texts 2, 4 and 6 |
| 39 | ○ | ▲ | ○ | ▼ | ▼ | ▼ | Read texts 2, 4, 5 and 6 |
| 40 | ○ | ▲ | ○ | ○ | ▼ | ▼ | Read texts 2, 5 and 6 |
| 41 | ○ | □ | ▼ | ▼ | ○ | ○ | Read texts 3 and 4 |
| 42 | ○ | □ | ▼ | ○ | ▼ | ○ | Read texts 3 and 5 |
| 43 | ○ | □ | ▼ | ○ | ○ | ▼ | Read texts 3 and 6 |
| 44 | ○ | □ | ▼ | ▼ | ▼ | ○ | Read texts 3, 4 and 5 |
| 45 | ○ | □ | ▼ | ▼ | ○ | ▼ | Read texts 3, 4 and 6 |
| 46 | ○ | □ | ▼ | ○ | ▼ | ▼ | Read texts 3, 5 and 6 |
| 47 | ○ | □ | ▼ | ▼ | ▼ | ▼ | Read texts 3, 4, 5 and 6 |
| 48 | ○ | □ | ○ | ▼ | ▼ | ○ | Read texts 4 and 5 |
| 49 | ○ | □ | ○ | ▼ | ○ | ▼ | Read texts 4 and 6 |
| 50 | ○ | □ | ○ | ▼ | ▼ | ▼ | Read texts 4, 5 and 6 |
| 51 | ○ | □ | ○ | ○ | ▼ | ▼ | Read texts 5 and 6 |
| 52 | ▼ | □ | ○ | ○ | ○ | ○ | Read text 1 |
| 53 | ○ | ▲ | ○ | ○ | ○ | ○ | Read text 2 |
| 54 | ○ | □ | ▼ | ○ | ○ | ○ | Read text 3 |
| 55 | ○ | □ | ○ | ▼ | ○ | ○ | Read text 4 |
| 56 | ○ | □ | ○ | ○ | ▼ | ○ | Read text 5 |
| 57 | ○ | □ | ○ | ○ | ○ | ▼ | Read text 6 |

**8th combination**

| fig. | | | | | | | Read |
|---|---|---|---|---|---|---|---|
| 1 | ▼ | ▼ | ○ | ○ | □ | ○ | Read texts 1 and 2 |
| 2 | ▼ | ○ | ▼ | ○ | □ | ○ | Read texts 1 and 3 |
| 3 | ▼ | ○ | ○ | ▼ | □ | ○ | Read texts 1 and 4 |
| 4 | ▼ | ○ | ○ | ○ | ▲ | ○ | Read texts 1 and 5 |
| 5 | ▼ | ○ | ○ | ○ | □ | ▼ | Read texts 1 and 6 |
| 6 | ▼ | ▼ | ▼ | ○ | □ | ○ | Read texts 1, 2 and 3 |
| 7 | ▼ | ▼ | ○ | ▼ | □ | ○ | Read texts 1, 2 and 4 |
| 8 | ▼ | ▼ | ○ | ○ | ▲ | ○ | Read texts 1, 2 and 5 |
| 9 | ▼ | ▼ | ○ | ○ | □ | ▼ | Read texts 1, 2 and 6 |
| 10 | ▼ | ▼ | ▼ | ▼ | □ | ○ | Read texts 1, 2, 3 and 4 |
| 11 | ▼ | ▼ | ▼ | ○ | ▲ | ○ | Read texts 1, 2, 3 and 5 |
| 12 | ▼ | ▼ | ▼ | ○ | □ | ▼ | Read texts 1, 2, 3 and 6 |
| 13 | ▼ | ▼ | ▼ | ▼ | ▲ | ○ | Read texts 1, 2, 3, 4 and 5 |
| 14 | ▼ | ▼ | ▼ | ▼ | □ | ▼ | Read texts 1, 2, 3, 4 and 6 |
| 15 | ▼ | ▼ | ▼ | ▼ | ▲ | ▼ | Read texts 1, 2, 3, 4, 5 and 6 |
| 16 | ▼ | ○ | ▼ | ▼ | □ | ○ | Read texts 1, 3 and 4 |
| 17 | ▼ | ○ | ▼ | ○ | ▲ | ○ | Read texts 1, 3 and 5 |
| 18 | ▼ | ○ | ▼ | ○ | □ | ▼ | Read texts 1, 3 and 6 |
| 19 | ▼ | ○ | ▼ | ▼ | ▲ | ○ | Read texts 1, 3, 4 and 5 |
| 20 | ▼ | ○ | ▼ | ▼ | □ | ▼ | Read texts 1, 3, 4 and 6 |
| 21 | ▼ | ○ | ▼ | ○ | ▲ | ▼ | Read texts 1, 3, 5 and 6 |
| 22 | ▼ | ○ | ▼ | ▼ | ▲ | ▼ | Read texts 1, 3, 4, 5 and 6 |
| 23 | ▼ | ○ | ○ | ▼ | ▲ | ○ | Read texts 1, 4 and 5 |
| 24 | ▼ | ○ | ○ | ▼ | □ | ▼ | Read texts 1, 4 and 6 |
| 25 | ▼ | ○ | ○ | ▼ | ▲ | ▼ | Read texts 1, 4, 5 and 6 |
| 26 | ▼ | ○ | ○ | ○ | ▲ | ▼ | Read texts 1, 5 and 6 |
| 27 | ○ | ▼ | ▼ | ○ | □ | ○ | Read texts 2 and 3 |
| 28 | ○ | ▼ | ○ | ▼ | □ | ○ | Read texts 2 and 4 |
| 29 | ○ | ▼ | ○ | ○ | ▲ | ○ | Read texts 2 and 5 |
| 30 | ○ | ▼ | ○ | ○ | □ | ▼ | Read texts 2 and 6 |
| 31 | ○ | ▼ | ▼ | ▼ | □ | ○ | Read texts 2, 3 and 4 |
| 32 | ○ | ▼ | ▼ | ○ | ▲ | ○ | Read texts 2, 3 and 5 |
| 33 | ○ | ▼ | ▼ | ○ | □ | ▼ | Read texts 2, 3 and 6 |
| 34 | ○ | ▼ | ▼ | ▼ | ▲ | ○ | Read texts 1, 3 and 6 |
| 35 | ○ | ▼ | ▼ | ▼ | □ | ▼ | Read texts 2, 3, 4 and 5 |
| 36 | ○ | ▼ | ▼ | ▼ | ▲ | ▼ | Read texts 2, 3, 4 and 6 |
| 37 | ○ | ▼ | ○ | ▼ | ▲ | ○ | Read texts 2, 4 and 5 |
| 38 | ○ | ▼ | ○ | ▼ | □ | ▼ | Read texts 2, 4 and 6 |
| 39 | ○ | ▼ | ○ | ▼ | ▲ | ▼ | Read texts 2, 4, 5 and 6 |
| 40 | ○ | ▼ | ○ | ○ | ▲ | ▼ | Read texts 2, 5 and 6 |
| 41 | ○ | ○ | ▼ | ▼ | □ | ○ | Read texts 3 and 4 |
| 42 | ○ | ○ | ▼ | ○ | ▲ | ○ | Read texts 3 and 5 |
| 43 | ○ | ○ | ▼ | ○ | □ | ▼ | Read texts 3 and 6 |
| 44 | ○ | ○ | ▼ | ▼ | ▲ | ○ | Read texts 3, 4 and 5 |
| 45 | ○ | ○ | ▼ | ▼ | □ | ▼ | Read texts 3, 4 and 6 |
| 46 | ○ | ○ | ▼ | ○ | ▲ | ▼ | Read texts 3, 5 and 6 |
| 47 | ○ | ○ | ▼ | ▼ | ▲ | ▼ | Read texts 3, 4, 5 and 6 |
| 48 | ○ | ○ | ○ | ▼ | ▲ | ○ | Read texts 4 and 5 |
| 49 | ○ | ○ | ○ | ▼ | □ | ▼ | Read texts 4 and 6 |
| 50 | ○ | ○ | ○ | ▼ | ▲ | ▼ | Read texts 4, 5 and 6 |
| 51 | ○ | ○ | ○ | ○ | ▲ | ▼ | Read texts 5 and 6 |
| 52 | ▼ | ○ | ○ | ○ | □ | ○ | Read text 1 |
| 53 | ○ | ▼ | ○ | ○ | □ | ○ | Read text 2 |
| 54 | ○ | ○ | ▼ | ○ | □ | ○ | Read text 3 |
| 55 | ○ | ○ | ○ | ▼ | □ | ○ | Read text 4 |
| 56 | ○ | ○ | ○ | ○ | ▲ | ○ | Read text 5 |
| 57 | ○ | ○ | ○ | ○ | □ | ▼ | Read text 6 |

desired outcome you will suffer the consequences, as will anyone else directly or indirectly involved in this affair. It would be a wise move to abandon this futile battle and everyone would be grateful.

**5** You have no choice but to defend yourself against attacks you can no longer ignore. You must act firmly and consistently, with complete clarity. It is essential to put a proper strategy in place, so that everyone knows and agrees the part they have to play in the scheme of things. That way, your resistance will not be futile.

**6** By putting up a tough fight you have ended a conflict and been vindicated. It is good to show your gratitude to those who helped you in this delicate and dangerous task. However, you must not feel that you owe them more than is legitimate and necessary. Otherwise they may take advantage and you will be responsible for this ambivalent situation.

# 8<sup>th</sup> combination ○ ○ ● ○ □ ○

Your natural qualities, talents, skills and experience give you two choices: either to surround yourself with those who share your feelings and interests, guiding and encouraging them by fully accepting this responsibility, or you can join an existing group, devote yourself to their cause and help them achieve their objectives.

**1** You aspire to become part of a group with whom you feel a natural affinity, or else you are about to come into contact with somebody who shares your vision. In either case you wonder what stance to adopt. Simple: just express your desires and feelings sincerely and spontaneously, and show yourself exactly as you are.

2   If you are driven to form or maintain certain key relationships by calculation or self-interest, sooner or later you risk discredit and bitter disappointment. On the other hand, if you simply respond to the interests or feelings others show towards you, your relationships will be enriching, stimulating and sincere.

3   Circumstances have thrown you together with people who do not share your interests, or with whom you have nothing in common. Don't get any closer to these people than is absolutely necessary. Do what you have to do with them, but do not expect to form tighter bonds.

4   You are in contact with a fairly influential person, on whose support you can rely. To this end, do not be shy about making clear what you expect of him or her, and about demonstrating decisively that your situation or future depends on their choices and decisions. In this way you will get what you want.

5   Do not strive for others' recognition, respect or interest at any price. Instead, work to develop the qualities you have – sooner or later they are bound to be noticed by those with whom you can live and work as you would wish, and will be appreciated and considered as you deserve.

6   Learn how to prove your devotion, kindness, loyalty, and even helpfulness, if needs be. If you hesitate before carrying out the duties expected of you, or if you do not

show solidarity with those around you, you will bitterly regret not having seized the opportunity to work together for a common cause, or not committing yourself wholly and spontaneously.

# 9th combination □ □ □ ○ □ □

You are not yet in a position to get what you want or to act entirely independently. That doesn't mean there is nothing you can do, or that the future is not bright. For the moment, be content to accept your situation within this restricted framework and to assume your tasks and responsibilities with patience and diligence.

1   You have taken an initiative that is not in itself incorrect, but it cannot succeed as things stand now. You are therefore resigned to taking a step back, in order to reflect on and contemplate the situation as a whole. This is actually the only position you can take, because it would be futile to try to force events, or to attempt to reach your goal at any cost, without carefully considering the obstacles or resistance you will meet along the way.

2   You are determined to get straight to the point, not to put off until tomorrow what you think you can do, or acquire, today. However, a quick assessment of the situation will show you that others, who felt as you do, encountered insurmountable obstacles along the way. This observation should lead you to postpone your own initiatives and to link up with others with whom you can jointly succeed.

**9th combination**

fig. 1

```
 1   ▲ ▲ □ ○ □ □   Read texts 1 and 2
 2   ▲ □ ▲ ○ □ □   Read texts 1 and 3
 3   ▲ □ □ ▼ □ □   Read texts 1 and 4
 4   ▲ □ □ ○ ▲ □   Read texts 1 and 5
 5   ▲ □ □ ○ □ ▲   Read texts 1 and 6
 6   ▲ ▲ ▲ ○ □ □   Read texts 1, 2 and 3
 7   ▲ □ ▲ ▼ □ □   Read texts 1, 3 and 4
 8   ▲ □ □ ▼ ▲ □   Read texts 1, 4 and 5
 9   ▲ □ □ ○ ▲ ▲   Read texts 1, 5 and 6
10   ▲ ▲ ▲ ▼ □ □   Read texts 1, 2, 3 and 4
11   ▲ □ ▲ ▼ ▲ □   Read texts 1, 3, 4 and 5
12   ▲ □ ▲ ▼ □ ▲   Read texts 1, 3, 4 and 6
13   ▲ □ □ ▼ ▲ ▲   Read texts 1, 4, 5 and 6
14   ▲ ▲ ▲ ▼ ▲ □   Read texts 1, 2, 3, 4 and 5
15   ▲ □ ▲ ▼ ▲ ▲   Read texts 1, 3, 4, 5 and 6
16   ▲ ▲ ▲ ▲ ▲ ▲   Read texts 1, 2, 3, 4, 5 and 6
17   □ ▲ ▲ ○ □ □   Read texts 2 and 3
18   □ ▲ □ ▼ □ □   Read texts 2 and 4
19   □ ▲ □ ○ ▲ □   Read texts 2 and 5
20   □ ▲ □ ○ □ ▲   Read texts 2 and 6
21   □ ▲ ▲ ▼ □ □   Read texts 2, 3 and 4
22   □ ▲ □ ▼ ▲ □   Read texts 2, 4 and 5
23   □ ▲ □ ○ ▲ ▲   Read texts 2, 5 and 6
24   □ ▲ ▲ ▼ ▲ □   Read texts 2, 3, 4 and 5
25   □ ▲ □ ▼ ▲ ▲   Read texts 2, 4, 5 and 6
26   □ ▲ ▲ ▼ ▲ ▲   Read texts 2, 3, 4, 5 and 6
27   ▲ ▲ □ ▼ □ □   Read texts 1, 2 and 4
28   ▲ ▲ □ ○ ▲ □   Read texts 1, 2 and 5
29   ▲ ▲ □ ○ □ ▲   Read texts 1, 2 and 6
30   ▲ ▲ ▲ ○ ▲ □   Read texts 1, 2, 3 and 5
31   ▲ ▲ ▲ ○ □ ▲   Read texts 1, 2, 3 and 6
32   ▲ ▲ ▲ ▼ □ ▲   Read texts 1, 2, 3, 4 and 6
33   ▲ □ ▲ ○ ▲ □   Read texts 1, 3 and 5
34   ▲ □ ▲ ○ □ ▲   Read texts 1, 3 and 6
35   ▲ □ ▲ ○ ▲ ▲   Read texts 1, 3, 5 and 6
36   ▲ □ □ ▼ □ ▲   Read texts 1, 4 and 6
37   □ ▲ ▲ ○ ▲ □   Read texts 2, 3 and 5
38   □ ▲ ▲ ○ □ ▲   Read texts 2, 3 and 6
39   □ ▲ ▲ ▼ □ ▲   Read texts 2, 3, 4 and 6
40   □ ▲ □ ▼ □ ▲   Read texts 2, 4 and 6
41   □ □ ▲ ▼ □ □   Read texts 3 and 4
42   □ □ ▲ ○ ▲ □   Read texts 3 and 5
43   □ □ ▲ ○ □ ▲   Read texts 3 and 6
44   □ □ ▲ ▼ ▲ □   Read texts 3, 4 and 5
45   □ □ ▲ ▼ □ ▲   Read texts 3, 4 and 6
46   □ □ ▲ ○ ▲ ▲   Read texts 3, 5 and 6
47   □ □ ▲ ▼ ▲ ▲   Read texts 3, 4, 5 and 6
48   □ □ □ ▼ ▲ □   Read texts 4 and 5
49   □ □ □ ▼ □ ▲   Read texts 4 and 6
50   □ □ □ ▼ ▲ ▲   Read texts 4, 5 and 6
51   □ □ □ ○ ▲ ▲   Read texts 5 and 6
52   ▲ □ □ ○ □ □   Read text 1
53   □ ▲ □ ○ □ □   Read text 2
54   □ □ ▲ ○ □ □   Read text 3
55   □ □ □ ▼ □ □   Read text 4
56   □ □ □ ○ ▲ □   Read text 5
57   □ □ □ ○ □ ▲   Read text 6
```

**3** You made an incorrect assessment of your chances of success, and this error of judgment has led you to act prematurely, or to try to force something through at an inappropriate moment. By acting or reacting too quickly and not taking circumstances into account, you have caused a clash that has not helped matters. Because of this, things will go badly for you, even though by rights you should have succeeded.

**4** You are involved with somebody hot-tempered, who refuses to listen to reason or take any notice of appeals for calm. However, if you demonstrate your sincerity, devotion and concern, this person will come over to your way of thinking, and the situation will not worsen.

**5** Someone close to you is unquestionably upright and honest, so you can be sure that his or her devotion to you is entirely sincere. In exchange, be sure to show your unconditional loyalty, in order to work together and to share equally the good things to come.

**6** You have certainly achieved a result to be proud of, as your current success is entirely due to your own merits. Nevertheless, do not let this go to your head and, for now, be content to reinforce and stabilize your position, because if, flushed with success, you tried to push things even further, your attempts would end in failure and you would lose all you have gained.

# 10<sup>th</sup> combination □ □ ○ □ □ □

You are currently involved with people who are difficult, unsociable, oversensitive or defensive. All you have to do to win them over is to remain polite. However, it is important that everyone should be in a position that suits his or her own particular abilities, skills and merits: otherwise demands, disagreements and conflicts are almost inevitable.

1   You are now in a position to exercise your independence fully, and to express your wishes as you see fit. Do not automatically consider your humble situation or your lack of assets to be a handicap. On the contrary, think of them as critical elements in your progress, as factors stimulating you to take on challenges or tasks of which you can be proud.

2   Whatever your circumstances, stay on track and remain constant in your choices. Follow your own path without worrying about what is happening elsewhere, and resist any tempting offers that may come along. In this way you will reach your goal and, more importantly, you will spare yourself many problems and difficulties.

3   Before taking on anything daring or risky, learn to assess your strengths, chances and capabilities. If you overestimate your own, or underestimate those of your opponents, you will inevitably come off worst and will find it difficult to get back on your feet. If this happens, you will have only yourself to blame.

| | | | | | | | |
|---|---|---|---|---|---|---|---|
| fig. 1 | ▲ | ▲ | ○ | □ | □ | □ | Read texts 1 and 2 |
| 2 | ▲ | □ | ▼ | □ | □ | □ | Read texts 1 and 3 |
| 3 | ▲ | □ | ○ | ▲ | □ | □ | Read texts 1 and 4 |
| 4 | ▲ | □ | ○ | □ | ▲ | □ | Read texts 1 and 5 |
| 5 | ▲ | □ | ○ | □ | □ | ▲ | Read texts 1 and 6 |
| 6 | ▲ | ▲ | ▼ | □ | □ | □ | Read texts 1, 2 and 3 |
| 7 | ▲ | □ | ▼ | ▲ | □ | □ | Read texts 1, 3 and 4 |
| 8 | ▲ | □ | ○ | ▲ | ▲ | □ | Read texts 1, 4 and 5 |
| 9 | ▲ | □ | ○ | □ | ▲ | ▲ | Read texts 1, 5 and 6 |
| 10 | ▲ | ▲ | ▼ | ▲ | □ | □ | Read texts 1, 2, 3 and 4 |
| 11 | ▲ | □ | ▼ | ▲ | ▲ | □ | Read texts 1, 3, 4 and 5 |
| 12 | ▲ | □ | ▼ | ▲ | □ | ▲ | Read texts 1, 3, 4 and 6 |
| 13 | ▲ | □ | ○ | ▲ | ▲ | ▲ | Read texts 1, 4, 5 and 6 |
| 14 | ▲ | ▲ | ▼ | ▲ | ▲ | □ | Read texts 1, 2, 3, 4 and 5 |
| 15 | ▲ | □ | ▼ | ▲ | ▲ | ▲ | Read texts 1, 3, 4, 5 and 6 |
| 16 | ▲ | ▲ | ▼ | ▲ | ▲ | ▲ | Read texts 1, 2, 3, 4, 5 and 6 |
| 17 | □ | ▲ | ▼ | □ | □ | □ | Read texts 2 and 3 |
| 18 | □ | ▲ | ○ | ▲ | □ | □ | Read texts 2 and 4 |
| 19 | □ | ▲ | ○ | □ | ▲ | □ | Read texts 2 and 5 |
| 20 | □ | ▲ | ○ | □ | □ | ▲ | Read texts 2 and 6 |
| 21 | □ | ▲ | ▼ | ▲ | □ | □ | Read texts 2, 3 and 4 |
| 22 | □ | ▲ | ○ | ▲ | ▲ | □ | Read texts 2, 4 and 5 |
| 23 | □ | ▲ | ○ | ▲ | □ | ▲ | Read texts 2, 5 and 6 |
| 24 | □ | ▲ | ▼ | ▲ | ▲ | □ | Read texts 2, 3, 4 and 5 |
| 25 | □ | ▲ | ○ | ▲ | ▲ | ▲ | Read texts 2, 4, 5 and 6 |
| 26 | □ | ▲ | ▼ | ▲ | ▲ | ▲ | Read texts 2, 3, 4, 5 and 6 |
| 27 | ▲ | ▲ | ○ | ▲ | □ | □ | Read texts 1, 2 and 4 |
| 28 | ▲ | ▲ | ○ | □ | ▲ | □ | Read texts 1, 2 and 5 |
| 29 | ▲ | ▲ | ○ | □ | □ | ▲ | Read texts 1, 2 and 6 |
| 30 | ▲ | ▲ | ▼ | □ | ▲ | □ | Read texts 1, 2, 3 and 5 |
| 31 | ▲ | ▲ | ▼ | □ | □ | ▲ | Read texts 1, 2, 3 and 6 |
| 32 | ▲ | ▲ | ▼ | ▲ | □ | ▲ | Read texts 1, 2, 3, 4 and 6 |
| 33 | ▲ | □ | ▼ | □ | ▲ | □ | Read texts 1, 3 and 5 |
| 34 | ▲ | □ | ▼ | □ | □ | ▲ | Read texts 1, 3 and 6 |
| 35 | ▲ | □ | ▼ | □ | ▲ | ▲ | Read texts 1, 3, 5 and 6 |
| 36 | ▲ | □ | ○ | ▲ | □ | ▲ | Read texts 1, 4 and 6 |
| 37 | □ | ▲ | ▼ | □ | ▲ | □ | Read texts 2, 3 and 5 |
| 38 | □ | ▲ | ▼ | □ | □ | ▲ | Read texts 2, 3 and 6 |
| 39 | □ | ▲ | ▼ | ▲ | □ | ▲ | Read texts 2, 3, 4 and 6 |
| 40 | □ | ▲ | ○ | ▲ | □ | ▲ | Read texts 2, 4 and 6 |
| 41 | □ | □ | ▼ | ▲ | □ | □ | Read texts 3 and 4 |
| 42 | □ | □ | ▼ | □ | ▲ | □ | Read texts 3 and 5 |
| 43 | □ | □ | ▼ | □ | □ | ▲ | Read texts 3 and 6 |
| 44 | □ | □ | ▼ | ▲ | ▲ | □ | Read texts 3, 4 and 5 |
| 45 | □ | □ | ▼ | ▲ | □ | ▲ | Read texts 3, 4 and 6 |
| 46 | □ | □ | ▼ | □ | ▲ | ▲ | Read texts 3, 5 and 6 |
| 47 | □ | □ | ▼ | ▲ | ▲ | ▲ | Read texts 3, 4, 5 and 6 |
| 48 | □ | □ | ○ | ▲ | ▲ | □ | Read texts 4 and 5 |
| 49 | □ | □ | ○ | ▲ | □ | ▲ | Read texts 4 and 6 |
| 50 | □ | □ | ○ | ▲ | ▲ | ▲ | Read texts 4, 5 and 6 |
| 51 | □ | □ | ○ | □ | ▲ | ▲ | Read texts 5 and 6 |
| 52 | ▲ | □ | ○ | □ | □ | □ | Read text 1 |
| 53 | □ | ▲ | ○ | □ | □ | □ | Read text 2 |
| 54 | □ | □ | ▼ | □ | □ | □ | Read text 3 |
| 55 | □ | □ | ○ | ▲ | □ | □ | Read text 4 |
| 56 | □ | □ | ○ | □ | ▲ | □ | Read text 5 |
| 57 | □ | □ | ○ | □ | □ | ▲ | Read text 6 |

10th combination □ □ ○ □ □ □

273

**11th combination**

| | | | | | | | | |
|---|---|---|---|---|---|---|---|---|
| fig. 1 | ▲ | ▲ | □ | ○ | ○ | ○ | Read texts 1 and 2 |
| 2 | ▲ | □ | ▲ | ○ | ○ | ○ | Read texts 1 and 3 |
| 3 | ▲ | □ | □ | ▼ | ○ | ○ | Read texts 1 and 4 |
| 4 | ▲ | □ | □ | ○ | ▼ | ○ | Read texts 1 and 5 |
| 5 | ▲ | □ | □ | ○ | ○ | ▼ | Read texts 1 and 6 |
| 6 | ▲ | ▲ | ▲ | ○ | ○ | ○ | Read texts 1, 2 and 3 |
| 7 | ▲ | □ | ▲ | ▼ | ○ | ○ | Read texts 1, 3 and 4 |
| 8 | ▲ | □ | □ | ▼ | ▼ | ○ | Read texts 1, 4 and 5 |
| 9 | ▲ | □ | □ | ○ | ▼ | ▼ | Read texts 1, 5 and 6 |
| 10 | ▲ | ▲ | ▲ | ▼ | ○ | ○ | Read texts 1, 2, 3 and 4 |
| 11 | ▲ | □ | ▲ | ▼ | ▼ | ○ | Read texts 1, 3, 4 and 5 |
| 12 | ▲ | □ | ▲ | ▼ | ○ | ▼ | Read texts 1, 3, 4 and 6 |
| 13 | ▲ | □ | □ | ▼ | ▼ | ▼ | Read texts 1, 4, 5 and 6 |
| 14 | ▲ | ▲ | ▲ | ▼ | ▼ | ○ | Read texts 1, 2, 3, 4 and 5 |
| 15 | ▲ | □ | ▲ | ▼ | ▼ | ▼ | Read texts 1, 3, 4, 5 and 6 |
| 16 | ▲ | ▲ | ▲ | ▼ | ▼ | ▼ | Read texts 1, 2, 3, 4, 5 and 6 |
| 17 | □ | ▲ | ▲ | ○ | ○ | ○ | Read texts 2 and 3 |
| 18 | □ | ▲ | □ | ▼ | ○ | ○ | Read texts 2 and 4 |
| 19 | □ | ▲ | □ | ○ | ▼ | ○ | Read texts 2 and 5 |
| 20 | □ | ▲ | □ | ○ | ○ | ▼ | Read texts 2 and 6 |
| 21 | □ | ▲ | ▲ | ▼ | ○ | ○ | Read texts 2, 3 and 4 |
| 22 | □ | ▲ | □ | ▼ | ▼ | ○ | Read texts 2, 4 and 5 |
| 23 | □ | ▲ | □ | ○ | ▼ | ▼ | Read texts 2, 5 and 6 |
| 24 | □ | ▲ | ▲ | ▼ | ▼ | ○ | Read texts 2, 3, 4 and 5 |
| 25 | □ | ▲ | □ | ▼ | ▼ | ▼ | Read texts 2, 4, 5 and 6 |
| 26 | □ | ▲ | ▲ | ▼ | ▼ | ▼ | Read texts 2, 3, 4, 5 and 6 |
| 27 | ▲ | ▲ | □ | ▼ | ○ | ○ | Read texts 1, 2 and 4 |
| 28 | ▲ | ▲ | □ | ○ | ▼ | ○ | Read texts 1, 2 and 5 |
| 29 | ▲ | ▲ | □ | ○ | ○ | ▼ | Read texts 1, 2 and 6 |
| 30 | ▲ | ▲ | ▲ | ○ | ▼ | ○ | Read texts 1, 2, 3 and 5 |
| 31 | ▲ | ▲ | ▲ | ○ | ○ | ▼ | Read texts 1, 2, 3 and 6 |
| 32 | ▲ | ▲ | ▲ | ▼ | ○ | ▼ | Read texts 1, 2, 3, 4 and 6 |
| 33 | ▲ | □ | ▲ | ○ | ▼ | ○ | Read texts 1, 3 and 5 |
| 34 | ▲ | □ | ▲ | ○ | ○ | ▼ | Read texts 1, 3 and 6 |
| 35 | ▲ | □ | ▲ | ○ | ▼ | ▼ | Read texts 1, 3, 5 and 6 |
| 36 | ▲ | □ | □ | ▼ | ○ | ▼ | Read texts 1, 4 and 6 |
| 37 | □ | ▲ | ▲ | ○ | ▼ | ○ | Read texts 2, 3 and 5 |
| 38 | □ | ▲ | ▲ | ○ | ○ | ▼ | Read texts 2, 3 and 6 |
| 39 | □ | ▲ | ▲ | ▼ | ○ | ▼ | Read texts 2, 3, 4 and 6 |
| 40 | □ | ▲ | □ | ▼ | ○ | ▼ | Read texts 2, 4 and 6 |
| 41 | □ | □ | ▲ | ▼ | ○ | ○ | Read texts 3 and 4 |
| 42 | □ | □ | ▲ | ○ | ▼ | ○ | Read texts 3 and 5 |
| 43 | □ | □ | ▲ | ○ | ○ | ▼ | Read texts 3 and 6 |
| 44 | □ | □ | ▲ | ▼ | ▼ | ○ | Read texts 3, 4 and 5 |
| 45 | □ | □ | ▲ | ▼ | ○ | ▼ | Read texts 3, 4 and 6 |
| 46 | □ | □ | ▲ | ○ | ▼ | ▼ | Read texts 3, 5 and 6 |
| 47 | □ | □ | ▲ | ▼ | ▼ | ▼ | Read texts 3, 4, 5 and 6 |
| 48 | □ | □ | □ | ▼ | ▼ | ○ | Read texts 4 and 5 |
| 49 | □ | □ | □ | ▼ | ○ | ▼ | Read texts 4 and 6 |
| 50 | □ | □ | □ | ▼ | ▼ | ▼ | Read texts 4, 5 and 6 |
| 51 | □ | □ | □ | ○ | ▼ | ▼ | Read texts 5 and 6 |
| 52 | ▲ | □ | □ | ○ | ○ | ○ | Read text 1 |
| 53 | □ | ▲ | □ | ○ | ○ | ○ | Read text 2 |
| 54 | □ | □ | ▲ | ○ | ○ | ○ | Read text 3 |
| 55 | □ | □ | □ | ▼ | ○ | ○ | Read text 4 |
| 56 | □ | □ | □ | ○ | ▼ | ○ | Read text 5 |
| 57 | □ | □ | □ | ○ | ○ | ▼ | Read text 6 |

**4**  You are about to do something that is dangerous, daring or not without risk. However, you are not blindly hurling yourself into a foolhardy venture; you are taking the time to think, in order to evaluate your best chances of success. This is clearly a very positive attitude that promises a happy conclusion.

**5**  You are determined to forge ahead, and see your actions through to the end, whatever obstacles or difficulties you encounter en route. This determination will ensure that you reach your goals, provided that you remain constantly aware of the risks you are taking and the dangers you will meet along the way.

**6**  Now that you have reached your goals, in order to make sure of your success consider the means you employed to achieve them. If you believe that you did the right thing in all circumstances, that your actions were worthy of respect and that you have achieved your objective, then your success is genuine. The things we do, and the results we achieve, tell us about the quality of our future.

# 11<sup>th</sup> combination □ □ □ ○ ○ ○

To obtain the best possible results in every situation, all you have to do is work in harmony with the people around you, with your environment and with circumstances, and to choose the appropriate moment. If you bear these things in mind, your activities will be productive.

**1**   Your current situation is just about as good as it gets. Stop wondering when and whether to take action or to start something ambitious. The answer lies under your nose: these circumstances are highly favourable, and are clearly giving you the green light.

**2**   You hold all the trump cards you need to succeed and to profit from the current, highly advantageous circumstances. All the same, you should be firm but fair in dealing with those you think are not up to the job, and must not give in to pressure from those who may be worthy but are rather clannish. This is a good attitude to adopt and will ensure your success.

**3**   Circumstances are constantly changing. You should certainly take this into account, but do not let yourself be influenced or thrown off course by the ever-changing vagaries of destiny. Instead, learn to develop and cultivate your inner qualities, aptitudes and talents, which are resistant to and unaffected by external matters. For this reason, positive or negative developments in any situation will have not the slightest affect on your state of mind or your behaviour.

**4**   You are entirely at ease with yourself, true to your principles and to your ideas. This happy disposition enables you to associate with people who are better off than you are, and who spontaneously offer to help or support you. You can accept their assistance without hesitation.

**5**   At present you enjoy extremely advantageous circumstances, or are in an ideal situation. At times like these, everything you do or acquire will turn to your advantage and prove entirely satisfactory.

**6**   It would be pointless to fight against the negative circumstances that confront you, and might even be dangerous for you and for your future. Indecision or a refusal to accept the truth of the matter would only make things worse. Accept this and adopt an attitude of withdrawal. This is the only way to avoid more serious damage.

# 12<sup>th</sup> combination ○ ○ ○ ❑ ❑ ❑

You are in contact with people whose life rules are totally at odds with your own. To curry favour, take part in their activities or to collude with them would go against your deepest convictions and would catapult you into an ambiguous and dangerous situation. Therefore avoid all dealings with them.

**1**   You must proceed with extreme caution, because of your current situation or associates. The correct attitude to adopt in circumstances like these is one of withdrawal. Take no decision that is not in keeping with your deepest convictions. Instead, retreat as far as is necessary.

**2**   Someone will probably try to involve you or to exploit your skills and qualities. But do not give in to pressure or temptation to put yourself at the disposal of others. You will only become a pawn in someone else's affair, one that does not match your own deeply held convictions. Do not get involved, even if this inertia or impasse means that you too could suffer the consequences.

| fig. 1 | ▼ | ▼ | ○ | □ | □ | □ | Read texts 1 and 2 |
|---|---|---|---|---|---|---|---|
| 2 | ▼ | ○ | ▼ | □ | □ | □ | Read texts 1 and 3 |
| 3 | ▼ | ○ | ○ | ▲ | □ | □ | Read texts 1 and 4 |
| 4 | ▼ | ○ | ○ | □ | ▲ | □ | Read texts 1 and 5 |
| 5 | ▼ | ○ | ○ | □ | □ | ▲ | Read texts 1 and 6 |
| 6 | ▼ | ▼ | ▼ | □ | □ | □ | Read texts 1, 2 and 3 |
| 7 | ▼ | ○ | ▼ | ▲ | □ | □ | Read texts 1, 3 and 4 |
| 8 | ▼ | ○ | ▲ | ▲ | □ | □ | Read texts 1, 4 and 5 |
| 9 | ▼ | ○ | ○ | □ | ▲ | ▲ | Read texts 1, 5 and 6 |
| 10 | ▼ | ▼ | ▼ | ▲ | □ | □ | Read texts 1, 2, 3 and 4 |
| 11 | ▼ | ○ | ▼ | ▲ | ▲ | □ | Read texts 1, 3, 4 and 5 |
| 12 | ▼ | ○ | ▼ | ▲ | □ | ▲ | Read texts 1, 3, 4 and 6 |
| 13 | ▼ | ○ | ○ | ▲ | ▲ | ▲ | Read texts 1, 4, 5 and 6 |
| 14 | ▼ | ▼ | ▼ | ▲ | ▲ | □ | Read texts 1, 2, 3, 4 and 5 |
| 15 | ▼ | ○ | ▼ | ▲ | ▲ | ▲ | Read texts 1, 3, 4, 5 and 6 |
| 16 | ▼ | ▼ | ▼ | ▲ | ▲ | ▲ | Read texts 1, 2, 3, 4, 5 and 6 |
| 17 | ○ | ▼ | ▼ | □ | □ | □ | Read texts 2 and 3 |
| 18 | ○ | ▼ | ○ | ▲ | □ | □ | Read texts 2 and 4 |
| 19 | ○ | ▼ | ○ | □ | ▲ | □ | Read texts 2 and 5 |
| 20 | ○ | ▼ | ○ | □ | □ | ▲ | Read texts 2 and 6 |
| 21 | ○ | ▼ | ▼ | ▲ | □ | □ | Read texts 2, 3 and 4 |
| 22 | ○ | ▼ | ○ | ▲ | ▲ | □ | Read texts 2, 4 and 5 |
| 23 | ○ | ▼ | ○ | □ | ▲ | ▲ | Read texts 2, 5 and 6 |
| 24 | ○ | ▼ | ▼ | ▲ | ▲ | □ | Read texts 2, 3, 4 and 5 |
| 25 | ○ | ▼ | ○ | ▲ | ▲ | ▲ | Read texts 2, 4, 5 and 6 |
| 26 | ○ | ▼ | ▼ | ▲ | ▲ | ▲ | Read texts 2, 3, 4, 5 and 6 |
| 27 | ▼ | ▼ | ○ | ▲ | □ | □ | Read texts 1, 2 and 4 |
| 28 | ▼ | ▼ | ○ | □ | ▲ | □ | Read texts 1, 2 and 5 |
| 29 | ▼ | ▼ | ○ | □ | □ | ▲ | Read texts 1, 2 and 6 |
| 30 | ▼ | ▼ | ▼ | □ | ▲ | □ | Read texts 1, 2, 3 and 5 |
| 31 | ▼ | ▼ | ▼ | □ | □ | ▲ | Read texts 1, 2, 3 and 6 |
| 32 | ▼ | ▼ | ▼ | ▲ | □ | ▲ | Read texts 1, 2, 3, 4 and 6 |
| 33 | ▼ | ○ | ▼ | □ | ▲ | □ | Read texts 1, 3 and 5 |
| 34 | ▼ | ○ | ▼ | □ | □ | ▲ | Read texts 1, 3 and 6 |
| 35 | ▼ | ○ | ▼ | □ | ▲ | ▲ | Read texts 1, 3, 5 and 6 |
| 36 | ▼ | ○ | ○ | ▲ | □ | ▲ | Read texts 1, 4 and 6 |
| 37 | ○ | ▼ | ▼ | □ | ▲ | □ | Read texts 2, 3 and 5 |
| 38 | ○ | ▼ | ▼ | □ | □ | ▲ | Read texts 2, 3 and 6 |
| 39 | ○ | ▼ | ▼ | ▲ | □ | ▲ | Read texts 2, 3, 4 and 6 |
| 40 | ○ | ▼ | ○ | ▲ | □ | ▲ | Read texts 2, 4 and 6 |
| 41 | ○ | ○ | ▼ | ▲ | □ | □ | Read texts 3 and 4 |
| 42 | ○ | ○ | ▼ | □ | ▲ | □ | Read texts 3 and 5 |
| 43 | ○ | ○ | ▼ | □ | □ | ▲ | Read texts 3 and 6 |
| 44 | ○ | ○ | ▼ | ▲ | ▲ | □ | Read texts 3, 4 and 5 |
| 45 | ○ | ○ | ▼ | ▲ | □ | ▲ | Read texts 3, 4 and 6 |
| 46 | ○ | ○ | ▼ | □ | ▲ | ▲ | Read texts 3, 5 and 6 |
| 47 | ○ | ○ | ▼ | ▲ | ▲ | ▲ | Read texts 3, 4, 5 and 6 |
| 48 | ○ | ○ | ○ | ▲ | ▲ | □ | Read texts 4 and 5 |
| 49 | ○ | ○ | ○ | ▲ | □ | ▲ | Read texts 4 and 6 |
| 50 | ○ | ○ | ○ | ▲ | ▲ | ▲ | Read texts 4, 5 and 6 |
| 51 | ○ | ○ | ○ | □ | ▲ | ▲ | Read texts 5 and 6 |
| 52 | ▼ | ○ | ○ | □ | □ | □ | Read text 1 |
| 53 | ○ | ▼ | ○ | □ | □ | □ | Read text 2 |
| 54 | ○ | ○ | ▼ | □ | □ | □ | Read text 3 |
| 55 | ○ | ○ | ○ | ▲ | □ | □ | Read text 4 |
| 56 | ○ | ○ | ○ | □ | ▲ | □ | Read text 5 |
| 57 | ○ | ○ | ○ | □ | □ | ▲ | Read text 6 |

**12th combination**

**3** You are involved with people who may wield considerable power or influence, although they are neither worthy nor competent. But things are developing to the point where they can no longer ignore their limitations, and their pride is already shattered. This is the first sign of a positive development in your favour.

**4** You are on the brink of an important and necessary change. However, in order to succeed, you must be equal to the situation and gain the approval or support of everyone concerned. Failing this, your initiatives or vague impulses towards change will end in failure.

**5** Your situation is stable and everything seems to be ticking along nicely. However you should not rest on your laurels or think you are finally out of the woods because it is always possible that a reversal of fortune or adverse circumstances may be lurking around the corner. For this reason you are advised to remain vigilant, persevering and well prepared, in order to preserve your security, whatever happens.

**6** You are in a prosperous situation or your life is quite calm and harmonious. However, at times like these, the first signs of a decline often make their appearance. Don't neglect any such signs and take preventive action before they grow bigger and cause real problems.

# 13th combination ❒ ❍ ❒ ❒ ❒ ❒

If you associate with people whose aspirations and ambitions are identical to your own, you must not be motivated by petty self-interest. Furthermore, for the objectives of the group to be met, every member should have an appropriate place within it and must fully accept his or her responsibilities.

1 You are in a new position, or else you are associated with a new venture involving a number of people. In this kind of situation it is important for everyone to be kept informed about the role they have to play. If arrangements are made without the agreement of everyone concerned, conflict is sure to ensue.

2 You are in some way involved with people who care only about their own advancement and personal gain, and who do not give a moment's thought to the needs or desires of others. They will do anything to achieve their ends. You should be aware that an attitude like this, unilateral and self-centred, is doomed to failure sooner or later.

3 Your relationships are breaking down. You suspect others of harbouring ill intentions towards you, and they think exactly the same about you. Misunderstandings and things left unsaid are becoming ever-greater barriers to communication. You are therefore advised to take immediate action and to clear up these misconceptions, whose origins or causes may not be as serious as they seem.

| | | | | | | | |
|---|---|---|---|---|---|---|---|
| fig. 1 | ▲ | ▼ | ❒ | ❒ | ❒ | ❒ | Read texts 1 and 2 |
| 2 | ▲ | ❍ | ▲ | ❒ | ❒ | ❒ | Read texts 1 and 3 |
| 3 | ▲ | ❍ | ❒ | ▲ | ❒ | ❒ | Read texts 1 and 4 |
| 4 | ▲ | ❍ | ❒ | ❒ | ▲ | ❒ | Read texts 1 and 5 |
| 5 | ▲ | ❍ | ❒ | ❒ | ❒ | ▲ | Read texts 1 and 6 |
| 6 | ▲ | ▼ | ▲ | ❒ | ❒ | ❒ | Read texts 1, 2 and 3 |
| 7 | ▲ | ❍ | ▲ | ▲ | ❒ | ❒ | Read texts 1, 3 and 4 |
| 8 | ▲ | ❍ | ❒ | ▲ | ▲ | ❒ | Read texts 1, 4 and 5 |
| 9 | ▲ | ❍ | ❒ | ❒ | ▲ | ▲ | Read texts 1, 5 and 6 |
| 10 | ▲ | ▼ | ▲ | ▲ | ❒ | ❒ | Read texts 1, 2, 3 and 4 |
| 11 | ▲ | ❍ | ▲ | ▲ | ▲ | ❒ | Read texts 1, 3, 4 and 5 |
| 12 | ▲ | ❍ | ▲ | ▲ | ❒ | ▲ | Read texts 1, 3, 4 and 6 |
| 13 | ▲ | ❍ | ❒ | ▲ | ▲ | ▲ | Read texts 1, 4, 5 and 6 |
| 14 | ▲ | ▼ | ▲ | ▲ | ▲ | ❒ | Read texts 1, 2, 3, 4 and 5 |
| 15 | ▲ | ❍ | ▲ | ▲ | ▲ | ▲ | Read texts 1, 3, 4, 5 and 6 |
| 16 | ▲ | ▼ | ▲ | ▲ | ▲ | ▲ | Read texts 1, 2, 3, 4, 5 and 6 |
| 17 | ❒ | ▼ | ▲ | ❒ | ❒ | ❒ | Read texts 2 and 3 |
| 18 | ❒ | ▼ | ❒ | ▲ | ❒ | ❒ | Read texts 2 and 4 |
| 19 | ❒ | ▼ | ❒ | ❒ | ▲ | ❒ | Read texts 2 and 5 |
| 20 | ❒ | ▼ | ❒ | ❒ | ❒ | ▲ | Read texts 2 and 6 |
| 21 | ❒ | ▼ | ▲ | ▲ | ❒ | ❒ | Read texts 2, 3 and 4 |
| 22 | ❒ | ▼ | ❒ | ▲ | ▲ | ❒ | Read texts 2, 4 and 5 |
| 23 | ❒ | ▼ | ❒ | ❒ | ▲ | ▲ | Read texts 2, 5 and 6 |
| 24 | ❒ | ▼ | ▲ | ▲ | ▲ | ❒ | Read texts 2, 3, 4 and 5 |
| 25 | ❒ | ▼ | ❒ | ▲ | ▲ | ▲ | Read texts 2, 4, 5 and 6 |
| 26 | ❒ | ▼ | ▲ | ▲ | ▲ | ▲ | Read texts 2, 3, 4, 5 and 6 |
| 27 | ▲ | ▼ | ❒ | ▲ | ❒ | ❒ | Read texts 1, 2 and 4 |
| 28 | ▲ | ▼ | ❒ | ❒ | ▲ | ❒ | Read texts 1, 2 and 5 |
| 29 | ▲ | ▼ | ❒ | ❒ | ❒ | ▲ | Read texts 1, 2 and 6 |
| 30 | ▲ | ▼ | ▲ | ❒ | ▲ | ❒ | Read texts 1, 2, 3 and 5 |
| 31 | ▲ | ▼ | ▲ | ❒ | ❒ | ▲ | Read texts 1, 2, 3 and 6 |
| 32 | ▲ | ▼ | ▲ | ▲ | ❒ | ▲ | Read texts 1, 2, 3, 4 and 6 |
| 33 | ▲ | ❍ | ▲ | ❒ | ▲ | ❒ | Read texts 1, 3 and 5 |
| 34 | ▲ | ❍ | ▲ | ❒ | ❒ | ▲ | Read texts 1, 3 and 6 |
| 35 | ▲ | ❍ | ▲ | ❒ | ▲ | ▲ | Read texts 1, 3, 5 and 6 |
| 36 | ▲ | ❍ | ❒ | ▲ | ❒ | ▲ | Read texts 1, 4 and 6 |
| 37 | ❒ | ▼ | ▲ | ❒ | ▲ | ❒ | Read texts 2, 3 and 5 |
| 38 | ❒ | ▼ | ▲ | ❒ | ❒ | ▲ | Read texts 2, 3 and 6 |
| 39 | ❒ | ▼ | ▲ | ▲ | ❒ | ▲ | Read texts 2, 3, 4 and 6 |
| 40 | ❒ | ▼ | ❒ | ▲ | ❒ | ▲ | Read texts 2, 4 and 6 |
| 41 | ❒ | ❍ | ▲ | ▲ | ❒ | ❒ | Read texts 3 and 4 |
| 42 | ❒ | ❍ | ▲ | ❒ | ▲ | ❒ | Read texts 3 and 5 |
| 43 | ❒ | ❍ | ▲ | ❒ | ❒ | ▲ | Read texts 3 and 6 |
| 44 | ❒ | ❍ | ▲ | ▲ | ▲ | ❒ | Read texts 3, 4 and 5 |
| 45 | ❒ | ❍ | ▲ | ▲ | ❒ | ▲ | Read texts 3, 4 and 6 |
| 46 | ❒ | ❍ | ▲ | ❒ | ▲ | ▲ | Read texts 3, 5 and 6 |
| 47 | ❒ | ❍ | ▲ | ▲ | ▲ | ▲ | Read texts 3, 4, 5 and 6 |
| 48 | ❒ | ❍ | ❒ | ▲ | ▲ | ❒ | Read texts 4 and 5 |
| 49 | ❒ | ❍ | ❒ | ▲ | ❒ | ▲ | Read texts 4 and 6 |
| 50 | ❒ | ❍ | ❒ | ▲ | ▲ | ▲ | Read texts 4, 5 and 6 |
| 51 | ❒ | ❍ | ❒ | ❒ | ▲ | ▲ | Read texts 5 and 6 |
| 52 | ▲ | ❍ | ❒ | ❒ | ❒ | ❒ | Read text 1 |
| 53 | ❒ | ▼ | ❒ | ❒ | ❒ | ❒ | Read text 2 |
| 54 | ❒ | ❍ | ▲ | ❒ | ❒ | ❒ | Read text 3 |
| 55 | ❒ | ❍ | ❒ | ▲ | ❒ | ❒ | Read text 4 |
| 56 | ❒ | ❍ | ❒ | ❒ | ▲ | ❒ | Read text 5 |
| 57 | ❒ | ❍ | ❒ | ❒ | ❒ | ▲ | Read text 6 |

| | | | | | | | | |
|---|---|---|---|---|---|---|---|---|
| fig. 1 | ▲ | ▲ | □ | □ | ○ | □ | Read texts 1 and 2 |
| 2 | ▲ | □ | ▲ | □ | ○ | □ | Read texts 1 and 3 |
| 3 | ▲ | □ | □ | ▲ | ○ | □ | Read texts 1 and 4 |
| 4 | ▲ | □ | □ | □ | ▼ | □ | Read texts 1 and 5 |
| 5 | ▲ | □ | □ | □ | ○ | ▲ | Read texts 1 and 6 |
| 6 | ▲ | ▲ | ▲ | □ | ○ | □ | Read texts 1, 2 and 3 |
| 7 | ▲ | □ | ▲ | ▲ | ○ | □ | Read texts 1, 3 and 4 |
| 8 | ▲ | □ | ▲ | □ | ▼ | □ | Read texts 1, 4 and 5 |
| 9 | ▲ | □ | □ | □ | ▼ | ▲ | Read texts 1, 5 and 6 |
| 10 | ▲ | ▲ | ▲ | ▲ | ○ | □ | Read texts 1, 2, 3 and 4 |
| 11 | ▲ | □ | ▲ | ▲ | ▼ | □ | Read texts 1, 3, 4 and 5 |
| 12 | ▲ | □ | ▲ | ▲ | ○ | ▲ | Read texts 1, 3, 4 and 6 |
| 13 | ▲ | □ | □ | ▲ | ▼ | ▲ | Read texts 1, 4, 5 and 6 |
| 14 | ▲ | ▲ | ▲ | ▲ | ▼ | □ | Read texts 1, 2, 3, 4 and 5 |
| 15 | ▲ | □ | ▲ | ▲ | ▼ | ▲ | Read texts 1, 3, 4, 5 and 6 |
| 16 | ▲ | ▲ | ▲ | ▲ | ▼ | ▲ | Read texts 1, 2, 3, 4, 5 and 6 |
| 17 | □ | ▲ | ▲ | □ | ○ | □ | Read texts 2 and 3 |
| 18 | □ | ▲ | □ | ▲ | ○ | □ | Read texts 2 and 4 |
| 19 | □ | ▲ | □ | □ | ▼ | □ | Read texts 2 and 5 |
| 20 | □ | ▲ | □ | □ | ○ | ▲ | Read texts 2 and 6 |
| 21 | □ | ▲ | ▲ | ▲ | ○ | □ | Read texts 2, 3 and 4 |
| 22 | □ | ▲ | □ | ▲ | ▼ | □ | Read texts 2, 4 and 5 |
| 23 | □ | ▲ | □ | □ | ▼ | ▲ | Read texts 2, 5 and 6 |
| 24 | □ | ▲ | ▲ | ▲ | ▼ | □ | Read texts 2, 3, 4 and 5 |
| 25 | □ | ▲ | □ | ▲ | ▼ | ▲ | Read texts 2, 4, 5 and 6 |
| 26 | □ | ▲ | ▲ | ▲ | ▼ | ▲ | Read texts 2, 3, 4, 5 and 6 |
| 27 | ▲ | ▲ | □ | ▲ | ○ | □ | Read texts 1, 2 and 4 |
| 28 | ▲ | ▲ | □ | □ | ▼ | □ | Read texts 1, 2 and 5 |
| 29 | ▲ | ▲ | □ | □ | ○ | ▲ | Read texts 1, 2 and 6 |
| 30 | ▲ | ▲ | ▲ | □ | ▼ | □ | Read texts 1, 2, 3 and 5 |
| 31 | ▲ | ▲ | ▲ | □ | ○ | ▲ | Read texts 1, 2, 3 and 6 |
| 32 | ▲ | ▲ | ▲ | ▲ | ○ | ▲ | Read texts 1, 2, 3, 4 and 6 |
| 33 | ▲ | □ | ▲ | □ | ▼ | □ | Read texts 1, 3 and 5 |
| 34 | ▲ | □ | ▲ | □ | ○ | ▲ | Read texts 1, 3 and 6 |
| 35 | ▲ | □ | ▲ | □ | ▼ | ▲ | Read texts 1, 3, 5 and 6 |
| 36 | ▲ | □ | □ | ▲ | ○ | ▲ | Read texts 1, 4 and 6 |
| 37 | □ | ▲ | ▲ | □ | ▼ | □ | Read texts 2, 3 and 5 |
| 38 | □ | ▲ | ▲ | □ | ○ | ▲ | Read texts 2, 3 and 6 |
| 39 | □ | ▲ | ▲ | ▲ | ○ | ▲ | Read texts 2, 3, 4 and 6 |
| 40 | □ | ▲ | □ | ▲ | ○ | ▲ | Read texts 2, 4 and 6 |
| 41 | □ | □ | ▲ | ▲ | ○ | □ | Read texts 3 and 4 |
| 42 | □ | □ | ▲ | □ | ▼ | □ | Read texts 3 and 5 |
| 43 | □ | □ | ▲ | □ | ○ | ▲ | Read texts 3 and 6 |
| 44 | □ | □ | ▲ | ▲ | ▼ | □ | Read texts 3, 4 and 5 |
| 45 | □ | □ | ▲ | ▲ | ○ | ▲ | Read texts 3, 4 and 6 |
| 46 | □ | □ | ▲ | □ | ▼ | ▲ | Read texts 3, 5 and 6 |
| 47 | □ | □ | ▲ | ▲ | ▼ | ▲ | Read texts 3, 4, 5 and 6 |
| 48 | □ | □ | □ | ▲ | ▼ | □ | Read texts 4 and 5 |
| 49 | □ | □ | □ | ▲ | ○ | ▲ | Read texts 4 and 6 |
| 50 | □ | □ | □ | ▲ | ▼ | ▲ | Read texts 4, 5 and 6 |
| 51 | □ | □ | □ | □ | ▼ | ▲ | Read texts 5 and 6 |
| 52 | ▲ | □ | □ | □ | ○ | □ | Read text 1 |
| 53 | □ | ▲ | □ | □ | ○ | □ | Read text 2 |
| 54 | □ | □ | ▲ | □ | ○ | □ | Read text 3 |
| 55 | □ | □ | □ | ▲ | ○ | □ | Read text 4 |
| 56 | □ | □ | □ | □ | ▼ | □ | Read text 5 |
| 57 | □ | □ | □ | □ | ○ | ▲ | Read text 6 |

**14th combination**

**4**   Tension and discord are making you feel as if you have reached the point of no return. But it is precisely this feeling of being trapped in a situation that will help you find a solution to your problems. By letting go, and giving up this desperate battle, you can put an end to this difficult situation.

**5**   At present you are having difficulty finding or connecting with somebody who also wishes to meet or join forces with you. This is painful, but all is not lost if you both have the will to surmount all the obstacles that currently stand between you. When you do succeed, you will experience great happiness.

**6**   In terms of shared beliefs and principles, you do not feel particularly close to the people with whom you are currently involved. However, your relationship with them is straightforward with no ulterior motive. Be content with this for now, and wait until you can connect with others who share your preoccupations or sympathies more closely.

# 14th combination □ □ □ □ ○ □

You are now in a position to gather all the help and influential support you need to see your plans through. This is possible only because you know how to ally modesty and generosity with a determination to achieve positive action and to eliminate negative factors.

**1** You will benefit from potential riches that you have not yet tapped into, although your troubles are not quite over and it will take some time before you can enjoy them. However, if you do remain modest about your qualities and concentrate on the road left to travel, there is no reason why you should not obtain what is rightfully yours and which you deserve.

**2** You are lucky enough to have efficient, competent and reliable friends, partners or associates, whom you can entrust with delicate assignments in complete confidence. Not only will they discharge them fully, but they will also relieve you of the weight of certain obligations that you could not bear alone.

**3** Learn how to show generosity. Share your privileges or blessings freely but sensibly so that others may enjoy them. If you are tempted to keep them to yourself, or to use them selfishly, you are bound to suffer unfortunate consequences.

**4** However privileged the situation of someone close to you may be, you must not envy or feel jealous of them. It is futile to hanker after something that does not belong to you, or that is not appropriate to your merits or your means. Be content with what you have and do not allow yourself to be distracted by other people's possessions.

**5** Your sympathetic, easy-going and uncomplicated personality makes you very popular, and rightly so. However, you need to draw a line between indulgence and permissiveness, otherwise certain people could treat you improperly or disrespectfully. To strike the right balance in your relationships, an element of distance might also be appropriate.

**6** You can continue as you are with total confidence. Your frank and honest nature, your receptivity to those around you and your genuine and spontaneous consideration for those who are talented or worthy ensure that you are successful in everything you do.

# 15<sup>th</sup> combination ○ ○ ❑ ○ ○ ○

If you have set your sights on a job that will bring you no personal glory whatsoever, you are setting a very good example. If, on the other hand, you hold a more humble position, but one in which you carry out your tasks – or your duty – with dignity, then sooner or later your merits will be recognized. Alternatively, if you encounter unjust or ill-advised behaviour, you will do everything in your power to judge impartially and to restore equilibrium. In each case, you know what you have to do.

**1** Whatever difficulties you encounter, or whatever action you have to take in the near future, just respond to the demands of the moment, nothing more. All other considerations are irrelevant. Act swiftly and efficiently, don't take too much time to think about it but do what your instinct dictates. In this fashion you will speedily achieve the desired results, and possibly more besides.

**2** Your words are perfectly in tune with your actions – so much so that you do not

**15th combination**

| | | | | | | | | |
|---|---|---|---|---|---|---|---|---|
| fig. 1 | ▼ | ▼ | □ | ○ | ○ | ○ | Read texts 1 and 2 |
| 2 | ▼ | ○ | ▲ | ○ | ○ | ○ | Read texts 1 and 3 |
| 3 | ▼ | ○ | □ | ▼ | ○ | ○ | Read texts 1 and 4 |
| 4 | ▼ | ○ | □ | ○ | ▼ | ○ | Read texts 1 and 5 |
| 5 | ▼ | ○ | □ | ○ | ○ | ▼ | Read texts 1 and 6 |
| 6 | ▼ | ▼ | ▲ | ○ | ○ | ○ | Read texts 1, 2 and 3 |
| 7 | ▼ | ▼ | □ | ▼ | ○ | ○ | Read texts 1, 2 and 4 |
| 8 | ▼ | ▼ | □ | ○ | ▼ | ○ | Read texts 1, 2 and 5 |
| 9 | ▼ | ▼ | □ | ○ | ○ | ▼ | Read texts 1, 2 and 6 |
| 10 | ▼ | ▼ | ▲ | ▼ | ○ | ○ | Read texts 1, 2, 3 and 4 |
| 11 | ▼ | ▼ | ▲ | ○ | ▼ | ○ | Read texts 1, 2, 3 and 5 |
| 12 | ▼ | ▼ | ▲ | ○ | ○ | ▼ | Read texts 1, 2, 3 and 6 |
| 13 | ▼ | ▼ | ▲ | ▼ | ▼ | ○ | Read texts 1, 2, 3, 4 and 5 |
| 14 | ▼ | ▼ | ▲ | ▼ | ○ | ▼ | Read texts 1, 2, 3, 4 and 6 |
| 15 | ▼ | ▼ | ▲ | ▼ | ▼ | ▼ | Read texts 1, 2, 3, 4, 5 and 6 |
| 16 | ▼ | ○ | ▲ | ▼ | ○ | ○ | Read texts 1, 3 and 4 |
| 17 | ▼ | ○ | ▲ | ○ | ▼ | ○ | Read texts 1, 3 and 5 |
| 18 | ▼ | ○ | ▲ | ○ | ○ | ▼ | Read texts 1, 3 and 6 |
| 19 | ▼ | ○ | ▲ | ▼ | ▼ | ○ | Read texts 1, 3, 4 and 5 |
| 20 | ▼ | ○ | ▲ | ▼ | ○ | ▼ | Read texts 1, 3, 4 and 6 |
| 21 | ▼ | ○ | ▲ | ○ | ▼ | ▼ | Read texts 1, 3, 5 and 6 |
| 22 | ▼ | ○ | ▲ | ▼ | ▼ | ▼ | Read texts 1, 3, 4, 5 and 6 |
| 23 | ▼ | ○ | □ | ▼ | ▼ | ○ | Read texts 1, 4 and 5 |
| 24 | ▼ | ○ | □ | ▼ | ○ | ▼ | Read texts 1, 4 and 6 |
| 25 | ▼ | ○ | □ | ▼ | ▼ | ▼ | Read texts 1, 4, 5 and 6 |
| 26 | ▼ | ○ | □ | ○ | ▼ | ▼ | Read texts 1, 5 and 6 |
| 27 | ○ | ▼ | ▲ | ○ | ○ | ○ | Read texts 2 and 3 |
| 28 | ○ | ▼ | □ | ▼ | ○ | ○ | Read texts 2 and 4 |
| 29 | ○ | ▼ | □ | ○ | ▼ | ○ | Read texts 2 and 5 |
| 30 | ○ | ▼ | □ | ○ | ○ | ▼ | Read texts 2 and 6 |
| 31 | ○ | ▼ | ▲ | ▼ | ○ | ○ | Read texts 2, 3 and 4 |
| 32 | ○ | ▼ | ▲ | ○ | ▼ | ○ | Read texts 2, 3 and 5 |
| 33 | ○ | ▼ | ▲ | ○ | ○ | ▼ | Read texts 2, 3 and 6 |
| 34 | ○ | ▼ | ▲ | ▼ | ▼ | ○ | Read texts 2, 3, 4 and 5 |
| 35 | ○ | ▼ | ▲ | ▼ | ○ | ▼ | Read texts 2, 3, 4 and 6 |
| 36 | ○ | ▼ | ▲ | ▼ | ▼ | ▼ | Read texts 2, 3, 4, 5 and 6 |
| 37 | ○ | ▼ | □ | ▼ | ▼ | ○ | Read texts 2, 4 and 5 |
| 38 | ○ | ▼ | □ | ▼ | ○ | ▼ | Read texts 2, 4 and 6 |
| 39 | ○ | ▼ | □ | ▼ | ▼ | ▼ | Read texts 2, 4, 5 and 6 |
| 40 | ○ | ▼ | □ | ○ | ▼ | ▼ | Read texts 2, 5 and 6 |
| 41 | ○ | ○ | ▲ | ▼ | ○ | ○ | Read texts 3 and 4 |
| 42 | ○ | ○ | ▲ | ○ | ▼ | ○ | Read texts 3 and 5 |
| 43 | ○ | ○ | ▲ | ○ | ○ | ▼ | Read texts 3 and 6 |
| 44 | ○ | ○ | ▲ | ▼ | ▼ | ○ | Read texts 3, 4 and 5 |
| 45 | ○ | ○ | ▲ | ▼ | ○ | ▼ | Read texts 3, 4 and 6 |
| 46 | ○ | ○ | ▲ | ○ | ▼ | ▼ | Read texts 3, 5 and 6 |
| 47 | ○ | ○ | ▲ | ▼ | ▼ | ▼ | Read texts 3, 4, 5 and 6 |
| 48 | ○ | ○ | □ | ▼ | ▼ | ○ | Read texts 4 and 5 |
| 49 | ○ | ○ | □ | ▼ | ○ | ▼ | Read texts 4 and 6 |
| 50 | ○ | ○ | □ | ▼ | ▼ | ▼ | Read texts 4, 5 and 6 |
| 51 | ○ | ○ | □ | ○ | ▼ | ▼ | Read texts 5 and 6 |
| 52 | ▼ | ○ | □ | ○ | ○ | ○ | Read text 1 |
| 53 | ○ | ▼ | □ | ○ | ○ | ○ | Read text 2 |
| 54 | ○ | ○ | ▲ | ○ | ○ | ○ | Read text 3 |
| 55 | ○ | ○ | □ | ▼ | ○ | ○ | Read text 4 |
| 56 | ○ | ○ | □ | ○ | ▼ | ○ | Read text 5 |
| 57 | ○ | ○ | □ | ○ | ○ | ▼ | Read text 6 |

need to explain what you are doing, or what you intend to do, in order for your actions to be understood. This clarity in your behaviour and thinking has a very positive effect on the people around you.

3    Your past actions have earned you the respect of others. However if you seem too proud or too susceptible to flattery you will be blamed or rejected. If, on the other hand, your recognition does not affect your outlook, you will receive whatever help you need to implement your plans or ambitions.

4    Whatever your position or your work, it is important to concentrate on what you are doing and to devote to it whatever time and energy are necessary. In this way, you will obtain excellent results and your merits will not go unnoticed.

5    Do not confuse modesty and simplicity with weakness. If you occupy an important position or have obligations and duties to perform, you probably need to act firmly from time to time. Nevertheless, if you have to be tough in certain circumstances, be careful to be impartial.

6    In cases of conflict or disagreement with those around you, do not be too quick to blame others for the difficulties you encounter. Learn to question yourself as well, to see yourself clearly and to be tough with yourself, so that you are not deceived either by your weaknesses or your strengths.

# 16th combination ○ ○ ○ ○ □ ○ ○

Nature and the universe are subject to immutable laws and cycles that give purpose and harmony to everything. The energy that turns the wheels of life can be found in joy, cheerfulness and in healthy competition between all the elements involved. The same goes for relationships between people, and what they do: passion unites them, motivates them and galvanizes them.

**1** You have a special relationship with certain people, whom you regard as important, but it is making you snobbish and scornful towards others. This is not a good attitude; it actually distances you from sincere and genuine friendships. If you enjoy the company of these important people, share them with your friends.

**2** Your powers of perception and insight give you advance warning of good and bad things to come, allowing you to react at the right moment. This clear-sightedness and your firm, discreet determination give you a stable, praiseworthy position; you know when to act and when to leave well alone.

**3** You get easily worked up, but are slow to get involved, to make choices or to forge ahead. You need to overcome your indecision; otherwise opportunities may pass you by. If you feel that the time has come to act, or to put yourself forward, do not hesitate.

**4** You have self-confidence and faith in life and destiny; you are also independent, good-humoured and a great communicator. These qualities are admired and have

| fig. | | | | | | | |
|---|---|---|---|---|---|---|---|
| fig. 1 | ▼ | ▼ | ○ | □ | ○ | ○ | Read texts 1 and 2 |
| 2 | ▼ | ○ | ▼ | □ | ○ | ○ | Read texts 1 and 3 |
| 3 | ▼ | ○ | ○ | ▲ | ○ | ○ | Read texts 1 and 4 |
| 4 | ▼ | ○ | ○ | □ | ▼ | ○ | Read texts 1 and 5 |
| 5 | ▼ | ○ | ○ | □ | ○ | ▼ | Read texts 1 and 6 |
| 6 | ▼ | ▼ | ▼ | □ | ○ | ○ | Read texts 1, 2 and 3 |
| 7 | ▼ | ▼ | ○ | ▲ | ○ | ○ | Read texts 1, 2 and 4 |
| 8 | ▼ | ▼ | ○ | □ | ▼ | ○ | Read texts 1, 2 and 5 |
| 9 | ▼ | ▼ | ○ | □ | ○ | ▼ | Read texts 1, 2 and 6 |
| 10 | ▼ | ▼ | ▼ | ▲ | ○ | ○ | Read texts 1, 2, 3 and 4 |
| 11 | ▼ | ▼ | ▼ | □ | ▼ | ○ | Read texts 1, 2, 3 and 5 |
| 12 | ▼ | ▼ | ▼ | □ | ○ | ▼ | Read texts 1, 2, 3 and 6 |
| 13 | ▼ | ▼ | ▼ | ▲ | ▼ | ○ | Read texts 1, 2, 3, 4 and 5 |
| 14 | ▼ | ▼ | ▼ | ▲ | ○ | ▼ | Read texts 1, 2, 3, 4 and 6 |
| 15 | ▼ | ▼ | ▼ | ▲ | ▼ | ▼ | Read texts 1, 2, 3, 4, 5 and 6 |
| 16 | ▼ | ○ | ▼ | ▲ | ○ | ○ | Read texts 1, 3 and 4 |
| 17 | ▼ | ○ | ▼ | □ | ▼ | ○ | Read texts 1, 3 and 5 |
| 18 | ▼ | ○ | ▼ | □ | ○ | ▼ | Read texts 1, 3 and 6 |
| 19 | ▼ | ○ | ▼ | ▲ | ▼ | ○ | Read texts 1, 3, 4 and 5 |
| 20 | ▼ | ○ | ▼ | ▲ | ○ | ▼ | Read texts 1, 3, 4 and 6 |
| 21 | ▼ | ○ | ▼ | □ | ▼ | ▼ | Read texts 1, 3, 5 and 6 |
| 22 | ▼ | ○ | ▼ | ▲ | ▼ | ▼ | Read texts 1, 3, 4, 5 and 6 |
| 23 | ▼ | ○ | ○ | ▲ | ▼ | ○ | Read texts 1, 4 and 5 |
| 24 | ▼ | ○ | ○ | ▲ | ○ | ▼ | Read texts 1, 4 and 6 |
| 25 | ▼ | ○ | ○ | ▲ | ▼ | ▼ | Read texts 1, 4, 5 and 6 |
| 26 | ▼ | ○ | ○ | □ | ▼ | ▼ | Read texts 1, 5 and 6 |
| 27 | ○ | ▼ | ▼ | □ | ○ | ○ | Read texts 2 and 3 |
| 28 | ○ | ▼ | ○ | ▲ | ○ | ○ | Read texts 2 and 4 |
| 29 | ○ | ▼ | ○ | □ | ▼ | ○ | Read texts 2 and 5 |
| 30 | ○ | ▼ | ○ | □ | ○ | ▼ | Read texts 2 and 6 |
| 31 | ○ | ▼ | ▼ | ▲ | ○ | ○ | Read texts 2, 3 and 4 |
| 32 | ○ | ▼ | ▼ | □ | ▼ | ○ | Read texts 2, 3 and 5 |
| 33 | ○ | ▼ | ▼ | □ | ○ | ▼ | Read texts 2, 3 and 6 |
| 34 | ○ | ▼ | ▼ | ▲ | ▼ | ○ | Read texts 2, 3, 4 and 5 |
| 35 | ○ | ▼ | ▼ | ▲ | ○ | ▼ | Read texts 2, 3, 4 and 6 |
| 36 | ○ | ▼ | ▼ | ▲ | ▼ | ▼ | Read texts 2, 3, 4, 5 and 6 |
| 37 | ○ | ▼ | ○ | ▲ | ▼ | ○ | Read texts 2, 4 and 5 |
| 38 | ○ | ▼ | ○ | ▲ | ○ | ▼ | Read texts 2, 4 and 6 |
| 39 | ○ | ▼ | ○ | ▲ | ▼ | ▼ | Read texts 2, 4, 5 and 6 |
| 40 | ○ | ▼ | ○ | □ | ▼ | ▼ | Read texts 2, 5 and 6 |
| 41 | ○ | ○ | ▼ | ▲ | ○ | ○ | Read texts 3 and 4 |
| 42 | ○ | ○ | ▼ | □ | ▼ | ○ | Read texts 3 and 5 |
| 43 | ○ | ○ | ▼ | □ | ○ | ▼ | Read texts 3 and 6 |
| 44 | ○ | ○ | ▼ | ▲ | ▼ | ○ | Read texts 3, 4 and 5 |
| 45 | ○ | ○ | ▼ | ▲ | ○ | ▼ | Read texts 3, 4 and 6 |
| 46 | ○ | ○ | ▼ | □ | ▼ | ▼ | Read texts 3, 5 and 6 |
| 47 | ○ | ○ | ▼ | ▲ | ▼ | ▼ | Read texts 3, 4, 5 and 6 |
| 48 | ○ | ○ | ○ | ▲ | ▼ | ○ | Read texts 4 and 5 |
| 49 | ○ | ○ | ○ | ▲ | ○ | ▼ | Read texts 4 and 6 |
| 50 | ○ | ○ | ○ | ▲ | ▼ | ▼ | Read texts 4, 5 and 6 |
| 51 | ○ | ○ | ○ | □ | ▼ | ▼ | Read texts 5 and 6 |
| 52 | ▼ | ○ | ○ | □ | ○ | ○ | Read text 1 |
| 53 | ○ | ▼ | ○ | □ | ○ | ○ | Read text 2 |
| 54 | ○ | ○ | ▼ | □ | ○ | ○ | Read text 3 |
| 55 | ○ | ○ | ○ | ▲ | ○ | ○ | Read text 4 |
| 56 | ○ | ○ | ○ | □ | ▼ | ○ | Read text 5 |
| 57 | ○ | ○ | ○ | □ | ○ | ▼ | Read text 6 |

**17th combination**

| fig. | 1 | 2 | 3 | 4 | 5 | 6 | |
|---|---|---|---|---|---|---|---|
| 1 | ▲ | ▼ | ○ | □ | □ | ○ | Read texts 1 and 2 |
| 2 | ▲ | ○ | ▼ | □ | □ | ○ | Read texts 1 and 3 |
| 3 | ▲ | ○ | ○ | ▲ | □ | ○ | Read texts 1 and 4 |
| 4 | ▲ | ○ | ○ | □ | ▲ | ○ | Read texts 1 and 5 |
| 5 | ▲ | ○ | ○ | □ | □ | ▼ | Read texts 1 and 6 |
| 6 | ▲ | ▼ | ▼ | □ | □ | ○ | Read texts 1, 2 and 3 |
| 7 | ▲ | ○ | ▼ | ▲ | □ | ○ | Read texts 1, 3 and 4 |
| 8 | ▲ | ○ | ○ | ▲ | □ | ○ | Read texts 1, 4 and 5 |
| 9 | ▲ | ○ | ○ | □ | ▲ | ▼ | Read texts 1, 5 and 6 |
| 10 | ▲ | ▼ | ▼ | ▲ | □ | ○ | Read texts 1, 2, 3 and 4 |
| 11 | ▲ | ○ | ▼ | ▲ | ▲ | ○ | Read texts 1, 3, 4 and 5 |
| 12 | ▲ | ○ | ▼ | ▲ | □ | ▼ | Read texts 1, 3, 4 and 6 |
| 13 | ▲ | ○ | ○ | ▲ | ▲ | ▼ | Read texts 1, 4, 5 and 6 |
| 14 | ▲ | ▼ | ▼ | ▲ | ▲ | ○ | Read texts 1, 2, 3, 4 and 5 |
| 15 | ▲ | ○ | ▼ | ▲ | ▲ | ▼ | Read texts 1, 3, 4, 5 and 6 |
| 16 | ▲ | ▼ | ▼ | ▲ | ▲ | ▼ | Read texts 1, 2, 3, 4, 5 and 6 |
| 17 | □ | ▼ | ▼ | □ | □ | ○ | Read texts 2 and 3 |
| 18 | □ | ▼ | ○ | ▲ | □ | ○ | Read texts 2 and 4 |
| 19 | □ | ▼ | ○ | □ | ▲ | ○ | Read texts 2 and 5 |
| 20 | □ | ▼ | ○ | □ | □ | ▼ | Read texts 2 and 6 |
| 21 | □ | ▼ | ▼ | ▲ | □ | ○ | Read texts 2, 3 and 4 |
| 22 | □ | ▼ | ○ | ▲ | ▲ | ○ | Read texts 2, 4 and 5 |
| 23 | □ | ▼ | ○ | □ | ▲ | ▼ | Read texts 2, 5 and 6 |
| 24 | □ | ▼ | ▼ | ▲ | ▲ | ○ | Read texts 2, 3, 4 and 5 |
| 25 | □ | ▼ | ○ | ▲ | ▲ | ▼ | Read texts 2, 4, 5 and 6 |
| 26 | □ | ▼ | ▼ | ▲ | ▲ | ▼ | Read texts 2, 3, 4, 5 and 6 |
| 27 | ▲ | ▼ | ○ | ▲ | □ | ○ | Read texts 1, 2 and 4 |
| 28 | ▲ | ▼ | ○ | □ | ▲ | ○ | Read texts 1, 2 and 5 |
| 29 | ▲ | ▼ | ○ | □ | □ | ▼ | Read texts 1, 2 and 6 |
| 30 | ▲ | ▼ | ▼ | □ | ▲ | ○ | Read texts 1, 2, 3 and 5 |
| 31 | ▲ | ▼ | ▼ | □ | □ | ▼ | Read texts 1, 2, 3 and 6 |
| 32 | ▲ | ▼ | ▼ | ▲ | □ | ▼ | Read texts 1, 2, 3, 4 and 6 |
| 33 | ▲ | ○ | ▼ | □ | ▲ | ○ | Read texts 1, 3 and 5 |
| 34 | ▲ | ○ | ▼ | □ | □ | ▼ | Read texts 1, 3 and 6 |
| 35 | ▲ | ○ | ▼ | □ | ▲ | ▼ | Read texts 1, 3, 5 and 6 |
| 36 | ▲ | ○ | ○ | ▲ | □ | ▼ | Read texts 1, 4 and 6 |
| 37 | □ | ▼ | ▼ | □ | ▲ | ○ | Read texts 2, 3 and 5 |
| 38 | □ | ▼ | ▼ | □ | □ | ▼ | Read texts 2, 3 and 6 |
| 39 | □ | ▼ | ▼ | ▲ | □ | ▼ | Read texts 2, 3, 4 and 6 |
| 40 | □ | ▼ | ○ | ▲ | □ | ▼ | Read texts 2, 4 and 6 |
| 41 | □ | ○ | ▼ | ▲ | □ | ○ | Read texts 3 and 4 |
| 42 | □ | ○ | ▼ | □ | ▲ | ○ | Read texts 3 and 5 |
| 43 | □ | ○ | ▼ | □ | □ | ▼ | Read texts 3 and 6 |
| 44 | □ | ○ | ▼ | ▲ | ▲ | ○ | Read texts 3, 4 and 5 |
| 45 | □ | ○ | ▼ | ▲ | □ | ▼ | Read texts 3, 4 and 6 |
| 46 | □ | ○ | ▼ | □ | ▲ | ▼ | Read texts 3, 5 and 6 |
| 47 | □ | ○ | ▼ | ▲ | ▲ | ▼ | Read texts 3, 4, 5 and 6 |
| 48 | □ | ○ | ○ | ▲ | ▲ | ○ | Read texts 4 and 5 |
| 49 | □ | ○ | ○ | ▲ | □ | ▼ | Read texts 4 and 6 |
| 50 | □ | ○ | ○ | ▲ | ▲ | ▼ | Read texts 4, 5 and 6 |
| 51 | □ | ○ | ○ | □ | ▲ | ▼ | Read texts 5 and 6 |
| 52 | ▲ | ○ | ○ | □ | □ | ○ | Read text 1 |
| 53 | □ | ▼ | ○ | □ | □ | ○ | Read text 2 |
| 54 | □ | ○ | ▼ | □ | □ | ○ | Read text 3 |
| 55 | □ | ○ | ○ | ▲ | □ | ○ | Read text 4 |
| 56 | □ | ○ | ○ | □ | ▲ | ○ | Read text 5 |
| 57 | □ | ○ | ○ | □ | □ | ▼ | Read text 6 |

earned you the approval of certain people who are ready to offer help or support. Your happy disposition wins you friends and allies with whom you can achieve your objectives.

**5** You are under pressure at the moment. You feel as though you cannot act freely, that you are constantly subject to different influences, and are weighed down by constraint and obligation. But since by nature you tend to get carried away rather easily, these impediments could turn out to be a positive thing in the end. In fact they stop you wasting your energy on futile speculation or building castles in the air.

**6** It seems that you have been involved with some half-baked project or feather-brained idea. Fortunately, you have realized this in time and it is not too late to take appropriate action. Much better to drop something halfway through than to stick to the bitter end with a project that is doomed to failure and disappointment.

# 17th combination □ ○ ○ □ □ ○

If you find colleagues or partners to help you put a plan into action, it is important that their support is given freely and willingly. Furthermore, it is essential that you build in time to rest and reflect in order to remain aware of what is happening around you and to the people you are involved with.

**1** Avoid taking sides and being cliquey. Be open to contradiction and differences of opinion, and give equal consideration to all possible objections. Playing devil's advocate helps to anticipate or prevent pitfalls and to see a project through to a successful conclusion.

2   You need to be particularly careful when choosing those with whom you spend time: you can either associate with those who enrich and stimulate you, or with those who debase and demean you – but you cannot keep company with both at the same time.

3   You like to associate with interesting people whom you can trust. Nevertheless you are sometimes charmed by, or attracted to, a weaker character, or by people of dubious qualities. Resist these passing attractions and do not attach too much importance to such ephemeral relationships.

4   You are in contact with people who seem keen to help you or get involved in what you are doing. However, appearances can be deceptive so do not trust them fully. You will soon learn that their first priority is to take advantage of the circumstances, or to use you for their own ends. When dealing with people like this, stay clear-sighted and vigilant.

5   Faith can move mountains. You need to have a goal, an ambition or an aspiration that drives you to act, to achieve and to surpass yourself. If your motivations are honourable, and your ideas, feelings and wishes are clear, there is no reason why you should not get what you want.

6   You feel that your task has been accomplished, and that you have achieved all your desires and ambitions, so you have stepped back a bit. But suddenly you encounter someone with whom you have a natural affinity, and whose aspirations or endeavours seem to be a continuation of your own. This unexpected association now inspires you to support this person's efforts and projects, which is an excellent thing.

# 18th combination ○ ☐ ☐ ○ ○ ☐

Your current difficulties are essentially due to your past mistakes. Nevertheless, you are now in a position to understand the nature and origin of these mistakes, and can take the appropriate action to rectify them, to ensure that they do not happen again. Just make sure you take all necessary precautions first.

1   Negligence, entrenched ideas and inability to adapt to changing circumstances are the root causes of your current problems and difficulties. They are not insoluble but if you really want to change the situation you must be fully aware of the risks you are taking.

2   Mistakes have been made because you, or someone close to you, has not been firm enough, or has been too complacent, indulgent or indecisive. You can now put this right by acting firmly, but make sure you are not too extreme or blunt.

3   Mistakes have led you to overreact, or to react too severely. Nevertheless, in certain circumstances a firm hand is necessary, even if it gives rise to conflict. Your reaction, although harsh, is justified.

**18th combination**

| fig. | | | | | | | |
|---|---|---|---|---|---|---|---|
| 1 | ▼ | ▲ | □ | ○ | ○ | □ | Read texts 1 and 2 |
| 2 | ▼ | □ | ▲ | ○ | ○ | □ | Read texts 1 and 3 |
| 3 | ▼ | □ | □ | ▼ | ○ | □ | Read texts 1 and 4 |
| 4 | ▼ | □ | □ | ○ | ▼ | □ | Read texts 1 and 5 |
| 5 | ▼ | □ | □ | ○ | ○ | ▲ | Read texts 1 and 6 |
| 6 | ▼ | ▲ | ▲ | ○ | ○ | □ | Read texts 1, 2 and 3 |
| 7 | ▼ | □ | ▲ | ▼ | ○ | □ | Read texts 1, 3 and 4 |
| 8 | ▼ | □ | □ | ▼ | ▼ | □ | Read texts 1, 4 and 5 |
| 9 | ▼ | □ | □ | ▼ | ○ | ▲ | Read texts 1, 5 and 6 |
| 10 | ▼ | ▲ | ▲ | ▼ | ○ | □ | Read texts 1, 2, 3 and 4 |
| 11 | ▼ | □ | ▲ | ▼ | ▼ | □ | Read texts 1, 3, 4 and 5 |
| 12 | ▼ | □ | ▲ | ▼ | ○ | ▲ | Read texts 1, 3, 4 and 6 |
| 13 | ▼ | □ | □ | ▼ | ▼ | ▲ | Read texts 1, 4, 5 and 6 |
| 14 | ▼ | ▲ | ▲ | ▼ | ▼ | □ | Read texts 1, 2, 3, 4 and 5 |
| 15 | ▼ | □ | ▲ | ▼ | ▼ | ▲ | Read texts 1, 3, 4, 5 and 6 |
| 16 | ▼ | ▲ | ▲ | ▼ | ▼ | ▲ | Read texts 1, 2, 3, 4, 5 and 6 |
| 17 | ○ | ▲ | □ | ○ | ○ | □ | Read texts 2 and 3 |
| 18 | ○ | ▲ | □ | ▼ | ○ | □ | Read texts 2 and 4 |
| 19 | ○ | ▲ | □ | ○ | ▼ | □ | Read texts 2 and 5 |
| 20 | ○ | ▲ | □ | ○ | ○ | ▲ | Read texts 2 and 6 |
| 21 | ○ | ▲ | ▲ | ▼ | ○ | □ | Read texts 2, 3 and 4 |
| 22 | ○ | ▲ | □ | ▼ | ▼ | □ | Read texts 2, 4 and 5 |
| 23 | ○ | ▲ | □ | ○ | ▼ | ▲ | Read texts 2, 5 and 6 |
| 24 | ○ | ▲ | ▲ | ▼ | ▼ | □ | Read texts 2, 3, 4 and 5 |
| 25 | ○ | ▲ | □ | ▼ | ▼ | ▲ | Read texts 2, 4, 5 and 6 |
| 26 | ○ | ▲ | ▲ | ▼ | ▼ | ▲ | Read texts 2, 3, 4, 5 and 6 |
| 27 | ▼ | ▲ | □ | ▼ | ○ | □ | Read texts 1, 2 and 4 |
| 28 | ▼ | ▲ | □ | ○ | ▼ | □ | Read texts 1, 2 and 5 |
| 29 | ▼ | ▲ | □ | ○ | ○ | ▲ | Read texts 1, 2 and 6 |
| 30 | ▼ | ▲ | ▲ | ○ | ▼ | □ | Read texts 1, 2, 3 and 5 |
| 31 | ▼ | ▲ | ▲ | ○ | ○ | ▲ | Read texts 1, 2, 3 and 6 |
| 32 | ▼ | ▲ | ▲ | ▼ | ○ | ▲ | Read texts 1, 2, 3, 4 and 6 |
| 33 | ▼ | □ | ▲ | ○ | ▼ | □ | Read texts 1, 3 and 5 |
| 34 | ▼ | □ | ▲ | ○ | ○ | ▲ | Read texts 1, 3 and 6 |
| 35 | ▼ | □ | ▲ | ○ | ▼ | ▲ | Read texts 1, 3, 5 and 6 |
| 36 | ▼ | □ | □ | ▼ | ○ | ▲ | Read texts 1, 4 and 6 |
| 37 | ○ | ▲ | ▲ | ○ | ▼ | □ | Read texts 2, 3 and 5 |
| 38 | ○ | ▲ | ▲ | ○ | ○ | ▲ | Read texts 2, 3 and 6 |
| 39 | ○ | ▲ | ▲ | ▼ | ○ | ▲ | Read texts 2, 3, 4 and 6 |
| 40 | ○ | ▲ | □ | ▼ | ○ | ▲ | Read texts 2, 4 and 6 |
| 41 | ○ | □ | ▲ | ▼ | ○ | □ | Read texts 3 and 4 |
| 42 | ○ | □ | ▲ | ○ | ▼ | □ | Read texts 3 and 5 |
| 43 | ○ | □ | ▲ | ○ | ○ | ▲ | Read texts 3 and 6 |
| 44 | ○ | □ | ▲ | ▼ | ▼ | □ | Read texts 3, 4 and 5 |
| 45 | ○ | □ | ▲ | ▼ | ○ | ▲ | Read texts 3, 4 and 6 |
| 46 | ○ | □ | ▲ | ○ | ▼ | ▲ | Read texts 3, 5 and 6 |
| 47 | ○ | □ | ▲ | ▼ | ▼ | ▲ | Read texts 3, 4, 5 and 6 |
| 48 | ○ | □ | □ | ▼ | ▼ | □ | Read texts 4 and 5 |
| 49 | ○ | □ | □ | ▼ | ○ | ▲ | Read texts 4 and 6 |
| 50 | ○ | □ | □ | ▼ | ▼ | ▲ | Read texts 4, 5 and 6 |
| 51 | ○ | □ | □ | ○ | ▼ | ▲ | Read texts 5 and 6 |
| 52 | ▼ | □ | □ | ○ | ○ | □ | Read text 1 |
| 53 | ○ | ▲ | □ | ○ | ○ | □ | Read text 2 |
| 54 | ○ | □ | ▲ | ○ | ○ | □ | Read text 3 |
| 55 | ○ | □ | □ | ▼ | ○ | □ | Read text 4 |
| 56 | ○ | □ | □ | ○ | ▼ | □ | Read text 5 |
| 57 | ○ | □ | □ | ○ | ○ | ▲ | Read text 6 |

**4**   Mistakes have been made and errors have been committed. You are aware of them, but you are not reacting firmly enough and are allowing matters to deteriorate through complacency or negligence. If you do not change your attitude and set things straight immediately, you will suffer the consequences.

**5**   You are well aware of the mistakes or slip-ups that have been made. However, you are not in a position to act as you would wish in order to put a stop to it all. Do not hesitate to ask for the help or support you need, because you must not let this situation get any worse.

**6**   You are not obliged to share the concerns or activities of your social circle. A certain distance or withdrawal will gain their respect and, ironically, get you closer to them; you will be open to new ways of thinking and behaving.

# 19<sup>th</sup> combination □ □ ○ ○ ○ ○

You are entering an extremely positive period of your life from many points of view, during which your wishes and dreams will come true. Enjoy it to the full, but keep a cool head in order to spot any signs of a deterioration or reversal of fortune, which will happen sooner or later.

**1**   Your ideas, plans or wishes will be carefully considered by those who have the power to help you realize them. So press on with them, resolutely and in good faith. Nevertheless, whatever kind of reception you get, do not be distracted from your highest aspirations or objectives.

2    Doors are opening. This is the moment to act, to forge ahead and to dare to achieve your goals or make your wishes or plans come true. The circumstances are highly favourable and you will be completely successful.

3    Excellent circumstances favour progress in your situation and you can be sure of an advantageous outcome. However, although you are having an easy time, do not relax your efforts. Accept your duties and obligations fully, and remain attentive to the nature and quality of your relationships.

4    Your talents or professional qualities will soon be given full expression, thanks to the dynamic and positive intervention of an influential person whom you have already met or will soon consult.

5    For your ventures to succeed, it is essential that you surround yourself with reliable and competent partners whom you can trust. When the time comes, you must be able to delegate some of your powers or responsibilities to them, if necessary.

6    You will probably have to issue sound advice and offer certain people the benefit of your experience; you will either resume a project in which you did not think you were really involved or take up an abandoned activity. Alternatively, you are considering whether to consult an experienced person about a plan or aspiration. You would be right to do so, because this person can give you all the information and advice you need.

| fig. | 1 | ▲ ▲ ○ ○ ○ ○ | Read texts 1 and 2 |
|---|---|---|---|
| | 2 | ▲ □ ▼ ○ ○ ○ | Read texts 1 and 3 |
| | 3 | ▲ □ ○ ▼ ○ ○ | Read texts 1 and 4 |
| | 4 | ▲ □ ○ ○ ▼ ○ | Read texts 1 and 5 |
| | 5 | ▲ □ ○ ○ ○ ▼ | Read texts 1 and 6 |
| | 6 | ▲ ▲ ▼ ○ ○ ○ | Read texts 1, 2 and 3 |
| | 7 | ▲ ▲ ○ ▼ ○ ○ | Read texts 1, 2 and 4 |
| | 8 | ▲ ▲ ○ ○ ▼ ○ | Read texts 1, 2 and 5 |
| | 9 | ▲ ▲ ○ ○ ○ ▼ | Read texts 1, 2 and 6 |
| | 10 | ▲ ▲ ▼ ▼ ○ ○ | Read texts 1, 2, 3 and 4 |
| | 11 | ▲ ▲ ▼ ○ ▼ ○ | Read texts 1, 2, 3 and 5 |
| | 12 | ▲ ▲ ▼ ○ ○ ▼ | Read texts 1, 2, 3 and 6 |
| | 13 | ▲ ▲ ▼ ▼ ▼ ○ | Read texts 1, 2, 3, 4 and 5 |
| | 14 | ▲ ▲ ▼ ▼ ○ ▼ | Read texts 1, 2, 3, 4 and 6 |
| | 15 | ▲ ▲ ▼ ▼ ▼ ▼ | Read texts 1, 2, 3, 4, 5 and 6 |
| | 16 | ▲ □ ▼ ▼ ○ ○ | Read texts 1, 3 and 4 |
| | 17 | ▲ □ ▼ ○ ▼ ○ | Read texts 1, 3 and 5 |
| | 18 | ▲ □ ▼ ○ ○ ▼ | Read texts 1, 3 and 6 |
| | 19 | ▲ □ ▼ ▼ ▼ ○ | Read texts 1, 3, 4 and 5 |
| | 20 | ▲ □ ▼ ▼ ○ ▼ | Read texts 1, 3, 4 and 6 |
| | 21 | ▲ □ ▼ ○ ▼ ▼ | Read texts 1, 3, 5 and 6 |
| | 22 | ▲ □ ▼ ▼ ▼ ▼ | Read texts 1, 3, 4, 5 and 6 |
| | 23 | ▲ □ ○ ▼ ▼ ○ | Read texts 1, 4 and 5 |
| | 24 | ▲ □ ○ ▼ ○ ▼ | Read texts 1, 4 and 6 |
| | 25 | ▲ □ ○ ▼ ▼ ▼ | Read texts 1, 4, 5 and 6 |
| | 26 | ▲ □ ○ ○ ▼ ▼ | Read texts 1, 5 and 6 |
| | 27 | □ ▲ ▼ ○ ○ ○ | Read texts 2 and 3 |
| | 28 | □ ▲ ○ ▼ ○ ○ | Read texts 2 and 4 |
| | 29 | □ ▲ ○ ○ ▼ ○ | Read texts 2 and 5 |
| | 30 | □ ▲ ○ ○ ○ ▼ | Read texts 2 and 6 |
| | 31 | □ ▲ ▼ ▼ ○ ○ | Read texts 2, 3 and 4 |
| | 32 | □ ▲ ▼ ○ ▼ ○ | Read texts 2, 3 and 5 |
| | 33 | □ ▲ ▼ ○ ○ ▼ | Read texts 2, 3 and 6 |
| | 34 | □ ▲ ▼ ▼ ▼ ○ | Read texts 2, 3, 4 and 5 |
| | 35 | □ ▲ ▼ ▼ ○ ▼ | Read texts 2, 3, 4 and 6 |
| | 36 | □ ▲ ▼ ▼ ▼ ▼ | Read texts 2, 3, 4, 5 and 6 |
| | 37 | □ ▲ ○ ▼ ▼ ○ | Read texts 2, 4 and 5 |
| | 38 | □ ▲ ○ ▼ ○ ▼ | Read texts 2, 4 and 6 |
| | 39 | □ ▲ ○ ▼ ▼ ▼ | Read texts 2, 4, 5 and 6 |
| | 40 | □ ▲ ○ ○ ▼ ▼ | Read texts 2, 5 and 6 |
| | 41 | □ □ ▼ ▼ ○ ○ | Read texts 3 and 4 |
| | 42 | □ □ ▼ ○ ▼ ○ | Read texts 3 and 5 |
| | 43 | □ □ ▼ ○ ○ ▼ | Read texts 3 and 6 |
| | 44 | □ □ ▼ ▼ ▼ ○ | Read texts 3, 4 and 5 |
| | 45 | □ □ ▼ ▼ ○ ▼ | Read texts 3, 4 and 6 |
| | 46 | □ □ ▼ ○ ▼ ▼ | Read texts 3, 5 and 6 |
| | 47 | □ □ ▼ ▼ ▼ ▼ | Read texts 3, 4, 5 and 6 |
| | 48 | □ □ ○ ▼ ▼ ○ | Read texts 4 and 5 |
| | 49 | □ □ ○ ▼ ○ ▼ | Read texts 4 and 6 |
| | 50 | □ □ ○ ▼ ▼ ▼ | Read texts 4, 5 and 6 |
| | 51 | □ □ ○ ○ ▼ ▼ | Read texts 5 and 6 |
| | 52 | ▲ □ ○ ○ ○ ○ | Read text 1 |
| | 53 | □ ▲ ○ ○ ○ ○ | Read text 2 |
| | 54 | □ □ ▼ ○ ○ ○ | Read text 3 |
| | 55 | □ □ ○ ▼ ○ ○ | Read text 4 |
| | 56 | □ □ ○ ○ ▼ ○ | Read text 5 |
| | 57 | □ □ ○ ○ ○ ▼ | Read text 6 |

**19th combination**  □ □ ○ ○ ○ ○

## 20th combination

| fig. 1 | ▼ ▼ ○ ○ □ □ | Read texts 1 and 2 |
|---|---|---|
| 2 | ▼ ○ ▼ ○ □ □ | Read texts 1 and 3 |
| 3 | ▼ ○ ○ ▼ □ □ | Read texts 1 and 4 |
| 4 | ▼ ○ ○ ○ ▲ □ | Read texts 1 and 5 |
| 5 | ▼ ○ ○ ○ □ ▲ | Read texts 1 and 6 |
| 6 | ▼ ▼ ▼ ○ □ □ | Read texts 1, 2 and 3 |
| 7 | ▼ ▼ ○ ▼ □ □ | Read texts 1, 2 and 4 |
| 8 | ▼ ▼ ○ ○ ▲ □ | Read texts 1, 2 and 5 |
| 9 | ▼ ▼ ○ ○ □ ▲ | Read texts 1, 2 and 6 |
| 10 | ▼ ▼ ▼ ▼ □ □ | Read texts 1, 2, 3 and 4 |
| 11 | ▼ ▼ ▼ ○ ▲ □ | Read texts 1, 2, 3 and 5 |
| 12 | ▼ ▼ ▼ ○ □ ▲ | Read texts 1, 2, 3 and 6 |
| 13 | ▼ ▼ ▼ ▼ ▲ □ | Read texts 1, 2, 3, 4 and 5 |
| 14 | ▼ ▼ ▼ ▼ □ ▲ | Read texts 1, 2, 3, 4 and 6 |
| 15 | ▼ ▼ ▼ ▼ ▲ ▲ | Read texts 1, 2, 3, 4, 5 and 6 |
| 16 | ▼ ○ ▼ ▼ □ □ | Read texts 1, 3 and 4 |
| 17 | ▼ ○ ▼ ○ ▲ □ | Read texts 1, 3 and 5 |
| 18 | ▼ ○ ▼ ○ □ ▲ | Read texts 1, 3 and 6 |
| 19 | ▼ ○ ▼ ▼ ▲ □ | Read texts 1, 3, 4 and 5 |
| 20 | ▼ ○ ▼ ▼ □ ▲ | Read texts 1, 3, 4 and 6 |
| 21 | ▼ ○ ▼ ○ ▲ ▲ | Read texts 1, 3, 5 and 6 |
| 22 | ▼ ○ ▼ ▼ ▲ ▲ | Read texts 1, 3, 4, 5 and 6 |
| 23 | ▼ ○ ○ ▼ ▲ □ | Read texts 1, 4 and 5 |
| 24 | ▼ ○ ○ ▼ □ ▲ | Read texts 1, 4 and 6 |
| 25 | ▼ ○ ○ ▼ ▲ ▲ | Read texts 1, 4, 5 and 6 |
| 26 | ▼ ○ ○ ○ ▲ ▲ | Read texts 1, 5 and 6 |
| 27 | ○ ▼ ▼ ○ □ □ | Read texts 2 and 3 |
| 28 | ○ ▼ ○ ▼ □ □ | Read texts 2 and 4 |
| 29 | ○ ▼ ○ ○ ▲ □ | Read texts 2 and 5 |
| 30 | ○ ▼ ○ ○ □ ▲ | Read texts 2 and 6 |
| 31 | ○ ▼ ▼ ▼ □ □ | Read texts 2, 3 and 4 |
| 32 | ○ ▼ ▼ ○ ▲ □ | Read texts 2, 3 and 5 |
| 33 | ○ ▼ ▼ ○ □ ▲ | Read texts 2, 3 and 6 |
| 34 | ○ ▼ ▼ ▼ ▲ □ | Read texts 2, 3, 4 and 5 |
| 35 | ○ ▼ ▼ ▼ □ ▲ | Read texts 2, 3, 4 and 6 |
| 36 | ○ ▼ ▼ ▼ ▲ ▲ | Read texts 2, 3, 4, 5 and 6 |
| 37 | ○ ▼ ○ ▼ ▲ □ | Read texts 2, 4 and 5 |
| 38 | ○ ▼ ○ ▼ □ ▲ | Read texts 2, 4 and 6 |
| 39 | ○ ▼ ○ ▼ ▲ ▲ | Read texts 2, 4, 5 and 6 |
| 40 | ○ ▼ ○ ○ ▲ ▲ | Read texts 2, 5 and 6 |
| 41 | ○ ○ ▼ ▼ □ □ | Read texts 3 and 4 |
| 42 | ○ ○ ▼ ○ ▲ □ | Read texts 3 and 5 |
| 43 | ○ ○ ▼ ○ □ ▲ | Read texts 3 and 6 |
| 44 | ○ ○ ▼ ▼ ▲ □ | Read texts 3, 4 and 5 |
| 45 | ○ ○ ▼ ▼ □ ▲ | Read texts 3, 4 and 6 |
| 46 | ○ ○ ▼ ○ ▲ ▲ | Read texts 3, 5 and 6 |
| 47 | ○ ○ ▼ ▼ ▲ ▲ | Read texts 3, 4, 5 and 6 |
| 48 | ○ ○ ○ ▼ ▲ □ | Read texts 4 and 5 |
| 49 | ○ ○ ○ ▼ □ ▲ | Read texts 4 and 6 |
| 50 | ○ ○ ○ ▼ ▲ ▲ | Read texts 4, 5 and 6 |
| 51 | ○ ○ ○ ○ ▲ ▲ | Read texts 5 and 6 |
| 52 | ▼ ○ ○ ○ □ □ | Read text 1 |
| 53 | ○ ▼ ○ ○ □ □ | Read text 2 |
| 54 | ○ ○ ▼ ○ □ □ | Read text 3 |
| 55 | ○ ○ ○ ▼ □ □ | Read text 4 |
| 56 | ○ ○ ○ ○ ▲ □ | Read text 5 |
| 57 | ○ ○ ○ ○ □ ▲ | Read text 6 |

# 20th combination ○ ○ ○ ○ □ □

True, deep faith does not need visible signs or tangible proofs to manifest or express it. Furthermore, inner faith gives those who have it a global vision, a broad and generous view of people and things, which makes them attractive to others. Try to cultivate this kind of faith within yourself.

**1** You have a shallow, blinkered or one-sided view of events around you or of your present circumstances. Your situation or position should encourage you to be more serious, and to understand and interpret things more liberally and more consistently. You should try to be more objective and broad-minded about the actions of those who are in a position of influence or responsibility.

**2** You must understand and interpret other people's actions with greater objectivity, and not judge them arbitrarily or rigidly, even if you disagree with them. Arbitrary or exclusive judgements simply impede you from carrying out a project that requires the support of all.

**3** You sincerely aspire to know yourself better, not to deceive yourself. This clear-sighted attitude is an excellent one but you must learn to assess the consequences of your actions with equal care. These will indicate just how well you are getting on, and will show you how honest you are being about yourself.

**4** You must not remain content to play the role of intermediary, nor allow your skills or qualities to be exploited for ends that do not concern you. In fact, this is essential in order to preserve your autonomy, keep the initiative, remain free to act and have your merits recognized, as they deserve.

5  You have a healthy and confident desire to know yourself better. This is often a useful or necessary aspiration, particularly when taking on an important responsibility, or when you are in a highly visible position. However, if you want to take stock and see yourself clearly, it is most important to judge your successes and failures with equal objectivity, and to assess correctly the way others see you. In this fashion you will not be pulling the wool over your eyes.

6  Selfish considerations are no longer a concern of yours. Naturally, they still surface within and around you, but you are no longer at their mercy. You can observe them with a hint of irony when they relate to you, or a certain indulgence when they relate to other people. In this fashion, as far as possible, you avoid getting involved in this game of ownership, which does you credit.

# 21st combination □ ○ ○ □ ○ □

If you cannot achieve the union or association to which you aspire, it is because you have been betrayed or wrongly accused. You must act swiftly to put a stop to this kind of situation, if necessary punishing those responsible, speedily and firmly.

| fig. | 1 | 2 | 3 | 4 | 5 | 6 | |
|---|---|---|---|---|---|---|---|
| 1 | ▲ | ▼ | ○ | □ | ○ | □ | Read texts 1 and 2 |
| 2 | ▲ | ○ | ▼ | □ | ○ | □ | Read texts 1 and 3 |
| 3 | ▲ | ○ | ○ | ▲ | ○ | □ | Read texts 1 and 4 |
| 4 | ▲ | ○ | ○ | □ | ▼ | □ | Read texts 1 and 5 |
| 5 | ▲ | ○ | ○ | □ | ○ | ▲ | Read texts 1 and 6 |
| 6 | ▲ | ▼ | ▼ | □ | ○ | □ | Read texts 1, 2 and 3 |
| 7 | ▲ | ○ | ▼ | ▲ | ○ | □ | Read texts 1, 3 and 4 |
| 8 | ▲ | ○ | ○ | ▲ | ▼ | □ | Read texts 1, 4 and 5 |
| 9 | ▲ | ○ | ○ | □ | ▼ | ▲ | Read texts 1, 5 and 6 |
| 10 | ▲ | ▼ | ▼ | ▲ | ○ | □ | Read texts 1, 2, 3 and 4 |
| 11 | ▲ | ○ | ▼ | ▲ | ▼ | □ | Read texts 1, 3, 4 and 5 |
| 12 | ▲ | ○ | ▼ | ▲ | ○ | ▲ | Read texts 1, 3, 4 and 6 |
| 13 | ▲ | ○ | ○ | ▲ | ▼ | ▲ | Read texts 1, 4, 5 and 6 |
| 14 | ▲ | ▼ | ▼ | ▲ | ▼ | □ | Read texts 1, 2, 3, 4 and 5 |
| 15 | ▲ | ○ | ▼ | ▲ | ▼ | ▲ | Read texts 1, 3, 4, 5 and 6 |
| 16 | ▲ | ▼ | ▼ | ▲ | ▼ | ▲ | Read texts 1, 2, 3, 4, 5 and 6 |
| 17 | □ | ▼ | ▼ | □ | ○ | □ | Read texts 2 and 3 |
| 18 | □ | ▼ | ○ | ▲ | ○ | □ | Read texts 2 and 4 |
| 19 | □ | ▼ | ○ | □ | ▼ | □ | Read texts 2 and 5 |
| 20 | □ | ▼ | ○ | □ | ○ | ▲ | Read texts 2 and 6 |
| 21 | □ | ▼ | ▼ | ▲ | ○ | □ | Read texts 2, 3 and 4 |
| 22 | □ | ▼ | ○ | ▲ | ▼ | □ | Read texts 2, 4 and 5 |
| 23 | □ | ▼ | ○ | □ | ▼ | ▲ | Read texts 2, 5 and 6 |
| 24 | □ | ▼ | ▼ | ▲ | ▼ | □ | Read texts 2, 3, 4 and 5 |
| 25 | □ | ▼ | ○ | ▲ | ▼ | ▲ | Read texts 2, 4, 5 and 6 |
| 26 | □ | ▼ | ▼ | ▲ | ▼ | ▲ | Read texts 2, 3, 4, 5 and 6 |
| 27 | ▲ | ▼ | ○ | ▲ | ○ | □ | Read texts 1, 2 and 4 |
| 28 | ▲ | ▼ | ○ | □ | ▼ | □ | Read texts 1, 2 and 5 |
| 29 | ▲ | ▼ | ○ | □ | ○ | ▲ | Read texts 1, 2 and 6 |
| 30 | ▲ | ▼ | ▼ | □ | ▼ | □ | Read texts 1, 2, 3 and 5 |
| 31 | ▲ | ▼ | ▼ | □ | ○ | ▲ | Read texts 1, 2, 3 and 6 |
| 32 | ▲ | ▼ | ▼ | ▲ | ○ | ▲ | Read texts 1, 2, 3, 4 and 6 |
| 33 | ▲ | ○ | ▼ | □ | ▼ | □ | Read texts 1, 3 and 5 |
| 34 | ▲ | ○ | ▼ | □ | ○ | ▲ | Read texts 1, 3 and 6 |
| 35 | ▲ | ○ | ▼ | □ | ▼ | ▲ | Read texts 1, 3, 5 and 6 |
| 36 | ▲ | ○ | ○ | ▲ | ○ | ▲ | Read texts 1, 4 and 6 |
| 37 | □ | ▼ | ▼ | □ | ▼ | □ | Read texts 2, 3 and 5 |
| 38 | □ | ▼ | ▼ | □ | ○ | ▲ | Read texts 2, 3 and 6 |
| 39 | □ | ▼ | ▼ | ▲ | ○ | ▲ | Read texts 2, 3, 4 and 6 |
| 40 | □ | ▼ | ○ | ▲ | ○ | ▲ | Read texts 2, 4 and 6 |
| 41 | □ | ○ | ▼ | ▲ | ○ | □ | Read texts 3 and 4 |
| 42 | □ | ○ | ▼ | □ | ▼ | □ | Read texts 3 and 5 |
| 43 | □ | ○ | ▼ | □ | ○ | ▲ | Read texts 3 and 6 |
| 44 | □ | ○ | ▼ | ▲ | ▼ | □ | Read texts 3, 4 and 5 |
| 45 | □ | ○ | ▼ | ▲ | ○ | ▲ | Read texts 3, 4 and 6 |
| 46 | □ | ○ | ▼ | ▲ | ▼ | ▲ | Read texts 3, 4 and 6 |
| 47 | □ | ○ | ▼ | ▲ | ▼ | ▲ | Read texts 3, 4, 5 and 6 |
| 48 | □ | ○ | ○ | ▲ | ▼ | □ | Read texts 4 and 5 |
| 49 | □ | ○ | ○ | ▲ | ○ | ▲ | Read texts 4 and 6 |
| 50 | □ | ○ | ○ | ▲ | ▼ | ▲ | Read texts 4, 5 and 6 |
| 51 | □ | ○ | ○ | □ | ▼ | ▲ | Read texts 5 and 6 |
| 52 | ▲ | ○ | ○ | □ | ○ | □ | Read text 1 |
| 53 | □ | ▼ | ○ | □ | ○ | □ | Read text 2 |
| 54 | □ | ○ | ▼ | □ | ○ | □ | Read text 3 |
| 55 | □ | ○ | ○ | ▲ | ○ | □ | Read text 4 |
| 56 | □ | ○ | ○ | □ | ▼ | □ | Read text 5 |
| 57 | □ | ○ | ○ | □ | ○ | ▲ | Read text 6 |

**1** If someone goes astray or makes a serious mistake, it's normal to take steps to prevent a recurrence. The same goes for you. If you have slipped up or blundered, the victims or those concerned will be forced to take decisive action.

**2** You are involved with someone who will not listen and who stubbornly persists in making mistakes or behaving irresponsibly. Your reaction to this attitude is no doubt disproportionate, but that does not really matter. The main thing is that you have reacted decisively.

**3** You need to sort out a long-standing problem or conflict. However you do not seem to be in a strong enough position to do so, nor do you have the means at your disposal. The fact that some people refuse to take notice does not help. Nevertheless, do not be discouraged: keep up the pressure and maintain your position until you get the desired results.

**4** You have major problems that need to be resolved. Worse still, you have some very determined enemies or rivals. You must be tough, persistent and supremely confident to win through. This is essential if you want to succeed and achieve your ends.

**5** You are in a delicate situation, and you have it in your power to solve your current problems. However, your natural tendency is to be overindulgent, or to wish to reconcile the irreconcilable. This attitude is not appropriate to the gravity of the situation. It is imperative that you act with greater firmness.

**6** Either you are involved with someone who persists in making mistakes – and it would be futile to think you can help this person get back on track, or change their behaviour – or you are clinging to a misplaced attitude or one that is ill-suited to your situation, and you refuse to listen to reason. Either way, you need to be clearer.

# 22<sup>nd</sup> combination ❑ ○ ❑ ○ ○ ❑

You are inclined to be reflective and to trust more to appearances than to the essence of things. This is not a bad attitude per se, but it is ill suited to critical circumstances and to the important decisions you may need to make in your life; these demand a more serious outlook.

**1** You have an opportunity to avoid taking certain initiatives or making certain efforts. However, do not let yourself be tempted by this privilege, as it would be inappropriate to your situation and merits. Use your own abilities to stay on track, and your qualities and skills will get you what you want.

**2** You attach too much importance to appearances and your own image, to the detriment of your true nature and motivations. This superficial behaviour could cause misunderstandings and disappointments in your life. Therefore you need to change your attitude so that there is no longer any discrepancy between how you appear and how you really are.

**3** Things are going very well for you at the moment – or perhaps you feel that everything is plain sailing and that nothing can go wrong. But beware of complacency;

if carelessness or recklessness set in, you could well be headed for some bitter disappointments.

**4**   Your current relationships, while pleasant and carefree, are also superficial and evanescent. If it has not already happened, you are about to meet a soul mate who will offer you deeper bonds. If you respond to the sincere and spontaneous impulses of this person, it will be good for you, and will enrich your life.

**5**   You are involved with people who are superficial, or whose concerns seem uninteresting or worthless to you. However you are attracted to someone who interests you, and whom you would like to get to know better, but you do not know how to go about making this attraction mutual. Very simple: all you have to do is be spontaneous and open. If you are sincere, you will be welcomed with open arms.

**6**   You are completely at one with yourself. Your actions are in harmony with your thoughts, desires and words, and you are achieving your deepest wishes. There is no discrepancy between what you are and what you do, and so you can have complete confidence in your actions.

# 23<sup>rd</sup> combination ○ ○ ○ ○ ○ ❑

Your current circumstances are very difficult but resistance would be futile. These conflicts or difficulties have sprung up through no fault of your own. This is just a testing time in your life that you must resolve to accept. Consequently, you are

**22nd combination** ❑ ○ ❑ ○ ○ ❑

fig. 1   ▲ ▼ ❑ ○ ○ ❑   Read texts 1 and 2
2   ▲ ○ ▲ ○ ○ ❑   Read texts 1 and 3
3   ▲ ○ ❑ ▼ ○ ❑   Read texts 1 and 4
4   ▲ ○ ❑ ○ ▼ ❑   Read texts 1 and 5
5   ▲ ○ ❑ ○ ○ ▲   Read texts 1 and 6
6   ▲ ▼ ▲ ○ ○ ❑   Read texts 1, 2 and 3
7   ▲ ○ ▲ ▼ ○ ❑   Read texts 1, 3 and 4
8   ▲ ○ ❑ ▼ ▼ ❑   Read texts 1, 4 and 5
9   ▲ ○ ❑ ○ ▼ ▲   Read texts 1, 5 and 6
10   ▲ ▼ ▲ ▼ ○ ❑   Read texts 1, 2, 3 and 4
11   ▲ ○ ▲ ▼ ▼ ❑   Read texts 1, 3, 4 and 5
12   ▲ ○ ▲ ▼ ○ ▲   Read texts 1, 3, 4 and 6
13   ▲ ○ ❑ ▼ ▼ ▲   Read texts 1, 4, 5 and 6
14   ▲ ▼ ▲ ▼ ▼ ❑   Read texts 1, 2, 3, 4 and 5
15   ▲ ○ ▲ ▼ ▼ ▲   Read texts 1, 3, 4, 5 and 6
16   ▲ ▼ ▲ ▼ ▼ ▲   Read texts 1, 2, 3, 4, 5 and 6
17   ❑ ▼ ▲ ○ ○ ❑   Read texts 2 and 3
18   ❑ ▼ ❑ ▼ ○ ❑   Read texts 2 and 4
19   ❑ ▼ ❑ ○ ▼ ❑   Read texts 2 and 5
20   ❑ ▼ ❑ ○ ○ ▲   Read texts 2 and 6
21   ❑ ▼ ▲ ▼ ○ ❑   Read texts 2, 3 and 4
22   ❑ ▼ ❑ ▼ ▼ ❑   Read texts 2, 4 and 5
23   ❑ ▼ ❑ ○ ▼ ▲   Read texts 2, 5 and 6
24   ❑ ▼ ▲ ▼ ▼ ❑   Read texts 2, 3, 4 and 5
25   ❑ ▼ ❑ ▼ ▼ ▲   Read texts 2, 4, 5 and 6
26   ❑ ▼ ▲ ▼ ▼ ▲   Read texts 2, 3, 4, 5 and 6
27   ▲ ▼ ❑ ▼ ○ ❑   Read texts 1, 2 and 4
28   ▲ ▼ ❑ ○ ▼ ❑   Read texts 1, 2 and 5
29   ▲ ▼ ❑ ○ ○ ▲   Read texts 1, 2 and 6
30   ▲ ▼ ▲ ○ ▼ ❑   Read texts 1, 2, 3 and 5
31   ▲ ▼ ▲ ○ ○ ▲   Read texts 1, 2, 3 and 6
32   ▲ ▼ ▲ ▼ ○ ▲   Read texts 1, 2, 3, 4 and 6
33   ▲ ○ ▲ ○ ▼ ❑   Read texts 1, 3 and 5
34   ▲ ○ ▲ ○ ○ ▲   Read texts 1, 3 and 6
35   ▲ ○ ▲ ○ ▼ ▲   Read texts 1, 3, 5 and 6
36   ▲ ○ ❑ ▼ ○ ▲   Read texts 1, 4 and 6
37   ❑ ▼ ▲ ○ ▼ ❑   Read texts 2, 3 and 5
38   ❑ ▼ ▲ ❑ ○ ▲   Read texts 2, 3 and 6
39   ❑ ▼ ▲ ▼ ○ ▲   Read texts 2, 3, 4 and 6
40   ❑ ▼ ❑ ▼ ○ ▲   Read texts 2, 4 and 6
41   ❑ ○ ▲ ▼ ○ ❑   Read texts 3 and 4
42   ❑ ○ ▲ ○ ▼ ❑   Read texts 3 and 5
43   ❑ ○ ▲ ○ ○ ▲   Read texts 3 and 6
44   ❑ ○ ▲ ▼ ▼ ❑   Read texts 3, 4 and 5
45   ❑ ○ ▲ ▼ ○ ▲   Read texts 3, 4 and 6
46   ❑ ○ ▲ ○ ▼ ▲   Read texts 3, 5 and 6
47   ❑ ○ ▲ ▼ ▼ ▲   Read texts 3, 4, 5 and 6
48   ❑ ○ ❑ ▼ ▼ ❑   Read texts 4 and 5
49   ❑ ○ ❑ ▼ ○ ▲   Read texts 4 and 6
50   ❑ ○ ❑ ▼ ▼ ▲   Read texts 4, 5 and 6
51   ❑ ○ ❑ ○ ▼ ▲   Read texts 5 and 6
52   ▲ ○ ❑ ○ ○ ❑   Read text 1
53   ❑ ▼ ❑ ○ ○ ❑   Read text 2
54   ❑ ○ ▲ ○ ○ ❑   Read text 3
55   ❑ ○ ❑ ▼ ○ ❑   Read text 4
56   ❑ ○ ❑ ○ ▼ ❑   Read text 5
57   ❑ ○ ❑ ○ ○ ▲   Read text 6

289

**23rd combination**

| fig. | | | | | | | |
|---|---|---|---|---|---|---|---|
| 1 | ▼ | ▼ | ○ | ○ | ○ | □ | Read texts 1 and 2 |
| 2 | ▼ | ○ | ▼ | ○ | ○ | □ | Read texts 1 and 3 |
| 3 | ▼ | ○ | ○ | ▼ | ○ | □ | Read texts 1 and 4 |
| 4 | ▼ | ○ | ○ | ○ | ▼ | □ | Read texts 1 and 5 |
| 5 | ▼ | ○ | ○ | ○ | ○ | ▲ | Read texts 1 and 6 |
| 6 | ▼ | ▼ | ▼ | ○ | ○ | □ | Read texts 1, 2 and 3 |
| 7 | ▼ | ▼ | ○ | ▼ | ○ | □ | Read texts 1, 2 and 4 |
| 8 | ▼ | ▼ | ○ | ○ | ▼ | □ | Read texts 1, 2 and 5 |
| 9 | ▼ | ▼ | ○ | ○ | ○ | ▲ | Read texts 1, 2 and 6 |
| 10 | ▼ | ▼ | ▼ | ▼ | ○ | □ | Read texts 1, 2, 3 and 4 |
| 11 | ▼ | ▼ | ▼ | ○ | ▼ | □ | Read texts 1, 2, 3 and 5 |
| 12 | ▼ | ▼ | ▼ | ○ | ○ | ▲ | Read texts 1, 2, 3 and 6 |
| 13 | ▼ | ▼ | ▼ | ▼ | ▼ | □ | Read texts 1, 2, 3, 4 and 5 |
| 14 | ▼ | ▼ | ▼ | ▼ | ○ | ▲ | Read texts 1, 2, 3, 4 and 6 |
| 15 | ▼ | ▼ | ▼ | ▼ | ▼ | ▲ | Read texts 1, 2, 3, 4, 5 and 6 |
| 16 | ▼ | ○ | ▼ | ▼ | ○ | □ | Read texts 1, 3 and 4 |
| 17 | ▼ | ○ | ▼ | ○ | ▼ | □ | Read texts 1, 3 and 5 |
| 18 | ▼ | ○ | ▼ | ○ | ○ | ▲ | Read texts 1, 3 and 6 |
| 19 | ▼ | ○ | ▼ | ▼ | ▼ | □ | Read texts 1, 3, 4 and 5 |
| 20 | ▼ | ○ | ▼ | ▼ | ○ | ▲ | Read texts 1, 3, 4 and 6 |
| 21 | ▼ | ○ | ▼ | ○ | ▼ | ▲ | Read texts 1, 3, 5 and 6 |
| 22 | ▼ | ○ | ▼ | ▼ | ▼ | ▲ | Read texts 1, 3, 4, 5 and 6 |
| 23 | ▼ | ○ | ○ | ▼ | ▼ | □ | Read texts 1, 4 and 5 |
| 24 | ▼ | ○ | ○ | ▼ | ○ | ▲ | Read texts 1, 4 and 6 |
| 25 | ▼ | ○ | ○ | ▼ | ▼ | ▲ | Read texts 1, 4, 5 and 6 |
| 26 | ▼ | ○ | ○ | ○ | ▼ | ▲ | Read texts 1, 5 and 6 |
| 27 | ○ | ▼ | ▼ | ○ | ○ | □ | Read texts 2 and 3 |
| 28 | ○ | ▼ | ○ | ▼ | ○ | □ | Read texts 2 and 4 |
| 29 | ○ | ▼ | ○ | ○ | ▼ | □ | Read texts 2 and 5 |
| 30 | ○ | ▼ | ○ | ○ | ○ | ▲ | Read texts 2 and 6 |
| 31 | ○ | ▼ | ▼ | ▼ | ○ | □ | Read texts 2, 3 and 4 |
| 32 | ○ | ▼ | ▼ | ○ | ▼ | □ | Read texts 2, 3 and 5 |
| 33 | ○ | ▼ | ▼ | ○ | ○ | ▲ | Read texts 2, 3 and 6 |
| 34 | ○ | ▼ | ▼ | ▼ | ▼ | □ | Read texts 2, 3, 4 and 5 |
| 35 | ○ | ▼ | ▼ | ▼ | ○ | ▲ | Read texts 2, 3, 4 and 6 |
| 36 | ○ | ▼ | ▼ | ▼ | ▼ | ▲ | Read texts 2, 3, 4, 5 and 6 |
| 37 | ○ | ▼ | ○ | ▼ | ▼ | □ | Read texts 2, 4 and 5 |
| 38 | ○ | ▼ | ○ | ▼ | ○ | ▲ | Read texts 2, 4 and 6 |
| 39 | ○ | ▼ | ○ | ▼ | ▼ | ▲ | Read texts 2, 4, 5 and 6 |
| 40 | ○ | ▼ | ○ | ○ | ▼ | ▲ | Read texts 2, 5 and 6 |
| 41 | ○ | ○ | ▼ | ▼ | ○ | □ | Read texts 3 and 4 |
| 42 | ○ | ○ | ▼ | ○ | ▼ | □ | Read texts 3 and 5 |
| 43 | ○ | ○ | ▼ | ○ | ○ | ▲ | Read texts 3 and 6 |
| 44 | ○ | ○ | ▼ | ▼ | ▼ | □ | Read texts 3, 4 and 5 |
| 45 | ○ | ○ | ▼ | ▼ | ○ | ▲ | Read texts 3, 4 and 6 |
| 46 | ○ | ○ | ▼ | ○ | ▼ | ▲ | Read texts 3, 5 and 6 |
| 47 | ○ | ○ | ▼ | ▼ | ▼ | ▲ | Read texts 3, 4, 5 and 6 |
| 48 | ○ | ○ | ○ | ▼ | ▼ | □ | Read texts 4 and 5 |
| 49 | ○ | ○ | ○ | ▼ | ○ | ▲ | Read texts 4 and 6 |
| 50 | ○ | ○ | ○ | ▼ | ▼ | ▲ | Read texts 4, 5 and 6 |
| 51 | ○ | ○ | ○ | ○ | ▼ | ▲ | Read texts 5 and 6 |
| 52 | ▼ | ○ | ○ | ○ | ○ | □ | Read text 1 |
| 53 | ○ | ▼ | ○ | ○ | ○ | □ | Read text 2 |
| 54 | ○ | ○ | ▼ | ○ | ○ | □ | Read text 3 |
| 55 | ○ | ○ | ○ | ▼ | ○ | □ | Read text 4 |
| 56 | ○ | ○ | ○ | ○ | ▼ | □ | Read text 5 |
| 57 | ○ | ○ | ○ | ○ | ○ | ▲ | Read text 6 |

advised to do nothing for the moment; wait instead for more favourable circumstances.

**1**  You are in a difficult and dangerous situation. Any intervention or reaction on your part would only make things worse. Ill-intentioned people are being manipulative and spreading gossip, and misunderstandings are building up as a result. In circumstances like these you must resign yourself to sitting it out.

**2**  You are up against some tough adversaries and can no longer ignore the fact that they are determined to harm you or put you in danger. It would be risky to try and maintain your position at any cost. Instead, be wary and suspicious or relinquish your prerogatives for as long as is necessary.

**3**  You are involved with people whose intentions are dishonest, or who behave in a negative fashion. However there is someone among them worthy of your interest and respect, towards whom you are inexorably drawn. You are actually in opposition to those around you, and this will cause an unavoidable clash. But you can rest assured that you have made the correct choice, because you will permanently shake off those harmful relationships.

**4**  You are in a difficult and dangerous situation and can no longer avoid immediate, unfortunate consequences – so you will have to face up to them with courage and clear-sightedness.

**5**  The opinion that certain people held of you has caused you plenty of problems but you are about to discover that one of them is ready to revise his viewpoint. This sudden U-turn will enable you not only to sort everything out but also, with his help or intervention, to gain the approval and support of everyone who previously opposed you.

**6**  You have finally escaped a very difficult and trying situation, which came about in part because somebody in your circle had a particularly vicious and negative attitude towards you. But you have emerged victorious, and from now on you can act with complete freedom and integrity. This cannot be said for the culprit, who is now paying for his or her mistakes.

# 24th combination □ ○ ○ ○ ○ ○

Order and harmony are returning to your life. In order to ensure lasting positive and beneficial results, you must take certain precautions and let events take their natural course. Nevertheless, if you get the opportunity to link up with like-minded people, you should do so honestly and openly, but with caution.

**1**  Human nature is not without weakness. So do not feel guilty if you cannot resist certain temptations, and do not exaggerate your bad ideas or negative thoughts. The main thing is to avoid such thoughts and to remain aware of your shortcomings and failings when necessary. That way you will avoid making any serious errors.

**2**  You are surrounded by excellent people who exert a positive influence on your character and help you to develop positively. You can therefore trust their advice

| fig. | | | | | | | |
|---|---|---|---|---|---|---|---|
| 1 | ▲ | ▼ | ○ | ○ | ○ | ○ | Read texts 1 and 2 |
| 2 | ▲ | ○ | ▼ | ○ | ○ | ○ | Read texts 1 and 3 |
| 3 | ▲ | ○ | ○ | ▼ | ○ | ○ | Read texts 1 and 4 |
| 4 | ▲ | ○ | ○ | ○ | ▼ | ○ | Read texts 1 and 5 |
| 5 | ▲ | ○ | ○ | ○ | ○ | ▼ | Read texts 1 and 6 |
| 6 | ▲ | ▼ | ▼ | ○ | ○ | ○ | Read texts 1, 2 and 3 |
| 7 | ▲ | ▼ | ○ | ▼ | ○ | ○ | Read texts 1, 2 and 4 |
| 8 | ▲ | ▼ | ○ | ○ | ▼ | ○ | Read texts 1, 2 and 5 |
| 9 | ▲ | ▼ | ○ | ○ | ○ | ▼ | Read texts 1, 2 and 6 |
| 10 | ▲ | ▼ | ▼ | ▼ | ○ | ○ | Read texts 1, 2, 3 and 4 |
| 11 | ▲ | ▼ | ▼ | ○ | ▼ | ○ | Read texts 1, 2, 3 and 5 |
| 12 | ▲ | ▼ | ▼ | ○ | ○ | ▼ | Read texts 1, 2, 3 and 6 |
| 13 | ▲ | ▼ | ▼ | ▼ | ▼ | ○ | Read texts 1, 2, 3, 4 and 5 |
| 14 | ▲ | ▼ | ▼ | ▼ | ○ | ▼ | Read texts 1, 2, 3, 4 and 6 |
| 15 | ▲ | ▼ | ▼ | ▼ | ▼ | ▼ | Read texts 1, 2, 3, 4, 5 and 6 |
| 16 | ▲ | ○ | ▼ | ▼ | ○ | ○ | Read texts 1, 3 and 4 |
| 17 | ▲ | ○ | ▼ | ○ | ▼ | ○ | Read texts 1, 3 and 5 |
| 18 | ▲ | ○ | ▼ | ○ | ○ | ▼ | Read texts 1, 3 and 6 |
| 19 | ▲ | ○ | ▼ | ▼ | ▼ | ○ | Read texts 1, 3, 4 and 5 |
| 20 | ▲ | ○ | ▼ | ▼ | ○ | ▼ | Read texts 1, 3, 4 and 6 |
| 21 | ▲ | ○ | ▼ | ○ | ▼ | ▼ | Read texts 1, 3, 5 and 6 |
| 22 | ▲ | ○ | ▼ | ▼ | ▼ | ▼ | Read texts 1, 3, 4, 5 and 6 |
| 23 | ▲ | ○ | ○ | ▼ | ▼ | ○ | Read texts 1, 4 and 5 |
| 24 | ▲ | ○ | ○ | ▼ | ○ | ▼ | Read texts 1, 4 and 6 |
| 25 | ▲ | ○ | ○ | ▼ | ▼ | ▼ | Read texts 1, 4, 5 and 6 |
| 26 | ▲ | ○ | ○ | ○ | ▼ | ▼ | Read texts 1, 5 and 6 |
| 27 | □ | ▼ | ▼ | ○ | ○ | ○ | Read texts 2 and 3 |
| 28 | □ | ▼ | ○ | ▼ | ○ | ○ | Read texts 2 and 4 |
| 29 | □ | ▼ | ○ | ○ | ▼ | ○ | Read texts 2 and 5 |
| 30 | □ | ▼ | ○ | ○ | ○ | ▼ | Read texts 2 and 6 |
| 31 | □ | ▼ | ▼ | ▼ | ○ | ○ | Read texts 2, 3 and 4 |
| 32 | □ | ▼ | ▼ | ○ | ▼ | ○ | Read texts 2, 3 and 5 |
| 33 | □ | ▼ | ▼ | ○ | ○ | ▼ | Read texts 2, 3 and 6 |
| 34 | □ | ▼ | ▼ | ▼ | ▼ | ○ | Read texts 2, 3, 4 and 5 |
| 35 | □ | ▼ | ▼ | ▼ | ○ | ▼ | Read texts 2, 3, 4 and 6 |
| 36 | □ | ▼ | ▼ | ▼ | ▼ | ▼ | Read texts 2, 3, 4, 5 and 6 |
| 37 | □ | ▼ | ○ | ▼ | ▼ | ○ | Read texts 2, 4 and 5 |
| 38 | □ | ▼ | ○ | ▼ | ○ | ▼ | Read texts 2, 4 and 6 |
| 39 | □ | ▼ | ○ | ▼ | ▼ | ▼ | Read texts 2, 4, 5 and 6 |
| 40 | □ | ▼ | ○ | ○ | ▼ | ▼ | Read texts 2, 5 and 6 |
| 41 | □ | ○ | ▼ | ▼ | ○ | ○ | Read texts 3 and 4 |
| 42 | □ | ○ | ▼ | ○ | ▼ | ○ | Read texts 3 and 5 |
| 43 | □ | ○ | ▼ | ○ | ○ | ▼ | Read texts 3 and 6 |
| 44 | □ | ○ | ▼ | ▼ | ▼ | ○ | Read texts 3, 4 and 5 |
| 45 | □ | ○ | ▼ | ▼ | ○ | ▼ | Read texts 3, 4 and 6 |
| 46 | □ | ○ | ▼ | ○ | ▼ | ▼ | Read texts 3, 5 and 6 |
| 47 | □ | ○ | ▼ | ▼ | ▼ | ▼ | Read texts 3, 4, 5 and 6 |
| 48 | □ | ○ | ○ | ▼ | ▼ | ○ | Read texts 4 and 5 |
| 49 | □ | ○ | ○ | ▼ | ○ | ▼ | Read texts 4 and 6 |
| 50 | □ | ○ | ○ | ▼ | ▼ | ▼ | Read texts 4, 5 and 6 |
| 51 | □ | ○ | ○ | ○ | ▼ | ▼ | Read texts 5 and 6 |
| 52 | ▲ | ○ | ○ | ○ | ○ | ○ | Read text 1 |
| 53 | □ | ▼ | ○ | ○ | ○ | ○ | Read text 2 |
| 54 | □ | ○ | ▼ | ○ | ○ | ○ | Read text 3 |
| 55 | □ | ○ | ○ | ▼ | ○ | ○ | Read text 4 |
| 56 | □ | ○ | ○ | ○ | ▼ | ○ | Read text 5 |
| 57 | □ | ○ | ○ | ○ | ○ | ▼ | Read text 6 |

24th combination □ ○ ○ ○ ○ ○

and alter aspects of your attitude or character that sometimes cause problems in your life. A happy state of mind can only do you good.

**3** You are probably guilty of indecision and inconsistency in your behaviour, choices and ideas. However, this does mean that you never stick with misplaced choices or bad ideas that could have permanent or unfortunate consequences for you. For this reason, if you want to, you can improve yourself and take decisive action with a positive approach.

**4** You associate with people who lack refinement, intelligence or subtlety. However, you are privileged to know somebody with a far superior mind and soul, with whom you enjoy a special relationship. This is why you have decided to have no further dealings with these superficial people, and to turn unreservedly towards the person who is in your thoughts. This decision is obviously the correct one.

**5** If you have made a mistake, deceived yourself or allowed someone to take advantage of you, admit the facts quite openly and apologize immediately. After all, a sin confessed is a sin half pardoned. By doing so, you can make up for a mistake of which you are only too aware and for which you have assumed full responsibility.

**6** If pride prevents you from recognizing or admitting your mistakes or weaknesses, and if you persist with inappropriate behaviour and utter irresponsibility, then you will continue to suffer the consequences. You will also be fooling yourself and turning a blind eye to the causes of your problems.

# 25<sup>th</sup> combination ❑ ○ ○ ❑ ❑ ❑

In all circumstances we should do what instinct and good sense dictate. However, instinct is not automatically innately good: everything depends on the use that you make of it, your inner motivations and the justice of your actions. This is why you must be careful to maintain a certain purity of intention and action.

**1** Sincere impulses and spontaneous, heartfelt feelings are always a pure and simple expression of our inner being, which we can trust implicitly. If this describes your current emotions and feelings, you can abandon yourself to them with complete confidence.

**2** Instead of anticipating the likely outcomes or advantages of a particular venture, think first of giving it your wholehearted attention, bearing in mind your circumstances and the means at your disposal. That way, everything you do will succeed.

**3** You are letting yourself be guided by the wrong instincts. You are actually in danger of forfeiting the potential advantages of a particular situation, and somebody else could benefit. Alternatively, you may suffer the consequences of somebody else's mistake. Either way, try to be more cautious and clear-sighted in future.

**4** Whatever your current circumstances or situation, understand that no one can take away what is yours and yours alone. This is why, as far as possible, you should avoid being influenced by those around you, and should remain faithful to yourself.

5   If you are confronted with a delicate situation or a problem that is not your responsibility, do not go all out to try and fix things. Let events take their course, and all will be resolved, without the need for justification or intervention.

6   Do not give in to reckless impulses or reactions. Your current situation does not lend itself well to bold initiatives or enterprises. Indeed, if you force things without considering your unfavourable circumstances, you will lay yourself open to failure.

# 26<sup>th</sup> combination ❑ ❑ ❑ ○ ○ ❑

This is an auspicious time for putting large-scale, ambitious projects into action, and you have all the qualities necessary to overcome the difficulties that lie in wait. In order to reinforce your power of action and chances of success, learn from certain lessons of the past and adapt them to your present circumstances.

1   You are in a hurry to push forward or get what you want. But circumstances do not favour bold initiatives, and so your enthusiasm has taken a sharp knock. Avoid anything that does not suit the conditions of the moment, or you risk failure.

2   You may have been tempted to forge ahead without further hesitation, but you know that to try and force events would be futile; consequently you have decided to sit tight and wait for the right moment before taking action. This wise resolve means that

| fig. | | | | | | | |
|---|---|---|---|---|---|---|---|
| 1 | ▲ | ▼ | ○ | □ | □ | □ | Read texts 1 and 2 |
| 2 | ▲ | ○ | ▼ | □ | □ | □ | Read texts 1 and 3 |
| 3 | ▲ | ○ | ○ | ▲ | □ | □ | Read texts 1 and 4 |
| 4 | ▲ | ○ | ○ | □ | ▲ | □ | Read texts 1 and 5 |
| 5 | ▲ | ○ | ○ | □ | □ | ▲ | Read texts 1 and 6 |
| 6 | ▲ | ▼ | ▼ | □ | □ | □ | Read texts 1, 2 and 3 |
| 7 | ▲ | ○ | ▼ | ▲ | □ | □ | Read texts 1, 3 and 4 |
| 8 | ▲ | ○ | ○ | ▲ | ▲ | □ | Read texts 1, 4 and 5 |
| 9 | ▲ | ○ | ○ | □ | ▲ | ▲ | Read texts 1, 5 and 6 |
| 10 | ▲ | ▼ | ▼ | ▲ | □ | □ | Read texts 1, 2, 3 and 4 |
| 11 | ▲ | ○ | ▼ | ▲ | ▲ | □ | Read texts 1, 3, 4 and 5 |
| 12 | ▲ | ○ | ▼ | ▲ | □ | ▲ | Read texts 1, 3, 4 and 6 |
| 13 | ▲ | ○ | ○ | ▲ | ▲ | ▲ | Read texts 1, 4, 5 and 6 |
| 14 | ▲ | ▼ | ▼ | ▲ | ▲ | □ | Read texts 1, 2, 3, 4 and 5 |
| 15 | ▲ | ○ | ▼ | ▲ | ▲ | ▲ | Read texts 1, 3, 4, 5 and 6 |
| 16 | ▲ | ▼ | ▼ | ▲ | ▲ | ▲ | Read texts 1, 2, 3, 4, 5 and 6 |
| 17 | □ | ▼ | ▼ | □ | □ | □ | Read texts 2 and 3 |
| 18 | □ | ▼ | ○ | ▲ | □ | □ | Read texts 2 and 4 |
| 19 | □ | ▼ | ○ | □ | ▲ | □ | Read texts 2 and 5 |
| 20 | □ | ▼ | ○ | □ | □ | ▲ | Read texts 2 and 6 |
| 21 | □ | ▼ | ▼ | ▲ | □ | □ | Read texts 2, 3 and 4 |
| 22 | □ | ▼ | ○ | ▲ | ▲ | □ | Read texts 2, 4 and 5 |
| 23 | □ | ▼ | ○ | □ | ▲ | ▲ | Read texts 2, 5 and 6 |
| 24 | □ | ▼ | ▼ | ▲ | ▲ | □ | Read texts 2, 3, 4 and 5 |
| 25 | □ | ▼ | ○ | ▲ | ▲ | ▲ | Read texts 2, 4, 5 and 6 |
| 26 | □ | ▼ | ▼ | ▲ | ▲ | ▲ | Read texts 2, 3, 4, 5 and 6 |
| 27 | ▲ | ▼ | ○ | ▲ | □ | □ | Read texts 1, 2 and 4 |
| 28 | ▲ | ▼ | ○ | □ | ▲ | □ | Read texts 1, 2 and 5 |
| 29 | ▲ | ▼ | ○ | □ | □ | ▲ | Read texts 1, 2 and 6 |
| 30 | ▲ | ▼ | ▼ | □ | ▲ | □ | Read texts 1, 2, 3 and 5 |
| 31 | ▲ | ▼ | ▼ | □ | □ | ▲ | Read texts 1, 2, 3 and 6 |
| 32 | ▲ | ▼ | ▼ | ▲ | □ | ▲ | Read texts 1, 2, 3, 4 and 6 |
| 33 | ▲ | ○ | ▼ | □ | ▲ | □ | Read texts 1, 3 and 5 |
| 34 | ▲ | ○ | ▼ | □ | □ | ▲ | Read texts 1, 3 and 6 |
| 35 | ▲ | ○ | ▼ | □ | ▲ | ▲ | Read texts 1, 3, 5 and 6 |
| 36 | ▲ | ○ | ○ | ▲ | □ | ▲ | Read texts 1, 4 and 6 |
| 37 | □ | ▼ | ▼ | □ | ▲ | □ | Read texts 2, 3 and 5 |
| 38 | □ | ▼ | ▼ | □ | □ | ▲ | Read texts 2, 3 and 6 |
| 39 | □ | ▼ | ▼ | ▲ | □ | ▲ | Read texts 2, 3, 4 and 6 |
| 40 | □ | ▼ | ○ | ▲ | □ | ▲ | Read texts 2, 4 and 6 |
| 41 | □ | ○ | ▼ | ▲ | □ | □ | Read texts 3 and 4 |
| 42 | □ | ○ | ▼ | □ | ▲ | □ | Read texts 3 and 5 |
| 43 | □ | ○ | ▼ | □ | □ | ▲ | Read texts 3 and 6 |
| 44 | □ | ○ | ▼ | ▲ | ▲ | □ | Read texts 3, 4 and 5 |
| 45 | □ | ○ | ▼ | ▲ | □ | ▲ | Read texts 3, 4 and 6 |
| 46 | □ | ○ | ▼ | □ | ▲ | ▲ | Read texts 3, 5 and 6 |
| 47 | □ | ○ | ▼ | ▲ | ▲ | ▲ | Read texts 3, 4, 5 and 6 |
| 48 | □ | ○ | ○ | ▲ | ▲ | □ | Read texts 4 and 5 |
| 49 | □ | ○ | ○ | ▲ | □ | ▲ | Read texts 4 and 6 |
| 50 | □ | ○ | ○ | ▲ | ▲ | ▲ | Read texts 4, 5 and 6 |
| 51 | □ | ○ | ○ | □ | ▲ | ▲ | Read texts 5 and 6 |
| 52 | ▲ | ○ | ○ | □ | □ | □ | Read text 1 |
| 53 | □ | ▼ | ○ | □ | □ | □ | Read text 2 |
| 54 | □ | ○ | ▼ | □ | □ | □ | Read text 3 |
| 55 | □ | ○ | ○ | ▲ | □ | □ | Read text 4 |
| 56 | □ | ○ | ○ | □ | ▲ | □ | Read text 5 |
| 57 | □ | ○ | ○ | □ | □ | ▲ | Read text 6 |

25th combination ❑ ○ ○ ❑ ❑ ❑

293

**26th combination**

| | | symbols | | | | | text |
|---|---|---|---|---|---|---|---|
| fig. 1 | ▲ | ▲ | □ | ○ | ○ | □ | Read texts 1 and 2 |
| 2 | ▲ | □ | ▲ | ○ | ○ | □ | Read texts 1 and 3 |
| 3 | ▲ | □ | □ | ▼ | ○ | □ | Read texts 1 and 4 |
| 4 | ▲ | □ | □ | ○ | ▼ | □ | Read texts 1 and 5 |
| 5 | ▲ | □ | □ | ○ | ○ | ▲ | Read texts 1 and 6 |
| 6 | ▲ | ▲ | ▲ | ○ | ○ | □ | Read texts 1, 2 and 3 |
| 7 | ▲ | □ | ▲ | ▼ | ○ | □ | Read texts 1, 3 and 4 |
| 8 | ▲ | □ | □ | ▼ | ▼ | □ | Read texts 1, 4 and 5 |
| 9 | ▲ | □ | □ | ○ | ▼ | ▲ | Read texts 1, 5 and 6 |
| 10 | ▲ | ▲ | ▲ | ▼ | ○ | □ | Read texts 1, 2, 3 and 4 |
| 11 | ▲ | □ | ▲ | ▼ | ▼ | □ | Read texts 1, 3, 4 and 5 |
| 12 | ▲ | □ | ▲ | ▼ | ○ | ▲ | Read texts 1, 3, 4 and 6 |
| 13 | ▲ | □ | □ | ▼ | ▼ | ▲ | Read texts 1, 4, 5 and 6 |
| 14 | ▲ | ▲ | ▲ | ▼ | ▼ | □ | Read texts 1, 2, 3, 4 and 5 |
| 15 | ▲ | □ | ▲ | ▼ | ▼ | ▲ | Read texts 1, 3, 4, 5 and 6 |
| 16 | ▲ | ▲ | ▲ | ▼ | ▼ | ▲ | Read texts 1, 2, 3, 4, 5 and 6 |
| 17 | □ | ▲ | ▲ | ○ | ○ | □ | Read texts 2 and 3 |
| 18 | □ | ▲ | □ | ▼ | ○ | □ | Read texts 2 and 4 |
| 19 | □ | ▲ | □ | ○ | ▼ | □ | Read texts 2 and 5 |
| 20 | □ | ▲ | □ | ○ | ○ | ▲ | Read texts 2 and 6 |
| 21 | □ | ▲ | ▲ | ▼ | ○ | □ | Read texts 2, 3 and 4 |
| 22 | □ | ▲ | □ | ▼ | ▼ | □ | Read texts 2, 4 and 5 |
| 23 | □ | ▲ | □ | ▼ | ○ | ▲ | Read texts 2, 5 and 6 |
| 24 | □ | ▲ | ▲ | ▼ | ▼ | □ | Read texts 2, 3, 4 and 5 |
| 25 | □ | ▲ | □ | ▼ | ▼ | ▲ | Read texts 2, 4, 5 and 6 |
| 26 | □ | ▲ | ▲ | ▼ | ▼ | ▲ | Read texts 2, 3, 4, 5 and 6 |
| 27 | ▲ | ▲ | □ | ▼ | ○ | □ | Read texts 1, 2 and 4 |
| 28 | ▲ | ▲ | □ | ○ | ▼ | □ | Read texts 1, 2 and 5 |
| 29 | ▲ | ▲ | □ | ○ | ○ | ▲ | Read texts 1, 2 and 6 |
| 30 | ▲ | ▲ | ▲ | ○ | ▼ | □ | Read texts 1, 2, 3 and 5 |
| 31 | ▲ | ▲ | ▲ | ○ | ○ | ▲ | Read texts 1, 2, 3 and 6 |
| 32 | ▲ | ▲ | ▲ | ▼ | ○ | ▲ | Read texts 1, 2, 3, 4 and 6 |
| 33 | ▲ | □ | ▲ | ○ | ▼ | □ | Read texts 1, 3 and 5 |
| 34 | ▲ | □ | ▲ | ○ | ○ | ▲ | Read texts 1, 3 and 6 |
| 35 | ▲ | □ | ▲ | ○ | ▼ | ▲ | Read texts 1, 3, 5 and 6 |
| 36 | ▲ | □ | □ | ▼ | ○ | ▲ | Read texts 1, 4 and 6 |
| 37 | □ | ▲ | ▲ | ○ | ▼ | □ | Read texts 2, 3 and 5 |
| 38 | □ | ▲ | ▲ | ○ | ○ | ▲ | Read texts 2, 3 and 6 |
| 39 | □ | ▲ | ▲ | ▼ | ○ | ▲ | Read texts 2, 3, 4 and 6 |
| 40 | □ | ▲ | □ | ▼ | ○ | ▲ | Read texts 2, 4 and 6 |
| 41 | □ | □ | ▲ | ▼ | ○ | □ | Read texts 3 and 4 |
| 42 | □ | □ | ▲ | ○ | ▼ | □ | Read texts 3 and 5 |
| 43 | □ | □ | ▲ | ○ | ○ | ▲ | Read texts 3 and 6 |
| 44 | □ | □ | ▲ | ▼ | ▼ | □ | Read texts 3, 4 and 5 |
| 45 | □ | □ | ▲ | ▼ | ○ | ▲ | Read texts 3, 4 and 6 |
| 46 | □ | □ | ▲ | ○ | ▼ | ▲ | Read texts 3, 5 and 6 |
| 47 | □ | □ | ▲ | ▼ | ▼ | ▲ | Read texts 3, 4, 5 and 6 |
| 48 | □ | □ | □ | ▼ | ▼ | □ | Read texts 4 and 5 |
| 49 | □ | □ | □ | ▼ | ○ | ▲ | Read texts 4 and 6 |
| 50 | □ | □ | □ | ▼ | ▼ | ▲ | Read texts 4, 5 and 6 |
| 51 | □ | □ | □ | ○ | ▼ | ▲ | Read texts 5 and 6 |
| 52 | ▲ | □ | □ | ○ | ○ | □ | Read text 1 |
| 53 | □ | ▲ | □ | ○ | ○ | □ | Read text 2 |
| 54 | □ | □ | ▲ | ○ | ○ | □ | Read text 3 |
| 55 | □ | □ | □ | ▼ | ○ | □ | Read text 4 |
| 56 | □ | □ | □ | ○ | ▼ | □ | Read text 5 |
| 57 | □ | □ | □ | ○ | ○ | ▲ | Read text 6 |

you will soon be able to make a big leap forward, and will attain the goal you have in view.

**3** All tensions and barriers are about to be overcome. You know that you will soon be able to act swiftly to obtain what you want. However, even though the obstacles have faded away, the situation is not yet without danger, and you should remain cautious, because there is still a long way to go before you reach your objective.

**4** So long as you are aware of what is going on inside your head, you can take preventive action against your reckless impulses, drastic reactions or impatience, thereby sparing yourself any risk of disappointment and failure. This kind of self-control will ensure success in all you do.

**5** By curbing your impulses, your anxious or nervous nature and your premature or abrupt reactions, you delay or intensify their effects, but you do not control them. Instead of refusing to allow yourself to act like this it would be better to seek out the root causes of your behaviour. This is the only way to bring about change and self-improvement.

**6** All the obstacles in your way have finally disappeared, and the tension that has been building up for so long now propels you forward, along the road to success. You can stride confidently down that road, safe in the knowledge that your merits will be valued as they deserve.

# 27<sup>th</sup> combination □ ○ ○ ○ ○ □

If you seek to question the true nature and moral qualities of certain people, pay close attention to their preoccupations, their interests and their motivations. Think about their ideas, words and actions. If all these aspects are in harmony, then you can trust them. On the other hand, if their feelings, thoughts and desires are petty and mean, beware!

**1** You are now in a position to provide for yourself, and to obtain unaided all that you need. However you cannot resist the temptation to compare yourself with those who are better off than you. This envious behaviour will only cause others to mock you or treat you with disdain.

**2** It is time to take your courage in both hands and stand on your own two feet. Those who are in a position to help you, or who have obligations towards you, will probably do what they can. Be that as it may, it's not up to others to look after you: it is up to you to earn your living and assume your responsibilities all on your own.

**3** You are in the grip of insatiable desires, unappeasable longings and ever-increasing wants. These are making your life a hotbed of frustration. Learn to temper your voracious sensuality and your frantic lust for pleasure; otherwise, sooner or later, you are going to feel painfully unfulfilled.

**4** To get what you want, or to reach the lofty ambition you have set yourself, you need competent and motivated helpers. This

| fig. 1 | ▲ ▼ ○ ○ ○ □ | Read texts 1 and 2 |
|---|---|---|
| 2 | ▲ ○ ▼ ○ ○ □ | Read texts 1 and 3 |
| 3 | ▲ ○ ○ ▼ ○ □ | Read texts 1 and 4 |
| 4 | ▲ ○ ○ ○ ▼ □ | Read texts 1 and 5 |
| 5 | ▲ ○ ○ ○ ○ ▲ | Read texts 1 and 6 |
| 6 | ▲ ▼ ▼ ○ ○ □ | Read texts 1, 2 and 3 |
| 7 | ▲ ▼ ○ ▼ ○ □ | Read texts 1, 2 and 4 |
| 8 | ▲ ▼ ○ ○ ▼ □ | Read texts 1, 2 and 5 |
| 9 | ▲ ▼ ○ ○ ○ ▲ | Read texts 1, 2 and 6 |
| 10 | ▲ ▼ ▼ ▼ ○ □ | Read texts 1, 2, 3 and 4 |
| 11 | ▲ ▼ ▼ ○ ▼ □ | Read texts 1, 2, 3 and 5 |
| 12 | ▲ ▼ ▼ ○ ○ ▲ | Read texts 1, 2, 3 and 6 |
| 13 | ▲ ▼ ▼ ▼ ▼ □ | Read texts 1, 2, 3, 4 and 5 |
| 14 | ▲ ▼ ▼ ▼ ○ ▲ | Read texts 1, 2, 3, 4 and 6 |
| 15 | ▲ ▼ ▼ ▼ ▼ ▲ | Read texts 1, 2, 3, 4, 5 and 6 |
| 16 | ▲ ○ ▼ ▼ ○ □ | Read texts 1, 3 and 4 |
| 17 | ▲ ○ ▼ ○ ▼ □ | Read texts 1, 3 and 5 |
| 18 | ▲ ○ ▼ ○ ○ ▲ | Read texts 1, 3 and 6 |
| 19 | ▲ ○ ▼ ▼ ▼ □ | Read texts 1, 3, 4 and 5 |
| 20 | ▲ ○ ▼ ▼ ○ ▲ | Read texts 1, 3, 4 and 6 |
| 21 | ▲ ○ ▼ ○ ▼ ▲ | Read texts 1, 3, 5 and 6 |
| 22 | ▲ ○ ▼ ▼ ▼ ▲ | Read texts 1, 3, 4, 5 and 6 |
| 23 | ▲ ○ ○ ▼ ▼ □ | Read texts 1, 4 and 5 |
| 24 | ▲ ○ ○ ▼ ○ ▲ | Read texts 1, 4 and 6 |
| 25 | ▲ ○ ○ ▼ ▼ ▲ | Read texts 1, 4, 5 and 6 |
| 26 | ▲ ○ ○ ○ ▼ ▲ | Read texts 1, 5 and 6 |
| 27 | □ ▼ ▼ ○ ○ □ | Read texts 2 and 3 |
| 28 | □ ▼ ○ ▼ ○ □ | Read texts 2 and 4 |
| 29 | □ ▼ ○ ○ ▼ □ | Read texts 2 and 5 |
| 30 | □ ▼ ○ ○ ○ ▲ | Read texts 2 and 6 |
| 31 | □ ▼ ▼ ▼ ○ □ | Read texts 2, 3 and 4 |
| 32 | □ ▼ ▼ ○ ▼ □ | Read texts 2, 3 and 5 |
| 33 | □ ▼ ▼ ○ ○ ▲ | Read texts 2, 3 and 6 |
| 34 | □ ▼ ▼ ▼ ▼ □ | Read texts 2, 3, 4 and 5 |
| 35 | □ ▼ ▼ ▼ ○ ▲ | Read texts 2, 3, 4 and 6 |
| 36 | □ ▼ ▼ ▼ ▼ ▲ | Read texts 2, 3, 4, 5 and 6 |
| 37 | □ ▼ ○ ▼ ▼ □ | Read texts 2, 4 and 5 |
| 38 | □ ▼ ○ ▼ ○ ▲ | Read texts 2, 4 and 6 |
| 39 | □ ▼ ○ ▼ ▼ ▲ | Read texts 2, 4, 5 and 6 |
| 40 | □ ▼ ○ ○ ▼ ▲ | Read texts 2, 5 and 6 |
| 41 | □ ○ ▼ ▼ ○ □ | Read texts 3 and 4 |
| 42 | □ ○ ▼ ○ ▼ □ | Read texts 3 and 5 |
| 43 | □ ○ ▼ ○ ○ ▲ | Read texts 3 and 6 |
| 44 | □ ○ ▼ ▼ ▼ □ | Read texts 3, 4 and 5 |
| 45 | □ ○ ▼ ▼ ○ ▲ | Read texts 3, 4 and 6 |
| 46 | □ ○ ▼ ○ ▼ ▲ | Read texts 3, 5 and 6 |
| 47 | □ ○ ▼ ▼ ▼ ▲ | Read texts 3, 4, 5 and 6 |
| 48 | □ ○ ○ ▼ ▼ □ | Read texts 4 and 5 |
| 49 | □ ○ ○ ▼ ○ ▲ | Read texts 4 and 6 |
| 50 | □ ○ ○ ▼ ▼ ▲ | Read texts 4, 5 and 6 |
| 51 | □ ○ ○ ○ ▼ ▲ | Read texts 5 and 6 |
| 52 | ▲ ○ ○ ○ ○ □ | Read text 1 |
| 53 | □ ▼ ○ ○ ○ □ | Read text 2 |
| 54 | □ ○ ▼ ○ ○ □ | Read text 3 |
| 55 | □ ○ ○ ▼ ○ □ | Read text 4 |
| 56 | □ ○ ○ ○ ▼ □ | Read text 5 |
| 57 | □ ○ ○ ○ ○ ▲ | Read text 6 |

**28th combination**

| fig. | | | | | | | |
|---|---|---|---|---|---|---|---|
| 1 | ▼ | ▲ | □ | □ | □ | ○ | Read texts 1 and 2 |
| 2 | ▼ | □ | ▲ | □ | □ | ○ | Read texts 1 and 3 |
| 3 | ▼ | □ | □ | ▲ | □ | ○ | Read texts 1 and 4 |
| 4 | ▼ | □ | □ | □ | ▲ | ○ | Read texts 1 and 5 |
| 5 | ▼ | □ | □ | □ | □ | ▼ | Read texts 1 and 6 |
| 6 | ▼ | ▲ | ▲ | □ | □ | ○ | Read texts 1, 2 and 3 |
| 7 | ▼ | □ | ▲ | ▲ | □ | ○ | Read texts 1, 3 and 4 |
| 8 | ▼ | □ | □ | ▲ | ▲ | ○ | Read texts 1, 4 and 5 |
| 9 | ▼ | □ | □ | □ | ▲ | ▼ | Read texts 1, 5 and 6 |
| 10 | ▼ | ▲ | ▲ | ▲ | □ | ○ | Read texts 1, 2, 3 and 4 |
| 11 | ▼ | □ | ▲ | ▲ | ▲ | ○ | Read texts 1, 3, 4 and 5 |
| 12 | ▼ | □ | ▲ | ▲ | □ | ▼ | Read texts 1, 3, 4 and 6 |
| 13 | ▼ | □ | □ | ▲ | ▲ | ▼ | Read texts 1, 4, 5 and 6 |
| 14 | ▼ | ▲ | ▲ | ▲ | ▲ | ○ | Read texts 1, 2, 3, 4 and 5 |
| 15 | ▼ | □ | ▲ | ▲ | ▲ | ▼ | Read texts 1, 3, 4, 5 and 6 |
| 16 | ▼ | ▲ | ▲ | ▲ | ▲ | ▼ | Read texts 1, 2, 3, 4, 5 and 6 |
| 17 | ○ | ▲ | ▲ | □ | □ | ○ | Read texts 2 and 3 |
| 18 | ○ | ▲ | □ | ▲ | □ | ○ | Read texts 2 and 4 |
| 19 | ○ | ▲ | □ | □ | ▲ | ○ | Read texts 2 and 5 |
| 20 | ○ | ▲ | □ | □ | □ | ▼ | Read texts 2 and 6 |
| 21 | ○ | ▲ | ▲ | ▲ | □ | ○ | Read texts 2, 3 and 4 |
| 22 | ○ | ▲ | □ | ▲ | ▲ | ○ | Read texts 2, 4 and 5 |
| 23 | ○ | ▲ | □ | □ | ▲ | ▼ | Read texts 2, 5 and 6 |
| 24 | ○ | ▲ | ▲ | ▲ | ▲ | ○ | Read texts 2, 3, 4 and 5 |
| 25 | ○ | ▲ | □ | ▲ | ▲ | ▼ | Read texts 2, 4, 5 and 6 |
| 26 | ○ | ▲ | ▲ | ▲ | ▲ | ▼ | Read texts 2, 3, 4, 5 and 6 |
| 27 | ▼ | ▲ | □ | ▲ | □ | ○ | Read texts 1, 2 and 4 |
| 28 | ▼ | ▲ | □ | □ | ▲ | ○ | Read texts 1, 2 and 5 |
| 29 | ▼ | ▲ | □ | □ | □ | ▼ | Read texts 1, 2 and 6 |
| 30 | ▼ | ▲ | ▲ | □ | ▲ | ○ | Read texts 1, 2, 3 and 5 |
| 31 | ▼ | ▲ | ▲ | □ | □ | ▼ | Read texts 1, 2, 3 and 6 |
| 32 | ▼ | ▲ | ▲ | ▲ | □ | ▼ | Read texts 1, 2, 3, 4 and 6 |
| 33 | ▼ | □ | ▲ | □ | ▲ | ○ | Read texts 1, 3 and 5 |
| 34 | ▼ | □ | ▲ | □ | □ | ▼ | Read texts 1, 3 and 6 |
| 35 | ▼ | □ | ▲ | □ | ▲ | ▼ | Read texts 1, 3, 5 and 6 |
| 36 | ▼ | □ | □ | ▲ | □ | ▼ | Read texts 1, 4 and 6 |
| 37 | ○ | ▲ | ▲ | □ | ▲ | ○ | Read texts 2, 3 and 5 |
| 38 | ○ | ▲ | ▲ | □ | □ | ▼ | Read texts 2, 3 and 6 |
| 39 | ○ | ▲ | ▲ | □ | ▲ | ▼ | Read texts 2, 3, 4 and 6 |
| 40 | ○ | ▲ | □ | ▲ | □ | ▼ | Read texts 2, 4 and 6 |
| 41 | ○ | □ | ▲ | ▲ | □ | ○ | Read texts 3 and 4 |
| 42 | ○ | □ | ▲ | □ | ▲ | ○ | Read texts 3 and 5 |
| 43 | ○ | □ | ▲ | □ | □ | ▼ | Read texts 3 and 6 |
| 44 | ○ | □ | ▲ | ▲ | ▲ | ○ | Read texts 3, 4 and 5 |
| 45 | ○ | □ | ▲ | ▲ | □ | ▼ | Read texts 3, 4 and 6 |
| 46 | ○ | □ | ▲ | □ | ▲ | ▼ | Read texts 3, 5 and 6 |
| 47 | ○ | □ | ▲ | ▲ | ▲ | ▼ | Read texts 3, 4, 5 and 6 |
| 48 | ○ | □ | □ | ▲ | ▲ | ○ | Read texts 4 and 5 |
| 49 | ○ | □ | □ | ▲ | □ | ▼ | Read texts 4 and 6 |
| 50 | ○ | □ | □ | ▲ | ▲ | ▼ | Read texts 4, 5 and 6 |
| 51 | ○ | □ | □ | □ | ▲ | ▼ | Read texts 5 and 6 |
| 52 | ▼ | □ | □ | □ | □ | ○ | Read text 1 |
| 53 | ○ | ▲ | □ | □ | □ | ○ | Read text 2 |
| 54 | ○ | □ | ▲ | □ | □ | ○ | Read text 3 |
| 55 | ○ | □ | □ | ▲ | □ | ○ | Read text 4 |
| 56 | ○ | □ | □ | □ | ▲ | ○ | Read text 5 |
| 57 | ○ | □ | □ | □ | □ | ▼ | Read text 6 |

is why you are in such a hurry to find them. Your impatience augurs well, for your intentions are generous and the objectives you have in mind will benefit everybody.

**5** You have to take on heavy responsibilities, or put up with material and moral obligations that you know to be beyond your strength or your means. To ameliorate this tricky situation you have decided to seek the advice of a wise person. This will probably lead to a lack of autonomy but, if you accept this as such, everything will work out well.

**6** You are taking on heavy responsibilities, but this has not dampened your initiative, your ambitions or your wish to broaden your horizons or improve your situation. A disposition as generous and dynamic as this will ensure success sooner or later.

# 28<sup>th</sup> combination ○ □ □ □ □ ○

At first glance your situation may seem to offer no way out, and could lead you to react swiftly or violently. However, this sort of behaviour would be completely inappropriate to the circumstances. As things stand, it would be better to untangle and clarify the situation patiently, without becoming downhearted.

**1** Before taking up a daring venture, or one that is extremely important to you, show how circumspect and sensible you are. Do nothing until you have carefully examined all the angles, weighed up the pros and cons and anticipated all the likely outcomes. With the stakes as they are, you would be well advised to take all possible precautions.

**2** Your current circumstances are unusual. At times like these we often feel the need to reassert our position. In order to do this, do not hesitate to appeal to people of more modest means. Their support or intervention will help you implement the changes you wish to make.

**3** You are faced with serious or dangerous circumstances that you refuse to take into consideration, and you persist in carrying on regardless of the difficulties and obstacles in your way. You are determined to press ahead without heeding any warnings. Be aware that this fecklessness is a sure-fire route to failure, so call a halt for as long as is necessary.

**4** You are in a position to exert influence over others or to dominate events, thanks to the privileged relationships you currently enjoy. However, if you abuse this situation to impose your choices and decisions, and to achieve your ambitions without regard for the needs and desires of those around you or those who help you, you will not reach your goals and will spoil your chances of success.

**5** Whichever way you look at it, you are in a comfortable and lucrative situation. All the same, you are not yet on firm ground and there is no guarantee that these favourable circumstances will continue. You need to associate with people who are in a more modest position, because they can offer you valuable support. Without them you will not be able to consolidate your position.

**6** You are facing exceptional circumstances and you need to go to extraordinary lengths, albeit with no guarantee of success or of meeting your objectives. However, if the intentions or motivations that spur you on are honourable, you are right to take such risks. Sometimes it is necessary to take risks.

# 29<sup>th</sup> combination ○ ❑ ○ ○ ❑ ○

You are so used to living through difficult or dangerous situations that you cannot imagine ever being able to escape them. However, it would be a good idea to analyse the causes of the problems you have been facing for so long, so that you can eventually find adequate solutions and take appropriate action.

**1** Difficulties and obstacles have become such a way of life for you that they are now almost second nature. You almost seem to cultivate painful or complicated situations. It is imperative to drop this negative attitude, and to make a determined effort to be dynamic, positive and productive.

**2** At present your situation is too difficult, possibly even too dangerous, for you to expect to extricate yourself quickly or to realize any ambitious plans. In circumstances like these all you can do is tackle the issues one at a time, and settle for modest results. That way, little by little, you will eventually get what you want.

**3** Your current situation offers no result, progress or retreat. Naturally you are

**29th combination**

○
□
○
○
□
○

| fig. 1 | | | | | | | |
|---|---|---|---|---|---|---|---|
| 1 | ▼ | ▲ | ○ | ○ | □ | ○ | Read texts 1 and 2 |
| 2 | ▼ | ○ | ▼ | ○ | □ | ○ | Read texts 1 and 3 |
| 3 | ▼ | □ | ○ | ▼ | □ | ○ | Read texts 1 and 4 |
| 4 | ▼ | □ | ○ | ○ | ▲ | ○ | Read texts 1 and 5 |
| 5 | ▼ | □ | ○ | ○ | □ | ▼ | Read texts 1 and 6 |
| 6 | ▼ | ▲ | ▼ | ○ | □ | ○ | Read texts 1, 2 and 3 |
| 7 | ▼ | ▲ | ○ | ▼ | □ | ○ | Read texts 1, 2 and 4 |
| 8 | ▼ | ▲ | ○ | ○ | ▲ | ○ | Read texts 1, 2 and 5 |
| 9 | ▼ | ▲ | ○ | ○ | □ | ▼ | Read texts 1, 2 and 6 |
| 10 | ▼ | ▲ | ▼ | ▼ | □ | ○ | Read texts 1, 2, 3 and 4 |
| 11 | ▼ | ▲ | ▼ | ○ | ▲ | ○ | Read texts 1, 2, 3 and 5 |
| 12 | ▼ | ▲ | ▼ | ○ | □ | ▼ | Read texts 1, 2, 3 and 6 |
| 13 | ▼ | ▲ | ▼ | ▼ | ▲ | ○ | Read texts 1, 2, 3, 4 and 5 |
| 14 | ▼ | ▲ | ▼ | ▼ | □ | ▼ | Read texts 1, 2, 3, 4 and 6 |
| 15 | ▼ | ▲ | ▼ | ▼ | ▲ | ▼ | Read texts 1, 2, 3, 4, 5 and 6 |
| 16 | ▼ | □ | ▼ | ▼ | □ | ○ | Read texts 1, 3 and 4 |
| 17 | ▼ | □ | ▼ | ○ | ▲ | ○ | Read texts 1, 3 and 5 |
| 18 | ▼ | □ | ▼ | ○ | □ | ▼ | Read texts 1, 3 and 6 |
| 19 | ▼ | □ | ▼ | ▼ | ▲ | ○ | Read texts 1, 3, 4 and 5 |
| 20 | ▼ | □ | ▼ | ▼ | □ | ▼ | Read texts 1, 3, 4 and 6 |
| 21 | ▼ | □ | ▼ | ○ | ▲ | ▼ | Read texts 1, 3, 5 and 6 |
| 22 | ▼ | □ | ▼ | ▼ | ▲ | ▼ | Read texts 1, 3, 4, 5 and 6 |
| 23 | ▼ | □ | ○ | ▼ | ▲ | ○ | Read texts 1, 4 and 5 |
| 24 | ▼ | □ | ○ | ▼ | □ | ▼ | Read texts 1, 4 and 6 |
| 25 | ▼ | □ | ○ | ▼ | ▲ | ▼ | Read texts 1, 4, 5 and 6 |
| 26 | ▼ | □ | ○ | ○ | ▲ | ▼ | Read texts 1, 5 and 6 |
| 27 | ○ | ▲ | ▼ | ○ | □ | ○ | Read texts 2 and 3 |
| 28 | ○ | ▲ | ○ | ▼ | □ | ○ | Read texts 2 and 4 |
| 29 | ○ | ▲ | ○ | ○ | ▲ | ○ | Read texts 2 and 5 |
| 30 | ○ | ▲ | ○ | ○ | □ | ▼ | Read texts 2 and 6 |
| 31 | ○ | ▲ | ▼ | ▼ | □ | ○ | Read texts 2, 3 and 4 |
| 32 | ○ | ▲ | ▼ | ○ | ▲ | ○ | Read texts 2, 3 and 5 |
| 33 | ○ | ▲ | ▼ | ○ | □ | ▼ | Read texts 2, 3 and 6 |
| 34 | ○ | ▲ | ▼ | ▼ | ▲ | ○ | Read texts 2, 3, 4 and 5 |
| 35 | ○ | ▲ | ▼ | ▼ | □ | ▼ | Read texts 2, 3, 4 and 6 |
| 36 | ○ | ▲ | ▼ | ▼ | ▲ | ▼ | Read texts 2, 3, 4, 5 and 6 |
| 37 | ○ | ▲ | ○ | ▼ | ▲ | ○ | Read texts 2, 4 and 5 |
| 38 | ○ | ▲ | ○ | ▼ | □ | ▼ | Read texts 2, 4 and 6 |
| 39 | ○ | ▲ | ○ | ▼ | ▲ | ▼ | Read texts 2, 4, 5 and 6 |
| 40 | ○ | ▲ | ○ | ○ | ▲ | ▼ | Read texts 2, 5 and 6 |
| 41 | ○ | □ | ▼ | ▼ | □ | ○ | Read texts 3 and 4 |
| 42 | ○ | □ | ▼ | ○ | ▲ | ○ | Read texts 3 and 5 |
| 43 | ○ | □ | ▼ | ○ | □ | ▼ | Read texts 3 and 6 |
| 44 | ○ | □ | ▼ | ▼ | ▲ | ○ | Read texts 3, 4 and 5 |
| 45 | ○ | □ | ▼ | ▼ | □ | ▼ | Read texts 3, 4 and 6 |
| 46 | ○ | □ | ▼ | ○ | ▲ | ▼ | Read texts 3, 5 and 6 |
| 47 | ○ | □ | ▼ | ▼ | ▲ | ▼ | Read texts 3, 4, 5 and 6 |
| 48 | ○ | □ | ○ | ▼ | ▲ | ○ | Read texts 4 and 5 |
| 49 | ○ | □ | ○ | ▼ | □ | ▼ | Read texts 4 and 6 |
| 50 | ○ | □ | ○ | ▼ | ▲ | ▼ | Read texts 4, 5 and 6 |
| 51 | ○ | □ | ○ | ○ | ▲ | ▼ | Read texts 5 and 6 |
| 52 | ▼ | □ | ○ | ○ | □ | ○ | Read text 1 |
| 53 | ○ | ▲ | ○ | ○ | □ | ○ | Read text 2 |
| 54 | ○ | □ | ▼ | ○ | □ | ○ | Read text 3 |
| 55 | ○ | □ | ○ | ▼ | □ | ○ | Read text 4 |
| 56 | ○ | □ | ○ | ○ | ▲ | ○ | Read text 5 |
| 57 | ○ | □ | ○ | ○ | □ | ▼ | Read text 6 |

tempted to take drastic action or to try to escape these difficulties by any means possible – but you would be making a serious mistake. However painful it may be, wait patiently for a solution to present itself or an escape route to open up, something which is bound to happen sooner or later.

4   You are in a difficult situation, but you know that you are not alone. You now understand that solidarity is the key, and that if everybody in the same boat got together to help each other, all would benefit. This is obviously the best attitude to take, and you should adopt it straightaway. However, to overcome any obstacles in your path your actions must be unambiguous and you need to have a clear and accurate sense of what or whom you are dealing with.

5   You would be in less danger and better equipped to solve the situation speedily if you were able to demonstrate more restraint and less ambition. In situations like this you need to begin at the beginning, not to expect immediate results, if you want to keep trouble at bay.

6   You have ignored the sound advice and warnings you have been given, or the early signs that your situation was deteriorating. Therefore you must now resign yourself to the consequences of your mistakes.

# 30th combination □ ○ □ □ ○ □

To be clear-sighted – in other words to see yourself, your situation and your life clearly – you must let your powers of perception take over and trust your intuition. This implies some degree of dependence on other people, on nature and on life in general. But this dependence is useful, because it will increase your awareness and give you greater freedom of action.

**1** A new cycle of your life is just beginning – or perhaps you are taking up a new activity or starting a new job. The future looks bright, albeit still hazy and imprecise, because many possibilities are opening up. In circumstances like these, be calm and clear-sighted so that you are not overcome by your emotions and contradictory feelings. In this way you will know how to separate truth from fiction, both in and around you.

**2** You have all the assets and qualities you need to make your dreams come true. You have complete control over everything destiny throws your way, and are poised to make full use of your talents and capabilities. Success is sure to follow.

**3** Your life is a bit of a roller coaster: sometimes you are happy or enthusiastic and sometimes despairing or disillusioned for no apparent reason. This is essentially due to a lack of inner balance. You would be well advised to moderate your changeable, suggestible nature and to have more faith in life and in destiny.

**4** By nature you are inclined to be over-enthusiastic or impatient, and to aim for

| fig. | | | | | | | |
|---|---|---|---|---|---|---|---|
| 1 | ▲ | ▼ | □ | □ | ○ | □ | Read texts 1 and 2 |
| 2 | ▲ | ○ | ▲ | □ | ○ | □ | Read texts 1 and 3 |
| 3 | ▲ | ○ | □ | ▲ | ○ | □ | Read texts 1 and 4 |
| 4 | ▲ | ○ | □ | □ | ▼ | □ | Read texts 1 and 5 |
| 5 | ▲ | ○ | □ | □ | ○ | ▲ | Read texts 1 and 6 |
| 6 | ▲ | ▼ | ▲ | □ | ○ | □ | Read texts 1, 2 and 3 |
| 7 | ▲ | ○ | ▲ | ▲ | ○ | □ | Read texts 1, 3 and 4 |
| 8 | ▲ | ○ | □ | ▲ | ▼ | □ | Read texts 1, 4 and 5 |
| 9 | ▲ | ○ | □ | □ | ▼ | ▲ | Read texts 1, 5 and 6 |
| 10 | ▲ | ▼ | ▲ | ▲ | ○ | □ | Read texts 1, 2, 3 and 4 |
| 11 | ▲ | ○ | ▲ | ▲ | ▼ | □ | Read texts 1, 3, 4 and 5 |
| 12 | ▲ | ○ | ▲ | ▲ | ▼ | ▲ | Read texts 1, 3, 4 and 6 |
| 13 | ▲ | ○ | □ | ▲ | ▼ | ▲ | Read texts 1, 4, 5 and 6 |
| 14 | ▲ | ▼ | ▲ | ▲ | ▼ | □ | Read texts 1, 2, 3, 4 and 5 |
| 15 | ▲ | ○ | ▲ | ▲ | ▼ | ▲ | Read texts 1, 3, 4, 5 and 6 |
| 16 | ▲ | ▼ | ▲ | ▲ | ▼ | ▲ | Read texts 1, 2, 3, 4, 5 and 6 |
| 17 | □ | ▼ | ▲ | □ | ○ | □ | Read texts 2 and 3 |
| 18 | □ | ▼ | □ | ▲ | ○ | □ | Read texts 2 and 4 |
| 19 | □ | ▼ | □ | □ | ○ | □ | Read texts 2 and 5 |
| 20 | □ | ▼ | □ | □ | ○ | ▲ | Read texts 2 and 6 |
| 21 | □ | ▼ | ▲ | ▲ | ○ | □ | Read texts 2, 3 and 4 |
| 22 | □ | ▼ | □ | ▲ | ▼ | □ | Read texts 2, 4 and 5 |
| 23 | □ | ▼ | □ | □ | ▼ | ▲ | Read texts 2, 5 and 6 |
| 24 | □ | ▼ | ▲ | ▲ | ▼ | □ | Read texts 2, 3, 4 and 5 |
| 25 | □ | ▼ | □ | ▲ | ▼ | ▲ | Read texts 2, 4, 5 and 6 |
| 26 | □ | ▼ | ▲ | ▲ | ▼ | ▲ | Read texts 2, 3, 4, 5 and 6 |
| 27 | ▲ | ▼ | □ | ▲ | ○ | ▲ | Read texts 1, 2 and 4 |
| 28 | ▲ | ▼ | □ | □ | ▼ | □ | Read texts 1, 2 and 5 |
| 29 | ▲ | ▼ | □ | □ | ○ | ▲ | Read texts 1, 2 and 6 |
| 30 | ▲ | ▼ | ▲ | □ | ▼ | □ | Read texts 1, 2, 3 and 5 |
| 31 | ▲ | ▼ | ▲ | □ | ○ | ▲ | Read texts 1, 2, 3 and 6 |
| 32 | ▲ | ▼ | ▲ | ▲ | ○ | ▲ | Read texts 1, 2, 3, 4 and 6 |
| 33 | ▲ | ○ | ▲ | □ | ▼ | □ | Read texts 1, 3 and 5 |
| 34 | ▲ | ○ | ▲ | □ | ○ | ▲ | Read texts 1, 3 and 6 |
| 35 | ▲ | ○ | ▲ | □ | ▼ | ▲ | Read texts 1, 3, 5 and 6 |
| 36 | ▲ | ○ | □ | ▲ | ○ | ▲ | Read texts 1, 4 and 6 |
| 37 | □ | ▼ | ▲ | □ | ▼ | □ | Read texts 2, 3 and 5 |
| 38 | □ | ▼ | ▲ | □ | ○ | ▲ | Read texts 2, 3 and 6 |
| 39 | □ | ▼ | ▲ | ▲ | ○ | ▲ | Read texts 2, 3, 4 and 6 |
| 40 | □ | ▼ | □ | ▲ | ○ | ▲ | Read texts 2, 4 and 6 |
| 41 | □ | ○ | ▲ | ▲ | ○ | □ | Read texts 3 and 4 |
| 42 | □ | ○ | ▲ | □ | ▼ | □ | Read texts 3 and 5 |
| 43 | □ | ○ | ▲ | □ | ○ | ▲ | Read texts 3 and 6 |
| 44 | □ | ○ | ▲ | ▲ | ▼ | □ | Read texts 3, 4 and 5 |
| 45 | □ | ○ | ▲ | ▲ | ○ | ▲ | Read texts 3, 4 and 6 |
| 46 | □ | ○ | ▲ | □ | ▼ | ▲ | Read texts 3, 5 and 6 |
| 47 | □ | ○ | ▲ | ▲ | ▼ | ▲ | Read texts 3, 4, 5 and 6 |
| 48 | □ | □ | ○ | ▲ | ▼ | □ | Read texts 4 and 5 |
| 49 | □ | □ | □ | ▲ | ○ | ▲ | Read texts 4 and 6 |
| 50 | □ | □ | □ | ▲ | ▼ | ▲ | Read texts 4, 5 and 6 |
| 51 | □ | □ | □ | □ | ▼ | ▲ | Read texts 5 and 6 |
| 52 | ▲ | ○ | □ | □ | ○ | □ | Read text 1 |
| 53 | □ | ▼ | □ | □ | ○ | □ | Read text 2 |
| 54 | □ | ○ | ▲ | □ | ○ | □ | Read text 3 |
| 55 | □ | □ | ○ | ▲ | ○ | □ | Read text 4 |
| 56 | □ | □ | □ | □ | ▼ | □ | Read text 5 |
| 57 | □ | □ | □ | □ | ○ | ▲ | Read text 6 |

**31st combination**

| fig. | | | | | | | |
|---|---|---|---|---|---|---|---|
| 1 | ▼ | ▼ | □ | □ | □ | ○ | Read texts 1 and 2 |
| 2 | ▼ | ○ | ▲ | □ | □ | ○ | Read texts 1 and 3 |
| 3 | ▼ | ○ | □ | ▲ | □ | ○ | Read texts 1 and 4 |
| 4 | ▼ | ○ | □ | □ | ▲ | ○ | Read texts 1 and 5 |
| 5 | ▼ | ○ | □ | □ | □ | ▼ | Read texts 1 and 6 |
| 6 | ▼ | ▼ | ▲ | □ | □ | ○ | Read texts 1, 2 and 3 |
| 7 | ▼ | ○ | ▲ | ▲ | □ | ○ | Read texts 1, 3 and 4 |
| 8 | ▼ | ○ | □ | ▲ | ▲ | ○ | Read texts 1, 4 and 5 |
| 9 | ▼ | ○ | □ | □ | ▲ | ▼ | Read texts 1, 5 and 6 |
| 10 | ▼ | ▼ | ▲ | ▲ | □ | ○ | Read texts 1, 2, 3 and 4 |
| 11 | ▼ | ○ | ▲ | ▲ | ▲ | ○ | Read texts 1, 3, 4 and 5 |
| 12 | ▼ | ○ | ▲ | ▲ | □ | ▼ | Read texts 1, 3, 4 and 6 |
| 13 | ▼ | ○ | □ | ▲ | ▲ | ▼ | Read texts 1, 4, 5 and 6 |
| 14 | ▼ | ▼ | ▲ | ▲ | ▲ | ○ | Read texts 1, 2, 3, 4 and 5 |
| 15 | ▼ | ○ | ▲ | ▲ | ▲ | ▼ | Read texts 1, 3, 4, 5 and 6 |
| 16 | ▼ | ▼ | ▲ | ▲ | ▲ | ▼ | Read texts 1, 2, 3, 4, 5 and 6 |
| 17 | ○ | ▼ | ▲ | □ | □ | ○ | Read texts 2 and 3 |
| 18 | ○ | ▼ | □ | ▲ | □ | ○ | Read texts 2 and 4 |
| 19 | ○ | ▼ | □ | □ | ▲ | ○ | Read texts 2 and 5 |
| 20 | ○ | ▼ | □ | □ | □ | ▼ | Read texts 2 and 6 |
| 21 | ○ | ▼ | ▲ | ▲ | □ | ○ | Read texts 2, 3 and 4 |
| 22 | ○ | ▼ | □ | ▲ | ▲ | ○ | Read texts 2, 4 and 5 |
| 23 | ○ | ▼ | □ | □ | ▲ | ▼ | Read texts 2, 5 and 6 |
| 24 | ○ | ▼ | ▲ | ▲ | ▲ | ○ | Read texts 2, 3, 4 and 5 |
| 25 | ○ | ▼ | □ | ▲ | ▲ | ▼ | Read texts 2, 4, 5 and 6 |
| 26 | ○ | ▼ | ▲ | ▲ | ▲ | ▼ | Read texts 2, 3, 4, 5 and 6 |
| 27 | ▼ | ▼ | □ | ▲ | □ | ○ | Read texts 1, 2 and 4 |
| 28 | ▼ | ▼ | □ | □ | ▲ | ○ | Read texts 1, 2 and 5 |
| 29 | ▼ | ▼ | □ | □ | □ | ▼ | Read texts 1, 2 and 6 |
| 30 | ▼ | ▼ | ▲ | □ | ▲ | ○ | Read texts 1, 2, 3 and 5 |
| 31 | ▼ | ▼ | ▲ | □ | □ | ▼ | Read texts 1, 2, 3 and 6 |
| 32 | ▼ | ▼ | ▲ | ▲ | □ | ▼ | Read texts 1, 2, 3, 4 and 6 |
| 33 | ▼ | ○ | ▲ | □ | ▲ | ○ | Read texts 1, 3 and 5 |
| 34 | ▼ | ○ | ▲ | □ | □ | ▼ | Read texts 1, 3 and 6 |
| 35 | ▼ | ○ | ▲ | □ | ▲ | ▼ | Read texts 1, 3, 5 and 6 |
| 36 | ▼ | ○ | □ | ▲ | □ | ▼ | Read texts 1, 4 and 6 |
| 37 | ○ | ▼ | ▲ | □ | ▲ | ○ | Read texts 2, 3 and 5 |
| 38 | ○ | ▼ | ▲ | □ | □ | ▼ | Read texts 2, 3 and 6 |
| 39 | ○ | ▼ | ▲ | ▲ | □ | ▼ | Read texts 2, 3, 4 and 6 |
| 40 | ○ | ▼ | □ | ▲ | □ | ▼ | Read texts 2, 4 and 6 |
| 41 | ○ | ○ | ▲ | ▲ | □ | ○ | Read texts 3 and 4 |
| 42 | ○ | ○ | ▲ | □ | ▲ | ○ | Read texts 3 and 5 |
| 43 | ○ | ○ | ▲ | □ | □ | ▼ | Read texts 3 and 6 |
| 44 | ○ | ○ | ▲ | ▲ | ▲ | ○ | Read texts 3, 4 and 5 |
| 45 | ○ | ○ | ▲ | ▲ | □ | ▼ | Read texts 3, 4 and 6 |
| 46 | ○ | ○ | ▲ | □ | ▲ | ▼ | Read texts 3, 5 and 6 |
| 47 | ○ | ○ | ▲ | ▲ | ▲ | ▼ | Read texts 3, 4, 5 and 6 |
| 48 | ○ | ○ | □ | ▲ | ▲ | ○ | Read texts 4 and 5 |
| 49 | ○ | ○ | □ | ▲ | □ | ▼ | Read texts 4 and 6 |
| 50 | ○ | ○ | □ | ▲ | ▲ | ▼ | Read texts 4, 5 and 6 |
| 51 | ○ | ○ | □ | □ | ▲ | ▼ | Read texts 5 and 6 |
| 52 | ▼ | ○ | □ | □ | □ | ○ | Read text 1 |
| 53 | ○ | ▼ | □ | □ | □ | ○ | Read text 2 |
| 54 | ○ | ○ | ▲ | □ | □ | ○ | Read text 3 |
| 55 | ○ | ○ | □ | ▲ | □ | ○ | Read text 4 |
| 56 | ○ | ○ | □ | □ | ▲ | ○ | Read text 5 |
| 57 | ○ | ○ | □ | □ | □ | ▼ | Read text 6 |

immediate, spectacular results. However your impassioned nature makes you unable to appreciate the long-term perspective or to maintain continuity or consistency. It would be advisable to temper the anxiety that drives you to rush ahead without taking account of changing circumstances and events.

5    You are too easily influenced by whatever circumstances you encounter, be they favourable or unfavourable. As a result you are constantly buffeted between hope and fear, never reaching the happy medium that would allow you to see things objectively. Nevertheless, if you take note of this weakness in your character and the difficulties it brings, you will be able to do something about it.

6    You are perfectly aware of your weaknesses and negative impulses, but you react against them a little too violently or severely, with no distinction between those that have unfortunate consequences and those that do not matter. A willingness to change is a good thing, but only if you know what to take into account and how to be tolerant and patient.

# 31st combination ○ ○ □ □ □ ○

If you are receptive to what is going on around you, and to the people around you, you will discover two positive effects: firstly, you will benefit from the sound advice that will be available to you when needed and secondly, you will be certain to meet people with whom you can feel in tune.

**1** Sooner or later your disposition and your natural abilities will lead you either to influence those around you in some way, or to assume certain responsibilities. This has not happened yet, but there is no reason why it should not happen sooner or later if you know how to develop your personality.

**2** You are guilty of impatience, or of being too quick to push yourself forward and impose your will or your power. This is not a good trait; wait until you are asked, until your services or skills are needed, or until circumstances call for your skills. Only then will they be accepted as authoritative.

**3** You are naturally too emotional and impulsive. Just as it is wrong to give in to the wishes or whims of others automatically, it is equally undesirable to be at the mercy of one's own contradictory emotions. You must therefore make more of an effort to control your emotions and your actions.

**4** Do not use your energy, determination and power to exert a subtle but constant influence on certain people around you. Not only is this a superficial and restrictive kind of domination but it might also give rise to contradictory emotions and feelings that could cause confusion in your own mind and in your relationships.

**5** You seem self-assured, extremely determined and completely aware of your own powers of self-mastery. You know what you are capable of, what you want, and how to get it. Nevertheless, you should also be aware that this attitude makes you insensitive to the advice and feelings of others, and prevents you from being able to exert any influence over the circumstances in your life.

**6** Your intentions and words are often more lofty, ambitious and remarkable than your actions. If you really want to bring people over to your way of thinking, or to make your advice or opinions count, it would be wise to pay more attention to what you do and stop your mouth running away with you.

# 32<sup>nd</sup> combination ○ ☐ ☐ ☐ ○ ○

If you want to give continuity to your actions, maintain your position and keep what you have acquired, in all areas of your life, it is essential that you adapt to changing circumstances. Furthermore, you must take account of unfolding events, while pursuing your objectives and remaining true to yourself.

**1** Do not be too demanding, choosy or uncompromising. By being in too much of a hurry, or by trying to force events in order to get what you want as quickly as possible, you risk overlooking present circumstances and requirements. If you carry on like this you will not get what you want, and will find yourself right back where you started.

**2** Your current situation and circumstances do little to encourage the free expression of your talents and skills, and do not help you to embark on the plans and ambitions that you are certainly capable of implementing. You are perfectly aware of this state of things, but you sensibly resist the temptation to force events.

**32nd combination**

| fig. | | | | | | | |
|---|---|---|---|---|---|---|---|
| 1 | ▼ | ▲ | □ | □ | ○ | ○ | Read texts 1 and 2 |
| 2 | ▼ | □ | ▲ | □ | ○ | ○ | Read texts 1 and 3 |
| 3 | ▼ | □ | □ | ▲ | ○ | ○ | Read texts 1 and 4 |
| 4 | ▼ | □ | □ | □ | ▼ | ○ | Read texts 1 and 5 |
| 5 | ▼ | □ | □ | □ | ○ | ▼ | Read texts 1 and 6 |
| 6 | ▼ | ▲ | ▲ | □ | ○ | ○ | Read texts 1, 2 and 3 |
| 7 | ▼ | □ | ▲ | ▲ | ○ | ○ | Read texts 1, 3 and 4 |
| 8 | ▼ | □ | □ | ▲ | ▼ | ○ | Read texts 1, 4 and 5 |
| 9 | ▼ | □ | □ | □ | ▼ | ▼ | Read texts 1, 5 and 6 |
| 10 | ▼ | ▲ | ▲ | ▲ | ○ | ○ | Read texts 1, 2, 3 and 4 |
| 11 | ▼ | □ | ▲ | ▲ | ▼ | ○ | Read texts 1, 3, 4 and 5 |
| 12 | ▼ | □ | ▲ | ▲ | ○ | ▼ | Read texts 1, 3, 4 and 6 |
| 13 | ▼ | □ | □ | ▲ | ▼ | ▼ | Read texts 1, 4, 5 and 6 |
| 14 | ▼ | ▲ | ▲ | ▲ | ▼ | ○ | Read texts 1, 2, 3, 4 and 5 |
| 15 | ▼ | □ | ▲ | ▲ | ▼ | ▼ | Read texts 1, 3, 4, 5 and 6 |
| 16 | ▼ | ▲ | ▲ | ▲ | ▼ | ▼ | Read texts 1, 2, 3, 4, 5 and 6 |
| 17 | ○ | ▲ | ▲ | □ | ○ | ○ | Read texts 2 and 3 |
| 18 | ○ | ▲ | □ | ▲ | ○ | ○ | Read texts 2 and 4 |
| 19 | ○ | ▲ | □ | □ | ▼ | ○ | Read texts 2 and 5 |
| 20 | ○ | ▲ | □ | □ | ○ | ▼ | Read texts 2 and 6 |
| 21 | ○ | ▲ | ▲ | ▲ | ○ | ○ | Read texts 2, 3 and 4 |
| 22 | ○ | ▲ | ▲ | ▲ | ▼ | ○ | Read texts 2, 4 and 5 |
| 23 | ○ | ▲ | □ | ▲ | ▼ | ▼ | Read texts 2, 5 and 6 |
| 24 | ○ | ▲ | ▲ | ▲ | ▼ | ○ | Read texts 2, 3, 4 and 5 |
| 25 | ○ | ▲ | □ | ▲ | ▼ | ▼ | Read texts 2, 4, 5 and 6 |
| 26 | ○ | ▲ | ▲ | ▲ | ▼ | ▼ | Read texts 2, 3, 4, 5 and 6 |
| 27 | ▼ | ▲ | □ | ▲ | ○ | ○ | Read texts 1, 2 and 4 |
| 28 | ▼ | ▲ | □ | □ | ▼ | ○ | Read texts 1, 2 and 5 |
| 29 | ▼ | ▲ | □ | □ | ○ | ▼ | Read texts 1, 2 and 6 |
| 30 | ▼ | ▲ | ▲ | □ | ▼ | ○ | Read texts 1, 2, 3 and 5 |
| 31 | ▼ | ▲ | ▲ | □ | ○ | ▼ | Read texts 1, 2, 3 and 6 |
| 32 | ▼ | ▲ | ▲ | ▲ | ○ | ▼ | Read texts 1, 2, 3, 4 and 6 |
| 33 | ▼ | □ | ▲ | □ | ▼ | ○ | Read texts 1, 3 and 5 |
| 34 | ▼ | □ | ▲ | □ | ○ | ▼ | Read texts 1, 3 and 6 |
| 35 | ▼ | □ | ▲ | □ | ▼ | ▼ | Read texts 1, 3, 5 and 6 |
| 36 | ▼ | □ | □ | ▲ | ○ | ▼ | Read texts 1, 4 and 6 |
| 37 | ○ | ▲ | ▲ | □ | ▼ | ○ | Read texts 2, 3 and 5 |
| 38 | ○ | ▲ | ▲ | □ | ▼ | ○ | Read texts 2, 3 and 6 |
| 39 | ○ | ▲ | ▲ | ▲ | ○ | ▼ | Read texts 2, 3, 4 and 6 |
| 40 | ○ | ▲ | □ | ▲ | ○ | ▼ | Read texts 2, 4 and 6 |
| 41 | ○ | □ | ▲ | ▲ | ○ | ○ | Read texts 3 and 4 |
| 42 | ○ | □ | ▲ | □ | ▼ | ○ | Read texts 3 and 5 |
| 43 | ○ | □ | ▲ | □ | ○ | ▼ | Read texts 3 and 6 |
| 44 | ○ | □ | ▲ | ▲ | ▼ | ○ | Read texts 3, 4 and 5 |
| 45 | ○ | □ | ▲ | ▲ | ○ | ▼ | Read texts 3, 4 and 6 |
| 46 | ○ | □ | ▲ | □ | ▼ | ▼ | Read texts 3, 5 and 6 |
| 47 | ○ | □ | ▲ | ▲ | ▼ | ▼ | Read texts 3, 4, 5 and 6 |
| 48 | ○ | □ | □ | ▲ | ▼ | ○ | Read texts 4 and 5 |
| 49 | ○ | □ | □ | ▲ | ○ | ▼ | Read texts 4 and 6 |
| 50 | ○ | □ | □ | ▲ | ▼ | ▼ | Read texts 4, 5 and 6 |
| 51 | ○ | □ | □ | □ | ▼ | ▼ | Read texts 5 and 6 |
| 52 | ▼ | □ | □ | □ | ○ | ○ | Read text 1 |
| 53 | ○ | ▲ | □ | □ | ○ | ○ | Read text 2 |
| 54 | ○ | □ | ▲ | □ | ○ | ○ | Read text 3 |
| 55 | ○ | □ | □ | ▲ | ○ | ○ | Read text 4 |
| 56 | ○ | □ | □ | □ | ▼ | ○ | Read text 5 |
| 57 | ○ | □ | □ | □ | ○ | ▼ | Read text 6 |

**3** Your inner serenity and personal development are too much at the mercy of the things that happen to you. Someone so easily influenced can only expect disappointment or moments of unhappiness that, although you do not realize it, are the direct result of your state of mind.

**4** If you do not give yourself every opportunity to find what you seek or to obtain the results you count upon – or if you are looking for something in completely the wrong place – you will get nowhere. Neither your determination nor your strength of character will help you achieve your ends.

**5** It is vital that you meet the demands of your responsibilities and current obligations, whether material or moral. Do not allow yourself to be distracted by anything or anyone. Nevertheless, your sense of duty should not prevent you from being flexible and adaptable. This will only make you more effective.

**6** You are probably not fully aware that a state of chronic anxiety drives you to rush things, and makes you too impatient when planning projects or following your objectives. This disruptive behaviour pattern must be broken before it causes you to fail.

# 33rd combination ○ ○ □ □ □ □

Your situation is such that, if you insist on seeing this struggle through to the bitter end, you are sure to lose. It would be better to pull out – but without dropping your guard – and wait for a better moment or more favourable circumstances before you return to the fray. By the same token, if you are up against a malicious person, do not put up a fight, and do not let the attacks bother you. In this way he or she will be powerless to hurt you.

1   In times of retreat or withdrawal, or when your options are limited, you find yourself unprotected and unable to avoid dangerous situations or unforeseen circumstances. In moments like these it is better to do nothing. Your sole concern should be to escape this negative situation or turn it around.

2   Although your circumstances and environment are unfavourable, and your relationships provide no support, you are trying so hard to obtain something, and are persevering so doggedly and with such faith, that you will undoubtedly reach your goal, and your revenge.

3   It is clear that your only solution is to take a step back, to give up certain things or to do nothing at all. However, your situation or current circumstances prevent you from doing so. Therefore you have to come to terms with the fact that, like it or not, your partners seem to need you but are not up to the job.

4   Since you realize that the only way out is to break off all contact with somebody in your circle, it should be done immediately, dispassionately and with no reservations. The person in question will have more trouble accepting the severance than you, because your relationship provided him/her with the strength necessary for balance and well-being.

| | | | | | | | |
|---|---|---|---|---|---|---|---|
| fig. 1 | ▼ | ▼ | □ | □ | □ | □ | Read texts 1 and 2 |
| 2 | ▼ | ○ | ▲ | □ | □ | □ | Read texts 1 and 3 |
| 3 | ▼ | ○ | □ | ▲ | □ | □ | Read texts 1 and 4 |
| 4 | ▼ | ○ | □ | □ | ▲ | □ | Read texts 1 and 5 |
| 5 | ▼ | ○ | □ | □ | □ | ▲ | Read texts 1 and 6 |
| 6 | ▼ | ▼ | ▲ | □ | □ | □ | Read texts 1, 2 and 3 |
| 7 | ▼ | ○ | ▲ | ▲ | □ | □ | Read texts 1, 3 and 4 |
| 8 | ▼ | ○ | □ | ▲ | ▲ | □ | Read texts 1, 4 and 5 |
| 9 | ▼ | ○ | □ | ▲ | □ | ▲ | Read texts 1, 5 and 6 |
| 10 | ▼ | ▼ | ▲ | ▲ | □ | □ | Read texts 1, 2, 3 and 4 |
| 11 | ▼ | ○ | ▲ | ▲ | ▲ | □ | Read texts 1, 3, 4 and 5 |
| 12 | ▼ | ○ | ▲ | ▲ | □ | ▲ | Read texts 1, 3, 4 and 6 |
| 13 | ▼ | ○ | □ | ▲ | ▲ | ▲ | Read texts 1, 4, 5 and 6 |
| 14 | ▼ | ▼ | ▲ | ▲ | ▲ | □ | Read texts 1, 2, 3, 4 and 5 |
| 15 | ▼ | ○ | ▲ | ▲ | ▲ | ▲ | Read texts 1, 3, 4, 5 and 6 |
| 16 | ▼ | ▼ | ▲ | ▲ | ▲ | ▲ | Read texts 1, 2, 3, 4, 5 and 6 |
| 17 | ○ | ▼ | ▲ | □ | □ | □ | Read texts 2 and 3 |
| 18 | ○ | ▼ | □ | ▲ | □ | □ | Read texts 2 and 4 |
| 19 | ○ | ▼ | □ | □ | ▲ | □ | Read texts 2 and 5 |
| 20 | ○ | ▼ | □ | □ | □ | ▲ | Read texts 2 and 6 |
| 21 | ○ | ▼ | ▲ | ▲ | □ | □ | Read texts 2, 3 and 4 |
| 22 | ○ | ▼ | □ | ▲ | ▲ | □ | Read texts 2, 4 and 5 |
| 23 | ○ | ▼ | □ | □ | ▲ | ▲ | Read texts 2, 5 and 6 |
| 24 | ○ | ▼ | ▲ | ▲ | ▲ | □ | Read texts 2, 3, 4 and 5 |
| 25 | ○ | ▼ | ▲ | ▲ | □ | ▲ | Read texts 2, 4, 5 and 6 |
| 26 | ○ | ▼ | ▲ | ▲ | ▲ | ▲ | Read texts 2, 3, 4, 5 and 6 |
| 27 | ▼ | ▼ | □ | ▲ | □ | □ | Read texts 1, 2 and 4 |
| 28 | ▼ | ▼ | □ | □ | ▲ | □ | Read texts 1, 2 and 5 |
| 29 | ▼ | ▼ | □ | □ | □ | ▲ | Read texts 1, 2 and 6 |
| 30 | ▼ | ▼ | ▲ | □ | ▲ | □ | Read texts 1, 2, 3 and 5 |
| 31 | ▼ | ▼ | ▲ | □ | □ | ▲ | Read texts 1, 2, 3 and 6 |
| 32 | ▼ | ▼ | ▲ | ▲ | □ | ▲ | Read texts 1, 2, 3, 4 and 6 |
| 33 | ▼ | ○ | ▲ | □ | ▲ | □ | Read texts 1, 3 and 5 |
| 34 | ▼ | ○ | ▲ | □ | □ | ▲ | Read texts 1, 3 and 6 |
| 35 | ▼ | ○ | ▲ | □ | ▲ | ▲ | Read texts 1, 3, 5 and 6 |
| 36 | ▼ | ○ | □ | ▲ | □ | ▲ | Read texts 1, 4 and 6 |
| 37 | ○ | ▼ | ▲ | □ | ▲ | □ | Read texts 2, 3 and 5 |
| 38 | ○ | ▼ | ▲ | □ | □ | ▲ | Read texts 2, 3 and 6 |
| 39 | ○ | ▼ | ▲ | ▲ | □ | ▲ | Read texts 2, 3, 4 and 6 |
| 40 | ○ | ▼ | □ | ▲ | □ | ▲ | Read texts 2, 4 and 6 |
| 41 | ○ | ○ | ▲ | ▲ | □ | □ | Read texts 3 and 4 |
| 42 | ○ | ○ | ▲ | □ | ▲ | □ | Read texts 3 and 5 |
| 43 | ○ | ○ | ▲ | □ | □ | ▲ | Read texts 3 and 6 |
| 44 | ○ | ○ | ▲ | ▲ | ▲ | □ | Read texts 3, 4 and 5 |
| 45 | ○ | ○ | ▲ | ▲ | □ | ▲ | Read texts 3, 4 and 6 |
| 46 | ○ | ○ | ▲ | □ | ▲ | ▲ | Read texts 3, 5 and 6 |
| 47 | ○ | ○ | ▲ | ▲ | ▲ | ▲ | Read texts 3, 4, 5 and 6 |
| 48 | ○ | ○ | □ | ▲ | ▲ | □ | Read texts 4 and 5 |
| 49 | ○ | ○ | □ | ▲ | □ | ▲ | Read texts 4 and 6 |
| 50 | ○ | ○ | □ | ▲ | ▲ | ▲ | Read texts 4, 5 and 6 |
| 51 | ○ | ○ | □ | □ | ▲ | ▲ | Read texts 5 and 6 |
| 52 | ▼ | ○ | □ | □ | □ | □ | Read text 1 |
| 53 | ○ | ▼ | □ | □ | □ | □ | Read text 2 |
| 54 | ○ | ○ | ▲ | □ | □ | □ | Read text 3 |
| 55 | ○ | ○ | □ | ▲ | □ | □ | Read text 4 |
| 56 | ○ | ○ | □ | □ | ▲ | □ | Read text 5 |
| 57 | ○ | ○ | □ | □ | □ | ▲ | Read text 6 |

**33rd combination**   ○ ○ □ □ □ □

303

**34th combination**

| fig. | | | | | | | |
|---|---|---|---|---|---|---|---|
| 1 | ▲ | ▲ | □ | □ | ○ | ○ | Read texts 1 and 2 |
| 2 | ▲ | □ | ▲ | □ | ○ | ○ | Read texts 1 and 3 |
| 3 | ▲ | □ | □ | ▲ | ○ | ○ | Read texts 1 and 4 |
| 4 | ▲ | □ | □ | □ | ▼ | ○ | Read texts 1 and 5 |
| 5 | ▲ | □ | □ | □ | ○ | ▼ | Read texts 1 and 6 |
| 6 | ▲ | ▲ | ▲ | □ | ○ | ○ | Read texts 1, 2 and 3 |
| 7 | ▲ | □ | ▲ | ▲ | ○ | ○ | Read texts 1, 3 and 4 |
| 8 | ▲ | □ | □ | ▲ | ▼ | ○ | Read texts 1, 4 and 5 |
| 9 | ▲ | □ | □ | □ | ▼ | ▼ | Read texts 1, 5 and 6 |
| 10 | ▲ | ▲ | ▲ | ▲ | ○ | ○ | Read texts 1, 2, 3 and 4 |
| 11 | ▲ | □ | ▲ | ▲ | ▼ | ○ | Read texts 1, 3, 4 and 5 |
| 12 | ▲ | □ | ▲ | ▲ | ○ | ▼ | Read texts 1, 3, 4 and 6 |
| 13 | ▲ | □ | □ | ▲ | ▼ | ▼ | Read texts 1, 4, 5 and 6 |
| 14 | ▲ | ▲ | ▲ | ▲ | ▼ | ○ | Read texts 1, 2, 3, 4 and 5 |
| 15 | ▲ | □ | ▲ | ▲ | ▼ | ▼ | Read texts 1, 3, 4, 5 and 6 |
| 16 | ▲ | ▲ | ▲ | ▲ | ▼ | ▼ | Read texts 1, 2, 3, 4, 5 and 6 |
| 17 | □ | ▲ | ▲ | □ | ○ | ○ | Read texts 2 and 3 |
| 18 | □ | ▲ | □ | ▲ | ○ | ○ | Read texts 2 and 4 |
| 19 | □ | ▲ | □ | □ | ▼ | ○ | Read texts 2 and 5 |
| 20 | □ | ▲ | □ | □ | ○ | ▼ | Read texts 2 and 6 |
| 21 | □ | ▲ | ▲ | ▲ | ○ | ○ | Read texts 2, 3 and 4 |
| 22 | □ | ▲ | □ | ▲ | ▼ | ○ | Read texts 2, 4 and 5 |
| 23 | □ | ▲ | □ | □ | ▼ | ▼ | Read texts 2, 5 and 6 |
| 24 | □ | ▲ | ▲ | ▲ | ▼ | ○ | Read texts 2, 3, 4 and 5 |
| 25 | □ | ▲ | □ | ▲ | ▼ | ▼ | Read texts 2, 4, 5 and 6 |
| 26 | □ | ▲ | ▲ | ▲ | ▼ | ▼ | Read texts 2, 3, 4, 5 and 6 |
| 27 | ▲ | ▲ | □ | ▲ | ○ | ○ | Read texts 1, 2 and 4 |
| 28 | ▲ | ▲ | □ | □ | ▼ | ○ | Read texts 1, 2 and 5 |
| 29 | ▲ | ▲ | □ | □ | ○ | ▼ | Read texts 1, 2 and 6 |
| 30 | ▲ | ▲ | ▲ | □ | ▼ | ○ | Read texts 1, 2, 3 and 5 |
| 31 | ▲ | ▲ | ▲ | □ | ○ | ▼ | Read texts 1, 2, 3 and 6 |
| 32 | ▲ | ▲ | ▲ | ▲ | ○ | ▼ | Read texts 1, 2, 3, 4 and 6 |
| 33 | ▲ | □ | ▲ | □ | ▼ | ○ | Read texts 1, 3 and 5 |
| 34 | ▲ | □ | ▲ | □ | ○ | ▼ | Read texts 1, 3 and 6 |
| 35 | ▲ | □ | ▲ | □ | ▼ | ▼ | Read texts 1, 3, 5 and 6 |
| 36 | ▲ | □ | □ | ▲ | ○ | ▼ | Read texts 1, 4 and 6 |
| 37 | □ | ▲ | ▲ | □ | ▼ | ○ | Read texts 2, 3 and 5 |
| 38 | □ | ▲ | ▲ | □ | ○ | ▼ | Read texts 2, 3 and 6 |
| 39 | □ | ▲ | ▲ | ▲ | ○ | ▼ | Read texts 2, 3, 4 and 6 |
| 40 | □ | ▲ | □ | ▲ | ○ | ▼ | Read texts 2, 4 and 6 |
| 41 | □ | □ | ▲ | ▲ | ○ | ○ | Read texts 3 and 4 |
| 42 | □ | □ | ▲ | □ | ▼ | ○ | Read texts 3 and 5 |
| 43 | □ | □ | ▲ | □ | ○ | ▼ | Read texts 3 and 6 |
| 44 | □ | □ | ▲ | ▲ | ▼ | ○ | Read texts 3, 4 and 5 |
| 45 | □ | □ | ▲ | ▲ | ○ | ▼ | Read texts 3, 4 and 6 |
| 46 | □ | □ | ▲ | □ | ▼ | ▼ | Read texts 3, 5 and 6 |
| 47 | □ | □ | ▲ | ▲ | ▼ | ▼ | Read texts 3, 4, 5 and 6 |
| 48 | □ | □ | □ | ▲ | ▼ | ○ | Read texts 4 and 5 |
| 49 | □ | □ | □ | ▲ | ○ | ▼ | Read texts 4 and 6 |
| 50 | □ | □ | □ | ▲ | ▼ | ▼ | Read texts 4, 5 and 6 |
| 51 | □ | □ | □ | □ | ▼ | ▼ | Read texts 5 and 6 |
| 52 | ▲ | □ | □ | □ | ○ | ○ | Read text 1 |
| 53 | □ | ▲ | □ | □ | ○ | ○ | Read text 2 |
| 54 | □ | □ | ▲ | □ | ○ | ○ | Read text 3 |
| 55 | □ | □ | □ | ▲ | ○ | ○ | Read text 4 |
| 56 | □ | □ | □ | □ | ▼ | ○ | Read text 5 |
| 57 | □ | □ | □ | □ | ○ | ▼ | Read text 6 |

**5** All things considered, you now know that the only thing to do is to relinquish a situation, to step back or to withdraw. Since this is clear in your mind, you can effect this transition or separation smoothly and gracefully; above all do not let yourself be influenced by irrelevant emotions, needs or objections.

**6** You see clearly what remains to be done. You have no doubts, regrets or remorse. When everything is this straight-forward and obvious, both in your own mind and around you, there is no sense in hanging around. From now on you can act with complete independence and break from whatever was hampering your actions, desires and wishes – for good.

# 34th combination □ □ □ □ ○ ○

Your current situation is a green light to act as you wish, without having to answer to anybody. However, this kind of liberty demands discipline, a sense of duty and fairness, and a knack for picking the ideal moment to act in conjunction with everything around you. If you can manage this, you will obtain the best possible results.

**1** You have all the power you need to push forward, and are strong and determined enough to do it, once you have made up your mind. Nevertheless, be aware that, as things stand, it would be a big mistake to force events or defy destiny. You are advised here and now not to press ahead, because the time is not right.

2    You are on the road to success. It is not yet staring you in the face, but you sense that it is within your grasp. Nevertheless, do not overestimate your strength or your luck, and do not think of it as a done deal. After all, this success is still only an objective or an opportunity along your way. You still have some way to go before you reach your final goal or can find satisfaction.

3    Instead of boasting about your strength, power or prerogatives in order to get what you want, when you want it – as certain people you know are perhaps tempted to do – it is wiser to show moderation and restraint when exercising your power or authority. This means waiting for the right moment to push ahead.

4    Do not seek automatically to defend yourself, nor to insist on overcoming the obstacles and difficulties in your way by force or at all costs. This kind of attitude causes unavoidable tension and opposition. When your inner resources are concentrated and focused firmly on a particular goal you can be sure to reach it when the time is right, without drastic action. Inner strength is the most powerful strength of all.

5    You can easily restrain your gratuitous aggression, or the temptation to act or to push yourself forward at the wrong time. Self-control can only be helpful right now, as it will prevent you from making a serious mistake and also because you will soon learn the power of this control over yourself.

6    You are stuck in a dead-end situation with no means of turning back. The only solution is to wait for an exit to present itself. In the meantime, there is no use in being agitated, in getting impatient or stubbornly trying to escape, because the time is not ripe. Calm down, take time to reflect and all will turn out well.

# 35th combination ○ ○ ○ ❑ ○ ❑

Professionally and socially, this is a time for progress and evolution. Therefore the mission, task or job entrusted to you is your authority to take steps to develop and broaden the whole picture.

1    Your determination to improve your situation, or to make changes to your professional or social life, has weakened. You feel that your initiatives have been misinterpreted or have been approved by very few people. But keep calm and pursue your objectives without letting other people's reactions get to you. You will reach your goal in the end.

2    You are in contact with an influential man who has power or considerable authority in his own field. You would like to associate with and possibly work with him, which would give your career a boost. Even though present circumstances make this unlikely in the near future, you are destined to work together, and you can be sure that he will make you a proposition soon.

3    You are doing anything and everything to move your situation forward, and you have the support of certain people who trust you and encourage your efforts. Obviously their support does, to some extent, compromise your independence and puts you in

**35th combination**

| fig. | | | | | | | |
|---|---|---|---|---|---|---|---|
| 1 | ▼ | ▼ | ○ | □ | ○ | □ | Read texts 1 and 2 |
| 2 | ▼ | ○ | ▼ | □ | ○ | □ | Read texts 1 and 3 |
| 3 | ▼ | ○ | ○ | ▲ | ○ | □ | Read texts 1 and 4 |
| 4 | ▼ | ○ | ○ | □ | ▼ | □ | Read texts 1 and 5 |
| 5 | ▼ | ○ | ○ | □ | ○ | ▲ | Read texts 1 and 6 |
| 6 | ▼ | ▼ | ▼ | ○ | □ | □ | Read texts 1, 2 and 3 |
| 7 | ▼ | ▼ | ○ | ▲ | ○ | □ | Read texts 1, 2 and 4 |
| 8 | ▼ | ▼ | ○ | □ | ▼ | □ | Read texts 1, 2 and 5 |
| 9 | ▼ | ▼ | ○ | □ | ○ | ▲ | Read texts 1, 2 and 6 |
| 10 | ▼ | ▼ | ▼ | ▲ | ○ | □ | Read texts 1, 2, 3 and 4 |
| 11 | ▼ | ▼ | ▼ | □ | ▼ | □ | Read texts 1, 2, 3 and 5 |
| 12 | ▼ | ▼ | ▼ | □ | ○ | ▲ | Read texts 1, 2, 3 and 6 |
| 13 | ▼ | ▼ | ▼ | ▲ | ▼ | □ | Read texts 1, 2, 3, 4 and 5 |
| 14 | ▼ | ▼ | ▼ | ▲ | ○ | ▲ | Read texts 1, 2, 3, 4 and 6 |
| 15 | ▼ | ▼ | ▼ | ▲ | ▼ | ▲ | Read texts 1, 2, 3, 4, 5 and 6 |
| 16 | ▼ | ○ | ▼ | ▲ | ○ | □ | Read texts 1, 3 and 4 |
| 17 | ▼ | ○ | ▼ | □ | ▼ | □ | Read texts 1, 3 and 5 |
| 18 | ▼ | ○ | ▼ | □ | ○ | ▲ | Read texts 1, 3 and 6 |
| 19 | ▼ | ○ | ▼ | ▲ | ▼ | □ | Read texts 1, 3, 4 and 5 |
| 20 | ▼ | ○ | ▼ | ▲ | ○ | ▲ | Read texts 1, 3, 4 and 6 |
| 21 | ▼ | ○ | ▼ | □ | ▼ | ▲ | Read texts 1, 3, 5 and 6 |
| 22 | ▼ | ○ | ▼ | ▲ | ▼ | ▲ | Read texts 1, 3, 4, 5 and 6 |
| 23 | ▼ | ○ | ○ | ▲ | ▼ | □ | Read texts 1, 4 and 5 |
| 24 | ▼ | ○ | ○ | ▲ | ○ | ▲ | Read texts 1, 4 and 6 |
| 25 | ▼ | ○ | ○ | ▲ | ▼ | ▲ | Read texts 1, 4, 5 and 6 |
| 26 | ▼ | ○ | ○ | □ | ▼ | ▲ | Read texts 1, 5 and 6 |
| 27 | ○ | ▼ | ▼ | □ | ○ | □ | Read texts 2 and 3 |
| 28 | ○ | ▼ | ○ | ▲ | ○ | □ | Read texts 2 and 4 |
| 29 | ○ | ▼ | ○ | □ | ▼ | □ | Read texts 2 and 5 |
| 30 | ○ | ▼ | ○ | □ | ○ | ▲ | Read texts 2 and 6 |
| 31 | ○ | ▼ | ▼ | ▲ | ○ | □ | Read texts 2, 3 and 4 |
| 32 | ○ | ▼ | ▼ | □ | ▼ | □ | Read texts 2, 3 and 5 |
| 33 | ○ | ▼ | ▼ | □ | ○ | ▲ | Read texts 2, 3 and 6 |
| 34 | ○ | ▼ | ▼ | ▲ | ▼ | □ | Read texts 2, 3, 4 and 5 |
| 35 | ○ | ▼ | ▼ | ▲ | ○ | ▲ | Read texts 2, 3, 4 and 6 |
| 36 | ○ | ▼ | ▼ | ▲ | ▼ | ▲ | Read texts 2, 3, 4, 5 and 6 |
| 37 | ○ | ▼ | ○ | ▲ | ▼ | □ | Read texts 2, 4 and 5 |
| 38 | ○ | ▼ | ○ | ▲ | ○ | ▲ | Read texts 2, 4 and 6 |
| 39 | ○ | ▼ | ○ | ▲ | ▼ | ▲ | Read texts 2, 4, 5 and 6 |
| 40 | ○ | ▼ | ○ | □ | ▼ | ▲ | Read texts 2, 5 and 6 |
| 41 | ○ | ○ | ▼ | ▲ | ○ | □ | Read texts 3 and 4 |
| 42 | ○ | ○ | ▼ | □ | ▼ | □ | Read texts 3 and 5 |
| 43 | ○ | ○ | ▼ | □ | ○ | ▲ | Read texts 3 and 6 |
| 44 | ○ | ○ | ▼ | ▲ | ▼ | □ | Read texts 3, 4 and 5 |
| 45 | ○ | ○ | ▼ | ▲ | ○ | ▲ | Read texts 3, 4 and 6 |
| 46 | ○ | ○ | ▼ | □ | ▼ | ▲ | Read texts 3, 5 and 6 |
| 47 | ○ | ○ | ▼ | ▲ | ▼ | ▲ | Read texts 3, 4, 5 and 6 |
| 48 | ○ | ○ | ○ | ▲ | ▼ | □ | Read texts 4 and 5 |
| 49 | ○ | ○ | ○ | ▲ | ○ | ▲ | Read texts 4 and 6 |
| 50 | ○ | ○ | ○ | ▲ | ▼ | ▲ | Read texts 4, 5 and 6 |
| 51 | ○ | ○ | ○ | □ | ▼ | ▲ | Read texts 5 and 6 |
| 52 | ▼ | ○ | ○ | □ | ○ | □ | Read text 1 |
| 53 | ○ | ▼ | ○ | □ | ○ | □ | Read text 2 |
| 54 | ○ | ○ | ▼ | □ | ○ | □ | Read text 3 |
| 55 | ○ | ○ | ○ | ▲ | ○ | □ | Read text 4 |
| 56 | ○ | ○ | ○ | □ | ▼ | □ | Read text 5 |
| 57 | ○ | ○ | ○ | □ | ○ | ▲ | Read text 6 |

their debt. However this will not have any negative repercussions, but will actually help you reach your goals.

4   In times like these, when things are changing and opening up, the powerful or strong-willed know how to exploit the situation to their own advantage. Nevertheless, if the means utilized are not good, this will soon become known and those responsible will suffer the consequences.

5   Things are looking rosy, although it has never occurred to you to exploit the situation for your own personal gain. But your natural selflessness is an excellent thing. It shows that you attach more importance to what you do than to the results you obtain, and are more concerned with substance than appearance. It also shows that doing something of which you can be proud matters more to you than any personal benefits you might gain from a given situation.

6   At the moment you are tempted to act aggressively, even brutally, to impose order around you or to dispense justice. Nevertheless, you must realize that this attitude is not without danger, particularly if you turn against strangers. On the other hand, if those close to you have made mistakes, such reactions can be justified – provided that you seek satisfaction in a more balanced manner.

# 36<sup>th</sup>


# 36th combination □ ○ □ ○ ○ ○

Your current circumstances or situation do not put you in a strong position to expose what needs to be exposed, or to take dynamic action to escape your difficulties. This is undoubtedly regrettable, but you must resign yourself to maintaining a degree of restraint without getting sidetracked or thrown off course, while trying not to be taken in by what is going on around you.

**1** You are in an uncomfortable, precarious position that makes you feel insecure. To achieve your ideas, ambitions or cherished plans, you must accept certain constraints, which have actually caused your present unfavourable circumstances. Whatever people think or say about you, you are guided by your ideals and follow a clear objective with perseverance and tenacity.

**2** You have suffered a rebuff or someone has tried to harm you or get in your way. However, your quick and determined reaction is the appropriate response and will stave off any serious consequences for you and the people around you. Your sense of responsibility dictates this reaction, which is the fairest way to behave in circumstances like these.

**3** Fortuitous circumstances will reveal the person, or hidden causes, behind the difficulties or obstacles you have been facing for some time. You will therefore be able to disarm the person in question or solve your problems. However, do not expect things to

| fig. 1 | ▲ | ▼ | □ | ○ | ○ | ○ | Read texts 1 and 2 |
|---|---|---|---|---|---|---|---|
| 2 | ▲ | ○ | ▲ | ○ | ○ | ○ | Read texts 1 and 3 |
| 3 | ▲ | ○ | □ | ▼ | ○ | ○ | Read texts 1 and 4 |
| 4 | ▲ | ○ | □ | ○ | ▼ | ○ | Read texts 1 and 5 |
| 5 | ▲ | ○ | □ | ○ | ○ | ▼ | Read texts 1 and 6 |
| 6 | ▲ | ▼ | ▲ | ○ | ○ | ○ | Read texts 1, 2 and 3 |
| 7 | ▲ | ▼ | □ | ▼ | ○ | ○ | Read texts 1, 2 and 4 |
| 8 | ▲ | ▼ | □ | ○ | ▼ | ○ | Read texts 1, 2 and 5 |
| 9 | ▲ | ▼ | □ | ○ | ○ | ▼ | Read texts 1, 2 and 6 |
| 10 | ▲ | ▼ | ▲ | ▼ | ○ | ○ | Read texts 1, 2, 3 and 4 |
| 11 | ▲ | ▼ | ▲ | ○ | ▼ | ○ | Read texts 1, 2, 3 and 5 |
| 12 | ▲ | ▼ | ▲ | ○ | ○ | ▼ | Read texts 1, 2, 3 and 6 |
| 13 | ▲ | ▼ | ▲ | ▼ | ▼ | ○ | Read texts 1, 2, 3, 4 and 5 |
| 14 | ▲ | ▼ | ▲ | ▼ | ○ | ▼ | Read texts 1, 2, 3, 4 and 6 |
| 15 | ▲ | ▼ | ▲ | ▼ | ▼ | ▼ | Read texts 1, 2, 3, 4, 5 and 6 |
| 16 | ▲ | ○ | ▲ | ▼ | ○ | ○ | Read texts 1, 3 and 4 |
| 17 | ▲ | ○ | ▲ | ○ | ▼ | ○ | Read texts 1, 3 and 5 |
| 18 | ▲ | ○ | ▲ | ○ | ○ | ▼ | Read texts 1, 3 and 6 |
| 19 | ▲ | ○ | ▲ | ▼ | ▼ | ○ | Read texts 1, 3, 4 and 5 |
| 20 | ▲ | ○ | ▲ | ▼ | ○ | ▼ | Read texts 1, 3, 4 and 6 |
| 21 | ▲ | ○ | ▲ | ○ | ▼ | ▼ | Read texts 1, 3, 5 and 6 |
| 22 | ▲ | ○ | ▲ | ▼ | ▼ | ▼ | Read texts 1, 3, 4, 5 and 6 |
| 23 | ▲ | ○ | □ | ▼ | ▼ | ○ | Read texts 1, 4 and 5 |
| 24 | ▲ | ○ | □ | ▼ | ○ | ▼ | Read texts 1, 4 and 6 |
| 25 | ▲ | ○ | □ | ▼ | ▼ | ▼ | Read texts 1, 4, 5 and 6 |
| 26 | ▲ | ○ | □ | ○ | ▼ | ▼ | Read texts 1, 5 and 6 |
| 27 | □ | ▼ | ▲ | ○ | ○ | ○ | Read texts 2 and 3 |
| 28 | □ | ▼ | □ | ▼ | ○ | ○ | Read texts 2 and 4 |
| 29 | □ | ▼ | □ | ○ | ▼ | ○ | Read texts 2 and 5 |
| 30 | □ | ▼ | □ | ○ | ○ | ▼ | Read texts 2 and 6 |
| 31 | □ | ▼ | ▲ | ▼ | ○ | ○ | Read texts 2, 3 and 4 |
| 32 | □ | ▼ | ▲ | ○ | ▼ | ○ | Read texts 2, 3 and 5 |
| 33 | □ | ▼ | ▲ | ○ | ○ | ▼ | Read texts 2, 3 and 6 |
| 34 | □ | ▼ | ▲ | ▼ | ▼ | ○ | Read texts 2, 3, 4 and 5 |
| 35 | □ | ▼ | ▲ | ▼ | ○ | ▼ | Read texts 2, 3, 4 and 6 |
| 36 | □ | ▼ | ▲ | ▼ | ▼ | ▼ | Read texts 2, 3, 4, 5 and 6 |
| 37 | □ | ▼ | □ | ▼ | ▼ | ○ | Read texts 2, 4 and 5 |
| 38 | □ | ▼ | □ | ▼ | ○ | ▼ | Read texts 2, 4 and 6 |
| 39 | □ | ▼ | □ | ▼ | ▼ | ▼ | Read texts 2, 4, 5 and 6 |
| 40 | □ | ▼ | □ | ○ | ▼ | ▼ | Read texts 2, 5 and 6 |
| 41 | □ | ○ | ▲ | ▼ | ○ | ○ | Read texts 3 and 4 |
| 42 | □ | ○ | ▲ | ○ | ▼ | ○ | Read texts 3 and 5 |
| 43 | □ | ○ | ▲ | ○ | ○ | ▼ | Read texts 3 and 6 |
| 44 | □ | ○ | ▲ | ▼ | ▼ | ○ | Read texts 3, 4 and 5 |
| 45 | □ | ○ | ▲ | ▼ | ○ | ▼ | Read texts 3, 4 and 6 |
| 46 | □ | ○ | ▲ | ○ | ▼ | ▼ | Read texts 3, 5 and 6 |
| 47 | □ | ○ | ▲ | ▼ | ▼ | ▼ | Read texts 3, 4, 5 and 6 |
| 48 | □ | ○ | □ | ▼ | ▼ | ○ | Read texts 4 and 5 |
| 49 | □ | ○ | □ | ▼ | ○ | ▼ | Read texts 4 and 6 |
| 50 | □ | ○ | □ | ▼ | ▼ | ▼ | Read texts 4, 5 and 6 |
| 51 | □ | ○ | □ | ○ | ▼ | ▼ | Read texts 5 and 6 |
| 52 | ▲ | ○ | □ | ○ | ○ | ○ | Read text 1 |
| 53 | □ | ▼ | □ | ○ | ○ | ○ | Read text 2 |
| 54 | □ | ○ | ▲ | ○ | ○ | ○ | Read text 3 |
| 55 | □ | ○ | □ | ▼ | ○ | ○ | Read text 4 |
| 56 | □ | ○ | □ | ○ | ▼ | ○ | Read text 5 |
| 57 | □ | ○ | □ | ○ | ○ | ▼ | Read text 6 |

**37th combination**

| fig. 1 | ▲ | ▼ | □ | ○ | □ | □ | Read texts 1 and 2 |
|---|---|---|---|---|---|---|---|
| 2 | ▲ | ○ | ▲ | ○ | □ | □ | Read texts 1 and 3 |
| 3 | ▲ | ○ | □ | ▼ | ○ | □ | Read texts 1 and 4 |
| 4 | ▲ | ○ | □ | ○ | ▲ | □ | Read texts 1 and 5 |
| 5 | ▲ | ○ | □ | ○ | □ | ▲ | Read texts 1 and 6 |
| 6 | ▲ | ▼ | ▲ | ○ | □ | □ | Read texts 1, 2 and 3 |
| 7 | ▲ | ○ | ▲ | ▼ | □ | □ | Read texts 1, 3 and 4 |
| 8 | ▲ | ○ | ▼ | ▲ | □ | □ | Read texts 1, 4 and 5 |
| 9 | ▲ | ○ | □ | ○ | ▲ | ▲ | Read texts 1, 5 and 6 |
| 10 | ▲ | ▼ | ▲ | ▼ | □ | □ | Read texts 1, 2, 3 and 4 |
| 11 | ▲ | ○ | ▲ | ▼ | ▲ | □ | Read texts 1, 3, 4 and 5 |
| 12 | ▲ | ○ | ▲ | ▼ | □ | ▲ | Read texts 1, 3, 4 and 6 |
| 13 | ▲ | ○ | □ | ▼ | ▲ | ▲ | Read texts 1, 4, 5 and 6 |
| 14 | ▲ | ▼ | ▲ | ▼ | ▲ | □ | Read texts 1, 2, 3, 4 and 5 |
| 15 | ▲ | ○ | ▲ | ▼ | ▲ | ▲ | Read texts 1, 3, 4, 5 and 6 |
| 16 | ▲ | ▼ | ▲ | ▼ | ▲ | ▲ | Read texts 1, 2, 3, 4, 5 and 6 |
| 17 | □ | ▼ | ▲ | ○ | □ | □ | Read texts 2 and 3 |
| 18 | □ | ▼ | □ | ▼ | □ | □ | Read texts 2 and 4 |
| 19 | □ | ▼ | □ | ○ | ▲ | □ | Read texts 2 and 5 |
| 20 | □ | ▼ | □ | ○ | □ | ▲ | Read texts 2 and 6 |
| 21 | □ | ▼ | ▲ | ▼ | □ | □ | Read texts 2, 3 and 4 |
| 22 | □ | ▼ | □ | ▼ | ▲ | □ | Read texts 2, 4 and 5 |
| 23 | □ | ▼ | □ | ○ | ▲ | ▲ | Read texts 2, 5 and 6 |
| 24 | □ | ▼ | ▲ | ▼ | ▲ | □ | Read texts 2, 3, 4 and 5 |
| 25 | □ | ▼ | □ | ▼ | ▲ | ▲ | Read texts 2, 4, 5 and 6 |
| 26 | □ | ▼ | ▲ | ▼ | ▲ | ▲ | Read texts 2, 3, 4, 5 and 6 |
| 27 | ▲ | ▼ | □ | ▼ | □ | □ | Read texts 1, 2 and 4 |
| 28 | ▲ | ▼ | □ | ○ | ▲ | □ | Read texts 1, 2 and 5 |
| 29 | ▲ | ▼ | □ | ○ | □ | ▲ | Read texts 1, 2 and 6 |
| 30 | ▲ | ▼ | ▲ | ○ | ▲ | □ | Read texts 1, 2, 3 and 5 |
| 31 | ▲ | ▼ | ▲ | ○ | □ | ▲ | Read texts 1, 2, 3 and 6 |
| 32 | ▲ | ▼ | ▲ | ▼ | □ | ▲ | Read texts 1, 2, 3, 4 and 6 |
| 33 | ▲ | ○ | ▲ | ○ | ▲ | □ | Read texts 1, 3 and 5 |
| 34 | ▲ | ○ | ▲ | ○ | □ | ▲ | Read texts 1, 3 and 6 |
| 35 | ▲ | ○ | ▲ | ○ | ▲ | ▲ | Read texts 1, 3, 5 and 6 |
| 36 | ▲ | ○ | □ | ▼ | □ | ▲ | Read texts 1, 4 and 6 |
| 37 | □ | ▼ | ▲ | ○ | ▲ | □ | Read texts 2, 3 and 5 |
| 38 | □ | ▼ | ▲ | ○ | □ | ▲ | Read texts 2, 3 and 6 |
| 39 | □ | ▼ | ▲ | ▼ | □ | ▲ | Read texts 2, 3, 4 and 6 |
| 40 | □ | ▼ | □ | ▼ | □ | ▲ | Read texts 2, 4 and 6 |
| 41 | □ | ○ | ▲ | ▼ | □ | □ | Read texts 3 and 4 |
| 42 | □ | ○ | ▲ | ○ | ▲ | □ | Read texts 3 and 5 |
| 43 | □ | ○ | ▲ | ○ | □ | ▲ | Read texts 3 and 6 |
| 44 | □ | ○ | ▲ | ▼ | ▲ | □ | Read texts 3, 4 and 5 |
| 45 | □ | ○ | ▲ | ▼ | □ | ▲ | Read texts 3, 4 and 6 |
| 46 | □ | ○ | ▲ | ○ | ▲ | ▲ | Read texts 3, 5 and 6 |
| 47 | □ | ○ | ▲ | ▼ | ▲ | ▲ | Read texts 3, 4, 5 and 6 |
| 48 | □ | ○ | □ | ▼ | ▲ | □ | Read texts 4 and 5 |
| 49 | □ | ○ | □ | ▼ | □ | ▲ | Read texts 4 and 6 |
| 50 | □ | ○ | □ | ▼ | ▲ | ▲ | Read texts 4, 5 and 6 |
| 51 | □ | ○ | □ | ○ | ▲ | ▲ | Read texts 5 and 6 |
| 52 | ▲ | ○ | □ | ○ | □ | □ | Read text 1 |
| 53 | □ | ▼ | □ | ○ | □ | □ | Read text 2 |
| 54 | □ | ○ | ▲ | ○ | □ | □ | Read text 3 |
| 55 | □ | ○ | □ | ▼ | □ | □ | Read text 4 |
| 56 | □ | ○ | □ | ○ | ▲ | □ | Read text 5 |
| 57 | □ | ○ | □ | ○ | □ | ▲ | Read text 6 |

get back to normal immediately because these problems have been around for quite a while.

**4** You are in direct contact with the person responsible for the major problems, difficulties or obstacles you are currently facing. Nevertheless, you realize that this person will not listen to reason, or that he or she is resistant to any possibility of change. Consequently, all you can do is abandon the situation before it degenerates or causes more damage.

**5** You are involved with a group of people who are difficult or hostile, or else you are in a very delicate position. Either way, you are not able to defend yourself or to free yourself from this restrictive and painful situation. In circumstances like these you are advised to proceed with extreme caution, so you can manage things in order to escape when the right moment arrives.

**6** It seems that hostile elements or adversaries are giving you no peace, and are gradually wearing away your patience and defences. However, their negative behaviour will harm them in the end. In other words, they will autodestruct and will crumble without you having to do anything at all.

# 37<sup>th</sup> combination □ ○ □ □ □ □

Your relations with your family affect all your other social and professional relationships. Thus, coherence, logic and harmony between your ideas, words and actions is essential, so that others see you as a balanced individual, one who is true to themself and to their commitments.

1   To maintain balance in your home life, and harmony in your relationships, it is crucial that everyone knows their place, plays their part and fully assumes their responsibilities. If each goes their own way, chaos sets in. This is why, in all communities, to prevent relationships breaking down, there must always be a few general rules that are respected by all.

2   The best thing to do, given your current situation and the nature of your relationships, is to refrain from taking any bold or arbitrary initiatives. Nor should you try and force things: just be content to carry out your tasks and accept your obligations.

3   You need to resolve a very delicate problem concerning someone close to you, and you are tempted to act with extreme firmness. It is always difficult to be harsh with someone you care about. However, if the circumstances demand it or the fault is serious it is better to be too strict than too soft: otherwise there will be unfortunate consequences sooner or later.

4   If you are prudent and vigilant when managing your income and expenditure, you will achieve perfect balance in your financial affairs. You can then look forward to a secure and comfortable future for yourself and those for whom you are responsible.

5   You are, or you have dealings with, a person who is trustworthy, with a strong, kindly character that inspires universal sympathy and approval. This person's motivations and actions are based on generous, spontaneous feelings. Whether this is yourself or somebody close to you who gives you support, such positive behaviour is a guarantee of happiness.

6   From now on you must stop questioning the nature of your relationships and, instead, assume your moral and material obligations in full, in order that your dependants or those for whom you are responsible can understand your motivations and actions. In this way, you will be able to exercise gentle authority.

# 38<sup>th</sup> combination ❏ ❏ ◯ ❏ ◯ ❏

Contradictions and antagonism can either create discord between people or make them aware of the richness and diversity of their mutual qualities and the stimulating and enriching contrasts these provide. So, if individuals in opposition can happily accept these differences and peculiarities they will no longer be at odds with each other – on the contrary, they will complement each other.

1   If, because of a disagreement or misunderstanding, somebody you know has turned their back on you, or refuses to speak to you or offer any explanation, do not seek to make them listen to reason at any price. If your relationship is genuine and sincere, things will come right in due course. Similarly, if people with whom you are unconnected make approaches to you, do not try to push them away. They will soon realize their mistake and leave you alone.

**38th combination**

| fig. | | | | | | | |
|---|---|---|---|---|---|---|---|
| 1 | ▲ | ▲ | ○ | □ | ○ | □ | Read texts 1 and 2 |
| 2 | ▲ | □ | ▼ | □ | ○ | □ | Read texts 1 and 3 |
| 3 | ▲ | □ | ○ | ▲ | ○ | □ | Read texts 1 and 4 |
| 4 | ▲ | □ | ○ | □ | ▼ | □ | Read texts 1 and 5 |
| 5 | ▲ | □ | ○ | □ | ○ | ▲ | Read texts 1 and 6 |
| 6 | ▲ | ▲ | ▼ | □ | ○ | □ | Read texts 1, 2 and 3 |
| 7 | ▲ | □ | ▼ | ▲ | ○ | □ | Read texts 1, 3 and 4 |
| 8 | ▲ | □ | ▼ | □ | ▲ | □ | Read texts 1, 4 and 5 |
| 9 | ▲ | □ | ○ | □ | ▼ | ▲ | Read texts 1, 5 and 6 |
| 10 | ▲ | ▲ | ▼ | ▲ | ○ | □ | Read texts 1, 2, 3 and 4 |
| 11 | ▲ | □ | ▼ | ▲ | ▼ | □ | Read texts 1, 3, 4 and 5 |
| 12 | ▲ | □ | ▼ | ▲ | ○ | ▲ | Read texts 1, 3, 4 and 6 |
| 13 | ▲ | □ | ○ | ▲ | ▼ | ▲ | Read texts 1, 4, 5 and 6 |
| 14 | ▲ | ▲ | ▼ | ▲ | ▼ | □ | Read texts 1, 2, 3, 4 and 5 |
| 15 | ▲ | □ | ▼ | ▲ | ▼ | ▲ | Read texts 1, 3, 4, 5 and 6 |
| 16 | ▲ | ▲ | ▼ | ▲ | ▼ | ▲ | Read texts 1, 2, 3, 4, 5 and 6 |
| 17 | □ | ▲ | ▼ | □ | ○ | □ | Read texts 2 and 3 |
| 18 | □ | ▲ | ○ | ▲ | ○ | □ | Read texts 2 and 4 |
| 19 | □ | ▲ | ○ | □ | ▼ | □ | Read texts 2 and 5 |
| 20 | □ | ▲ | ○ | □ | ○ | ▲ | Read texts 2 and 6 |
| 21 | □ | ▲ | ▼ | ▲ | ○ | □ | Read texts 2, 3 and 4 |
| 22 | □ | ▲ | ○ | ▲ | ▼ | □ | Read texts 2, 4 and 5 |
| 23 | □ | ▲ | ○ | □ | ▼ | ▲ | Read texts 2, 5 and 6 |
| 24 | □ | ▲ | ▼ | ▲ | ▼ | □ | Read texts 2, 3, 4 and 5 |
| 25 | □ | ▲ | ○ | ▲ | ▼ | ▲ | Read texts 2, 4, 5 and 6 |
| 26 | □ | ▲ | ▼ | ▲ | ▼ | ▲ | Read texts 2, 3, 4, 5 and 6 |
| 27 | ▲ | ▲ | ○ | ▲ | ○ | □ | Read texts 1, 2 and 4 |
| 28 | ▲ | ▲ | ○ | □ | ▼ | □ | Read texts 1, 2 and 5 |
| 29 | ▲ | ▲ | ○ | □ | ○ | ▲ | Read texts 1, 2 and 6 |
| 30 | ▲ | ▲ | ▼ | □ | ▼ | □ | Read texts 1, 2, 3 and 5 |
| 31 | ▲ | ▲ | ▼ | □ | ○ | ▲ | Read texts 1, 2, 3 and 6 |
| 32 | ▲ | ▲ | ▼ | ▲ | ○ | ▲ | Read texts 1, 2, 3, 4 and 6 |
| 33 | ▲ | □ | ▼ | □ | ▼ | □ | Read texts 1, 3 and 5 |
| 34 | ▲ | □ | ▼ | □ | ○ | ▲ | Read texts 1, 3 and 6 |
| 35 | ▲ | □ | ▼ | □ | ▼ | ▲ | Read texts 1, 3, 5 and 6 |
| 36 | ▲ | □ | ○ | ▲ | ○ | ▲ | Read texts 1, 4 and 6 |
| 37 | □ | ▲ | ▼ | □ | ▼ | □ | Read texts 2, 3 and 5 |
| 38 | □ | ▲ | ▼ | □ | ○ | ▲ | Read texts 2, 3 and 6 |
| 39 | □ | ▲ | ▼ | ▲ | ○ | ▲ | Read texts 2, 3, 4 and 6 |
| 40 | □ | ▲ | ○ | ▲ | ○ | ▲ | Read texts 2, 4 and 6 |
| 41 | □ | □ | ▼ | ▲ | ○ | □ | Read texts 3 and 4 |
| 42 | □ | □ | ▼ | □ | ▼ | □ | Read texts 3 and 5 |
| 43 | □ | □ | ▼ | □ | ○ | ▲ | Read texts 3 and 6 |
| 44 | □ | □ | ▼ | ▲ | ▼ | □ | Read texts 3, 4 and 5 |
| 45 | □ | □ | ▼ | ▲ | ○ | ▲ | Read texts 3, 4 and 6 |
| 46 | □ | □ | ▼ | □ | ▼ | ▲ | Read texts 3, 5 and 6 |
| 47 | □ | □ | ▼ | ▲ | ▼ | ▲ | Read texts 3, 4, 5 and 6 |
| 48 | □ | □ | ○ | ▲ | ▼ | □ | Read texts 4 and 5 |
| 49 | □ | □ | ○ | ▲ | ○ | ▲ | Read texts 4 and 6 |
| 50 | □ | □ | ○ | ▲ | ▼ | ▲ | Read texts 4, 5 and 6 |
| 51 | □ | □ | ○ | □ | ▼ | ▲ | Read texts 5 and 6 |
| 52 | ▲ | □ | ○ | □ | ○ | □ | Read text 1 |
| 53 | □ | ▲ | ○ | □ | ○ | □ | Read text 2 |
| 54 | □ | □ | ▼ | □ | ○ | □ | Read text 3 |
| 55 | □ | □ | ○ | ▲ | ○ | □ | Read text 4 |
| 56 | □ | □ | ○ | □ | ▼ | □ | Read text 5 |
| 57 | □ | □ | ○ | □ | ○ | ▲ | Read text 6 |

**2**  Awkwardness, misunderstandings, things left unsaid or disagreements with no real substance have caused a split with someone in your circle. Nevertheless your differences can be quickly settled, as long as you both agree to meet and talk with no hidden agenda or ulterior motive.

**3**  Your current circumstances make you feel that everything conspires against you. Whether things are going badly or your plans are being opposed, everything seems to be blocking your path. However you are fortunate to enjoy a special relationship with somebody you can trust, and you can rely on this person to help you or provide moral support.

**4**  You have two problems at the moment. Firstly, your circumstances, and those around you do not facilitate your initiatives or plans; secondly, you see no immediate prospect, if not of making close ties, at least of improving your relationship with these people. However, in spite of your scepticism and reticence, if you come across somebody with whom you instinctively bond, this will be a sure sign that a positive change is on the way.

**5**  Your situation is so complex or so painful that everything tells you to withdraw into your shell, to trust no one. However someone with whom you may have lost contact, or no longer think about, will come back into your life. This person will propose a partnership or association that you must accept with complete confidence and no hesitation.

**6**  Whether through weakness, negligence or pride, you have let a disagreement drive a wedge between you and someone close to you, which has caused you to go your separate ways. Since then you have withdrawn into your shell and are always on the defensive with regard to this person. However, as you will soon find out, this person is very well disposed towards you so everything will work out and things will get back to normal between you.

# 39th combination ○ ○ □ ○ □ ○

You are in a difficult situation that appears to have no exit, but there are two things you can do to escape it. Firstly, surround yourself with efficient people whose help or support will be useful to you. Secondly, challenge your own thinking and ask yourself about the real, deep-rooted causes of these problems. If you can correctly assess your share of responsibility in this matter, you will learn precious lessons for the future.

**1**  A major obstacle has put the brakes on your efforts and halted your progress. It would be dangerous to try to skirt round it, or ignore it and continue on your way, which would certainly cause even more disarray. Instead, have a break and take time to think about the nature of the problem. Find appropriate solutions and wait for an opportune moment before taking any action.

**2**  You have been stopped in your tracks by a major difficulty that you cannot ignore. The wise thing to do would be to take time out to think, and to react appropriately at the right moment. But you do not

| fig. | | | | | | | |
|---|---|---|---|---|---|---|---|
| 1 | ▼ | ▼ | □ | ○ | □ | ○ | Read texts 1 and 2 |
| 2 | ▼ | ○ | ▲ | ○ | □ | ○ | Read texts 1 and 3 |
| 3 | ▼ | ○ | □ | ▼ | □ | ○ | Read texts 1 and 4 |
| 4 | ▼ | ○ | □ | ○ | ▲ | ○ | Read texts 1 and 5 |
| 5 | ▼ | ○ | □ | ○ | □ | ▼ | Read texts 1 and 6 |
| 6 | ▼ | ▼ | ▲ | ○ | □ | ○ | Read texts 1, 2 and 3 |
| 7 | ▼ | ▼ | □ | ▼ | □ | ○ | Read texts 1, 2 and 4 |
| 8 | ▼ | ▼ | □ | ○ | ▲ | ○ | Read texts 1, 2 and 5 |
| 9 | ▼ | ▼ | □ | ○ | □ | ▼ | Read texts 1, 2 and 6 |
| 10 | ▼ | ▼ | ▲ | ▼ | □ | ○ | Read texts 1, 2, 3 and 4 |
| 11 | ▼ | ▼ | ▲ | ○ | ▲ | ○ | Read texts 1, 2, 3 and 5 |
| 12 | ▼ | ▼ | ▲ | ○ | □ | ▼ | Read texts 1, 2, 3 and 6 |
| 13 | ▼ | ▼ | ▲ | ▼ | ▲ | ○ | Read texts 1, 2, 3, 4 and 5 |
| 14 | ▼ | ▼ | ▲ | ▼ | □ | ▼ | Read texts 1, 2, 3, 4 and 6 |
| 15 | ▼ | ▼ | ▲ | ▼ | ▲ | ▼ | Read texts 1, 2, 3, 4, 5 and 6 |
| 16 | ▼ | ○ | ▲ | ▼ | □ | ○ | Read texts 1, 3 and 4 |
| 17 | ▼ | ○ | ▲ | ○ | ▲ | ○ | Read texts 1, 3 and 5 |
| 18 | ▼ | ○ | ▲ | ○ | □ | ▼ | Read texts 1, 3 and 6 |
| 19 | ▼ | ○ | ▲ | ▼ | ▲ | ○ | Read texts 1, 3, 4 and 5 |
| 20 | ▼ | ○ | ▲ | ▼ | □ | ▼ | Read texts 1, 3, 4 and 6 |
| 21 | ▼ | ○ | ▲ | ○ | ▲ | ▼ | Read texts 1, 3, 5 and 6 |
| 22 | ▼ | ○ | ▲ | ▼ | ▲ | ▼ | Read texts 1, 3, 4, 5 and 6 |
| 23 | ▼ | ○ | □ | ▼ | ▲ | ○ | Read texts 1, 4 and 5 |
| 24 | ▼ | ○ | □ | ▼ | □ | ▼ | Read texts 1, 4 and 6 |
| 25 | ▼ | ○ | □ | ▼ | ▲ | ▼ | Read texts 1, 4, 5 and 6 |
| 26 | ▼ | ○ | □ | ○ | ▲ | ▼ | Read texts 1, 5 and 6 |
| 27 | ○ | ▼ | ▲ | ○ | □ | ○ | Read texts 2 and 3 |
| 28 | ○ | ▼ | □ | ▼ | □ | ○ | Read texts 2 and 4 |
| 29 | ○ | ▼ | □ | ○ | ▲ | ○ | Read texts 2 and 5 |
| 30 | ○ | ▼ | □ | ○ | □ | ▼ | Read texts 2 and 6 |
| 31 | ○ | ▼ | ▲ | ▼ | □ | ○ | Read texts 2, 3 and 4 |
| 32 | ○ | ▼ | ▲ | ○ | ▲ | ○ | Read texts 2, 3 and 5 |
| 33 | ○ | ▼ | ▲ | ○ | □ | ▼ | Read texts 2, 3 and 6 |
| 34 | ○ | ▼ | ▲ | ▼ | ▲ | ○ | Read texts 2, 3, 4 and 5 |
| 35 | ○ | ▼ | ▲ | ▼ | □ | ▼ | Read texts 2, 3, 4 and 6 |
| 36 | ○ | ▼ | ▲ | ▼ | ▲ | ▼ | Read texts 2, 3, 4, 5 and 6 |
| 37 | ○ | ▼ | □ | ▼ | ▲ | ○ | Read texts 2, 4 and 5 |
| 38 | ○ | ▼ | □ | ▼ | □ | ▼ | Read texts 2, 4 and 6 |
| 39 | ○ | ▼ | □ | ▼ | ▲ | ▼ | Read texts 2, 4, 5 and 6 |
| 40 | ○ | ▼ | □ | ○ | ▲ | ▼ | Read texts 2, 5 and 6 |
| 41 | ○ | ○ | ▲ | ▼ | □ | ○ | Read texts 3 and 4 |
| 42 | ○ | ○ | ▲ | ○ | ▲ | ○ | Read texts 3 and 5 |
| 43 | ○ | ○ | ▲ | ○ | □ | ▼ | Read texts 3 and 6 |
| 44 | ○ | ○ | ▲ | ▼ | ▲ | ○ | Read texts 3, 4 and 5 |
| 45 | ○ | ○ | ▲ | ▼ | □ | ▼ | Read texts 3, 4 and 6 |
| 46 | ○ | ○ | ▲ | ○ | ▲ | ▼ | Read texts 3, 5 and 6 |
| 47 | ○ | ○ | ▲ | ▼ | ▲ | ▼ | Read texts 3, 4, 5 and 6 |
| 48 | ○ | ○ | □ | ▼ | ▲ | ○ | Read texts 4 and 5 |
| 49 | ○ | ○ | □ | ▼ | □ | ▼ | Read texts 4 and 6 |
| 50 | ○ | ○ | □ | ▼ | ▲ | ▼ | Read texts 4, 5 and 6 |
| 51 | ○ | ○ | □ | ○ | ▲ | ▼ | Read texts 5 and 6 |
| 52 | ▼ | ○ | □ | ○ | □ | ○ | Read text 1 |
| 53 | ○ | ▼ | □ | ○ | □ | ○ | Read text 2 |
| 54 | ○ | ○ | ▲ | ○ | □ | ○ | Read text 3 |
| 55 | ○ | ○ | □ | ▼ | □ | ○ | Read text 4 |
| 56 | ○ | ○ | □ | ○ | ▲ | ○ | Read text 5 |
| 57 | ○ | ○ | □ | ○ | □ | ▼ | Read text 6 |

39th combination ○ ○ □ ○ □ ○

have time for that, and must forge ahead somehow. Therefore you will probably be unable to avoid incurring some damage, but you have no choice in the matter.

3   Should you decide to tackle your current difficulties, alone and unprepared, not only would you endanger your own situation but also the security and peace of mind of those for whom you are responsible. This is why it would be best to refrain from acting recklessly or charging in with your head down. Take refuge among those close to you, who will be happy with your wise decision.

4   You are facing problems and difficulties that you will never be able to solve alone. Furthermore, there is no guarantee that circumstances will develop favourably; this is pure speculation on your part. This situation should automatically prompt you to seek help and support from competent, sincere and efficient people.

5   You have to face up to some serious difficulties and you know very well that if you do not intervene or take urgent action the situation will deteriorate. Those around you respect your goodwill and wise determination and you can count on them: every one of them is ready to follow you and to play a direct role in your victory and success.

6   You are facing some difficulties or problems that concern you only indirectly, but affect the whole community to which you belong. You are not obliged to help resolve them. However your experience and your kindly, generous nature incline you to do so. You find yourself intervening once again to help those who need support in overcoming their difficulties.

# 40<sup>th</sup> combination ○ ▢ ○ ▢ ○ ○

The problems and obstacles that you have met along your way are about to disappear for good. Quite rightly, you feel an enormous sense of relief; nonetheless, resist any temptation to be self-satisfied or careless. Above all, you must not overlook any minor problems that may still remain. On the other hand, when considering other people's mistakes, make allowances and wipe the slate clean.

1   Having conquered many obstacles and difficulties you are now enjoying a lull, so you can regroup and recharge your batteries in tranquillity. Take full advantage of this moment of respite to recover your energies and to prepare yourself for new challenges.

2   You are involved with people who are not openly malevolent but operate sneakily behind the scenes in order to scupper your initiatives or to make what you do seem useless or unjustified in the eyes of others. However, you also have a few tricks up your sleeve and if you react with equal subtlety you will triumph in the end.

3   Having overcome plenty of obstacles and difficulties you have finally reached a position that, if not enviable, at least makes you feel secure and comfortable. Nevertheless, avoid smugness and over-confidence, or you could endanger yourself without noticing it or excite the envy of ill-intentioned people.

4   You are on very intimate terms with people who seem to be part of your life. However, in reality you have absolutely

nothing in common with them – aside from having undertaken a common project at some point. If you want to cultivate deeper, more genuine relationships with like-minded people, you need to distance yourself from these passing acquaintances, or else worthwhile people will keep their distance.

5    If it is your intention or desire to break off all contact with certain people, don't oppose them openly or show them any hostility. A wiser and more effective way of demonstrating that you are determined to sever all ties would be to detach yourself mentally, by eliminating all trace of feeling for them. Your indifference will put them off in the end, and they will decide to leave you alone.

6    You are faced with a situation to which there is a perfectly obvious solution. You know that without prompt and drastic action your enemy will stand in the way of your goals and allow you no peace. Act now to disarm this person.

# 41<sup>st</sup> combination □ □ ○ ○ ○ □

You are probably not in a very favourable position, or one in which you can shine, but it would be wrong to feel ashamed or hung up about it. Your true motives and your heartfelt impulses are all that count. The authenticity of these feelings goes a long way towards compensating for your slender means.

1    Your natural inclination towards kindness and solidarity to others prompts you to

| fig. | 1 | 2 | 3 | 4 | 5 | 6 | |
|---|---|---|---|---|---|---|---|
| fig. 1 | ▼ | ▲ | ○ | □ | ○ | ○ | Read texts 1 and 2 |
| 2 | ▼ | □ | ▼ | □ | ○ | ○ | Read texts 1 and 3 |
| 3 | ▼ | □ | ○ | ▲ | ○ | ○ | Read texts 1 and 4 |
| 4 | ▼ | □ | ○ | □ | ▼ | ○ | Read texts 1 and 5 |
| 5 | ▼ | □ | ○ | □ | ○ | ▼ | Read texts 1 and 6 |
| 6 | ▼ | ▲ | ▼ | □ | ○ | ○ | Read texts 1, 2 and 3 |
| 7 | ▼ | ▲ | ○ | ▲ | ○ | ○ | Read texts 1, 2 and 4 |
| 8 | ▼ | ▲ | ○ | □ | ▼ | ○ | Read texts 1, 2 and 5 |
| 9 | ▼ | ▲ | ○ | □ | ○ | ▼ | Read texts 1, 2 and 6 |
| 10 | ▼ | ▲ | ▼ | ▲ | ○ | ○ | Read texts 1, 2, 3 and 4 |
| 11 | ▼ | ▲ | ▼ | □ | ▼ | ○ | Read texts 1, 2, 3 and 5 |
| 12 | ▼ | ▲ | ▼ | □ | ○ | ▼ | Read texts 1, 2, 3 and 6 |
| 13 | ▼ | ▲ | ▼ | ▲ | ▼ | ○ | Read texts 1, 2, 3, 4 and 5 |
| 14 | ▼ | ▲ | ▼ | ▲ | ○ | ▼ | Read texts 1, 2, 3, 4 and 6 |
| 15 | ▼ | ▲ | ▼ | ▲ | ▼ | ▼ | Read texts 1, 2, 3, 4, 5 and 6 |
| 16 | ▼ | □ | ▼ | ▲ | ○ | ○ | Read texts 1, 3 and 4 |
| 17 | ▼ | □ | ▼ | □ | ▼ | ○ | Read texts 1, 3 and 5 |
| 18 | ▼ | □ | ▼ | □ | ○ | ▼ | Read texts 1, 3 and 6 |
| 19 | ▼ | □ | ▼ | ▲ | ▼ | ○ | Read texts 1, 3, 4 and 5 |
| 20 | ▼ | □ | ▼ | ▲ | ○ | ▼ | Read texts 1, 3, 4 and 6 |
| 21 | ▼ | □ | ▼ | □ | ▼ | ▼ | Read texts 1, 3, 5 and 6 |
| 22 | ▼ | □ | ▼ | ▲ | ▼ | ▼ | Read texts 1, 3, 4, 5 and 6 |
| 23 | ▼ | □ | ○ | ▲ | ▼ | ○ | Read texts 1, 4 and 5 |
| 24 | ▼ | □ | ○ | ▲ | ○ | ▼ | Read texts 1, 4 and 6 |
| 25 | ▼ | □ | ○ | ▲ | ▼ | ▼ | Read texts 1, 4, 5 and 6 |
| 26 | ▼ | □ | ○ | □ | ▼ | ▼ | Read texts 1, 5 and 6 |
| 27 | ○ | ▲ | ▼ | □ | ○ | ○ | Read texts 2 and 3 |
| 28 | ○ | ▲ | ○ | ▲ | ○ | ○ | Read texts 2 and 4 |
| 29 | ○ | ▲ | ○ | □ | ▼ | ○ | Read texts 2 and 5 |
| 30 | ○ | ▲ | ○ | □ | ○ | ▼ | Read texts 2 and 6 |
| 31 | ○ | ▲ | ▼ | ▲ | ○ | ○ | Read texts 2, 3 and 4 |
| 32 | ○ | ▲ | ▼ | □ | ▼ | ○ | Read texts 2, 3 and 5 |
| 33 | ○ | ▲ | ▼ | □ | ○ | ▼ | Read texts 2, 3 and 6 |
| 34 | ○ | ▲ | ▼ | ▲ | ▼ | ○ | Read texts 2, 3, 4 and 5 |
| 35 | ○ | ▲ | ▼ | ▲ | ○ | ▼ | Read texts 2, 3, 4 and 6 |
| 36 | ○ | ▲ | ▼ | ▲ | ▼ | ▼ | Read texts 2, 3, 4, 5 and 6 |
| 37 | ○ | ▲ | ○ | ▲ | ▼ | ○ | Read texts 2, 4 and 5 |
| 38 | ○ | ▲ | ○ | ▲ | ○ | ▼ | Read texts 2, 4 and 6 |
| 39 | ○ | ▲ | ○ | ▲ | ▼ | ▼ | Read texts 2, 4, 5 and 6 |
| 40 | ○ | ▲ | ○ | □ | ▼ | ▼ | Read texts 2, 5 and 6 |
| 41 | ○ | □ | ▼ | ▲ | ○ | ○ | Read texts 3 and 4 |
| 42 | ○ | □ | ▼ | □ | ▼ | ○ | Read texts 3 and 5 |
| 43 | ○ | □ | ▼ | □ | ○ | ▼ | Read texts 3 and 6 |
| 44 | ○ | □ | ▼ | ▲ | ▼ | ○ | Read texts 3, 4 and 5 |
| 45 | ○ | □ | ▼ | ▲ | ○ | ▼ | Read texts 3, 4 and 6 |
| 46 | ○ | □ | ▼ | □ | ▼ | ▼ | Read texts 3, 5 and 6 |
| 47 | ○ | □ | ▼ | ▲ | ▼ | ▼ | Read texts 3, 4, 5 and 6 |
| 48 | ○ | □ | ○ | ▲ | ▼ | ○ | Read texts 4 and 5 |
| 49 | ○ | □ | ○ | ▲ | ○ | ▼ | Read texts 4 and 6 |
| 50 | ○ | □ | ○ | ▲ | ▼ | ▼ | Read texts 4, 5 and 6 |
| 51 | ○ | □ | ○ | □ | ▼ | ▼ | Read texts 5 and 6 |
| 52 | ▼ | □ | ○ | □ | ○ | ○ | Read text 1 |
| 53 | ○ | ▲ | ○ | □ | ○ | ○ | Read text 2 |
| 54 | ○ | □ | ▼ | □ | ○ | ○ | Read text 3 |
| 55 | ○ | □ | ○ | ▲ | ○ | ○ | Read text 4 |
| 56 | ○ | □ | ○ | □ | ▼ | ○ | Read text 5 |
| 57 | ○ | □ | ○ | □ | ○ | ▼ | Read text 6 |

40th combination ○ □ ○ □ ○

313

**41st combination**

| fig. | 1 | 2 | 3 | 4 | 5 | 6 | |
|---|---|---|---|---|---|---|---|
| 1 | ▲ | ▲ | ○ | ○ | ○ | □ | Read texts 1 and 2 |
| 2 | ▲ | □ | ▼ | ○ | ○ | □ | Read texts 1 and 3 |
| 3 | ▲ | □ | ○ | ▼ | ○ | □ | Read texts 1 and 4 |
| 4 | ▲ | □ | ○ | ○ | ▼ | □ | Read texts 1 and 5 |
| 5 | ▲ | □ | ○ | ○ | ○ | ▲ | Read texts 1 and 6 |
| 6 | ▲ | ▲ | ▼ | ○ | ○ | □ | Read texts 1, 2 and 3 |
| 7 | ▲ | □ | ▼ | ▼ | ○ | □ | Read texts 1, 3 and 4 |
| 8 | ▲ | □ | ○ | ▼ | ▼ | □ | Read texts 1, 4 and 5 |
| 9 | ▲ | □ | ○ | ○ | ▼ | ▲ | Read texts 1, 5 and 6 |
| 10 | ▲ | ▲ | ▼ | ▼ | ○ | □ | Read texts 1, 2, 3 and 4 |
| 11 | ▲ | □ | ▼ | ▼ | ▼ | □ | Read texts 1, 3, 4 and 5 |
| 12 | ▲ | □ | ▼ | ▼ | ○ | ▲ | Read texts 1, 3, 4 and 6 |
| 13 | ▲ | □ | ○ | ▼ | ▼ | ▲ | Read texts 1, 4, 5 and 6 |
| 14 | ▲ | ▲ | ▼ | ▼ | ▼ | □ | Read texts 1, 2, 3, 4 and 5 |
| 15 | ▲ | □ | ▼ | ▼ | ▼ | ▲ | Read texts 1, 3, 4, 5 and 6 |
| 16 | ▲ | ▲ | ▼ | ▼ | ▼ | ▲ | Read texts 1, 2, 3, 4, 5 and 6 |
| 17 | □ | ▲ | ▼ | ○ | ○ | □ | Read texts 2 and 3 |
| 18 | □ | ▲ | ○ | ▼ | ○ | □ | Read texts 2 and 4 |
| 19 | □ | ▲ | ○ | ○ | ▼ | □ | Read texts 2 and 5 |
| 20 | □ | ▲ | ○ | ○ | ○ | ▲ | Read texts 2 and 6 |
| 21 | □ | ▲ | ▼ | ▼ | ○ | □ | Read texts 2, 3 and 4 |
| 22 | □ | ▲ | ○ | ▼ | ▼ | □ | Read texts 2, 4 and 5 |
| 23 | □ | ▲ | ○ | ○ | ▼ | ▲ | Read texts 2, 5 and 6 |
| 24 | □ | ▲ | ▼ | ▼ | ▼ | □ | Read texts 2, 3, 4 and 5 |
| 25 | □ | ▲ | ○ | ▼ | ▼ | ▲ | Read texts 2, 4, 5 and 6 |
| 26 | □ | ▲ | ▼ | ▼ | ▼ | ▲ | Read texts 2, 3, 4, 5 and 6 |
| 27 | ▲ | ▲ | ○ | ▼ | ○ | □ | Read texts 1, 2 and 4 |
| 28 | ▲ | ▲ | ○ | ○ | ▼ | □ | Read texts 1, 2 and 5 |
| 29 | ▲ | ▲ | ○ | ○ | ○ | ▲ | Read texts 1, 2 and 6 |
| 30 | ▲ | ▲ | ▼ | ○ | ▼ | □ | Read texts 1, 2, 3 and 5 |
| 31 | ▲ | ▲ | ▼ | ○ | ○ | ▲ | Read texts 1, 2, 3 and 6 |
| 32 | ▲ | ▲ | ▼ | ▼ | ○ | ▲ | Read texts 1, 2, 3, 4 and 6 |
| 33 | ▲ | □ | ▼ | ○ | ▼ | □ | Read texts 1, 3 and 5 |
| 34 | ▲ | □ | ▼ | ○ | ○ | ▲ | Read texts 1, 3 and 6 |
| 35 | ▲ | □ | ▼ | ○ | ▼ | ▲ | Read texts 1, 3, 5 and 6 |
| 36 | ▲ | □ | ○ | ▼ | ○ | ▲ | Read texts 1, 4 and 6 |
| 37 | □ | ▲ | ▼ | ○ | ▼ | □ | Read texts 2, 3 and 5 |
| 38 | □ | ▲ | ▼ | ○ | ○ | ▲ | Read texts 2, 3 and 6 |
| 39 | □ | ▲ | ▼ | ▼ | ○ | ▲ | Read texts 2, 3, 4 and 6 |
| 40 | □ | ▲ | ○ | ▼ | ○ | ▲ | Read texts 2, 4 and 6 |
| 41 | □ | □ | ▼ | ▼ | ○ | □ | Read texts 3 and 4 |
| 42 | □ | □ | ▼ | ○ | ▼ | □ | Read texts 3 and 5 |
| 43 | □ | □ | ▼ | ○ | ○ | ▲ | Read texts 3 and 6 |
| 44 | □ | □ | ▼ | ▼ | ▼ | □ | Read texts 3, 4 and 5 |
| 45 | □ | □ | ▼ | ▼ | ○ | ▲ | Read texts 3, 4 and 6 |
| 46 | □ | □ | ▼ | ○ | ▼ | ▲ | Read texts 3, 5 and 6 |
| 47 | □ | □ | ▼ | ▼ | ▼ | ▲ | Read texts 3, 4, 5 and 6 |
| 48 | □ | □ | ○ | ▼ | ▼ | □ | Read texts 4 and 5 |
| 49 | □ | □ | ○ | ▼ | ○ | ▲ | Read texts 4 and 6 |
| 50 | □ | □ | ○ | ▼ | ▼ | ▲ | Read texts 4, 5 and 6 |
| 51 | □ | □ | ○ | ○ | ▼ | ▲ | Read texts 5 and 6 |
| 52 | ▲ | □ | ○ | ○ | ○ | □ | Read text 1 |
| 53 | □ | ▲ | ○ | ○ | ○ | □ | Read text 2 |
| 54 | □ | □ | ▼ | ○ | ○ | □ | Read text 3 |
| 55 | □ | □ | ○ | ▼ | ○ | □ | Read text 4 |
| 56 | □ | □ | ○ | ○ | ▼ | □ | Read text 5 |
| 57 | □ | □ | ○ | ○ | ○ | ▲ | Read text 6 |

help someone who is actually better off than you. If this person truly appreciates what you are doing, you can go ahead in complete confidence, but if he or she does not deserve your help, or considers it their due, do not get involved.

**2** Do not confuse helpfulness with servility. A helpful person is responsible and devoted, and offers help willingly. A servile person suppresses his own personality in deference to those who are stronger or better placed. Helpfulness reveals nobility and strength of character. Servility reveals low and petty motives that can only invite disdain or discredit.

**3** Any three-way relationship will give rise to passion, tension and jealousy sooner or later. This is why one of the three must retire from the situation; a special relationship can only move to a deeper level if it involves two people. If you are in this situation, you know what you have to do. Moreover if you are, or feel, alone, take heart because you will soon meet somebody who is meant for you.

**4** Your weaknesses or inflexibility do not encourage others to approach you openly and sincerely. In addition, you associate with people who encourage these negative attitudes. However it is not too late to wake up to this and to react in such a way that those who are well disposed towards you can show their feelings.

**5** Whether you realize it or not, great happiness is definitely coming your way soon, particularly in your love life.

**6** Your kind and generous nature instinctively prompts you to share your good fortune with others and to redistribute your wealth or reinvest what you have earned, to the advantage of everybody. Such a positive attitude can only earn you universal respect and gratitude.

# 42<sup>nd</sup> combination □ ○ ○ ○ □ □

Share your assets willingly with those close to you. Not only will they be grateful but they will also be devoted to you, and your affairs will continue to prosper and bear fruit. Similarly, be quick to correct your weaknesses and to draw inspiration from the qualities shown by those around you: this will benefit you greatly.

**1** Your present circumstances are so favourable that you have the chance to do something important and ambitious, which probably did not feature in your plans. You would be wrong to pass up this opportunity or fail to take advantage of this auspicious situation.

**2** Your motives and actions are perfectly in keeping with your current encouraging circumstances. You can therefore take advantage of them, knowing that you are sure to reach your goals or do what you want to do. Such an overwhelmingly positive situation is a guarantee of success in all areas of your life.

**3** Highly favourable circumstances, in conjunction with your equable and consistent behaviour, make it easy for you to resolve the problems and difficulties you are facing. You can also draw from them valuable lessons that are useful, not only for you

| fig. | | | | | | | |
|---|---|---|---|---|---|---|---|
| 1 | ▲ | ▼ | ○ | ○ | □ | □ | Read texts 1 and 2 |
| 2 | ▲ | ○ | ▼ | ○ | □ | □ | Read texts 1 and 3 |
| 3 | ▲ | ○ | ○ | ▼ | □ | □ | Read texts 1 and 4 |
| 4 | ▲ | ○ | ○ | ○ | ▲ | □ | Read texts 1 and 5 |
| 5 | ▲ | ○ | ○ | ○ | □ | ▲ | Read texts 1 and 6 |
| 6 | ▲ | ▼ | ▼ | ○ | □ | □ | Read texts 1, 2 and 3 |
| 7 | ▲ | ○ | ▼ | ▼ | □ | □ | Read texts 1, 3 and 4 |
| 8 | ▲ | ○ | ○ | ▼ | ▲ | □ | Read texts 1, 4 and 5 |
| 9 | ▲ | ○ | ○ | ○ | ▲ | ▲ | Read texts 1, 5 and 6 |
| 10 | ▲ | ▼ | ▼ | ▼ | □ | □ | Read texts 1, 2, 3 and 4 |
| 11 | ▲ | ○ | ▼ | ▼ | ▲ | □ | Read texts 1, 3, 4 and 5 |
| 12 | ▲ | ○ | ▼ | ▼ | □ | ▲ | Read texts 1, 3, 4 and 6 |
| 13 | ▲ | ○ | ○ | ▼ | ▲ | ▲ | Read texts 1, 4, 5 and 6 |
| 14 | ▲ | ▼ | ▼ | ▼ | ▲ | □ | Read texts 1, 2, 3, 4 and 5 |
| 15 | ▲ | ○ | ▼ | ▼ | ▲ | ▲ | Read texts 1, 3, 4, 5 and 6 |
| 16 | ▲ | ▼ | ▼ | ▼ | ▲ | ▲ | Read texts 1, 2, 3, 4, 5 and 6 |
| 17 | □ | ▼ | ▼ | ○ | □ | □ | Read texts 2 and 3 |
| 18 | □ | ▼ | ○ | ▼ | □ | □ | Read texts 2 and 4 |
| 19 | □ | ▼ | ○ | ○ | ▲ | □ | Read texts 2 and 5 |
| 20 | □ | ▼ | ○ | ○ | □ | ▲ | Read texts 2 and 6 |
| 21 | □ | ▼ | ▼ | ▼ | □ | □ | Read texts 2, 3 and 4 |
| 22 | □ | ▼ | ○ | ▼ | ▲ | □ | Read texts 2, 4 and 5 |
| 23 | □ | ▼ | ○ | ▼ | □ | ▲ | Read texts 2, 5 and 6 |
| 24 | □ | ▼ | ▼ | ▼ | ▲ | □ | Read texts 2, 3, 4 and 5 |
| 25 | □ | ▼ | ○ | ▼ | ▲ | ▲ | Read texts 2, 4, 5 and 6 |
| 26 | □ | ▼ | ▼ | ▼ | ▲ | ▲ | Read texts 2, 3, 4, 5 and 6 |
| 27 | ▲ | ▼ | ○ | ▼ | □ | □ | Read texts 1, 2 and 4 |
| 28 | ▲ | ▼ | ○ | ○ | ▲ | □ | Read texts 1, 2 and 5 |
| 29 | ▲ | ▼ | ○ | ○ | □ | ▲ | Read texts 1, 2 and 6 |
| 30 | ▲ | ▼ | ▼ | ○ | ▲ | □ | Read texts 1, 2, 3 and 5 |
| 31 | ▲ | ▼ | ▼ | ○ | □ | ▲ | Read texts 1, 2, 3 and 6 |
| 32 | ▲ | ▼ | ▼ | ▼ | □ | ▲ | Read texts 1, 2, 3, 4 and 6 |
| 33 | ▲ | ○ | ▼ | ○ | ▲ | □ | Read texts 1, 3 and 5 |
| 34 | ▲ | ○ | ▼ | ○ | □ | ▲ | Read texts 1, 3 and 6 |
| 35 | ▲ | ○ | ▼ | ○ | ▲ | ▲ | Read texts 1, 3, 5 and 6 |
| 36 | ▲ | ○ | ○ | ▼ | □ | ▲ | Read texts 1, 4 and 6 |
| 37 | □ | ▼ | ▼ | ○ | ▲ | □ | Read texts 2, 3 and 5 |
| 38 | □ | ▼ | ▼ | ○ | □ | ▲ | Read texts 2, 3 and 6 |
| 39 | □ | ▼ | ▼ | ○ | ▲ | ▲ | Read texts 2, 3, 4 and 6 |
| 40 | □ | ▼ | ○ | ▼ | □ | ▲ | Read texts 2, 4 and 6 |
| 41 | □ | ○ | ▼ | ▼ | □ | □ | Read texts 3 and 4 |
| 42 | □ | ○ | ▼ | ○ | ▲ | □ | Read texts 3 and 5 |
| 43 | □ | ○ | ▼ | ○ | □ | ▲ | Read texts 3 and 6 |
| 44 | □ | ○ | ▼ | ▼ | ▲ | □ | Read texts 3, 4 and 5 |
| 45 | □ | ○ | ▼ | ▼ | □ | ▲ | Read texts 3, 4 and 6 |
| 46 | □ | ○ | ▼ | ○ | ▲ | ▲ | Read texts 3, 5 and 6 |
| 47 | □ | ○ | ▼ | ▼ | ▲ | ▲ | Read texts 3, 4, 5 and 6 |
| 48 | □ | ○ | ○ | ▼ | ▲ | □ | Read texts 4 and 5 |
| 49 | □ | ○ | ○ | ▼ | □ | ▲ | Read texts 4 and 6 |
| 50 | □ | ○ | ○ | ▼ | ▲ | ▲ | Read texts 4, 5 and 6 |
| 51 | □ | ○ | ○ | ○ | ▲ | ▲ | Read texts 5 and 6 |
| 52 | ▲ | ○ | ○ | ○ | □ | □ | Read text 1 |
| 53 | □ | ▼ | ○ | ○ | □ | □ | Read text 2 |
| 54 | □ | ○ | ▼ | ○ | □ | □ | Read text 3 |
| 55 | □ | ○ | ○ | ▼ | □ | □ | Read text 4 |
| 56 | □ | ○ | ○ | ○ | ▲ | □ | Read text 5 |
| 57 | □ | ○ | ○ | ○ | □ | ▲ | Read text 6 |

42nd combination □ ○ ○ ○ □ □

**43rd combination**

| fig. 1 | ▲ ▲ □ □ □ ○ | Read texts 1 and 2 |
|---|---|---|
| 2 | ▲ □ ▲ □ □ ○ | Read texts 1 and 3 |
| 3 | ▲ □ □ ▲ □ ○ | Read texts 1 and 4 |
| 4 | ▲ □ □ □ ▲ ○ | Read texts 1 and 5 |
| 5 | ▲ □ □ □ □ ▼ | Read texts 1 and 6 |
| 6 | ▲ ▲ ▲ □ □ ○ | Read texts 1, 2 and 3 |
| 7 | ▲ ▲ □ ▲ □ ○ | Read texts 1, 3 and 4 |
| 8 | ▲ □ ▲ ▲ □ ○ | Read texts 1, 4 and 5 |
| 9 | ▲ □ □ □ ▲ ▼ | Read texts 1, 5 and 6 |
| 10 | ▲ ▲ ▲ ▲ □ ○ | Read texts 1, 2, 3 and 4 |
| 11 | ▲ □ ▲ ▲ ▲ ○ | Read texts 1, 3, 4 and 5 |
| 12 | ▲ □ ▲ ▲ □ ▼ | Read texts 1, 3, 4 and 6 |
| 13 | ▲ □ □ ▲ ▲ ▼ | Read texts 1, 4, 5 and 6 |
| 14 | ▲ ▲ ▲ ▲ ▲ ○ | Read texts 1, 2, 3, 4 and 5 |
| 15 | ▲ □ ▲ ▲ ▲ ▼ | Read texts 1, 3, 4, 5 and 6 |
| 16 | ▲ ▲ ▲ ▲ ▲ ▼ | Read texts 1, 2, 3, 4, 5 and 6 |
| 17 | □ ▲ ▲ □ □ ○ | Read texts 2 and 3 |
| 18 | □ ▲ □ ▲ □ ○ | Read texts 2 and 4 |
| 19 | □ ▲ □ □ ▲ ○ | Read texts 2 and 5 |
| 20 | □ ▲ □ □ □ ▼ | Read texts 2 and 6 |
| 21 | □ ▲ ▲ ▲ □ ○ | Read texts 2, 3 and 4 |
| 22 | □ ▲ □ ▲ ▲ ○ | Read texts 2, 4 and 5 |
| 23 | □ ▲ □ □ ▲ ▼ | Read texts 2, 5 and 6 |
| 24 | □ ▲ ▲ ▲ ▲ ○ | Read texts 2, 3, 4 and 5 |
| 25 | □ ▲ □ ▲ ▲ ▼ | Read texts 2, 4, 5 and 6 |
| 26 | □ ▲ ▲ ▲ ▲ ▼ | Read texts 2, 3, 4, 5 and 6 |
| 27 | ▲ ▲ □ ▲ □ ○ | Read texts 1, 2 and 4 |
| 28 | ▲ ▲ □ □ ▲ ○ | Read texts 1, 2 and 5 |
| 29 | ▲ ▲ □ □ □ ▼ | Read texts 1, 2 and 6 |
| 30 | ▲ ▲ ▲ □ ▲ ▼ | Read texts 1, 2, 3 and 5 |
| 31 | ▲ ▲ ▲ □ □ ▼ | Read texts 1, 2, 3 and 6 |
| 32 | ▲ ▲ ▲ ▲ □ ▼ | Read texts 1, 2, 3, 4 and 6 |
| 33 | ▲ □ ▲ □ ▲ ○ | Read texts 1, 3 and 5 |
| 34 | ▲ □ ▲ □ □ ▼ | Read texts 1, 3 and 6 |
| 35 | ▲ □ ▲ □ ▲ ▼ | Read texts 1, 3, 5 and 6 |
| 36 | ▲ □ □ ▲ □ ▼ | Read texts 1, 4 and 6 |
| 37 | □ ▲ ▲ □ ▲ ○ | Read texts 2, 3 and 5 |
| 38 | □ ▲ ▲ □ □ ▼ | Read texts 2, 3 and 6 |
| 39 | □ ▲ ▲ ▲ □ ▼ | Read texts 2, 3, 4 and 6 |
| 40 | □ ▲ □ ▲ □ ▼ | Read texts 2, 4 and 6 |
| 41 | □ □ ▲ ▲ □ ○ | Read texts 3 and 4 |
| 42 | □ □ ▲ □ ▲ ○ | Read texts 3 and 5 |
| 43 | □ □ ▲ □ □ ▼ | Read texts 3 and 6 |
| 44 | □ □ ▲ ▲ ▲ ○ | Read texts 3, 4 and 5 |
| 45 | □ □ ▲ ▲ □ ▼ | Read texts 3, 4 and 6 |
| 46 | □ □ ▲ □ ▲ ▼ | Read texts 3, 5 and 6 |
| 47 | □ □ ▲ ▲ ▲ ▼ | Read texts 3, 4, 5 and 6 |
| 48 | □ □ □ ▲ ▲ ○ | Read texts 4 and 5 |
| 49 | □ □ □ ▲ □ ▼ | Read texts 4 and 6 |
| 50 | □ □ □ ▲ ▲ ▼ | Read texts 4, 5 and 6 |
| 51 | □ □ □ □ ▲ ▼ | Read texts 5 and 6 |
| 52 | ▲ □ □ □ □ ○ | Read text 1 |
| 53 | □ ▲ □ □ □ ○ | Read text 2 |
| 54 | □ □ ▲ □ □ ○ | Read text 3 |
| 55 | □ □ □ ▲ □ ○ | Read text 4 |
| 56 | □ □ □ □ ▲ ○ | Read text 5 |
| 57 | □ □ □ □ □ ▼ | Read text 6 |

but also for those around you and for your situation in general.

4   You have an opportunity to play the role of mediator or messenger. Do not underestimate the importance of a mission like this. To prove yourself worthy to carry out this task properly you must be able to demonstrate objectivity, honesty and neutrality, qualities that are relatively rare and demand a clear and rigorous mental attitude.

5   There are no limits to truth and fairness; acting according to these principles, with sincere and generous-spirited motives, will ensure positive results for all your undertakings.

6   If you succumb to your impulses, talk without thinking or try at all costs to acquire something without help or support, you will have poor results. On the other hand if you think before you act, weigh up the pros and cons before expressing yourself and make sure of those whose help you seek, everything you do will succeed.

# 43rd combination □ □ □ □ □ ○

Instinct and reason rarely make good bedfellows; neither do passion and wisdom. Nevertheless, whether it is a question of denouncing your own weaknesses or those of others or of ending a harmful situation, you must act with great firmness. Furthermore, it is important to remember that your ideas and actions must not be inflexible or automatic; you should remain receptive to the opinions or objections of others, questioning your own if necessary.

**1** You are determined to forge ahead, but here and there pockets of resistance or tension still slow you down or hold you back. For this reason it is wiser to stay within your known limits rather than risk the consequences of premature action.

**2** If you show prudence and caution in all circumstances, you will gain the respect and interest of others. If your clear-sightedness enables you to exert true control over yourself and your instincts, you will never fall victim to your emotions, excesses or indiscretions. Lastly, if you take all necessary precautions before starting any endeavour, you will avoid all risks and ensure success.

**3** Special circumstances force you to associate or collaborate with somebody who is not held in high regard by your colleagues. They think you are his or her accomplice or that you share the same viewpoint. Neither of these assumptions is true, but you cannot disprove them. You just have to get the job done, sticking to your principles, while waiting for the right moment to distance yourself from this person.

**4** Your anxious nature drives you to constant activity. But by forcing events and manipulating circumstances as you do, you generate messy situations and endless obstacles and difficulties, without even realizing it. You would be well advised to calm down and stop stubbornly insisting on intervening in everything. But will you be able to take this advice on board?

**5** You are up against some tough adversaries or those with the means to exert considerable power, influence or pressure against you. But do not give up: keep fighting for what you want, even if the relationship you are forced to maintain with these people may seem discouraging or without hope of improvement.

**6** You are to be applauded if you have made efforts to resolve serious difficulties, to put a stop to a negative situation, or to correct or improve yourself. However, make sure that you have gone into everything in great depth and have not overlooked a detail that could turn out to be critical and dangerous. Only then can you be satisfied and sure of your results.

# 44<sup>th</sup> combination ○ □ □ □ □ □

Attraction and repulsion are the strongest poles of all. When two people are attracted to each other nothing can prevent them from coming together. On the other hand, beware of those with whom you have no particular affinity, whom you tend to trust or value too much.

**1** Somebody you did not think dangerous, or whose actions seemed harmless, has finally achieved a position that strengthens their power and intrigues. If you continue to allow this to happen without intervening, you will find yourself in serious trouble.

**2** You are involved with somebody whom you trust very little, and rightly so. Your relationship is such that you can try to exert a subtle, positive influence, to prevent any mistakes. But it is obvious that you have to remain vigilant unless you want to see this person go astray through clumsiness or lack of tact.

**44th combination**

| fig. 1 | ▼ | ▲ | □ | □ | □ | □ | Read texts 1 and 2 |
|---|---|---|---|---|---|---|---|
| 2 | ▼ | □ | ▲ | □ | □ | □ | Read texts 1 and 3 |
| 3 | ▼ | □ | □ | ▲ | □ | □ | Read texts 1 and 4 |
| 4 | ▼ | □ | □ | □ | ▲ | □ | Read texts 1 and 5 |
| 5 | ▼ | □ | □ | □ | □ | ▲ | Read texts 1 and 6 |
| 6 | ▼ | ▲ | ▲ | □ | □ | □ | Read texts 1, 2 and 3 |
| 7 | ▼ | □ | ▲ | ▲ | □ | □ | Read texts 1, 3 and 4 |
| 8 | ▼ | □ | □ | ▲ | ▲ | □ | Read texts 1, 4 and 5 |
| 9 | ▼ | □ | □ | □ | ▲ | ▲ | Read texts 1, 5 and 6 |
| 10 | ▼ | ▲ | ▲ | ▲ | □ | □ | Read texts 1, 2, 3 and 4 |
| 11 | ▼ | □ | ▲ | ▲ | ▲ | □ | Read texts 1, 3, 4 and 5 |
| 12 | ▼ | □ | ▲ | ▲ | □ | ▲ | Read texts 1, 3, 4 and 6 |
| 13 | ▼ | □ | □ | ▲ | ▲ | ▲ | Read texts 1, 4, 5 and 6 |
| 14 | ▼ | ▲ | ▲ | ▲ | ▲ | □ | Read texts 1, 2, 3, 4 and 5 |
| 15 | ▼ | □ | ▲ | ▲ | ▲ | ▲ | Read texts 1, 3, 4, 5 and 6 |
| 16 | ▼ | ▲ | ▲ | ▲ | ▲ | ▲ | Read texts 1, 2, 3, 4, 5 and 6 |
| 17 | ○ | ▲ | ▲ | □ | □ | □ | Read texts 2 and 3 |
| 18 | ○ | ▲ | □ | ▲ | □ | □ | Read texts 2 and 4 |
| 19 | ○ | ▲ | □ | □ | ▲ | □ | Read texts 2 and 5 |
| 20 | ○ | ▲ | □ | □ | □ | ▲ | Read texts 2 and 6 |
| 21 | ○ | ▲ | ▲ | ▲ | □ | □ | Read texts 2, 3 and 4 |
| 22 | ○ | ▲ | □ | ▲ | ▲ | □ | Read texts 2, 4 and 5 |
| 23 | ○ | ▲ | □ | □ | ▲ | ▲ | Read texts 2, 5 and 6 |
| 24 | ○ | ▲ | ▲ | ▲ | ▲ | □ | Read texts 2, 3, 4 and 5 |
| 25 | ○ | ▲ | □ | ▲ | ▲ | ▲ | Read texts 2, 4, 5 and 6 |
| 26 | ○ | ▲ | ▲ | ▲ | ▲ | ▲ | Read texts 2, 3, 4, 5 and 6 |
| 27 | ▼ | ▲ | □ | ▲ | □ | □ | Read texts 1 and 2 and 4 |
| 28 | ▼ | ▲ | □ | □ | ▲ | □ | Read texts 1, 2 and 5 |
| 29 | ▼ | ▲ | □ | □ | □ | ▲ | Read texts 1, 2 and 6 |
| 30 | ▼ | ▲ | ▲ | □ | ▲ | □ | Read texts 1, 2, 3 and 5 |
| 31 | ▼ | ▲ | ▲ | □ | □ | ▲ | Read texts 1, 2, 3 and 6 |
| 32 | ▼ | ▲ | ▲ | ▲ | □ | ▲ | Read texts 1, 2, 3, 4 and 6 |
| 33 | ▼ | □ | ▲ | □ | ▲ | □ | Read texts 1, 3 and 5 |
| 34 | ▼ | □ | ▲ | □ | □ | ▲ | Read texts 1, 3 and 6 |
| 35 | ▼ | □ | ▲ | □ | ▲ | ▲ | Read texts 1, 3, 5 and 6 |
| 36 | ▼ | □ | □ | ▲ | □ | ▲ | Read texts 1, 4 and 6 |
| 37 | ○ | ▲ | ▲ | □ | ▲ | □ | Read texts 2, 3 and 5 |
| 38 | ○ | ▲ | ▲ | □ | □ | ▲ | Read texts 2, 3 and 6 |
| 39 | ○ | ▲ | ▲ | ▲ | □ | ▲ | Read texts 2, 3, 4 and 6 |
| 40 | ○ | ▲ | □ | ▲ | □ | ▲ | Read texts 2, 4 and 6 |
| 41 | ○ | □ | ▲ | ▲ | □ | □ | Read texts 3 and 4 |
| 42 | ○ | □ | ▲ | □ | ▲ | □ | Read texts 3 and 5 |
| 43 | ○ | □ | ▲ | □ | □ | ▲ | Read texts 3 and 6 |
| 44 | ○ | □ | ▲ | ▲ | ▲ | □ | Read texts 3, 4 and 5 |
| 45 | ○ | □ | ▲ | ▲ | □ | ▲ | Read texts 3, 4 and 6 |
| 46 | ○ | □ | ▲ | □ | ▲ | ▲ | Read texts 3, 5 and 6 |
| 47 | ○ | □ | ▲ | ▲ | ▲ | ▲ | Read texts 3, 4, 5 and 6 |
| 48 | ○ | □ | □ | ▲ | ▲ | □ | Read texts 4 and 5 |
| 49 | ○ | □ | □ | ▲ | □ | ▲ | Read texts 4 and 6 |
| 50 | ○ | □ | □ | ▲ | ▲ | ▲ | Read texts 4, 5 and 6 |
| 51 | ○ | □ | □ | □ | ▲ | ▲ | Read texts 5 and 6 |
| 52 | ▼ | □ | □ | □ | □ | □ | Read text 1 |
| 53 | ○ | ▲ | □ | □ | □ | □ | Read text 2 |
| 54 | ○ | □ | ▲ | □ | □ | □ | Read text 3 |
| 55 | ○ | □ | □ | ▲ | □ | □ | Read text 4 |
| 56 | ○ | □ | □ | □ | ▲ | □ | Read text 5 |
| 57 | ○ | □ | □ | □ | □ | ▲ | Read text 6 |

**3** You are tempted to get involved with somebody whose intentions or connections, while not necessarily questionable, are at least at odds with your convictions and principles. However, particular circumstances will stand in the way of any involvement, thereby acting in your favour. Despite any disappointment or frustration you may feel, this is an excellent result because it will prevent you from making a serious mistake.

**4** Always remember to maintain good relations with those who are less well off than yourself, or whose financial situation does not reflect their true worth. What matters most are people's intentions and motives, not their social position. One day you may need them as much as they seem to need you now.

**5** You are not in complete agreement with certain people around you, nor are you fully satisfied with their behaviour and actions. Nevertheless, you do not interfere in their lives, choices or decisions: you leave them to it without saying a word. This is probably the right attitude to take, because in due course they will change their way of thinking and come to agree with you.

**6** You have stepped back, and put some distance between yourself and the outside world and social relationships in general. This does not always go down too well with the people around you, who see it as pride, indifference or a superiority complex. Nevertheless this does not change your attitude, or your inner calm, one iota; you know full well that this behaviour is best for you, and that you could not do otherwise.

# 45th combination ○ ○ ○ □ □ ○

For any community to form a lasting and harmonious bond, it is important that all members share the same motivation and feelings. In every group there is a risk of tension, disagreement and conflict. However this can be avoided – or at least defused – by taking preventive action, and by being prepared for all eventualities.

**1** You are irresistibly drawn to a certain person and would like to get closer to him or her. However your intimate relationships with other people hold you back and are making you confused and indecisive. Trust this person, who is worthy of respect and will help you see yourself clearly and make the right decisions.

**2** Do not waste your energy or willpower trying to go in one direction rather than another. If you meet somebody who shares your feelings and principles, you can spontaneously give them your trust, open your heart to them and let yourself be guided by the laws of attraction. In this type of situation, if one is sincere, then everything is simple and straightforward.

**3** You feel lonely, isolated and out of the game. You are also having some difficulty, due either to shyness or pride, in fitting in with people whom you would like to get to know better. All you have to do is approach one of them, who will introduce you to the others.

**4** You take up a duty or responsibility, or through natural ability you bring people together. This encourages the people around

| fig. | | | | | | | |
|---|---|---|---|---|---|---|---|
| 1 | ▼ | ▼ | ○ | □ | □ | ○ | Read texts 1 and 2 |
| 2 | ▼ | ○ | ▼ | □ | □ | ○ | Read texts 1 and 3 |
| 3 | ▼ | ○ | ○ | ▲ | □ | ○ | Read texts 1 and 4 |
| 4 | ▼ | ○ | ○ | □ | ▲ | ○ | Read texts 1 and 5 |
| 5 | ▼ | ○ | ○ | □ | □ | ▼ | Read texts 1 and 6 |
| 6 | ▼ | ▼ | ▼ | □ | □ | ○ | Read texts 1, 2 and 3 |
| 7 | ▼ | ▼ | ○ | ▲ | □ | ○ | Read texts 1, 2 and 4 |
| 8 | ▼ | ▼ | ○ | □ | ▲ | ○ | Read texts 1, 2 and 5 |
| 9 | ▼ | ▼ | ○ | □ | □ | ▼ | Read texts 1, 2 and 6 |
| 10 | ▼ | ▼ | ▼ | ▲ | □ | ○ | Read texts 1, 2, 3 and 4 |
| 11 | ▼ | ▼ | ▼ | □ | ▲ | ○ | Read texts 1, 2, 3 and 5 |
| 12 | ▼ | ▼ | ▼ | □ | □ | ▼ | Read texts 1, 2, 3 and 6 |
| 13 | ▼ | ▼ | ▼ | ▲ | ▲ | ○ | Read texts 1, 2, 3, 4 and 5 |
| 14 | ▼ | ▼ | ▼ | ▲ | □ | ▼ | Read texts 1, 2, 3, 4 and 6 |
| 15 | ▼ | ▼ | ▼ | ▲ | ▲ | ▼ | Read texts 1, 2, 3, 4, 5 and 6 |
| 16 | ▼ | ○ | ▼ | ▲ | □ | ○ | Read texts 1, 3 and 4 |
| 17 | ▼ | ○ | ▼ | □ | ▲ | ○ | Read texts 1, 3 and 5 |
| 18 | ▼ | ○ | ▼ | □ | □ | ▼ | Read texts 1, 3 and 6 |
| 19 | ▼ | ○ | ▼ | ▲ | ▲ | ○ | Read texts 1, 3, 4 and 5 |
| 20 | ▼ | ○ | ▼ | ▲ | □ | ▼ | Read texts 1, 3, 4 and 6 |
| 21 | ▼ | ○ | ▼ | □ | ▲ | ▼ | Read texts 1, 3, 5 and 6 |
| 22 | ▼ | ○ | ▼ | ▲ | ▲ | ▼ | Read texts 1, 3, 4, 5 and 6 |
| 23 | ▼ | ○ | ○ | ▲ | ▲ | ○ | Read texts 1, 4 and 5 |
| 24 | ▼ | ○ | ○ | ▲ | □ | ▼ | Read texts 1, 4 and 6 |
| 25 | ▼ | ○ | ○ | ▲ | ▲ | ▼ | Read texts 1, 4, 5 and 6 |
| 26 | ▼ | ○ | ○ | □ | ▲ | ▼ | Read texts 1, 5 and 6 |
| 27 | ○ | ▼ | ▼ | □ | □ | ○ | Read texts 2 and 3 |
| 28 | ○ | ▼ | ○ | ▲ | □ | ○ | Read texts 2 and 4 |
| 29 | ○ | ▼ | ○ | □ | ▲ | ○ | Read texts 2 and 5 |
| 30 | ○ | ▼ | ○ | □ | □ | ▼ | Read texts 2 and 6 |
| 31 | ○ | ▼ | ▼ | ▲ | □ | ○ | Read texts 2, 3 and 4 |
| 32 | ○ | ▼ | ▼ | □ | ▲ | ○ | Read texts 2, 3 and 5 |
| 33 | ○ | ▼ | ▼ | □ | □ | ▼ | Read texts 2, 3 and 6 |
| 34 | ○ | ▼ | ▼ | ▲ | ▲ | ○ | Read texts 2, 3, 4 and 5 |
| 35 | ○ | ▼ | ▼ | ▲ | □ | ▼ | Read texts 2, 3, 4 and 6 |
| 36 | ○ | ▼ | ▼ | ▲ | ▲ | ▼ | Read texts 2, 3, 4, 5 and 6 |
| 37 | ○ | ▼ | ○ | ▲ | ▲ | ○ | Read texts 2, 4 and 5 |
| 38 | ○ | ▼ | ○ | ▲ | □ | ▼ | Read texts 2, 4 and 6 |
| 39 | ○ | ▼ | ○ | ▲ | ▲ | ▼ | Read texts 2, 4, 5 and 6 |
| 40 | ○ | ▼ | ○ | □ | ▲ | ▼ | Read texts 2, 5 and 6 |
| 41 | ○ | ○ | ▼ | ▲ | □ | ○ | Read texts 3 and 4 |
| 42 | ○ | ○ | ▼ | □ | ▲ | ○ | Read texts 3 and 5 |
| 43 | ○ | ○ | ▼ | □ | □ | ▼ | Read texts 3 and 6 |
| 44 | ○ | ○ | ▼ | ▲ | ▲ | ○ | Read texts 3, 4 and 5 |
| 45 | ○ | ○ | ▼ | ▲ | □ | ▼ | Read texts 3, 4 and 6 |
| 46 | ○ | ○ | ▼ | □ | ▲ | ▼ | Read texts 3, 5 and 6 |
| 47 | ○ | ○ | ▼ | ▲ | ▲ | ▼ | Read texts 3, 4, 5 and 6 |
| 48 | ○ | ○ | ○ | ▲ | ▲ | ○ | Read texts 4 and 5 |
| 49 | ○ | ○ | ○ | ▲ | □ | ▼ | Read texts 4 and 6 |
| 50 | ○ | ○ | ○ | ▲ | ▲ | ▼ | Read texts 4, 5 and 6 |
| 51 | ○ | ○ | ○ | □ | ▲ | ▼ | Read texts 5 and 6 |
| 52 | ▼ | ○ | ○ | □ | □ | ○ | Read text 1 |
| 53 | ○ | ▼ | ○ | □ | □ | ○ | Read text 2 |
| 54 | ○ | ○ | ▼ | □ | □ | ○ | Read text 3 |
| 55 | ○ | ○ | ○ | ▲ | □ | ○ | Read text 4 |
| 56 | ○ | ○ | ○ | □ | ▲ | ○ | Read text 5 |
| 57 | ○ | ○ | ○ | □ | □ | ▼ | Read text 6 |

**46th combination**

| | | | | | | |
|---|---|---|---|---|---|---|
| fig. 1 | ▼ ▲ □ ○ ○ ○ | Read texts 1 and 2 |
| 2 | ▼ □ ▲ ○ ○ ○ | Read texts 1 and 3 |
| 3 | ▼ □ □ ▼ ○ ○ | Read texts 1 and 4 |
| 4 | ▼ □ □ ○ ▼ ○ | Read texts 1 and 5 |
| 5 | ▼ □ □ ○ ○ ▼ | Read texts 1 and 6 |
| 6 | ▼ ▲ ▲ ○ ○ ○ | Read texts 1, 2 and 3 |
| 7 | ▼ ▲ □ ▼ ○ ○ | Read texts 1, 2 and 4 |
| 8 | ▼ ▲ □ ○ ▼ ○ | Read texts 1, 2 and 5 |
| 9 | ▼ ▲ □ ○ ○ ▼ | Read texts 1, 2 and 6 |
| 10 | ▼ ▲ ▲ ▼ ○ ○ | Read texts 1, 2, 3 and 4 |
| 11 | ▼ ▲ ▲ ○ ▼ ○ | Read texts 1, 2, 3 and 5 |
| 12 | ▼ ▲ ▲ ○ ○ ▼ | Read texts 1, 2, 3 and 6 |
| 13 | ▼ ▲ ▲ ▼ ▼ ○ | Read texts 1, 2, 3, 4 and 5 |
| 14 | ▼ ▲ ▲ ▼ ○ ▼ | Read texts 1, 2, 3, 4 and 6 |
| 15 | ▼ ▲ ▲ ▼ ▼ ▼ | Read texts 1, 2, 3, 4, 5 and 6 |
| 16 | ▼ □ ▲ ▼ ○ ○ | Read texts 1, 3 and 4 |
| 17 | ▼ □ ▲ ○ ▼ ○ | Read texts 1, 3 and 5 |
| 18 | ▼ □ ▲ ○ ○ ▼ | Read texts 1, 3 and 6 |
| 19 | ▼ □ ▲ ▼ ▼ ○ | Read texts 1, 3, 4 and 5 |
| 20 | ▼ □ ▲ ▼ ○ ▼ | Read texts 1, 3, 4 and 6 |
| 21 | ▼ □ ▲ ○ ▼ ▼ | Read texts 1, 3, 5 and 6 |
| 22 | ▼ □ ▲ ▼ ▼ ▼ | Read texts 1, 3, 4, 5 and 6 |
| 23 | ▼ □ □ ▼ ▼ ○ | Read texts 1, 4 and 5 |
| 24 | ▼ □ □ ▼ ○ ▼ | Read texts 1, 4 and 6 |
| 25 | ▼ □ □ ▼ ▼ ▼ | Read texts 1, 4, 5 and 6 |
| 26 | ▼ □ □ ○ ▼ ▼ | Read texts 1, 5 and 6 |
| 27 | ○ ▲ ▲ ○ ○ ○ | Read texts 2 and 3 |
| 28 | ○ ▲ □ ▼ ○ ○ | Read texts 2 and 4 |
| 29 | ○ ▲ □ ○ ▼ ○ | Read texts 2 and 5 |
| 30 | ○ ▲ □ ○ ○ ▼ | Read texts 2 and 6 |
| 31 | ○ ▲ ▲ ▼ ○ ○ | Read texts 2, 3 and 4 |
| 32 | ○ ▲ ▲ ○ ▼ ○ | Read texts 2, 3 and 5 |
| 33 | ○ ▲ ▲ ○ ○ ▼ | Read texts 2, 3 and 6 |
| 34 | ○ ▲ ▲ ▼ ▼ ○ | Read texts 2, 3, 4 and 5 |
| 35 | ○ ▲ ▲ ▼ ○ ▼ | Read texts 2, 3, 4 and 6 |
| 36 | ○ ▲ ▲ ▼ ▼ ▼ | Read texts 2, 3, 4, 5 and 6 |
| 37 | ○ ▲ □ ▼ ▼ ○ | Read texts 2, 4 and 5 |
| 38 | ○ ▲ □ ▼ ○ ▼ | Read texts 2, 4 and 6 |
| 39 | ○ ▲ □ ▼ ▼ ▼ | Read texts 2, 4, 5 and 6 |
| 40 | ○ ▲ □ ○ ▼ ▼ | Read texts 2, 5 and 6 |
| 41 | ○ □ ▲ ▼ ○ ○ | Read texts 3 and 4 |
| 42 | ○ □ ▲ ○ ▼ ○ | Read texts 3 and 5 |
| 43 | ○ □ ▲ ○ ○ ▼ | Read texts 3 and 6 |
| 44 | ○ □ ▲ ▼ ▼ ○ | Read texts 3, 4 and 5 |
| 45 | ○ □ ▲ ▼ ○ ▼ | Read texts 3, 4 and 6 |
| 46 | ○ □ ▲ ○ ▼ ▼ | Read texts 3, 5 and 6 |
| 47 | ○ □ ▲ ▼ ▼ ▼ | Read texts 3, 4, 5 and 6 |
| 48 | ○ □ □ ▼ ▼ ○ | Read texts 4 and 5 |
| 49 | ○ □ □ ▼ ○ ▼ | Read texts 4 and 6 |
| 50 | ○ □ □ ▼ ▼ ▼ | Read texts 4, 5 and 6 |
| 51 | ○ □ □ ○ ▼ ▼ | Read texts 5 and 6 |
| 52 | ▼ □ □ ○ ○ ○ | Read text 1 |
| 53 | ○ ▲ □ ○ ○ ○ | Read text 2 |
| 54 | ○ □ ▲ ○ ○ ○ | Read text 3 |
| 55 | ○ □ □ ▼ ○ ○ | Read text 4 |
| 56 | ○ □ □ ○ ▼ ○ | Read text 5 |
| 57 | ○ □ □ ○ ○ ▼ | Read text 6 |

you to dedicate themselves to a common goal, for which you deserve praise.

**5**   If your colleagues voluntarily associate with you or support you willingly and sincerely, without you having to ask for anything, all well and good. On the other hand, if others express the same intentions with ulterior motives or simply wish to benefit from your situation and its privileges and advantages, be vigilant and demanding.

**6**   You sincerely wish to get close to someone, or to unite with them, but either they do not know this, or you have not made your intentions clear. Clear up this misunderstanding by expressing your disappointment and confusion – this person will certainly not remain indifferent to your feelings.

# 46<sup>th</sup> combination ○ □ □ □ ○ ○

The circumstances you enjoy at the moment should encourage you to act, to take up new endeavours and to progress. Therefore you should not delay in pushing yourself forward or putting your plans into action and do not be afraid to take bold initiatives, because you have every chance of success.

**1**   You are planning to start something that requires the approval or support of somebody influential or in a position of authority and power. However, because you have no references, you are afraid you will not be heard, but when you approach this person you will very quickly realize that he/she is extremely well disposed towards you.

2    At times you lack flexibility and tact in your relations with those around you, although you are trustworthy and extremely honest. These qualities have won you the respect and interest of all, and make them overlook your scant regard for convention, and your occasionally severe or unsubtle reactions.

3    The obstacles and difficulties you experienced, or that you might have encountered, which others are currently facing, have disappeared as if by magic. Do not expect to understand why, but continue to forge ahead without a second thought. Just make the most of these exceptional circumstances!

4    Your goal is within reach; you have achieved or acquired what you wanted or you will do so very soon. Savour the sweet taste of victory without reservation, because your success will allow you to reinforce your position and improve your situation.

5    You are on the road to success. Do not relax your efforts. Prove yourself worthy. Do not manipulate events; just climb the ladder one step at a time, remaining tenacious, vigilant, modest and alert, whatever happens. Do all these things and success and victory will be yours.

6    Do not go all out to get what you want regardless of your circumstances means or opportunities. Your lack of scruples and consistency could actually have unfortunate or dangerous consequences.

# 47th combination ○ ▢ ○ ▢ ▢ ○

If fate is against you or you encounter setbacks or feel that you are confronting insurmountable obstacles, call on your inner strength; this will give you the power to overcome all your difficulties while remaining true to yourself, your principles and your beliefs, whatever happens.

1    If you just bemoan your fate, give up or despair of ever finding a way out of your problems, not only will you solve nothing but your situation may quite possibly deteriorate. You are therefore recommended to react more vigorously and not to let yourself go.

2    You feel extremely weary at the moment because of the monotony of your current existence. It is true that your present position does not match your capabilities but a better job is on the horizon. In the meantime, cultivate your personality and have faith in yourself and in life.

3    Faced with your current obstacles and difficulties, you show yourself to be indecisive or reliant on other people's help, or else your projected solutions are completely unrealistic, illusory or unsuited to the circumstances. You need to react more vigorously and take firm decisions.

4    You sincerely want to help certain people you know, who are experiencing real difficulties and truly need support. Those who are in a position to help them are not doing so. But your kind, generous nature and your powers of persuasion should eventually overcome these tempo-

○
□
□
○
○
□
○

**47th combination**

| | | | | | | | | |
|---|---|---|---|---|---|---|---|---|
| fig. 1 | ▼ | ▲ | ○ | □ | □ | ○ | Read texts 1 and 2 |
| 2 | ▼ | □ | ▼ | □ | □ | ○ | Read texts 1 and 3 |
| 3 | ▼ | □ | ○ | ▲ | □ | ○ | Read texts 1 and 4 |
| 4 | ▼ | □ | ○ | □ | ▲ | ○ | Read texts 1 and 5 |
| 5 | ▼ | □ | ○ | □ | □ | ▼ | Read texts 1 and 6 |
| 6 | ▼ | ▲ | ▼ | □ | □ | ○ | Read texts 1, 2 and 3 |
| 7 | ▼ | □ | ▼ | ▲ | □ | ○ | Read texts 1, 3 and 4 |
| 8 | ▼ | □ | ○ | ▲ | ▲ | ○ | Read texts 1, 4 and 5 |
| 9 | ▼ | □ | ○ | □ | ▲ | ▼ | Read texts 1, 5 and 6 |
| 10 | ▼ | ▲ | ▼ | ▲ | □ | ○ | Read texts 1, 2, 3 and 4 |
| 11 | ▼ | □ | ▼ | ▲ | ▲ | ○ | Read texts 1, 3, 4 and 5 |
| 12 | ▼ | □ | ▼ | ▲ | □ | ▼ | Read texts 1, 3, 4 and 6 |
| 13 | ▼ | □ | ○ | ▲ | ▲ | ▼ | Read texts 1, 4, 5 and 6 |
| 14 | ▼ | ▲ | ▼ | ▲ | ▲ | ○ | Read texts 1, 2, 3, 4 and 5 |
| 15 | ▼ | □ | ▼ | ▲ | ▲ | ▼ | Read texts 1, 3, 4, 5 and 6 |
| 16 | ▼ | ▲ | ▼ | ▲ | ▲ | ▼ | Read texts 1, 2, 3, 4, 5 and 6 |
| 17 | ○ | ▲ | ▼ | □ | □ | ○ | Read texts 2 and 3 |
| 18 | ○ | ▲ | ○ | ▲ | □ | ○ | Read texts 2 and 4 |
| 19 | ○ | ▲ | ○ | □ | ▲ | ○ | Read texts 2 and 5 |
| 20 | ○ | ▲ | ○ | □ | □ | ▼ | Read texts 2 and 6 |
| 21 | ○ | ▲ | ▼ | ▲ | □ | ○ | Read texts 2, 3 and 4 |
| 22 | ○ | ▲ | ○ | ▲ | ▲ | ○ | Read texts 2, 4 and 5 |
| 23 | ○ | ▲ | ○ | □ | ▲ | ▼ | Read texts 2, 5 and 6 |
| 24 | ○ | ▲ | ▼ | ▲ | ▲ | ○ | Read texts 2, 3, 4 and 5 |
| 25 | ○ | ▲ | ○ | ▲ | ▲ | ▼ | Read texts 2, 4, 5 and 6 |
| 26 | ○ | ▲ | ▼ | ▲ | ▲ | ▼ | Read texts 2, 3, 4, 5 and 6 |
| 27 | ▼ | ▲ | ○ | ▲ | □ | ○ | Read texts 1, 2 and 4 |
| 28 | ▼ | ▲ | ○ | □ | ▲ | ○ | Read texts 1, 2 and 5 |
| 29 | ▼ | ▲ | ○ | □ | □ | ▼ | Read texts 1, 2 and 6 |
| 30 | ▼ | ▲ | ▼ | □ | ▲ | ○ | Read texts 1, 2, 3 and 5 |
| 31 | ▼ | ▲ | ▼ | □ | □ | ▼ | Read texts 1, 2, 3 and 6 |
| 32 | ▼ | ▲ | ▼ | ▲ | □ | ▼ | Read texts 1, 2, 3, 4 and 6 |
| 33 | ▼ | □ | ▼ | □ | ▲ | ○ | Read texts 1, 3 and 5 |
| 34 | ▼ | □ | ▼ | □ | □ | ▼ | Read texts 1, 3 and 6 |
| 35 | ▼ | □ | ▼ | □ | ▲ | ▼ | Read texts 1, 3, 5 and 6 |
| 36 | ▼ | □ | ○ | ▲ | □ | ▼ | Read texts 1, 4 and 6 |
| 37 | ○ | ▲ | ▼ | □ | ▲ | ○ | Read texts 2, 3 and 5 |
| 38 | ○ | ▲ | ▼ | □ | □ | ▼ | Read texts 2, 3 and 6 |
| 39 | ○ | ▲ | ▼ | ▲ | □ | ▼ | Read texts 2, 3, 4 and 6 |
| 40 | ○ | ▲ | ○ | ▲ | □ | ▼ | Read texts 2, 4 and 6 |
| 41 | ○ | □ | ▼ | ▲ | □ | ○ | Read texts 3 and 4 |
| 42 | ○ | □ | ▼ | □ | ▲ | ○ | Read texts 3 and 5 |
| 43 | ○ | □ | ▼ | □ | □ | ▼ | Read texts 3 and 6 |
| 44 | ○ | □ | ▼ | ▲ | ▲ | ○ | Read texts 3, 4 and 5 |
| 45 | ○ | □ | ▼ | ▲ | □ | ▼ | Read texts 3, 4 and 6 |
| 46 | ○ | □ | ▼ | □ | ▲ | ▼ | Read texts 3, 5 and 6 |
| 47 | ○ | □ | ▼ | ▲ | ▲ | ▼ | Read texts 3, 4, 5 and 6 |
| 48 | ○ | □ | ○ | ▲ | ▲ | ○ | Read texts 4 and 5 |
| 49 | ○ | □ | ○ | ▲ | □ | ▼ | Read texts 4 and 6 |
| 50 | ○ | □ | ○ | ▲ | ▲ | ▼ | Read texts 4, 5 and 6 |
| 51 | ○ | □ | ○ | □ | ▲ | ▼ | Read texts 5 and 6 |
| 52 | ▼ | □ | ○ | □ | □ | ○ | Read text 1 |
| 53 | ○ | ▲ | ○ | □ | □ | ○ | Read text 2 |
| 54 | ○ | □ | ▼ | □ | □ | ○ | Read text 3 |
| 55 | ○ | □ | ○ | ▲ | □ | ○ | Read text 4 |
| 56 | ○ | □ | ○ | □ | ▲ | ○ | Read text 5 |
| 57 | ○ | □ | ○ | □ | □ | ▼ | Read text 6 |

rary obstacles. There will soon be a show of solidarity around you.

**5** You are not in a strong position and are therefore unable to gain the necessary means to help those in need or to avoid a catastrophe. However, given the way events are unfolding, you can expect a positive change from those responsible. You will do better to remain faithful to your convictions and carry on as you are.

**6** You are having trouble making a complete break from a situation or relationship that no longer has any reason to exist. You must therefore react firmly, take the obvious decision and stop shilly-shallying; above all, do not be discouraged.

# 48<sup>th</sup> combination ○ □ □ ○ □ ○

You must understand clearly that the principles and convictions you have been taught or have acquired are merely useful tools for expressing your inner personality and true nature. This also holds true for those around you. Therefore do not attach too much importance to form and convention but draw as often as possible from the wealth of resources within you.

**1** Your loneliness or isolation is causing you suffering. It seems clear that, because you lack self-respect, you are neglecting your personal qualities and inner resources while ignoring or rejecting those of others. This is the root cause of your isolation; be aware of it in order to put things right.

2   You have many good qualities and great potential, but you do not give them enough consideration or else you do not develop or exploit them. Thus you surround yourself with people who do not stimulate you or enhance your status. Respect yourself more and seek out those whose interests will stimulate and enrich you.

3   You have many good qualities, but either you are unaware of them, you refuse to acknowledge them or you have an innate tendency to underestimate yourself and put yourself down in front of other people. However there is close to you a kind and attentive person whose example and advice you should follow. In fact, it seems that this person deplores your attitude and is ready to help and encourage you.

4   You are at a point in your life where you feel the need to put things in order and see yourself more clearly. You are not very responsive to other people and you cannot start anything new. But this will not matter in the end, because a period of introspection will be beneficial and you will act more effectively and live more harmoniously as a result.

5   You have some excellent qualities but do not exploit them enough and, above all, your relationships with other people lack generosity and simplicity. As a result you are not sharing your gifts or talents with anyone, something you should take on board. If one's abilities are not developed as they should be, they remain sterile and useless.

6   If you allow those around you to share in your qualities, abilities or gifts, you always enrich yourself as well. Acting in a

| fig. | | | | | | | |
|---|---|---|---|---|---|---|---|
| fig. 1 | ▼ | ▲ | □ | ○ | □ | ○ | Read texts 1 and 2 |
| 2 | ▼ | □ | ▲ | ○ | □ | ○ | Read texts 1 and 3 |
| 3 | ▼ | □ | □ | ▲ | ○ | ○ | Read texts 1 and 4 |
| 4 | ▼ | □ | □ | ○ | ▲ | ○ | Read texts 1 and 5 |
| 5 | ▼ | □ | □ | ○ | □ | ▼ | Read texts 1 and 6 |
| 6 | ▼ | ▲ | ▲ | ○ | □ | ○ | Read texts 1, 2 and 3 |
| 7 | ▼ | □ | ▲ | ▼ | □ | ○ | Read texts 1, 3 and 4 |
| 8 | ▼ | □ | □ | ▼ | ▲ | ○ | Read texts 1, 4 and 5 |
| 9 | ▼ | □ | □ | ○ | ▲ | ▼ | Read texts 1, 5 and 6 |
| 10 | ▼ | ▲ | ▲ | ▼ | □ | ○ | Read texts 1, 2, 3 and 4 |
| 11 | ▼ | □ | ▲ | ▼ | ▲ | ○ | Read texts 1, 3, 4 and 5 |
| 12 | ▼ | □ | ▲ | ▼ | □ | ▼ | Read texts 1, 3, 4 and 6 |
| 13 | ▼ | □ | □ | ▼ | ▲ | ▼ | Read texts 1, 4, 5 and 6 |
| 14 | ▼ | ▲ | ▲ | ▼ | ▲ | ○ | Read texts 1, 2, 3, 4 and 5 |
| 15 | ▼ | □ | ▲ | ▼ | ▲ | ▼ | Read texts 1, 3, 4, 5 and 6 |
| 16 | ▼ | ▲ | ▲ | ▼ | ▲ | ▼ | Read texts 1, 2, 3, 4, 5 and 6 |
| 17 | ○ | ▲ | ▲ | ○ | □ | ○ | Read texts 2 and 3 |
| 18 | ○ | ▲ | □ | ▼ | ○ | ○ | Read texts 2 and 4 |
| 19 | ○ | ▲ | □ | ○ | ▲ | ○ | Read texts 2 and 5 |
| 20 | ○ | ▲ | □ | ○ | □ | ▼ | Read texts 2 and 6 |
| 21 | ○ | ▲ | ▲ | ▼ | □ | ○ | Read texts 2, 3 and 4 |
| 22 | ○ | ▲ | □ | ▼ | ▲ | ○ | Read texts 2, 4 and 5 |
| 23 | ○ | ▲ | □ | ○ | ▲ | ▼ | Read texts 2, 5 and 6 |
| 24 | ○ | ▲ | ▲ | ▼ | ▲ | ○ | Read texts 2, 3, 4 and 5 |
| 25 | ○ | ▲ | □ | ▼ | ▲ | ▼ | Read texts 2, 4, 5 and 6 |
| 26 | ○ | ▲ | ▲ | ▼ | ▲ | ▼ | Read texts 2, 3, 4, 5 and 6 |
| 27 | ▼ | ▲ | □ | ▼ | □ | ○ | Read texts 1, 2 and 4 |
| 28 | ▼ | ▲ | □ | ○ | ▲ | ○ | Read texts 1, 2 and 5 |
| 29 | ▼ | ▲ | □ | ○ | □ | ▼ | Read texts 1, 2 and 6 |
| 30 | ▼ | ▲ | ▲ | ○ | ▲ | ○ | Read texts 1, 2, 3 and 5 |
| 31 | ▼ | ▲ | ▲ | ○ | □ | ▼ | Read texts 1, 2, 3 and 6 |
| 32 | ▼ | ▲ | ▲ | ▼ | □ | ▼ | Read texts 1, 2, 3, 4 and 6 |
| 33 | ▼ | □ | ▲ | ○ | □ | ▼ | Read texts 1, 3 and 5 |
| 34 | ▼ | □ | ▲ | ○ | □ | ▼ | Read texts 1, 3 and 6 |
| 35 | ▼ | □ | ▲ | ○ | ▲ | ▼ | Read texts 1, 3, 5 and 6 |
| 36 | ▼ | □ | □ | ▼ | □ | ▼ | Read texts 1, 4 and 6 |
| 37 | ○ | ▲ | ▲ | ○ | ▲ | ○ | Read texts 2, 3 and 5 |
| 38 | ○ | ▲ | ▲ | ○ | □ | ▼ | Read texts 2, 3 and 6 |
| 39 | ○ | ▲ | ▲ | ▼ | □ | ▼ | Read texts 2, 3, 4 and 6 |
| 40 | ○ | ▲ | □ | ▼ | □ | ▼ | Read texts 2, 4 and 6 |
| 41 | ○ | □ | □ | ▲ | ▼ | ○ | Read texts 3 and 4 |
| 42 | ○ | □ | ▲ | ○ | ▲ | ○ | Read texts 3 and 5 |
| 43 | ○ | □ | ▲ | ○ | □ | ▼ | Read texts 3 and 6 |
| 44 | ○ | □ | ▲ | ▼ | ▲ | ○ | Read texts 3, 4 and 5 |
| 45 | ○ | □ | ▲ | ▼ | □ | ▼ | Read texts 3, 4 and 6 |
| 46 | ○ | □ | ▲ | ○ | ▲ | ▼ | Read texts 3, 5 and 6 |
| 47 | ○ | □ | ▲ | ▼ | ▲ | ▼ | Read texts 3, 4, 5 and 6 |
| 48 | ○ | □ | □ | ▼ | ▲ | ○ | Read texts 4 and 5 |
| 49 | ○ | □ | □ | ▼ | □ | ▼ | Read texts 4 and 6 |
| 50 | ○ | □ | □ | ▼ | ▲ | ▼ | Read texts 4, 5 and 6 |
| 51 | ○ | □ | □ | ○ | ▲ | ▼ | Read texts 5 and 6 |
| 52 | ▼ | □ | □ | ○ | □ | ○ | Read text 1 |
| 53 | ○ | ▲ | □ | ○ | □ | ○ | Read text 2 |
| 54 | ○ | □ | ▲ | ○ | □ | ○ | Read text 3 |
| 55 | ○ | □ | □ | ▼ | □ | ○ | Read text 4 |
| 56 | ○ | □ | □ | ○ | ▲ | ○ | Read text 5 |
| 57 | ○ | □ | □ | ○ | □ | ▼ | Read text 6 |

**48th combination**  ○ □ □ ○ ○

323

**49th combination**

| | | | | | | | |
|---|---|---|---|---|---|---|---|
| fig. 1 | ▲ | ▼ | □ | □ | □ | ○ | Read texts 1 and 2 |
| 2 | ▲ | ○ | ▲ | □ | □ | ○ | Read texts 1 and 3 |
| 3 | ▲ | ○ | □ | ▲ | □ | ○ | Read texts 1 and 4 |
| 4 | ▲ | ○ | □ | □ | ▲ | ○ | Read texts 1 and 5 |
| 5 | ▲ | ○ | □ | □ | □ | ▼ | Read texts 1 and 6 |
| 6 | ▲ | ▼ | ▲ | □ | □ | ○ | Read texts 1, 2 and 3 |
| 7 | ▲ | ○ | ▲ | ▲ | □ | ○ | Read texts 1, 3 and 4 |
| 8 | ▲ | ○ | □ | ▲ | ▲ | ○ | Read texts 1, 4 and 5 |
| 9 | ▲ | ○ | □ | □ | ▲ | ▼ | Read texts 1, 5 and 6 |
| 10 | ▲ | ▼ | ▲ | ▲ | □ | ○ | Read texts 1, 2, 3 and 4 |
| 11 | ▲ | ○ | ▲ | ▲ | ▲ | ○ | Read texts 1, 3, 4 and 5 |
| 12 | ▲ | ○ | ▲ | ▲ | □ | ▼ | Read texts 1, 3, 4 and 6 |
| 13 | ▲ | ○ | □ | ▲ | ▲ | ▼ | Read texts 1, 4, 5 and 6 |
| 14 | ▲ | ▼ | ▲ | ▲ | ▲ | ○ | Read texts 1, 2, 3, 4 and 5 |
| 15 | ▲ | ○ | ▲ | ▲ | ▲ | ▼ | Read texts 1, 3, 4, 5 and 6 |
| 16 | ▲ | ▼ | ▲ | ▲ | ▲ | ▼ | Read texts 1, 2, 3, 4, 5 and 6 |
| 17 | □ | ▼ | ▲ | □ | □ | ○ | Read texts 2 and 3 |
| 18 | □ | ▼ | □ | ▲ | □ | ○ | Read texts 2 and 4 |
| 19 | □ | ▼ | □ | □ | ▲ | ○ | Read texts 2 and 5 |
| 20 | □ | ▼ | □ | □ | □ | ▼ | Read texts 2 and 6 |
| 21 | □ | ▼ | ▲ | ▲ | □ | ○ | Read texts 2, 3 and 4 |
| 22 | □ | ▼ | □ | ▲ | ▲ | ○ | Read texts 2, 4 and 5 |
| 23 | □ | ▼ | □ | □ | ▲ | ▼ | Read texts 2, 5 and 6 |
| 24 | □ | ▼ | ▲ | ▲ | ▲ | ○ | Read texts 2, 3, 4 and 5 |
| 25 | □ | ▼ | □ | ▲ | ▲ | ▼ | Read texts 2, 4, 5 and 6 |
| 26 | □ | ▼ | ▲ | ▲ | ▲ | ▼ | Read texts 2, 3, 4, 5 and 6 |
| 27 | ▲ | ▼ | □ | ▲ | □ | ○ | Read texts 1, 2 and 4 |
| 28 | ▲ | ▼ | □ | □ | ▲ | ○ | Read texts 1, 2 and 5 |
| 29 | ▲ | ▼ | □ | □ | □ | ▼ | Read texts 1, 2 and 6 |
| 30 | ▲ | ▼ | ▲ | □ | ▲ | ○ | Read texts 1, 2, 3 and 5 |
| 31 | ▲ | ▼ | ▲ | ▲ | □ | ▼ | Read texts 1, 2, 3 and 6 |
| 32 | ▲ | ▼ | ▲ | ▲ | ▲ | ○ | Read texts 1, 2, 3, 4 and 6 |
| 33 | ▲ | ○ | ▲ | □ | ▲ | ○ | Read texts 1, 3 and 5 |
| 34 | ▲ | ○ | ▲ | □ | □ | ▼ | Read texts 1, 3 and 6 |
| 35 | ▲ | ○ | ▲ | □ | ▲ | ▼ | Read texts 1, 3, 5 and 6 |
| 36 | ▲ | ○ | □ | ▲ | □ | ▼ | Read texts 1, 4 and 6 |
| 37 | □ | ▼ | ▲ | □ | ▲ | ○ | Read texts 2, 3 and 5 |
| 38 | □ | ▼ | ▲ | □ | □ | ▼ | Read texts 2, 3 and 6 |
| 39 | □ | ▼ | ▲ | ▲ | □ | ▼ | Read texts 2, 3, 4 and 6 |
| 40 | □ | ▼ | □ | ▲ | □ | ▼ | Read texts 2, 4 and 6 |
| 41 | □ | ○ | ▲ | ▲ | □ | ○ | Read texts 3 and 4 |
| 42 | □ | ○ | ▲ | □ | ▲ | ○ | Read texts 3 and 5 |
| 43 | □ | ○ | ▲ | □ | □ | ▼ | Read texts 3 and 6 |
| 44 | □ | ○ | ▲ | ▲ | ▲ | ○ | Read texts 3, 4 and 5 |
| 45 | □ | ○ | ▲ | ▲ | □ | ▼ | Read texts 3, 4 and 6 |
| 46 | □ | ○ | ▲ | □ | ▲ | ▼ | Read texts 3, 5 and 6 |
| 47 | □ | ○ | ▲ | ▲ | ▲ | ▼ | Read texts 3, 4, 5 and 6 |
| 48 | □ | ○ | □ | ▲ | ▲ | ○ | Read texts 4 and 5 |
| 49 | □ | ○ | □ | ▲ | □ | ▼ | Read texts 4 and 6 |
| 50 | □ | ○ | □ | ▲ | ▲ | ▼ | Read texts 4, 5 and 6 |
| 51 | □ | ○ | □ | □ | ▲ | ▼ | Read texts 5 and 6 |
| 52 | ▲ | ○ | □ | □ | □ | ○ | Read text 1 |
| 53 | □ | ▼ | □ | □ | □ | ○ | Read text 2 |
| 54 | □ | ○ | ▲ | □ | □ | ○ | Read text 3 |
| 55 | □ | ○ | □ | ▲ | □ | ○ | Read text 4 |
| 56 | □ | ○ | □ | □ | ▲ | ○ | Read text 5 |
| 57 | □ | ○ | □ | □ | □ | ▼ | Read text 6 |

fair and honourable way always earns respect and will bring you a wonderful and lasting sense of fulfilment. Make sure you preserve it, whatever happens.

# 49th combination □ ○ □ □ □ ○

You have tried everything to work things out but, in spite of all, you still come up against the same obstacles and the same difficulties. This means a more radical and profound life change is required. However, implement this change in a dynamic and positive way, in order that everybody will welcome it and encourage it.

**1** If you have really examined the situation from every angle, and exhausted all possibilities and resources at your disposal, with nothing to show for it, a radical change is needed. However, do not take any action unsuited to the demands of the moment. Do not act prematurely or without preparation; wait for the right time – otherwise you risk spoiling or losing everything.

**2** It is now obvious to you that a radical, decisive change is needed, one that must be implemented with great firmness and due respect for the rules. This is the only way to renew and improve your position. However, to gain the approval of all concerned, it is important that you have a clear picture of the transformations you are going to make, and that you have the unconditional support of someone trusted by all.

**3** If a profound change appears to be a vital necessity that cannot be ignored, do not rush to implement it; conversely, do not try to obstruct it at any cost – either through fear, or because you do not want to change your ways. If you have examined the situation from every angle and consulted all those concerned, and have their encouragement, you must now make a firm decision to this effect.

4   In order to achieve the important life change you are planning or discussing, your motives must be completely objective and generous, taking account of everybody's interests and position; otherwise you will not be given the confidence you need to see it through.

5   You know precisely what changes you want to make. Everybody around you understands the need for these changes and, what is more, they are all ready to support you, and join forces with you, so that you can get started as quickly as possible. This way, you will reach your goals with ease.

6   Having reorganized your life in a radical or major way, a few details remain to be settled. However, do not be too demanding about the progress that others can achieve. The essential thing is that the change has been made and that, from now on, everybody can live and work in peace.

# 50<sup>th</sup> combination ○ ▢ ▢ ▢ ○ ▢

Your destiny is what gives your life all its meaning, shape and strength. This is why it is necessary to understand it and submit to it if you want a better life. In knowing your destiny you know yourself and you can improve your life. In other words, your destiny always works in harmony with your life.

1   Are you sincere, alert, receptive and ready to make changes within yourself? Do you question yourself when necessary and make every possible effort to achieve the tasks you have been set, or to assume your responsibilities? If so, there is no doubt that sooner or later your qualities and merits will be recognized and appreciated.

2   As far as is possible, do not focus solely on tangible, material results, to the exclusion of all other considerations. You will probably be unable to avoid the jealousy of those around you, but tell yourself that, by concentrating on your most productive work, you will make yourself impervious to attack.

3   Your current job or position does not allow you to utilize your qualities, gifts or talents in any way whatsoever. Naturally this is frustrating, and you feel that everything you do is pointless. However do not worry about this any more; instead, cultivate these qualities until circumstances are in your favour when you can make full use of them.

4   You have to take on important responsibilities or obligations, but are not sure you are up to the job. You doubt yourself and your abilities. What is more, you are not devoting yourself to them as fully as you should, and your relationships are making you lose sight of your main objective that, for these reasons, you will certainly not reach.

5   You have responsibilities to assume, or are in a position of some power, but you are

**50th combination** ○

| # | | | | | | | Read texts |
|---|---|---|---|---|---|---|---|
| fig. 1 | ▼ | ▲ | □ | □ | ○ | □ | Read texts 1 and 2 |
| 2 | ▼ | □ | ▲ | □ | ○ | □ | Read texts 1 and 3 |
| 3 | ▼ | □ | □ | ▲ | ○ | □ | Read texts 1 and 4 |
| 4 | ▼ | □ | □ | □ | ▼ | □ | Read texts 1 and 5 |
| 5 | ▼ | □ | □ | □ | ○ | ▲ | Read texts 1 and 6 |
| 6 | ▼ | ▲ | ▲ | □ | ○ | □ | Read texts 1, 2 and 3 |
| 7 | ▼ | □ | ▲ | ▲ | ○ | □ | Read texts 1, 3 and 4 |
| 8 | ▼ | □ | □ | ▲ | ▼ | □ | Read texts 1, 4 and 5 |
| 9 | ▼ | □ | □ | □ | ▼ | ▲ | Read texts 1, 5 and 6 |
| 10 | ▼ | ▲ | ▲ | ▲ | ○ | □ | Read texts 1, 2, 3 and 4 |
| 11 | ▼ | □ | ▲ | ▲ | ▼ | □ | Read texts 1, 3, 4 and 5 |
| 12 | ▼ | □ | ▲ | ▲ | ○ | ▲ | Read texts 1, 3, 4 and 6 |
| 13 | ▼ | □ | □ | ▲ | ▼ | ▲ | Read texts 1, 4, 5 and 6 |
| 14 | ▼ | ▲ | ▲ | ▲ | ▼ | □ | Read texts 1, 2, 3, 4 and 5 |
| 15 | ▼ | □ | ▲ | ▲ | ▼ | ▲ | Read texts 1, 3, 4, 5 and 6 |
| 16 | ▼ | ▲ | ▲ | ▲ | ▼ | ▲ | Read texts 1, 2, 3, 4, 5 and 6 |
| 17 | ○ | ▲ | ▲ | □ | ○ | □ | Read texts 2 and 3 |
| 18 | ○ | ▲ | □ | ▲ | ○ | □ | Read texts 2 and 4 |
| 19 | ○ | ▲ | □ | □ | ▼ | □ | Read texts 2 and 5 |
| 20 | ○ | ▲ | □ | □ | ○ | ▲ | Read texts 2 and 6 |
| 21 | ○ | ▲ | ▲ | ▲ | ○ | □ | Read texts 2, 3 and 4 |
| 22 | ○ | ▲ | □ | ▲ | ▼ | □ | Read texts 2, 4 and 5 |
| 23 | ○ | ▲ | □ | □ | ▼ | ▲ | Read texts 2, 5 and 6 |
| 24 | ○ | ▲ | ▲ | ▲ | ▼ | □ | Read texts 2, 3, 4 and 5 |
| 25 | ○ | ▲ | □ | ▲ | ▼ | ▲ | Read texts 2, 4, 5 and 6 |
| 26 | ○ | ▲ | ▲ | ▲ | ▼ | ▲ | Read texts 2, 3, 4, 5 and 6 |
| 27 | ▼ | ▲ | □ | ▲ | ○ | □ | Read texts 1, 2 and 4 |
| 28 | ▼ | ▲ | □ | □ | ▼ | □ | Read texts 1, 2 and 5 |
| 29 | ▼ | ▲ | □ | □ | ○ | ▲ | Read texts 1, 2 and 6 |
| 30 | ▼ | ▲ | ▲ | □ | ▼ | □ | Read texts 1, 2, 3 and 5 |
| 31 | ▼ | ▲ | ▲ | □ | ○ | ▲ | Read texts 1, 2, 3 and 6 |
| 32 | ▼ | ▲ | ▲ | ▲ | ○ | ▲ | Read texts 1, 2, 3, 4 and 6 |
| 33 | ▼ | □ | ▲ | □ | ▼ | □ | Read texts 1, 3 and 5 |
| 34 | ▼ | □ | ▲ | □ | ○ | ▲ | Read texts 1, 3 and 6 |
| 35 | ▼ | □ | ▲ | □ | ▼ | ▲ | Read texts 1, 3, 5 and 6 |
| 36 | ▼ | □ | □ | ▲ | ○ | ▲ | Read texts 1, 4 and 6 |
| 37 | ○ | ▲ | ▲ | □ | ▼ | □ | Read texts 2, 3 and 5 |
| 38 | ○ | ▲ | ▲ | □ | ○ | ▲ | Read texts 2, 3 and 6 |
| 39 | ○ | ▲ | ▲ | ▲ | ○ | ▲ | Read texts 2, 3, 4 and 6 |
| 40 | ○ | ▲ | □ | ▲ | ○ | ▲ | Read texts 2, 4 and 6 |
| 41 | ○ | □ | ▲ | ▲ | ○ | □ | Read texts 3 and 4 |
| 42 | ○ | □ | ▲ | □ | ▼ | □ | Read texts 3 and 5 |
| 43 | ○ | □ | ▲ | □ | ○ | ▲ | Read texts 3 and 6 |
| 44 | ○ | □ | ▲ | ▲ | ▼ | □ | Read texts 3, 4 and 5 |
| 45 | ○ | □ | ▲ | ▲ | ○ | ▲ | Read texts 3, 4 and 6 |
| 46 | ○ | □ | ▲ | □ | ▼ | ▲ | Read texts 3, 5 and 6 |
| 47 | ○ | □ | ▲ | ▲ | ▼ | ▲ | Read texts 3, 4, 5 and 6 |
| 48 | ○ | □ | □ | ▲ | ▼ | □ | Read texts 4 and 5 |
| 49 | ○ | □ | □ | ▲ | ○ | ▲ | Read texts 4 and 6 |
| 50 | ○ | □ | □ | ▲ | ▼ | ▲ | Read texts 4, 5 and 6 |
| 51 | ○ | □ | □ | □ | ▼ | ▲ | Read texts 5 and 6 |
| 52 | ▼ | □ | □ | □ | ○ | □ | Read text 1 |
| 53 | ○ | ▲ | □ | □ | ○ | □ | Read text 2 |
| 54 | ○ | □ | ▲ | □ | ○ | □ | Read text 3 |
| 55 | ○ | □ | □ | ▲ | ○ | □ | Read text 4 |
| 56 | ○ | □ | □ | □ | ▼ | □ | Read text 5 |
| 57 | ○ | □ | □ | □ | ○ | ▲ | Read text 6 |

still mindful of the opinions and needs of those around you or in your charge. This is why you can count on the unconditional support of efficient and competent assistants or colleagues. Keep up this attitude and your excellent disposition.

**6** You have a reputation for being firm and determined, but also generous and kind when you want to be. These qualities make you popular with the people around you, and often give you the opportunity to issue good advice when asked. Such a positive attitude – looking out for the greater good – can only work in your favour.

# 51st combination □ ○ ○ □ ○ ○

Whatever unforeseen or unavoidable upsets shake your life, if you are mentally prepared, or have been able to cultivate deep and fundamental qualities, you will remain steadfast, true to yourself and perfectly serene.

**1** There has been such upheaval in your life or your job that you fear the worst, and have a deep and uncontrollable conviction that you will be unable to cope or react as necessary. But if you take a good look at the situation you will realize, once the shock has passed, that this shake-up is actually for the best.

**2** You have suffered such an upheaval that you have probably not been able to protect yourself, or those around you, from the fall-out or unfortunate consequences. However, you must not worry too much or over-dramatize the situation. Even if you have suffered some losses, you will recover what is yours in due course.

**3** You are not to blame for the current upset in your life, because it is due to outside circumstances and is also a feature of your destiny. This is a real test that can benefit your personal development enormously, if you are able to exploit it skilfully and intelligently.

**4** Your present circumstances prevent you from engaging openly in pitched battle to get what you want; nor do they give you the chance to confront some visible obstacle that would impel you to impose your will actively and resolutely. The situation is actually so confused and unclear that your best bet is to sit tight and do nothing to escape it – for the moment, at least.

**5** The upheavals in your life leave you no peace or respite. Nevertheless you were prepared for this, and so you are fully focused, right at the heart of the situation, and will not let yourself be overtaken by events. This means you are sure to win, and to master your destiny.

**6** The recent upheavals in your life, or in the lives of others around you, have, first and foremost, had a negative effect on your mental equilibrium. But you have managed to pull yourself together and judge the situation objectively. You have urged those close to you, or those equally affected by the upheavals, to stay calm. However it seems that they did not listen or that no one understood your attitude. Take no notice and, whatever is said about you, do not join in the general panic.

| fig. | | | | | | | |
|---|---|---|---|---|---|---|---|
| 1 | ▲ ▼ ○ □ ○ ○ | Read texts 1 and 2 |
| 2 | ▲ ○ ▼ □ ○ ○ | Read texts 1 and 3 |
| 3 | ▲ ○ ○ ▲ ○ ○ | Read texts 1 and 4 |
| 4 | ▲ ○ ○ □ ▼ ○ | Read texts 1 and 5 |
| 5 | ▲ ○ ○ □ ○ ▼ | Read texts 1 and 6 |
| 6 | ▲ ▼ ▼ □ ○ ○ | Read texts 1, 2 and 3 |
| 7 | ▲ ▼ ○ ▲ ○ ○ | Read texts 1, 2 and 4 |
| 8 | ▲ ▼ ○ □ ▼ ○ | Read texts 1, 2 and 5 |
| 9 | ▲ ▼ ○ □ ○ ▼ | Read texts 1, 2 and 6 |
| 10 | ▲ ▼ ▼ ▲ ○ ○ | Read texts 1, 2, 3 and 4 |
| 11 | ▲ ▼ ▼ □ ▼ ○ | Read texts 1, 2, 3 and 5 |
| 12 | ▲ ▼ ▼ □ ○ ▼ | Read texts 1, 2, 3 and 6 |
| 13 | ▲ ▼ ▼ ▲ ▼ ○ | Read texts 1, 2, 3, 4 and 5 |
| 14 | ▲ ▼ ▼ ▲ ○ ▼ | Read texts 1, 2, 3, 4 and 6 |
| 15 | ▲ ▼ ▼ ▲ ▼ ▼ | Read texts 1, 2, 3, 4, 5 and 6 |
| 16 | ▲ ○ ▼ ▲ ○ ○ | Read texts 1, 3 and 4 |
| 17 | ▲ ○ ▼ □ ▼ ○ | Read texts 1, 3 and 5 |
| 18 | ▲ ○ ▼ □ ○ ▼ | Read texts 1, 3 and 6 |
| 19 | ▲ ○ ▼ ▲ ▼ ○ | Read texts 1, 3, 4 and 5 |
| 20 | ▲ ○ ▼ ▲ ○ ▼ | Read texts 1, 3, 4 and 6 |
| 21 | ▲ ○ ▼ □ ▼ ▼ | Read texts 1, 3, 5 and 6 |
| 22 | ▲ ○ ▼ ▲ ▼ ▼ | Read texts 1, 3, 4, 5 and 6 |
| 23 | ▲ ○ ○ ▲ ▼ ○ | Read texts 1, 4 and 5 |
| 24 | ▲ ○ ○ ▲ ○ ▼ | Read texts 1, 4 and 6 |
| 25 | ▲ ○ ○ ▲ ▼ ▼ | Read texts 1, 4, 5 and 6 |
| 26 | ▲ ○ ○ □ ▼ ▼ | Read texts 1, 5 and 6 |
| 27 | □ ▼ ▼ □ ○ ○ | Read texts 2 and 3 |
| 28 | □ ▼ ○ ▲ ○ ○ | Read texts 2 and 4 |
| 29 | □ ▼ ○ □ ▼ ○ | Read texts 2 and 5 |
| 30 | □ ▼ ○ □ ○ ▼ | Read texts 2 and 6 |
| 31 | □ ▼ ▼ ▲ ○ ○ | Read texts 2, 3 and 4 |
| 32 | □ ▼ ▼ □ ▼ ○ | Read texts 2, 3 and 5 |
| 33 | □ ▼ ▼ □ ○ ▼ | Read texts 2, 3 and 6 |
| 34 | □ ▼ ▼ ▲ ▼ ○ | Read texts 2, 3, 4 and 5 |
| 35 | □ ▼ ▼ ▲ ○ ▼ | Read texts 2, 3, 4 and 6 |
| 36 | □ ▼ ▼ ▲ ▼ ▼ | Read texts 2, 3, 4, 5 and 6 |
| 37 | □ ▼ ○ ▲ ▼ ○ | Read texts 2, 4 and 5 |
| 38 | □ ▼ ○ ▲ ○ ▼ | Read texts 2, 4 and 6 |
| 39 | □ ▼ ○ ▲ ▼ ▼ | Read texts 2, 4, 5 and 6 |
| 40 | □ ▼ ○ □ ▼ ▼ | Read texts 2, 5 and 6 |
| 41 | □ ○ ▼ ▲ ○ ○ | Read texts 3 and 4 |
| 42 | □ ○ ▼ □ ▼ ○ | Read texts 3 and 5 |
| 43 | □ ○ ▼ □ ○ ▼ | Read texts 3 and 6 |
| 44 | □ ○ ▼ ▲ ▼ ○ | Read texts 3, 4 and 5 |
| 45 | □ ○ ▼ ▲ ○ ▼ | Read texts 3, 4 and 6 |
| 46 | □ ○ ▼ □ ▼ ▼ | Read texts 3, 5 and 6 |
| 47 | □ ○ ▼ ▲ ▼ ▼ | Read texts 3, 4, 5 and 6 |
| 48 | □ ○ ○ ▲ ▼ ○ | Read texts 4 and 5 |
| 49 | □ ○ ○ ▲ ○ ▼ | Read texts 4 and 6 |
| 50 | □ ○ ○ ▲ ▼ ▼ | Read texts 4, 5 and 6 |
| 51 | □ ○ ○ □ ▼ ▼ | Read texts 5 and 6 |
| 52 | ▲ ○ ○ □ ○ ○ | Read text 1 |
| 53 | □ ▼ ○ □ ○ ○ | Read text 2 |
| 54 | □ ○ ▼ □ ○ ○ | Read text 3 |
| 55 | □ ○ ○ ▲ ○ ○ | Read text 4 |
| 56 | □ ○ ○ □ ▼ ○ | Read text 5 |
| 57 | □ ○ ○ □ ○ ▼ | Read text 6 |

**51st combination** □ ○ ○ □ ○ ○

| fig. | | | | | | | |
|---|---|---|---|---|---|---|---|
| 1 | ▼ | ▼ | □ | ○ | ○ | □ | Read texts 1 and 2 |
| 2 | ▼ | ○ | ▲ | ○ | ○ | □ | Read texts 1 and 3 |
| 3 | ▼ | ○ | □ | ▼ | ○ | □ | Read texts 1 and 4 |
| 4 | ▼ | ○ | □ | ○ | ▼ | □ | Read texts 1 and 5 |
| 5 | ▼ | ○ | □ | ○ | ○ | ▲ | Read texts 1 and 6 |
| 6 | ▼ | ▼ | ▲ | ○ | ○ | □ | Read texts 1, 2 and 3 |
| 7 | ▼ | ▼ | □ | ▼ | ○ | □ | Read texts 1, 2 and 4 |
| 8 | ▼ | ▼ | □ | ○ | ▼ | □ | Read texts 1, 2 and 5 |
| 9 | ▼ | ▼ | □ | ○ | ○ | ▲ | Read texts 1, 2 and 6 |
| 10 | ▼ | ▼ | ▲ | ▼ | ○ | □ | Read texts 1, 2, 3 and 4 |
| 11 | ▼ | ▼ | ▲ | ○ | ▼ | □ | Read texts 1, 2, 3 and 5 |
| 12 | ▼ | ▼ | ▲ | ○ | ○ | ▲ | Read texts 1, 2, 3 and 6 |
| 13 | ▼ | ▼ | ▲ | ▼ | ▼ | □ | Read texts 1, 2, 3, 4 and 5 |
| 14 | ▼ | ▼ | ▲ | ▼ | ○ | ▲ | Read texts 1, 2, 3, 4 and 6 |
| 15 | ▼ | ▼ | ▲ | ▼ | ▼ | ▲ | Read texts 1, 2, 3, 4, 5 and 6 |
| 16 | ▼ | ○ | ▲ | ▼ | ○ | □ | Read texts 1, 3 and 4 |
| 17 | ▼ | ○ | ▲ | ○ | ▼ | □ | Read texts 1, 3 and 5 |
| 18 | ▼ | ○ | ▲ | ○ | ○ | ▲ | Read texts 1, 3 and 6 |
| 19 | ▼ | ○ | ▲ | ▼ | ▼ | □ | Read texts 1, 3, 4 and 5 |
| 20 | ▼ | ○ | ▲ | ▼ | ○ | ▲ | Read texts 1, 3, 4 and 6 |
| 21 | ▼ | ○ | ▲ | ○ | ▼ | ▲ | Read texts 1, 3, 5 and 6 |
| 22 | ▼ | ○ | ▲ | ▼ | ▼ | ▲ | Read texts 1, 3, 4, 5 and 6 |
| 23 | ▼ | ○ | □ | ▼ | ▼ | □ | Read texts 1, 4 and 5 |
| 24 | ▼ | ○ | □ | ▼ | ○ | ▲ | Read texts 1, 4 and 6 |
| 25 | ▼ | ○ | □ | ▼ | ▼ | ▲ | Read texts 1, 4, 5 and 6 |
| 26 | ▼ | ○ | □ | ○ | ▼ | ▲ | Read texts 1, 5 and 6 |
| 27 | ○ | ▼ | ▲ | ○ | ○ | □ | Read texts 2 and 3 |
| 28 | ○ | ▼ | □ | ▼ | ○ | □ | Read texts 2 and 4 |
| 29 | ○ | ▼ | □ | ○ | ▼ | □ | Read texts 2 and 5 |
| 30 | ○ | ▼ | □ | ○ | ○ | ▲ | Read texts 2 and 6 |
| 31 | ○ | ▼ | ▲ | ▼ | ○ | □ | Read texts 2, 3 and 4 |
| 32 | ○ | ▼ | ▲ | ○ | ▼ | □ | Read texts 2, 3 and 5 |
| 33 | ○ | ▼ | ▲ | ○ | ○ | ▲ | Read texts 2, 3 and 6 |
| 34 | ○ | ▼ | ▲ | ▼ | ▼ | □ | Read texts 2, 3, 4 and 5 |
| 35 | ○ | ▼ | ▲ | ▼ | ○ | ▲ | Read texts 2, 3, 4 and 6 |
| 36 | ○ | ▼ | ▲ | ▼ | ▼ | ▲ | Read texts 2, 3, 4, 5 and 6 |
| 37 | ○ | ▼ | □ | ▼ | ▼ | □ | Read texts 2, 4 and 5 |
| 38 | ○ | ▼ | □ | ▼ | ○ | ▲ | Read texts 2, 4 and 6 |
| 39 | ○ | ▼ | □ | ▼ | ▼ | ▲ | Read texts 2, 4, 5 and 6 |
| 40 | ○ | ▼ | □ | ○ | ▼ | ▲ | Read texts 2, 5 and 6 |
| 41 | ○ | ○ | ▲ | ▼ | ○ | □ | Read texts 3 and 4 |
| 42 | ○ | ○ | ▲ | ○ | ▼ | □ | Read texts 3 and 5 |
| 43 | ○ | ○ | ▲ | ○ | ○ | ▲ | Read texts 3 and 6 |
| 44 | ○ | ○ | ▲ | ▼ | ▼ | □ | Read texts 3, 4 and 5 |
| 45 | ○ | ○ | ▲ | ▼ | ○ | ▲ | Read texts 3, 4 and 6 |
| 46 | ○ | ○ | ▲ | ○ | ▼ | ▲ | Read texts 3, 5 and 6 |
| 47 | ○ | ○ | ▲ | ▼ | ▼ | ▲ | Read texts 3, 4, 5 and 6 |
| 48 | ○ | ○ | □ | ▼ | ▼ | □ | Read texts 4 and 5 |
| 49 | ○ | ○ | □ | ▼ | ○ | ▲ | Read texts 4 and 6 |
| 50 | ○ | ○ | □ | ▼ | ▼ | ▲ | Read texts 4, 5 and 6 |
| 51 | ○ | ○ | □ | ○ | ▼ | ▲ | Read texts 5 and 6 |
| 52 | ▼ | ○ | □ | ○ | ○ | □ | Read text 1 |
| 53 | ○ | ▼ | □ | ○ | ○ | □ | Read text 2 |
| 54 | ○ | ○ | ▲ | ○ | ○ | □ | Read text 3 |
| 55 | ○ | ○ | □ | ▼ | ○ | □ | Read text 4 |
| 56 | ○ | ○ | □ | ○ | ▼ | □ | Read text 5 |
| 57 | ○ | ○ | □ | ○ | ○ | ▲ | Read text 6 |

**52nd combination**

# 52<sup>nd</sup> combination ○ ○ □ ○ ○ □

If you want to live an untroubled life in peace and tranquillity, learn when to act and when not to act, according to the circumstances. Thus, if you feel that you can go ahead, do so. If, on the other hand, you know that it would be better to do nothing, then do nothing. All other considerations or inferences would be inappropriate and only lead to disappointment.

**1** You have taken a step forward, but one cannot say that you have really got anything underway. In moments like these, when you are about to take significant decisions and make crucial choices for your future, it is important to trust your intuition and not to be influenced by the changing circumstances you encounter.

**2** You have allowed yourself to be drawn into a bad situation, or possibly you are being forced to follow a determined person down a perilous or dead-end path. Fortunately you scented danger and stopped in your tracks, so you will escape unharmed. On the other hand, this probably will not be the case for the other person, particularly if he or she obstinately refuses to listen to reason.

**3** You are in the grip of acute anxiety, which is making you impatient, nervous and feverish, and you are trying everything and anything to control it, using artificial methods or drastic measures. But by acting this way you are working against yourself, and against your vital balance and well-being. You must therefore stop suppressing your anxiety and give your anguish free expression, so that you can understand it better and find inner peace in a natural way.

4   You have not yet mastered your impulses, emotions or desires, and all the cyclical anxieties – big and small – that unavoidably stem from these, but at least you are not fooled by them, and you even know how to avoid being their victim. This means you are on the right road to deeper inner balance and greater harmony and serenity.

5   You have a plan in mind, a task to complete or a mission to accomplish that is probably beyond your capabilities; nevertheless you boast wildly about your chances of success. You will soon realize that you have overestimated your strengths and resources, and you will see that it is always unwise or dangerous to count your chickens before they are hatched.

6   You do what you have to do, when you have to do it. You demand nothing else from yourself, from other people, or from life. A serene and measured attitude like this ensures success in everything you do.

# 53rd combination ○ ○ ▢ ○ ▢ ▢

If you aspire to exert a certain influence within your environment, or to play an important role in your field, you must progress slowly but surely, step by step, so that solid foundations and principles may underpin your influence.

1   You are about to start something new or take the first steps down an important road. But you are moving forward cautiously, not too sure about where you are going or how to begin; furthermore, you have no support or point of reference to help you reach your goal. Caution is the watchword here, because caution makes you take your time and will enable you to succeed in everything you do.

2   You are currently in a stable, comfortable situation that offers the security you need to embark upon projects that are close to your heart or to contemplate new opportunities in your personal and professional life. In addition, you know how to share with others the benefit of your own advantages – all of which, of course, bodes very well for your present and your future.

3   Try not to force events, burn bridges or abandon the rules and objectives you have set yourself when only halfway through; otherwise you risk spoiling everything that you have undertaken or achieved up to now, and may also lead those around you into a disastrous situation. Stay calmly where you are, do not intervene or try to sway events, and all will be well.

4   Given the stage you are at, you have no choice but to run for cover. Granted, you may have to drop anchor somewhere inconvenient or rather hostile but, on the plus side, you will have a chance to rest and wait for better days. This situation is probably not an end in itself but at least it offers guaranteed, if temporary, security, given your present circumstances.

5   Misunderstandings and silent reproaches are building between you and

**53rd combination**

| fig. | | | | | | | |
|---|---|---|---|---|---|---|---|
| 1 | ▼ | ▼ | □ | ○ | □ | □ | Read texts 1 and 2 |
| 2 | ▼ | ○ | ▲ | ○ | □ | □ | Read texts 1 and 3 |
| 3 | ▼ | ○ | □ | ▼ | □ | □ | Read texts 1 and 4 |
| 4 | ▼ | ○ | □ | ○ | ▲ | □ | Read texts 1 and 5 |
| 5 | ▼ | ○ | □ | ○ | □ | ▲ | Read texts 1 and 6 |
| 6 | ▼ | ▼ | ▲ | ○ | □ | □ | Read texts 1, 2 and 3 |
| 7 | ▼ | ○ | ▲ | ▼ | □ | □ | Read texts 1, 3 and 4 |
| 8 | ▼ | ○ | □ | ▼ | ▲ | □ | Read texts 1, 4 and 5 |
| 9 | ▼ | ○ | □ | ▲ | ▲ | □ | Read texts 1, 5 and 6 |
| 10 | ▼ | ▼ | ▲ | ▼ | □ | □ | Read texts 1, 2, 3 and 4 |
| 11 | ▼ | ○ | ▲ | ▼ | ▲ | □ | Read texts 1, 3, 4 and 5 |
| 12 | ▼ | ○ | ▲ | ▼ | □ | ▲ | Read texts 1, 3, 4 and 6 |
| 13 | ▼ | ○ | □ | ▼ | ▲ | ▲ | Read texts 1, 4, 5 and 6 |
| 14 | ▼ | ▼ | ▲ | ▼ | ▲ | □ | Read texts 1, 2, 3, 4 and 5 |
| 15 | ▼ | ○ | ▲ | ▼ | ▲ | ▲ | Read texts 1, 3, 4, 5 and 6 |
| 16 | ▼ | ▼ | ▲ | ▼ | ▲ | ▲ | Read texts 1, 2, 3, 4, 5 and 6 |
| 17 | ○ | ▼ | ▲ | ○ | □ | □ | Read texts 2 and 3 |
| 18 | ○ | ▼ | □ | ▼ | □ | □ | Read texts 2 and 4 |
| 19 | ○ | ▼ | □ | ○ | ▲ | □ | Read texts 2 and 5 |
| 20 | ○ | ▼ | □ | ○ | □ | ▲ | Read texts 2 and 6 |
| 21 | ○ | ▼ | ▲ | ▼ | □ | □ | Read texts 2, 3 and 4 |
| 22 | ○ | ▼ | □ | ▼ | ▲ | □ | Read texts 2, 4 and 5 |
| 23 | ○ | ▼ | □ | ○ | ▲ | ▲ | Read texts 2, 5 and 6 |
| 24 | ○ | ▼ | ▲ | ▼ | ▲ | □ | Read texts 2, 3, 4 and 5 |
| 25 | ○ | ▼ | □ | ▼ | ▲ | ▲ | Read texts 2, 4, 5 and 6 |
| 26 | ○ | ▼ | ▲ | ▼ | ▲ | ▲ | Read texts 2, 3, 4, 5 and 6 |
| 27 | ▼ | ▼ | □ | ▼ | □ | □ | Read texts 1, 2 and 4 |
| 28 | ▼ | ▼ | □ | ○ | ▲ | □ | Read texts 1, 2 and 5 |
| 29 | ▼ | ▼ | □ | ○ | □ | ▲ | Read texts 1, 2 and 6 |
| 30 | ▼ | ▼ | ▲ | ○ | ▲ | □ | Read texts 1, 2, 3 and 5 |
| 31 | ▼ | ▼ | ▲ | ○ | □ | ▲ | Read texts 1, 2, 3 and 6 |
| 32 | ▼ | ▼ | ▲ | ▼ | □ | ▲ | Read texts 1, 2, 3, 4 and 6 |
| 33 | ▼ | ○ | ▲ | ○ | □ | ▲ | Read texts 1, 3 and 5 |
| 34 | ▼ | ○ | ▲ | ○ | □ | ▲ | Read texts 1, 3 and 6 |
| 35 | ▼ | ○ | ▲ | ○ | ▲ | ▲ | Read texts 1, 3, 5 and 6 |
| 36 | ▼ | ○ | □ | ▼ | □ | ▲ | Read texts 1, 4 and 6 |
| 37 | ○ | ▼ | ▲ | ○ | ▲ | □ | Read texts 2, 3 and 5 |
| 38 | ○ | ▼ | ▲ | ○ | □ | ▲ | Read texts 2, 3 and 6 |
| 39 | ○ | ▼ | ▲ | ▼ | □ | ▲ | Read texts 2, 3, 4 and 6 |
| 40 | ○ | ▼ | □ | ▼ | □ | ▲ | Read texts 2, 4 and 6 |
| 41 | ○ | ○ | ▲ | ▼ | □ | □ | Read texts 3 and 4 |
| 42 | ○ | ○ | ▲ | ○ | ▲ | □ | Read texts 3 and 5 |
| 43 | ○ | ○ | ▲ | ○ | □ | ▲ | Read texts 3 and 6 |
| 44 | ○ | ○ | ▲ | ▼ | ▲ | □ | Read texts 3, 4 and 5 |
| 45 | ○ | ○ | ▲ | ▼ | □ | ▲ | Read texts 3, 4 and 6 |
| 46 | ○ | ○ | ▲ | ○ | ▲ | ▲ | Read texts 3, 5 and 6 |
| 47 | ○ | ○ | ▲ | ▼ | ▲ | ▲ | Read texts 3, 4, 5 and 6 |
| 48 | ○ | ○ | □ | ▼ | ▲ | □ | Read texts 4 and 5 |
| 49 | ○ | ○ | □ | ▼ | □ | ▲ | Read texts 4 and 6 |
| 50 | ○ | ○ | □ | ▼ | ▲ | ▲ | Read texts 4, 5 and 6 |
| 51 | ○ | ○ | □ | ○ | ▲ | ▲ | Read texts 5 and 6 |
| 52 | ▼ | ○ | □ | ○ | □ | □ | Read text 1 |
| 53 | ○ | ▼ | □ | ○ | □ | □ | Read text 2 |
| 54 | ○ | ○ | ▲ | ○ | □ | □ | Read text 3 |
| 55 | ○ | ○ | □ | ▼ | □ | □ | Read text 4 |
| 56 | ○ | ○ | □ | ○ | ▲ | □ | Read text 5 |
| 57 | ○ | ○ | □ | ○ | □ | ▲ | Read text 6 |

someone who is close to you, or with whom you might have a special relationship. But you are less to blame than underhand ill wishers who seem to have had a bad influence on the person in question. Nevertheless you can and must take tough action as quickly as possible to stamp out this malaise.

**6** You are in an ideal situation that allows you to blossom and shine, and to share the benefits you enjoy with as many people as possible. Do not hold back – this is a moment to cherish.

# 54th combination □ □ ○ □ □ ○ ○

The feeling of being in sympathy with someone is a free and spontaneous emotion to which you can abandon yourself unreservedly. To become something deeper and more lasting, it must be left to develop naturally. In fact, violent emotions rarely lead to solid relationships, but to break-ups and an unstable and turbulent emotional life.

**1** An influential, experienced person with a certain power or authority is very fond of you. However, this relationship is not sufficient to put you in a position where you too can exercise influence or take your place. In circumstances like these, therefore, you must be very discreet and act, if not behind the scenes, then at least with some reserve.

**2** Somebody you know is currently behaving in a way that disappoints you, or that goes against the way things used to be between you. Despite the bitterness you feel, you will remain loyal and sincere, and faithful to your commitments.

3   Your aspirations and desires don't match or suit your current position or the environment you are in. To satisfy them you need to come out of your shell, take risks, make concessions or act in a manner that is unconventional or out of the ordinary. Take note of this and act accordingly, in order to achieve your goals.

4   If you can wait patiently for the right moment, remaining true to your principles and – whatever happens – true to the real nature of the feelings and relationships you would like to experience, there is no reason why your patience should not be rewarded and you should not meet the person destined for you.

5   An association or union based on deep attraction, genuine feelings and sincere relations, unencumbered by convention and propriety, has greater value than an alliance that appears lucrative or flamboyant but has no real foundation.

6   Your emotional relationships lack depth, sincerity and authenticity. If you fail to modify your behaviour and persist in avoiding the truth about yourself and the nature of your relationships, you will be heading for disappointment or failure. However this type of misplaced attitude can, of course, be easily corrected.

| fig. | | | | | | | |
|---|---|---|---|---|---|---|---|
| 1 | ▲ | ▲ | ○ | □ | ○ | ○ | Read texts 1 and 2 |
| 2 | ▲ | □ | ▼ | □ | ○ | ○ | Read texts 1 and 3 |
| 3 | ▲ | □ | ○ | ▲ | ○ | ○ | Read texts 1 and 4 |
| 4 | ▲ | □ | ○ | □ | ▼ | ○ | Read texts 1 and 5 |
| 5 | ▲ | □ | ○ | □ | ○ | ▼ | Read texts 1 and 6 |
| 6 | ▲ | ▲ | ▼ | □ | ○ | ○ | Read texts 1, 2 and 3 |
| 7 | ▲ | □ | ▼ | ▲ | ○ | ○ | Read texts 1, 3 and 4 |
| 8 | ▲ | □ | ○ | ▲ | ▼ | ○ | Read texts 1, 4 and 5 |
| 9 | ▲ | □ | ○ | □ | ▼ | ▼ | Read texts 1, 5 and 6 |
| 10 | ▲ | ▲ | ▼ | ▲ | ○ | ○ | Read texts 1, 2, 3 and 4 |
| 11 | ▲ | □ | ▼ | ▲ | ▼ | ○ | Read texts 1, 3, 4 and 5 |
| 12 | ▲ | □ | ▼ | ▲ | ○ | ▼ | Read texts 1, 3, 4 and 6 |
| 13 | ▲ | □ | ○ | ▲ | ▼ | ▼ | Read texts 1, 4, 5 and 6 |
| 14 | ▲ | ▲ | ▼ | ▲ | ▼ | ○ | Read texts 1, 2, 3, 4 and 5 |
| 15 | ▲ | □ | ▼ | ▲ | ▼ | ▼ | Read texts 1, 3, 4, 5 and 6 |
| 16 | ▲ | ▲ | ▼ | ▲ | ▼ | ▼ | Read texts 1, 2, 3, 4, 5 and 6 |
| 17 | □ | ▲ | ▼ | □ | ○ | ○ | Read texts 2 and 3 |
| 18 | □ | ▲ | ○ | ▲ | ○ | ○ | Read texts 2 and 4 |
| 19 | □ | ▲ | ○ | □ | ▼ | ○ | Read texts 2 and 5 |
| 20 | □ | ▲ | ○ | □ | ○ | ▼ | Read texts 2 and 6 |
| 21 | □ | ▲ | ▼ | ▲ | ○ | ○ | Read texts 2, 3 and 4 |
| 22 | □ | ▲ | ○ | ▲ | ▼ | ○ | Read texts 2, 4 and 5 |
| 23 | □ | ▲ | ○ | □ | ▼ | ▼ | Read texts 2, 5 and 6 |
| 24 | □ | ▲ | ▼ | ▲ | ▼ | ○ | Read texts 2, 3, 4 and 5 |
| 25 | □ | ▲ | ○ | ▲ | ▼ | ▼ | Read texts 2, 4, 5 and 6 |
| 26 | □ | ▲ | ▼ | ▲ | ▼ | ▼ | Read texts 2, 3, 4, 5 and 6 |
| 27 | ▲ | ▲ | ○ | ▲ | ○ | ○ | Read texts 1, 2 and 4 |
| 28 | ▲ | ▲ | ○ | □ | ▼ | ○ | Read texts 1, 2 and 5 |
| 29 | ▲ | ▲ | ○ | □ | ○ | ▼ | Read texts 1, 2 and 6 |
| 30 | ▲ | ▲ | ▼ | □ | ▼ | ○ | Read texts 1, 2, 3 and 5 |
| 31 | ▲ | ▲ | ▼ | □ | ○ | ▼ | Read texts 1, 2, 3 and 6 |
| 32 | ▲ | ▲ | ▼ | ▲ | ○ | ▼ | Read texts 1, 2, 3, 4 and 6 |
| 33 | ▲ | □ | ▼ | □ | ▼ | ○ | Read texts 1, 3 and 5 |
| 34 | ▲ | □ | ▼ | □ | ○ | ▼ | Read texts 1, 3 and 6 |
| 35 | ▲ | □ | ▼ | □ | ▼ | ▼ | Read texts 1, 3, 5 and 6 |
| 36 | ▲ | □ | ○ | ▲ | ○ | ▼ | Read texts 1, 4 and 6 |
| 37 | □ | ▲ | ▼ | □ | ▼ | ○ | Read texts 2, 3 and 5 |
| 38 | □ | ▲ | ▼ | □ | ○ | ▼ | Read texts 2, 3 and 6 |
| 39 | □ | ▲ | ▼ | ▲ | ○ | ▼ | Read texts 2, 3, 4 and 6 |
| 40 | □ | ▲ | ○ | ▲ | ○ | ▼ | Read texts 2, 4 and 6 |
| 41 | □ | □ | ▼ | ▲ | ○ | ○ | Read texts 3 and 4 |
| 42 | □ | □ | ▼ | □ | ▼ | ○ | Read texts 3 and 5 |
| 43 | □ | □ | ▼ | □ | ○ | ▼ | Read texts 3 and 6 |
| 44 | □ | □ | ▼ | ▲ | ▼ | ○ | Read texts 3, 4 and 5 |
| 45 | □ | □ | ▼ | ▲ | ○ | ▼ | Read texts 3, 4 and 6 |
| 46 | □ | □ | ▼ | □ | ▼ | ▼ | Read texts 3, 5 and 6 |
| 47 | □ | □ | ▼ | ▲ | ▼ | ▼ | Read texts 3, 4, 5 and 6 |
| 48 | □ | □ | ○ | ▲ | ▼ | ○ | Read texts 4 and 5 |
| 49 | □ | □ | ○ | ▲ | ○ | ▼ | Read texts 4 and 6 |
| 50 | □ | □ | ○ | ▲ | ▼ | ▼ | Read texts 4, 5 and 6 |
| 51 | □ | □ | ○ | □ | ▼ | ▼ | Read texts 5 and 6 |
| 52 | ▲ | □ | ○ | □ | ○ | ○ | Read text 1 |
| 53 | □ | ▲ | ○ | □ | ○ | ○ | Read text 2 |
| 54 | □ | □ | ▼ | □ | ○ | ○ | Read text 3 |
| 55 | □ | □ | ○ | ▲ | ○ | ○ | Read text 4 |
| 56 | □ | □ | ○ | □ | ▼ | ○ | Read text 5 |
| 57 | □ | □ | ○ | □ | ○ | ▼ | Read text 6 |

54th combination □ □ ○ □ ○ ○

**55th combination**

| fig. | 1 | 2 | 3 | 4 | 5 | 6 | |
|---|---|---|---|---|---|---|---|
| 1 | ▲ | ▼ | □ | □ | ○ | ○ | Read texts 1 and 2 |
| 2 | ▲ | ○ | ▲ | □ | ○ | ○ | Read texts 1 and 3 |
| 3 | ▲ | ○ | □ | ▲ | ○ | ○ | Read texts 1 and 4 |
| 4 | ▲ | ○ | □ | □ | ▼ | ○ | Read texts 1 and 5 |
| 5 | ▲ | ○ | □ | □ | ○ | ▼ | Read texts 1 and 6 |
| 6 | ▲ | ▼ | ▲ | □ | ○ | ○ | Read texts 1, 2 and 3 |
| 7 | ▲ | ○ | ▲ | ▲ | ○ | ○ | Read texts 1, 3 and 4 |
| 8 | ▲ | ○ | □ | ▲ | ▼ | ○ | Read texts 1, 4 and 5 |
| 9 | ▲ | ○ | □ | □ | ▼ | ▼ | Read texts 1, 5 and 6 |
| 10 | ▲ | ▼ | ▲ | ▲ | ○ | ○ | Read texts 1, 2, 3 and 4 |
| 11 | ▲ | ○ | ▲ | ▲ | ▼ | ○ | Read texts 1, 3, 4 and 5 |
| 12 | ▲ | ○ | ▲ | ▲ | ○ | ▼ | Read texts 1, 3, 4 and 6 |
| 13 | ▲ | ○ | □ | ▲ | ▼ | ▼ | Read texts 1, 4, 5 and 6 |
| 14 | ▲ | ▼ | ▲ | ▲ | ▼ | ○ | Read texts 1, 2, 3, 4 and 5 |
| 15 | ▲ | ○ | ▲ | ▲ | ▼ | ▼ | Read texts 1, 3, 4, 5 and 6 |
| 16 | ▲ | ▼ | ▲ | ▲ | ▼ | ▼ | Read texts 1, 2, 3, 4, 5 and 6 |
| 17 | □ | ▼ | ▲ | □ | ○ | ○ | Read texts 2 and 3 |
| 18 | □ | ▼ | □ | ▲ | ○ | ○ | Read texts 2 and 4 |
| 19 | □ | ▼ | □ | □ | ▼ | ○ | Read texts 2 and 5 |
| 20 | □ | ▼ | □ | □ | ○ | ▼ | Read texts 2 and 6 |
| 21 | □ | ▼ | ▲ | ▲ | ○ | ○ | Read texts 2, 3 and 4 |
| 22 | □ | ▼ | □ | ▲ | ▼ | ○ | Read texts 2, 4 and 5 |
| 23 | □ | ▼ | □ | □ | ▼ | ▼ | Read texts 2, 5 and 6 |
| 24 | □ | ▼ | ▲ | ▲ | ▼ | ○ | Read texts 2, 3, 4 and 5 |
| 25 | □ | ▼ | □ | ▲ | ▼ | ▼ | Read texts 2, 4, 5 and 6 |
| 26 | □ | ▼ | ▲ | ▲ | ▼ | ▼ | Read texts 2, 3, 4, 5 and 6 |
| 27 | ▲ | ▼ | □ | ▲ | ○ | ○ | Read texts 1, 2 and 4 |
| 28 | ▲ | ▼ | □ | □ | ▼ | ○ | Read texts 1, 2 and 5 |
| 29 | ▲ | ▼ | □ | □ | ○ | ▼ | Read texts 1, 2 and 6 |
| 30 | ▲ | ▼ | ▲ | □ | ▼ | ○ | Read texts 1, 2, 3 and 5 |
| 31 | ▲ | ▼ | ▲ | □ | ○ | ▼ | Read texts 1, 2, 3 and 6 |
| 32 | ▲ | ▼ | ▲ | ▲ | ○ | ▼ | Read texts 1, 2, 3, 4 and 6 |
| 33 | ▲ | ○ | ▲ | □ | ▼ | ○ | Read texts 1, 3 and 5 |
| 34 | ▲ | ○ | ▲ | □ | ○ | ▼ | Read texts 1, 3 and 6 |
| 35 | ▲ | ○ | ▲ | □ | ▼ | ▼ | Read texts 1, 3, 5 and 6 |
| 36 | ▲ | ○ | □ | ▲ | ○ | ▼ | Read texts 1, 4 and 6 |
| 37 | □ | ▼ | ▲ | □ | ▼ | ○ | Read texts 2, 3 and 5 |
| 38 | □ | ▼ | ▲ | □ | ○ | ▼ | Read texts 2, 3 and 6 |
| 39 | □ | ▼ | ▲ | ▲ | ○ | ▼ | Read texts 2, 3, 4 and 6 |
| 40 | □ | ▼ | □ | ▲ | ○ | ▼ | Read texts 2, 4 and 6 |
| 41 | □ | ○ | ▲ | ▲ | ○ | ○ | Read texts 3 and 4 |
| 42 | □ | ○ | ▲ | □ | ▼ | ○ | Read texts 3 and 5 |
| 43 | □ | ○ | ▲ | □ | ○ | ▼ | Read texts 3 and 6 |
| 44 | □ | ○ | ▲ | ▲ | ▼ | ○ | Read texts 3, 4 and 5 |
| 45 | □ | ○ | ▲ | ▲ | ○ | ▼ | Read texts 3, 4 and 6 |
| 46 | □ | ○ | ▲ | □ | ▼ | ▼ | Read texts 3, 5 and 6 |
| 47 | □ | ○ | ▲ | ▲ | ▼ | ▼ | Read texts 3, 4, 5 and 6 |
| 48 | □ | ○ | □ | ▲ | ▼ | ○ | Read texts 4 and 5 |
| 49 | □ | ○ | □ | ▲ | ○ | ▼ | Read texts 4 and 6 |
| 50 | □ | ○ | □ | ▲ | ▼ | ▼ | Read texts 4, 5 and 6 |
| 51 | □ | ○ | □ | □ | ▼ | ▼ | Read texts 5 and 6 |
| 52 | ▲ | ○ | □ | □ | ○ | ○ | Read text 1 |
| 53 | □ | ▼ | □ | □ | ○ | ○ | Read text 2 |
| 54 | □ | ○ | ▲ | □ | ○ | ○ | Read text 3 |
| 55 | □ | ○ | □ | ▲ | ○ | ○ | Read text 4 |
| 56 | □ | ○ | □ | □ | ▼ | ○ | Read text 5 |
| 57 | □ | ○ | □ | □ | ○ | ▼ | Read text 6 |

# 55th combination □ ○ □ □ ○ ○

You are about to enter a period of fulfilment and abundance, when you will feel in control of your situation and in perfect harmony with your surroundings. However be aware that moments like these are fleeting, so enjoy them to the full without worrying about what tomorrow will bring.

**1** To achieve all that you want to achieve – plans you hold dear, or more ambitious ventures – you must join forces unreservedly with somebody whose energy and decisiveness will help you to succeed in your enterprises. You will gain both confidence and excellent results.

**2** You are in a situation where your intentions, initiatives and actions – however positive or rational they may be – risk being misinterpreted. What has happened is that mistrustful, envious people have come between you and someone in authority to such a degree that all your current projects seem bound to fail. When faced with such adverse circumstances, the most important thing is to stay true to yourself. Your merits will be recognized in the end.

**3** Your present situation and surroundings make it impossible for you to benefit your environment or community. The person responsible for this is actually so deeply confused that he or she no longer has a clear perspective on life or the situation, and is prey to all sorts of influences. In circumstances like these, therefore, it is wiser to do nothing.

**4**  The time has come to join forces with somebody whose clear thinking and experience can help you to operate more effectively in order to achieve your goal. Moments like these – when one meets somebody whose qualities complement our own – are significant, because they often herald a period of success and abundance.

**5**  Whatever your current situation or position, you remain attentive and receptive to the sound advice offered by those around you, and to their concerns and suggestions. Such a benevolent and inspired attitude will bring affluence to you and your relatives.

**6**  Your aspirations, desires and ambitions are too selfish. In fact you seem more concerned with your own profit, and how you and your close allies can benefit most, than with the good or development of your social milieu. What is more, you insist on being lord and master at home, and even your close relatives will end up turning their backs on you. You need to change your behaviour!

# 56th combination ○ ○ ○ □ □ ○ □

It is not yet time for you to settle down, put down roots and integrate yourself permanently in a particular milieu. There's no need to slow your pace but do keep a certain distance in your relationships with other people. If possible, associate only with congenial and welcoming folk: this way, sooner or later, you will find the ideal place to settle down.

| fig. | | | | | | | |
|---|---|---|---|---|---|---|---|
| 1 | ▼ ▼ □ □ ○ ○ □ | Read texts 1 and 2 |
| 2 | ▼ ○ ▲ □ ○ □ | Read texts 1 and 3 |
| 3 | ▼ ○ □ ▲ ○ □ | Read texts 1 and 4 |
| 4 | ▼ ○ □ □ ▼ □ | Read texts 1 and 5 |
| 5 | ▼ ○ □ □ ○ ▲ | Read texts 1 and 6 |
| 6 | ▼ ▼ ▲ □ ○ □ | Read texts 1, 2 and 3 |
| 7 | ▼ ○ ▲ ▲ ○ □ | Read texts 1, 3 and 4 |
| 8 | ▼ ○ □ ▲ ▼ □ | Read texts 1, 4 and 5 |
| 9 | ▼ ○ □ □ ▼ ▲ | Read texts 1, 5 and 6 |
| 10 | ▼ ▼ ▲ ▲ ○ □ | Read texts 1, 2, 3 and 4 |
| 11 | ▼ ○ ▲ ▲ ▼ □ | Read texts 1, 3, 4 and 5 |
| 12 | ▼ ○ ▲ ▲ ○ ▲ | Read texts 1, 3, 4 and 6 |
| 13 | ▼ ○ □ ▲ ▼ ▲ | Read texts 1, 4, 5 and 6 |
| 14 | ▼ ▼ ▲ ▲ ▼ □ | Read texts 1, 2, 3, 4 and 5 |
| 15 | ▼ ○ ▲ ▲ ▼ ▲ | Read texts 1, 3, 4, 5 and 6 |
| 16 | ▼ ▼ ▲ ▲ ▼ ▲ | Read texts 1, 2, 3, 4, 5 and 6 |
| 17 | ○ ▼ ▲ □ ○ □ | Read texts 2 and 3 |
| 18 | ○ ▼ □ ▲ ○ □ | Read texts 2 and 4 |
| 19 | ○ ▼ □ □ ▼ □ | Read texts 2 and 5 |
| 20 | ○ ▼ □ □ ○ ▲ | Read texts 2 and 6 |
| 21 | ○ ▼ ▲ ▲ ○ □ | Read texts 2, 3 and 4 |
| 22 | ○ ▼ □ ▲ ▼ □ | Read texts 2, 4 and 5 |
| 23 | ○ ▼ □ □ ▼ ▲ | Read texts 2, 5 and 6 |
| 24 | ○ ▼ ▲ ▲ ▼ □ | Read texts 2, 3, 4 and 5 |
| 25 | ○ ▼ □ ▲ ▼ ▲ | Read texts 2, 4, 5 and 6 |
| 26 | ○ ▼ ▲ ▲ ▼ ▲ | Read texts 2, 3, 4, 5 and 6 |
| 27 | ▼ ▼ □ ▲ ○ □ | Read texts 1, 2 and 4 |
| 28 | ▼ ▼ □ □ ▼ □ | Read texts 1, 2 and 5 |
| 29 | ▼ ▼ □ □ ○ ▲ | Read texts 1, 2 and 6 |
| 30 | ▼ ▼ ▲ □ ▼ □ | Read texts 1, 2, 3 and 5 |
| 31 | ▼ ▼ ▲ □ ○ ▲ | Read texts 1, 2, 3 and 6 |
| 32 | ▼ ▼ ▲ ▲ ○ ▲ | Read texts 1, 2, 3, 4 and 6 |
| 33 | ▼ ○ ▲ □ ▼ □ | Read texts 1, 3 and 5 |
| 34 | ▼ ○ ▲ □ ○ ▲ | Read texts 1, 3 and 6 |
| 35 | ▼ ○ ▲ □ ▼ ▲ | Read texts 1, 3, 5 and 6 |
| 36 | ▼ ○ □ ▲ ○ ▲ | Read texts 1, 4 and 6 |
| 37 | ○ ▼ ▲ □ ▼ □ | Read texts 2, 3 and 5 |
| 38 | ○ ▼ ▲ □ ○ ▲ | Read texts 2, 3 and 6 |
| 39 | ○ ▼ ▲ ▲ ○ ▲ | Read texts 2, 3, 4 and 6 |
| 40 | ○ ▼ □ ▲ ○ ▲ | Read texts 2, 4 and 6 |
| 41 | ○ ○ ▲ ▲ ○ □ | Read texts 3 and 4 |
| 42 | ○ ○ ▲ □ ▼ □ | Read texts 3 and 5 |
| 43 | ○ ○ ▲ □ ○ ▲ | Read texts 3 and 6 |
| 44 | ○ ○ ▲ ▲ ▼ □ | Read texts 3, 4 and 5 |
| 45 | ○ ○ ▲ ▲ ○ ▲ | Read texts 3, 4 and 6 |
| 46 | ○ ○ ▲ □ ▼ ▲ | Read texts 3, 5 and 6 |
| 47 | ○ ○ ▲ ▲ ▼ ▲ | Read texts 3, 4, 5 and 6 |
| 48 | ○ ○ □ ▲ ▼ □ | Read texts 4 and 5 |
| 49 | ○ ○ □ ▲ ○ ▲ | Read texts 4 and 6 |
| 50 | ○ ○ □ ▲ ▼ ▲ | Read texts 4, 5 and 6 |
| 51 | ○ ○ □ □ ▼ ▲ | Read texts 5 and 6 |
| 52 | ▼ ○ □ □ ○ □ | Read text 1 |
| 53 | ○ ▼ □ □ ○ □ | Read text 2 |
| 54 | ○ ○ ▲ □ ○ □ | Read text 3 |
| 55 | ○ ○ □ ▲ ○ □ | Read text 4 |
| 56 | ○ ○ □ □ ▼ □ | Read text 5 |
| 57 | ○ ○ □ □ ○ ▲ | Read text 6 |

**1** Your position means that you cannot play the fool; if you do, sooner or later you will pay for it, since your associates will stop taking you seriously and will show you no consideration or respect.

**2** You have probably not yet settled down permanently, but at least you are in a comfortable and satisfying situation. Furthermore, you are attentive and receptive to other people and, in return, they appreciate you and encourage or protect you. But your greatest asset is someone close to you who is loyal and faithful and devoted to you, body and soul.

**3** Your abrupt manner and your propensity to meddle in other people's business will bring trouble or hostility from your acquaintances sooner or later. Moreover, you neither understand nor respect the faithful, devoted person who is close to you. If you do not change your attitude and radically modify your behaviour the situation will very soon turn dangerous.

**4** You give the impression of being mild-mannered, understanding and attentive. In reality you conceal fierce ambition or voracious greed that secretly urges you to push yourself forward, and makes you ready to do anything to achieve your ends and improve your position. However this attitude makes you insecure and ever fearful of losing what you have acquired.

**5** Special circumstances are forcing you to move house or change your place of work. Initially you will feel worried and awkward. However, if you can remain adaptable, flexible and open-minded, you will be able to forge new and very satisfying relationships and to integrate into an environment that previously seemed strange or hostile.

**6** Whatever happens, always remain flexible in your attitude to your environment or in your dealings with others. If not, sooner or later you will lose your peace of mind and not know what to do or where to go.

# 57<sup>th</sup> combination ○ ▢ ▢ ○ ▢ ▢

If you wish to examine an issue in depth, to understand the root causes and inner workings of a situation or penetrate the hidden meaning of a given event, a softly-softly approach is vital. Ensure that you make use of your psychic abilities rather than your external strength. To do this your objective should be precise and worthy, so that you can see the investigation through, and it can be useful to you.

**1** You are in a state of complete and uncontrollable indecision that, if it continues, is likely to put you in danger. In such a case, when one no longer knows to whom to appeal or what choice to make, the best course is just to plunge in without further ado or hesitation: in other words, to decide, firmly and finally, which way to go.

**2** You are encountering vague obstacles and difficulties that are essentially due to ill wishers working behind the scenes, unknown to you. However you must not allow yourself to be discouraged by these hostile ploys. Instead, go after your enemies, even as they retreat, so you can flush them out, unmask them and disarm them.

**3** You are in a position to find out precisely where you are and what you have to do. However, by constantly seeking to investigate things in more depth, you get bogged down in the detail and cannot decide on a course of action. Bear in mind that the more we think, the less we act, and the more we doubt.

**4** You assume your responsibilities and your moral and material obligations wholeheartedly. You are also sensible enough to learn from your past actions, and from the circumstances you have encountered. Such a well-balanced outlook guarantees success in your life and in everything you do.

**5** You are on the threshold of a positive turning point in your life, and have the opportunity to make the right decisions about your situation. To achieve the best possible outcome, take time to reflect before embarking on this new path and, once you have set forth, think again about the methods necessary to achieve your objectives. If you take care, you will undoubtedly make a praiseworthy change.

**6** You are 100 per cent clear about the source of your weaknesses, difficulties and negative influences. But you have expended so much energy trying to combat them and flush them out that you are unable to overcome them fully and finally. This being the case, it is better to abandon any premature offensives: get back your strength, and save the situation as soon as you are back on top form.

| fig. 1 | | | | | | |
|---|---|---|---|---|---|---|
| 1 | ▼ ▲ □ ○ □ □ | Read texts 1 and 2 |
| 2 | ▼ □ ▲ ○ □ □ | Read texts 1 and 3 |
| 3 | ▼ □ □ ▼ □ □ | Read texts 1 and 4 |
| 4 | ▼ □ □ ○ ▲ □ | Read texts 1 and 5 |
| 5 | ▼ □ □ ○ □ ▲ | Read texts 1 and 6 |
| 6 | ▼ ▲ ▲ ○ □ □ | Read texts 1, 2 and 3 |
| 7 | ▼ □ ▲ ▼ □ □ | Read texts 1, 3 and 4 |
| 8 | ▼ □ □ ▼ ▲ □ | Read texts 1, 4 and 5 |
| 9 | ▼ □ □ ○ ▲ ▲ | Read texts 1, 5 and 6 |
| 10 | ▼ ▲ ▲ ▼ □ □ | Read texts 1, 2, 3 and 4 |
| 11 | ▼ □ ▲ ▼ ▲ □ | Read texts 1, 3, 4 and 5 |
| 12 | ▼ □ ▲ ▼ □ ▲ | Read texts 1, 3, 4 and 6 |
| 13 | ▼ □ □ ▼ ▲ ▲ | Read texts 1, 4, 5 and 6 |
| 14 | ▼ ▲ ▲ ▼ ▲ □ | Read texts 1, 2, 3, 4 and 5 |
| 15 | ▼ □ ▲ ▼ ▲ ▲ | Read texts 1, 3, 4, 5 and 6 |
| 16 | ▼ ▲ ▲ ▼ ▲ ▲ | Read texts 1, 2, 3, 4, 5 and 6 |
| 17 | ○ ▲ ▲ ○ □ □ | Read texts 2 and 3 |
| 18 | ○ ▲ □ ▼ □ □ | Read texts 2 and 4 |
| 19 | ○ ▲ □ ○ ▲ □ | Read texts 2 and 5 |
| 20 | ○ ▲ □ ○ □ ▲ | Read texts 2 and 6 |
| 21 | ○ ▲ ▲ ▼ □ □ | Read texts 2, 3 and 4 |
| 22 | ○ ▲ □ ▼ ▲ □ | Read texts 2, 4 and 5 |
| 23 | ○ ▲ □ ○ ▲ ▲ | Read texts 2, 5 and 6 |
| 24 | ○ ▲ ▲ ▼ ▲ □ | Read texts 2, 3, 4 and 5 |
| 25 | ○ ▲ □ ▼ ▲ ▲ | Read texts 2, 4, 5 and 6 |
| 26 | ○ ▲ ▲ ▼ ▲ ▲ | Read texts 2, 3, 4, 5 and 6 |
| 27 | ▼ ▲ □ ▼ □ □ | Read texts 1, 2 and 4 |
| 28 | ▼ ▲ □ ○ ▲ □ | Read texts 1, 2 and 5 |
| 29 | ▼ ▲ □ ○ □ ▲ | Read texts 1, 2 and 6 |
| 30 | ▼ ▲ ▲ ○ ▲ □ | Read texts 1, 2, 3 and 5 |
| 31 | ▼ ▲ ▲ ○ □ ▲ | Read texts 1, 2, 3 and 6 |
| 32 | ▼ ▲ ▲ ▼ □ ▲ | Read texts 1, 2, 3, 4 and 6 |
| 33 | ▼ □ ▲ ○ □ ▲ | Read texts 1, 3 and 5 |
| 34 | ▼ □ ▲ ○ □ ▲ | Read texts 1, 3 and 6 |
| 35 | ▼ □ ▲ ○ ▲ ▲ | Read texts 1, 3, 5 and 6 |
| 36 | ▼ □ □ ▼ □ ▲ | Read texts 1, 4 and 6 |
| 37 | ○ ▲ ▲ ○ ▲ □ | Read texts 2, 3 and 5 |
| 38 | ○ ▲ ▲ ○ □ ▲ | Read texts 2, 3 and 6 |
| 39 | ○ ▲ ▲ ▼ □ ▲ | Read texts 2, 3, 4 and 6 |
| 40 | ○ ▲ □ ▼ □ ▲ | Read texts 2, 4 and 6 |
| 41 | ○ □ ▲ ▼ □ □ | Read texts 3 and 4 |
| 42 | ○ □ ▲ ○ ▲ □ | Read texts 3 and 5 |
| 43 | ○ □ ▲ ○ □ ▲ | Read texts 3 and 6 |
| 44 | ○ □ ▲ ▼ ▲ □ | Read texts 3, 4 and 5 |
| 45 | ○ □ ▲ ▼ □ ▲ | Read texts 3, 4 and 6 |
| 46 | ○ □ ▲ ○ ▲ ▲ | Read texts 3, 5 and 6 |
| 47 | ○ □ ▲ ▼ ▲ ▲ | Read texts 3, 4, 5 and 6 |
| 48 | ○ □ □ ▼ ▲ □ | Read texts 4 and 5 |
| 49 | ○ □ □ ▼ □ ▲ | Read texts 4 and 6 |
| 50 | ○ □ □ ▼ ▲ ▲ | Read texts 4, 5 and 6 |
| 51 | ○ □ □ ○ ▲ ▲ | Read texts 5 and 6 |
| 52 | ▼ □ □ ○ □ □ | Read text 1 |
| 53 | ○ ▲ □ ○ □ □ | Read text 2 |
| 54 | ○ □ ▲ ○ □ □ | Read text 3 |
| 55 | ○ □ □ ▼ □ □ | Read text 4 |
| 56 | ○ □ □ ○ ▲ □ | Read text 5 |
| 57 | ○ □ □ ○ □ ▲ | Read text 6 |

**57th combination** ○ □ □ ○ □ □

335

○
□
□
○
□ □
□

**58th combination**

| | | | | | | | |
|---|---|---|---|---|---|---|---|
| fig. 1 | ▲ | ▲ | ○ | □ | □ | ○ | Read texts 1 and 2 |
| 2 | ▲ | □ | ▼ | □ | □ | ○ | Read texts 1 and 3 |
| 3 | ▲ | □ | ○ | ▲ | □ | ○ | Read texts 1 and 4 |
| 4 | ▲ | □ | ○ | □ | ▲ | ○ | Read texts 1 and 5 |
| 5 | ▲ | □ | ○ | □ | □ | ▼ | Read texts 1 and 6 |
| 6 | ▲ | ▲ | ▼ | □ | □ | ○ | Read texts 1, 2 and 3 |
| 7 | ▲ | □ | ▼ | ▲ | □ | ○ | Read texts 1, 3 and 4 |
| 8 | ▲ | □ | ○ | ▲ | ▲ | ○ | Read texts 1, 4 and 5 |
| 9 | ▲ | □ | ○ | □ | ▲ | ▼ | Read texts 1, 5 and 6 |
| 10 | ▲ | ▲ | ▼ | ▲ | □ | ○ | Read texts 1, 2, 3 and 4 |
| 11 | ▲ | □ | ▼ | ▲ | ▲ | ○ | Read texts 1, 3, 4 and 5 |
| 12 | ▲ | □ | ▼ | ▲ | □ | ▼ | Read texts 1, 3, 4 and 6 |
| 13 | ▲ | □ | ○ | ▲ | ▲ | ▼ | Read texts 1, 4, 5 and 6 |
| 14 | ▲ | ▲ | ▼ | ▲ | ▲ | ○ | Read texts 1, 2, 3, 4 and 5 |
| 15 | ▲ | □ | ▼ | ▲ | ▲ | ▼ | Read texts 1, 3, 4, 5 and 6 |
| 16 | ▲ | ▲ | ▼ | ▲ | ▲ | ▼ | Read texts 1, 2, 3, 4, 5 and 6 |
| 17 | □ | ▲ | ▼ | □ | □ | ○ | Read texts 2 and 3 |
| 18 | □ | ▲ | ○ | ▲ | □ | ○ | Read texts 2 and 4 |
| 19 | □ | ▲ | ○ | □ | ▲ | ○ | Read texts 2 and 5 |
| 20 | □ | ▲ | ○ | □ | □ | ▼ | Read texts 2 and 6 |
| 21 | □ | ▲ | ▼ | ▲ | □ | ○ | Read texts 2, 3 and 4 |
| 22 | □ | ▲ | ○ | ▲ | ▲ | ○ | Read texts 2, 4 and 5 |
| 23 | □ | ▲ | ○ | □ | ▲ | ▼ | Read texts 2, 5 and 6 |
| 24 | □ | ▲ | ▼ | ▲ | ▲ | ○ | Read texts 2, 3, 4 and 5 |
| 25 | □ | ▲ | ○ | ▲ | ▲ | ▼ | Read texts 2, 4, 5 and 6 |
| 26 | □ | ▲ | ▼ | ▲ | ▲ | ▼ | Read texts 2, 3, 4, 5 and 6 |
| 27 | ▲ | ▲ | ○ | ▲ | □ | ○ | Read texts 1, 2 and 4 |
| 28 | ▲ | ▲ | ○ | □ | ▲ | ○ | Read texts 1, 2 and 5 |
| 29 | ▲ | ▲ | ○ | □ | □ | ▼ | Read texts 1, 2 and 6 |
| 30 | ▲ | ▲ | ▼ | □ | ▲ | ○ | Read texts 1, 2, 3 and 5 |
| 31 | ▲ | ▲ | ▼ | □ | □ | ▼ | Read texts 1, 2, 3 and 6 |
| 32 | ▲ | ▲ | ▼ | ▲ | □ | ▼ | Read texts 1, 2, 3, 4 and 6 |
| 33 | ▲ | □ | ▼ | □ | ▲ | ○ | Read texts 1, 3 and 5 |
| 34 | ▲ | □ | ▼ | □ | □ | ▼ | Read texts 1, 3 and 6 |
| 35 | ▲ | □ | ▼ | □ | ▲ | ▼ | Read texts 1, 3, 5 and 6 |
| 36 | ▲ | □ | ○ | ▲ | □ | ▼ | Read texts 1, 4 and 6 |
| 37 | □ | ▲ | ▼ | □ | ▲ | ○ | Read texts 2, 3 and 5 |
| 38 | □ | ▲ | ▼ | □ | □ | ▼ | Read texts 2, 3 and 6 |
| 39 | □ | ▲ | ▼ | ▲ | □ | ▼ | Read texts 2, 3, 4 and 6 |
| 40 | □ | ▲ | ○ | ▲ | □ | ▼ | Read texts 2, 4 and 6 |
| 41 | □ | □ | ▼ | ▲ | □ | ○ | Read texts 3 and 4 |
| 42 | □ | □ | ▼ | □ | ▲ | ○ | Read texts 3 and 5 |
| 43 | □ | □ | ▼ | □ | □ | ▼ | Read texts 3 and 6 |
| 44 | □ | □ | ▼ | ▲ | ▲ | ○ | Read texts 3, 4 and 5 |
| 45 | □ | □ | ▼ | ▲ | □ | ▼ | Read texts 3, 4 and 6 |
| 46 | □ | □ | ▼ | □ | ▲ | ▼ | Read texts 3, 5 and 6 |
| 47 | □ | □ | ▼ | ▲ | ▲ | ▼ | Read texts 3, 4, 5 and 6 |
| 48 | □ | □ | ○ | ▲ | ▲ | ○ | Read texts 4 and 5 |
| 49 | □ | □ | ○ | ▲ | □ | ▼ | Read texts 4 and 6 |
| 50 | □ | □ | ○ | ▲ | ▲ | ▼ | Read texts 4, 5 and 6 |
| 51 | □ | □ | ○ | □ | ▲ | ▼ | Read texts 5 and 6 |
| 52 | ▲ | □ | ○ | □ | □ | ○ | Read text 1 |
| 53 | □ | ▲ | ○ | □ | □ | ○ | Read text 2 |
| 54 | □ | □ | ▼ | □ | □ | ○ | Read text 3 |
| 55 | □ | □ | ○ | ▲ | □ | ○ | Read text 4 |
| 56 | □ | □ | ○ | □ | ▲ | ○ | Read text 5 |
| 57 | □ | □ | ○ | □ | □ | ▼ | Read text 6 |

# 58th combination □ □ ○ □ □ ○

Joy comes from instinctual serenity, deep faith and inner truth, whereas gaiety is always rather superficial and ephemeral. This is why a joyful attitude is always infectious and can help naturally through painful or difficult times. By the same token, knowledge is stimulating and inclusive, while science is austere and exclusive.

**1** You feel at peace with yourself and with those close to you. You do not exclusively favour one particular person over another, and you reject no one. Such an open, dispassionate attitude makes you serene, self assured and confident about your future.

**2** You are involved with people of dubious morality or intentions, and there is reason to fear that you are not entirely indifferent to their advances or proposals. However you will stop yourself in time, being careful not to give them a definite answer. Consequently, their bad influence will not affect you again in any way.

**3** When one cannot find the source of everlasting joy within – the pure and simple joy of being alive, and the joy of love – there may arise an urgent need to indulge in worldly pleasures. But such dependency is dangerous in the long run: not only does it drain inner resources, but it also leads to despair, ridicule, bitterness and remorse.

**4** You constantly waver between a desire to experience deep, spiritual, lasting joy and an eagerness to enjoy ephemeral, selfish or base pleasures. You must make a decisive choice between the two; furthermore, you should bear in mind that desire begets pleasure that, in turn, engenders new desires... all of which plunges us into a never-ending cycle of passion and frustration. Only if you are aware of this can you hope to make the right choice.

5   You are involved with people who, despite appearances, could well upset your psychological balance and inner serenity or send you astray. Do not discount their insidious and destructive influence and guard against it, before they attempt to get to you in any way.

6   Since you have been unable to cultivate core values, inner truth and elemental joy, you are now swept up in a flurry of ephemeral pleasures and distractions and superficial gratification. This means you are no longer in control of your future but are at the mercy of external circumstances, which, when favourable, will make you happy, but unhappy when they are against you.

# 59<sup>th</sup>combination ○ □ ○ ○ □ □

Selfishness, individualism, pride and self-interest are at the root of all disagreements, dissension and conflict between people. To make up for these all too human frailties, people need to come together to experience universal faith or defend a common cause. In this way, petty feelings can be overcome.

1   You are well aware that differences of opinion or conflicting views are about to

| fig. 1 | | | | | | | |
|---|---|---|---|---|---|---|---|
| 1 | ▼ | ▲ | ○ | ○ | □ | □ | Read texts 1 and 2 |
| 2 | ▼ | □ | ▼ | ○ | □ | □ | Read texts 1 and 3 |
| 3 | ▼ | □ | ○ | ▼ | □ | □ | Read texts 1 and 4 |
| 4 | ▼ | □ | ○ | ○ | ▲ | □ | Read texts 1 and 5 |
| 5 | ▼ | □ | ○ | ○ | □ | ▲ | Read texts 1 and 6 |
| 6 | ▼ | ▲ | ▼ | ○ | □ | □ | Read texts 1, 2 and 3 |
| 7 | ▼ | □ | ▼ | ▼ | □ | □ | Read texts 1, 3 and 4 |
| 8 | ▼ | □ | ○ | ▼ | ▲ | □ | Read texts 1, 4 and 5 |
| 9 | ▼ | □ | ○ | ○ | ▲ | □ | Read texts 1, 5 and 6 |
| 10 | ▼ | ▲ | ▼ | ▼ | □ | □ | Read texts 1, 2, 3 and 4 |
| 11 | ▼ | □ | ▼ | ▼ | ▲ | □ | Read texts 1, 3, 4 and 5 |
| 12 | ▼ | □ | ▼ | ▼ | □ | ▲ | Read texts 1, 3, 4 and 6 |
| 13 | ▼ | □ | ○ | ▼ | ▲ | ▲ | Read texts 1, 4, 5 and 6 |
| 14 | ▼ | ▲ | ▼ | ▼ | ▲ | □ | Read texts 1, 2, 3, 4 and 5 |
| 15 | ▼ | □ | ▼ | ▼ | ▲ | ▲ | Read texts 1, 3, 4, 5 and 6 |
| 16 | ▼ | ▲ | ▼ | ▼ | ▲ | ▲ | Read texts 1, 2, 3, 4, 5 and 6 |
| 17 | ○ | ▲ | ▼ | ○ | □ | □ | Read texts 2 and 3 |
| 18 | ○ | ▲ | ○ | ▼ | □ | □ | Read texts 2 and 4 |
| 19 | ○ | ▲ | ○ | ○ | ▲ | □ | Read texts 2 and 5 |
| 20 | ○ | ▲ | ○ | ○ | □ | ▲ | Read texts 2 and 6 |
| 21 | ○ | ▲ | ▼ | ▼ | □ | □ | Read texts 2, 3 and 4 |
| 22 | ○ | ▲ | ○ | ▼ | ▲ | □ | Read texts 2, 4 and 5 |
| 23 | ○ | ▲ | ○ | ○ | ▲ | ▲ | Read texts 2, 5 and 6 |
| 24 | ○ | ▲ | ▼ | ▼ | ▲ | □ | Read texts 2, 3, 4 and 5 |
| 25 | ○ | ▲ | ○ | ▼ | ▲ | ▲ | Read texts 2, 4, 5 and 6 |
| 26 | ○ | ▲ | ▼ | ▼ | ▲ | ▲ | Read texts 2, 3, 4, 5 and 6 |
| 27 | ▼ | ▲ | ○ | ▼ | □ | □ | Read texts 1, 2 and 4 |
| 28 | ▼ | ▲ | ○ | ○ | ▲ | □ | Read texts 1, 2 and 5 |
| 29 | ▼ | ▲ | ○ | ○ | □ | ▲ | Read texts 1, 2 and 6 |
| 30 | ▼ | ▲ | ▼ | ○ | ▲ | □ | Read texts 1, 2, 3 and 5 |
| 31 | ▼ | ▲ | ▼ | ○ | □ | ▲ | Read texts 1, 2, 3 and 6 |
| 32 | ▼ | ▲ | ▼ | ▼ | ▲ | □ | Read texts 1, 2, 3, 4 and 6 |
| 33 | ▼ | □ | ▼ | ○ | ▲ | □ | Read texts 1, 3 and 5 |
| 34 | ▼ | □ | ▼ | ○ | □ | ▲ | Read texts 1, 3 and 6 |
| 35 | ▼ | □ | ▼ | ○ | ▲ | ▲ | Read texts 1, 3, 5 and 6 |
| 36 | ▼ | □ | ○ | ▼ | □ | ▲ | Read texts 1, 4 and 6 |
| 37 | ○ | ▲ | ▼ | ○ | ▲ | □ | Read texts 2, 3 and 5 |
| 38 | ○ | ▲ | ▼ | ○ | □ | ▲ | Read texts 2, 3 and 6 |
| 39 | ○ | ▲ | ▼ | ▼ | □ | ▲ | Read texts 2, 3, 4 and 6 |
| 40 | ○ | ▲ | ○ | ▼ | ▲ | □ | Read texts 2, 4 and 6 |
| 41 | ○ | □ | ▼ | ▼ | □ | □ | Read texts 3 and 4 |
| 42 | ○ | □ | ▼ | ○ | ▲ | □ | Read texts 3 and 5 |
| 43 | ○ | □ | ▼ | ○ | □ | ▲ | Read texts 3 and 6 |
| 44 | ○ | □ | ▼ | ▼ | ▲ | □ | Read texts 3, 4 and 5 |
| 45 | ○ | □ | ▼ | ▼ | □ | ▲ | Read texts 3, 4 and 6 |
| 46 | ○ | □ | ▼ | ○ | ▲ | ▲ | Read texts 3, 5 and 6 |
| 47 | ○ | □ | ▼ | ▼ | ▲ | ▲ | Read texts 3, 4, 5 and 6 |
| 48 | ○ | □ | ○ | ▼ | ▲ | □ | Read texts 4 and 5 |
| 49 | ○ | □ | ○ | ▼ | □ | ▲ | Read texts 4 and 6 |
| 50 | ○ | □ | ○ | ▼ | ▲ | ▲ | Read texts 4, 5 and 6 |
| 51 | ○ | □ | ○ | ○ | ▲ | ▲ | Read texts 5 and 6 |
| 52 | ▼ | □ | ○ | ○ | □ | □ | Read text 1 |
| 53 | ○ | ▲ | ○ | ○ | □ | □ | Read text 2 |
| 54 | ○ | □ | ▼ | ○ | □ | □ | Read text 3 |
| 55 | ○ | □ | ○ | ▼ | □ | □ | Read text 4 |
| 56 | ○ | □ | ○ | ○ | ▲ | □ | Read text 5 |
| 57 | ○ | □ | ○ | ○ | □ | ▲ | Read text 6 |

**59th combination** ○ □ ○ ○ □ □

drive a wedge between you and somebody close to you, or between you and others in your circle. You must therefore take firm action and put a stop to these unfounded misunderstandings or differences that could lead to a split.

**2** You judge those around you, and people in general, in an inflexible, exclusive and arbitrary way. Your refusal to show any objective understanding or make any concessions is likely to result in your isolation. You must therefore work hard at making measured, tempered judgments that are more in keeping with reality and circumstances.

**3** Your present circumstances require you to set aside your personal preoccupations or selfish designs, and to throw yourself wholeheartedly into an ambitious project. This actually means giving up some of your prerogatives, so that you can broaden your horizons and your sphere of activities.

**4** The way you are operating at the moment means that you cannot afford to be distracted or to waste time focussing precious attention on certain people rather than those who deserve it. In fact, by cutting back on contact with certain people you actually free yourself to meet others and to enlarge your social circle. The more ambitious a project is, the more you need to be open to the possibilities offered by other people and by the many and various elements in life – if you want to see it through.

**5** When it seems that there is no option and that everything is leading up to a final, complete separation or split, we need to call upon the great principles, sublime feelings and eternal values that unite people. A person with moral strength and good judgment can annihilate all misunderstandings, and bring people together peaceably.

**6** You are in a situation that appears to offer no recourse and requires immediate action, so that you can protect those close to you, or in your charge, from damage or harm. By sheltering and saving those around you, you assume your full responsibilities and act as you ought.

# 60<sup>th</sup> combination ❏ ❏ ○ ○ ❏ ○

In everything, it is good to know how to set limits – precise measures that allow you to operate on firm foundations and within a clearly defined framework. Otherwise you risk spreading yourself too thinly or wasting your energies. Nevertheless, you must not allow your responsibilities or your obligations to become a straitjacket for you or for those around you.

**1** You would like to push ahead or act decisively, but you are prevented from doing so by adverse circumstances or insurmountable obstacles. If you accept this and wait for the right moment to act, your willpower and strength will be so well consolidated that you will easily and instantly reach your goal.

**2** The time has come for you to act, take the initiative and go full steam ahead to turn your good intentions and ideas into clear and concrete actions. This is not the time to hesitate or to indulge in irrelevant thoughts, because you might miss the opportunity to obtain what you want or reach your objectives rapidly.

3 You succumb too readily to excess in all areas of your life – to unbridled pleasure, reckless expenditure or extravagance. Such thoughtless behaviour can only lead, sooner or later, to a reversal of fortune or to a shock, which will be nobody's fault but your own.

4 Any measures intended to save you from excess or from making mistakes must be accepted voluntarily, without causing constant tension or resistance; otherwise you will achieve the exact opposite of what you were hoping for. If, on the other hand, you calmly set your own limits, you are sure to benefit from them.

5 Do not expect others to follow your advice or bend to your will if you set a bad example. To get positive results and to ensure that those around you submit to certain necessary restrictions, you must first of all impose them on yourself, and adhere to them firmly and without hesitation.

6 It is not a good idea to impose ruthless or excessive restrictions on yourself, because sooner or later they will cause moral and physical tension that could compromise your inner equilibrium. Nevertheless, if you feel there is no other choice or alternative way to guard against the risks caused by your own weakness or lack of self-control, then you are right to do so.

| fig. | | | | | | | |
|---|---|---|---|---|---|---|---|
| 1 | ▲ | ▲ | ○ | ○ | □ | ○ | Read texts 1 and 2 |
| 2 | ▲ | □ | ▼ | ○ | ○ | ○ | Read texts 1 and 3 |
| 3 | ▲ | □ | ○ | ▼ | ○ | ○ | Read texts 1 and 4 |
| 4 | ▲ | □ | ○ | ○ | ▲ | ○ | Read texts 1 and 5 |
| 5 | ▲ | □ | ○ | ○ | □ | ▼ | Read texts 1 and 6 |
| 6 | ▲ | ▲ | ▼ | ○ | ○ | ○ | Read texts 1, 2 and 3 |
| 7 | ▲ | □ | ▼ | ▼ | ○ | ○ | Read texts 1, 3 and 4 |
| 8 | ▲ | □ | ○ | ▼ | ▲ | ○ | Read texts 1, 4 and 5 |
| 9 | ▲ | □ | ○ | ○ | ▲ | ▼ | Read texts 1, 5 and 6 |
| 10 | ▲ | ▲ | ▼ | ▼ | □ | ○ | Read texts 1, 2, 3 and 4 |
| 11 | ▲ | □ | ▼ | ▼ | ▲ | ○ | Read texts 1, 3, 4 and 5 |
| 12 | ▲ | □ | ▼ | ▼ | □ | ▼ | Read texts 1, 3, 4 and 6 |
| 13 | ▲ | □ | ○ | ▼ | ▲ | ▼ | Read texts 1, 4, 5 and 6 |
| 14 | ▲ | ▲ | ▼ | ▼ | ▲ | ○ | Read texts 1, 2, 3, 4 and 5 |
| 15 | ▲ | □ | ▼ | ▼ | ▲ | ▼ | Read texts 1, 3, 4, 5 and 6 |
| 16 | ▲ | ▲ | ▼ | ▼ | ▲ | ▼ | Read texts 1, 2, 3, 4, 5 and 6 |
| 17 | □ | ▲ | ▼ | ○ | □ | ○ | Read texts 2 and 3 |
| 18 | □ | ▲ | ○ | ▼ | ○ | ○ | Read texts 2 and 4 |
| 19 | □ | ▲ | ○ | ○ | ▲ | ○ | Read texts 2 and 5 |
| 20 | □ | ▲ | ○ | ○ | □ | ▼ | Read texts 2 and 6 |
| 21 | □ | ▲ | ▼ | ▼ | ○ | ○ | Read texts 2, 3 and 4 |
| 22 | □ | ▲ | ○ | ▼ | ▲ | ○ | Read texts 2, 4 and 5 |
| 23 | □ | ▲ | ○ | ○ | ▲ | ▼ | Read texts 2, 5 and 6 |
| 24 | □ | ▲ | ▼ | ▼ | ▲ | ○ | Read texts 2, 3, 4 and 5 |
| 25 | □ | ▲ | ○ | ▼ | ▲ | ▼ | Read texts 2, 4, 5 and 6 |
| 26 | □ | ▲ | ▼ | ▼ | ▲ | ▼ | Read texts 2, 3, 4, 5 and 6 |
| 27 | ▲ | ▲ | ○ | ▼ | □ | ○ | Read texts 1, 2 and 4 |
| 28 | ▲ | ▲ | ○ | ○ | ▲ | ○ | Read texts 1, 2 and 5 |
| 29 | ▲ | ▲ | ○ | ○ | □ | ▼ | Read texts 1, 2 and 6 |
| 30 | ▲ | ▲ | ▼ | ○ | ▲ | ○ | Read texts 1, 2, 3 and 5 |
| 31 | ▲ | ▲ | ▼ | ○ | □ | ▼ | Read texts 1, 2, 3 and 6 |
| 32 | ▲ | ▲ | ▼ | ▼ | □ | ▼ | Read texts 1, 2, 3, 4 and 6 |
| 33 | ▲ | □ | ▼ | ○ | ▲ | ○ | Read texts 1, 3 and 5 |
| 34 | ▲ | □ | ▼ | ○ | □ | ▼ | Read texts 1, 3 and 6 |
| 35 | ▲ | □ | ▼ | ○ | ▲ | ▼ | Read texts 1, 3, 5 and 6 |
| 36 | ▲ | □ | ○ | ▼ | □ | ▼ | Read texts 1, 4 and 6 |
| 37 | □ | ▲ | ▼ | ○ | ▲ | ○ | Read texts 2, 3 and 5 |
| 38 | □ | ▲ | ▼ | ○ | □ | ▼ | Read texts 2, 3 and 6 |
| 39 | □ | ▲ | ▼ | ▼ | □ | ▼ | Read texts 2, 3, 4 and 6 |
| 40 | □ | ▲ | ○ | ▼ | □ | ▼ | Read texts 2, 4 and 6 |
| 41 | □ | □ | ▼ | ▼ | □ | ○ | Read texts 3 and 4 |
| 42 | □ | □ | ▼ | ○ | ▲ | ○ | Read texts 3 and 5 |
| 43 | □ | □ | ▼ | ○ | □ | ▼ | Read texts 3 and 6 |
| 44 | □ | □ | ▼ | ▼ | ▲ | ○ | Read texts 3, 4 and 5 |
| 45 | □ | □ | ▼ | ▼ | □ | ▼ | Read texts 3, 4 and 6 |
| 46 | □ | □ | ▼ | ○ | ▲ | ▼ | Read texts 3, 5 and 6 |
| 47 | □ | □ | ▼ | ▼ | ▲ | ▼ | Read texts 3, 4, 5 and 6 |
| 48 | □ | □ | ○ | ▼ | ▲ | ○ | Read texts 4 and 5 |
| 49 | □ | □ | ○ | ▼ | □ | ▼ | Read texts 4 and 6 |
| 50 | □ | □ | ▼ | ▼ | ▲ | ▼ | Read texts 4, 5 and 6 |
| 51 | □ | □ | ○ | ○ | ▲ | ▼ | Read texts 5 and 6 |
| 52 | ▲ | □ | ○ | ○ | □ | ○ | Read text 1 |
| 53 | □ | ▲ | ○ | ○ | □ | ○ | Read text 2 |
| 54 | □ | □ | ▼ | ○ | □ | ○ | Read text 3 |
| 55 | □ | □ | ○ | ▼ | □ | ○ | Read text 4 |
| 56 | □ | □ | ○ | ○ | ▲ | ○ | Read text 5 |
| 57 | □ | □ | ○ | ○ | □ | ▼ | Read text 6 |

**60th combination** □ □ ○ ○ □ ○

**61st combination**

| | fig. 1 | ▲ ▲ ○ ○ □ □ | Read texts 1 and 2 |
|---|---|---|---|
| | 2 | ▲ □ ▼ ○ □ □ | Read texts 1 and 3 |
| | 3 | ▲ □ ○ ▼ □ □ | Read texts 1 and 4 |
| | 4 | ▲ □ ○ ○ ▲ □ | Read texts 1 and 5 |
| | 5 | ▲ □ ○ ○ □ ▲ | Read texts 1 and 6 |
| | 6 | ▲ ▲ ▼ ○ □ □ | Read texts 1, 2 and 3 |
| | 7 | ▲ □ ▼ ▼ □ □ | Read texts 1, 3 and 4 |
| | 8 | ▲ □ ○ ▼ ▲ □ | Read texts 1, 4 and 5 |
| | 9 | ▲ □ ○ ○ ▲ ▲ | Read texts 1, 5 and 6 |
| | 10 | ▲ ▲ ▼ ▼ ▲ □ | Read texts 1, 2, 3 and 4 |
| | 11 | ▲ □ ▼ ▼ ▲ □ | Read texts 1, 3, 4 and 5 |
| | 12 | ▲ □ ▼ ▼ □ ▲ | Read texts 1, 3, 4 and 6 |
| | 13 | ▲ □ ○ ▼ ▲ ▲ | Read texts 1, 4, 5 and 6 |
| | 14 | ▲ ▲ ▼ ▼ ▲ □ | Read texts 1, 2, 3, 4 and 5 |
| | 15 | ▲ □ ▼ ▼ ▲ ▲ | Read texts 1, 3, 4, 5 and 6 |
| | 16 | ▲ ▲ ▼ ▼ ▲ ▲ | Read texts 1, 2, 3, 4, 5 and 6 |
| | 17 | □ ▲ ▼ ○ □ □ | Read texts 2 and 3 |
| | 18 | □ ▲ ○ ▼ □ □ | Read texts 2 and 4 |
| | 19 | □ ▲ ○ ○ ▲ □ | Read texts 2 and 5 |
| | 20 | □ ▲ ○ ○ □ ▲ | Read texts 2 and 6 |
| | 21 | □ ▲ ▼ ▼ □ □ | Read texts 2, 3 and 4 |
| | 22 | □ ▲ ○ ▼ ▲ □ | Read texts 2, 4 and 5 |
| | 23 | □ ▲ ○ ○ ▲ ▲ | Read texts 2, 5 and 6 |
| | 24 | □ ▲ ▼ ▼ ▲ □ | Read texts 2, 3, 4 and 5 |
| | 25 | □ ▲ ○ ▼ ▲ ▲ | Read texts 2, 4, 5 and 6 |
| | 26 | □ ▲ ▼ ▼ ▲ ▲ | Read texts 2, 3, 4, 5 and 6 |
| | 27 | ▲ ▲ ○ ▼ □ □ | Read texts 1, 2 and 4 |
| | 28 | ▲ ▲ ○ ○ ▲ □ | Read texts 1, 2 and 5 |
| | 29 | ▲ ▲ ○ ○ □ ▲ | Read texts 1, 2 and 6 |
| | 30 | ▲ ▲ ▼ ○ ▲ □ | Read texts 1, 2, 3 and 5 |
| | 31 | ▲ ▲ ▼ ○ □ ▲ | Read texts 1, 2, 3 and 6 |
| | 32 | ▲ ▲ ▼ ▼ □ ▲ | Read texts 1, 2, 3, 4 and 6 |
| | 33 | ▲ □ ▼ ○ ▲ □ | Read texts 1, 3 and 5 |
| | 34 | ▲ □ ▼ ○ □ ▲ | Read texts 1, 3 and 6 |
| | 35 | ▲ □ ▼ ○ ▲ ▲ | Read texts 1, 3, 5 and 6 |
| | 36 | ▲ □ ○ ▼ □ ▲ | Read texts 1, 4 and 6 |
| | 37 | □ ▲ ▼ ○ ▲ □ | Read texts 2, 3 and 5 |
| | 38 | □ ▲ ▼ ○ □ ▲ | Read texts 2, 3 and 6 |
| | 39 | □ ▲ ▼ ▼ □ ▲ | Read texts 2, 3, 4 and 6 |
| | 40 | □ ▲ ○ ▼ □ ▲ | Read texts 2, 4 and 6 |
| | 41 | □ □ ▼ ▼ □ □ | Read texts 3 and 4 |
| | 42 | □ □ ▼ ○ ▲ □ | Read texts 3 and 5 |
| | 43 | □ □ ▼ ○ □ ▲ | Read texts 3 and 6 |
| | 44 | □ □ ▼ ▼ ▲ □ | Read texts 3, 4 and 5 |
| | 45 | □ □ ▼ ▼ □ ▲ | Read texts 3, 4 and 6 |
| | 46 | □ □ ▼ ○ ▲ ▲ | Read texts 3, 5 and 6 |
| | 47 | □ □ ▼ ▼ ▲ ▲ | Read texts 3, 4, 5 and 6 |
| | 48 | □ □ ○ ▼ ▲ □ | Read texts 4 and 5 |
| | 49 | □ □ ○ ▼ □ ▲ | Read texts 4 and 6 |
| | 50 | □ □ ○ ▼ ▲ ▲ | Read texts 4, 5 and 6 |
| | 51 | □ □ ○ ○ ▲ ▲ | Read texts 5 and 6 |
| | 52 | ▲ □ ○ ○ □ □ | Read text 1 |
| | 53 | □ ▲ ○ ○ □ □ | Read text 2 |
| | 54 | □ □ ▼ ○ □ □ | Read text 3 |
| | 55 | □ □ ○ ▼ □ □ | Read text 4 |
| | 56 | □ □ ○ ○ ▲ □ | Read text 5 |
| | 57 | □ □ ○ ○ □ ▲ | Read text 6 |

# 61st combination □ □ ○ ○ □ □

Your relationships with certain people do not stem from within, and are not based on true inclinations or profound affinities, but merely on common interests. Relationships like these can only be temporary. If you want to forge more authentic bonds with people, you must act with integrity and energy and without equivocation. Nor should you condemn other people, but show yourself to be perceptive and understanding.

**1** Clear-sightedness and inner balance depend on a constant and responsible character, and on being alert, attentive and prepared. However, if you seek relationships only with those who praise and flatter you, you will lose not only your independence and integrity, but also any objectivity in your actions and judgments.

**2** If your actions match your thoughts and your motives clearly express your will – in other words, if your feelings are truly sincere – you will get exactly what you want; this is the way you exert your inner power over the circumstances of your life. On the other hand, if you attempt to interfere arbitrarily with the course of events, you will achieve precisely the opposite result.

**3** You depend too much on your social relationships and the feelings others have for you, and on the good and bad moods of those around you. This is not a bad thing in itself, but it is important for you to realize that this deprives you of your spiritual autonomy.

**4**   As far as is possible, avoid being too dependent on close friendships or on your tight social circle. Similarly, in your relationship with your partner, try to retain your autonomy and originality and your own personality. Do not identify yourself with your partner's personality and, likewise, allow him or her a separate identity. In this way both of you can work together in the pursuit of a common goal.

**5**   Any union or association must be based on natural inclinations, genuine principles, solid foundations and profound truth. If this is not the case, the relationship will be temporary or will not turn out as you wish.

**6**   You seem to enjoy formidable powers of seduction or persuasion that allow you to exert a strong influence on your entourage. Nevertheless, if your words do not derive from deep convictions or personal experience, they will cause confusion and serious disappointment in your relationships.

# 62<sup>nd</sup> combination ○ ○ □ □ ○ ○

You lack the necessary qualities or means to carry out some ambitious projects. However if you behave with sensitivity, discretion, skill and genuine humility you will achieve perfectly respectable results. Do not worry about what other people think of you, but remain true to yourself at all costs.

**1**   It is not yet time to pull out all the stops to get what you want, nor should your wishes and plans be too ambitious. If you act prematurely or without preparation, or

| fig. | 1 | | | | | | |
|---|---|---|---|---|---|---|---|
| 1 | ▼ | ▼ | □ | □ | ○ | ○ | Read texts 1 and 2 |
| 2 | ▼ | ○ | ▲ | □ | ○ | ○ | Read texts 1 and 3 |
| 3 | ▼ | ○ | □ | ▲ | ○ | ○ | Read texts 1 and 4 |
| 4 | ▼ | ○ | □ | □ | ▼ | ○ | Read texts 1 and 5 |
| 5 | ▼ | ○ | □ | □ | ○ | ▼ | Read texts 1 and 6 |
| 6 | ▼ | ▼ | ▲ | □ | ○ | ○ | Read texts 1, 2 and 3 |
| 7 | ▼ | ▼ | □ | ▲ | ○ | ○ | Read texts 1, 2 and 4 |
| 8 | ▼ | ▼ | □ | □ | ▲ | ○ | Read texts 1, 2 and 5 |
| 9 | ▼ | ▼ | □ | □ | ○ | ▼ | Read texts 1, 2 and 6 |
| 10 | ▼ | ▼ | ▲ | ▲ | ○ | ○ | Read texts 1, 2, 3 and 4 |
| 11 | ▼ | ▼ | ▲ | □ | ▼ | ○ | Read texts 1, 2, 3 and 5 |
| 12 | ▼ | ▼ | ▲ | □ | ○ | ▼ | Read texts 1, 2, 3 and 6 |
| 13 | ▼ | ▼ | ▲ | ▲ | ▼ | ○ | Read texts 1, 2, 3, 4 and 5 |
| 14 | ▼ | ▼ | ▲ | ▲ | ○ | ▼ | Read texts 1, 2, 3, 4 and 6 |
| 15 | ▼ | ▼ | ▲ | ▲ | ▼ | ▼ | Read texts 1, 2, 3, 4, 5 and 6 |
| 16 | ▼ | ○ | ▲ | ▲ | ○ | ○ | Read texts 1, 3 and 4 |
| 17 | ▼ | ○ | ▲ | □ | ▼ | ○ | Read texts 1, 3 and 5 |
| 18 | ▼ | ○ | ▲ | □ | ○ | ▼ | Read texts 1, 3 and 6 |
| 19 | ▼ | ○ | ▲ | ▲ | ▼ | ○ | Read texts 1, 3, 4 and 5 |
| 20 | ▼ | ○ | ▲ | ▲ | ○ | ▼ | Read texts 1, 3, 4 and 6 |
| 21 | ▼ | ○ | ▲ | □ | ▼ | ▼ | Read texts 1, 3, 5 and 6 |
| 22 | ▼ | ○ | ▲ | ▲ | ▼ | ▼ | Read texts 1, 3, 4, 5 and 6 |
| 23 | ▼ | ○ | □ | ▲ | ▼ | ○ | Read texts 1, 4 and 5 |
| 24 | ▼ | ○ | □ | ▲ | ○ | ▼ | Read texts 1, 4 and 6 |
| 25 | ▼ | ○ | □ | ▲ | ▼ | ▼ | Read texts 1, 4, 5 and 6 |
| 26 | ▼ | ○ | □ | □ | ▼ | ▼ | Read texts 1, 5 and 6 |
| 27 | ○ | ▼ | ▲ | □ | ○ | ○ | Read texts 2 and 3 |
| 28 | ○ | ▼ | □ | ▲ | ○ | ○ | Read texts 2 and 4 |
| 29 | ○ | ▼ | □ | □ | ▼ | ○ | Read texts 2 and 5 |
| 30 | ○ | ▼ | □ | □ | ○ | ▼ | Read texts 2 and 6 |
| 31 | ○ | ▼ | ▲ | ▲ | ○ | ○ | Read texts 2, 3 and 4 |
| 32 | ○ | ▼ | ▲ | □ | ▼ | ○ | Read texts 2, 3 and 5 |
| 33 | ○ | ▼ | ▲ | □ | ○ | ▼ | Read texts 2, 3 and 6 |
| 34 | ○ | ▼ | ▲ | ▲ | ▼ | ○ | Read texts 2, 3, 4 and 5 |
| 35 | ○ | ▼ | ▲ | ▲ | ○ | ▼ | Read texts 2, 3, 4 and 6 |
| 36 | ○ | ▼ | ▲ | ▲ | ▼ | ▼ | Read texts 2, 3, 4, 5 and 6 |
| 37 | ○ | ▼ | □ | ▲ | ▼ | ○ | Read texts 2, 4 and 5 |
| 38 | ○ | ▼ | □ | ▲ | ○ | ▼ | Read texts 2, 4 and 6 |
| 39 | ○ | ▼ | □ | ▲ | ▼ | ▼ | Read texts 2, 4, 5 and 6 |
| 40 | ○ | ▼ | □ | □ | ▼ | ▼ | Read texts 2, 5 and 6 |
| 41 | ○ | ○ | ▲ | ▲ | ○ | ○ | Read texts 3 and 4 |
| 42 | ○ | ○ | ▲ | □ | ▼ | ○ | Read texts 3 and 5 |
| 43 | ○ | ○ | ▲ | □ | ○ | ▼ | Read texts 3 and 6 |
| 44 | ○ | ○ | ▲ | ▲ | ▼ | ○ | Read texts 3, 4 and 5 |
| 45 | ○ | ○ | ▲ | ▲ | ○ | ▼ | Read texts 3, 4 and 6 |
| 46 | ○ | ○ | ▲ | □ | ▼ | ○ | Read texts 3, 5 and 6 |
| 47 | ○ | ○ | ▲ | ▲ | ▼ | ▼ | Read texts 3, 4, 5 and 6 |
| 48 | ○ | ○ | □ | ▲ | ▼ | ○ | Read texts 4 and 5 |
| 49 | ○ | ○ | □ | ▲ | ○ | ▼ | Read texts 4 and 6 |
| 50 | ○ | ○ | □ | ▲ | ▼ | ▼ | Read texts 4, 5 and 6 |
| 51 | ○ | ○ | □ | □ | ▼ | ▼ | Read texts 5 and 6 |
| 52 | ▼ | ○ | □ | □ | ○ | ○ | Read text 1 |
| 53 | ○ | ▼ | □ | □ | ○ | ○ | Read text 2 |
| 54 | ○ | ○ | ▲ | □ | ○ | ○ | Read text 3 |
| 55 | ○ | ○ | □ | ▲ | ○ | ○ | Read text 4 |
| 56 | ○ | ○ | □ | □ | ▼ | ○ | Read text 5 |
| 57 | ○ | ○ | □ | □ | ○ | ▼ | Read text 6 |

**62nd combination** ○ ○ □ □ ○ ○

aim for something beyond your true capabilities, you will fail mightily.

2   You seek to gain something or to meet somebody in a key position whose influence or support could help you. You will not succeed, although your request will be taken into consideration. Be content with that for the moment, because this represents an important step.

3   You think it would be unworthy or undignified to give up, not to take all the risks that you feel yourself able or entitled to take. However, it would be wise to show more caution and not to overlook even the smallest detail before throwing yourself into this dangerous venture. Accept this and the goals will be within your reach. Ignore it and anything might happen.

4   You must refrain from imprudent behaviour and not seek to impose your will or your wishes, given the way things are at the moment. In circumstances like these, extreme vigilance is in order. It is a question of keeping your eyes fixed on the objective you have set yourself, and of holding to it with patience, persistence and tenacity. Then, when the right moment comes, you can take action.

5   You want to carry out an ambitious plan, or to accomplish something that is dear to your heart. However, you are having trouble finding the partners or the support you need. Without question the answer lies with somebody who is underrated or unknown, but who will prove to have exceptional qualities. This person will undoubtedly help you see your task through. If you have not already met, you soon will.

6   You are too impatient, agitated and feverish. You insist on trying to reach the inaccessible. You are in danger of suffering disastrous consequences or losing everything if you do not calm down, temper your anxiety and control your impulsive behaviour.

# 63rd combination ☐ ○ ☐ ○ ☐ ○

Your present situation seems satisfactory in every way. Your difficulties have passed and you have managed to solve your problems. Everything appears perfectly normal. However it is often in circumstances like these that we become overconfident and fail to notice the apparently insignificant signs of possible deterioration in the situation. It would be prudent not to underestimate these signs in order to prevent any risk of destabilization.

1   You are being swept along on a tide of generosity and encouragement that naturally encourages your optimism and enthusiasm. However, do not lose your powers of perception and trust your intuition, which tells you to be doubly cautious and not to act too soon. Those around you will probably not take such advice seriously, but the main thing is that you yourself should bear it in mind.

2   You want to carry out an ambitious plan or to accomplish something that is dear to your heart, but those with the necessary power and authority give you no help or support at all. But you have not given up, and you are doing everything and anything

to gain recognition or be taken into consideration. It would be wiser just to be patient, knowing that what is yours can never be taken away, and that sooner or later this will earn you universal respect.

**3**  You have obtained excellent results and now things are getting better and better. This is, of course, a very good thing. Nevertheless, you must be rigorous and selective when choosing the partners you need to broaden your sphere of activity or move your situation along. Those with whom you achieved the current results are not necessarily those whom you will take with you to the next level.

**4**  You are in a comfortable position that is going from strength to strength. Granted, a troubling passage came along, but you knew how to deal with it promptly and effectively and everything quickly returned to normal. All the same, be mindful of episodes like this so that they do not recur; in the long run they could put your situation in danger.

**5**  You are in such an advantageous situation that you are forgetting something: namely, that everything you do should be rooted in sincerity and authenticity. Do not be content just to respect principles and convention, but make sure that they are deep and true, for otherwise they have no value.

**6**  You have managed to overcome the difficulties and obstacles in your way, and you have reached your goals. Naturally you can be proud of this, but avoid looking back with complacency and fix your attention firmly on the future; otherwise you risk being trapped by the events of the past.

| fig. | | | | | | | |
|---|---|---|---|---|---|---|---|
| 1 | ▲ | ▼ | □ | ○ | □ | ○ | Read texts 1 and 2 |
| 2 | ▲ | ○ | ▲ | ○ | □ | ○ | Read texts 1 and 3 |
| 3 | ▲ | ○ | □ | ▼ | □ | ○ | Read texts 1 and 4 |
| 4 | ▲ | ○ | □ | ○ | ▲ | ○ | Read texts 1 and 5 |
| 5 | ▲ | ○ | □ | ○ | □ | ▼ | Read texts 1 and 6 |
| 6 | ▲ | ▼ | ▲ | ○ | □ | ○ | Read texts 1, 2 and 3 |
| 7 | ▲ | ○ | ▲ | ▼ | □ | ○ | Read texts 1, 3 and 4 |
| 8 | ▲ | ○ | □ | ▼ | ▲ | ○ | Read texts 1, 4 and 5 |
| 9 | ▲ | ○ | □ | ○ | ▲ | ▼ | Read texts 1, 5 and 6 |
| 10 | ▲ | ▼ | ▲ | ▼ | □ | ○ | Read texts 1, 2, 3 and 4 |
| 11 | ▲ | ○ | ▲ | ▼ | ▲ | ○ | Read texts 1, 3, 4 and 5 |
| 12 | ▲ | ○ | ▲ | ▼ | □ | ▼ | Read texts 1, 3, 4 and 6 |
| 13 | ▲ | ○ | □ | ▼ | ▲ | ▼ | Read texts 1, 4, 5 and 6 |
| 14 | ▲ | ▼ | ▲ | ▼ | ▲ | ○ | Read texts 1, 2, 3, 4 and 5 |
| 15 | ▲ | ○ | ▲ | ▼ | ▲ | ▼ | Read texts 1, 3, 4, 5 and 6 |
| 16 | ▲ | ▼ | ▲ | ▼ | ▲ | ▼ | Read texts 1, 2, 3, 4, 5 and 6 |
| 17 | □ | ▼ | ▲ | ○ | □ | ○ | Read texts 2 and 3 |
| 18 | □ | ▼ | □ | ▼ | □ | ○ | Read texts 2 and 4 |
| 19 | □ | ▼ | □ | ○ | ▲ | ○ | Read texts 2 and 5 |
| 20 | □ | ▼ | □ | ○ | □ | ▼ | Read texts 2 and 6 |
| 21 | □ | ▼ | ▲ | ▼ | □ | ○ | Read texts 2, 3 and 4 |
| 22 | □ | ▼ | □ | ▼ | ▲ | ○ | Read texts 2, 4 and 5 |
| 23 | □ | ▼ | □ | ▼ | ▲ | ○ | Read texts 2, 5 and 6 |
| 24 | □ | ▼ | ▲ | ▼ | ▲ | ○ | Read texts 2, 3, 4 and 5 |
| 25 | □ | ▼ | □ | ▼ | ▲ | ▼ | Read texts 2, 4, 5 and 6 |
| 26 | □ | ▼ | ▲ | ▼ | ▲ | ▼ | Read texts 2, 3, 4, 5 and 6 |
| 27 | ▲ | ▼ | □ | ▼ | □ | ○ | Read texts 1, 2 and 4 |
| 28 | ▲ | ▼ | □ | ○ | ▲ | ○ | Read texts 1, 2 and 5 |
| 29 | ▲ | ▼ | □ | ○ | □ | ▼ | Read texts 1, 2 and 6 |
| 30 | ▲ | ▼ | ▲ | ○ | ▲ | ○ | Read texts 1, 2, 3 and 5 |
| 31 | ▲ | ▼ | ▲ | ○ | □ | ▼ | Read texts 1, 2, 3 and 6 |
| 32 | ▲ | ▼ | ▲ | ▼ | □ | ▼ | Read texts 1, 2, 3, 4 and 6 |
| 33 | ▲ | ○ | ▲ | ○ | ▲ | ○ | Read texts 1, 3 and 5 |
| 34 | ▲ | ○ | ▲ | ○ | □ | ▼ | Read texts 1, 3 and 6 |
| 35 | ▲ | ○ | ▲ | ○ | ▲ | ▼ | Read texts 1, 3, 5 and 6 |
| 36 | ▲ | ○ | □ | ▼ | □ | ▼ | Read texts 1, 4 and 6 |
| 37 | □ | ▼ | ▲ | ○ | ▲ | ○ | Read texts 2, 3 and 5 |
| 38 | □ | ▼ | ▲ | ○ | □ | ▼ | Read texts 2, 3 and 6 |
| 39 | □ | ▼ | ▲ | ▼ | □ | ▼ | Read texts 2, 3, 4 and 6 |
| 40 | □ | ▼ | □ | ▼ | □ | ▼ | Read texts 2, 4 and 6 |
| 41 | □ | ○ | ▲ | ▼ | □ | ○ | Read texts 3 and 4 |
| 42 | □ | ○ | ▲ | ○ | ▲ | ○ | Read texts 3 and 5 |
| 43 | □ | ○ | ▲ | ○ | □ | ▼ | Read texts 3 and 6 |
| 44 | □ | ○ | ▲ | ▼ | ▲ | ○ | Read texts 3, 4 and 5 |
| 45 | □ | ○ | ▲ | ▼ | □ | ▼ | Read texts 3, 4 and 6 |
| 46 | □ | ○ | ▲ | ○ | ▲ | ▼ | Read texts 3, 5 and 6 |
| 47 | □ | ○ | ▲ | ▼ | ▲ | ▼ | Read texts 3, 4, 5 and 6 |
| 48 | □ | ○ | □ | ▼ | ▲ | ○ | Read texts 4 and 5 |
| 49 | □ | ○ | □ | ▼ | □ | ▼ | Read texts 4 and 6 |
| 50 | □ | ○ | □ | ▼ | ▲ | ▼ | Read texts 4, 5 and 6 |
| 51 | □ | ○ | □ | ○ | ▲ | ▼ | Read texts 5 and 6 |
| 52 | ▲ | ○ | □ | ○ | □ | ○ | Read text 1 |
| 53 | □ | ▼ | □ | ○ | □ | ○ | Read text 2 |
| 54 | □ | ○ | ▲ | ○ | □ | ○ | Read text 3 |
| 55 | □ | ○ | □ | ▼ | □ | ○ | Read text 4 |
| 56 | □ | ○ | □ | ○ | ▲ | ○ | Read text 5 |
| 57 | □ | ○ | □ | ○ | □ | ▼ | Read text 6 |

63rd combination  □ ○ □ ○ □ ○

| | | | | | | | | |
|---|---|---|---|---|---|---|---|---|
| fig. 1 | ▼ | ▲ | ○ | □ | ○ | □ | Read texts 1 and 2 |
| 2 | ▼ | □ | ▼ | □ | ○ | □ | Read texts 1 and 3 |
| 3 | ▼ | □ | ○ | ▲ | ○ | □ | Read texts 1 and 4 |
| 4 | ▼ | □ | ○ | □ | ▼ | □ | Read texts 1 and 5 |
| 5 | ▼ | □ | ○ | □ | ○ | ▲ | Read texts 1 and 6 |
| 6 | ▼ | ▲ | ▼ | □ | ○ | □ | Read texts 1, 2 and 3 |
| 7 | ▼ | □ | ▼ | ▲ | ○ | □ | Read texts 1, 3 and 4 |
| 8 | ▼ | □ | ○ | ▲ | ▼ | □ | Read texts 1, 4 and 5 |
| 9 | ▼ | □ | ○ | □ | ▼ | ▲ | Read texts 1, 5 and 6 |
| 10 | ▼ | ▲ | ▼ | ▲ | ○ | □ | Read texts 1, 2, 3 and 4 |
| 11 | ▼ | □ | ▼ | ▲ | ▼ | □ | Read texts 1, 3, 4 and 5 |
| 12 | ▼ | □ | ▼ | ▲ | ○ | ▲ | Read texts 1, 3, 4 and 6 |
| 13 | ▼ | □ | ○ | ▲ | ▼ | ▲ | Read texts 1, 4, 5 and 6 |
| 14 | ▼ | ▲ | ▼ | ▲ | ▼ | □ | Read texts 1, 2, 3, 4 and 5 |
| 15 | ▼ | □ | ▼ | ▲ | ▼ | ▲ | Read texts 1, 3, 4, 5 and 6 |
| 16 | ▼ | ▲ | ▼ | ▲ | ▼ | ▲ | Read texts 1, 2, 3, 4, 5 and 6 |
| 17 | ○ | ▲ | ▼ | □ | ○ | □ | Read texts 2 and 3 |
| 18 | ○ | ▲ | ○ | ▲ | ○ | □ | Read texts 2 and 4 |
| 19 | ○ | ▲ | ○ | □ | ▼ | □ | Read texts 2 and 5 |
| 20 | ○ | ▲ | ○ | □ | ○ | ▲ | Read texts 2 and 6 |
| 21 | ○ | ▲ | ▼ | ▲ | ○ | □ | Read texts 2, 3 and 4 |
| 22 | ○ | ▲ | ○ | ▲ | ▼ | □ | Read texts 2, 4 and 5 |
| 23 | ○ | ▲ | □ | ▼ | ▲ | □ | Read texts 2, 5 and 6 |
| 24 | ○ | ▲ | ▼ | ▲ | ▼ | □ | Read texts 2, 3, 4 and 5 |
| 25 | ○ | ▲ | ○ | ▲ | ▼ | ▲ | Read texts 2, 4, 5 and 6 |
| 26 | ○ | ▲ | ▼ | ▲ | ▼ | ▲ | Read texts 2, 3, 4, 5 and 6 |
| 27 | ▼ | ▲ | ○ | ▲ | ○ | □ | Read texts 1, 2 and 4 |
| 28 | ▼ | ▲ | ○ | □ | ▼ | □ | Read texts 1, 2 and 5 |
| 29 | ▼ | ▲ | ○ | □ | ○ | ▲ | Read texts 1, 2 and 6 |
| 30 | ▼ | ▲ | ▼ | □ | ▼ | □ | Read texts 1, 2, 3 and 5 |
| 31 | ▼ | ▲ | ▼ | ▲ | ○ | ▲ | Read texts 1, 2, 3 and 6 |
| 32 | ▼ | ▲ | ▼ | ▲ | ○ | ▲ | Read texts 1, 2, 3, 4 and 6 |
| 33 | ▼ | □ | ▼ | □ | ▼ | □ | Read texts 1, 3 and 5 |
| 34 | ▼ | □ | ▼ | □ | ○ | ▲ | Read texts 1, 3 and 6 |
| 35 | ▼ | □ | ▼ | □ | ▼ | ▲ | Read texts 1, 3, 5 and 6 |
| 36 | ▼ | □ | ○ | ▲ | ○ | ▲ | Read texts 1, 4 and 6 |
| 37 | ○ | ▲ | ▼ | □ | ▼ | □ | Read texts 2, 3 and 5 |
| 38 | ○ | ▲ | ▼ | □ | ○ | ▲ | Read texts 2, 3 and 6 |
| 39 | ○ | ▲ | ▼ | ▲ | ○ | ▲ | Read texts 2, 3, 4 and 6 |
| 40 | ○ | ▲ | ○ | ▲ | ○ | ▲ | Read texts 2, 4 and 6 |
| 41 | ○ | □ | ▼ | ▲ | ○ | □ | Read texts 3 and 4 |
| 42 | ○ | □ | ▼ | □ | ▼ | □ | Read texts 3 and 5 |
| 43 | ○ | □ | ▼ | □ | ○ | ▲ | Read texts 3 and 6 |
| 44 | ○ | □ | ▼ | ▲ | ▼ | □ | Read texts 3, 4 and 5 |
| 45 | ○ | □ | ▼ | ▲ | ○ | ▲ | Read texts 3, 4 and 6 |
| 46 | ○ | □ | ▼ | □ | ▼ | ▲ | Read texts 3, 5 and 6 |
| 47 | ○ | □ | ▼ | ▲ | ▼ | ▲ | Read texts 3, 4, 5 and 6 |
| 48 | ○ | □ | ○ | ▲ | ▼ | □ | Read texts 4 and 5 |
| 49 | ○ | □ | ○ | ▲ | ○ | ▲ | Read texts 4 and 6 |
| 50 | ○ | □ | ○ | ▲ | ▼ | ▲ | Read texts 4, 5 and 6 |
| 51 | ○ | □ | ○ | □ | ▼ | ▲ | Read texts 5 and 6 |
| 52 | ▼ | □ | ○ | □ | ○ | □ | Read text 1 |
| 53 | ○ | ▲ | ○ | □ | ○ | □ | Read text 2 |
| 54 | ○ | □ | ▼ | □ | ○ | □ | Read text 3 |
| 55 | ○ | □ | ○ | ▲ | ○ | □ | Read text 4 |
| 56 | ○ | □ | ○ | □ | ▼ | □ | Read text 5 |
| 57 | ○ | □ | ○ | □ | ○ | ▲ | Read text 6 |

# 64th combination ○ □ □ ○ □ ○

You are in a troubled, difficult and dangerous situation. The slightest error could prove fatal. However, if you are aware of this, and if you take all the time you need to think carefully about it and to make the most intelligent use of the means at your disposal, you are certain to break free.

**1** Right now there is an air of confusion all around you, and you are gripped by deep uncertainty. You are therefore thinking about making an honest, straightforward and all-out effort to escape this troubled climate, but the time is not favourable for such a decision. It is better to refrain from action for the immediate future.

**2** Your position is uncomfortable, and of course you want to escape it as quickly as possible. However, it is not yet time to make your move. You must therefore prepare yourself patiently and focus firmly on your aim; thus when the time is right, you will be ready to free yourself from your shackles.

**3** The time has come to escape a confused or muddled situation that is hampering your actions and initiatives. You cannot act alone, but you cannot wait much longer. You must therefore seek help and support from competent and effective people who will enable you to solve this delicate problem and go forward.

**4** The time for thinking, for futile reflection and idle speculation has passed. You must act with the greatest determination in order to put a stop to a confused and unsatisfactory situation. As soon as this is done, you can contemplate building on more healthy and solid foundations.

5   You have done exactly what your duty and responsibilities required you to do, and everything has turned out well. The situation has improved and you got what you wanted. From now on you can turn firmly towards the future and make full use of the advantages at your disposal, which are a far cry from the obstacles and difficulties you previously faced.

6   You have achieved all that you wished and your situation is now healthy, prosperous and going from strength to strength. You are confident about the future, and past events have helped you to assess your abilities and talents. Nevertheless, do not be too careless or too confident, because nobody can ever be immune to a reversal of fortune.

*'It is the same with prophecies, miracles, divination by dreams, sorceries, &c. For if there had been nothing true in all this, men would have believed nothing of them; and thus, instead of concluding that there are no true miracles because there are so many false, we must, on the contrary, say that there certainly are true miracles, since there are false, and that there are false miracles only because some are true.'*

Blaise Pascal,
*Pensées*, On Miracles

# Bibliography

Alliance Mondiale des Religions *Les Songes et les Rêves,* Désiris 1992.

Eliade, M *Histoire des Croyances et des Idées Religieuses* vols. 1, 2 and 3, Payot 1976.

Franz, M-L von *Rêves d'Hier et d'Aujourd'hui,* Jacqueline-Renard (eds), Collection La Fontaine de Pierre 1990.

Gheerbrant, J C-A *Dictionnaire des Symboles,* Robert Laffont 1969.

Rocherie, J. de la *La Symbologie des Rêves,* Imago 1984.

Sîrîn, I *L'Interprétation des Rêves dans la Tradition Islamique,* Alif 1992.

Sources Orientales, *Les Songes et leur Interprétation,* Du Scuil 1959.

Souzenelle, A. de *Le Symbolisme du Corps Humain ou De l'Arbre de Vie au Schéma Corporel,* Danglès 1984.

Eliade, Mircea *A History of Religious Ideas: From Gautama Buddha to the Triumph of Christianity* (trs. Willard Trask), 1985.

Frazer, Sir James George *The Golden Bough,* Oxford Paperbacks, 1998.

Hall, John *Dictionary of Subjects and Symbols in Art,* John Murray, 1989.

Jung, C G *Memories, Dreams, Reflections,* Vintage, 1989.

Jung, C G *Man and His Symbols,* Dell Publishing, 1970.

Seligmann, Kurt Magic, *Supernaturalism and Religion,* Pantheon Books, 1948.

Shepherd, Rupert (ed.) *1000 Symbols,* Thames & Hudson, 2002.